# Here I Stand

# Here I Stand

*My Struggle for a Christianity of*
*Integrity, Love, and Equality*

✳

## JOHN SHELBY SPONG

HarperSanFrancisco
*A Division of HarperCollinsPublishers*

HarperCollins books may be purchased for educational, business, or sales promotional use. For information please write: Special Markets Department, HarperCollins Publishers Inc., 10 East 53rd Street, New York, NY 10022.

For further educational resources exploring ideas and issues addressed in this and other books by John Shelby Spong or to communicate with the author contact:
Christianity for the Third Millennium
P.O. Box 69
Morristown, NJ 07963–0069
Telephone: (908) 813–2954, Fax (973) 540–9584
email: CMSCTM@AOL.com

HarperCollins Web Site: http://www.harpercollins.com
HarperCollins®, ▇®, and HarperSanFrancisco™ are trademarks of
HarperCollins Publishers Inc.

FIRST HARPERCOLLINS PAPERBACK EDITION PUBLISHED IN 2001
*Designed by Joseph Rutt*

Library of Congress Cataloging-in-Publication Data
Spong, John Shelby.
Here I stand : my struggle for a Christianity of integrity, love, and equality /
John Shelby Spong. — 1st ed.
p.   cm.
Includes index.
ISBN 0–06–067538–1 (cloth).
ISBN 0–06–067539–X (pbk.)
ISBN 0–06–067544–6 (international pbk.)
1. Spong, John Shelby.   2. Episcopal Church — Bishops Biography.
I. Title.
BX5995.S77A3   1999
283'.092—dc21      99–41160

04 05 ❖/RRD 10 9 8 7 6 5 4 3 2

This book is dedicated to those who shaped my life personally:

My parents, John Shelby Spong (1889–1943) and
Doolie Boyce Griffith Spong (1907–1999)
My first wife, Joan Lydia Ketner Spong (1929–1988)
Our children, Ellen Elizabeth, Mary Katharine, and
Jaquelin Ketner Spong
My second wife, Christine Mary Spong
My stepchildren, Brian Yancy and Rachel Elizabeth Barney
Our grandchildren, Shelby and Jay Catlett, and John and Lydia Hylton

And to those who shaped my life professionally:
William Wall Whiddit, choirmaster
Robert Littlefield Crandall, rector
Janet Robinson, teacher
William H. Poteat, teacher
Edwin Anderson Penick, bishop
William Belser Spong, Jr., cousin, senator
David Watt Yates, college rector
Richard Henry Baker, bishop
Marian Alston Bourne, mentor
John A. T. Robinson, mentor
William Henry Marmion, bishop
John Elbridge Hines, bishop and ultimate role model
Desmond Tutu, bishop and Nobel Prize winner
Jack Daniel Spiro, rabbi
Don Cupitt, mentor
Michael Donald Goulder, mentor
Jack Marston McKelvey, bishop
John Palmer Croneberger, bishop

Trusted advisers:

Ward J. Herbert

Eliot S. Knight

Michael F. Rehill

William L. Heick

E. Louie Crew

Phillip C. Cato

Dale Gruner

Marjorie L. Christie

Harry E. Smith

Gerrie H. Jeter

John E. Lynch

John G. Zinn

Michael P. Francaviglia

Marilyn Conrad

# CONTENTS

# PREFACE

※

I N MANY WAYS, writing an autobiography has a touch of arrogance about it. The author has to assume that his or her life will be of interest to a reading public. This is true, I suspect, only if that life has been involved in issues that have helped determine and shape the lives of others. Otherwise, reading it is like watching someone's home movies. When my editors at HarperCollins first broached the idea of this book, I was both flattered and filled with hesitancy, perhaps even fear. It was, however, a task that also appealed to me, not for reasons of serving an ever present ego, but rather because it afforded me an opportunity to review my life, to reassess major decisions, to make new judgments, and to revisit both the valleys through which I have walked and the mountaintops where I have been enabled to see visions not always discernible to others.

An autobiography is by definition subjective. This book is my view of the experiences through which I have lived. I have worked hard to make certain I have both my facts and my dates correct, though I suspect in time someone will demonstrate that in one or two places I was mistaken. My major emphasis, however, was to share my personal interpretations of the experiences associated with those facts and dates. Inevitably, I have been forced to make judgments about people and events. That is the nature of an autobiography. I hope I have not been unfair in doing so, but I suspect that those not flattered by my descriptions of them will think I have been. My goal has been to hold up a mirror to friend and foe alike and, when the reflection was visible, to say this is how you looked to me. That is not to claim objective truth for my perception, nor is it to assert that my version is, in fact, who anyone is. Rather, it is to say that, given who I am and the values I represent, this is how I have experienced you. I have tried in these descriptions to be scrupulously honest, yet avoid as much as possible any small-minded pettiness.

I have loved revisiting the various episodes of my life and the terrain over which I have been privileged to walk. In some sense this has helped me to bring about some closures that might never otherwise have been available to me. I had to recreate and thus to relive, for example, my childhood feelings for such primary people as my father, who died when I was twelve and who left me with lots of unhealed wounds from our incomplete relationship. But I also could chronicle the healing that occurred when I found a surrogate father in the person of my rector, Robert Crandall, who helped me discover my own call to the priesthood. I visited anew the experience I had with my first shaping undergraduate professor, named William H. Poteat, at the University of North Carolina, who taught me how to think as he taught me philosophy, and later with gigantic heroes like John E. Hines and John A. T. Robinson, both bishops, who modeled for me in very different ways what an episcopal career based on a vision of the future could look like.

I also had great fun reliving my days in the various congregations I served: St. Joseph's, Durham, North Carolina; Calvary Parish, Tarboro, North Carolina; St. John's, Lynchburg, Virginia; and St. Paul's in Richmond. To add to these opportunities a professional life of almost a quarter of a century as a bishop in that part of northern New Jersey known as the Diocese of Newark, a very special, open, and honest community of faith, was more than any person might have expected in a lifetime. I have been touched by some incredible people, both men and women, over these years who have helped to create the person I now am. Many, but obviously not all, of their names will appear in these pages.

The actual physical work on this book consumed three years of my writing career. From the time I signed the contract to do it, in 1994, it has been present, even if just in the back of my mind. I first began to put my thoughts on paper while in New Zealand in 1997. Fortunately for the completion of this task, I have over the years thrown away almost nothing! I have kept massive files, scrapbooks, date books, and calendars for every year of my professional career, which began with my ordination in 1955 and continued until my retirement forty-five years later in 2000. Clearing out those files when this book was complete was not the easiest emotional task I have ever faced.

The thing that frightened me most in preparing this volume was how would I tell the story of my wife, Joan, who died of cancer in 1988. Not only did I love her very much, but I did not want in any way to diminish either her memory or her gifts to the world, to me, or to our daughters. But her mental illness, which she endured overtly for fifteen years, was such a major piece of our family's history and provided so powerful a background to both my personal and my professional life that I could not omit it. I hope, for her sake and for the sake of our daughters, in whom she still lives so obviously and so beautifully, I have done this with sensitivity, kindness, and the love I still have for her. I wanted this recounting to be both realistic and a contribution to the joy of her memory.

I am particularly indebted to the clergy and people of our diocese, who called me to be their bishop in 1976 and who have lived with me in that wonderful, mature, and creative tension in which we sought together to affirm diversity, to respect differences, and to create an environment in which each person can be called and empowered to be the deepest, fullest self possible, for that is what I believe the church, known as the Body of Christ, is designed to do.

Many people helped me in researching this book. Harold (Packy) Morris, a boxing fan in our church in Jersey City, helped me get the details of the Louis-Braddock, Louis-Schmeling, and Louis-Conn heavyweight championship fights that enabled me to frame the issues of racism in my early life. The Reverend Lawrence Falkowski, our priest in West Orange, went on the Internet to get me details of historical events in the public arena around which my own life revolved. Marilyn (Lyn) Conrad, my executive secretary, got the dates from the library reference department when obscure people served in Congress and in the Senate so that my story would have an accurate factual basis. My wife, Christine, ran down details in a variety of places that fleshed out my narrative. Each of my daughters challenged my memory of certain events in which they had shared and forced me to investigate further until I usually discovered that they were right and I was wrong. I would have sworn, for example, that I was in Charlottesville, Virginia, watching a basketball game the night before I was elected bishop, but they demonstrated conclusively that I was in Landover, Maryland, and my daughters Ellen and Katharine were with me. So I corrected that. I could not correct, however, the fact that the University of Virginia, their alma mater, defeated the University of North Carolina, my alma mater, on that particular night.

I deeply appreciate those research assistants who have helped me with various chapters of this book. In Tarboro, North Carolina, Gray Procter Clark worked for over a year on verifying certain facts. I am also grateful to Peter J. Long and Jacksie Berwick Aycock for their assistance, to say nothing of the staff at the Edgecombe County Public Library.

In Lynchburg, Evelyn Stickley and her husband, Bob, got details from the newspaper archives, the library, the parish records, and even from the Diocese of Southwestern Virginia. The bishop of that diocese, Neff Powell, and his staff were also helpful. Bishop William H. Marmion, who is still the finest bishop under whom I have ever served, was also a great source of information.

In Richmond, Carter McDowell and the Reverend Canon Robert Hetherington looked things up for me in lots of places. Thomas Gordon, former member of the Virginia Supreme Court, verified political facts, and Earl Dunford went into the microfilm files of the *Richmond Times-Dispatch* especially to recapture the flavor of the Carwile episode. My cousin, Martha Spong, provided me with corroborative data about her father, William Belser Spong, Jr.

In the Diocese of Newark I had a host of helpers. My chancellor, Michael Rehill, obtained the exact texts from the minutes of the church, both locally and nationally. Others, like Jack McKelvey, John Zinn, Michael Francaviglia, Jack Croneberger, Dale Gruner, Gerrie Jeter, Deborah Brown, and Eliot Knight, made this effort a community one.

At the Office of the Archives of the Episcopal Church in Austin, Texas, I found ready and competent help every time I requested it. I thank Jennifer Peters in particular.

In running down details that involved my life in the Diocese of North Carolina, Sarah Jo Manning was a wonder, even though her research forced me to rewrite two chapters to correct an error in my dating.

Lyn Conrad has put these pages, from first draft to final editing, on her computer. I don't know how she has managed to do that with everything else she has to do and with the phone interrupting her about fifty times a day. I have been blessed with wonderful secretaries through the years, and Lyn is among the finest. This is the third book I have done with her. This book was also different. All of my other books were lectures first, given in the diocese, which I later prepared for publication. This one was never spoken anywhere. So the diocese has benefited very little from this manuscript except to have a record of a piece of its history placed into written form. For that reason I have made a major monetary contribution to the Diocese of Newark for allowing so much of Lyn's time to be used on this project. But I am still in her personal debt tremendously. She chose her retirement to coincide with mine. I don't think either of us wanted to work with anybody else.

My chief editor on this manuscript other than John Loudon at HarperCollins has been my unique wife, Christine Mary Spong. What a remarkable gift she is to me and what talent resides in her incredible head. She is the best primary editor with whom I have ever worked in my entire career. She can spell better than Spell Check. She recognizes a poor grammatical construction from twenty paces. She knows when a passage sings and when it does not. She will say cut this, expand this, edit this, develop this, and almost always she is absolutely correct. I love this lady passionately, but even if she were not my wife, I would have enormous respect for her incredible abilities. Our marriage has been the absolute wonder of my life, a privilege beyond my ability to articulate adequately.

I also thank that community of people who have shared life with me in Episcopal House in downtown Newark. My writing career and high-profile life made their lives a bit more complicated, but I hope also a bit more exciting.

Finally, I thank my family. Beyond Christine, there are our daughters, Ellen, Katharine, Jaquelin, and Rachel; our son, Brian; our grandchildren, Shelby, Jay, John, and Lydia; our sons-in-law, Gus Epps and Jack Catlett; our mothers, Ina Bridger and Doolie Boyce Spong (though I need to note that my mother died before this book came fully to life); our brothers, Will Spong and Bill Bridger; and our sisters, Betty Spong Marshall, Nancy Whitworth, and Doris Bridger. Such a talented person each one is and how deeply Chris and I love them all. I am a happy and fulfilled man. In addition to being a bishop, I am a husband, a father, a stepfather, a father-in-law, a grandfather, a brother, a brother-in-law, a son, and a son-in-law. I have enjoyed every role. For the gifts I have received from so many, I give thanks to the God my life has sought to serve and to the people through whom this God has been revealed.

Shalom,

John S. Spong
Newark, New Jersey
February 1, 2000

# Here I Stand

# Setting the Stage:
# The Parameters of the Debate

※

*"Your words are not just heresy, they are apostasy. Burning you at the stake would be too kind!"*

Pittsburgh, Pennsylvania

*"Your book was like manna from heaven—God-sent! I cannot adequately express my gratitude."*

Richmond, Virginia

*"You rail against the Church's doctrines and core beliefs while you accept wages from her. Even whores appreciate their clients. You, sir, have less integrity than a whore!"*

Selma, Alabama

*"You have made it possible for me to remain in the Church and have taught me how to believe honestly its creeds even in the twentieth century."*

Boston, Massachusetts

*"Bishop Spong, you are full of sh–t. We are going to clean you up."*
An orthodox Christian

*"Reading your book is like eating a delicious Black Forest cherry birthday cake. It has made me vulnerable while increasing my desire to worship."*

British Columbia, Canada

*"Remember, as you prance about disguised as a minister of the gospel, that you will pay for your sins eternally in the lake of fire."*
Charleston, South Carolina

*"Your book is a transcendent work of brilliance and, I am sure, permanence."*
Pasadena, California

*"I hope the next plane on which you fly crashes. You are not worthy of life. If all else fails, I will try to rid the world of your evil presence personally."*
Orlando, Florida

*"I believe you are a prophet and I will strive with you to answer God's call to live fully, love wastefully, and be all that I can be. Thank you, thank you, and may your life continue to be blessed."*
Grosse Point, Michigan

THESE ARE excerpts from but a tiny few of literally thousands of letters I have received in my career as a bishop. They clearly reveal the diversity of responses my life, ministry, and writings have elicited over the years. If someone had told me years ago that I would create these enormous levels of both appreciation and hostility in my ordained life, I would have been dumbfounded, shocked, and probably deeply hurt. How did it happen? What created these twin emotions of praise and anger, of gratitude and fear? What forces pushed me, compelled me, or led me to play my particular role in the struggle to make the Christian Church respond to the issues of our century, and indeed to open new dimensions of spirituality to the citizens of this century? That is the story I seek to tell.

March 6, 1976, was a crisp, sunny late winter Saturday in Richmond, Virginia. It fell in the midst of a busy weekend in my life. On Friday, the fifth, I had indulged my passion for sports and secured, through my politically well connected cousin, tickets to the semifinals of the Atlantic Coast Conference basketball tournament, which was being played in Landover, Maryland. My alma mater, the University of North Carolina, was playing my daughters' alma mater, the University of Virginia, in one of the two semifinal games on that date. To be a Tar Heel while living in Virginia and serving St. Paul's Episcopal Church, the historic "Cathedral of the

Confederacy," in downtown Richmond made me about as popular as Kentucky Fried Chicken's Colonel Sanders at a chicken farm. The commitment of old-line Virginians to the Cavaliers of the University of Virginia was deep. Even my two older daughters would choose to go to the University of Virginia and to be grafted into the Virginia tradition. So I watched this particular game in a sea of Virginia alumni. One of them, sitting just behind me, was my friend Sidney Buford Scott, whose family had given Scott Stadium to the University of Virginia and Scott Lounge to the Virginia Theological Seminary. He was one of the few in those stands who was aware that I was at that moment a nominee for the position of bishop coadjutor of the Diocese of Newark in the state of New Jersey and the choice would be made the next morning. That night, as my university was being eliminated by his, he inquired about that process.

"Any chance you'll be elected?" he asked.

"Somewhere between slim and none." I replied. "I believe I'll get enough votes not to be embarrassed, but not nearly enough to be elected. It's not something in which I have any great investment."

That was an honest assessment. That was also the only time that evening that the Newark election entered my consciousness.

The Sunday of that same weekend was also to be a big day in my life. I was engaged in a series of dialogue sermons that were to last for three Sundays on the wide-ranging subject of medical ethics. This was my attempt to address theologically a concern that had been brought to the public's attention by the case of one Karen Quinlan, who had been in a coma for months, kept alive by mechanical devices. Her parents had petitioned the courts for permission to remove these artificial support systems and allow this young woman, their child, to die. The courts had refused this request, and a national debate had ensued.

St. Paul's Church in Richmond was only three blocks from the Medical College of Virginia. We had over eighty doctors in the congregation. Occasionally I used the sermon period for a dialogue on vital public issues. This allowed me to invite people who possessed an expertise that I did not to engage both me and the congregation in debate. Whether a hopelessly brain-dead young woman should be kept breathing by medical devices seemed tailor-made for such an approach. A young internist associated with the Medical College of Virginia and active at St. Paul's named Daniel Gregory had agreed to be the medical member for this dialogue. I was cast in the role of the Christian ethicist. Using the Karen Quinlan case as the point of entry, we hoped to extend the debate to the beginning of life, addressing abortion and birth control, as well as to the far side of life, where we hoped to examine active and passive euthanasia and physician-assisted suicide. There had been good response to these initiatives as the dialogue unfolded. These Sunday events were widely covered by the local press, radio, and television and had succeeded in what was always my primary agenda as a priest, namely, to move the theological debate out of the structures of sacred space and into the homes and professional lives of our people. To have a sermon discussed during the week in offices and hospitals, on golf courses, at bridge tables, and at cocktail parties was my measure of successful preaching. This dialogue had been particularly engaging, since Dan Gregory was a thoughtful and articulate representative of the medical community.

At about 11:45 on that Saturday morning I was in my office at the church with Dan Gregory and Lucy Boswell Negus working on the details of the Sunday presentation. Lucy Negus, our administrative assistant, was a particularly gifted and helpful member of my staff who had assisted me in every book I had written. She was an exquisite editor and a published poet who had just that previous fall transformed about two years of my sermons into free verse for publication by a local Richmond publisher in an elegant coffee-table book entitled *Christpower*. She was there to help Dan and me put the final literary touches on the dialogue so that it would stimulate the debate we desired. It was a comfortable, easy, exciting, fun morning with two people whose company I thoroughly enjoyed. That was the setting interrupted by the telephone message that would redirect the balance of my life.

"Hi, Jack! This is Joe Herring," was the cheery greeting of the interrupter. Joe Herring was a priest in the Diocese of Newark, serving as the rector of St. Stephen's Church in Millburn. I had not known him prior to my nomination. For reasons not altogether clear to me, he and another priest, Phillip Cato, had decided that I was the person they wanted to be elected bishop, and so they had become my unofficial "campaign managers." Indeed, they were far more eager to elect me than I was to be elected, but I was touched by their interest and did not object to their doing what I thought was tilting at windmills. Joe's voice on the other end of the line was now noticeably excited. His words poured out.

"We've just completed the sixth ballot," he stated. "You have been elected in the lay order since the fourth ballot. In the clergy order you are one vote short of an election. Herbert Donovan has just asked to have his name withdrawn from further consideration and has stated publicly his intention to vote for you on the seventh ballot. That means you will be elected, Jack!"

It was more than I could register at that moment. Herb Donovan was the rector of St. Luke's Church in Montclair, New Jersey. He was one of the three clergy in the Diocese of Newark I had known prior to the nomination, a friend since seminary days. My impression was that he was the clear clergy leader of the diocese. He was an elected member of the Standing Committee, the highest governing body in the diocese. He was also an elected deputy to the general convention, a prestige position for clergy, and he had been one of two official "in diocese" nominees for bishop coadjutor. He was supported by both the retired bishop of Newark, Leland Stark, and the diocesan bishop, George E. Rath. When I had gone to New Jersey to be interviewed by the nominating committee, I had stayed with Herb. He and his wife, Mary, were gracious hosts and lovely people. On those visits he and I had discussed the election. I knew almost nothing about the inner dynamics of diocesan life in Newark. He was obviously well informed, and I was convinced that he would be elected. He loved church politics and was destined to play a significant role in the life of our church in the following years.

With Herb so clearly the favorite in my mind, I had allowed myself to develop little emotional energy during the election process. That was easy for me to do, since I was happy and fulfilled in my life in Richmond. I had written four books and a fifth one was at that moment under contract and in preparation. My orbit of travel as an invited lecturer and guest preacher was expanding. I was eager to be not a bishop, but another Walter Russell Bowie or Theodore Parker Ferris, two men I greatly admired for their shaping of the church through their writing and preaching as priests. For that reason I had been reluctant for some time to enter the episcopal process.

In 1975 I had agreed to be nominated in the Diocese of Delaware, but had withdrawn the night before the election. I had not been able to develop any enthusiasm for that position and thought it unfair to the people in Delaware to allow them to consider and even to vote for so reluctant a candidate. Part of my willingness to enter the Newark process a year later came from my conviction that I had no chance of being elected in that diocese, and I thought it would cleanse me of the negativity that always surrounds the withdrawal of a publicly acknowledged nominee for the office of bishop.

Yet, as I put the phone down that Saturday morning, it seemed obvious that, whether I wanted it or not, this was now to be my destiny. I tried to call my wife, Joan, but there was no answer. I then shared the call with my two office companions, Lucy and Dan. How they reacted inside I do not know. I do know that this news put an end to our preparation for the next day. We talked about what it might mean. They were both kind and gentle. We kept reminding ourselves that it was still quite unofficial, but it didn't work. In less than twenty minutes the phone rang again.

"Jack, this is George Rath. I want to congratulate you on being elected bishop coadjutor. I look forward to working with you." There were other words that passed between us that morning, I am sure, but they were lost in the fog of what was for me a kind of swirling of emotions and a surprising sense of depression. I placed the phone down. I did not have to say a word to my good friends. They understood that this was the confirming call. I shook Dan's hand and embraced Lucy. They both departed quickly and left me alone to sort out my thoughts.

I then called my closest friend, John Elbridge Hines. He was the retired presiding bishop of our church. I visited with him weekly by phone and had spent a considerable portion each of the preceding three summers with him at his home in Highlands, North Carolina. A deep bond between us had developed. He now was the primary person with whom I wanted to discuss this matter. He answered the phone himself, not with "Hello," but with the familiar words, "John Hines."

"John, this is Jack," I stammered. "I've just been elected bishop coadjutor of the Diocese of Newark."

John was pleased. I had clearly become his protégé, and he knew the Diocese of Newark well. He did not pull his punches, however.

"Jack, that may be the most difficult position in the whole church. The urban areas of New Jersey—Newark, Paterson, Jersey City, Camden, and Trenton—are among the most desperate in America. The social fabric of those cities is all but dysfunctional. You will succeed two good bishops in Leland Stark and George Rath, and yet Leland's health was broken by that position and George survived by not engaging the issues. You are a strong person, Jack, but this position will test everything you have. You also need to recognize that the New York area is the communications center of the world. If you do this task well in that location, everyone will know it. If you stumble and fall, everyone will know that also. But I'm very pleased for you and for the church!"

It was a typical John Hines statement—straightforward, honest, blunt, and helpful.

A couple of hours later I had a call from John Maury Allin, the present presiding bishop. I was an elected member of the executive council, the highest governing body, of the national church, so I knew this man well. Jack Allin was a radically different person from John Hines. He had been chosen for this position as a strong reaction to John's fearless and aggressive leadership. He was far more an institutional-maintenance bishop than a prophet. His self-projection was that of a pastor to a divided and hurting church. I experienced him as a deeply partisan person with little or no capacity to embrace reality beyond his perception of it. He also had tremendous control needs. He had positioned himself as the chief voice opposing John Hines and had ridden that image to win the election as John's successor.

To say the least, we were not close. To his credit, in his first conversation with me as a bishop-elect, honesty prevailed over duplicity. With false laughter designed to cover his negativity, he said, "When I heard the news, I said, 'Dear God, the church does not need this!'" It was a bit startling, even for him. I did not help the situation with my response.

"That's interesting, Jack," I said, returning the false laughter. "That's exactly what I said when I heard you had been chosen presiding bishop."

I had, in fact, been part of the three-hour debate in the House of Deputies over whether to confirm his election. I voted against confirmation, but I did not prevail. The lines were clear. The same church that had elected him had now also elected me. It had to be a church big enough to embrace us both, but we would always march to the beat of different drummers. We represented two diametrically opposite approaches to ministry in the twentieth century. Jack would leave the primate's office in 1985. I would depart the episcopal office in 2000. Yet, though the content of the debate would shift, the points of view we each represented would contend through all of those years and would define the life and role of the church as we entered the third millennium. I clearly came to represent one polarity and Jack Allin the other in the church's struggle for relevance, life, and meaning. The dance we were to conduct, bound together by our love for the church, yet seeking to pull that church in very different directions, was the result of many, many factors over which neither of us had ultimate control. Both of us had deep Southern roots. He was born in Arkansas and I was a child of North Carolina. He was the bishop of Mississippi before moving to the national scene as the presiding bishop, a role that inevitably gave him an international stage. I was a Southern rector elected to be the bishop of Newark in the metropolitan New York area, but my life as an author also gave me both a national and even an international stage. Let me begin at the beginning.

# 2

# Beginnings in the
# Segregated South

❋

PERHAPS the very place in which I was born was an omen. St. Peter's Hospital was one of two hospitals related to the Episcopal Church in Charlotte, North Carolina. It served the white population. The other, Good Samaritan Hospital, some fifteen blocks away, served the black community. Neither was a first-rate facility, but Good Samaritan was woefully inadequate, with a death rate far above the norm. Racial prejudice was the only reason there were two Episcopal hospitals in this mid-sized Southern city. So it was that I began my journey on June 16, 1931, under the aegis of church-sponsored segregation and as the beneficiary of a presumed white superiority. It occurred neither to me nor to many others even to notice, much less to protest. It was reality. One does not debate reality.

St. Peter's Hospital had been founded by St. Peter's Episcopal Church, a red brick structure in the heart of Charlotte. It was a venerable church, built in a modified cruciform pattern, that seated perhaps five hundred worshipers. It possessed a quite impressive history and was the mother church of all the suburban Episcopal congregations in that city, of which there were five when I was born. Despite this outpouring of its life, St. Peter's retained for itself, at least until World War II, the status of being not just the largest, but the most socially prominent Episcopal church in town.

Strangely enough, St. Peter's Church, which would play a crucial role in my life, was not at the time of my birth the church to which my family belonged. It had been my father's church when he migrated to Charlotte and settled in a midtown house nearby. The family had later moved into the Dilworth section and transferred to one of those daughter churches,

8

the Church of the Holy Comforter, on South Boulevard. So it seemed fitting that I would be born in an Episcopal hospital and one identified with the church in which the Spong family's earliest days in this city were spent.

I was the second child and the first son of my mother and father. My sister, Betty Boyce, was two years and four months older. I was destined to have a brother, William Conwell, who would be born two years and four months after me. It was exact if, I gather, not fully planned spacing.

The year 1931 was not an easy one in which to enter the world. Herbert Hoover was still president. The Great Depression was two years old. Political unrest was rampant. The reform-minded governor of New York, Democrat Franklin Delano Roosevelt, was making his candidacy for the presidency known, which was creating political tension within the Democratic party. Al Smith, New York's former governor and the 1928 Democratic standard bearer against Hoover, believed that he had earned a second run at the top prize, since all his criticisms of Hoover had come true.

Governor Smith had lost to President Hoover by an overwhelming margin, and his Roman Catholicism, as well as his stand in favor of legalizing alcohol, had caused the Protestant fundamentalist southland of my birth to break its solid Democratic voting record for the first time since the days of Reconstruction following the Civil War. Racial and religious politics were the emotional issues of this region. The religious right of my adult life is the direct descendant of that evangelical, moralistic mentality that turned its back on the first Roman Catholic candidate for president.

I do not know how my parents voted in 1928, the first election in which my mother was old enough to vote. It was only the second presidential election in which any woman in America had been allowed to vote. I do know that following what was called the "Hoover Depression" few people admitted to having been a supporter of Hoover. I also know that the Democrat, Roosevelt, when he gained the presidency, had the intense loyalty of my parents. "Happy Days Are Here Again" was their theme song as the nation slowly emerged out of hard times.

My father did not lose his job during the depression. He did, however, have his salary reduced on two or three occasions. We were, by the standards of the day, a middle-class family. We lived in a large house on three and a half acres outside Charlotte. We had two cars, a 1932 Chevrolet used by my mother and a company-owned Ford supplied to my father annually as a perk of his traveling job.

How we happened to be a family in Charlotte, North Carolina, is one of those fateful accidents that occur in all of life. So far as we are able to reconstruct the history, my mother's family had lived there for generations. In 1760 Aaron Wilson left Scotland to come to Mecklinburg County, in which Charlotte was the major city. Farming and working in the textile industry in the Piedmont section of the Carolinas were the principal occupations attracting immigrants over the years. The Wilsons brought with them a fierce Calvinistic Presbyterian religion, both fundamentalistic and repressive. The Griffith part of my mother's family came from Wales, and the two families intermarried over several generations. My mother was a Griffith, but most of her relatives were Wilsons.

On my father's side, the Spongs originated in the East Anglia section of England in the county of Norfolk, where they farmed the spongy bottomland from which the name derived. The family spread from Norfolk to Kent, but never became large. Some member of this family had been knighted by the king of England at a time before we have any records, and so we possess and pass on to each generation an official coat of arms. The Latin slogan under the seal reads *Vox emissa,* which translates "The voice going forth," but which might equally well be read as "Loud-mouthed." There were clergy in that family history,[1] as well as politicians and salesmen. The one thing all three professions have in common is that their members talk for a living.

Somewhere in the early 1800s my great-great-grandfather, the firstborn son of John Spong and Letitia Halfhead, set off to seek his fortune in the new world. Also named John, he left his native England from Southampton for the dangerous voyage across the Atlantic to the "new world." The American Revolution had occurred some thirty-five to forty years earlier, and opportunity knocked for the sons of English farming families when the crops had bad years. Many of them in this new land retained their connection with the mother country by remaining Anglicans. Through the *Book of Common Prayer* and the familiar, mostly Victorian, hymns of the Church of England, the Episcopal Church in America provided them with a touch of identification with their ancestral home. The place of landing for this first Spong immigrant appears to have been the port of Mobile, Alabama, and over the next two generations members of the family migrated northward to the state capital of Montgomery. At some point in this migration a member of the Spong family, probably the first namesake immigrant, married a member of the Shelby family, who have been among Alabama's leading citizens and politicians for generations. That Shelby name was important to the

Spong family, so it was given to two of the seven children in my grandfather's family. My father was one of them.

This family also took on the prejudices and the cause of the South. There were several brothers in my grandfather's family. Born in 1860, my grandfather, Augustus Maye Spong, was not old enough to fight on the side of the South in the Civil War. According to family stories, only he and one of his older brothers, John Rowen Spong, survived that war. Stories of the slaughter at Gettysburg reverberated through family folklore.

After the war, John Rowan moved to New York and became an Episcopal priest. Augustus Maye stayed in Alabama and became a salesman and the Southern representative of a coffee and tea company in Boston, Massachusetts. In 1899 with his wife, Jimmie Marie Dillehay, and their six children, Augustus Marian, Laura Shelby, John Shelby, William Belser, Louise Bibb, and Jean Douglas, he left Montgomery for Atlanta. A year later, he packed up his family once again and headed for Charlotte. In Charlotte a seventh child, Ernest Maye Spong, was born in 1900. They all joined St. Peter's Church shortly thereafter.

My father was now eleven years old. Of his siblings, he was closest to his nearest younger brother, William Belser. They were good athletes and played semiprofessional baseball together. They even dreamed of making it to the major leagues. They never did. They also excelled at playing pool. All sports seemed to fascinate these two boys—football, baseball, basketball, and even boxing. They also enjoyed competing in checkers, dominoes, and card games, especially bridge.

The first and third sons of my grandfather became newspaper people, one in Richmond and the other in Portsmouth. So my grandfather groomed his second son, Shelby, to take his job selling coffee and tea across the South. When my grandfather died in 1918, a victim of the influenza epidemic that followed World War I, my father inherited not only his job, but primary responsibility for the care of his mother. When his mother died in 1921, my father, acting as the head of the family that remained in Charlotte, built a house with rooms in it for him, but primarily intended for his youngest brother, Ernest, who had just married a bubbly woman named Catherine. She would assume the role of "woman of the house." In my father's mind a woman's role was clear. She was to cook, clean, wash, iron, and sew. The man was to earn the living, and the expectation was that he would be treated as a king in his own home. So long as either his mother or his sister-in-law provided the necessary female care, my father appeared content not to be married. But when first the death of his mother and then Catherine's pregnancy, which produced twins, took away his primary female caregivers, he decided, at the age of thirty-eight, that perhaps the time had come to form his own family.

A young man named John Hunter Griffith, Jr., was working for him. Johnny, as he was called, had a mother who ran a boardinghouse about ten blocks from where my father lived. So Johnny invited his boss to dinner. There he met the twenty-year-old "little sister" of Johnny Griffith named Doolie Boyce. During their brief courtship, which lasted less than a year, only one story emerged that casts light upon my father. He was dining as a guest of his fiancée's family at that boardinghouse table on one occasion when the conversation took a rather negative, anti-Semitic turn. After listening to the openly expressed prejudice for a few moments, my father stopped the conversation cold by saying, "Didn't you folks know that I'm Jewish? My original name was Spongberg, but we shortened it to Spong." It brought the conversation to a halt. To my knowledge, not an ounce of Jewish blood flowed in his veins, but a sense of decency, at least on this issue, did. I have always been proud of that episode and encouraged my mother to tell it to me on several occasions.

The two of them were married by the pastor of Chalmers Memorial Associate Reformed Presbyterian Church in the family home at 8:30 A.M. on April 18, 1928. After a wedding trip, the newlyweds settled into what was to become my home on Park Road in Charlotte, a mile or so beyond the city limits. The land on which the house stood was subdivided, and Ernest and his wife, Catherine, built a home for themselves on the new lot. So I would grow up next door to relatives, and those twins, whose birth seemed to force my father into holy matrimony, would be my admired older playmates. The two families would always be close.

The family's religious fervor, which had sent my father's Uncle John Rowan Spong into the priesthood, had clearly faded in my father by the time he arrived at his adult years. I know of nothing specific that might either explain or have caused that. I can only make a judgment based on observed behavior. He had each of his children baptized at the Church of the Holy Comforter by a tall austere Episcopal rector named Robert Bruce Owens, a Scotsman with distinct evangelical leanings, and we were taken regularly to Sunday school. But his own church attendance was limited to Christmas and/or Easter and then only under duress. He would sing the hymns, a custom derived from his boyhood choir days at St. Peter's, but he participated in little else in the service and complained bitterly when he was asked to donate a case of coffee to the church bazaar. It was clear to me that he had little use for the church.

Yet, strange as it might seem, I never saw him retire for the night without kneeling at his bed to pray. He never talked with me about that prayer time or its meaning to him, and though I did not experience him as a religious man, that symbol of kneeling made a powerful impression on me. In my world a religious man would not do the things my father did. He drank whiskey, mostly bourbon, he used profanity with enthusiasm, he played poker for money, and on the church's every-member canvass Sunday, he pretended not to be at home when the canvasser called so that he would not be asked to pledge. I learned that when he dropped us off at Sunday school, he sometimes went to his private Elks Club to gamble at slot machines and cards. I even prevailed on him once in a while to let me skip Sunday school and go with him. The whirl of the cylinders on the slots and the hope of hitting a jackpot were exciting to me. It also felt like something a man would do. There was an agreed upon conspiracy of silence between my father and me about these adventures, and my mother was never the wiser for it.

My mother's religious viewpoint was quite different. Both the Scottish stock through her mother and Welsh stock through her father fed an evangelical nonconformist piety. The religion of her household was a brand of rigorous fundamentalist Calvinism. Her family members were part of a very strict splinter Presbyterian Church that was known for its intense moralistic code. She joined the Episcopal Church only after her marriage because she thought Dad might attend if she were confirmed and went with him. It was, in her mind, a woman's duty. It did not work, however, and she wound up going alone. But the religion of our home was quite clearly the religion of my Presbyterian mother. Sunday was called the "Sabbath," and one did not work or cause others to work on that day. The Lord's name was never to be taken in vain, not even by saying "My goodness," for that was a clear reference to God, and the phrase "For crying out loud" was said to be a direct reference to the cross. I can recall having my mouth washed out with soap for saying "gosh" and "darn." Alcohol was a proper beverage only for the devil. Cards and gambling were bad to their core, and she was convinced children were born evil. It was therefore the duty of the parent to tame them, to break their spirit. Corporal punishment was the discipline of choice.

God, as I was introduced to this deity through my mother, was very much like a punishing parent, male to be sure. This God had heaven as a place of reward and hell as the place of punishment, and I was taught to fear him.

No hymns were allowed to be sung in my mother's church, because hymns were composed of human words. Only the words of God were thought to be appropriate for worship, so they sang the 150 Psalms set to music. The Sabbath day, set aside by God himself, was grim indeed, at least as grim as John Calvin must have been. So frequently was Calvin mentioned that I thought he might have been the fourth person of the Holy Trinity. On the "Sabbath" I had to comply with my mother's value system by keeping on my Sunday clothes. I could not play marbles, go to a baseball game, or even read the comics. We visited relatives on Sundays, very boring relatives, I might add. I was encouraged to spend a part of that day reading the Bible, but biblical words and phrases like "thinketh" and "believest thou this," combined with those tissue-thin pages that my little fingers could not turn easily, made Bible reading a chore. I was also fearful that I might accidentally tear one of those sacred pages and thus have the wrath of God descend upon me. I hated Sundays.

Yet to be fair to my mother's religious viewpoint, she did represent the moderate or liberal wing of her family's rigorous fundamentalist background. My mother's uncle was the Reverend Eli Griffith, once the pastor of Chalmers Memorial Associate Reformed Presbyterian Church, where the family attended. His fundamentalistic fervor was so intense and his zealous hostility so uncomfortable that it created a split in the church, and his own brother, John Hunter Griffith, Sr., my grandfather, actually sided with those who opposed him. My mother, encouraged by this family split, conspired with her cousins, the daughters of this same preacher, to get together, roll up the rug, and dance to recorded music on their primitive Victrola of such popular songs as "Red Lips Kiss My Blues Away" or "Side by Side." So there was some flexibility and distancing from religious excesses in her attitude.

Another illustration was that the family Bible sat on the coffee table in the living room in clear view of everyone, yet it was seldom read and indeed was hardly ever opened except to insert family data like births, baptisms, confirmations, marriages, or the burials of various relatives. It was, however, treated with awe and respect, as I discovered one day when I placed my Coca Cola on top of the Holy Book. The things I learned about the Bible in my early life, however, came from my Episcopal Sunday school, not my family.

Sunday school appealed to me for reasons I cannot actually state. Perhaps it was the perfect-attendance pin and the annual bars that I so eagerly sought for their status appeal. Perhaps it was holding the American flag for the pledge of allegiance in front of the assembly that captured me. Patriotism and religion were two sides of the same coin in my mind. Perhaps it was Lent, with its mite boxes, or the Lenten contests our church would have, or the romantic discipline of giving up candy, ice cream, or whatever my particular Lenten vow was for that year. Perhaps it was the gentle love of my church-school kindergarten teacher, a woman named Estelle Darrow. I do not really know wherein its attraction lay, but I do know that I looked forward to it on most Sundays. As a matter of fact, that willingness made things easier, since I do not recall that I was given any choice in the matter.

I am certain I began to gain in Sunday school not only a knowledge of, but also a love for, the biblical stories. Yet I cannot bring to mind any specific learning experience involving any biblical content. My knowledge of the Bible was helped perhaps by the fact that it permeated the culture. I also must have been affected by those times I went to church, for I remember while being alone at home actually playing church games. My moments of "Let's Pretend" included sermons I preached with much fervor, hymns I sang, prayers I offered, and communion elements I gave out. I do not remember what I used for wine. I am confident the real thing was not available to me. Since at that time I had never received communion, I am not sure I even knew that wine was the appropriate beverage.

When I try now to recall specific moments in my Sunday-school life, only two come to mind. I recall being slapped for misbehavior by my fourth-grade teacher. I do not remember what my misbehavior was; I only remember the shock and the embarrassment of her slap. I do not even remember that teacher's name, but I thought of her as a pretty young woman, and somehow that made her hostile action more distressing. Perhaps I had already equated attractiveness with niceness.

The other episode occurred in the fifth grade. My teacher was Herbert Darrow, Estelle's husband, and a man of some girth with a booming singing voice. The subject matter for that fifth-grade year was the Ten Commandments. It was pretty tedious going through those Sundays in which we dealt with idols, graven images, the sacred name of God, and the Sabbath day observance. Then we journeyed through the honoring of our parents and the prohibition against murder, by which time more than half of the year had elapsed. Next, to my surprise and with no explanation whatsoever, we leaped over commandment number seven and started dealing with number eight and the meaning of stealing.

I was a precocious but uninformed lad, and so I raised my hand. "But Mr. Darrow," I protested, "we skipped the seventh commandment. What does it mean to commit adultery?" I had not the slightest idea that this would prove to be an embarrassing or difficult question, but it soon became obvious that my query had caused Mr. Darrow great distress. He sputtered, looked away, mopped his brow, and then blurted out, "You'll learn about that when you get older." What he communicated to me was that whatever adultery was, it was clearly the worst of all sins. That, too, was part of the code of the South. I would learn that Southerners committed adultery as much as anyone else, but they did not seem to enjoy it. Sex was something that was not to be enjoyed. It was a kind of duty of married life and a prohibition outside of it. I had disturbed that uneasy repression.

This was also an all-white church, which meant that neither sex nor race was allowed to be discussed. These realities would come together, however, in the racist jargon used in the social order as the reductio ad absurdum of all race conversations, at least as I began to hear those conversations in my teenage years, "Do you want your sister or daughter to marry a Negro?" The answer was assumed to be so obviously "no" that the argument for justice or equal opportunity was supposed to be stopped in its tracks.

I did not understand at that time this strange intersection between sexual attraction and racial fear. I was not then aware of how frequently in the days of both slavery and segregation in the South black women had been sexually violated by white men. That is why there are so many shades of black people in the United States to this day. Nor did I understand that the emotional castration of black men was a prerequisite to this violent sexual behavior. So black men were whipped, physically castrated, or even hanged for looking at a white woman in a way that might express desire, and keeping black people uneducated, dependent, servile, and powerless was necessary to enable this sexual pattern to continue to exist. It also meant that the deepest subliminal racial fear that white males had was that if black men ever got real power and escaped the intimidation of fear, they might well do to white women the same thing that white men had done to black women for generations.

There was also in this Southern white male shibboleth the not so subtle implication and dread that if white women ever had a choice, they might actually choose the sexually virile black male over the sexually sedate white male. This was an expression of what I would later call the "Othello factor." But the fact remains that I did not at that time know any more about sex than I knew about race or segregation. I was simply picking up the vibrations of a way of life that even then was doomed, although its adherents did not yet know it. Racism was and is an omnipresent irrational force. So were the sexual fears that were deeply entwined with that racism. So deep were these fears that even my fifth-grade Sunday-school teacher felt he had to skip over the commandment on adultery. It is also a fact that when that class talked about murder, neither the dehumanization of blacks nor the activity of lynching ever came up. Nor did we talk about how we stole the labor of the black people by conspiring to keep wages at rock bottom when we discussed the prohibition about stealing. Never were sex and race allowed to meet in a religious setting.

In my overtly pious home, racism was an operative assumption. I do not believe anyone could have been raised in that society without being a racist. We would, however, never have pled guilty to that charge. In my home we had "colored" help in the house and in the yard, but black people were not allowed to enter our house by the front door. Public parks and the public library were available only to white taxpayers. Drinking fountains and public toilets were clearly marked "white" and "colored." No black people ate in public restaurants, slept in public hotels, or used the rest rooms of commercial gas stations. In department stores no black woman could try on a dress before purchasing it. The economic system kept many of these things from being too obvious a problem, however, since the standard wage of five dollars a week for full-time domestic help did not lend itself to the ability to eat out, travel far, or wear "store bought" clothes. It was a cruel system, and I was one of the unknowing beneficiaries of it. Once again, I profited from this evil, though at that point in my life I remained blissfully ignorant of it.

The first dawning on my consciousness that there might be something out of sync about the way of life I accepted as normal occurred when I was no more than three or four. Yet it settled into my memory bank and over the years acted like a pebble in my shoe. For me it marked the first moment of self-actualization, the first step out of my Southern upbringing.

A decorative brick wall was being constructed on the side of our home. Two black men whom I presumed to have been bricklayers were employed to assist my father in the construction. One of them was an older man whose heavy head of hair had turned gray. The other was a much younger man, perhaps in his late twenties. My father had told me about this project and that he would need my help, and I had anticipated the day we would get the new brick wall with excitement. During the day, I stirred cement, carried bricks, got in the way, and asked hundreds of questions, all of which started with "How come?" For the two bricklayers I must have been a chore indeed.

My parents had drilled into me their understanding of Southern manners. The first rule in that Southern code was that a child never responded to his or her elders without saying "ma'am" to a woman or "sir" to a man. "Yes sir," "no sir," "yes ma'am," "no ma'am" were essential ingredients of politeness. If I, as a child, were ever to say either a simple "yes" or a simple "no" to my parents, they would respond "yes what?" or "no what?" Their voices would have that kind of animation that convinced me to blurt out the appropriate "sir" or "ma'am" quickly for fear of the consequences. I had learned this lesson well, probably at some cost to my personal comfort.

On this particular Saturday morning, however, the elderly black man had asked me a question, and I had responded just as I had been taught with a proper "yes sir" or "no sir," whichever was appropriate. My father stopped what he was doing and took me forcibly into the house, where he lectured me sternly on the fact that "you do not say 'sir' to a Negro." I was crushed. I did not understand why doing what I had been taught to do was a cause for discipline. There must be something different, I concluded, about my elders if they were black. The rules somehow did not apply to them. There were unstated assumptions in the sacred code of Southern etiquette, and I had clearly violated one of them. I remember feeling deeply conflicted over this episode for days or even weeks. The fact that I can still recall it vividly at this moment indicates its even deeper, indelible quality. I tried to process my father's hostility internally, but it made no real sense to me. I felt wronged, and although I could not articulate it at the time, I was certain that my father had been unfair. I learned that day that my father was not always right. That does not seem like a revolutionary thought today. Human fallibility is a universal assumption, but for me, as a three- or four-year-old boy, to decide in a deep and significant way that my father was wrong, morally wrong, in what he had done opened doors in me to a radical new self-consciousness that would never go away.

I was also told that I must not play with black children. I did not understand why. There were no black athletes in my childhood. The Jackie Robinsons, Hank Aarons, Wilt Chamberlains, Bill Russells, and Michael Jordans were not yet icons of the young.

I went to segregated schools all my life. It did not occur to me to wonder why there were no black children in my school. Perhaps black children did not have to go to school, I might have reasoned with some envy. The question, however, simply never arose. An all-white school was just the way it was for me.

A partial answer to this unasked question, however, did come to me in the fifth grade in a strange manner. I was then ten years old, and through some process I was chosen to be one of four students who would visit another school in our city for a special assembly program. Perhaps that invitation had something to do with the war. Patriotism is a mighty force, and World War II had begun for America a little before this time. The invitation did not appear to be reciprocal. No one came from that other school to visit us. Perhaps this other school had simply invited my school to send four representatives to their program and our principal, in an act that must have required some courage in that day, decided to accept.

Whatever the circumstances, the four of us were driven by one of our teachers to a school in another section of Charlotte. To my utter amazement the place was filled with black children. I had never before in my life seen so many black children in one place. The teachers and the principal were also black. I had never before seen black adults in any role outside of menial labor or domestic service. One of the black female teachers drove a car. I had never seen a black woman driving a car. It was as if my world expanded in quantum leaps on that day. At least my view of reality was opened to new possibilities. I responded to this experience by simply keeping my eyes open and my mouth shut.

The assembly program that morning in that strange school was equally expansive. These black children also pledged allegiance to the flag of our country, I discovered, and they also said the same Lord's Prayer. That was quite legal in 1942 in North Carolina, where the public schools were opened each day with prayer and a Bible story. I was pleased and proud that I could join in both of these familiar activities. I even felt a growing sense of belonging. Then someone announced that we would stand to sing "our national anthem." Like a toy soldier I rose, placed my small hand over my heart and stood ready to sing, "O, say, can you see . . ." To my amazement that was not "our national anthem." Instead, the assembly rose and without any prompting sang from memory the words to what I discovered was called the black national anthem, "Lift every voice and sing till heaven's arches ring, ring with the harmony of liberty." It was the first time I had ever heard the words that gave expression to the history of a painful slavery, the memory of the master's lash, and the impact of the blood of the black martyrs. I was still invested with the myth of slavery as a benign system that had been a great benefit for Africans. "Lift Every Voice and Sing" was also a song of hope that a new day would dawn—a day of freedom and justice. I was not aware that freedom and justice were not equally available in the black community. But years later when I next heard an assembly of black people sing "Lift Every Voice and Sing," the memories of that day in 1942 came tumbling back into my mind in vivid pictures.

I recall only one other episode that tempered my racial upbringing. It had to do with the one sport in which black men were allowed to compete on an equal basis—boxing. Indeed, this sport had all kinds of historical racial overtones; the heavyweight champion Jim Jeffries, in a previous generation, had been described as "the great white hope."

However, in my childhood the big hero was a young heavyweight from Detroit, Joseph Louis Barrow, who fought under the ring name of Joe Louis. With his nickname, the "Brown Bomber," he had broken upon the world scene like a shooting star, winning the world title from Jimmy Braddock in June 1937. On his rise to that title fight, he had been defeated only once. On June 19, 1936, he was knocked out in the twelfth round by a German heavyweight named Max Schmeling. It had been a bruising battle until the knockout occurred. When Louis won the world heavyweight title, there was a desire on his and his handlers' part to remove that single defeat from his record in a rematch with Schmeling.

This boxing match, however, got caught up in the drama of international politics and became entangled with the master-race theories of Adolf Hitler. Schmeling was perceived to be carrying the banner for Nazi Germany and white superiority. He was a specimen of that Aryan master-race manhood about which Hitler spoke so frequently. The propaganda of Joseph Goebbels was at work throughout the world proclaiming it to be the destiny of Aryan civilization to rule the human race. Joe Louis was an obscure poor black man until he captured the heavyweight crown, but he was also an American. The advance publicity must have been sensational. If it were not, then my father's enthusiasm for boxing made it seem to me like this was the match of the century.

We anticipated the match for weeks in our household. On June 22, 1938, the members of my family, with great expectations, gathered around the large cabinet radio in our living room with all of its mysterious knobs to listen to the blow-by-blow description from ringside. It was a short but spectacular evening. Schmeling hardly landed a punch. The "Brown Bomber" destroyed the representative of Aryan manhood in just over two minutes of the first round. White America was proud of a black fighter. That was a new thing. Patriotism had won out over prejudice, at least for the moment. But it would not last.

Another white hope, but this time an American of Irish descent named Billy Conn, emerged even before the war was over to carry the banner of white superiority against Joe Louis in two memorable bouts. The first fight occurred in June 1941, just before the United States was actively at war. In this bout Conn, even though well ahead on points, miscalculated his opponent's weakness and in the closing rounds elected to slug it out with Louis in search of a knockout. It did not work, and Conn was himself knocked out in the thirteenth round. However, Conn had indicated that a skillful white boxer could neutralize the power of the Brown Bomber, and so the great rematch, which came after the war was over, was said to be certain to put the championship belt around Conn's waist. Those racist dreams died in June 1946 when Louis, winning just about every round, knocked out his challenger in the eighth round.

That regression into a racist mentality, however, could not destroy my memory of that transcendent moment in 1938 when even my father put aside his racism in favor of his patriotism to cheer a black American to victory over a white German. The Louis-Schmeling fight became one more episode in a subconscious filing system that told me that something was wrong with the values I was learning and that, finally, they could not be my values. That was not easy in a world where even the values of my church seemed to affirm the values of my racist and sexuality-denying society.

1. There is a window in a parish church near the cathedral in Rochester, United Kingdom, that was given in memory of the Reverend John Spong.

# 3
# *"The Man of the House":*
# *Shaping Memories*

✳

I N THOSE early years of my life, nothing seemed unusual in our family. We did not stand out from the norm in any noteworthy way. We appeared, I assume, to be a relatively healthy unit of a father, mother, older sister, and younger brother, with me in the middle. We had a dog, a cat, and an ample number of friends. The children in our family seemed to get along relatively well. I do not recall any sibling rivalry, at least with my older sister. As a little boy I only recall adoring her and thinking myself ever so fortunate when she would play with me, no matter what it was I had to play. I would outgrow that of course, especially when it became obvious to me that her baseball skills, both in throwing and batting, were lacking. My sense of her adequacy as an all-knowing older sibling was also compromised by her apparent desire to make me into a well-mannered eater of my food. To her, I gather, my table manners resembled those of a caveman. I gnawed on the bones of my pork chops, my fingers worked better than my fork on a variety of dishes, and apparently I made incredible noises while chewing celery. So I became her project; she was determined to teach me proper eating procedures. This, of course, only heightened my refusal to be couth at the table. After all, she was only my sister.

My greatest love as a child was baseball. It was not the major leagues that attracted my attention. I was only vaguely aware they existed. It was the Charlotte Hornets, a farm team of the Washington Senators, who played in the class B Piedmont League, who were the object of my affection. To go to Griffith Park, the home of the Hornets named for the owner, Calvin Griffith, was the sum total of bliss in my childhood. The Hornets were bigger than life to me. I listened to the radio broadcasts of every game I could. (Television did not yet exist.) I even convinced myself that if I dried the supper dishes without protest, which was my assigned duty, God would let the Hornets win. I kept massive scrapbooks of newspaper clippings of these heroes in action. I yearned for their autographs and always took my glove to the park in the hope of catching a foul ball. I never did. At that rather inelegant park I watched future big leaguers like Early Wynn, Jimmy Bloodworth, Al Evans, Jake Early, and Roberto Ortiz play, along with my all-time sentimental favorite, a Cuban center fielder who never made it big named Bobby Estallela. Despite my devotion to and interest in baseball, I was not myself a particularly good athlete. I think I peaked athletically at nine years of age when I made a hand-picked team of fourth-grade all stars who played and defeated a fifth-grade class team. I was sure the scouts were in the stands watching.

When football season came, the sentiments and loyalty of our household shifted from the Hornets to the Tar Heels of the University of North Carolina.

In my father's generation, a university degree was not a requirement for most jobs. On-the-job training still opened doors to success. My mother suffered from the sexism rampant in our society. She was pulled from school six weeks into her ninth-grade year to help support the family after the failure of one of my grandfather's entrepreneurial schemes that had to do with a cotton gin. The decision to take her out instead of her older brother, Johnny, was predicated on the "fact" that it was a waste of time to educate a girl. All that girls needed to learn were domestic chores, which their mothers could teach them better than any school. So into a music store my mother went, selling sheet music. Her ability to play that music on the piano added to her employability. She turned her salary over to her father and was allowed to keep only a few dollars a week for her personal use. It was a lesson in stereotyping that became quite vivid to me as life unfolded.

In some ways this behavior was replicated in my sister's life. Betty received no encouragement from my mother to go to a university since she was a girl. That may have been predicated on economic realities as much as sexism, but sexism was surely present. She was given instead a year at a business school to prepare her to enter the workforce as a secretary. Being a secretary, nurse, or schoolteacher represented the normal limits of female job opportunities in that day. Although being a secretary meant a young woman had a career, it had a distinct ceiling. Yet that seemed fair to me at the time. Once

again, it just was the way things were. It did not affect me as a male, so it was
not a big deal. Just as with cultural racism, I profited from cultural sexism.

But that kind of routine family life was destined not to last. The critical turn in our family history came in 1939, when I was but eight years
old. It was caused not by the beginning of World War II, even though
that is the thing most people associate with that year. The tragedy that
engulfed my family was far more personal than a European war and
involved the heightening of what had perhaps been a longtime unrecog-
nized problem. Increasingly it became apparent that my father was an
alcoholic.

He was not a constant drinker, but rather an episodic one. He would go
for five or six months in a perfectly normal fashion without a drop of alcohol. Then with no apparent warning he would start drinking, and once he
started, there was no stopping him. We would watch the long, intense, and
costly downhill spiral before he recovered, usually by means of hospitalization. To my knowledge he never sought counseling for this sickness or even
the help of Alcoholics Anonymous. The effect on our family emotionally
and financially was devastating. His behavior, or the constant fear of it, was
like a dark cloud that was always part of our lives. We spent the normal times
of his life wondering when the next dreadful episode would occur. Alcohol
brought with it a personality change in my father. The kind and generous
man I knew all but disappeared, and in his place appeared a man who denigrated me constantly. "You can't do anything right" is a theme I still can hear
him saying to me, even in my sleep.

His attitude toward my mother was scary. When sober, he was a loving if
patriarchal husband, but when he was drinking, she became his enemy, the
object of his scorn and wrath. I never saw him strike her, but I did see him
threaten her with physical harm. My most difficult moment was when he
held her over the stairwell, threatening to throw her down. It was accompanied by her screams and tears and by my horror. He was also physically
incompetent when under the influence of alcohol. I recall trying to pick him
up at the bottom of the stairs, which he had been unable to navigate. To see
this large man tumble down the flight of stairs and lie lifeless at the bottom
was a vision never to be forgotten.

His sickness also reduced our family's economic situation below the
level of security. He missed lots of time from his job, but it never appeared
to be in jeopardy. He had loyal salesmen working for him and loyal customers who must have been touched by his sober charm, so they continued

to do business with him even if he did not service them at some times quite as well as others.

The style of life his job represented was also in transition. The coffee and tea he sold depended on the existence of the corner grocer. The age of supermarkets and chain stores, with their house brands and the emergence of conglomerates—like Procter and Gamble, Heinz, Campbell Soup Company, and General Foods—that bought up the brand names of little, independent companies, was just beginning. My father's constant anger at and his refusal to allow my mother to shop at the new local supermarket was only the first sign of the collapse of the firm for which he and his father had worked.

Alcoholism was followed in a couple of years by the diagnosis of heart disease. After the attack on Pearl Harbor launched our nation into World War II in December of 1941, all families were encouraged to plant a victory garden to grow food. It was the patriotic thing to do. For those who had never had a garden, it was an enormous physical effort. My father, who weighed more than 220 pounds and never got any exercise, was not ready for the level of physical exertion that this project required. His first heart attack occurred as a result of planting that victory garden, but excessive drinking, an ample high-fat diet, and heavy smoking had taken their toll on his obese body. He deteriorated slowly, but surely. His drinking did not abate. His inability to work and the hospital and doctors' bills sent the whole family into financial depression. None of us children could quite understand the seriousness of the sickness or of the economic distress. We were impacted, however, by the fact that our home was reordered so that the living room became his bedroom since he could no longer climb the stairs. We also noticed that visits from his siblings increased.

Sister Laurie came from Pennsylvania in early spring 1943 and decided that I should be enrolled in the boys' choir at St. Peter's Church, in which my father had once sung. She was a powerful, manipulative woman, and before I quite knew what had happened, I found myself downtown being auditioned and accepted by choirmaster William Wall Whiddit. After a very short period of time, I decided to be confirmed at St. Peter's in April 1943. I learned at choir rehearsal on Wednesday that the bishop was coming on Sunday. The rector, an old priest named Willis Gaylord Clark, decided that if I attended a single class on Saturday morning following choir practice, I could be confirmed the next day. It was shoddy preparation that would have embarrassed me as a priest years later, but it did not embarrass me then. The one class amounted only to a definition of the word "confirm," but I had the distinct sense, in this decision, that I was moving out of my family's orbit and doing a dramatic and independent thing, yet I was in fact returning to my father's childhood church.

Little did I recognize that this decision would prove to be the single most determinative moment on which the story of my life would turn. In William Wall Whiddit, a stately old man with a head of snow-white hair, I found a caring male adult figure who took enormous interest in each of "his choir-boys." In this choir we were "paid" singers. We got fifty cents a month plus bus fare to and from rehearsals on Wednesdays and Saturdays. We sang every Sunday, except in July and August, and frequently did concerts and weddings, for which we received as much as a dollar. It was usually a silver dollar. It was also the first time that I had earned anything that was considered a reward for my contribution.

I will never forget the first two hymns I learned in that choir at my first Wednesday rehearsal. They were "Fight the Good Fight," to a tune that disappeared in the 1943 revision of the Episcopal hymnal, and "Awake My Soul, Stretch Every Nerve." A piece from the anthem "Stabat Mater," by G. Rossini, which we sang with the adult choir, was also my favorite. What this experience did for me emotionally was to give me a community other than my family to which I developed a deep sense of belonging.

When fall 1943 neared, it was apparent that Dad's health was fragile. My Uncle Ernest drove up from Columbia, South Carolina, for a long visit that included consultations with the doctors. I understand, in retrospect, that he was told that Dad's heart was enlarged to twice its normal size and that it was only a matter of days.

Sister Jean came from Florida to assist Mother with the home nursing duty. She was present on the night he died. The announcement of his death was made in an eerie scream that my mother uttered for Jean early in the morning of September 15. The reality of his death produced in me some strange psychological feelings.

I had bargained with God many times in my life. I do not know where this intimate God association came from, but I never doubted its reality in those early years. The bargain was straightforward. "If I do this for you, God, you will do this for me," was my convincing formula. In my attempt to make up for my inadequate confirmation preparation since I was now a member of the choir, I had decided that I must memorize the catechism found in the *Book of Common Prayer* in something called the Offices of Instruction. I said the prayers in the Offices of Instruction seven times each night. Why seven? I do not know. They also had to be said perfectly. If I got anything confused or stumbled over any word, I had to start all over from the beginning. My magic did not work if I made a mistake, or so I assumed. My bargain with God was that this formula faithfully executed each night, no matter how sleepy I was, would keep my father alive. That in itself, I recognize in retrospect, demonstrated that I was cognizant of how desperately ill he was.

I had been somewhere the night before his death that kept me out rather late. When I came in I went straight to bed. I did not go into the living room to tell him goodnight. My rationale was that he was already asleep. I also did not say my prayers. That was the first thing that came to my mind when I heard that scream before dawn had broken. I had failed God, and God had exacted the penalty! I hoped the scream did not mean what I feared. I hoped I would have a second chance. I was sure that my failure to do my prayers was responsible for his death. Emotions are strange in a young life confronting the death of a parent, especially a parent with whom the child has a conflicted and difficult relationship.

It felt like I had never pleased my father. I was quite sure that in his eyes I was at that time and was destined always to be a major disappointment. Both his drinking and his alcohol-related actions were repellent to me. I wanted some distance between us, to be free of what felt like oppressive behavior. I was seeking to establish my own identity, to resist his definition of me and his power over me. It was highly oedipal. I also saw myself as my mother's protector, usurping his role, if you will, and salving my conscience by keeping him alive with my prayers. But he had died, and I was told I had to play an adult role.

Boys in rebellion against their fathers do not really want to win. However, in the face of his death, I pulled myself to the fullest stature of manhood that I could muster and played the role of grieving son in a stoical manner. My newly acquired adult status was, however, then dealt a significant blow when my mother decided that both my brother and I were "too young" to attend the funeral, which was to be held in our home. So we were farmed out to neighbors to play and to have lunch while the funeral went on, and thus were forced to miss that essential bit of closure. I resented my demotion greatly. He was buried in Elmwood Cemetery, very near his first home in Charlotte. He had completed that full circle.

As All Saints' Day (November 1) approached in the 1943 church year, the boys' choir at St. Peter's began to practice T. Tertius Noble's anthem "Souls of the Righteous in the Hand of God." This anthem provided the opportunity for me to begin to deal with my father's death with the only person who seemed to understand, my choirmaster. So one Saturday in October I lingered to talk to Mr. Whiddit. Among my requests was that our singing of "Souls of the Righteous in the Hand of God" might be dedicated to my father. He said, "Of course." No notice of this dedication was ever published anywhere, but it was a powerful symbol to me. This was a funeral for my father that I could attend. Indeed, I would sing at it. I did so with a spiritual awareness and gusto I have known only a few times in my life.

My brother, Will, soon joined the choir and in time he too was confirmed at St. Peter's. Then Betty and my mother transferred so that they might be in the congregation where we were singing. The next few years would be very difficult years for me and for our family. This church was to prove a safe harbor in the swirling sea of those difficulties. I often wonder what the course of my life might have been apart from that church.

I should have been considered too young to have the responsibility of a dysfunctional family imposed upon me, but as my mother said more times than I wanted to hear it, "You are the man of this house now!" I was quaking in my boots as I listened to these words, which seemed to suggest that my mother, the only adult in our devastated family, was depending on me.

The first thing that became obvious to me was that our family finances were almost nonexistent. Dad had no pension. Eight thousand dollars in three life insurance policies and some stock in the company for which he worked, which proved to be worthless, were the sum of his assets. The company was in bankruptcy by the end of the war. The life insurance was used to pay off the final medical expenses and the costs of Dad's burial.

He was covered by Social Security and his widow and three dependent children qualified for his payments, but a family could not live on that alone. Altogether it amounted to less than a hundred dollars a month. Our large house was now an albatross. It was heated by a coal furnace, which burned some fifteen tons of coal a winter, the price of which we could no longer afford.

Clearly we needed more income. Within two weeks of Dad's death, Mother began looking for a job. She had not worked for fifteen years, and she had few marketable skills. After much searching, she finally landed a position as a salesperson in the baby department of Belk Brothers' Department Store—the Macy's of Charlotte. My mother had been a caring, concerned, and effective person with her own babies. Now she turned this experience into the job that must support her children aged fourteen, twelve, and nine, starting at less than $20 a week. We did not quite realize what her full-time job would do to us. She had always been available to meet our every need, but we would never know a full-time mother again. We had no inkling and clearly expected no diminution of her ability to cook breakfast, pack lunches, and come home to fix dinner for us each day. I suspect that Betty helped more than I was aware. I also know that my mother performed these duties when she was all but exhausted.

From some source I began to feel a tremendous responsibility to help, so I sought a job and was successful. That was not easy since a worker's permit required that one be fifteen years of age. We lived one house removed from a dairy farm owned by the Ashcraft family. The Ashcrafts knew me well, and when I earnestly pled my cause, Joe Ashcraft hired me to work for a couple of hours each night to strip the cows after the electric milkers had done their job, to hose down the barn after the cows had been taken out, and then to ride a horse in the pasture until the sun went down, making sure that the cows did not wander off. This latter chore was by far the most exciting. I had never milked a cow before, but I was a quick learner. My wages were to be three dollars a week, plus all the milk I could drink on the job. Fresh whole milk not yet either pasteurized or homogenized came through the dairy's cooling system so cold it had slivers of ice in it. It was absolutely delicious. I must have drunk a quart a day on the job. I seek to recreate that same taste today when I drink milk only over ice. People think this is a peculiar habit, but they have no idea what ancient memory it elicits.

I had the feeling, as bizarre as it seems, that my job and this new source of family income would save our family from starvation. At least that was my grand illusion. Imagine my distress when I received a message on Christmas Day that my services were no longer required by the dairy. Very few people experience being fired at age twelve, and on Christmas Day no less! I realize in retrospect that I probably was hired out of sympathy over the death of my father, and sympathy did not last more than three months.

That Christmas was unique in two other ways for me. I received two primary gifts from Santa (my mother sought to keep the myth alive). One was a large portrait of Jesus, perhaps two feet by three feet. It was the typical schmaltzy, pious, lowbrow picture of Jesus, complete with long blond hair, fair skin, and blue eyes. He also had a nimbus over his head and a heavenly light coming from heaven itself that seemed to illumine his face. Why my mother decided that this picture was my heart's desire I do not know. But I was thrilled with this gift, and it hung on the wall over my bed from that day till the day I went to the university.

My other Santa gift was a Bible. It was the King James Version, with Jesus' words in red letters. It had a variety of maps, a concordance, and a brief introduction to each book. The floppy leather cover and the gilt-edged, tissue-thin pages made it seem like a proper Bible. I remember being equally thrilled with this gift. That Bible went on my bed stand and on that day a lifetime love affair with that book was first born in me. It has never yet departed. I began on that Christmas Day the habit of daily Bible reading. I have missed very few days from that one to this in which I did not spend some part of that day reading and studying the Scriptures. I suspect I have read the Bible through twenty-five times by now. Where that early love came from I do not know. I only know that it was there and that it was intense. If I saw that behavior in a twelve-year-old boy today, I would probably think it strange. But it did not appear strange to me at that time, and my mother clearly picked up the signals and fed my growing religious consciousness. For me it would have been a completely perfect Christmas if only I had not lost my job.

I quickly reorganized myself to seek new profit-making enterprises. This time my efforts took the form of being a newspaper carrier, first for the *Charlotte News,* an afternoon paper, and by the time I had turned fifteen for the *Charlotte Observer,* the morning paper. I made six to eight dollars a week with the *News* and ten to twelve a week with the *Observer,* rather substantial increases over my dairy income. The morning paper, however, required my rising at 4:00 A.M. each morning—rain, snow, sleet, or hail. On more than one occasion when the weather was dreadful, my mother would get up and assist me before going on to her work. It never occurred to me on those days that I added another two to three hours to her already exhausting work schedule. As a newsboy I also had some primary lessons to learn about human nature. There were perennial customers who found it impossible ever to have money available when I did my weekly or monthly collections. They made my life miserable and it was so consistent as to seem intentional. I now bought my clothes, took care of my school and personal needs, and placed the balance into my savings account, which was designed to help me finance a university education, something I had determined I must receive.

I do not know whether this money rescued my family from financial distress, but I am certain it helped. It also created a financially conservative person in the heart of one who would be thought of as a liberal on most other issues. Money was precious because it stood between minimal security and emotional chaos.

The economic pain of our family, however, was destined to grow deeper. Mother, more out of ignorance than malevolence, did not report to the Social Security authorities that she had gone to work. Even with her meager paycheck she still made more than a Social Security recipient was allowed to make and still retain her Social Security check.

It took the people at the Social Security Agency about two years to catch this abnormality, but when they did, I gather that they reacted as if a crime had been committed. My mother, with less than a ninth-grade education, was to be punished, and the unwarranted payments would have to be returned. She had not a cent in the bank and no way to borrow this sum, amounting to more than a thousand dollars. She also could not have paid off a loan if she could have gotten one. Even with what turned out to be illegal income, we lived right on the edge. Mother sought the help of some of my father's friends and a compromise was worked out. Mother would not be prosecuted or penalized with back interest, but she would have to surrender the payments made to the children until the improper money had been restored. The income of our family would descend below the poverty level. The only alternative was to sell the house and seek a smaller, less expensive home. If it were inside the city limits of Charlotte, we could go to the schools we presently attended without paying tuition. The house was put on the market for $15,500. It sold for $12,500. We bought a house one and a half miles closer in, but on the same street for $7,500. After closing costs, realtors' fees, and moving expenses, there was a profit of about $2,000 that helped enormously, but the style of our living had been reduced significantly.

We were sheltered from most of these details, but I was powerfully aware of the hurtful calls from unpaid creditors, the bill collectors who rang our doorbell in the evening with regularity, the threat that no more fuel would be delivered to our home until the past due bill had been paid, and of my mother's tears, buckets of tears, that seemed to flow from her every day. I suspect her stress level was enormously high and her depression severe. I also know that deep in me resides a horror of having a bill of any size that I cannot pay in full at the end of the month it is charged. The only loans I have ever had were to purchase a car, the monthly payment on those loans was always met on time, and every credit card bill has been paid on the date due. The pain of not doing so is still too great. I have also had genuine difficulty in enjoying money even when I finally got above the subsistence level. I kept very tight reins on the family finances—far too tight, I suspect, for the well-being of either my wife or my children. The fear of financial misfortune was something I could never allow to come near me again.

It was also, inevitably, it seemed, my destiny to become aware of how my mother with her lack of business experience was abused by those upon whom she leaned. This abuse was not physical, but it was abuse just the same. I watched a "friend of the family" sell her twenty-year-payment life insurance policies on each of the three children when she hardly had the ability to put food on the table. This "friend" scared my susceptible mother with horror stories about her not being able to pay the funeral expenses if one of us should die. Of course, statistically the chances of that were remote. Having burial money always available remained a driving financial priority for her to the day she died. I still have that paid-up insurance policy. It remains for me a symbol of an unscrupulous man who feathered his own nest at the expense of a woman who counted on his wise counsel. It burned an indelible impression into me that made the cause of women, oppressed, harassed, and violated, one to which I would respond someday with energy and deep emotion.

It was not easy being forced to grow up before I was emotionally capable of doing so. I greatly resented my mother's emotional dependency on me. I did not want to be the man in the house, but my mother needed me in that role. To be as afraid as I was and to discover that the only adult in the family was seeking my counsel and asking for my support sent tremors of insecurity down my spine. In every way I could, I acted out the fact that I was not ready to be responsible. I kept looking for a way to rebel, to be a child, to elicit some strong word or action from my mother that would convince me that she was still in charge and that someone bigger than I was around on whom I could depend.

By the time I was thirteen I began smoking. I did it clandestinely for about six months, but finally began to take bigger and bigger risks of being discovered. Smoking in the bathroom is a dead giveaway. So I was discovered. My mother's response was not what I anticipated.

She told me that if I was going to smoke, she wanted me to do it openly. She did not like people being sneaky. She went so far as to put ashtrays around the house and even commented that it felt so good to have the "smell of a man" around the house once more. I was devastated, for now I had to find something worse than smoking to do. I actually remember planning more and more antisocial activities. I would steal porch furniture from the houses in our neighborhood and place it on top of a drugstore in our block that had an easily accessible flat roof. It was always returned and somehow I was never caught. I remember yearning to have my Aunt Marguerite for my mother. She had a reputation for running a tight ship with her children. In my disappointment at my mother's weakness, I treated her shamefully until I grew past this stage toward the end of my high-school years. She never understood that I was asking her to be strong for my sake. I never understood that she was being all that she was capable of being. I am glad that she lived long enough to enable me to demonstrate my ability to give her the care she needed when I was finally capable of doing so.

In fall 1944 and spring 1945 it became obvious that my days as a boy soprano were limited. By this time St. Peter's was so central to my life that I simply left the choir to become an acolyte. I was, in turn, a flag bearer, a crucifer, and finally a server at communion. Each step felt like a promotion in responsibility and in holiness. First I led the procession into the church, and then I became essential to the communion service itself. Our rector, Dr. Clark, was now past retirement age, but there was a shortage of clergy because of the war. With VE Day in May and VJ day in August 1945, the world was returning to normal. Chaplains and servicemen were coming out of the service to return to parish priesthood or to enter theological seminaries in record numbers. The church was headed into a fantastic period of growth that would not end until the early 1960s.

# 4

# *Rejection at School, Acceptance at Church*

✳

"H E WAS a navy chaplain on an aircraft carrier in the Pacific."
That was the first identification I received of the priest, the new
rector of St. Peter's, who would be instrumental in shaping the course of my
life. Other biographical details were sparse. I did learn, however, that he was
from Georgia and was married, but had no children. There was an excitement at the church anticipating his arrival. Dr. Clark had retired. Now a
younger priest was coming to our church, perhaps a war hero. As the war
came to an end, heroes seemed to be plentiful. The battles of the Pacific had
already entered the romantic nostalgia of the nation. We could recite knowingly and lovingly the names of places where battles had been fought, lifting
heretofore unknown sites into warm familiarity—Guam, Wake Island,
Midway, Saipan, Iwo Jima, Corregidor, Bataan. Perhaps this chaplain had
actually been to those places. Hopes were high, but nobody's hopes were
higher than mine.

When I first met him, I was astonished to find my hopes totally inadequate. Robert Littlefield Crandall was dapper, personable, articulate, and
charming. I could hardly believe the way he smashed every stereotype of a
priest I had ever known. He was thirty-two years old. I could not believe a
priest could be that young. Mr. Owens and Dr. Clark I presumed to be at
least eighty. In my mind being elderly was a prerequisite for priesthood.

Mr. Crandall wore white buck shoes. They may not be stylish today, but
in 1946 they were pretty spiffy indeed. He drove a Ford convertible! I
thought clergy only drove black hearses. When he would turn into the
church's parking lot in that convertible, with his skin tanned and the wind

blowing through his hair, leap out with verve, and almost run to the door wearing his white shoes, it was a vision I could barely believe. Bing Crosby as the priest in *Going My Way* was no match for Robert Crandall.

In fact, my new rector topped Bing Crosby in yet another category. His primary life companion was not Barry Fitzgerald. On his arm was the most amazing and even tantalizing woman I had ever seen. Erin Crandall, his wife, was what we in those days might have called a pure Georgia peach. She was from a well-to-do Southern family and her clothes, furs, and jewelry, to say nothing of her manner, made that quite obvious.

I will never forget the way she would retire to her husband's office after church on Sunday morning, sit down on the top of his desk, cross her legs in a most enticing manner, and then proceed to take from her purse a long golden cigarette holder and light a cigarette. Franklin D. Roosevelt, who had made cigarette holders fashionable, had nothing on Mrs. Crandall in terms of sophistication.

I was smitten by this woman at once, but I was even more captivated by her husband. He was such an immediate hero to me that I know I was a fawning groupie. I hung around him whenever I could. I volunteered for the acolyte duty that no one really wanted, the poorly attended 8:00 A.M. communion services. No crowd was there in front of which I could perform, but *he* was there and that was quite enough for me.

Mr. Crandall leaned toward what Episcopalians call the High Church side of our church's tradition. He really wanted to be called "Father" by his congregation, but that ran counter to the Southern Low Church tradition, and so he did not press it. But when he asked me not to call him Mr. Crandall, but "Padre," I felt as if I had been invited into his inner circle. That was what the sailors on the aircraft carrier had called him, he said. It sounded so grown up and so intimate. It did not occur to me that "Padre" meant "Father." It meant only that we were close and I was important to him.

He called himself an Anglo-Catholic. I hardly knew what that was, but my reasoning was that it must be something good since that is what my Padre said he was. He wore vestments I had never before seen, but I mastered their titles—alb, chasuble, and maniple. Vesting before the 8:00 A.M. service was ritualized. He prayed as he put on each liturgical piece. I was terribly impressed. This was the uniform of the Lord, and it conferred on him, I gathered, a hundred times more authority than my red acolyte's vestment conferred on me. Yet my uniform had also impressed me mightily with its power. Once he was vested, we went through a series of preparatory prayers together in the sacristy. In one of these prayers this larger-than-life man actually confessed to me his unworthiness to celebrate what I began to call the "Eucharist." The title "holy communion" now seemed so pedestrian, so lacking in dignity.

When the service itself began, Mr. Crandall did interesting and, I presumed, magical physical things. He, for example, always kept his thumb and his index finger pressed so tightly together that I feared they might become stuck irreparably. He made crosses in the air over the bread and wine at special times in the liturgy. He fell to one knee, then lifted the consecrated bread high above his head, and then fell to one knee again with bells ringing at each of these actions. At the end of the Eucharist, he made cleaning the vessels on the altar an elaborate activity. I asked him a thousand questions, and he painstakingly explained the absolute necessity of doing it exactly this way, for these procedures were designed to make sure that all of "the sacred blood of Jesus" was consumed, even that part of Jesus' blood that somehow attached itself to the side of the chalice. His understanding of the Eucharist was different from any I had ever known, but I adopted it without any hesitancy.

He soon asked me about my willingness to be enrolled in a national acolytes' program known as the Order of St. Vincent. I was thrilled. In time I received the training manual, which explained the cleansing procedures and countless numbers of others. It also gave me forms for self-examination prior to coming to the Eucharist. My prayer life was growing. I learned why the altar candles were lit and extinguished in the order that they were, what the Epistle side and the Gospel side of the altar were, why the missal was moved from one side to the other, and when and how to genuflect and cross oneself. I also learned that the only proper way to receive the sacred body and blood of Jesus was after fasting, lest the sacrament be corrupted by some undigested bits of matter still in my stomach. Twelve midnight was the cutoff time for eating, I discovered, whether one was having surgery or receiving communion. I also received my own St. Vincent's medal, which Mr. Crandall placed around my neck in a ceremony that could not have moved me more deeply if I had been knighted by the king or queen. I was a zealot, a Crandallite, and so I vowed to make myself into a perfect acolyte and a true believing Catholic churchman.

Following this regimen for holiness was not easy. Rising at 4:00 A.M. to deliver newspapers, returning home to dress, then catching a bus for downtown that allowed me to arrive with sufficient time to vest and go through the rituals with my Padre left me absolutely famished. That hunger combined with the service from the 1928 *Book of Common Prayer,* which required long periods of kneeling, made the burden intolerable. More often than not I began to feel queasy, wobble visibly, turn green around the edges, and sweat profusely. Before I learned the order and meaning of these symptoms and my inevitable responses, I actually fainted dead away and had to be carried bodily out of the sanctuary. The saving grace on this occasion was that I was unconscious when I departed. The other option, which also occurred from time to time, was to throw up all over the altar. Then I would be helped out of the sanctuary while still conscious, watching the mop-and-towel brigade come in to clean up my contribution to worship. I seldom made it to the end of the service. Most Sundays I did not even make it through the long monologue prayer known as the "Prayer for the Whole State of Christ's Church." Later in life some of my passion for prayer book revision, which included the demise of this prayer, would reflect memories born in these moments.

Despite this somewhat inadequate acolyte performance, Mr. Crandall's confidence in me did not seem to be diminished. When the service was over, by which time I was newly composed and cleaned up, this unique priest and I would walk half a block up North Tryon Street to a little Greek restaurant for breakfast. We would also talk. I hung on his every word. For years I did not realize what was a fact, namely, that in all my teenage years, this was the only adult who ever talked with me. Lots of adults talked at me and to me, but my Padre talked with me. I have no memory today of the content of those conversations. I suspect they were more trivial than profound, but the emotional sense of being taken seriously by a significant adult was powerful indeed. I doubt if Robert Crandall ever had a clue about how very important he was to me. I have no idea of what I might have meant to him. He and Erin remained childless until long after I had gone away to school, when they adopted first a girl and then a boy.

I adored this man, and quite obviously I fashioned my life on his in every way I could. I see his echoes in me even today. He was worldly-wise, fashionable, urbane, not pious, but rather secular in his outlook. He was fascinated by whatever affected the church and eager to speak what he perceived to be the church's word to the world. Those characteristics have also marked my career. I have also abandoned some of his traits. I long ago cut myself loose from his Anglo-Catholicism, his narrow view of the church as the source of all truth, and his conservative liturgical commitments. I care little today for the trivia of ablutions or hand motions and genuflections that once accompanied my celebration of the Eucharist, all of which I had adopted unquestioningly from my mentor.

However, because of that primary relationship, I determined then and there that I wanted to be a priest—not just any kind of priest, but one in the mold of Robert Crandall. Every other ambition paled when compared with this goal in life. Perhaps it is true that my childhood religious zeal, my love of Sunday school, my playing church at home, and my joy in having a framed picture of Jesus and my own personal Bible seemed to predispose me to walk in this direction. But all of those interests were focused and incarnated in my Padre, Robert Crandall.

My desire to be constantly in my Padre's company led me to join the church's Young People's Service League, or YPSL. It met every Sunday night for prayers, a light supper, and then a program. Sometimes the program was a talk, or a religious movie about Jesus or St. Paul, complete with dusty trails, sandals, and white tunics. The fellowship of that group was greatly enhanced by the guitar playing and singing of our multitalented Padre. We learned to sing such ditties as "A Dollar Down and a Dollar a Week" and "My Father Shot a Kangaroo." Every contact I had with this man seemed to expand my life.

My church life was a haven of warm security in my otherwise frightening and insecure world. Through the eighth and ninth grades I kept my school work up well enough to be elected to the honor society, and I had enough self-esteem to seek to win as my girlfriend a charming classmate named Peggy Hollingsworth. It was a strange courtship. Increasingly, I began to feel second class. My clothes were old. I had no car and little discretionary money, so I could not take a girl out on a date or go on field trips that cost anything. To save money I often rode my bicycle to school. But not looking where I was going one afternoon, I rode into the back of a bus and broke off my front tooth. The economic ramifications of this accident in the life of my family were severe.

When I arrived in high school in the tenth grade, social lines were forming and I did not rank very highly. My classwork was deteriorating. I had little athletic prowess. I also had to go to bed early to rise at 4:00 A.M. to deliver papers. In the eleventh grade, by which time I was finally old enough to have a work permit, I got an additional job at the Sanitary Laundry. I worked twenty hours a week—from 4:00 to 6:00 P.M. on Monday through

Friday and from 7:00 A.M. to 6:00 P.M. on Saturday—for thirty-five cents an
hour. It took all my free time and made playing sports or engaging in any
after-school social activities impossible. I was relegated by my peers to the
ranks of the "nerds." School became an increasingly unpleasant and unful-
filling place for me. My schoolwork showed my disdain and lack of fulfillment. I was a C student at best.

These two foci of my life—my church and my school—seemed to be carrying me in opposite directions. One opened doors for me; the other closed
them. One was a place of acceptance and success; the other was a place of
rejection and failure. One seemed to endow me with some sense of self-
worth; the other revealed all of my insecurities.

I was elected president of my church youth group at the start of the tenth
grade. I was eager to do a good job. We sponsored a Halloween party for the
little children of the parish. We fixed and delivered Thanksgiving baskets to
the poor. We sang Christmas carols at a couple of nursing homes. We organized and carried out a Shrove Tuesday pancake supper and hawked tickets
to the members of the church on Sunday morning, telling them that they
must support the youth of the parish. They did.

That youth group also forced me to broaden my Episcopal contacts, for
we had fall and spring district meetings of the Episcopal youth of the area.
Sometimes these meetings would be overnight Saturday and Sunday. I met
other clergy at these gatherings. We would sing camp songs, study the Bible,
and discuss the issues in our lives. These meetings also introduced me to
church camp at a place called Vade Mecum, where the young people gathered each summer.

This camp site was in Stokes County, North Carolina, between Winston
Salem and Mt. Airy or, as we said, just a mile from Mickey's Store. In 1947
at the diocesan youth convention, held over a weekend in June at Vade
Mecum, my work as president of our local church youth group was
rewarded. I was elected treasurer of the YPSL of the Diocese of North
Carolina. That convention was a wonderful, memorable event for me.
Teenagers from all over the diocese came, friendships were formed,
romances developed, and the clergy we met and enjoyed in our district
meetings seemed to multiply. A major feature of that convention was the
singing in the evening around a roaring campfire led by some of the younger
clergy of the diocese who became my new heroes. We also did skits, told
ghost stories, enjoyed square dances, and prepared for our youth banquet. It
was an ecstatic time and being elected treasurer was the first significant

honor to come to me in my life. Suddenly something called the Diocese of North Carolina became an entity to which I belonged. The bishop, a gifted and saintly man named Edwin Anderson Penick, even knew me by name. My church world was expanding.

My school world was, however, still contracting. My only real friends at school in the eleventh grade were low-status students, the ne'er-do-wells, and the rejected. My grades kept getting worse. I made three C's and two D's in my last semester that year.

With two of my friends I talked about dropping out of school that summer and joining the navy. It seemed an exciting thing to do. If the other two had been willing to do so, I would surely have joined them. It was a narrow escape.

Two things happened in the spring months of my junior year that were significant in turning my life in a new direction. One had to do with a girl named Cynthia Shelmire Cook. She was a member of St. Peter's and came, though not regularly, to the youth group. This connection meant, however, that she saw me as a leader, a role in which most of my school classmates would not see me. But she was also well connected in high school. If not on the top social tier, which was generally occupied by cheerleaders and class officers, she was certainly in the next highest rung of the ladder of status and acceptability. I was nowhere near that level. Cynthia was beautiful with a Snow White kind of effect, and had placed third in the Miss Charlotte contest in her junior year in high school. I do not recall how the relationship actually began, but I know I was flabbergasted when expressions of my interest were not rebuffed. We went to a movie or two. By now I had access to my mother's car. After the motion picture we would go to one of the popular drive-ins for a hamburger, a shake, or the coolest of all, a sour lemonade. Before the eleventh-grade year ended, people had begun to associate the two of us, giving my status a boost. I was so proud to be seen in her company. It amazes me even today how healing and enhancing it was that this wonderful person did not reject me outright.

The second event was, not surprisingly, church related. A twenty-nine-year-old priest from North Carolina, serving in the remote Alaskan village of Point Hope, was elected by the Episcopal House of Bishops to be bishop of the Missionary District of Alaska. In the election this particular clergyman was championed by Bishop Penick who, at that time, served as the vice president of the House of Bishops. Bishop Penick argued that the rugged life in Alaska required a young, vigorous, and athletic bishop to travel long distances by dogsled. Bishop Penick was persuasive and so, to the great surprise of Alaskans, this almost unknown young priest, William Jones Gordon, the son of a rector in Spray, North Carolina, was elected. I am sure it was a feather in Bishop Penick's cap. I suddenly became aware that it had interesting significance for the YPSL of the Diocese of North Carolina. This young priest had been diocesan president of this organization, and now his consecration, strangely enough, was to take place in North Carolina.

The Diocese of North Carolina decided to equip this new bishop for his episcopal duties, so one diocesan group agreed to buy his vestments, another his pectoral cross, and the young people of the diocese were asked to buy him his bishop's ring. The cost was five hundred dollars, a princely sum in those days, but we agreed, and I, as treasurer, was put in charge of the fund-raising drive. It was a tremendous honor, I felt, and it excited me greatly.

I got about my task quickly. After correspondence with Bishop-Elect Gordon, who was to become the first bishop I would ever address by his first name, I set about organizing the fund-raising campaign. Each youth group of the diocese was assigned a share based upon the group's level of activity and the wealth and size of its church. St. Peter's youth group made the first contribution, and I began to send out a weekly bulletin that had a thermometer with the symbol $500 at the top and the rising total painted in week by week. I also would list the youth groups who had contributed and, in a shameless use of coercive force, those who had "not yet sent their contribution to the treasurer."

A sense of excitement grew as we got closer and closer to a victory in our campaign. The day the check from the Church of the Messiah in Rockingham put us over the top was an occasion of great celebration. I called my Padre at once. He suggested that I call Bishop Penick in Raleigh. I was awestruck at this suggestion for two reasons. First, I could not imagine calling this enormously important man. Second, long-distance calls in that day were not commonplace, at least in my experience. They were expensive and usually carried with them some extreme news. As a child, whenever the phone had rung in our home and the operator had said, "I have a long-distance call for Mr. Shelby Spong," we would panic in relaying the message to my father, and he would react as if this were a moment of gravity. No long-distance call had come to our home since his death. But Mr. Crandall insisted I make that call, and promised to reimburse my mother for it.

Bishop Penick's secretary, Cicely Browne, answered the phone, and in a moment the dignified voice of the bishop was on the line. He called me by name and asked why I was calling. I blurted my story out quickly, since I feared this call would cost a fortune. The bishop's response was warm and congratulatory. Then he said the words I could never have anticipated. "Jack, would it be possible for you to come to Raleigh for Bishop Gordon's consecration and present the ring to him during the service on behalf of the young people of this diocese?" I responded that I would do everything I could to be present and would let him know.

I went. It was the first consecration of a bishop I had ever seen. Some fifteen to twenty bishops, including Bishop Penick, were in the procession following about a hundred of the clergy of the Diocese of North Carolina. At the time in the service following the laying on of the hands of all the bishops, Bishop Gordon was officially vested in the low church tradition of white rochet, black chimere, and tippet. Then the pectoral cross was placed around his neck, the pastoral staff was given into his hand, and I helped to put the bishop's ring on his finger. The glory of being among these luminaries of the church was lasting. I was a church romantic for sure.

One result on which I had not counted was that this campaign for funds for the bishop's ring made me well known among the young people of the diocese and at the convention of the YPSLs of the diocese at Vade Mecum that June, I was nominated and elected without opposition to be president of the young people of the diocese for a one-year term. Once again the church had been the place of affirmation and honor for me. It is no wonder I reveled in ecclesiastical things and entertained no other possibility for myself than the life of the priesthood. On the Sunday following the Vade Mecum convention, Mr. Crandall asked me to stand during the church service at St. Peter's, and in his comments he linked me with Bishop Gordon. "Eleven years ago," he began, "a young man was elected president of the Young People's Service League of this diocese at Vade Mecum. This year he was elected and consecrated bishop of Alaska. Last weekend another young man, Jack Spong, a member of this parish, was elected president of the young people of this diocese. I predict the day will come when he too will be elected one of the bishops of our church." My fantasies knew no bounds.

More and more I turned over my paper route to my brother, Will, so that I could pursue these fulfilling opportunities. I became senior acolyte. I preached on Youth Sunday, my first nonpretending sermon, and that summer I was chosen to be a delegate to the North American Christian Youth Conference held in Grand Rapids, Michigan. I had rarely been more than a short trip away from my home, yet from somewhere I managed to find the courage to catch a train, change twice, and get to Grand Rapids. The leader of the Episcopal part of this ecumenical venture was John E. Booty, a sophisticated college student active in the Canterbury Club movement nationally. This conference, because it was also racially integrated, was my first experience of meeting and talking to young black Christians as peers. We worshiped together, prayed together, sang together, and listened to the same speeches together. It was strangely refreshing. In the accompanying social activities, my eyes bulged at the sight of blacks and whites dancing together, holding each other closely. It was a new image that would be processed painstakingly as I moved out of the orbit of my family and region into what I perceived to be a Christ-centered world in which racial prejudices must surely be challenged.

When I returned home, I planned to speak about this conference at district meetings of the young people of our diocese and in any individual churches that would invite me. I worked hard on that speech and delivered it first at Christ Church in downtown Raleigh. I recall today only the first sentence of that sermon. "I went to Grand Rapids an Episcopalian. I returned united, committed to Christ." I extolled the virtues of the ecumenical movement and chided my elders for not working faster in this area. It was a cheeky sermon, but immaturity is frequently forgiven where passion and enthusiasm are displayed. It must have gone well, for I received congratulations from both my peers and my elders.

Entering my senior year I had more gusto for school than I had had in the last four years combined. The Social Security debt had now been paid off, and the financial burdens of our household had lessened. My sister had graduated, finished business school, and was preparing to marry our next-door neighbor.

One thing became clear to me as my senior year dawned. I would have to go to the university in order to become a priest, but my academic record was not college-worthy. No member of my high-school faculty would be willing to write a letter of reference on my behalf. One of my teachers had shared with me that my I.Q. scores were quite high. Perhaps evidence of that had been seen in my earlier years, but grades ten and eleven had been academic disasters. I knew that I would need to win some scholarships to manage a university career, and I could not do that without significant upgrading of my record. I was motivated in a way I had never been motivated before.

I started the year with a burst of energy. My teachers wondered at the change. My homework was always done on time. I got involved on the yearbook staff. I took five courses each semester plus a study hall and a lab—a heavy load. Two of those classes could be electives, so I chose to take two Bible courses.

The Bible teacher was a lovely unmarried woman, probably in her forties, whose name was Miss Janet Robinson. She wore her hair tight in a bun at the back of her head. She wore no makeup, since that was clearly prohibited by Scripture. She was sweet, not strident. She loved the Lord and talked about him as a living presence, but she was a biblical literalist to the core. She represented an interesting polarity with Mr. Crandall. Hers was very much the religious viewpoint of my mother and her family, away from which I had moved significantly. Her last word on every subject was, "The Bible says . . ." Mine had become "The church teaches . . ." Both were fundamentalist positions, but I did not recognize that truth at that moment. I thought of myself and the authority of the church as infinitely superior and far more sophisticated than Miss Robinson and her claim to the authority of Scripture. Miss Robinson was plain, pious, and somber. Mr. Crandall was electric, convincing, and exciting. But she had something I wanted—a knowledge of the Scriptures.

She was a genius at the art of storytelling. I reveled in her narratives of such biblical heroes as Cain and Abel, Noah, Abraham, Isaac, Jacob, Joseph, and Moses. I identified with Samuel, the boy called to the life of a prophet. She did not do much with the prophets, but the Gospel stories, the dramatic parables, and the travels of Paul thrilled me on a daily basis. Her love for the Bible fed my love for the Bible. I became her star pupil. Our assignments were to write new psalms, create new parables, and see the whole story of salvation, from the goodness of creation to the literal fall of Adam to rescue operations mounted by God in the person of his son Jesus in the acts of his crucifixion, his physical resuscitation, and his literal ascension back to the heavenly throne from which he had come. It was a magnificent overall scheme, but if any part of it proved to be less than literally true, the whole edifice came tumbling down. The thought of Charles Darwin had been in the public domain for eighty-nine years at this point, but it had not permeated Miss Robinson's thinking. She reduced Darwin to the simple proposition that we descended from apes—a proposition she rejected as absurd. In a real way Mr. Crandall's viewpoint was equally in denial. He only carved out a bigger role for the church in the post-ascension phase by suggesting that God's grace only operated through the sacraments of the catholic tradition, which of course bound them to being the gifts that only the ordained could offer.

My high-school status continued to rise during the year. I was frequently asked to lead devotions in assembly programs. I was the first nonfundamentalist student to be elected president of the Bible Club. When the class prophecy was written, it was said of me that I would be the chaplain of the U.S. Senate. Cynthia and I were by this time "going steady," as we said. It was probably the happiest year of my young life. Our relationship lasted through one semester of separation when I was away from Charlotte at the university. After that it died a natural death. We parted, recognizing that we had been special friends, but not lifelong partners. It is a category in human relationships I have come to respect.

To my amazement and that of my teachers, I was a straight-A student in my senior year. At graduation I won the Winkler Scholarship awarded on the basis of merit and need, the Bible award, and, best of all, admission to the University of North Carolina in Chapel Hill. I was a competent president of the diocesan YPSL and presided over our annual youth convention at Vade Mecum in summer 1949.

Only one note of great significance marked that final year of youth activities. It revolved around the ancient theme of race, to which that Grand Rapids conference had sensitized me. I became aware, I do not know how, that there was a second youth group in the Diocese of North Carolina, one for those who were then called "colored" young people. They too, I discovered, were organized and even had a president named Perry Leazer, from Salisbury. I had met Perry at the diocesan convention that spring. I was amazed that there was another Episcopal youth organization about which I had never heard. But racism builds very high walls. Armed with that new knowledge and my own expanding consciousness, I wrote to Bishop Penick requesting that we invite the black young people to our youth convention at Vade Mecum that June so that "this gathering would truly be the young people of the Episcopal Church in the Diocese of North Carolina."

His response was a quick and emphatic no. His reasoning was insightful about the depth and content of racial fear in the South in the late 1940s. "The people of the diocese are not yet ready for the vision of Negro boys and white girls swimming together in the pool at Vade Mecum." It was interesting that his image involved "Negro boys and white girls." Race and sex were never separated. Perry Leazer did not come. I never saw him again, although we did talk on the phone in 1998 when I led the clergy conference for the Diocese of North Carolina. He was an active layman in the diocese. But the church that was so life-giving and affirming of me was rejecting and death-dealing to him in this earlier moment. It was an anomaly so deep and so evil that it surely could not be allowed to endure. But for now it was deeply entrenched. Once more, I was the beneficiary. Jesus had said that to those "to whom much is given, shall much be required." The day would come when I would be required to act against these demeaning aspects of my church's life, but it would not be yet. As great as Bishop Penick had been, he would not be able to lead this church beyond its racism into a new world. He was too much a child of his era. Time has an incredible way of making ancient good uncouth.

# 5

# The University Years: Philosophy, St. Mark's, and Wedding Bells

❋

AS LATE August 1949 arrived, my life was consumed with preparation to move to Chapel Hill. I was the first member of my immediate family on either side to go to the university. It was to be a huge stretch for me financially. I would not draw on my mother's meager resources since that would have significantly diminished her life and my brother's. I had about eighteen hundred dollars saved from my paper routes and other jobs. I would be able to make that last through my degree aided by several supplementary sources, most of which were church-related.

The rector at the Chapel of the Cross in Chapel Hill, the Episcopal church on the campus of the university, provided rooms in the parish house to four Episcopal students a year. As in-kind rent for these rooms we did the Sunday bulletin, answered the phone at night, and were a presence in the building at night. Of eight roommates who came and went during my Chapel Hill years, three others also became priests. I am convinced that the primary person responsible for this phenomenon was David Watt Yates, the rector of Chapel of the Cross.

David was, strangely enough, also a child of St. Peter's Church in Charlotte. He was a unique human being, and a single man in every sense of the word. A militant low churchman, a courageous, if not always inspiring, preacher, and a man of deep convictions, he was a total abstainer from alcoholic beverages and a dedicated pacifist. He preached against war throughout World War II. It became relatively easy to be a Christian pacifist when the atomic era emerged or during the politically compromised wars in Korea, Vietnam, and Iraq, but World War II was thought of as a moral crusade against the likes of Adolf Hitler. To be a pacifist in that war took conviction and courage. David Yates had plenty of both. When the European phase ended on VE Day, and later when hostilities everywhere ceased on VJ Day, great crowds of celebrating citizens took to the streets and entered the churches of their downtown areas to give thanks. David met those worshipers in downtown Durham, where he was at this time rector at St. Phillip's, and led them not in prayers of thanksgiving that the war was over, but in prayers of penitence that we had ever taken up arms against other human beings. Some people that night came with gratitude in their hearts and left with enormous hostility. David Yates, however, was undeterred.

David also believed that racial integration was God's will and that segregation was evil, and he said so publicly and frequently. When accosted by irate parishioners, he quickly forced them to try to defend segregation and even slavery as God's will. I listened to this man preach, watched him live his life with incredible integrity, and learned from him something of the cost of discipleship. I later came to admire the people of the church in Chapel Hill for calling this uncompromising person to be their rector. They had to have known what they were getting.

Arriving on that campus alone, not knowing another soul or where anything was, being on a very tight budget, and having not the slightest idea what university life would be like, I was one frightened eighteen-year-old. When my mother and brother drove off, a sense of lostness overwhelmed me. When time for dinner on my first night arrived, I found myself absolutely alone. My roommate went off with his family. The guys in the other room left without thinking to include me. So I walked into the downtown section of Chapel Hill, found a Walgreen's with a food counter, and ordered a bowl of canned chicken noodle soup. It was both the low point and the first meal of my college career.

The chaos and fear soon disappeared, and order and familiarity replaced them. I enrolled in my classes, taking a basic liberal arts course of English, history, science, and math with philosophy as my major. The academic power I had discovered in my senior year in high school was still with me. I took to my studies like a duck to water. If I needed any external stimulus to become a good student, my new roommate supplied it. His name was John Schnorrenberg, from Asheville, North Carolina. He was a prep-school graduate, and my first impression of him was that he thought himself intellectually superior to any of the rest of us. He may well have been. Today he is a professor of art history at the University of Alabama at Birmingham and a leading layman in the Diocese of Alabama. But I was not ready to concede his superiority at that early moment, and so I vowed that I would beat him into Phi Beta Kappa. I did by a whole semester, but I doubt if he was aware that he was my competition. I was in the second semester of my second year before I failed to ace the final exam of one of my courses and thus made my first B. It was in trigonometry. I was elected to Phi Eta Sigma, the freshman academic fraternity, at the end of my first year and to Phi Beta Kappa at the end of my sophomore year. I went to summer school for a summer and a half and finished the university in three years in the class of 1952 at the ripe old age of twenty-one.

My minor was in Greek, where I studied with Dr. Preston Epps, accumulating twenty-five college hours of credit in that language. I also did a good bit of work in the zoology department, where my chief mentor was Dr. Claiborne Jones. He walked with two canes, a polio victim, I believe, and was an active member of the Chapel of the Cross. He was also an evolutionist, the first Darwinian Christian I had ever met. I took two classes with him as well as others in the zoology department. In those classes I tried to defend the literal creation story against Darwin's theory. Claiborne Jones was always gracious, but even I knew that I had lost that fight. But I was to need some help before I would be able to get my Christianity out of the realm of my childhood faith system and into engagement with the modern world. Claiborne Jones would provide that in great measure. I was delighted years later to discover that his daughter, who bears his name, had become a priest.

I have often wondered why I chose philosophy as my major. It is true that I have always loved to roam around in the world of ideas, but philosophy is so nebulous and it equips one for almost nothing. This department was chaired by Professor Louis Katsoff, who was a Jew by ethnic background and a self-proclaimed atheist by religious conviction. Other professors included Maynard Adams, once an ordained minister, but now another atheist dedicated to removing the superstition of religion from the life of our society; Stephen Emery, a philosophical, nonreligious pragmatist; and William H. Poteat, the son of a well-known enlightened Southern Baptist pastor in Raleigh, North Carolina. Dr. Poteat would ultimately become an Episcopalian, teach at the Episcopal Theological Seminary of the Southwest, and conclude his career as a professor of philosophy at Duke University. He was the only self-acknowledged Christian in the entire department. It was an interesting mix, but into its life I plunged eagerly.

I met with Dr. Katsoff to secure my major in the department. He wanted to know why I was interested in philosophy. I told him my ultimate goal was to be a priest. He was not ecstatic and conveyed to me that Christianity was a hopeless hangover from another age and that I should not waste my life. He would be a challenge for me. Years later, after being ordained, I was invited to return to Chapel Hill to speak to the men's club of the Chapel of the Cross. To my absolute amazement, Louis Katsoff was there and was now a baptized, confirmed, and active Christian.

After my talk I spoke with him and then went by his home for a visit, where he related the account of the changes in his life in the last decade. "David Yates finally got to me," he said. I was even more surprised at that.

"How could that be?" I asked. "You can think rings around him."

"David didn't outthink me," Dr. Katsoff countered quickly, "he just out-lived me." That I understood.

I had a couple of courses with Dr. Katsoff, one with Maynard Adams, and one with Stephen Emery. They were all fascinating, but Bill Poteat was my teacher of choice. I took every class of his I could fit into my schedule. Under his direction I founded and chaired a campus organization called the Young Pascalians. We met once a week to read and discuss the thinking of Blaise Pascal, especially his *Pensées*. We gloried in such gems as "The heart has its reasons which the reason knows not of." Immanuel Kant, Friedrich Schleiermacher, René Descartes, and Friedrich Nietzsche are to me even today real people whose thought I have engaged. Bill Poteat introduced me to each of them.

Other campus activities included being the leader of the United World Federalists and the campaign manager for a classmate's run for presidency of the student body. He lost. I also engaged a columnist named Harry Snook, who wrote for the *Daily Tar Heel*, in a debate through the Letters to the Editor column. Since he was the columnist, he had the final word, but it did whet my appetite for further debate. I was also elected to the campus leadership order known as the Order of the Old Well.

One other activity engaged my time. Through my youth group activities I had gotten to know a student at Duke Divinity School named Fred I. E. Ferris. Prior to ordination he was acting as lay reader in charge of a small Episcopal church in Roxboro, North Carolina, named St. Mark's. That was not an unusual pattern in that day, as lots of churches were run by laypeople with a priest coming in once a month to do the Eucharist. Fred was an energetic and deeply caring person and had won the affections of his small worshiping community. In the summer before I entered the university, Fred asked me to conduct services in Roxboro while he was on vacation in August. I was to be paid fifty dollars plus room and board. A few days before Fred's departure, I arrived in Roxboro so that he could acquaint me with my duties and introduce me to the town.

It was a fascinating community with all of the stereotypes found in small-town America: the wealthy but tight businessman, the elegant midlife divorcée, the village rake, the socially prominent woman of loose morals, the bedrock families such as the local druggist's or the local jeweler's, and a host of teenagers in varying states of maturity.

I took over Fred's room, ate my meals in a local boardinghouse, got to know the teenagers, and came to know the warts and glories of this little town. I knew the abusers and the abused, family secrets that were not as well guarded as the families thought, and ghosts that lived in the most prestigious of social settings. I entered deeply into the life of that community, conducted services each Sunday morning, preached sermons of questionable expertise, and organized and ran a daily vacation Bible school.

When Fred returned, he found me well ensconced in the affections of the people. He was planning to leave permanently in another year, so he and the church decided that I would succeed him the following September, my second year at the university. It never occurred to them or to me to think that the bishop needed to be consulted or that he had any knowledge of what was happening at one of his churches. I went to Roxboro about once a month during my first year just to stay in touch. When fall 1950 arrived, I became lay reader in charge. I was still paid fifty dollars a month, but now this also had to cover the cost of transportation. As an economy measure, each Saturday, I thumbed a ride the thirty miles to Roxboro, where I was given a room by Mrs. Carlyle Brooks, an eighty-year-old widow and mother of Roxboro's wealthiest citizen. My routine each weekend was to make one or two pastoral visits, organize and run Sunday school, and conduct morning prayer with sermon except for the Sunday the priest celebrated holy communion. I loved every minute of it. The church actually grew, an expansion of the parish house was built, a confirmation class was prepared, and I even presented these candidates to Bishop Penick on his official visitation. This new position now meant that I had fifty dollars a month to supplement my meager food budget. I could add an egg to breakfast and a ground beef patty to dinner. I finished my degree with no help from my mother, no indebtedness, and no bank balance.

In 1951 as I headed toward graduation, I was listening to the radio to hear the election returns in a bitterly fought primary for the Democratic nomination to the U.S. Senate between the incumbent Dr. Frank Graham, the former president of the University of North Carolina, who had been appointed to the Senate seat by Governor Kerr Scott upon the death of Senator J. Melville Broughton. His challenger was Willis Smith, an earlier generation's version of Jesse Helms or Strom Thurmond, who played on racial fears to gain votes. It had been a dirty campaign in which literature suggested that if Frank Graham were reelected, "race mixing and interracial marriage would ensue." My blood would boil when I saw these ads, but in North Carolina in the early 1950s they had enormous power. Dr. Graham was swept out of office. I vowed that my deepest ambition was to live long enough to cast my first vote against Willis Smith. I did not get that opportunity, since he died in office before his term expired.

While I was listening to those election results, I heard the first news of the invasion of South Korea by the army of North Korea. I had been fourteen when World War II was over. With victory won, the draft was ended. None of us were registered. I did not grasp the full implications of that news that night, but it unfolded in dramatic detail over the next few days.

The question this war posed was for me intensely personal—whether or not it should interrupt my pursuit of the priesthood. I sought the advice of one who would affect my destiny with his decision-making power. I made an appointment to see Bishop Penick in Raleigh at his earliest convenience.

There was no question in his mind, and it was his style to make decisions quickly. He made me a postulant for holy orders on the spot. There were no commissions on ministry for bishops to contend with in those days. I was to go to Virginia Theological Seminary in Alexandria, Virginia. Both Bishop Penick and Mr. Crandall were graduates of that institution, so that was fine with me. The bishop wrote my draft board and requested a 4D classification for a seminary student. He extracted from me a promise that if the war was still on when I graduated, I would seek a chaplain's position. My vocation was not to be deterred by the Korean war.

My university life was not all work and no play. Granted, I did not have much money, but both friends and romantic attachments were part of my social life, which was not surprisingly centered in the church.

Indeed, it was a Canterbury Club social event held at the church in my junior year that I met a recent transfer to the university named Joan Lydia Ketner. She was dating my roommate David Woodruff. The next time I saw Joan Ketner was when the Chapel Hill Glee Club presented Bach's *B Minor Mass* in concert. This magnificent music featured two soloists. Singing the soprano lead was none other than Joan Ketner. Singing the baritone lead was the Kenan Professor of Classical Language and Literature, a man named Urban Tignor Holmes, Jr. It was a moving performance and a group of us, including Joan, went out afterward for a celebratory party. Our spirits were high and Joan, having just completed a winning performance, was ecstatic. Her voice and her poise gave her new dimensions in my mind. I also learned that she sang in the regular Sunday choir at the Chapel of the Cross and was therefore an active Episcopalian. My church job in Roxboro took me away every Sunday, so I knew little about Sunday worship in Chapel Hill.

Joan had completed her first three academic years at Catawba College, a small liberal arts school in Rowan County, North Carolina, near her home. She was a commuter who lived at home, a situation made necessary, she told me, by her father's health.

Joan was a lovely young woman, extremely bright and very shy. She had brown hair, green eyes, and a winning smile. When I discovered that my roommate was not continuing to ask her out, I took a chance and invited her out for our first date. The relationship grew slowly. I visited her home briefly over that Christmas. It gave me an insight into her family that was slightly off-putting and served primarily to build anxiety.

James Ketner, her father, was a lawyer who had decided to opt for security instead of the risks of private practice. He had entered government service as an attorney in the Internal Revenue Service and had risen in the ranks. He traveled in a fairly small orbit that included Charlotte, Asheville, and Winston-Salem. His friends, however, were wealthy businessmen. They were the movers and shakers in Rowan County, and he seemed to be a tax adviser to many corporate CEOs in the furniture industry, a dominant industry in that section of North Carolina. He had come from a relatively poor German family, but had been industrious and ambitious. He had two other brothers who had been equally ambitious. One became a doctor and one a lawyer in private practice. Jim Ketner was the poorest of the three. He was politically very conservative, reflecting the political opinions of his friends, who believed that Franklin D. Roosevelt was a total disaster. Senator Robert Taft of Ohio was his political hero. He resented deeply the Dewey wing of the Republican party, and when that wing backed Dwight

Eisenhower to snatch the nomination from Senator Taft in 1952, he was enraged.

Joan's mother was Frances Baptista, whose father had been a member of John Philip Sousa's marching band. Frances was probably the most shy, repressed, and pious woman I had ever met. She was a loner who hated parties as much as her husband enjoyed them. She kept a fastidious house furnished in ice-blue shades that seemed to match her personality. She lived in semi-isolation. The Ketner home was on Route 52, about three miles east of the town of Salisbury. She did not drive, which guaranteed that she had few new experiences. She spent her time watching birds and reading religious books and tracts. Her favorite authors were Bonnell Spencer, a monk in the Order of the Holy Cross, and F. P. Harton, an English divine whose book *The Elements of the Spiritual Life* was significantly underlined and in which the placement of permanent bookmarks led her quickly to her favorite passages. Her world revolved around St. Luke's Episcopal Church in Salisbury, where she would go every Sunday at 8:00 A.M. and every Wednesday at 10:30 A.M. to attend services of holy communion. Those were her only two trips away from her house each week. When she was brought to church on Wednesday, either by a friend or by taxi, she would on her way home do her weekly grocery shopping.

When Jim Ketner attended parties, Frances would go with him. Jim and his friends would drink while Frances would sit demurely in a chair sipping a glass of water through the evening. Jim and his friends would dance, flirt, laugh, and occasionally pinch someone else's wife. Frances would keep her gaze directed at the floor and never enter into the frivolity. She was always the first wife who sought to leave. Since Jim was frequently the life of the party, the group endured Frances in order to have Jim around.

Shirley, Joan's older sister, was a very beautiful young woman who had recently received a degree in zoology and, following her father's pattern, had entered the service of the federal government. There she met and married another civil servant. I quickly became aware of a deep rivalry between Joan and her older sister. Shirley was clearly Jim's daughter. Joan was clearly Frances's daughter.

Their younger brother, Jimmy, was at that time a delicately wired teenager. Sure in all of his adolescent opinions and aggressive to a fault, he was an aficionado of speed, whether in cars or airplanes. He appeared not to be close to anyone in his family.

I took in all these impressions on that first visit and simply registered that this was not a home I would choose to visit with regularity. I had the impression that the feelings were mutual. It did not concern me greatly at the time, for my relationship with Joan could not then be called serious.

In spring 1951 that relationship did become an exclusive one, although she was not "pinned," as we said in college. Membership in a fraternity was simply outside my financial capability, but people thought of us as a couple.

Joan was supposed to graduate in June 1951, but a course in organic chemistry was not successfully completed and she had not received proper credit for all of her transferring Catawba courses. She needed to return for one more semester. Her father was displeased and suspected, I am sure, that there was something deliberate about the failed course. Perhaps there was, but it was not conscious. I was delighted. This would be my senior year, and Joan would be on campus at least half of that year. During that semester we saw each other daily. We walked to classes together, frequently ate together, studied together, and went to social functions together.

Joan, like her mother, did not enjoy parties or dancing. She simply fitted into our rather sedate church-oriented group of friends. I would leave for Roxboro late Saturday afternoon, usually after the UNC football game, and return on Sunday night, when I would tell her about my adventures at St. Mark's. She was a good listener, but had no desire to enter my Roxboro life. To my knowledge she never visited this little town that meant so much to me.

By Christmas 1951, I was as sure as any twenty-year-old can be that she was the one I wished to marry. I am certain it was not a mature decision, but I was a young man in a hurry. My father had died at the age of fifty-four and deep down I thought that an early death would also be my destiny. I dreaded the thought that, like my own father, I might leave young children in as fragile a state as my father had left me. Having children when I was young was a conscious priority. By this time I was officially enrolled in the Virginia Theological Seminary in Alexandria, which had a policy against marrying while enrolled in the program. So one either entered married or one waited three years to be married after graduation. I did not intend to wait three years. David Woodruff was also entering the Virginia Seminary that fall and planned to marry in the summer. The herd spirit was in play. Between Thanksgiving and Christmas I sought out the local jeweler in Roxboro and purchased an infinitesimally small diamond for two hundred dollars. I took the diamond home in its box, placed it under my pillow, and periodically opened it quickly in the hopes that it would look bigger. It never did. It was the tiniest mounted solitaire I have ever seen, more like diamond dust than a diamond. It was all I could afford. I planned to present it to Joan as her Christmas present. That of course meant another visit over the holidays with the Ketner family.

Joan was thrilled with my gift and all that it meant. We were out that night at dinner and did not return until the Ketners had gone to sleep. The next morning Joan went into their bedroom to show them the ring. It was embarrassing. Not only was the diamond painfully small, but I had incorrectly guessed her ring size, and it dangled on her finger.

When Mr. Ketner came down to breakfast, his only comment was, "That was a lovely ring you gave my daughter last night, Jack." He was neither congratulatory nor enthusiastic. I am quite sure he had hoped that Joan would marry into the family of one of his wealthy friends. He was active in St. Luke's Church, even serving as the warden of the vestry on one occasion, but had little respect for clergy. He felt they were lazy, nonproductive people. On one occasion he tried to get the vestry of St. Luke's to install a time clock in the parish house, so that the rector could punch in and out whenever he was working.

It was the former rector of St. Luke's that Mrs. Ketner particularly treasured. He was the Reverend W. Moultrie Moore, who had, just a year before, moved to Charlotte on a career path that would lead him into the House of Bishops. Moultrie tended toward the Anglo-Catholic side of our church, and his life was marked with a deep piety. He affirmed Mrs. Ketner's spiritual disciplines and did not threaten her strange religious habits. When our wedding day came, Moultrie would preside over the ceremony, assisted by David Yates.

Since they were now to be my in-laws, I thought it imperative to break down the barriers that seemed to divide us. I sought both the opportunity and the appropriate subjects by which I might engage this couple in some meaningful conversation. Mr. Ketner was not interested in talking about church issues, and he would begin his other conversations by making dogmatic assertions about race, or Harry Truman, or how evil the Democrats in Congress were, which would set up nothing but a debate. My choices were to absorb these aggressive statements or to offer a contrary point of view. I tried the silent route, but his racist comments were, to my ears, so outrageous that I could not in silence endure them without compromising my own integrity. So our relationship devolved into a rather tense one. I am confident he regarded me as immature and arrogant. He was undoubtedly correct on both counts. I am also sure he discussed this discomfort with his prospective son-in-law with his circle of friends, where his political and racial attitudes would be affirmed.

It was no better with Mrs. Ketner. Her ability to discuss any biblical or theological subject was limited to her wondering about how Mary had prepared Jesus' swaddling clothes with silk, satin, and lace so that his tender and holy baby's flesh would not be scratched by the hay in the manger. She also made no secret about her conviction that bodies were displeasing, unpleasant, and repellant, which meant that sex was at best a necessary evil, a woman's duty that was meant to be endured. I never saw Mrs. Ketner kiss her husband or demonstrate any physical affection at all. I am certain a more mature person would have recognized Mrs. Ketner's fragility and not confronted her. I was not that mature. But my primary experience in that house was the need for space in which to breathe. It was for me a stifling environment. When I would tell Joan my concerns about my relationships with her parents, I actually found her responses encouraging. She herself had interesting relationships with her parents. She courted her father, seeking his love and approval. She felt she never received it. Her relationship with her mother was compensatory; that is, she welcomed her mother's affection as a substitute for what her father did not give her.

In any event, we were engaged and we made plans to be married in the church in Salisbury on Saturday, September 5, 1952. I would enter the seminary along with my roommate, David Woodruff, as a married man.

The courtship would be long-distance in the final semester of my senior year. Joan planned to follow her sister's path and move to Washington, seeking a position in the government. I thought it strange that this family who excoriated the government as a bloated, incompetent, wasteful bureaucracy all sought their livelihood from it. At one time or another every employed member of this family received a federal government salary check. But I did have the grace not to point that out.

At the end of her final semester in January 1952, Joan moved to Washington, got a room in a house near the National Episcopal Cathedral, and began making job applications. She was not immediately successful and subsisted on a semi-volunteer job selling cards and religious effects in the cathedral's bookstore. Finally, around Easter she landed an entry-level position with the Central Intelligence Agency. She would be in the employ of the CIA until the beginning of our senior year in seminary, when pregnancy ended her working career.

I called seldom, for long-distance was still, in my mind, an expensive luxury. I wrote frequently. My life was filled with senior-year activities, and my work in Roxboro took care of my weekends. I was still thrilled at the learning experience I had at the university and would graduate with a 95 average. I was pleased with my academic success and believed that a life of scholarship was mine to possess.

During spring 1952, on the weekends the priest came to Roxboro, I made several trips to Washington to see Joan. They were happy times, as we made our wedding plans and prepared to move close to the seminary, where convenient bus service provided easy transportation to the CIA offices near the Lincoln Memorial.

As the summer and graduation drew near, my need to make money became dominant. I finished in Roxboro on the first of June and planned to return to Charlotte for those last three months before seminary. With Mr. Crandall's assistance, I obtained a summer job at a machine shop in Charlotte owned by Ralph Bouligny. He was an active layman in both his local Episcopal church and the diocese and was on the board of trustees at St. Mary's Junior College, an Episcopal institution in Raleigh, North Carolina. This school had just launched a capital-fund campaign, and Mr. Bouligny was chairing the Charlotte phase of that effort. He hired me to do two things. First, I worked forty-five hours a week operating a lathe in his machine shop. In obvious work clothes and carrying my lunch pail, I punched the time clock each day before 7:00 A.M. My first assignment was to ream out the end of each of ten thousand pieces of pipe. I remember seeing the carts lined up around my workplace. I had never seen so much pipe. When that job was over and I reported to my supervisor for my next assignment, I discovered that it was to turn each of the ten thousand pieces of pipe around and ream out the other end. It was my first experience with the drudging sameness of industrial labor. I left work at 4:00 P.M., went home, cleaned the formidable grime of an industrial sweatshop off my body, hands, and nails, and ate a quick dinner. Then I transformed myself into a proper middle-class American, putting on a suit and tie to undertake my second assignment. I called each night on alumni of St. Mary's Junior College, soliciting their pledges and contributions to the capital-fund campaign. I did that Sunday night through Thursday night, averaging three calls an evening. Each Friday after work I went into Mr. Bouligny's office to report on my progress. The two jobs together, plus living at home, meant that I could save money for the wedding.

The rehearsal party, usually the responsibility of the groom's family, was covered by my Uncle Ernest. I had to buy the wedding band, my wife's going-away corsage, decent wedding clothes for myself, and the honeymoon. I knew so little about where to go that I wound up making reservations for one week in the only place with which I was familiar, the Hanover Inn at Wrightsville Beach, North Carolina. This old beachfront hotel had been the place where, prior to my father's death, our family had gone on summer holidays. I had remembered it so fondly through my seven- to nine-year-old eyes that it seemed like a good, romantic place to go. The beach in September was not crowded, and the ocean water was still warm and lovely.

On my last visit to Washington prior to the wedding, however, an ominous note entered our relationship. By this time Joan had moved into a three-room apartment. I had not planned well for this trip and assumed I could get a hotel room for Friday night, but some national event was gathering in the capital city that night and there were no rooms to be had. I suggested I sleep on the sofa in her living room, but she felt that this would compromise her reputation. That seems like strange reasoning to me today, but in 1952 I was sympathetic and secretly admired her moral code. It was not different from my own. I, too, was a deeply repressed puritan who identified desire with sin and saw sex outside of marriage as simply wrong. Even as an engaged couple we had limited our physical relationship to holding hands and a goodnight kiss.

Confronted with that dilemma, we worked out what was, in both our minds, a morally acceptable compromise. We would go out to dinner, return to her apartment for dessert and coffee, talk together as late as we thought appropriate, and then I would leave. I would walk around Washington until early in the morning when I would return for breakfast. I smile now at our naïveté in thinking that leaving a girlfriend's apartment at 2:00 A.M. and returning at 5:00 or 5:30 protected her reputation. Nonetheless, I left her apartment at around 2:00 A.M. and walked around the National Zoo for three hours, sitting on a park bench from time to time. It was a long three hours. Perhaps I should have viewed Joan's insistence on this routine as abnormal, but we were both locked into our repressed pasts, and this was not the time to bring to consciousness that overwhelming guilt that had been employed for decades to keep our biological urges under control. I pressed the edges of our agreement by coming in nearer to 5:00 than 5:30 A.M., but the symbol had been preserved and that was deemed acceptable. I had a hotel room for Saturday night.

That next evening, however, was equally troubling. We went to an event at the National Cathedral. It was over about 11:00 P.M. Returning to our car, we did not drive away at once, but we began to talk in the car. We held hands as we talked, but when it was time to go, I pulled her close to me and kissed her passionately. It was certainly returned. She stayed in my arms and I held her tightly, kissing her many times. It seemed to me discreet enough, but I yearned to let her know that I loved her deeply.

We were in that parking lot for no more than an hour before driving back to Joan's apartment, where I again kissed her goodnight. She seemed troubled. I assumed she was just tired. I went to my hotel and to sleep.

Our plans were that I would pick her up in time for church the next morning. We were going to attend St. Alban's, the Episcopal parish on the cathedral grounds where Joan had worshiped regularly since moving to the District of Columbia. I arrived in plenty of time and greeted her warmly. She was attired in a dark, austere outfit with a skirt far longer than present styles mandated. She appeared to be dressed for mourning. My warm greeting was not returned. She was clearly unhappy. We walked out to the car and got in. Before I could get the key into the ignition, Joan announced that the engagement was off. She explained that she felt dirty and unclean because of our behavior the previous night. It was clear, she said, that I did not respect her, and that she was not respectable. She was in tears, angry, and quite distraught. My response was shock, followed by amazement and hurt. I tried to reason with her, to assure her that we had violated no rules, broken no taboos, and were, in fact, towers of moral correctness. She was not ready to hear such words. I suppressed a genuine desire to be angry and to say that if that was what she wanted, it was okay with me. Instead, I sank into silence. It was a heavy atmosphere as we drove to church with no further conversation.

Perhaps the service helped. Maybe when we said the confession, "We have done those things which we ought not to have done," and "There is no health in us," the guilt she felt began to be dispelled. I don't know, but when the service was over, we had lunch together and the engagement was back on. I left after lunch for the long trip home. I was troubled, but I set my anxieties aside. I would not see Joan again until she came home to Salisbury about two weeks before the wedding.

The wedding was fun. The families were on their best behavior. My best man was my brother, Will. Joan's best friend in Salisbury, Grace (Tillie) Woodson, was her maid of honor. Significantly, the choice for this role was not her sister, Shirley. Others in the wedding were our Chapel Hill friends, several of them future seminarians, plus Fred Ferris, who had started my Roxboro career. It was Fred who helped me more than anyone else to get ready for this wedding. I had no earthly idea what would be required of me.

The wedding over, we drove off to the North Carolina coast in a car provided by Mr. Ketner. I suppose that no two more naive, apprehensive, repressed, and fearful people ever got married before. The embarrassment of living together was overwhelming to us both. So was the need to conform to our expectations of what marriage was supposed to be. But over that week, in tender moments holding hands on the beach, talking over our after-dinner coffee, and holding each other as we fell asleep, the strangeness gradually diminished and the joy of married life began to emerge.

The honeymoon week was all too short and we began to turn our eyes toward the next phase of our life as members of the seminary community. It was still an era in which the man was the professional and the woman was the wife of the professional. We would learn together how to live into those roles as a graduate student at the Virginia Theological Seminary and as an employee of the Central Intelligence Agency. It was a fast-moving life for this now twenty-one-year-old young man.

# 6

# Priestly Formation on
# the Holy Hill

✳

VIRGINIA Theological Seminary in Alexandria is known to its alumni as the "Holy Hill." Established in the nineteenth century as a country retreat in which to train men in the evangelical tradition of the Anglican Communion, it had long ago been engulfed by the suburban sprawl of metropolitan Washington, D.C. Consequently, it is sitting on what arguably might be called the most expensive undeveloped piece of land in the United States.

The anchor and landmark of this campus was a strange looking building known as Aspinwall Hall, but called by faculty and alumni alike the "Chinese Revenge." From its tower one could see a panoramic view of our nation's capitol. A roughly oval-shaped drive linked the two halves of the campus. In my day the Aspinwall half contained all of the classrooms, the administrative building, the bookstore, and, for those who traded the austerity and inconvenience of an ancient building for the romance of tradition, there was a single dormitory. The other half of the campus contained more modern dormitories, the refectory, and Scott Lounge, a kind of campus living room where a piano, flowers, and overstuffed furniture created an inviting atmosphere. About midway around the oval drive was the seminary library and an auditorium where lectures were sometimes delivered and famous people, especially missionaries and successful alumni, were invited to speak.

Off to one side of Aspinwall was the seminary chapel, which was quite obviously the focal point of the community's life. A brick neo-Gothic structure, it housed a bare holy table that had visible legs so it would not be confused with an altar on which "the sacrifice of the Mass might be offered." No candles were allowed on this holy table, since they were believed to be a "popish" influence. All services here, whether morning prayer or holy communion, were conducted in the low church vestments of a black cassock, a white surplice, and a stole for communion services or a tippet for morning prayer. The faculty had assigned stalls in the choir or chancel section; the more ornate and impressive ones went to the senior endowed-chair professors, and the junior faculty and instructors claimed the rest. Once a student learned the seating pattern, he could know at a glance which of his teachers had missed worship on that occasion.

Each morning the community gathered to start the day in that chapel. The pattern was daily morning prayer except on Thursday, when the community's weekly communion service was held. Once a week the morning prayer service would feature a senior student who would preach his (there were no hers) senior sermon to what was probably the most critical congregation he would ever face.

Entering this campus for the first time, I was engulfed by the aura. People spoke of past professors and deans, like Cosby Bell or "Skinny" Rollins, in worshipful tones. The present faculty had men of enormous reputation in our faith community. Clifford Stanley and Albert Mollegen were thought to be giants of our time. Reuel Howe was also generally placed in that topmost tier. He was the one who had introduced clinical pastoral education to the curriculum as a requirement for graduation and thus had begun the psychological training for clergy aimed at making them effective counselors in their ministry. Clifford Stanley was the primary spokesman for traditional academic standards and was singularly unimpressed by Reuel Howe. The tension and antipathy between these two men was the polarizing reality in which all learning took place in that community. A man named Robert O. Kevin, who signed everything ROK and was known as the "Rok of Ages," completed the "big four" of the faculty. He was a professor of Old Testament and Hebrew and, though not the "name professor" of this faculty, would prove to be a tremendous influence on me.

A new dean, E. Felix Kloman, entered with my class in the fall of 1952. He was the former rector of St. Alban's Church on the cathedral grounds in Washington and who thus had been Joan's rector during that brief time when she lived in the capital city before our marriage. He was not a scholar in any primary sense, but he had great administrative and organizational skills, which were deemed to be the primary talents needed at that moment in the seminary's history.

Dr. Kloman presided over our opening orientation session, introduced the faculty, and said a few things about the history of the place. He also began this session by telling a story that dissipated the heavy levels of piety that infected me and, I gather, was normal for an incoming class of prospective clergy.

His story was about a clergyman who was calling on a man in the hospital suffering from a kidney stone. The first day this pastor called, the patient was in much pain and was sweating profusely. However, the next day when the pastor returned, the patient was dancing around the room singing an Easter song entitled "A Tisket, a Tasket, a Green and Yellow Basket." The pastor inquired about the meaning of this song. The patient countered by suggesting that the minister had not quite understood the words. What the patient was shouting was "I pissed it, I passed it. Ain't I a lucky bastard!" So much for that kidney stone. The assembly roared with laughter. My own laugh was tempered by shock that such language would be used in this holy place.

My first semester's classes provided me with access only to Dr. Kevin among the big four of the faculty. We were introduced mostly to the "Kiddie Korps," as we called them—Bill Clebsch in Church history, Jesse Trotter in apologetics, Bob Cox in New Testament, and Bart Lloyd in pastoral care.

It was three months past my twenty-first birthday when I joined this community as the youngest person in the seminary family. My class, still reflecting veterans returning from service in World War II, averaged thirty-two years of age and ranged from my youthfulness to a fifty-seven-year-old man who had been an auto executive in Detroit. We had a retired army colonel, former lawyers, businessmen, teachers, newspaper executives, and a football coach. We were all Anglo Saxon or at least of European descent. But the class ahead of me, which would produce a record number of future bishops, had the first American-born black student in this seminary's history. His name was John Walker, later to become bishop of Washington.

The thing that surprised me most about the seminary community was its open and nonhierarchical character. The faculty members lived in homes on the campus, and their homes were always open to us at any time of the day or night. Also, the students and faculty all called each other by their first names. I had, at this point in my life, rarely called any adult by his or her first name and here I was being invited into a peer relationship with men who were almost legendary in my mind. It was not an easy hurdle to get over, but in time the big four were Cliff, Molle, Reuel, and Bob to me. First names were not a problem with the junior faculty. I came to appreciate this practice, for it discouraged the parent-child games that marked most faculty-student relationships and it trained us by example not to play those games with our congregations or some version of that favorite ecclesiastical pastime known as "Father Knows Best." Indeed, the title "Father" was simply not in the lexicon of this seminary.

My academic success continued in graduate school, and I quickly was recognized as one of the top students in my class. I continued to revel in this new academic challenge. Bob Kevin made the Hebrew Scriptures live for me in wonderful ways and gave me a love for things Jewish. In time he would introduce me to the prophets in such a way as to enable them to become good friends. My other favorite first-semester course was apologetics with Jesse Trotter. Here we began to look at the dialogue between the thought forms of the world and the story of the Gospels. Both of these courses would open doors for me to themes that would dominate my ordained life and most especially my writing career.

One other memory from that first wonderful and growing year focused on the events surrounding the death of Cliff Stanley's wife, Helen. Her malady, which I later learned was leukemia, burst upon our community with startling suddenness. She was in a comatose state almost immediately. The members of my class had never taken a class with Cliff and knew him only slightly, yet we were the ones who seemed to be the most affected by Helen's sickness. Perhaps our naive religious zeal or heavy piety, those very emotions that had propelled us into seminary in the first place, were the realities that caused our more profound response and thus set us apart.

Our class decided corporately that this sickness was a struggle between light and darkness, or God and Satan. We were going to stand on God's side and do battle for her life, so we organized a prayer vigil. Members of our class signed the roster to keep the prayers bombarding the throne of God on a twenty-four-hour basis. Those of us who volunteered to stand watch and offer prayers alone in the dark seminary chapel in the wee hours of the morning thought of ourselves as the most virtuous, the most romantic, and the most stalwart of all of God's soldiers. I am sure we enjoyed the ego-filling experience of being visibly sleepy and exhausted in public the next day. But when one is in a battle for life, sleep becomes a minor consideration. We kept up the vigil for several days. I often wonder in retrospect how we would have sustained a long siege, but we never got to find out. Helen died in the hours before dawn of the fourth day of our heroic effort.

The news spread as we gathered that day for morning chapel. A simple announcement was made, and prayers for the departed and mourners were offered. Speaking to each other quietly as if still in church, we walked somberly to our first class, a required Old Testament course in which all the members of our first-year class would be present. When we entered the lecture hall, Cliff Stanley was sitting at the desk in front with Bob Kevin. We took our seats and wondered what would proceed. Bob opened the class by saying that Cliff had asked for the opportunity of addressing us this morning. I had not been this close to death since my father died about ten years earlier. I certainly had never listened to a grieving man who had just a few hours earlier lost his wife and the mother of his teenage children. I had never been part of a religious prayer vigil that had so clearly failed in its purpose of hurling back the forces of evil. All of these realities conspired to make this an indelible moment of high, unforgettable drama.

Cliff, his voice anything but steady, began by thanking us for our caring. His concern was that we might be disillusioned that our efforts on Helen's behalf had come to naught. He wanted to assure us that prayer did not always work the way we expected, that God was still God, and that what we had done was to unleash vast quantities of loving energy that had its effect in many ways. It had sustained him and his family, and perhaps it had eased Helen's transition or given peace to her soul. But it had not been able to turn around the destruction in her body that resulted in her death. He assured us that grief was neither inappropriate nor unmanly. Certainly it was not unchristian to shed tears or to experience a broken heart. He would smile again, he assured us; so would his children and so would we. This experience, he said, would bind him to our class and us to him in a way that would be different from the experience of any class that he had ever taught before. He would look forward to what that meant. He hoped we would too. He closed his remarks by asserting that he had trusted God for his entire lifetime and that trust would not be diminished by this death. He led us in prayer during which his wavering voice broke, but he managed to finish. He wiped the tears from his cheeks. Bob Kevin embraced him and, waving good-bye, Cliff departed. I and my classmates had a great deal of new reality to process. Bob Kevin could hardly move into the lecture for the day. The trials of David with his son Absalom simply did not touch where we were. He used the remaining time to allow us to talk together about Helen's death and what it meant, although words seemed inane. We soon adjourned that class and spent time with our own thoughts.

Helen's funeral two days later was in our packed chapel. The voices of students, faculty, alumni, and friends were raised to sing defiant songs of faith. There was no sermon, for in that day a eulogy was thought to be unepiscopal and was not provided for in the burial office of the 1928 prayer book. When the service was concluded, Helen's body was borne by members of the faculty to her grave on the seminary grounds to the accompaniment of hymns. It was a funeral the likes of which I had never seen. It had posed for me the ancient theological dilemma. Did God have the power to heal? If so, why did God not use it? If God did not have the power to heal, then could God still be said to be God? Was God malevolent? Was God impotent? Were there any other possibilities? One who is planning to be a pastor to those "in trouble, sorrow, need, sickness or any other adversity" must deal with these questions.

Our first class with Cliff Stanley, a required course entitled "The History of Christian Thought," began in the second term of our first year. This class would go through two semesters before we began two semesters of systematic theology. The thinking was that we needed first to understand how others dealt in their time with various theological issues before we began to build the way we would deal with those same issues. Cliff Stanley, the primary and only "name" theologian on our faculty, would be the teacher for all four of these units. There was a sense in which this would be the center of our theological education, and Cliff, as the theologian, was in fact the backbone of the faculty. He was the first among equals.

It was clear as we read the writings and listened to Cliff speak about the theologians of the past that he had particular favorites. Paul, Augustine, Luther, Schleiermacher, and Barth were his heroes. His primary and most influential teacher when he did the work for his Th.D. degree at Union Seminary in New York was Paul Tillich, a German Reformed theologian who had joined the faculty of Union and later of Harvard Divinity School in a flight from the horrors of Adolf Hitler's Nazi Germany. While at Union, Tillich was surrounded with what must have been the greatest assembly of scholars ever gathered onto one faculty in an American school of theology. Reinhold Niebuhr was there in social ethics, James Meilenburg in Hebrew/ Old Testament studies, Walter Russell Bowie in homiletics, and Frederick C. Grant in New Testament studies. Union was probably the mecca of theological education in the Western world.

It was Tillich, however, who was to shape Cliff Stanley theologically, and it was Cliff Stanley who was to shape me theologically. God was not a person to Tillich. God was the Ground of Being, unknowable, mysterious, without form. Most people do not worship God, said Tillich. They worship, rather, a human creation endowed with supernatural qualities. He spoke of the God beyond the gods of men and women. He correlated God with Being, Christ with existence, and Holy Spirit with church. I struggled with concepts I had never heard before. My personal God, a kind of divine father protector, a bit of a Mr. Fixit, what Dietrich Bonhoeffer would later call the God of the gaps, began to shake visibly, to wobble before my eyes, and to fade perceptibly. I had begun my long theological journey into maturity.

I became aware that these issues and debates about the nature of God were commonplace in the theological academy and were neither threatening nor controversial. Theologians discussed them in a quite matter-of-fact way, but seldom did they face, at least over a protracted period of time, a theologically untrained congregation. Tillich did preach in both the Union Seminary Chapel and the Harvard Chapel on a fairly regular basis,[1] but the audiences who heard him in these rarefied academic settings were hardly your typical pew sitters. These theologians never had to deal with the reactions of ordinary folks who felt that their spiritual leader was destroying their faith. That would be the job of graduates like myself. Most graduates, I was to learn, however, would not rise to this challenge. They would graduate, pack up their seminary notes, and revert to the piety of their youth, undergirding their preaching with traditional religious understandings. They would claim the power to explain the ways of God to their congregations, thus encouraging the unbelievable concepts of a manipulative, invasive, this-world-oriented deity who governed the intimate details of people's lives from a position just beyond the sky. I vowed that I would be different when I finally became a priest. Little did I know how difficult that would be. For now I was content simply to drink in this wondrous, disturbing new knowledge and to have my mind expand, sometimes to where it seemed about to explode.

The "name" professor in the New Testament department was Albert Mollegen. His course on the Gospel of John, which came late in our academic careers, was rumored to be the most important, perhaps the crown jewel of the seminary career. But when that much-hyped course finally arrived, it was a disappointment. Molle's yellowed lecture notes gave evidence of the lack of fresh thought.

The other person in the New Testament department was a young priest named Robert Cox. I did not find him to be an outstanding teacher and a few weeks after his course on Romans began, I became aware that I would never learn the New Testament adequately in his class. So I devised a study formula to compensate for this. I would get faculty recommendations on the best commentaries available in English on the various books of the New Testament and I would work through these commentaries, taking copious notes on each one of them. So Denis Nineham on Mark, Edwin Hoskyns on John, Karl Barth on Romans, and John McKay on Ephesians became my academic companions. I would revel in the dating controversies of the various books of the New Testament, the debates as to which of the Epistles were genuinely Pauline, and the actual identity of those who finally wrote the Gospels. I would enter into what were called the source theories of the New Testament, mastering the "Q" hypothesis, which I would reject some forty years later. Never has a weak professor done more to inspire a student to new heights than Bob Cox did for me.

In church history, we had a wonderful contrast between the older professor, Alexander C. Zabriskie, and the aspiring comer, William A. Clebsch. Zab was a bit of a mystic, standing humbly before the wonder and sweep of history, greatly admiring the heroes of the past. Bill Clebsch was brash, arrogant, and competent. He was an impressive scholar and lecturer. He would enter the room, put a brief outline of the day's lecture on the board, and proceed to cover his material with great skill. I was drawn to this young man and would elect to take my senior seminar with him on the philosophy of history, where Arnold Toynbee would become a key person in my thought processes. Bill Clebsch, however, could not deal with the confining life of the seminary career and left the Holy Hill for the challenge of a secular university. He wound up being a professor of history at Stanford University. In time he also found the church itself to be too confining and resigned from his ordination. I did not understand his reasoning for this step, but over the course of years I too came to grasp, as he must have, the need to escape the theological and ecclesiastical boundaries that had been placed on the pursuit of truth by a fearful hierarchy.

During that first year of our training we were encouraged to attend a wide variety of churches of all traditions. We were warned that this would be the last time we would have a Sunday free. In our second and third years we would be in supervised fieldwork on Sundays. After that, free weekends would never again be part of our priestly lives. So I went to Peter Marshall's Presbyterian church in Washington to hear his successor, another Scotsman, preach in that magnificent accent. I went to Methodist, Baptist, Pentecostal,

Roman Catholic, Unitarian, and Swedenborgian churches. I went once or twice
to synagogues on Friday evenings. But I also went to a variety of Episcopal
churches.

One of my two favorites was Grace Church on Russell Road in Alexandria, where Edward Merrow was rector. He was a massive hulk of a man who
had once played professional football as well as sought out a career in the
Metropolitan Opera. He was also an Anglo-Catholic and appealed to that
aspect of church life to which Mr. Crandall had introduced me. He was
called "Father." He referred to the Eucharist as the Mass. He sang the service with a resonant voice and had a self-confident aggressiveness about
him. He was known to announce that those persons who were not regularly
pledging members of Grace Church should remove their children from his
Sunday school at once. He was not going to educate them free of charge. In
the world of clergy so eager to please and so willing to accommodate, this
was an attention-getting and invigorating change of pace. I was, however,
destined very soon to abandon the Anglo-Catholic piety of Grace Church
and Father Merrow. It became for me just a new ecclesiastical form of
fundamentalism that I could tolerate no more than I could tolerate biblical
fundamentalism. Yet much of Ed Merrow's style I not only envied, but emu-
lated.

The other church to which I was particularly drawn was the Church of
the Epiphany in downtown Washington. The rector was the Reverend Leland
Stark, a rising ecclesiastical star who combined provocative, powerful
preaching with a low church, yet dignified, form of worship. He also had a
regular parade of outstanding world figures gracing his pulpit. I did not at
that time get to meet Dr. Stark except as one among many worshipers at his
door. But impressive he was. I was very pleased to learn in spring 1953 that
he had been elected the sixth bishop of the Diocese of Newark. That, of
course, meant nothing special to me then. It did, however, guarantee that in
time I would get to know him well.

As the first year drew to a close, the big decision on everyone's mind was
where each of us would go to do our institutional unit of clinical pastoral
education (CPE), that aspect of training that Virginia Seminary was to be
among the first to require as a prerequisite for ordination. This was the area
in which Reuel Howe was the dominant professor.

We had to receive this training in a mental institution, a hospital, or a
penitentiary. Since Joan was working in Washington, my choice was limited
to St. Elizabeth's Mental Hospital, the D.C. General Hospital in Wash-

ington, or the D.C. Federal Penitentiary fifteen miles south of Alexandria in
Lorton, Virginia. I was eager to go to either a mental hospital or a prison
because my understanding of life in either type of institution was almost
nonexistent. Also the directors of these programs at both St. Elizabeth's and
Lorton were highly regarded by upperclassmen. I applied to both and was
pleased to be appointed to Lorton, my first choice.

Each day a group of five students drove together to Lorton. Among the
five were two very close friends, Bill Moll, a former duck farmer from
Virginia, and Colley Bell, a candidate from the Diocese of Newark. This was
my second contact with that diocese, but that did not register as significant
at the time.

Our supervisor, Knox Kreutzer, had graduated from our seminary just a
few years earlier. He was a bit on the pudgy side, light-hearted, slightly
irreverent, and very well trained in both psychological and supervisory
skills. He would prove to be a major resource for my growth and development. The training consisted of our interviewing the newly arriving in-
mates, writing up the interviews verbatim, and then sharing them in a group
seminar with Knox. In the discussion we would analyze the interaction,
show where the conversation came to a dead end and why, ask questions
about the motivation of the questioning process, and try to understand the
self that was revealed in the interview. As we discussed each case, we also did
something called a process observation on our own interaction, so that we
could learn who we were to each other and what the quality of our interaction was. It was powerfully self-oriented.

In addition to this we had a one-on-one session with Knox at least three
times a week. Every word we spoke, every question we asked, every action
we took was scrutinized. I would welcome the return home on Fridays
because it meant the end of that pressure-cooker kind of atmosphere for at
least two days. I would also dread the coming of Sunday night, because it
meant that I would be returning for five more intensive days. At the same
time I relished the experience. For the first time I was being invited into a
deeply introspective mode. I began to understand how my interior life was
constructed and what motivated me. I got in touch with feelings about my
father's alcoholism, my mother's dependency, and my fears of being unable
to pay my bills. I even became able to discover the infantile aspects of my
understanding of God. Growth is painful. In those thirteen weeks I had to
integrate all that I believed about God into the new dimensions of my being
that were beginning to emerge within me. I came out of that experience a

vastly different person from the one who began it in June. It remains for me today the most intense growth opportunity I have ever known. I have championed a unit of clinical pastoral education for every prospective priest from that day to this.

When CPE was over, there was in me a sense of incompleteness, or at least a sense of wanting more. I discussed this desire with Bill Moll. Unknown to me, two of my close friends, Allan Zacher and Loren Mead, who had done their training at St. Elizabeth's Mental Hospital, were discussing the same issue. Allan had been an attorney and Loren had gotten a master's degree in English at the University of South Carolina prior to their arrival at seminary. A fifth classmate, Ken Taylor, had trained at the D.C. General Hospital, and he too was eager to deepen that particular learning curve. We became aware of each other's interest and sought a way to continue our experiences. Bill Moll suggested that we enter into a group therapy relationship with Knox Kreutzer serving as our therapist. He had talked with Knox and had received encouragement for the idea. It was also suggested that the five of us involve our wives in this project, making a group of ten people, or eleven with Knox. It was large for the standard group-therapy ideal, but we were confident we could make it work. Polly Mead, Loren's wife, was employed as a secretary to Reuel Howe, so we had a direct line to the guru of clinical training himself. We committed ourselves to this process for one evening a week beginning the first of October. It was group therapy in a fairly formal sense for that next academic year. When we reconvened in September of our senior year, Knox dropped out, but we decided to continue without him. We formed teams of one seminarian and one wife to build a rotating leadership for the final year.

It was, by that time, not group therapy technically speaking, but it was an intensely real experience in which we processed our learnings together and integrated them into our being. We certainly continued the therapeutic process of asking introspective questions and demanding of each other honest answers. This process also provided me with insight, growth, and counseling skills far beyond those of a typical theological school graduate. I leaned on that training for my counseling ministry as a priest and gave thanks for it constantly. It also enabled me to ask far deeper theological questions than I had ever asked before and to force those theological questions into dialogue with real life.

Of course, rumors spread in the seminary community about this group. There was enormous curiosity among faculty and students alike, who took shots at the group from time to time. We all had vowed not to repeat what was said in our group sessions outside those sessions. To my knowledge none of us ever violated that trust. That, of course, only served to enhance the mystery and intrigue. But all of us emerged from our seminary careers sitting rather loosely with the necessary distance to think independently of the line promulgated by the church. We also seemed to be aware that this institution we were eager to serve actually encouraged dependency and frequently sought to control rather than enhance life. Of the five of us, I was the only one who continued to serve as a parish priest and later as a bishop, part of whose responsibility it was to preserve and enhance the institution. Loren Mead, after two successful rectorships, founded the Alban Institute, which served the church, but he became, in fact, a business executive. Allan Zacher got a Ph.D. in psychology and spent his life running a counseling clinic. Bill Moll went back into farming, and Ken Taylor decided not to be ordained in the Episcopal Church. One wonders how much this group experience shaped the future of each of our careers.

Other than this major activity, that second year in seminary was just a deepening of the first. We finally got into systematic theology. We began to take more pastorally oriented courses on marriage, death, and teenage counseling. We began to practice preaching in homiletics classes. My homiletics teacher was Walter Russell Bowie, one of the giants of the liberal Protestant movement in America in the twentieth century. He was semiretired when he came to Virginia and had developed a serious and permanent speech impediment by this time. But we all knew that he had been a golden-throated orator and we still heard reports of his preaching power from both St. Paul's in Richmond and Grace Church in New York, where he had had long and significant pastorates. Five rectors after Dr. Bowie left St. Paul's in Richmond, I was destined to succeed him in that great downtown congregation. It was an intimate kind of association that I came to treasure years later. As the professor of preaching, he was a gentle critic and no matter how totally a sow's ear a student's sermon was, he always found some elements of a silk purse in it that he could praise. Whatever preaching gift I ever developed was due in no small way to Russell Bowie. When I wrote my second book, *This Hebrew Lord*, I paid my personal tribute to him in the preface.[2]

Another activity took place that year that had nothing to do with seminary per se, but it expressed a side of my life and a perennial interest that was never far from the surface. There was a not well organized intramural athletic program on campus that amounted to little more than a pick-up game of touch football in the fall and softball in the spring. I decided that many more people would participate if we had an organized league. So I set about to do just that. Using such names as Molle's Monsters, Kevin's Kuties, and Stanley's Steamrollers, I divided the student body into teams, asked people to serve as captains, drew up a schedule, and announced that games would begin the following week. After the first game, an unsigned write-up appeared on the bulletin board and garnered much attention. The article mentioned as many names as possible and included rather primitive statistics. As each game was played, new write-ups appeared. Now the students actually looked for them. When the season ended and the two top teams played for the championship of the Holy Hill, almost the entire seminary faculty and student body turned out for the occasion. We repeated this process with the softball season and that too created excitement. We actually had a banquet at the end of the season and named by secret ballot the "All Seminary Nine."

This athletic interest never died. It was destined to pop up again and again throughout my career. Though I had once been tempted to seek a career as a sportscaster, I did not let that ambition grow. The priesthood was the only ambition I ever had.

For my middle-year fieldwork assignment I applied for the seminarian's position at St. Paul's Church, a large, socially prominent congregation in downtown Alexandria. I was thrilled when the rector, William Henry Mead, chose me. He was a fascinating man whose wife, Kate, was the sister of Bart Lloyd, a member of the faculty at Virginia Seminary.

Bill Mead was a restless man, impatient with the structures of the church and with the pace of change. He tended to move from position to position every five years, but he was powerfully effective and did not know how to give less than his best. What attracted me to St. Paul's was Bill's preaching. Sunday in and Sunday out Bill had the capacity to move me and that congregation with his words. He may well have been the most effective preacher I had ever heard on a consistent basis.

With gusto, I threw myself into my Sunday assignment in this church. I taught a teenage Sunday-school class, including a sprinkling of the sons and daughters of high-ranking Pentagon officials. In the White House sat Dwight David Eisenhower. It was a time of the postwar return to normalcy, perhaps even benign neglect, in our country. America was at peace. Even the Korean war had finally stopped. Mr. Eisenhower played lots of golf while the social problems of our cities festered and the racial tensions in our country grew. I allowed my perception of Mr. Eisenhower's presidency to affect my Sunday-school class when I did a lecture on the book of Joshua. I dubbed Moses' successor as "another five-star general who didn't know how to run the country." The reaction from my Pentagon families was swift and shrill. It was a good lesson in sensitivity training. Bill Mead was later elected bishop of Delaware. In the fourth year of his career in Delaware, he invited me to lead his clergy conference in the Poconos. It was a great success. A year later Bill simply died in his sleep. The church lost a great leader and I lost a good friend. I will always be in his debt.

In May of my middle year, the Supreme Court issued its startling and unanimous opinion in the case known as *Brown vs. the Board of Education*. In that decision segregation was ruled to be inherently unequal and the public schools of the land were ordered to proceed "with all deliberate speed" to dismantle any system based on race. Segregation was now illegal. A way of life, particularly in the South, was passing away.

I rejoiced in this decision because it was right, but I knew full well that if I lived my life in the South, as I fully expected to do, I would deal with the implications of this decision for the balance of my career.

The political leaders of the South recoiled and sought ways to resist, which posed an interesting dilemma. A law-abiding person could not refuse to obey what had been declared to be the law of the land. Yet the political establishment of the South did just that and laid the seeds of the lack of respect for the law that appeared in urban areas a decade later when race-tinged riots engulfed our cities. Then these same conservative politicians called for "law and order." It was too late. There cannot be "massive resistance to the law of the land" in one era without teaching another generation that respect for the law is not a virtue.

More moderate politicians looked for wiggle room in the phrase "all deliberate speed." That meant, first, "as slowly as the law will tolerate" and, second, "in as token a way as we can manage."

The response of our church was not universally heroic in the South. There were exceptions, like Bishop Hines of Texas, but they were rare. My Bishop Penick sought to be statesmanlike by acknowledging that the law must be obeyed, but urging a policy of "gradualism" upon his region. "Gradualism" was defined as moving as quickly as the prejudice of the white majority could tolerate. It would not be the last time that I would see the church sacrifice truth and justice to the sensitivities of the majority of those who made up the ecclesiastical body politic.

In my second summer two things happened that would impact my life dramatically. One was that Richard H. Baker, the bishop coadjutor of North Carolina, who was destined to be Bishop Penick's successor, wanted me to return to the diocese to work at Vade Mecum, the summer camp that had always been very special to me. There I would get to know well the people and the clergy of the diocese.

The other factor was that Joan and I had just discovered that our first child was on the way. We were both ecstatic and frightened. The CIA was not friendly to pregnant employees and would not let her work beyond the fourth month of pregnancy. If she took the accumulated leave she possessed to go to Vade Mecum with me she would be four months pregnant when we returned in September, so she could not return to the CIA. Her salary was essential to our economic well-being. Yet I would not have been interested in going to Vade Mecum without her. Our marriage had grown in seminary. The group-therapy sessions had brought us even closer together. Our marriage was a source of deep satisfaction to me and, I believe, to her.

We had saved some money each month and lived quite frugally. But everyone lived this way in the seminary community, and it was fun trying to find new ways to prepare hamburger and canned tuna. After reviewing our financial resources, we decided we could, with part-time jobs including babysitting, make it until graduation and ordination in June 1955, after which the diocese would place me in a salaried position. So Joan resigned her position at the CIA and we went to Vade Mecum. Ellen Elizabeth Spong was born on February 1, 1955. We were a happy family and we finished seminary solvent, but with less than twenty-five dollars in the bank. It was a tight squeeze.

Senior year was a wonderful experience. We were a closely knit class. By this time the faculty members were generally our friends as well as our teachers. My academic work was still exciting. My grades put me on a course to be a cum laude graduate. My fieldwork assignment was as the seminarian on the staff of an area ministry called the Culpeper-Madison larger parish, made up of five congregations served by two priests. Under their direction I was, in effect, to be in charge of St. Paul's Church in Raccoon Ford, Virginia, a rural congregation I dearly loved. The rector, David Lewis, was a courageous man who, like my friend David Yates, engaged the issue of racial prejudice long before it was fashionable to do so, and the associate rector, Paul Heins, was a salt-of-the-earth, good human being. David would one day be elected bishop suffragan of Virginia. Sometimes the church does reward the very best it produces. David was an example of that.

In the second semester of that final year I turned away from my classes to concentrate on preparing for canonical exams. That paid off as I sailed through the exams, which were in that day given by a group of examining chaplains in our diocese. The examiner in Bible was the most feared. It was my old friend, David Yates. In the oral exam he began with the question, "List what happened on each of the seven days of creation as reported by the first chapter of Genesis." He concluded by asking us to "quote the closing verse of the book of Revelation." He missed very little in between. But my work with Bob Kevin on the Old Testament, as well as my copious notes on the books of the New Testament, a gift to me from Bob Cox, and my own fundamentalist background, including the work in high school with Janet Robinson, prepared me well.

However, the neglect of my classwork during my last semester saw my grades drop, not badly, but from A's to B's, sufficient to lose the chance to graduate cum laude. Academically, I finished third in our class behind Loren Mead and Charles Sheerin.

The day of graduation finally arrived. About May 1 I got the word that I would be assigned upon ordination to St. Joseph's Church in West Durham. The vicar, however, would not be leaving until September 1, so the bishop wanted me to move into the rectory of St. Saviour's Church in Raleigh, which was vacant, and to assist the interim priest, the Reverend Thaddeus Cheatham, who would come in to do Sunday services. I would be paid a full salary, but it would mean moving twice in three months. That was not convenient, but who was I to complain? We had our wonderful new daughter baptized by Dr. Kloman at the seminary chapel. Loren and Polly Mead, along with Charlie Browning, were the godparents. Our seminary career had come to an end. The realization of my ambition to be ordained was on the horizon.

I floated a loan. We bought a 1953 Dodge. We packed, we graduated, we moved. We were an ecstatically happy family of three.

1. Those sermons were published in a trilogy of books by Scribner: *The Shaking of the Foundations* (1948), *The New Being* (1965), and *The Eternal Now* (1963).

2. *This Hebrew Lord* (New York: Seabury Press, 1974).

# 7

# My Pastoral Education in Durham

※

I WAS QUITE sure that the whole world would be as excited about my ordination as I was. Seminarians develop that kind of pious exuberance about themselves. That exuberance, however, was quickly deflated by the small congregation that attended my ordination. I had not been involved in the life of St. Peter's Church in Charlotte for six full years and that congregation had gone on about its life rather well in my absence. A new rector, Gray Temple, was in place. He had not shared the struggles of my growing-up years. He knew me only as a young seminary graduate whom he had examined in moral and ascetical theology to determine his academic fitness to be ordained. Even from that slight acquaintance he recognized me as someone who would not be in his school of thought. The Anglican Communion was broad, however, and accommodated within it a wide variety of viewpoints. Mine was acceptable to Gray, if not one he could celebrate.

I invited Bob Crandall to come back to Charlotte to preach at the ordination service. No one else would have been appropriate in my mind. It was only the ordination to the diaconate, not the priesthood—that would come six months later—but this was the Rubicon moment for me, the great divide, and once I stepped over I would never be the same. From this day forward the world, for whom the difference between diaconate ordination and priestly ordination was blurred, would relate to me as a minister, for good or ill. Bishop Baker was to be the ordaining bishop.

This new bishop coadjutor for our diocese was an interesting contrast to Bishop Penick. Bishop Penick was a powerful orator. Bishop Baker never once, to my knowledge, delivered a memorable sermon; indeed most of them were dull and rambling. Bishop Penick was well organized, a genius at administration. Bishop Baker could never quite keep his schedule clear and on at least two occasions he was known to have shown up at the wrong church for confirmation, thereby creating mild anxiety in the places where he did not appear and enormous anxiety in those places where he did. Bishop Penick was a dominant, controlling "prince bishop" in the autocratic low church wing of our Communion. Bishop Baker was more like a comfortable neighbor who frequently would not even be noticed. Bishop Penick kept his own counsel and one had the impression that he was privy to all kinds of secrets and confidential information. Bishop Baker was an open book who shared information not malevolently, but as part of his understanding of the church as a community.

I, like most people in the diocese of North Carolina, admired Bishop Penick. He had been the thirty-four-year-old rector of my beloved church, St. Peter's in Charlotte, when he was chosen to succeed another long-term autocratic bishop of the old-school style, named Joseph Blount Cheshire, Jr., as North Carolina's Episcopal Church leader. Stories, most always flattering, circulated about Bishop Penick. He cut a large figure in ecumenical circles. Over the years this man had opened critical doors for me, and though I found myself worried about what I regarded as his compromised stand on racial justice, I held him in high regard.

Bishop Baker, however, remains in my mind as the most effective bishop under whom I ever served. That conclusion will, I am sure, come as a surprise to many, since I have just chronicled his list of glaring weaknesses, but Bishop Baker had one great gift. He recognized that he was not an especially gifted man. He did not try to pretend he had skills that were simply not his. He also had the grace to ask for help. The result was a phenomenal influx of talent into the service of the church during the Baker years. People thought the diocese did well in spite of Bishop Baker's weaknesses. I am convinced the diocese did well because of Bishop Baker's weaknesses and the way he related to those weaknesses.

Strong laypeople with business and financial skills who loved the church seemed horrified at Bishop Baker's lack of administrative competence, so they rushed to offer their talents in diocesan service. Clergy were called by this humble man to assume roles of leadership in various areas of diocesan life that had in years past been the prerogative of the bishop alone. Clergy talents expanded and a clergy sense of ownership began to be apparent. In his own way, aided by the clergy and lay leadership of the diocese, Bishop

Baker lived out the most successful episcopacy I have ever watched. The finances of the diocese grew in a healthy way. The quality of the clergy leadership grew more and more impressive. The great issues of our day were faced with integrity. New bishops for other dioceses were chosen with great regularity from those clergy who had been part of Bishop Baker's diocese. Thomas A. Fraser, O'Kelley Whitaker, Moultrie Moore, Clarence Haden, Robert Ladehoff, and myself are but a few of them. The positions of cathedral dean and cardinal rector were also filled time after time with one of "Bishop Baker's boys."

So I was pleased it would be his hands that would be laid upon my head. This ordination service was marred emotionally for me by the fact that my brother, Will, had been hospitalized and finally diagnosed with spinal meningitis. The crisis had passed by the time the ordination date actually arrived, but our anxieties had not yet disappeared. Following that ordination and dressed in my blackest suit and freshest new clerical collar, I went to the Charlotte Memorial Hospital to call on my brother. It was the first time that I, in the clothes of a pastor, had walked through a hospital door anywhere. I was terribly self-conscious. St. Peter's Hospital, the facility in which I was born, had been closed several years earlier and its assets had been folded into this new facility with its new name. So my first act as an ordained man was to roam inside the walls of the successor institution to the place where I was born. It seemed a fitting symbol.

Our little family of three had by this time actually moved to Raleigh and set up housekeeping for our first assignment. The rectory of St. Saviour's Church became our home on June 1. The church had graciously agreed to pay my first month's salary in advance so we could live without begging. I was pleased by that act and pleased to be finally at work. St. Saviour's took me first as a layperson for three weeks and then welcomed me back into their life as a deacon following the ordination on the feast of St. John the Baptist. My duties there were not unlike those in a glorified fieldwork assignment. I suspect now it was a made-up job to allow me to be placed somewhere. Bishops do that, I was to discover later. I was to run the youth group, organize and carry out the daily summer vacation Bible school, call on the sick and shut-ins, and then spend my Sundays reading the Gospel and administering the chalice while Dr. Thaddeus Cheatham, a retired priest in his seventies, was brought in to lead the worship and to preach at all services. He was a delightful elflike man whose understanding of the gospel was shaped by the same tradition that produced Norman Vincent Peale and, in a later generation, Robert Schuller. He never saw the dark side of life and his sermons were upbeat, self-help sermons, delivered with warmth and many smiles. I really admired him even as I resented the lack of confidence in me shown by the leadership of the church, who decided that I was too young to be given any real clerical responsibility.

When August came, Dr. Cheatham went on vacation and I finally got the opportunity to function liturgically and to preach. I reveled in that opportunity and began in that remaining month of my tenure to bond with the congregation. There was the inevitable talk of petitioning the bishop to allow me to stay and become rector. I was flattered by the suggestion, which Bishop Penick dismissed, and rightly so, without any consideration whatsoever.

The move to my first permanent assignment in Durham occurred on Labor Day weekend. St. Joseph's Church stood physically between the east campus of Duke University and the Erwin Cotton Mill in West Durham. Its congregation straddled both worlds. On one occasion my two wardens were Dr. Herman Salinger, head of the German department at Duke and a published poet, and Milton Barefoot, known as "Piggy," the child of an uneducated mill family and the salt of the earth.

Very quickly we developed at St. Joseph's two distinct congregations. It was not economic segregation so much as a divided interest that lay behind the division. The congregation made up of workers from the mill village tended to worship at 9:30 A.M. and to move on about their duties. The university congregation liked to sleep later, so they tended to come to the 11:00 A.M. service. Over time and driven by my need to communicate with these vastly different constituencies, I began to preach two quite distinct sermons, seeking to engage my two quite distinct congregations.

St. Joseph's was not a self-supporting church. It was named not for Joseph, the earthly father of Jesus, or even for Joseph of Arimathea, but for Joseph Erwin, the owner and the head of the cotton mill, who provided the money to build this place of worship for his workers. Joseph Erwin had long since died, but the heritage of his presence lingered on. The mill workers rented their homes and bought water, heat, and electricity from the mill; they even purchased most of their food and provisions from the "company store," to which they were constantly in debt. It was something close to white bondage, though it was not untypical of mill communities before the rise of the labor movement in the early years of the twentieth century. To Mr. Erwin's credit, he was a benevolent despot. Many a tale was told about his discovery of a bright or talented child in one of his employee families and how he would act on that discovery personally by giving that child a four-year university education. He also reserved for himself the starring role in the Christmas parade in West Durham. I was told by the older people who remembered that in the final float of the parade, the one that normally features Santa Claus, Mr. Erwin would ride on an elevated pedestal, not just waving to the crowd, but throwing dollar bills to the onlookers who, not surprisingly, always attended this event in great numbers.

Mr. Erwin also wanted his mill workers to attend his church. That was not easy in that community. Anglican worship, with its Elizabethan English prayer book and its stately Victorian hymns and Bach chorales, had little appeal to these relatively uneducated people. Their natural religious tastes ran toward far more emotional responses like the Southern Baptist or the Pentecostal traditions. Undeterred by that, Joseph Erwin himself taught the adult Bible class and was clearly known to look with favor on those employees who attended. People related to me the story of the biggest confirmation class in the history of the Diocese of North Carolina, because it occurred at St. Joseph's. In his effort to build the confirmed membership of his church, Mr. Erwin organized a contest among his employees to see which side could get the most new members. He picked two of his foremen to be captains of the respective blue and red teams. Every candidate for confirmation received a watch. The number of conversions to the Episcopal Church was stunning. Bishop Penick confronted a class of more than three hundred candidates. I doubt if that number has been topped in any confirmation service since.

By the time I arrived at St. Joseph's, Mr. Erwin was but a memory and most of these storied candidates for confirmation had, with watches on their arms, returned to the churches of their own preference, but a core of the mill community was still present. Piggy Barefoot was one of them, and he was their leader.

As the years went by, what began as a small Methodist school called Trinity College became, after coming into the vast tobacco wealth of the Duke family, a great university and changed its name. In time Duke University's size meant that it began to impinge upon the mill community. The women's campus was one block away from St. Joseph's and all that separated the two was a baseball diamond. In later days that was transformed by the development of a shopping center, which had the effect of cutting down dramatically on the number of home runs that shattered our stained-glass windows. The men's campus was about a mile away out Erwin Road. Duke

Chapel stood in the center of the men's campus and was the church of choice for most undergraduates.

However, as the university grew, its medical school and other graduate departments began to attract more and more young married graduate students, who occupied an increasingly dense ring of apartments and condominiums that grew up around the university. This community wanted a church with nursery and Sunday-school facilities and perhaps even young adult programs. Duke Chapel would never offer that. So St. Joseph's, which for seventy years had been a dependent mission congregation of mill workers, began to churn with the influx of new life from these seekers after a varied lot of graduate degrees. The 11:00 A.M. service began to grow.

Two people showed up on our doorstep in my first month at St. Joseph's who impacted our life dramatically. One was Deane Stubbs, whose husband, Bill, managed the old prestigious Washington Duke Hotel in downtown Durham. It was company policy that the head of the hotel must live on the site itself and a penthouse apartment was provided for that purpose. Deane, therefore, had a great need to get out of the hotel every day for her own mental health. Having heard of me or of St. Joseph's from an introductory story in the *Durham Sun,* she came by to volunteer to be my half-time unpaid secretary. I accepted her offer on the spot, and she became a vital part of our leadership team; both she and her husband became close friends with whom we stay in touch to this day.

The second person, a member of that graduate-school community, was June Eager Finney, a lovely, dark-eyed woman who had grown up in the church in Baltimore where Bishop Baker had been rector prior to his Episcopal election in North Carolina. Her husband, William H. M. Finney, was in the last couple of years of a residency in neurosurgery at Duke medical school. Both were from well-known families in Baltimore, and on the Finney side they were a family of outstanding surgeons. Bill would soon join them and enhance that reputation. June, having heard of St. Joseph's and me by word of mouth, had come by to volunteer to run the Sunday school and nursery and to be, in effect, our director of Christian education. It was a gracious offer. Suddenly we had a staff of three and things started bubbling in the church.

The total budget of St. Joseph's Church the previous year had been $3,500. The former priest had served as Episcopal chaplain at Duke University and had been paid most of his salary from a diocesan source. He left St. Joseph's to make his chaplaincy position a full-time job. St. Joseph's was thus required to receive a diocesan subsidy to be able to have me as a full-time vicar. My goal, even though I was still a deacon, was to achieve total self-support as quickly as possible. I determined that we would try to be enrolled in the diocese as an independent parish by spring 1956. This meant we had to quadruple the budget in four months. I shared this dream with no one, since it would have been scary and premature to most. By October, however, the 9:30 service was showing signs of steady growth and the 11:00 service was crowded. We had developed a covered-dish Sunday-night program in which graduate students in medicine, law, science, and the arts brought a dish and had supper together. For the program we discussed the morning sermon, which frequently I had to defend against this interdisciplinary gathering. My preaching became more and more issue-oriented to make the discussions on Sunday nights hotter and more engaging. I also began to share in that sermon hour many of the critical issues of biblical scholarship that had challenged me at the seminary. The students who made up my 11:00 worshiping community had never been introduced to a scholarly Christianity, and they responded with enthusiasm. A steady stream of people began to seek membership in our church. In the September 1955 to June 1956 year, I presented more than sixty candidates for confirmation to the bishop on four different episcopal visitations. All of them were young adults. Clearly something in this church was feeding them. It was for me a heady experience.

The bishops were also somewhat amazed at what was happening. At the congregational meeting in November 1955, I finally got the courage to announce publicly my intention to seek pledges of at least $12,500 in that year's canvass, which would be enough to make us a self-supporting parish. That figure seems impossibly low today, but in 1955 that was sufficient to run a church. My salary, for example, was only $3,600 a year. But this goal, though sounding modest to our ears, represented that fourfold increase I had determined was necessary to reach self-support. When I made this announcement, a fuse blew—literally—and the congregation sat in darkness. It was quipped that I asked them to raise so much money, the church itself had blinked! When light was restored, I introduced Major James Barnhill of the Army ROTC faculty at Duke, who had agreed to lead the every-member canvass. Jim was most enthusiastic and, as a newcomer, announced his own pledge, which immediately made him the highest giver in the church. The large number of graduate students who lived frugally also pledged generously, and by December 10 we had reached our goal. We petitioned the diocese immediately for parish status and received it at the convention the following spring. St. Joseph's became the talk of the diocese. We returned our subsidy to the diocese in 1956, and St. Joseph's newly constituted vestry celebrated the new status by making me their first rector.

I was ordained to the priesthood on Holy Innocents' Day, December 28, 1955, by Bishop Penick. The preacher was the Reverend David Lewis of Culpeper. It was a happy occasion. I was now equipped to do that for which I had yearned, prayed, planned, and worked. No one could have been more satisfied with life than I.

Our social life as a couple turned more and more toward the young graduate students who came in increasing numbers into our worship community. Many of them had been raised in small-town Christian churches that were significantly uncritical or fundamentalistic in their outlook. Their minds were being stretched in a great institution of higher learning. That learning challenged, day after day, the simple assumptions of their premodern religious upbringing, which still spoke of God as a personal being, supernatural in power, who invaded history periodically in a variety of miraculous ways. Such a view of God did not fit the concepts of life in their expanding postmodern world.

Before finding St. Joseph's, these graduate students had begun to feel that if they entered a house of worship, they were required to park their brains by the door in order to participate. They had not been encouraged in their churches to worship God with their minds. The ancient assumptions of their primitive religious past continued to come at them in worship. Among those assumptions were that they lived in a three-tiered universe, that God dwelled in that third tier beyond the sky, that human life was created good, but then fell into sin, and that Jesus was the divine rescuer who entered human history through a virgin birth and exited human history through a cosmic ascension. His death was a sacrifice required by our sins. That was the tradition! Their minds, however, could not translate these images or process their truth. So they had entered a crisis of the spirit and of faith itself. Either they had to give up the only religious heritage they knew or else they had to give up their modern education. Most of them had chosen with great reluctance to sacrifice their religious upbringing. They were the ones who were searching and they were the ones who found St. Joseph's and loved what we seemed to offer.

A few of their number had chosen to become anti-intellectual and to cling to their religious traditions in the face of all the odds. They became the religious fanatics of the campus who revealed anxiety, fear, and vulnerability beneath their closed minds and deep religious anger. St. Joseph's became to them a threat to a delicately balanced security system. They delighted in hurling hostile barbs at our church. More than anyone else, they did our advertising for us. Many of these people would find a place in the unthinking churches of my future life either as clergy or as laypeople.

The word spread quickly that St. Joseph's was a church that welcomed questions, that was not afraid of issues, that allowed debate, whose rector could be challenged. The Sunday-night suppers grew in popularity. In response, my sermon preparation became far more disciplined and careful than it had ever been before. I began to research my sermons and not just to depend on the things I remembered from my seminary days. This was a wonderful demonstration of that practice that I was destined to see more than once: a church creating a pastor to meet the needs of the people.

I was also at this time learning a great deal about how to be a pastor. That was the most mysterious, humbling, and new experience of my ordained life. Even a twenty-four-year-old, fresh-out-of-school parson would discover that somehow the One he represented in the minds of the people caused him to be entrusted with the secrets of many lives. Sometimes that experience had an amusing side, sometimes a somber and deeply emotional aspect.

The first couple who approached me about getting married will forever be etched in my memory. Marriage counseling had been a major area of my seminary preparation. Included in that study was a format for premarital counseling that covered issues from sex to the handling of money. There was an assumption abroad at that time, but probably only in the church, that sexual activity was actually begun on one's wedding night. So each graduate of my seminary had a notebook filled with guides to effective premarital counseling. I couldn't wait for my first opportunity to use these newly acquired skills.

When the call from my first couple came, I made the appointment to see them and looked forward to what I was sure would be an exciting experience. It was, but not exactly in the way I had anticipated.

At the appointed hour the couple arrived. I thought at first there must be some mistake. Perhaps the people my eyes fell upon were the grandparents of the couple who wished to be married. Perhaps they had come to make the arrangements, and the couple would come later. I actually wondered if this older couple might try to sit in on my premarital counseling sessions. I quickly learned, however, that there was no mistake. These were the prospective bride and groom.

They introduced themselves to me. I invited them to sit down and, following my forms for church records, I began to get some basic information such as their full names, the date and place of their births, their parents' full names, whether they had been baptized or not, and whether this was the first marriage for both of them. If it were not, then I had to know what brought the other marriage or marriages to termination. Remarrying was very difficult in the church at that time.

The bride was seventy years old. She had been married three times. All three of her husbands were deceased. The first one died in an automobile accident after about five years of marriage. The second succumbed to a heart attack in the prime of life, and the third, after a few years of marriage, had died of cancer. She was the mother of three grown children and the grandmother of five.

The groom was sixty-nine years old. He had been widowed twice. He was the father of two grown children and the grandfather of four. Somehow this image of a prospective married couple had never even entered my mind. Life has a way of confounding and challenging our stereotypes.

I looked at these two people who were somewhere between the age of my parents and my grandparents. I looked at my notes on premarital sexual counseling. Nothing fit. This couple, between them, had forgotten more about sex than I had ever known. I closed my seminary counseling notes and put them away. I have never looked at them since. "Tell me how you met and what your hopes and dreams for this marriage are," I said. Then I sat back and listened to their story, which was filled with moments of both beauty and pain. They shared some of their successes and failures, their anxieties about their children, and times when their children were hurt and they could not do anything about it. I interrupted their story from time to time only to ask them to amplify or go more deeply into an experience. Our images of older people most often prevent us from making what might well seem to us to be an inappropriate inquiry. Abundant wisdom and life experience is thus never released from its secret places. Two hours passed before this happy couple, holding hands, departed from my office. The date for their wedding was set, the church was reserved, and we had agreed to meet again in a week to go over some specific details. The education of Jack Spong as a priest had finally begun in that school that always meets outside the classroom. The wedding of this couple itself was one of the happiest liturgical events over which I have ever presided.

Another part of my postgraduate training came when a young couple transferred into the congregation. He was a well-known athlete in college whom I knew by name and reputation. His wife was the perfect complement, the campus beauty who had married the athletic hero. They were also very kind and sweet people and the parents of two adorable children. But a tragedy had invaded their seemingly idyllic lives. They had lost their first child. I was never quite sure how that death occurred, for they were still not capable of talking about it in great detail. I got the impression, however, that it was a sudden and unexpected trauma like that unexplained and thankfully infrequent phenomenon known as "crib death."

This death had sent this couple reeling, and they fell back on their rather fundamentalistic religious backgrounds. They consoled themselves with the idea that this child's death was somehow God's will. Life was thus neither as chaotic and irrational as it seemed, nor was it lived under the twin auspices of fate and chance. Their child's death, they had convinced themselves, was not meaningless, but was rather filled with an inscrutable divine purpose. They might not understand that purpose, but they had become convinced that it was their task to trust God and to believe without equivocation that this was so. This is, of course, a fairly standard way of explaining trauma in religious circles even today. To this explanation this wonderful young couple was clinging with emotional tenacity. Neither they nor the religious voices that led them to this particular resolution of their pain seemed to embrace what this solution did to the reality of God. The deity became a capricious, malevolent power who imposed a purpose on life that required a child's death. It also meant God was a Being who needed to be served and placated lest this capricious deity strike again.

As I developed my increasingly theological agenda in preaching, I could not long avoid facing the problem of human tragedy and the meaning of human suffering. When I did so, my thought processes and theological understanding collided directly with this family's delicate security system. In a sermon in my second year at St. Joseph's, I called the God who would will the death of an innocent child nothing but a demon who ought to be destroyed. I cited the fact that life just has tragic dimensions and that we must embrace that reality as mature adults and seek the meaning of God in all of life, including the dark side of tragedy and suffering. This was an early attempt to express a view of God that would someday come to be identified

,with my public theological life. This was not a sentimental, childish, and dependent view of God as the heavenly parent who knew best, who intervened often and watched over each of us in guarding, protective ways. That God I was prepared to jettison. After the sermon was over, I looked forward to the group that would gather with covered dishes to discuss it that night. I was confident it would be an invigorating conversation.

I did not have to wait for the evening. This young couple met me at the door. She had tears in her eyes. His face was grim. They asked if they could speak with me as soon as possible. Of course I agreed. It was for me a remarkable and learning conversation. They were hurt first, angry second, and confused third. It also made me aware of how deeply people listen to and care about the words of their designated spiritual leader. Preaching becomes, when one realizes that, an awesome responsibility. It was a lesson I would never forget.

I had unwittingly opened anew this couple's grief and pain. I had disturbed that emotional membrane that had been stretched rather thinly over their wounds. The fact that it was an inadequate membrane that would someday rupture anyway was not a consideration. If preachers are going to touch life significantly, they must be willing to live deeply with their people. That day I began a long conversation with my friends. We walked through their disturbed feelings and anger into their pain and grief. We built a relationship deep enough and trusting enough to allow their unresolved feelings to emerge and to find expression. The sense of their child and themselves as victims of God's unknowable plan emerged and so did their anger at this God, an anger that had been deeply suppressed by this couple for two primary reasons. First, they were personally uncomfortable raging at God. The anger they felt violated all of their religious training and sensitivities. Second, there was that dreadful, superstitious fear that if they ever did vent their intense anger at God, this divine, omnipotent, and powerful Being just might strike their family once more.

So I entered this realm of life and began to see that the roles of pastor, preacher, and priest are not separate. Each role affects the others, and ordained persons are to live in each of these roles simultaneously in a way that enables them to be agents of life for the people they serve. My vocation was to call people into being and to free them simultaneously from the clutches of those religious systems, including my own, that create a false security, provide a phony peace, and pretend to solve the profound questions of life with simplistic answers. I learned this lesson early as my priestly education continued. My teachers were these two hurting, grieving young parents.

Early in 1957 I experienced some strange physical symptoms, beginning with lower back pain. I paid little attention to it at first, but it not only did not go away, it became intense. It was always worse early in the morning, to the point where I could hardly get out of bed and walking sometimes was quite difficult. I sought medical help and had lots of tests. The preliminary diagnosis was rheumatoid arthritis of the spine, sometimes called spondylitis. Suddenly a very long shadow fell across my future. Unless this disease could be properly managed, my destiny was to be an almost immobilized poker-spined person. I was really frightened. I had only begun my career. My wife and daughter depended on me. Was I destined to fail them in the way my father had failed me? The symptoms came and went, but they became quite familiar. The first treatment was aspirin, four a day as maintenance, eight a day if acute. I went to the library to read about this disease. It had the effect of shortening my horizon. I must accomplish my life's work, I felt, in a very limited time span. The young man who was already in a hurry began to be even more driven to achieve. This back situation had to be kept in check. My career goals depended on it.

As we moved deeper into 1957, that shadow, combined with my own ego needs, caused me to be seduced by my own ambition. St. Joseph's was quite obviously a transformed place. People began to tell me I would not stay at St. Joseph's long, since I was destined to make my mark on the wider church. I secretly relished those comments, but outwardly denied them. Even in my own congregation those sentiments were expressed openly. In the university part of our church there was no anxiety attached to these comments. The students lived in a transitory world. They were at Duke and therefore at St. Joseph's for a short period of time, two to four years at most. They had learned to drink deeply from the fountains that were available without worrying about how long they would last. In June 1956 and again in June 1957, I would lose up to 25 percent of my university congregation. It was a way of life. If I were to leave St. Joseph's, I would be missed, but they would soon leave also, so it was no big deal to them.

That was not so, however, for the permanent members of the congregation. They were rooted people who had found something special in this church that they did not want to lose. So when they began to hear talk that I might be destined soon for some bigger responsibility than St. Joseph's, a sadness tinged with fear entered our relationships.

In September 1957 I had my first official visitation from a calling committee. Tarboro, North Carolina, was a small town of 7,500 people located on the Tar River in the rich agricultural belt of eastern North Carolina. It was roughly on a line connecting Raleigh with Norfolk, Virginia. Although quite small, this town could boast of one of the diocese's leading congregations. Calvary Church had been the congregation in which the former bishop of North Carolina, Joseph Blount Cheshire, Jr., had been raised. His father, Joseph Blount Cheshire, Sr., had been rector there for over fifty years.

Under Dr. Cheshire's rectorship and that of his most famous successor, Bertram E. Brown, this congregation had established parochial mission stations in every crossroads of the county. These parochial missions were served by lay readers from Calvary Church. The lay readers taught a Bible class on Sunday morning, led morning worship, preached, organized the Sunday school, and called on the people with regularity. When a member of the church died, they most often conducted the funeral. They prepared children for confirmation, infants and their parents for baptism, and young couples for marriage. The rector from Tarboro would come out to perform the sacramental services. The people in these rural communities, however, looked to these laypeople as their primary pastors. These lay readers in turn viewed their particular mission station as their primary church responsibility, even though they would complete their Sunday morning mission responsibilities in time to be present at the 11:00 A.M. service at Calvary, where they also served as vestry members and wardens.

This system provided two unique features in the parish. First, there was a tremendous sense of lay ownership and participation in the life of the church. Second, when people left these rural areas and moved to town, they were already Episcopalians and came easily and quickly into Calvary Church. The lay reader in charge of their mission church was present to welcome and introduce them. So this small town had an inordinately large Episcopal church. Calvary's congregation had between four and five hundred baptized members.

At the high-water mark of mission churches, Calvary directed eleven congregations in Edgecombe County other than itself. When I was introduced to this town, only five of them remained. It felt like a small diocese organized under the leadership of the cathedral. By the end of September 1957 I had become the rector-elect and we moved before November 1.

I was both enormously pleased and still guilt-ridden for leaving St. Joseph's before I had been there three years. It had been such a responsive congregation, I could not have asked for anything better or more exciting. It had challenged me deeply and introduced me to a ministry of relating the gospel to those who were searching for meaning. Far more than I realized then, the themes of my ministry at St. Joseph's would dominate my career. The audience I found in the postgraduate population of Duke University would be the audience toward which I would direct my future ministry. I would remember that congregation with great love for my entire lifetime. Those feelings, however, were not sufficient to prevent my accepting the call to Tarboro.

Considerations other than health worries and my overarching ambition also went into the decision. Joan was expecting our second child. Our family finances were stretched very thin. The yearly salary of $5,400, augmented by the $600 utility allowance and $500 travel allowance, that Tarboro offered would give us the first financial flexibility in our entire married lives. Children were expensive, I was discovering. We had no resources left at the end of a month. We would soon need a second car or else either my ministry or Joan's life would be restricted. All of these things put together were factors in the decision, but the compelling reality was I really wanted to be rector of this parish. So at age twenty-six I prepared to assume the responsibility of the rectorship of one of North Carolina's most unusual congregations.

# 8

# *Not Popular but Right:*
# *Racial Issues and Leadership*
# *Lessons in Tarboro*

IN THE last week of October 1957 the moving van deposited our earthly belongings at 1008 St. Patrick Street in Tarboro, a lovely white frame house on a corner lot of a tree-lined street. This house reminded me a great deal of the one in which I had begun life in Charlotte, and it meant a return to that more gracious style of life I had known prior to my father's death. We felt thrilled to be in this place, and I was eager to demonstrate that Calvary Church had chosen well, even though it had gambled on a very young and inexperienced new rector.

To live in a small town is a special opportunity. I am not surprised that many leaders of our nation have grown up in small towns like Independence, Missouri, Plains, Georgia, or Hope, Arkansas. Small towns give their citizens opportunities to develop leadership skills. One can embrace and manage the dynamics of a small town. The first thing I had to understand was that to be rector of Calvary Church meant a circuit-riding ministry, given its parochial missions. My liturgical schedule was that I would be at my major church, Calvary, at 8:00 and 11:00 A.M. each Sunday, but at 9:30 A.M. and 5:00 P.M. I would be at one of the parochial missions. My ministry in what I referred to as the Diocese of Edgecombe County, North Carolina, was to be a peripatetic calling.

The second thing I had to recognize was that every member of the twelve-person vestry of my principal parish was not only a male, but was also old enough to be my father. Beyond that, these vestrymen tended to be the dominant figures in the business and economic life of the town. This was a radical departure from the world of graduate students my own age who surrounded me in Durham, or even from the not very well educated members of the mill community.

Third, the dominant family, socially and economically, in the whole county was a major presence in Calvary Church. The Clarks began their rise to power and wealth a couple of generations earlier as the owners of a feed-and-seed hardware store. By the time I arrived in town, the members of the second generation of this family were nearing the end of their lives and the third generation was running the family empire, which now included well over 50 percent of the rich farmland of the county, to say nothing of other major business ventures in the town and extensive investments. The wealth of the Clarks dwarfed that of anyone else in the community. However, this family had over the generations become so extensive that it was actually broken into two segments that were competitive, but not hostile to each other.

One line was headed by William Grimes Clark, who had been a state senator and active in the political life of North Carolina. He was affectionately known as "Cousin Willie." The other branch of the family was headed by Cousin Willie's brother, Samuel Nash Clark, known as "Mr. Sam." He was principally identified with the store that bore his father's name, W. S. (which stood for William Samuel) Clark & Sons. Two other members of that senior generation, Nan Clark and Russell Clark, were also associated with the store. Much of the town's social life revolved around Clark family events. A Clark wedding was the high point of any season. Even the Clark funerals were spectacular. When Cousin Willie was buried, five former governors of North Carolina or their surviving spouses were in attendance. A party held afterward for out-of-town guests at Mr. Sam's house was discussed for years. Mr. Sam was quoted as having said after that party, "I had so much fun at Willie's funeral, I can't wait for Russell to die."

Beyond this dominant family, Calvary Church had more than its share of the other leading citizens of the town, including doctors, lawyers, and the top executives in the small, local Carolina Telephone and Telegraph Company, as well as the sheriff, mayor, and chief of police.

Tarboro's population of approximately 7,500 was marked by a well-organized social system. My own youthful looks and lack of significant experience were very obvious to me and I suspect to others. My immaturity demanded that I assert my leadership and independence immediately. In my first sermon I thundered, "I have not come to Tarboro to be a family chaplain to a contented few. I have come to preach a gospel that is challenging, not always comfortable, and to call us all into a growing sense of discipleship." There were two responses: A telephone public-relations man decided to call me "Slugger," and an elderly woman said to me, "Mr. Spong, we are distance runners in Tarboro, not sprinters. You'll get used to us in time." These responses were probably more gracious than I deserved.

Less than four months after our arrival, our second daughter, Mary Katharine Spong, was born. Her birth gave us the opportunity to become deeply invested in the community by choosing local people to be her godparents. Our choice was a childless couple, Thelma and Jack Denson, who, as it worked out, would shape our daughter's life beautifully and wondrously. Jack worked in the hardware department of W. S. Clark & Sons. Thelma was a homemaker who also served as the director of the altar guild at Calvary Church. These loving people were pleased to be asked and almost immediately began the tradition of having Kathy spend every Sunday from waking to sleeping with them. It would be godparenting as I had never seen before nor would I ever see again.

A key power in the community was a woman named Marian Alston Bourne. She was in her mid-sixties when I arrived. Early in my tenure I discovered that she had decided I was to be her project. She saw a potential in me that even I did not see, and she relished the opportunity to help shape this young priest in his intellectual and spiritual development. She was married to a local attorney, Henry Bourne. They possessed all the grace and style of the wealthiest citizens of the town, but they had other remarkable qualities as well—they were broad-minded and well-read people. While Henry practiced law as his profession, Marian saw her role in town to be that of keeping its citizens from becoming ingrown and thus perpetuating their prejudices.

She used three organizations to accomplish her purpose: the Magazine Club, the Episcopal Churchwomen, and the Edgecombe County Public Library. She forced standards into each of the three institutions that were remarkable indeed, but the Magazine Club was her special fiefdom. The Magazine Club was a "by invitation only" social club that met to hear papers presented by its members who had worked a minimum of two years to prepare them. The club got its name from the fact that they subscribed, as a group, to a series of superior magazines, such as *Harper's Review, Atlantic Monthly, National Geographic, Gourmet,* and many others. These magazines were then circulated to all the membership on a rotating basis so that each member had a chance at all of them once a month.

It was a highly coveted honor to be invited to join this unique body. New members were elected by the other members and only when a vacancy occurred. When a new member was elected, a committee of three, one of whom was Marian, would call dressed as if they were going to high tea in Buckingham Palace. No one ever declined membership.

The meetings of the club were held monthly. One person would present the paper, and another (probably the more anxious of the two) would host the event, which was clearly the Tarboro social event of the month. The silver was polished. The best china and crystal were brought out. The refreshments reflected meticulous personal effort. Each host tried to serve something more elegant than anyone had served before. The social standards and culinary delights of the town were thus stretched month by month, and Marian seemed to up the ante to ever higher levels whenever it was her turn.

The women would pick a theme for the year and then assign topics to the people who would present the individual papers. In one of my early years in Tarboro, under Marian's driving leadership, the members of the Magazine Club had adopted as their theme "major contemporary theologians." Marian opened the series with a paper on the thought of Dietrich Bonhoeffer. It was through her that I first heard of this man. His thought had not permeated the consciousness of my seminary faculty. I, of course, did not attend the Magazine Club meetings, but I was allowed to read Marian's paper after it had been presented. It caused me to begin to learn from this woman in a variety of ways.

Marian was liberal in her politics, which also caused her to be marked in Tarboro as a bit different. She was sufficiently open in her perspective to know that segregation, for example, was evil and could not be preserved. Her husband joined her in this understanding, which made the two of them stand out, not always comfortably, in this community.

The articulate political counterpoints to Marian and Henry Bourne in this community were two people who seemed to stand together on about every issue. They were Pembroke Nash, a man in his early fifties when I arrived, who ran one of the two savings and loan associations owned primarily by the Clarks, and his slightly younger soul mate, Francis Jenkins, called Tish, the quintessential Southerner of the old school, complete with straw hat, who was a Clark son-in-law. The Clarks, at least the senior members of the family, were above the battles of the town, but they clearly were aligned with Pem and Tish, who opposed change in almost every manifestation. But it was racial change that brought out their most negative feelings. They honestly believed that black people were by nature inferior and any effort at assimilation would destroy the white race. They treated black people as children, insisting that no title of respect, like "Mr." or "Mrs." ever be used in referring to those they called "colored people" or "Negroes."

I knew of only one black couple who managed to maintain their dignity and thus their titles of respect in this community. They were the Reverend and Mrs. Milton Moran Weston. He was tall, stately, and dignified—the epitome of a Southern gentleman—and former vicar of the black Episcopal church. Even in the atmosphere of this town they managed to raise a son, Milton Moran Weston, Jr., who would be one of the great priests of the Episcopal Church, serving St. Philip's Church in Harlem and forcing the Episcopal Church and people like me to confront our racism, conscious and unconscious.

The school system of Tarboro was radically segregated and grossly unequal. The Southern claim of "separate but equal" was a cruel lie. The black system used the textbooks of the white system when they were discarded and new ones purchased for the white children. The white system would graduate from high school 75 percent of those who started in the first grade. The black system had in my day never graduated 10 percent.

The one plus of this segregated system was that at least the black principal and black teachers received respectable middle-class employment. They represented the major percentage of educated black people in the community and, along with the black doctor, dentist, undertaker, and farm agent and their respective wives, constituted the top tier of black society. It was a minuscule number of people, but that same minuscule number existed in every little town in eastern North Carolina. This meant that for the educated black leaders, social life was regional. They did not constitute a critical mass locally.

St. Luke's was the only non-Pentecostal black church in the town. For this reason it seemed to attract the black leadership people and a significant number of the black high-school students. Although in many ways my ministry in Tarboro was not nearly so intellectually demanding as it has been at the Durham church, it did relate me to the whole community.

The years that I was in Tarboro were years in which the issue of race was never far from the surface. The world kept moving forward on this issue, and small Southern towns like Tarboro were carried by that tide somewhat reluctantly. The Supreme Court ruling against segregation was a three-year-old unimplemented ruling when I moved to this town. It represented to the white citizenry a ticking bomb people tried to ignore.

In my first two years I felt the need to establish my credentials in the town. My natural habits and interests served as springboards for that task. Since I got up early each morning to study, I began to go down to a restaurant on Main Street owned by Gus and Chris Pistolis, two Greek immigrant brothers, to drink coffee with the farmers at about 6:00 A.M. I gained a rare insight into local wisdom from these rustic members of the community. Because of my natural love of sports, I began to attend all of the high-school football, basketball, and baseball games. After a while I got to know Bob Harper, the manager of WCPS-FM, the "Coastal Plains Station" serving Tarboro and eastern North Carolina. He was a one-man gang who, with one assistant, tried both to run the station and to do play-by-play of all the games. I began to assist him at those games by doing the statistics and spotting for him, so he could say who made the tackle or who shot the basket. After a while he put me on the air to do the color and to give him a breather. Finally, I took over the play-by-play and for the balance of my life in that town I was the "Voice of the Tigers" on radio. My sponsors were "Wink, That Sassy Drink" and "Happy Dan, the TV Man." In the high school I was a welcomed personality and was invited by the coaches of the various sports to ride the team bus to out-of-town games so that I got to know the players well. I knew their parents, girlfriends, troubles, and triumphs. It made me aware of just how important athletics could be as a gateway into a significant pastoral ministry.

I moved from these arenas into wondering how we could provide an organized athletic program for the younger teenagers and preteens in our community. There was in this town no YMCA or YWCA, no Little League or police athletic league activities, indeed, nothing for our children except the junior varsity and varsity teams of the high schools, which touched a tiny percentage of kids. To solve this issue and to create this opportunity would be a challenge I would seek to address as part of Calvary Church's ministry.

At the congregational meeting less than a year after my arrival, I proposed that this parish family embark upon a massive capital-funds campaign to build a new educational building complete with a modern kitchen and an assembly hall. This hall would serve both as an auditorium for large church and community events and as a small gymnasium in which the younger teens and preteens of the town could play basketball and other sports and youth socials and dances could be held. I further suggested that we should aim to complete this project for dedication in 1960, when we celebrated the hundredth anniversary of the building of Calvary Church. Last but not least, to mark that anniversary celebration I urged the congregation to authorize its vestry to invite the convention of the Diocese of North Carolina to meet in Tarboro as part of our centennial observance. That invitation would have to be extended at the first convention I would attend as Tarboro's rector. It was a sweeping proposal people described as breathtaking, but the congregation responded with enthusiasm, and we launched a capital-fund drive for $180,000, an enormous sum in 1958. The drive was a success, thanks in no small measure to the generosity of the Clark family. Slowly, but surely, Memorial Hall began to rise. That project was to consume our energy for two years.

During this time two events occurred that added new dimensions to my life. One was that our third daughter, Jaquelin Ketner Spong, was born. The second was that my life in the Diocese of North Carolina expanded greatly. In 1958 the bishop had appointed me to membership on the State of the Diocese Committee, which was to report to the 1959 convention. It was the task of this committee to evaluate the health of the diocese and to bring resolutions to the floor of the diocesan convention to address these realities. It was frequently a time to pass out bouquets to the bishops and lay leaders and was not thought of as terribly significant. I was the second clergyman appointed to this committee. When the committee convened, I was asked to serve as vice chair to the senior priest, whom the bishop appointed to be chair. During the year, however, this senior priest had accepted a call to another diocese and since very little time remained before the convention, the bishop decided to allow this very junior vice chairman to head the committee and to bring its report to the convention. At that point the committee had done almost nothing. I took that assignment with great enthusiasm. If the state of the diocese was weak or destructive, then I wanted to have the convention address those issues. Two diocesan institutions, both in Charlotte and both well known to me, became the focus of our investigation. One was the segregated Good Samaritan Hospital. The other was the Thompson Orphanage, a facility run by an old-fashioned couple who believed in firm discipline for the orphans and the necessity of raising them in a proper work environment. For the managers of the Thompson Orphanage this meant running a dairy farm with forty cows.

My inquiries about both institutions turned up an enormous amount of data and were met with defensiveness by both administrations. The Good Samaritan Hospital was not only practicing segregated medicine, but was practicing it quite poorly. The standards were very lax, and both the medical competence and service were incredibly poor by almost any measure.

The orphanage farm was run with no sense of a proper ratio of expense to profit. The overhead per cow was twice that deemed profitable by farming authorities at the state level. It was clear that the farm was a hobby of the head of the orphanage and that the sentiment surrounding the orphanage was sufficiently romantic to keep the money pouring in. The cows seemed to me to benefit from this largess far more than the children. I also had real questions about the very philosophy of large institutional orphanages. They were passing out of existence throughout the land as social workers called for individual foster-care facilities to replace them.

The convention of the diocese was held in the spring of 1959 in St. Peter's Church in Charlotte, that venerable old church that had been so important to me. I was to make the report on the state of the diocese on the first day of that two-day gathering. This was the first time the convention delegates had heard this report, and it broke like a bombshell on the convention.

I challenged our wisdom as a diocese being identified with a segregated, low-quality medical facility and called for the closing of Good Samaritan Hospital, thus forcing white hospitals to open their doors to care for the black population. I also called for the diocese to examine whether or not we wanted to continue to be in the somewhat outdated orphanage business and, if we did, to oversee it so that the children and not the cows were the major recipients of our people's generosity. I had prepared copies of this report and handed them out when I finished presenting it. It was clearly the talk of the convention and the dullness of church business was now transformed into debates on segregated medicine and the efficacy of orphanages. The Charlotte newspapers made certain that these issues received proper coverage. Seldom did a church convention make front-page news, but we did that year.

The heads of the Good Samaritan Hospital and the Thompson Orphanage were present to defend their institutions the next day. After a good discussion, further investigation with the power to act was delegated to the elected executive council of the diocese, resulting in the closing of the Good Samaritan Hospital soon thereafter. In time the Thompson Orphanage got out of the dairy business and was transformed into a totally different kind of childcare facility. This had been my first venture into the power of a church convention to shape the thought, policy, and destiny of ecclesiastical life. I was well aware that I would not be unknown when we hosted the convention the following year.

When that 1960 diocesan convention neared, there was pride in our new building, a desire to show it off, and general excitement in the community. We also faced the prospect of hosting the five hundred lay and clergy delegates from churches across the diocese. Most of the delegates would be housed either in private homes or in motels some miles away. We did not have sufficient Episcopal homes to handle this load so, as is customary in small towns, the call went out to our Presbyterian, Methodist, Baptist, Roman Catholic, and Jewish neighbors to volunteer a guest room. Their response was terrific.

We planned a banquet on Tuesday night to be held in the gymnasium of our new parish house. Great bouquets of flowers would protrude from each goal on our basketball court. The banquet would be prepared in our new kitchen, which was the envy of every restaurant in town.

At this convention issues of race were destined to dominate both the agenda and the emotional energy of the delegates, since prior to this gathering the executive council of the Diocese of North Carolina had made a decision that the diocesan camp, Vade Mecum, could no longer refuse to admit black Episcopalians to its appropriate camps and conferences. The thing I had sought to do in 1949 with Perry Leazer was now to be achieved eleven years later. There was an immediate outcry among the conservative white lay leadership of North Carolina. Pembroke Nash and Francis Jenkins were among the more vocal critics of this action. There would clearly be a hotly contested debate at this convention with organized efforts on the parts of many delegates to reverse this decision. If this decision were not reversed, then integration was coming to the Episcopal Diocese of North Carolina. In 1960 that constituted a revolution.

One priest in the diocese, James Parker Dees, then the rector of Trinity Church in Statesville, played overtly to the conservative strain of racism. His rhetoric would be deeply embarrassing to the cause of Christ as he told of all the horrors that would ensue if "nigra children and white children were allowed to commingle." The positive side of the argument was carried by Thom Blair, the rector of Christ Church in Charlotte and a close personal friend. Indeed, Joan and I had made him godfather to our new baby girl. Thom argued for justice, for doing what was right. I shall never forget Jim

Dees gesturing to Thom with a finger across his throat suggesting that Thom was damaging the church and killing his own career.

It's funny, but predictions like that never really come true. When issues are being fought over in a changing world, those who risk rejection by embracing the future and moving beyond the barriers of past prejudices are never finally hurt. Those who cling to the insights of a dying world or a passing prejudice are the ones who will ultimately lose both credibility and integrity.

Jim Dees was the voice of a dying, but still powerful, racism. His first tactic was to get his church to withhold all financial support to the diocese and to urge others to do likewise. Those who adopt this tactic always try to perfume it by designating their money to other nonthreatening outreach ministries, so that they can hide this act of economic blackmail even from themselves. But it never works. Ultimately respect disappears, and their successors are left to try to find a way back into the fold, at least until the next issue emerges to drive them once again into the same threadbare, immature response.

When the convention adjourned, the camp was still integrated and the delegates had returned home, but the little town of Tarboro was in an uproar. Because delegates had been housed in the homes of all of our citizens, the desegregation battle at the Episcopal camp had been discussed around almost every breakfast table in the town. Tensions, anger, and the need to strike back were high. The vestry of our church, led by Pem Nash and Francis Jenkins, demanded that we call a congregational meeting to pass resolutions objecting to this decision and playing the blackmail card by withholding any funds from the diocese until this integration action was rescinded. That congregational meeting was held about two weeks later and it was clear from the turnout and the level of emotion that I would not be able to hold back the negativity. But I had decided I had to make my own witness whether it was popular or not.

I chaired the meeting as the rector. I called it to order, opened it with a prayer from the prayer book for the "Holy Catholic Church." That time-honored prayer said, "Where it is right, establish it. Where it is wrong, forgive it. Where it is divided, reunite it." Even that prayer was thought by some to be hostile and manipulative. Perhaps it was. I insisted on making some opening remarks to try to put the issues into perspective. I went over the history of Vade Mecum, the nonintegrated camp, the absolute injustice of having an Episcopal camp not available to some of the Episcopalians in the owning diocese, and my own efforts as early as 1949 to open this facility to the black members of the Young People's Service League. Finally I appealed to the higher instincts of our people, reminding them of the church's vocation to model inclusivity and above all to obey the law of the land. Can a segregated church have any moral credibility in a world where segregation has been ruled to be inherently unequal and therefore wrong? With that question left hanging, I added some rules that would govern this meeting and then concluded my remarks.

There was the barest polite applause after I finished my remarks, and then the emotions exploded. Jim Simmons, Jr., a member of the vestry, had been designated to offer two motions in the name of many members of the church whose signatures were on his list. This group had clearly come prepared. The first resolution denounced the action of "integrating the races." During the discussion on this motion both Pem Nash and Francis Jenkins denounced the diocese and the bishop vehemently. Others, given permission to be negative by the words of these two social leaders of the town, also vented their feelings. Marian Bourne and two women, Mary Wood Heydenreich and Dolores Pitt, were the three lone voices that tried to stand against the tide. It rolled over them and me too. That resolution was passed by a margin of 139 to 39. The second resolution, designed to split the pledge cards in the future so that people in our congregation could pledge to Calvary Church without any of their money going to the diocese, passed by a closer vote of 109 to 67. It would be the first and only time that a church or diocese I served would use this economic blackmail tactic.

I was crushed. I suppose I made my opposition to this action known. My reputation as the one white man in town who would "give in to the Negro demands" was enormously enhanced. Race-motivated hostility was rising to more and more frenzied levels. A short time later Tarboro had its first sit-ins at the food counter of the local drugstore. Rumors spread that I had trained these young people in the tactics of demonstrating. It was said that I conducted classes on how to tie up traffic by lying down in the streets before automobiles and that I was determined to lead the racial revolution in Tarboro.

The Ku Klux Klan decided that the time had come to hold a countywide rally in a field just outside of Tarboro, where they could burn a cross with impunity. I was denounced at this rally as public enemy number one of the KKK in Edgecombe County. It was among my highest compliments. A program of character assassination was also begun by this hate-filled organization. The common wisdom of the mentality present in the Klan assumed that there were only two possible reasons that a white man would assist what was at that time called "the Negro cause." Either he had some "nigger blood" in him or else he had a Negro mistress. My pale skin made the first assumption somewhat hard to defend, so they began to spread the word that the Episcopal preacher was keeping a "high yellah" in East Tarboro. For the benefit of those who did not grow up in the racist South, a "high yellah" was a light-skinned black woman. This would clearly be the major battlefield of my Tarboro years. In the succeeding months and years the racial temperature continued to rise, propelled more by the moving tide of events in the social and political order than by the church.

The Klan and others in the community awakened in this same period of time to the fact that I was also serving St. Luke's, a black Episcopal congregation. I supposed they assumed that this simply meant conducting Sunday worship services. Of course it meant that, but it also meant baptizing infants, marrying young couples, visiting the sick, and counseling the troubled. Since baptisms, marriages, and even funerals were normally associated with social activities, it suddenly dawned on my critics that I was a guest in the homes of the black people of St. Luke's with some frequency.

In Tarboro, and I suspect in most small Southern towns, the barrier of knowledge between the black community and the white community was firm from the white side. The white community used the services of the black community, but had no interest in and no knowledge of life in the black community. But since most black people worked either directly or indirectly in the white community and specifically in white homes, there was an enormous body of knowledge about the white community that was alive and available to the people in the black community. Blacks, for example, knew the tastes, habits, friends, enemies, and biases of almost every white person in town. They also knew something else that, if it had been known by the whites, would have caused a horrified response. The members of the black community knew who their white fathers and grandfathers were, who their white half brothers and sisters were, who their white cousins were. To the white boys and men, black women had been convenient sex objects, nothing more. Those sexual liaisons produced babies, however, and in the black community those relationships were part of the people's folk wisdom. When trust developed deeply enough between me and the people of St. Luke's, much of this knowledge was shared with me.

The small, black faith community at St. Luke's educated me in many ways. Its people also loved me, and by doing so helped to break open the residual racism of my childhood upbringing. The pastoral experiences I had there transformed my consciousness. There was the burial of a black child, not a year old, who had been left with her illiterate grandmother, while her mother and father, two schoolteachers, returned to their alma mater for a homecoming weekend. The child got into the medicine cabinet and ingested a substance that brought on convulsions. The grandmother had no phone to call for help and no car, so she gathered up the child in her arms and walked to the hospital about three miles away, where the child died within thirty minutes.

The religion of the grandmother and most of the extended family was a primitive form of black Pentecostalism. Only the mother and father, responding to their expanded educational opportunities, had become Episcopalians. The grief of this young couple was overwhelming. Not only was this their only child, but the mother had endured a very difficult delivery, which had resulted in a postnatal hysterectomy. Under the stress of this trauma, both of these schoolteachers reverted to their earlier religious heritage. There was not just weeping at this funeral; rather, earth-shattering wailing and primeval screams filled the air. Members of the extended family would come to the grave site, take this infant out of her casket, and lift her toward the sky while their eerie sounds reverberated throughout the cemetery. I am sure there was something of an ancient African ritual preserved in these acts, but it was an emotionally rending experience for me on several levels. I saw a picture of emerging people drawn back to their past by an experience that simply could not be dealt with by that way of life into which they had moved via education.

Dealing with the death of a child is the most difficult grief of all. Over the course of my forty-five-year ordained career, I faced that crisis on three other occasions. In one case, the marriage that produced that child came to separation in less than a year. In another case, alcohol became the major crutch on which the couple leaned. In the last case, obesity and depression resulted. This black couple made it through this trauma better than any other couple I had known. They continued their growing and creative lives. Perhaps those rituals I called primitive were more helpful, more therapeutic than the sanitized white rituals had been. But that did not occur to me then.

Another funeral I conducted at St. Luke's seemed to exacerbate the racist mentality of the Klan's constituency more than any other. The deceased man was not active in the church, but his wife was. She was a kind, warm, and lovely black woman perhaps in her late fifties or early sixties who, to my knowledge, had not an enemy in the world. Her home was actually on the "white side" of Panola Street, which divided the town racially. It was therefore literally across the side road from Calvary Church. This home was thus exposed to white surveillance in a way that most black homes were not, for white traffic seldom went east of Panola Street. When I got the message of the death of this woman's husband, I went over immediately. A crowd of black people had already gathered. I was the only white face visible in that yard and on that porch. I went immediately to the widow and embraced her, kissing her on the cheek. To my knowledge, that was the first time I had embraced and kissed a black woman. Racism is a deep divide. Since there was nothing romantic or sensual about this, I did not even think about what I did. This woman was some twenty-five to thirty years my senior, but she was a good friend and was in the vulnerable state of grief. I suppose I visited that home three or four times prior to the funeral and three or four times afterward. That also was normal. The prefuneral visits were for dealing with the trauma itself and planning the funeral. The visits afterward were for support and counseling as the shock settled into a living reality. Again on each visit, especially before the funeral, I would be seen in the yard or on the porch by whatever cars might pass. It never occurred to me that these visits, so natural in my profession, would create active hostility.

The funeral itself was at St. Luke's, and it was very crowded. As I preceded the body both in and out of the church, I was also quite visible to the cars driving up and down Panola Street. After the burial we all returned to the widow's house for a repast prepared by her friends. The mood was lighter, as it always is once the burial has been accomplished. We were served marvelous delicacies anchored, as was the custom in that region, by mounds of Southern fried chicken, which could only be eaten with one's fingers.

This close social contact between a white priest and a black community, and probably especially a black widow, was a violation of one of the basic laws of racism. Blacks and whites did not eat together. They did not socialize. Whites did not visit in black homes. Once again I was identified as the untrustworthy white man who was bending the rules, violating the town's value system, and pushing integration. It was more than the Klan leaders could manage, and so they struck back in a manner true to their mentality. They would seek to frighten and to intimidate in their time-tested patterns.

About 2:00 one morning I was awakened by a telephone call from the widow. She was alone in her house. Outside she heard strange noises that awakened her. Going to her window, she saw a couple of pickup trucks parked in front of her house. One of the pickup trucks had a shotgun in the back window of the cab. Both had Confederate flags emblazoned on them. Three or four men wearing hoods, but no sheets, were walking in her yard. They came on her porch to place some hate flyers in her mailbox. She was convinced that they intended to burn a cross in her yard. She was petrified.

The men made no effort to be quiet. Acting despite her fear, the widow turned on every light in her house as quickly as possible. The startled Klansmen returned to their trucks and drove away quickly. My friend called me immediately. When I heard the fear in her voice, I dressed quickly and was ready to drive the half mile to her home, when I heard noises outside my own house. I turned on the floodlights that illumined our yard and opened the front door almost simultaneously. It was faster action than the Klan had expected. Cowards always like to work in darkness and to engage in hit-and-run attacks. They also feared that a white man defending his house in the middle of the night might well be armed. So crosses were never burned, but we were both convinced they were scheduled at both houses.

When I arrived at the home of my friend I tried to reassure her. We notified the police. She had not wanted to do that. In a Southern town the police were not always trusted in the black community, but I never found that to be so in Tarboro. They did their duty of enforcing the law in what I regarded as a color-blind manner. The chief of police Harry Alderman's membership in Calvary Church, I like to think, made a difference. But as this story made its way across the town on both sides of Panola Street, the responses were quite different. East of Panola Street, in the black community, I was increasingly the most trusted white man in town. In the white community, however, west of Panola Street, I was the least trusted white man in town. The tensions were clearly rising.

I felt a tremendous need to focus the church's energy in a new direction, and our new parish house provided me with that opportunity. I moved to employ this resource for the young people of the town. I must say it was actually only for the white young people of the town. We had no official exclusionary policy, but a century of segregated customs did not die overnight. The black and white communities came together very seldom.

So the word went out in the white community that a boys' basketball league would be formed for boys in the fifth through eighth grades. We recruited eight coaches and six referees. The teams were picked by draft among the applicants. Names were chosen with a certain ecclesiastical flair, including the Bishops, the Deacons, the Saints, the Demons, and others borrowed from the National Basketball League. We named the league itself the Holy Hoopster League. Uniforms were T-shirts dyed a variety of colors: purple for the Bishops, orange for the Deacons, red for the Demons, green for the Celtics, and so on. Homer Zirkle, of Zirkle's Cleaners, in town, dyed the shirts for us so that they were uniform. Adhesive tape on the T-shirts created numbers. Practice sessions were held, and finally the day of the first game arrived. There was excitement in the town. The mayor, Herbert Bailey, came out to toss up the first ball at center court. The referees were two brothers, Noah and Dan Baker, who had once refereed high-school games and who wore official-looking striped shirts. The gymnasium was crowded. I handled the loudspeaker, and we opened the festivities by introducing the teams, first the five reserves and then the five starters from each squad, along with their coaches. The starters ran out to center court. Then we rolled in a piano to sing "The Star-Spangled Banner" and the first season of the Holy Hoopster year had begun.

It would be a tremendous success. Pastoral relationships grew between coaches and players. Competition was encouraged but within an environment of mutual support. We decided early that we would give a team championship award, but not individual awards based on athletic ability. The only individual awards would be for sportsmanship. The All Sportsmanship Team would be announced at the Hoopster Ball that would conclude the season. We would also elect the King and Queen of Hearts to preside over the Hoopster Ball. It was all great fun. I persuaded Mabrey Bass, Jr., the editor of the *Daily Southerner* to run stories of these games in the daily press. I wrote the games up with all of the flair of the big time. Since I had already begun to write up the high-school games for the *Daily Southerner*, I actually saw the time when my sports stories filled six of the eight columns of page one of that newspaper.

The season went off without a hitch. The championship game was a fitting conclusion. This activity brought me the deepest appreciation I was to receive in my ministry in this town. The only pressure I felt after this successful launch came from the girls of the town, who saw themselves as excluded. I must confess that my sexist upbringing did not naturally lead me to suggest a league for girls. My own daughters were not old enough to exert their influence. But when the demand was made, I was able to hear it, and the following year the Holy Hoopskirt League was born. It had now become more than I could manage on my own, so the tasks were handed out and duties delegated. I stayed in close touch, however, not because I had to, but because I enjoyed it so much. When the all-sportsmanship teams for both boys and girls were announced the following year, a photographer from the local newspaper was present to record that moment for posterity. The standards we were trying to inculcate began to reach down into the community itself.

No black child ever applied for a place on any Hoopster squad during my years in Tarboro. I look back now and think that was a pity, and my lack of aggressively inviting them to apply is a source of embarrassment and shame. But I was overjoyed when I went back to Tarboro some years later and discovered that Memorial Hall was filled with black and white kids playing together as if segregation had never existed. I was glad that I had helped to create the facility that would, within the decade after my departure, become a recreation center for all the children of Tarboro. But no matter what we did, escaping racial tension was all but impossible.

In the early 1960s Charlotte, Greensboro, and Winston-Salem had finally broken the color line in North Carolina's public schools with token integration of a few black children. Angry parents and townspeople had greeted these actions with public demonstrations, gathering at the affected schools to shout racial epithets, curse, and even spit at these black children. Those images filled the local news on television night after night. It was an appalling and disturbing look into the depths of racism in our region. The people in Tarboro, I am sure, hoped and some even seemed to believe that such a radical thing as desegregation would never come to them. Yet each year thereafter a larger number of school systems in ever smaller towns throughout the state took this step, and the pressure was clearly mounting. I engaged this issue in my preaching. It was neither heroic nor inflammatory preaching. I simply stated that we lived in a society of law, not anarchy. The highest court in the land had spoken. Desegregation was the law of the land. Whether we agreed or not, we had no choice but to obey. Jesus urged that we render to Caesar the things that are Caesar's, I recalled. Obedience to the laws of the state were part of what we owed to Caesar. I quoted Paul, who urged Christians to submit themselves to the higher authority. That was the tone of my preaching. These sermons were not popular, but because the issue had not yet been drawn in our community, the reaction was not overtly hostile. I was laying the groundwork for what I was sure was inevitable.

During this time Tarboro, like all small towns, was being carried inexorably by the history of the larger world. Part of my responsibility was to interpret that larger world to this community. One such inescapable moment came in 1961 when American reconnaissance planes discovered indisputable proof that Russian missile-launching facilities were being constructed ninety miles offshore in Communist Cuba. The Kennedy administration responded by ordering them to be dismantled and dispatching the U.S. Atlantic fleet to blockade Cuba with orders to intercept any Soviet ship or aircraft that might attempt to arm those missile sites. The world hovered closer and closer to the start of a nuclear holocaust that would become World War III. There was near hysteria in the nation, which the town of Tarboro did not escape.

In the midst of that crisis, I addressed the issue in the Sunday sermon, using as my key illustration a book called *The Plague* by Albert Camus. This book was the story of a town in North Africa that was infected by a plague, so it was quarantined. No one could go in; no one could get out. Supplies were dropped by air and everyone in the town believed they would die. It was a book about how doomed people would respond when they faced the inescapable reality of their own deaths. The world in which we lived in that moment seemed not unlike the North African village. Camus called for people to live with nobility and to affirm life and love in their actions even as they died. As I related this story to the Cuban missile showdown that was developing in the Atlantic, one woman began to scream and ran out of the church. When the crisis ended with Soviet withdrawal, there was a collective sigh of relief. The residual effect, however, was an experience of bonding in a crisis and the grudging recognition that I had been a strong interpreter of reality and thus a community leader in a critical moment.

The assassination of John Kennedy again brought me into a community leadership role. On the day of his funeral the only service held in Tarboro was at Calvary Church. Our sanctuary was packed with citizens from all parts of the community who needed an opportunity to mourn. Again I interpreted the events, articulating the anger, the grief, and the fear of our people and giving voice to the strength of this nation to survive the crisis and the reality of the God who rules history. A level of trust in my ability to speak to this community and to have my voice respected grew. This tempered the negative feelings that my role in Tarboro's racial struggle had produced. That leadership was tested in the local arena when the courts ordered the desegregation of Tarboro schools to commence the coming September 1964.

When the fateful date of school openings drew near, the intemperate racist language in some segments of the community became excessive. The political leadership was paralyzed. The other clergy in town were almost all beholden to their congregations and not free to assume leadership. The newspaper editorials were speaking only to the fears of the people. I felt, perhaps in a deluded manner, that I was the only one free enough to offer leadership. I knew it would be costly, but I also knew that the canons of the Episcopal Church protected the rector from dismissal by congregational vote. I also knew that my bishop would support me. The time had come, I said to myself, for me to see the stuff of which I was made. We needed to walk competently through the feared moment of integration, which represented to most white people the death of the only way of life they had ever known. I discussed my plans with no one, but I decided to act.

I first went to see the sheriff, Tom Bardin. I knew him well as a member of the parish. He would be a key person in providing security for the integrating children. He was, however, also an elected sheriff who had to face his countywide constituency once every four years. I asked him whether or not he was prepared to protect the lives and welfare of these few black children. He assured me that he was. To put a bit of firmness into his backbone, I told him that, if necessary, I would be there on that first day of school to escort those black children into the building. If an angry white crowd gathered with the intention of being abusive or hurtful, they would have to be abusive and hurtful to me before they could get to those children. I did not doubt that if those children were in danger, I would be also, but what I sought to do was to raise the price of unruly behavior. That potentially angry crowd of protesters knew that white people like me knew how to hire lawyers and take people to court for personal damages. They were used to being verbally or even physically abusive to black people and getting away with it. I also would know the people in the crowds and they would know me. It was a calculated gamble. Tom Bardin was a good man, and I trusted him to do the right thing. I never told a soul about this conversation. I am not sure Tom did either, but he urged me not to be there. He believed that my presence would simply exacerbate the tensions if a crowd gathered. He assured me that the law would be upheld. I was willing to trust his judgment, though I am confident I made his intention firmer.

On the Sunday before school opened I preached on the issue once more. It was again neither a heroic nor an inflammatory sermon. I urged the people to be calm. I suggested that street violence was illegal and should be prosecuted. I urged them to seek peaceful and legal means to redress their grievances. They knew as well as I that such efforts would be fruitless, since the highest court in the land had unanimously ruled that segregated schools were inherently unequal. So people spent their time and energy cursing the court. Chief Justice Earl Warren became the epitome of evil. Dwight Eisenhower, our president, actually aided and abetted the hard-line resisters. He never gave his personal approval to the Supreme Court decision. He described the nomination of Earl Warren as the "worst mistake of my presidency." What he was doing unwittingly was allowing racism to flow freely with no impediment from the president. It was not one of Eisenhower's greatest moments. It would also come back to haunt him when the governor of Arkansas, Orville Faubus, assuming he had the tacit consent of the president, or at least that the president would not act against him and "the sovereign state of Arkansas," defied the law of the land at Little Rock High School. Mr. Eisenhower then had to act in a crisis to uphold the law even though his personal behavior had encouraged lawlessness. To articulate firmly the power of the law was a function of leadership that I would note carefully.

When the morning of desegregation came to Tarboro, the small crowd at the school seemed more apprehensive than angry. There were also sufficient police. The sheriff and his deputies were in place. Only four black children were enrolled, a tolerable number to most people. I stayed more than a block away, trying to speak to individuals I knew as they walked toward the school. Even there I listened to abusive words, and if spitting not directly at me but clearly to express their feelings constitutes a hostile act, I endured hostile acts. Yet at the school when the black children arrived, the law enforcement personnel were quite professional. Those who were enraged limited their response to muttering to one another. I went into the school later that morning. I was the parent of a student there, so my presence was quite legitimate. All was quiet. I discovered, interestingly enough, that segregation was a bit like virginity. Once it is lost, there is no effort to restore it. After that one simply adjusts. That was the way it was in Tarboro. However, one thing was real. I had been identified once more throughout the town as "pro-Negro," or, in the more vulgar phrase, as a "nigger lover." When it is not effective to hate the Supreme Court or the government, one looks for a more available and convenient target. In the minds of many people in that little town, I was now the leading candidate to fill that role. Hostility began to be expressed quite overtly.

The people with whom I played golf every Monday decided that they would not play again with me. At Calvary Church the side door became more popular, since people exiting there did not have to greet me. In the downtown section of Tarboro I would notice people crossing the street when they saw me coming. The telephone began to ring at night with threatening calls, designed not just to harass and to disturb sleep, but also to frighten. The calls went on for weeks. We thought about getting an unlisted number, but I would not tolerate the idea that narrow-minded and mean-spirited people might separate me from those whose needs were legitimate. For me, part of the priesthood was making myself available and even vulnerable. So we endured the calls. Threats were made against me, my wife, and our children. One of the most memorable of these callers informed us that our daughters were going to be raped by "the biggest, blackest nigger we can find." Our girls were nine, six, and five at the time. We walked the older children to and from school each day for a long period of time. Racial concerns continued to affect the total life of this town, but now the area shifted from the school to the local political situation.

Tarboro was administered by a mayor and council form of government. The town council members were elected in geographical districts, five in all. They in turn elected one of themselves to be the mayor. Up until this moment the council had been composed exclusively of white males. Neither a woman nor a black male had ever served. The district in which I lived had a three-to-two black-to-white ratio. Most of the black citizens, however, had been discouraged from voting by the very barriers that the national civil rights laws were now sweeping away. A new sense of self-confidence entered the black community, along with their new sense of empowerment. My incumbent councilman was the local florist, Herman Creech. He was a Methodist, so I did not know him more than superficially. Herman was not an offensive person, but he was not a particularly broad-minded leader either, and he looked upon his role as a council member as something due to him for his willingness to serve. At this time the primary method of campaigning in the black community was to seek their votes with what politically came to be called "street money," aided by gifts of alcohol. The tactic was based upon a white definition of black people, who were thought to be willing do almost anything for money and cheap whiskey. It had seemed to work in a day when there was no black candidate to invigorate their political energy, and few of them bothered to register.

By 1964, with the passing of the Voting Rights law, many black voters were enrolled, and Dr. Moses Ray, the black dentist in town and a man of unquestioned ability, filed the necessary papers to run for the town council in my district. Herman Creech now had a black opponent in a majority black district. The foundations of the past began to shake visibly.

The typical racist campaign of hate and fear was launched. Dire predictions were heard of what would happen if the black people took over the town government. Dr. Ray was the first step, the foot in the door, it was said. If he were elected, the black tide would be unstoppable. Sexual politics also entered the fray, for anonymous posters appeared asserting that no white woman would be sexually safe if blacks achieved political power. I do not think that Herman Creech was directly responsible for these campaign tactics, but I do know they were used.

Dr. Ray, who had been an officer in the segregated armed forces during World War II, met these charges with magnificent decorum. He never dignified them with a response. Instead, he stuck to his positive themes. He promised not to play racial politics. He would seek to represent all the people of his district fairly. He contended that the town would be safer and healthier if the almost 50 percent of the population that was black had some representation. He sought to allay fears and to present his ideas positively and rationally. It was a brilliant campaign.

Dr. Ray's office was just across the street from my office, on the second floor of a black-owned drugstore. This meant that it was also on the "white" side of Panola Street and therefore in view of white traffic patterns. Several times a week I would go across the street to purchase something in that drugstore, like a Coke, cough drops, or aspirin. It was certainly convenient. From time to time I would meet Dr. Ray in that store. Occasionally we would have a Coke together. I liked him, but I knew him quite casually. To my knowledge he had never attended St. Luke's. Those facts, however, did not forestall the rumors.

The logic of white racism went something like this: Dr. Ray has run a brilliant campaign. Black people are not smart enough to conceive and run such a campaign. Therefore, some white person must be masterminding his political effort. There is in this town only one racially untrustworthy white man and he is the Episcopal rector. His office and Dr. Ray's office are across the street from each other. The two of them have been seen coming out of that "Negro drugstore" together.

The conclusion was clear. The Episcopal rector was the secret force behind Dr. Ray's political effort. His church office has the equipment to mimeograph all of Dr. Ray's flyers and political mailings. A high level of hostility once again invaded this little town.

This kind of talk did not reach crisis proportions immediately because no one could conceive of Dr. Ray actually winning. Lots of street money poured into the Creech campaign. His operatives began to make journeys into East Tarboro. In this election, both money and takers seemed plentiful. The assumption was that this time-honored tactic would work again as usual.

It did not! When the votes were counted, Dr. Ray had won by a bare handful of votes. He had gotten solid, almost unanimous, votes in the black polling places and, according to white analysis, there was a small core of white voters who had voted for Dr. Ray. If those turncoat white voters had stayed firmly in the white column, Dr. Ray would have been defeated. I do not know how that vote count was determined, but facts never matter much when racial fears are rampant. A vigilante mentality developed as attempts were made to identify the white turncoats. I was at the top of the list of suspects. The white fear erupted as rage. We were destined to ride another tide of racial hostility. The Klan once again became active.

Within days after that election, I received a call that a committee of citizens, including members of Calvary, wanted to see me that night. I did not have to guess what the problem was. Interestingly enough, they did not send the heavyweights. This was to be an attempt at reasoning. The three-person committee turned out to include two members of Calvary, Don Gilliam, Jr., and Jim Simmons, Jr. Don had a job in the courthouse. Jim had previously been the chosen spokesperson of the group that sought to fight the diocese financially. As things go, neither of these men was rabidly racist, but they were concerned, and with no middle ground on this issue in the community, they were clearly in league with those who wanted to retain white power and white control. The third person on this committee was a Presbyterian and a sitting member of the town council recently reelected. When they began the conversation, it became clear that the purpose of this visit was to violate my constitutional and civil rights. They actually asked me how I had voted in the election. I declined to tell them. In that climate, however, they took that declination as an admission of guilt. They began to tell me that my future in Tarboro was at stake and probably my career in the priesthood. The threat was clear and it was genuine.

I had the grace to remain calm. I informed them that an Episcopal rector enjoyed the protection of the canons and that I could not be removed from my position, nor was I willing to be intimidated. They could all vote to ask me to resign, and I would still refuse to do so. No matter how difficult it was, I would remain in Tarboro. If everyone left the church, I would remain. If they got to the place where they could no longer pay my salary, I would find a way to support myself and my family and I would remain as rector. That is,

I would conduct services every Sunday at the appointed hours even if no one attended. I further reminded them that they could not speak for the whole congregation. I knew by that time that I stood firmly in the affections and respect of a significant number of people in both the church and the town. I further stated that if they persisted in this attempt to identify and harass the white voters for Dr. Ray, I would expose their tactics and their names publicly and that they should expect those white citizens they were targeting to take legal action to protect their rights.

It was a tense conversation, but there was no mistaking the issues before us. The three almost apologized before they left my home. They tried to say that they had come to me as my friends to try to tell me what people were thinking. They wanted to warn me about the levels of anger. It was an ancient and dishonorable tactic that has never washed with me. They claimed not to be upset, but to be speaking, as my friends, for those who were. I told them that they had agreed to be the bearers of this message of intimidation and that I held them responsible for this action. They left with the balance of anger a bit more even. To my knowledge, that was the only intimidation of suspected white turncoats that was ever made. The vigilante mentality died as quickly as it had been born. It was one more lesson that a leader must learn. A leader does what he or she believes is right, does not compromise, and sees the issue through to the end without waffling. In the long run far less hostility accrues to the leader who does this than to the one who compromises his or her integrity in the search for accommodation, compromise, or popularity. No one will finally respect a frightened, pulse-feeling kind of leadership.

Dr. Ray took his seat on the council of the town of Tarboro and served with distinction. Herman Creech returned to the florist business a wiser man. A crucial moment of crisis had passed. The truth is I did vote for Dr. Ray. He was, in my opinion, the better candidate of the two. However, I did not advise, assist, or aid his campaign in any way. The brilliance in Dr. Ray's strategy was his own, and people came to recognize that in time. Another prejudiced racial stereotype had bitten the dust. Before he died, Dr. Ray became a popular and long-serving mayor of Tarboro.

Having five congregations in a kind of circuit-riding ministry had one other dramatic consequence I never considered until well into my Tarboro years. My frenetic schedule meant that I gave little time to the educational phase of any of these congregations and certainly had no time on Sunday for adult education. Mine was a hit-and-run schedule of liturgical activity. In later years I was very critical of those congregations that expected the Sunday sermon to provide an adequate amount of adult education. Yet I was, in Tarboro, guilty of that very thing. There always was a Lenten study for adults at Calvary Church. In this congregation for Lent the custom was to have evening prayer and a sermon Monday through Friday in the chapel, which would be attended by twenty to twenty-five people. I would take a book of the Bible, like Acts, divide it into forty segments, one for each day of Lent, and preach on it day by day, doubling up on Friday since we did not observe Saturday worship. I am not sure that this format meant a great deal to the people who attended, since they were not the same people each day, but for me it was a way to master one book of the Bible each year, and I loved the discipline of it.

Probably the best and most effective educational venture I launched in Tarboro came to be called "Give Up Saturday Night for Lent." I approached a group of young adults who were related to the church in varying ways, from average to tangential. I would guess that the church was not a central part of the lives of any of them, but they were the pace-setting group of young adults in the town as members of the dominant economic families. They were also quite clearly the next generation of Tarboro's civic leadership. "How about forming a study group among your closest friends," I suggested. "We could meet at each others homes each Saturday night, eat together, and work through a really good book in discussion. You all know each other well enough to talk freely. You have no hesitancy disagreeing and it just might be fun. It will take six Saturday nights. It has a clear beginning and ending. What do you think?"

I trotted out that proposal to three of the couples who were the leaders of the leaders in more or less those words. They were willing to talk to others. It was a go. Eight couples, including Joan and me, made the commitment. The book was picked, and the schedule arranged. I agreed to chair the first session, which was to meet at the home of one of our young attorneys. We agreed not to talk about this group publicly for fear that someone not included might be hurt, but we might just as well have advertised it on a public billboard.

On the first Saturday night of Lent the gathering of the young social set at Tarboro's Hilma Country Club was strangely smaller. As someone observed, "Only the Presbyterians were drinking at the club on that Saturday night." Since such a gathering was more or less a norm, inquiries were made to a number of our Saturday night groupers during the next week.

They each tried to suggest that they simply had other plans. But when the same faces were missing for the next two or three Saturday nights, the intrigue grew, the curiosity became boundless, and the rumors ran rampant. Small towns tolerate poorly what they do not understand, especially if it changes established social patterns. So the story was told and the Lenten discipline known as "Give Up Saturday Night for Lent" entered our vocabulary.

Each Saturday night was unique. Men who were unaccustomed to talking about much more than hunting, fishing, business, politics, and the University of North Carolina's football team began to discuss ideas that had been hidden even from their own consciousness for years. Spiritual yearnings, concepts of God, and strange religious words that were repeated by rote, but that made no sense to most of them like "Jesus died for my sins," were opened up and made acceptable to question. Most of us in the group were sorry to see Easter come, and the post-Easter party to celebrate our successful study was significantly different from social evenings that had involved these people before. They also looked forward to repeating this project next Lent. A tradition had been born.

There were two other serendipities of note that derived from this adventure. The future lay leadership of Calvary Church was in that group and in a very short period of time, they became vestry people, wardens, and the president of the Episcopal Churchwomen. When I left Tarboro, they were significant leaders in the search or calling committee that looked for a new rector.

Second, more than I realized at the time, this group was my primary doorway back into the full good graces of the community. The young leaders of this town had decided that my being "an integrationist" did not outweigh the other gifts I had to bring and their embrace of me made the town's embrace of me almost inevitable. That was never articulated. It just happened. The one who made that clearest to me and to the others was the wife of one of the Clarks. Her name was Gray Procter Clark. Her husband was Cousin Willie's grandson, William G. Clark III. The graceful embrace offered to me by Gray Clark was among the most healing gifts I have ever received. I was grateful to her and am devoted to her to this day.

My interest in significant adult Christian education as a major feature of the church's Sunday life was never able to find expression in Tarboro. Yet my experience in this area of life was growing and developing in a powerful way always, strangely enough, outside the boundaries of Tarboro. Because of this separation, I sometimes felt that I had two careers. As a rector in Tarboro, because of my peripatetic schedule to provide worship services in the parochial missions, I never functioned as a teacher in any church on Sunday morning. So the teaching side of my professional life, which would someday be the source of my books and of my pushing theological frontiers with radical new possibilities for the future of Christianity, had to be born somewhere else. That turned out to be a place called Kanuga.

As early as 1958, the Kanuga Conference Center in western North Carolina invited me to be a minor faculty member on the staff of something called the Adult Conference. This event would be attended by up to three hundred people from across the South. The conference would feature a keynote lecturer each morning whose class, held in the chapel, was attended by everyone. In that role were people like Stephen Bayne, the Anglican executive officer, Henry Knox Sherrill, the retired presiding bishop, William J. Gordon, the bishop of Alaska, and Carroll Simcox, editor of *The Living Church*. Underneath the keynoter would be a dozen or so secondary faculty members who would offer a variety of courses at the second and third hour of the day from which the people could choose. Each of us would describe our class with as much excitement as we could at the opening get-acquainted session with the hope that we would not be embarrassed by having no one choose our offering. Teaching was a great love of mine and after my first visit to Kanuga, I was invited back year after year.

A break to my future life and career occurred at one of those subsequent adult conferences. I was once again scheduled to be one of the junior faculty members to undergird the keynoter. This particular year, however, followed a slightly different format from that employed in the past. There would be two keynoters, one for each of the first two hours. Only at the third hour of the day would there be electives staffed by the younger faculty. One of the other junior faculty members that year was Robert W. Estill, a young priest who in his early thirties had recently become the rector of Christ Church in Lexington, the largest Episcopal congregation in Kentucky.

The first keynoter that year was the Very Reverend George Alexander, Dean of St. Luke's School of Theology at Sewanee and formerly the very popular rector of Trinity Church, Columbia, South Carolina. His topic was a biblical one. The second keynoter was Helen Shoemaker, the wife of Sam Shoemaker, the rector of Calvary Church, Pittsburgh, probably as well-known a rector as there was in the United States at that time. Helen was also a popular and much sought after lecturer in her own right on the subject of prayer.

When my family and I rolled into Kanuga that summer, I received the surprise of my young ordained life. In one of those flukes of conference planning, lightening had struck that conference not once, but twice. In the last couple of days, because of a sickness in one instance and a death in the family in the other, both George Alexander and Helen Shoemaker had been forced to cancel their appearances. It was too late to get substitutes. Some three hundred people, many of whom were drawn by the reputations of these two leaders, were arriving. The head of Kanuga, Bill Verduin, met me with the news that I was being moved into George Alexander's keynote hour. Bob Estill was soon to learn that he was being moved into Helen Shoemaker's place. This meant that we would speak to the whole conference rather than to the thirty to fifty people who might have elected our courses during the third hour. I was sorry I would not get to hear Dean Alexander and Helen Shoemaker, but I was thrilled at this opportunity.

That opening dinner, however, was not easy. Bill Verduin had to explain to the conference audience his dilemma. There were audible groans from the assembled crowd. Bill built Bob and me up the best he could, but the fact is that few people had ever heard of us and no one had come to Kanuga specifically to hear either of us. My ego was bruised and challenged simultaneously, and I retired early to make sure my preparation was complete. I was going to give this my best shot.

I met my disappointed class at 9:00 the next morning. It was probably the largest audience I had ever addressed in my young career. My topic was the Resurrection, and I treated it like a great detective story. I searched out the clues to Easter in the biblical texts. I assembled the evidence for the reality of the Easter moment as a lawyer might amass courtroom evidence in a trial. I placed it before my class, asking them to be the jury. I went into the changes in Peter, the transformation of the other disciples, the birth of Sunday as a day of worship, and those strange connections between the Resurrection and the sharing of a common meal, best symbolized by words attributed to Cleopas in Luke's Emmaus Road story, "He was known to us in the breaking of the bread." Then I tried to recreate what I believed actually happened. The people were intrigued and quickly got over their disappointment. The class was a rousing success. No one wanted his or her money back. Indeed, they congratulated Kanuga on having a secondary staff like Spong and Estill who could step in at the last minute and carry the conference to so positive a conclusion. I had also filled the keynoter role so well that I would be invited to do it again.

Another happy result occurred almost immediately. I began to get invitations to do lectures in Episcopal churches across the South, which was Kanuga's basic orbit. For the next few years I would be away from Tarboro at least once a month doing what we called "Teaching Missions." They would consist of three lectures on three successive evenings in a local church. Lenten noonday preaching opportunities at large urban churches in the South also flowed in. So did invitations to lead diocesan conferences of men, women, and families. There was no state in the South that I did not go to on one of these journeys. I was on my way to becoming a well-known figure across the region of my birth.

As a lecturer, I crisscrossed the South during my Tarboro years, from South Carolina through Georgia, Alabama, Mississippi, Arkansas, Florida, Tennessee, Louisiana, and Kentucky. I began to have growing contact with the leaders of the Southern Church, and frequently met my seminary classmates on these journeys. I was also learning that I was a good communicator and that there was enormous spiritual emptiness, even in the pious, religious South. A growing gap was developing between the work of the theological academy and the traditional preaching that took place in the congregations. Increasingly I began to reflect it, but at the same time, I started to experience what can only be called professional and spiritual restlessness. My teaching, lecture-circuit life, where my study could find outlet among responsive people, was not part of my regular parochial priesthood. I was in Tarboro cast as a liturgist rather than as an educator. Yet it was as a lecturer that I began to receive my greatest sense of fulfillment. I clearly had grown to the limits of what Tarboro seemed to offer. At the same time a certain closure seemed to be coming to my Tarboro years.

The Junior Chamber of Commerce named me "Man of the Year" in Tarboro early in 1965. The presentation was made by the mayor, who was a local surgeon. The citation referred to my work with the youth of the city through the high school and the two Hoopster leagues. It also made reference to some work I had done in the formation of a mental health association. But the thing that meant most to me was what the mayor said personally that was not in the citation. He proclaimed to his assembled audience that I had been courageous and helpful in the area of race relations in the town. "Not popular," he added, "but right." The willingness to be true to one's conviction, to take the heat of a disturbed prejudice, and to change people's fears through education had proved to be at long last not just the right way to go, but a successful way to go as well. It would be a lesson I would never forget.

Several months later I had my first contact with the search committee of St. John's Church in Lynchburg, Virginia. It was neither the church nor the geographical direction from which I had anticipated a move might someday come. Lynchburg was not part of the area that Kanuga served and into which I had moved so deeply. It was, in fact, my first step out of the South, as strange as that might sound to those who know Lynchburg as Jerry Falwell country. Virginia was in the mid-Atlantic area of the Episcopal Church and outside my orbit. St. John's was, however, a church that excited me from the very beginning. It was a large enough single responsibility so that I could be invested in adult education Sunday after Sunday. I could thus bring my two priestly vocations together. It was across the street from Randolph Macon Woman's College, so it had an academic interest. Finally, it would afford me my first opportunity to have a full-time assistant.

The call to be rector came before we left for our vacation on the Outer Banks of North Carolina. I was ecstatic and I knew I would accept, so on that vacation I was in some sense no longer in Tarboro and not yet in Lynchburg. That combination made this holiday completely tension free. We planned only to enjoy the sun and sand and to read. The book highest on my agenda to read that summer was a thin paperback by an English bishop that had been the source of great controversy in the church press. It was entitled *Honest to God*. Its author was John A. T. Robinson, the bishop of Woolwich, an area in the Diocese of Southwark that embraced part of the city of London south of the Thames. I had read a number of reviews of this book and had been singularly unimpressed. Robinson quoted at length from the writings of Paul Tillich, Dietrich Bonhoeffer, and Rudolf Bultmann. Each of these scholars was familiar to me, Tillich from seminary and Bonhoeffer from Tarboro. Bultmann, who had been generally ignored by my seminary, had begun to invade my consciousness through reading. None of them disturbed me. I could not understand what the debate was about, but Robinson's book had so permeated the public consciousness and I had been asked about it so often, I knew I had to read it. This book had been out for more than eighteen months so I had hardly rushed into the fray it was creating. The beach in the summer of 1965 was to be the time I put this book behind me.

Arriving at our rented home at Nag's Head, we settled in and watched the children make those obligatory first sand castles, see them be knocked down by the first waves, and step on the first jellyfish. After dinner we went for quick visits to favorite beach places the children had learned to love from previous visits: Newman's shell store, the amusement park with its many rides, and the sand dunes where Wilbur and Orville Wright had flown the first airplane for a hundred yards or so. Then a tired family went to bed. I got out *Honest to God*, read the cover, looked over the preface and table of contents, and turned off the light. That would be tomorrow's agenda.

Tomorrow came quickly and after pancakes and sausage, always our first vacation breakfast, we went to the beach armed with buckets, shovels, beach chairs, umbrellas, books, dark glasses, and suntan lotion. I would periodically rotate parental duty with Joan to go into the ocean with our daughters, search for shells, or play in the sand, and then I would read while she enjoyed the children. We would go inside from 11:00 to 3:00 to avoid the harmful rays of the sun and to nap. I would have uninterrupted reading time while they napped. In this setting I turned my attention fully to *Honest to God*.

I was riveted by this book! I could not put it down. I read it three times from cover to cover before I thought about picking up anything else to read. It was not that it was a great book. It revealed the rapidity with which it was written, but it was an honest book. It talked about issues I had not been willing to talk about or even to think about publicly. "Our image of God has got to go!" was the headline in the *Sunday Observer* of London that launched this book into public debate in 1963. The God above the sky had been obliterated by the insights of astrophysicists. The story of Jesus as the Son of this Divine Being just beyond the sky was equally shaky. The whole arena of situation ethics, which reflected the introduction of relativity, injected by Albert Einstein into every human consideration, had made ethics based on natural laws or the revealed will of God problematic. The monastic disciplines of prayer addressed to the God up there or out there were disappearing. John Robinson touched every issue about which I felt a general dis-ease in the church's life, and he showed me why. I knew from that moment on that my theological education had not prepared me to deal with the world in which all of us were now living. If I were honest, I could never again use the pious clichés of my profession as a substitute for hard study and effective scholarship. It was as if I knew that I could not continue to be the kind of priest I had been. It did not affect my political or sociological convictions, for those still seemed to have enormous integrity, but it did challenge radically my theological convictions, for increasingly I realized they did not have either depth or integrity. I could no longer pretend that the Bible had the answers when its verses were read literally. It was as if I had seen the future and must now equip myself to enter it. I began to see how my whole priestly career would change dramatically when we moved to Lynchburg. There I could engage my congregation intellectually and in depth. It felt as if my life was coming to a new sense of oneness. I recalled that many of the faculty of Randolph Macon Woman's College were members of St. John's. Indeed, the head of the religion department there was Edwin Anderson Penick, Jr., the son of my former bishop. It was as if people from my past were ushering me into a new place.

Returning home from Nag's Head, I announced my resignation. A month later we said our good-byes to a church and a town I had deeply loved. I received a wonderful welcoming letter from the bishop of Southwestern Virginia, William Henry Marmion. St. John's seemed to be a dream about to come true. In Tarboro I had gone through valleys and up mountains with the people who lived there. I had grown up in every way imaginable in years, in maturity, in faith, in personality, and in confidence. I had been there almost eight years, the longest tenure I would have anywhere as a priest. Separating was painful for me indeed, but separate we did.

One strange note, however, forced its way into my attention. I discovered that my wife, Joan, did not share my grief at leaving. Indeed, she was eager to leave. She had no regrets and stated with a strange vehemence that she never wanted to see Tarboro or its people again. For the first time she said to me that she had been miserably unhappy there. I could not believe what I was hearing. I had seen no sign of this distress in her. She had never mentioned those feelings. I wondered if I had become so insensitive that I had simply failed to notice. But no one else seemed to be aware of these feelings in her either.

I looked back, searching for something that might give me a clue to this response. All I could recall was that while living in Tarboro, Joan's only sister, Shirley, had died of cancer of the pancreas at age thirty-seven. That death was incredibly painful, especially since Shirley had two young daughters. Shirley and Joan had not been particularly close. Yet when the diagnosis was made, Joan made several trips to Shirley's home just outside Washington, D.C., to see her sister and to assist with the care of the two girls. Strangely enough, Joan's father had died of the same disease in 1955.

When Shirley's death came, Joan went through a strange personality change. It was as if Joan believed that everyone in her family, including her mother and brother, wished it could have been Joan who died rather than Shirley. She acted as if she almost had to apologize for the fact that she was still alive. After we returned from Shirley's burial, Joan began the habit of getting up early each morning to pray and to read the kind of devotional material that her mother read constantly. Slowly but surely she stopped seeing our social friends and began to be more and more in the company of those who were particularly needy, a mental patient, an obese woman, the wife of an alcoholic. I knew all of these people well. In some sense I applauded this, thinking in my naive way that her level of compassion and religious devotion was growing. Indeed, I even wanted to take some credit for this new devotion. Those in her new group of friends were highly motivated to reach out to the marginalized people in our community. Together they began a Head Start program in Princeville, a poor black community just east of Tarboro, that was one of the best programs of its sort I had ever seen. I was proud of her accomplishment and said so loudly and publicly. I did not know that the Saturday night group, which I had enjoyed so much, had been an absolute chore for her. I remembered going alone a couple of Saturdays, because she told me she did not feel well.

Yet as we followed the van in our family station wagon out of Tarboro headed toward Lynchburg, all of these feelings poured out of Joan. I could not easily put together my observations of her behavior with the words I heard her speaking. For now these troubling thoughts just lodged in my subconscious mind.

# 9

# *A Bible Class, the Press, and More Racial Conflict in Lynchburg*

※

ONE MOVES to a new position in the church by stepping into the living history of both congregation and diocese. As an elderly woman said to me in Tarboro when she was less than thrilled about some of my initiatives, "Son, this church was here long before you came and it will be here long after you have departed." That was certainly true of St. John's Church, Lynchburg, and of the Diocese of Southwestern Virginia. I was stepping into a moving stream of life, and therefore I was destined to be both victim and beneficiary of that living history.

A man named Robert C. Jett was chosen to be the first bishop of this diocese, serving from 1920 to 1938. He cast a mighty spell over the diocese, setting its tone, helping to get institutions like the Virginia Episcopal School in Lynchburg launched, and building a sense of diocesan identity and ownership. He came from a well-educated Virginia family of social standing with all the grace and manners that are a part of good breeding and gentility; yet accompanying them were all of the prejudices of his class and the values of the time in which he lived. His children and his grandchildren continued in this tradition and were active members of the Episcopal Church. One of his granddaughters, nicknamed "Bunny," married a well-known pediatrician named Ed Vaden, and they moved to Lynchburg to become social leaders of the town and active members of St. John's. Bunny was vibrant and alive, if rather provincial, in her attitudes. His other granddaughter, nicknamed "Jinx," married an attorney from Big Stone Gap, Virginia, named Linwood Holton, who was both a liberal and a Republican. This meant that she was a bit more rebellious and a bit less provincial. Bunny and Ed Vaden would be important parts of our life in Lynchburg and, strangely enough, Jinx and Linwood Holton would be important parts of our life in Richmond.

Robert Magill became rector of St. John's Church in 1929, so he stretched back literally to the days of Bishop Jett and reflected the values of the Jett era. In his thirty-five-year rectorship he had baptized, married, and buried the leading people of the city and was himself a fixture in the social world of Lynchburg, much loved as a pastor and cherished as a friend. Among his greatest admirers was Bunny Vaden. She was also one of many who could not imagine St. John's apart from the beloved Robert Magill. I think it is fair to say that Dr. Magill had a hard time imagining that himself.

In 1953 the Diocese of Southwestern Virginia was going to elect a new bishop to replace Henry D. Phillips, the not especially popular successor to Robert C. Jett. Probably no one who succeeded Bishop Jett would have been. It was now time for the Bishop Jett wing of the diocese to reclaim the bishop's office for those who really appreciated the way the Episcopal Church was intended to be. Since Bob Magill was just such a man, the descendants of Bishop Jett worked hard to secure his election. However, the world of both the church and society had changed far more than this group realized, and Dr. Magill's day had quite simply passed. He could not get the required votes, especially from among the younger clergy, and a compromise candidate, William Henry Marmion, from Delaware, was elected. Bishop Marmion, a graduate of Virginia Theological Seminary, had Southern roots, having been born in Texas and having served in Alabama. However, he had long ago emotionally moved miles away from the traditions and attitudes of the Old South. It was clear that this convention had not only elected William Marmion but had rejected Robert Magill. Following that defeat, Dr. Magill in some sense folded his tent, narrowed his world, and sank into the city of Lynchburg and the parish of St. John's as if they were both mere extensions of himself until his retirement in 1965.

Southwestern Virginia was a small diocese that depended financially on its two largest churches, St. John's Church in Roanoke and St. John's Church in Lynchburg. If these two churches were not supportive, the life of the sparsely populated, mountainous diocese was in jeopardy. Robert Magill's personal sense of having been rejected by the diocese to which he had given so great a part of his life made his ability to give that support to the new bishop difficult. His deepest admirers, including relatives of Bishop Jett who were active in both of those major churches, encouraged him in that direction.

Bishop Marmion was consecrated on May 13, 1954. The Supreme Court decision in the case of *Brown vs. the Board of Education,* outlawing segregation in public schools, was handed down on May 17, 1954. Virginia politics was at this time dominated by its Democratic U.S. senator, Harry Byrd, Sr., and what was called the Byrd Machine. A call went out from this political leadership to mount a vigorous, instantaneous, and total rejection of the Supreme Court ruling. The adopted stance of these Southern politicians would be to resist this law everywhere and forever. Public schools would be closed in Virginia before political leaders would allow integration to occur. The success of this strategy would lie, it was believed, in its totality. Any effort anywhere to respond to this ruling in any other manner would be opposed with the massive resources of the state's dominant political party.

The annual convention of the diocese of Southwestern Virginia was to assemble at St. John's Church in Bedford, Virginia, the very next day, on May 18.

The new bishop, in his first annual address to the diocese, did not dodge the controversial issue. It was one more sign to the conservative elements of the diocese that they had, in fact, lost their bid to reassert the leadership of a previous era. At his second diocesan gathering a year later, Bishop Marmion announced that the official policy of this diocese at meetings would be to make no distinction because of race or color. In that day it was a bold announcement. However, since it was still just talk without action, it was tolerated.

Over the next few years the tide continued to flow in favor of a new generation of leadership. New, younger clergy were recruited for the diocese, public issues continued to be engaged, and the tone of the diocese became more and more controversial and confrontational.

Things came to a head in 1957 when the diocese acquired Hemlock Haven, a camp and conference center adjacent to the Hungry Mother State Park in Marion, Virginia. It was a lovely, but rustic place consisting of camp-type cottages and a main building that housed the administrative offices, kitchen, dining room, and infirmary. A swimming pool, volleyball court, athletic field, and hiking trails made up the balance of the facilities.

It would certainly not be feasible to build a "separate but equal" center to service the camping and conference needs of the few black Episcopalians in this diocese. It was also impossible for Bishop Marmion to conceive of the possibility that any diocesan facility would not be open and available to every member of the diocese. That was so elemental to this young bishop's thinking that other options never occurred to him. He had told the people of his diocese what the operative principle would be. It should come as no surprise that he would act on what he had said.

The executive board of the diocese announced that Hemlock Haven would be open to all the communicants of the diocese. That announcement, when it was made public, sent shivers down the spines of those traditional members who felt that the world that they had known was about to disappear. They began to organize in one final attempt to turn back the clock at the coming annual convention of the diocese.

Some of the operatives of Senator Byrd's political organization were Episcopalians in this diocese. Their response was instantaneous and predictable. Enormous hostility began to be directed at the new bishop from many quarters. Bill Marmion and the diocesan executive board had seized enormous power when they announced the policy of full inclusion for a diocesan facility. This policy had never been prohibited, but that was because of the racist assumption that integration would never be the choice of white people. In the unusual way the Episcopal Church is organized, the laity and the clergy could vote by separate orders in diocesan conventions, which meant that for a resolution to be passed at the convention, it must receive a majority among both the clergy and the laity concurrently. When the convention met, the majority of the clergy consistently supported their bishop. The laity, aided and abetted by Dr. Magill, tried over and over to reverse the decision. When they failed, they vowed they would punish the bishop and the diocese in any way they could. Where a vote by orders was required, the conservative laity refused to give their consent. The budget of the diocese failed to be adopted, and authorization for the most mundane of diocesan responsibilities was withheld. If the old-line members of the diocese could not win on issues of preserving their segregated way of life, then they would express their fury by paralyzing the ability of the diocese to act in any way. Dr. Magill became the clergy rallying point for these laypeople. He was now cast as the ordained leader of the opposition to the new bishop.

Returning home from that diocesan gathering, the vestry of St. John's, Lynchburg, with the support of their rector, Robert Magill, prepared to act out their opposition to Bishop Marmion. They cut their financial support for the diocese to a token level. When the bishop would visit for confirmation, the congregation, except for those being confirmed, would boycott the service. No one would entertain the bishop at a meal. Bob Magill was too sweet a person to be overtly vicious, so he maintained a polite demeanor, but

he was also too conservative and too alienated to try to be helpful. This state
of cold war continued for the next few years. Bill Marmion simply vowed to
outlive his critics, and he did it with enormous integrity, never returning
insult for insult. He kept himself sane by playing the most vigorous game of
tennis one could imagine.

But as time rolled by, desegregation became an almost universal pattern,
and St. John's Church began to feel more and more isolated in its self-
imposed ghetto of prejudice. It also became more and more embarrassed
about the stand it had taken, but there was no way these attitudes could be
changed so long as Dr. Magill was active. Shortly before his retirement Dr.
Magill made a tactical mistake. He called an associate, the Reverend Kyle
Boeger, a dedicated pastor in his mid-thirties who shared his conservative
and increasingly out-of-date attitudes. There was little doubt in anyone's
mind that Dr. Magill was grooming his own successor for an eternal struggle that must go on even after he had stepped out of the role of its leader.
This was to be his final attempt to exercise local control over the world that
had rejected him.

The search committee was set up by the vestry, which Dr. Magill controlled. It was loaded with old Virginia conservatives. Bunny Vaden was
clearly its leader. Dr. Magill, however, had miscalculated on one essential
issue. He had not counted on the gentility and social sensitivity of those he
sought to lead. They were conservative indeed, but they did not respond
well to social coarseness and attitudes they identified with lower-class tastes.
Kyle Boeger did not measure up according to these unconscious standards.
They could not imagine him living in the context required of the rector of
Lynchburg's most socially prominent church. So the search was on, and it
was destined to be wide-ranging.

In a way that I did not anticipate, a family connection aided the search
committee to view me initially quite favorably. My first cousin, William
Belser Spong, Jr., who lived in Portsmouth, Virginia, had, a number of years
earlier, been elected first to membership in the state Assembly and then,
later, to the state Senate of Virginia. In that office he rose to statewide promi-
nence. He quickly identified himself with a group of Virginia politicians
known as the "Young Turks." It was an affectionate, not a hostile, designation. The Young Turks were still conservative enough to be in touch with
mainline Virginia values, but they were open enough to be able to represent
a new generation. Beginning in 1959 and continuing into the early 1960s a
statewide study of the problems facing public education was conducted. Bill

Spong was chosen to head this commission, so he presided over hearings across Virginia that focused on the quality of public education for both black and white students. The final report, when issued, was called the "Spong Report." It, by and large, sidestepped the issue of desegregation and confined its recommendations to how the state might address the quality issues in public education and improve the learning potential of Virginia's children. This report was well received politically, and it was commended in the conservative Virginia press from Norfolk through Richmond to Lynchburg and Roanoke. The editorials also hailed the chair of this report for his leadership. Bill Spong was, in many ways, a part of old Virginia, but he was increasingly identified as a major leader of a new generation of Virginians. He made the Spong name both recognized and respected. Somehow, in the minds of members of St. John's search committee, that carried over to his North Carolina cousin when they discovered an Old South church in Tarboro with a low church tradition similar to their own.

St. John's Church had large numbers of young families and a student body of young women, eighteen to twenty-two years old, who lived across the street at Randolph Macon Woman's College. The congregation took great pride in having the students present, but in recent years that student presence had almost disappeared. Dr. Magill's thirty-five years as rector had, from their point of view, ignored the needs of both young families and the college community.

Kyle Boeger's attitudes had made him appealing to Dr. Magill's elderly constituency, but not to the young couples, and certainly not to the students. So for these reasons the decision was made to seek a young leader who could meet the needs of younger families, communicate with the college students, concentrate on the church school and adult education, and, responding to an unstated but real concern, give this congregation a face-saving way to come out of its siege mentality and rejoin the diocese. So the chemistry—that irrational factor that moves more personnel decisions than most imagine—was right. I was to be their choice. The great appeal to me personally was that this parish would enable me to pull my teaching opportunities into my parish priesthood. This combination would become the defining aspect of my ministry from that day forward.

The first issue I had to face in my new responsibility was to find a way to bring St. John's and the diocese back together again. The congregation's share of the diocesan budget was still, by design, only a token amount. Hemlock Haven was still almost a profane word in the parish and Bishop

Marmion was still persona non grata. Yet I had, in the search process, been given enough hints the congregation wanted to change this mentality that I was confident the people would follow my lead in this area of their life. After much thought and some consultation, I decided on a strategy that would link all three issues dramatically in a pro-active way.

My wife, Joan, and I had been enthusiastically embraced by Bunny and Ed Vaden, which meant that we had been almost immediately adopted into their whirling, socially prominent lives. We were at most of their parties and other key civic functions in which they and their friends were cast in leadership roles. It was clear to me that they were willing to put that same energy into St. John's and into the diocese itself, if a way could be found and if I asked them to do so. And so I did.

I began, at Bunny Vaden's suggestion, by asking Wallace McKenna, one of the most bitter voices against the diocese, to head up the every-member canvass that fall. I was quite specific in calling for his better self by telling him that this would be his "penance" for the negative attitude he had fostered and wallowed in for so long. I insisted, as one aspect of this canvass, that the commitment of the parish to the program and budget of the diocese be raised back to the level of its pre–Hemlock Haven days. The second largest and second wealthiest congregation in the diocese needed to also be the second most generous congregation. It was a blatant appeal to their social pride. I also insisted and was supported by the vestry in the decision that the parish had to make a public act symbolizing its intention to be once again involved in the life of the diocese. The symbol we chose was an appropriate one. We would, as a congregation, build outdoor tennis courts at Hemlock Haven as a gift to the diocese. They would be named the Robert A. Magill Tennis Courts. No one would misunderstand the meaning of this act.

In regard to Bishop Marmion, I decided on two strategies. One would take place at his first confirmation visitation of my rectorship. The other would occur at the next annual diocesan convention. I would need help with the former. I could manage the latter alone.

I asked Bill Marmion and his wife, Blossom, to spend the Saturday night before that first confirmation Sunday in our home. We hosted a dinner party in their honor, the guests at which were primarily members of the social group of St. John's Church that revolved around Bunny Vaden. The evening was organized so that the ice that marked the relationships in the past would be broken. Bunny agreed to help. Her approval of the plans guaranteed that her friends would come and that the evening would be a success. Next,

I went to a local store and bought a newly popular parlor game called "Twister." This game forced the two people competing to place their hands and feet onto designated areas that adorned a five-by-seven-foot plastic floor mat as directed by the spin of a pointer until one or the other, unable to twist into a more distorted shape, would fall over. In the process the two persons would become significantly intertwined. It might have seemed a strange way to entertain our bishop, but it would make it impossible for all of the guests not to see Bill Marmion in a new way and to force them to laugh together. It worked! By the time the evening had progressed from cocktails, to dinner served with an elegant wine, to dessert served with another wine, to "Twister" in the living room, which had these young adults falling all over the floor with a bishop they had heretofore loathed, a whole new sense of community had been born. Before the evening was over, perhaps on his third fall, Bishop Marmion, always quick with the quip, commented, "Once this church beat up on me emotionally. Now they are doing it physically."

The next day the bishop saw the largest congregation he had ever seen in St. John's at a confirmation service. A covered-dish dinner after the service for all of the congregation welcomed him to the parish. All of these were signs of a new day.

When the diocesan convention arrived in January 1966, we had purchased a new red chimere[1] for Bishop Marmion. He was one of the last bishops of our church to wear only a black chimere, which, along with the white rochet, was the standard dress of low church bishops before the change instituted at the Lambeth Conference[2] of 1958. Indeed, by the end of that 1958 Lambeth Conference, the only bishops in the entire Communion still clad in black and white "penguin suits," as they came to be called, were Bishop Marmion of Southwestern Virginia and his brother, Gresham Marmion, the bishop of Kentucky. This prompted someone to approach the two of them walking in a procession and ask, "Are you two guys monks?"

Bishop Marmion privately indicated to me his willingness to change and so I ordered the red chimere, which would be presented to him at the convention. I also had a clerical vest made in a brilliant Scottish plaid to present to him at the same time to add to the festivities. The chimere he could put on only for show at the business session of the convention and then at the worship services, but the clerical vest he could wear while presiding over the entire meeting. It would be a visible sign of the fact that this bishop's integrity had won the day and that this recalcitrant congregation was now taking its place proudly as a loyal part of his team. Symbols sometimes tell their story far more powerfully than words. On being recognized by the chair, I made these presentations. The bishop responded, once again with his quick wit. "I have been dressed down by this congregation many times. Now," he said, "I am being dressed up." The applause told the story. Bill Marmion was destined to become a close personal friend. I treasure to this day the leadership he gave the diocese in those difficult years, and I admire even more the example of uncompromising courage he set for me.

My primary parochial task in that first year was to launch and establish the adult class as the focal point of St. John's Sunday program. It would not prove to be easy. A tradition of adult education had never been part of the life of this congregation. Their biblical knowledge was on a Sunday-school level. Christianity was, for most of them, simply part of their culture and was exhibited by showing decency, good manners, and good citizenship. I now had an opportunity to see if I could accomplish a modern Christian education revolution at a well-educated and socially prominent, but biblically childlike congregation. To avoid being perceived as simply a one-man wrecking crew, I would first have to demonstrate that there was in fact a vast audience present even in this conservative Southern community seeking a way to worship God with their minds. That would be essential when what I had to say became offensive to those who had vested their security in a set of literal religious propositions.

With absolute clarity of purpose I made a straightforward decision that would govern the life of this class. I would treat the members of this adult forum as if they were students in a theological-seminary or graduate-school course on the Bible. This adult class would, however, be developed as an adjunct to church life at St. John's. The regular worship services would still be there for the entire congregation. I would not be dishonest in sermons or in the liturgy, but I would not use the sermon period to raise biblical questions and provocative theological issues with which people were not equipped to deal. I would be gentle, loving, and encouraging in that setting, seeking primarily to enhance faith, to clarify issues, to enrich life, and to call people to a deeper devotion to the Christ I served.

But the adult class was to be another experience altogether. The people were to attend only if they wanted to and only if it met their needs. But in that class I would duck no issues, compromise no truth, and avoid no frontier to which my thought and study led me. I would resist no new insight out of some need to be defensive for God. I would adopt as my motto the words of my theology professor Clifford L. Stanley, "Any God who can be killed ought to be killed." I would allow every part of my faith system, its creeds, its Bible, its sacred traditions, to be examined and questioned openly and honestly. If I discovered that any traditional belief could not stand the test of this challenge, I would abandon it publicly. No protective barriers, no claim for inerrancy, infallibility, or divine revelation would be placed around any symbol of Christianity, including core doctrines like the Incarnation, the Trinity, the Resurrection. Orthodoxy was not orthodox because it was right, I would argue, it was orthodox only because it won. New data might at any time call into question the conclusions of yesterday. I would invite those who attended this class into a journey. I would test in a parish church arena whether or not the total education a priest receives in the academy, including the questions it raises, can be made available to a congregation of pew sitters even if it reveals that the Christianity to which they are attached is not intellectually credible. Could a contemporary religious leader do these things without being forced out of the life of organized religion by the security seekers? Those would be the questions this class would pose. This class would present quite a challenge for me. Ultimately, it would become a challenge for the church.

Lynchburg would be a fascinating place in which to test this hypothesis. It was a very conservative Southern city. It boasted a daily newspaper owned by a publisher named Carter Glass III, who was a member of St. John's. He was assumed by many to be closely identified with the John Birch Society. That paper, in both its editorials and news columns, tended to regard as a communist anyone who stepped out of the pack on any issue. All racial "agitators," that is, those who wanted to change the system of segregation, were communists. All academicians who did not work for or draw their salaries from the Lynchburg economic base and who therefore could not be intimidated or controlled by economic pressure were probably also communists. Of course, all clergy who worked for economic justice or who did not adhere to the rigidly orthodox and therefore noncontroversial traditions of the past were communists. The *Lynchburg News*, the flagship paper of the Carter Glass family, would regularly interrupt the stories on its front-page news column to announce in bold type, inside even bolder parentheses, that the person in the story "has on many occasions been identified with communist or communist-front organizations." Some of those "communist-front" organizations turned out to be almost every environmental group, labor unions, the Democratic party, The United Nations, and the National Council of the Churches of Christ in America.

People made fun of this newspaper, but it had a powerful effect on the total life of the community. Its morning and afternoon editions were not unlike Chinese water torture—constant, unrelenting, and ultimately distorting of its readers' sense of reality. This newspaper also made no excuses for its overt racism and absolute opposition to racial integration. So it seemed to me that if an intellectual banner could be raised in a church in this community, it could be raised anywhere. I welcomed the challenge. There were in both Lynchburg and St. John's outspoken critics of this newspaper and the issues it espoused, but they were so small a minority as to be dismissed from consideration. Yet in a real way they kept the waters troubled and made it possible for someone like me to build on their agitation.

On the first Sunday after Labor Day in 1965 the new program began at St. John's. The response was underwhelming to say the least. At the adult class there were about twenty-five adults whose attendance was motivated not by the high-sounding, challenging rhetoric of the new rector, but rather because their children's Sunday-school classes were not yet adjourned and there was nothing better to do. Besides, the coffee was good.

My subject matter for the first year was to be a survey of the whole Bible. I would discover that I would only scratch the surface of this resource in that first year. I leaned heavily on a book called *The Holy Scriptures* by Robert Denton, a professor at General Theological Seminary. What Denton's book allowed me to do was "to sweep and swoop" as a teacher. I would sweep over the terrain of the entire Bible itself and swoop down into the specific text whenever I wanted to examine a theme in more detail. Pretending I was addressing a veritable host of excited listeners, I began on that crisp September day this new adventure.

The idea that an adult Bible class on a Sunday morning at a Christian church in the United States would prove to be a revolutionary thing is almost a laughable suggestion, but in fact this class was exactly that for this congregation. I began by stating the obvious: The Bible did not drop from heaven fully written. It had human authors who reflected specific historical settings. Their stories were told in terms of the knowledge available to them in their era. The authors of the various books of the Bible were also limited by their prejudices, stereotypes, and unchallenged assumptions. I introduced the class to the four-document theory of the Graf-Wellhausen school of thought. Assisted by a book written by Fleming James entitled *Personalities of the Old Testament*, I brought to life the Jahwist writer (J), the Ehohist writer (E), the Deuteronomic writer (D), and the Priestly writer

(P). I grounded the individual authors in their own day. When that background was complete, I would swoop down on the text itself and go into the creation story, identifying the J, E, D, and P strands in that narrative. Without ever mentioning Charles Darwin, I removed any possibility of taking the creation story literally. I illustrated the human and psychological truths found in the story of Adam and Eve, the meaning of both temptation and alienation, the human capacity to feel pushed out of that for which we believed ourselves destined. I lingered over the symbols of the snake, the fruit of the tree of knowledge, called an apple by Jerome hundreds of years later, the flaming sword of the angel who guarded Eden so that the man and the woman could never return. I went into the meaning of guilt, the irrational but human tendency to blame others, and the meaning of work, childbirth, and death, which this ancient story said were the punishments for sin. I worked over Cain and Abel, sibling rivalry, and "brotherly love." I sought to lift into consciousness the ancient struggle between nomadic people and settled agricultural people that was reflected in these stories. I wandered into the brief story of the long-living Methuselah and raised questions about the meaning of life itself. Finally, I entered the story of Noah and the flood, revealing by the use of flood stories among other ancient peoples of the world, the mythological roots of this legend. I also exposed the irrational way the flood story had been used in the South to justify segregation. That story, in fact, contained one of the proof texts that fundamentalist Christians had used to prove that God had intended black people for a life of servitude as punishment for the sin of Ham, Noah's son. I know that sounds weird and distorted to modern ears, but that is the way all biblical texts that have been used to undergird historical prejudices sound after the new consensus has been built. In 1965 that new consciousness had not yet been secured.

The class attendance did grow, by November touching fifty. By January 1, 1966, we went over sixty. When it adjourned for the summer on the last Sunday in May, it had a solid core of around eighty, a 300-percent increase over its sad beginning and a good base on which to build the next year.

The class also became a conversation piece far beyond the boundaries of church life. The idea that this number of Episcopalians who were, by and large, community leaders were attending a Bible class every Sunday morning was noteworthy. I became aware that conversations about this class had entered boardrooms, city council meetings, and cocktail parties. It defined me and my ministry most specifically in the community. Civic clubs began to ask me to be their speaker. The departments of religion at Randolph

Macon and Lynchburg College in town and Sweet Briar College about ten miles out of Lynchburg began to draw me into their orbits. It was a wonderful start for a ministry that fulfilled me deeply.

However, this class did not escape controversy. Carter Glass III attended this class periodically, and some began to see a correlation between some of Carter's editorials and the content of the previous week's Bible class.

The particular favorite of the *Lynchburg News* was Jerry Falwell, the young pastor of the Thomas Roàd Baptist Church. As Falwell built his religious empire, his racist behavior was obvious. The school he founded, which grew into Liberty Baptist College, began as a means of providing a haven from integration. The justifying cover for this racism was always "giving our children biblical and religious values" that were being eroded in the public schools by secular humanists and communist sympathizers. The rhetoric of the younger Falwell vigorously supported the apartheid regime of South Africa and opposed the use of economic sanctions against that nation on the basis that the Republic of South Africa was a strong bulwark against communism on the African continent. He seemed to believe that every freedom movement of blacks in Africa was a communist-inspired insurrection. Falwell was regularly hailed for these anticommunist stands in the local press, which built him slowly but surely into a national figure. He was the town's one, certain, non-communist-sympathizing pastor. Yet if I had any doubts about the adverse impact of this newspaper on the life of this town, they were forever erased by an incident that occurred in the seventh month of the life of this class.

It had long been the policy of the *Lynchburg News* not to report on the engagements, marriages, or deaths of black people. Only white brides got newspaper attention and only white faces seemed to populate the obituary pages. If a black family wanted a newspaper announcement of the marriage or death of a family member or relative, its only option would be to buy a personal advertisement in the classified section. It was a bizarre policy started in an era in which racism was so entrenched that it was assumed to be proper, and it had become so frozen that it was made to feel normal, no matter how irrational.

It was also the policy of this paper to exaggerate race in a detrimental way wherever it could in its news stories. All murders, thefts, robberies, or acts of violence involving a black person had that fact noted very prominently. The achievements of members of the black community were seldom noted. The tensions in the black community were always close to the surface, and this newspaper was primarily responsible for that.

By this time desegregation had begun in the South, but it was as token as the authorities could get away with and it was one-way; that is, only a few black children were integrated into the white school system. The traditionally black schools were still all black and segregated. In Lynchburg one of these all black schools was a middle, or junior-high, facility named Dunbar.

During the night of March 23–24, 1966, a murder occurred at or near that school; at least the victim's body was discovered early that Thursday morning on the school grounds. Whether that had been the actual location of the murder or whether the victim was simply deposited there was not at that time determined. The police were called and the newspaper reporters who monitored the police radio for breaking stories rushed to the school. The press people, I gather, were quite aggressive, pushing their way onto the scene of the crime, as journalists are prone to do, and ignoring the principal and the teachers, who had the unenviable task of receiving the full quota of students and trying to conduct a day of school activities in what was becoming a circus atmosphere.

With this bias against anyone black, the reporter for the *Lynchburg News* was determined to get his story and his photographer was determined to get a picture of the body on the grounds of the black school. The police were equally concerned with keeping everyone away until they could get whatever clues might be available. Police photographers were taking pictures of the body from every angle. The school's black coach and gym teacher was assisting the police in keeping the curious away from the victim's body when a confrontation occurred between the reporter and the coach. No one was quite sure exactly how it came about, but the coach insisted he had been insulted by the reporter with some words like "Out of my way, boy!" So a minor shoving match occurred. No blows were struck. No harm was done. But the newspaper photographer was clicking away and captured every stage of this minor altercation.

The police acted quickly to restore order and treated the episode, in light of the murder investigation, as so inconsequential that no further action was deemed necessary. I am sure it was totally forgotten until the *Lynchburg News* was published the next day.

Suddenly this minor event had become a cause célèbre. The story of a person murdered on the grounds of a black school got the typical racially biased treatment. But the paper carried a series of photographs portraying every stage of the shoving match between the black coach and the newspaper reporter. The story line was that this black coach had violated the civil rights of this white reporter. Furthermore, the police of this city stood by passively while this violation had occurred. They had thus condoned this attack on the freedom of the press, which indicated that they were either unable or unwilling to protect the civil rights of Lynchburg's citizens. Anarchy was on the doorstep of this community, according to the newspaper. The paper demanded that the city manager, a man named Robert Morrison, apologize publicly and take quick and effective action to bring the offending police officer or officers to justice. The newspaper further stated that if the city manager did not take these steps, the newspaper would never again publish news about any black school in the Lynchburg school system. It was a response that was not only racist and irrational, but also enormously out of proportion to the incident.

Robert Morrison and his wife were active and committed members of St. John's. They were also across-the-street neighbors of Carter Glass III, and the two families knew each other well. This was to be a fight that would not only tear the town apart, but would have enormous ramifications in this small, immediate neighborhood.

Bob Morrison's preliminary investigation revealed that the incident was no more than what I have described. It became apparent that if the city manager acquiesced to the demands of the newspaper, there would be a major rebellion in the ranks of the police force. Their morale and reputation were at stake. So Bob Morrison stated that he regretted the incident, but that he believed the police operated professionally and no further action would be taken. The murder was all but forgotten in this furor. The newspaper, however, would not be satisfied that easily. It roared its anger editorially and kept repeating what it believed was the incriminating evidence pointed out in their photographs, which showed, as they interpreted them, how aggressively the coach had his arm drawn. With no apology forthcoming from the city administration, the newspaper began its boycott of black news from the schools of the city. Football scores, test results, school activities, and even bus schedules to the black schools disappeared from the pages of the paper. At first it was thought to be a minor nuisance, but as the weeks dragged on and the boycott grew, it became a major irritant. The editorial page of the newspaper would not let the issue die down, convinced it was a clear sign that the communist revolution was on the doorstep of this community. Making Bob Morrison an agent of a communist conspiracy was a bit far from reality. He came from a long line of respected Virginia ancestors and was a man of integrity. The newspaper would have a difficult time convincing those who knew him that he was either inept or evil, to say nothing of being a communist.

The tensions began to rise visibly in the black community. There was talk of an organized black boycott of the downtown merchants if the newspaper's attitude did not change. That threat got people's attention and the merchants, fearful of being caught in the middle of a struggle that was not their own, appealed to the elected town council members to do something to end this hostile stalemate. Several town councilmen tried, but were rebuffed. Pressure began to grow on Bob Morrison to give in to Carter Glass's excessive demands. There were a sufficient number of clear heads, however, who had reached the end of their ability to tolerate Carter Glass's abusive behavior, expressed through his newspaper, that they strengthened Bob Morrison's backbone. Weeks passed into months.

Finally, in desperation a member of the council, Eliot Schewel, a Jewish merchant, with the consent of the mayor, James Ould, called and asked me if I would try to negotiate a settlement by talking to both of the principals separately and then together. The reputation of the town was suffering as it became the butt of jokes throughout Virginia. The national press was becoming involved. Business was destined to suffer. I was chosen for this assignment because both Bob Morrison and Carter Glass were members of St. John's, and the Spong name had become one that was respected in political and social circles, primarily through Bill's work. It just might work. At least it was worth a try. I agreed to accept this assignment.

I talked first with Bob Morrison in his home. It was a pleasant, reasonable conversation. He told me that he would meet Carter on any level short of a public apology or a disciplinary action against a policeman. He would say how sorry he was that the incident occurred, that he regretted the pain that the newspaper had experienced, that he would certainly see that the civil rights of the press were always protected, but that the city would not and could not go beyond that. The irrationality of this conflict could not be allowed to violate the integrity of the city government or the police department. After this one conversation I knew where Bob's bottom line was. I hoped that some face-saving way could be worked out within those parameters that could allow Carter to feel that he had won without winning.

Carter Glass III agreed to see me, but only for thirty minutes and only in his office alone. The appointment was set, and I prepared to enter what increasingly felt like the lion's den. If I was to beard this lion, it would have to be in his own lair.

I arrived a few minutes early and was allowed to cool my heels in the corridor until the exact time of the appointment, when Carter's office door opened. I sat down on a single chair across the desk from Carter. I wasted little time with social amenities other than to thank him for agreeing to see me and to express the concern of the business and political leaders of the city that this conflict had reached the point where it was hurting the city and had to be resolved. That would be easy, Carter said. An apology, the proper disciplinary action, and the promise that the civil rights of the representatives of the press would be protected in the future was all that it would take.

The promise that his employees' civil rights would be protected in the future we can get, I told him, hoping to present that as a victory, but his first two demands had been dismissed and were not likely to be reopened. Before he could explode and end the conversation, I pressed on. "I really would like to hear the whole story from your perspective," I said. "Would you relate to me the episode as you believe it unfolded, and tell me why it is so important to you?"

He settled back in his chair and went over the details that I was confident he had rehearsed in his mind a thousand times. There appeared to me to be nothing new in his recitation that had not appeared in the newspaper numbers of times before. I listened patiently and then pressed the last part of my inquiry. "I understand that this is the way you see it. But what I don't understand is why this is so important to you. Could you go over that?" It was clearly the right question, and the most incredible story poured forth.

Its substance had to do with the international communist conspiracy. Carter was convinced that the communist strategy was to infiltrate structures like the educational processes and to encourage racial agitation and the breakdown of law and order. It was his responsibility, as a leader in Lynchburg and with the public voice of the newspaper, to resist this attack upon the freedoms of this nation with all of the power at his disposal. In his mind he really was standing between the Western world and a communist takeover. This story made Senator Joseph McCarthy of Wisconsin look almost normal. I listened with increasing incredulity. When he finished, I asked only one question. "Carter," I said, "if you were masterminding the international communist conspiracy would you make Lynchburg, Virginia, your primary target?"

Our town was a sleepy town of a few more than fifty thousand citizens. It was not at the crossroads of anything. The major state highways in Virginia connected Norfolk with Richmond, Washington, D.C., Charlottesville, and

Roanoke. Lynchburg was off the beaten trail, surrounded by such communities as Amherst, Forest, Bedford, and Alta Vista. It was a good town with good people, but most of the people of the world outside of Virginia had never heard of it. Indeed, the tiny village of Lynchburg, Tennessee, was better known, since it was the home of Jack Daniels sour mash whiskey. If pressed, people thought that our town might have been named for the uncivilized practice of lynching, instead of for its founder, John Lynch. The James River, on which this town was situated, was not navigable this far west except by very small craft. It would not have been a strategic center in anybody's bold plans for world domination. I thought my question would bring those facts into consciousness.

I think it did, for Carter stopped cold, stared at me with intensity for a moment while his face reddened, and then with cold politeness invited me out of his office immediately. My mission had failed, but it was also clear that the problem we faced in the city with that paper was not one that rationality would ever solve. We were dealing with apparent pathology in high places. In time a settlement of this dispute was forced on Carter by his family. His newspaper, of course, claimed victory, but the fact remains that no apology was ever given and no disciplinary action was ever taken, but the boycott of black school news ceased, and our community breathed a sigh of relief.

That struggle between the newspaper and the town, however, took enormous energy from the life of our city. It was destined to erupt again and again. Carter Glass III had in this episode clearly identified me as part of the enemy. We would meet again.

All of these activities were woven together to present a rich trapestry of memories in my first year in Lynchburg. As that year ended I took stock of my vocation. It had taken a dramatic turn toward teaching. The adult class, a midweek study group, two separate confirmation classes, and a Lenten study program were part of our regular menu. When one adds the Sunday sermon to this mix, it meant that almost three days of every work week went into preparation. I was gratified to learn that the vestry leaders of my congregation also began to recognize this and to raise these realities to a public awareness. This was done in two ways. First, my wardens began to say that the model this congregation needed to keep in mind for me was that of a college professor, not a traditional pastor. A college professor has the summer free to prepare for the following academic year. St. John's would move in that direction. Second, the vestry authorized me to begin at once a search for a full-time assistant who would be able to cover those things like youth work, college work, the support and training of our church-school teachers, and the whole area of pastoral care that I would never handle adequately with my teaching responsibility. I felt wonderfully supported by this affirmation.

Midway through the first program year, even before the Dunbar School incident, I began to hear the whispers that my cousin, Bill Spong, was going to be a candidate in the Democratic primary that coming June for the seat in the U.S. Senate held at that moment by a seventy-eight-year-old man named A. Willis Robertson. Senator Robertson had served three full terms, plus a two-year unfinished term, in the Senate and had actually surprised people by announcing his decision to run for a fourth term. By this time Harry Byrd, Sr., had been forced to resign from the Senate for reasons of age and health and had been replaced by his son, Harry Byrd, Jr., who in the words of one commentator "resembled his father in everything but courage, brains, and ability."[3] "Little Harry," as he was called, had had a lackluster career and his principal assets were that he looked like his father and bore his name. His appointment was only until the next election. To the Young Turks of the Virginia political scene, the time had come for a new generation of leaders, moderate in tone, but not outside Virginia's conservative tradition. They looked around to identify viable alternative candidates and finally settled on Armistead Boothe, a lawyer from northern Virginia, to run against Harry Byrd, Jr., and Bill Spong to run against Willis Robertson. It was a classic generational battle. Senator Robertson had a son named Pat, a Yale Law School graduate who was still in the "sowing wild oats" period of his life. He was not involved in this campaign. He was too busy settling some issues in his personal life. He had not yet "met the Lord," become a preacher, and built a television empire as part of the movement of the religious right in the United States that would in 1988 lead him to seek the presidential nomination of the Republican party. His father was a decent man, but without an outstanding image or record as a U.S. senator. To show how small a world it is, Robertson occupied the Senate seat once held by a man named Carter Glass from 1920 to 1946, who had also served as Secretary of the Treasury in the cabinet of Woodrow Wilson from 1918 to 1920. He was the grandfather of our newspaper publisher. It was and is an intimate little glimpse into the incestuousness of Virginia politics.

Spong and Boothe ran separate campaigns. They did, however, draw their strength from the same constituencies in the electorate. The campaign was fascinating to me; the Spong name now appeared daily in the newspaper and was spoken constantly on radio and television. Usually I had to pronounce my name and then spell it when I was doing some public transaction. Bill would also stay with us when he came to Lynchburg on a campaign trip. In those days in Virginia politics the winner of the Democratic primary was for all practical purposes elected. The Republicans would offer only token resistance in the fall election. Virginia was still part of the one-party, solid South.

This primary was a tense, vigorous, and hard-fought campaign. Indeed, all the polls found both races too close to call. The four candidates crisscrossed the state with enormous energy. Senator Robertson was, among other things, out to prove his vigor and good health at age seventy-eight.

Shortly before the polling date for the primary, Harry Byrd, Jr., called off his campaign to return to his home in Berryville, Virginia, to watch around the bed of what he described as "my dying father," the old revered senator. Whether his father was actually critically ill or not, I will never know. I do know that the former Senator Byrd did not die until much later that fall, many weeks after the primary election. I also know that this tactic made good theater, roused the sympathy vote, and put "Little Harry" on the television news each night at his father's home issuing medical bulletins. Armistead Boothe, in deference to the death watch of the former senator and because the politics of that moment demanded it, also called off his campaign. He certainly did not want to be pictured attacking Little Harry politically while the media was showing him grieving at his father's bedside. It may have been a political tactic without character, but it was an effective tactic nonetheless. State Senator Spong and U.S. Senator Robertson, however, continued their campaigns at full tilt until election day finally arrived. The results were interesting. Senator Byrd, Jr., defeated challenger Armistead Boothe by about eight thousand votes. If half of that small number of voters across Virginia were turned by sympathy, that would have been sufficient to elect "Little Harry." No one doubts that there were at least that many sympathy votes and probably a lot more. The tactic had worked.

In the other contest in what would now be the seat of Virginia's junior senator, William Spong defeated Willis Robertson by 611 votes out of approximately 800,000 cast. "Landslide Spong" we called him! Our suggestion that he get a license plate for his Virginia car with the number 611 on it was not fully appreciated. This election would add an interesting new dimension to my life, since I now would have a member of my family, and one to whom I was known to be quite close, in the public arena.

Yet the glare of that new public attention did not succeed in dislodging the increasingly dark and foreboding shadow that seemed to hover over my family. My wife, Joan, was clearly still deeply bothered by something. The symptom she manifested at this time was insomnia. She began to withdraw from Lynchburg's social world. As the months went by her insomnia and depression became more aggravated. I urged her to seek professional help and consulted my medical friends to get the name of a good psychiatrist. She shared with me that she had sought counseling from a well-known professor at my former seminary. His behavior appeared to me to be less than professional as she related it. Indeed it was so out of bounds that I confronted him about it. He did not deny the charges, but they were never made public. In that confrontation, however, this professor startled me with his assertion that Joan was a mentally sick woman who needed medical attention immediately. It was a diagnosis I was not yet prepared to accept, but it did set up in my mind a possibility that would never go away.

Things actually seemed to improve for Joan that fall. She got involved in some inner-city work sponsored by something called the Lynchburg Christian Fellowship. It was one-on-one activity not unlike what she had done in Princeville, North Carolina, several years earlier. She was quite good at it and derived much satisfaction from it. She also began to associate herself with an ecumenical organization of women and, through these contacts, to move outside the orbit of St. John's church family. A new set of friends came into her life. They were never couple friends, but they strengthened Joan and in a real sense they belonged to her alone. She needed to establish her own identity. She was an incredibly gifted woman, and having her identity limited to the role of being my wife in the minds of many must have been difficult for her. Joan always struggled with that designation. Issues that would someday be common in feminist thought were just dawning in my thick patriarchal brain, so I did not fully appreciate this. It would finally take my daughters to bring me into the twentieth century on women's issues.

When my second year as rector began, the Bible class was still at center stage. I picked up where I had left off, rejoicing that attendance rose above the one-hundred mark. I drove the narrative through the story of the patriarchs Abraham, Isaac, Jacob, and Joseph. Again, so many of the great themes of the Bible were present in these stories. With Abraham one can deal with the meaning of the covenant with that wondrous ability "to entertain angels unawares," which was a major theme in the Sodom and Gomorrah story. I also had the chance to deliteralize that Sodom story for the first time. I avoided confronting the issue of homosexuality and concentrated on such things as the immorality of Lot, who appeared to offer his virgin daughters to the men of the city "so that you may do to them whatever you will," and his later incestuous relationship with his daughters. Just to relate people to the whole story of Sodom and Gomorrah was to destabilize its literalness as a text that many use to condemn homosexuality. I also waxed eloquent on the story of Lot's wife who, because she was "looking backward," was turned into a pillar of salt. With great levity, receiving much laughter from the class, I related how those who face the past, not the future, will have similar experiences. It was a gratuitous shot at those tradition-bound people in St. John's who had finally decided that I might be taking them in a direction they did not want to go. But St. John's was growing, and college students and young married couples were finding their way into its doors in increasing numbers. So criticism was muted and minimal.

I also dealt with the history of child sacrifice and sacrifice in general when we came to the story of Abraham offering his son, Isaac. This class kept opening doors to new learning for me, and I kept walking through them into subjects I had never before thought much about. The themes I yearned to develop kept presenting themselves. Sibling rivalry came back in the story of Jacob and Esau. So did the willingness of parents to ally themselves with their children and against each other. In this story Jacob and Rebekkah were pitted against Esau and Isaac. We also could discuss the tension between meeting current needs and postponing gratification to achieve long-range goals later. The account of Esau selling his birthright for a bowl of red lentil soup became the starting place for that discussion. In the Jacob story the issues of using sex as a reward emerged, as did parental favoritism that set brother against brother, and finally the rich themes of forgiveness and restoration, to say nothing of sex and power that can be found in the Joseph saga. Once again I found the pace at which I was able to move in the class to be quite slow, but the material to be incredibly rich.

In the other aspects of my ministry, I continued to be involved in diocesan matters. Bishop Marmion asked me to try to revive our companion diocese relationship with Ecuador that had fallen into some state of neglect following a visit of the previous chairman to Ecuador. He was an older priest in the diocese who was, I gather, horrified with his experience in Ecuador. He returned to tell people that filthy children roamed the streets of the cities of Ecuador. "They would steal you blind," he said, and he brought back slides of Ecuadorian children whose primary activity seemed, from the pictures, to be that of urinating in the streets. His stories inspired no one to be involved in this mission project.

The Reverend Onell Soto, a priest in Quito, was coming to the diocese soon, and I would get a chance to meet with him and discuss some plans for the future. Onell was a gregarious, open-faced, smiling human being of Cuban background, who had been a missionary in Ecuador for two years. When he came to visit us, we mapped our plans in great detail. I would fly to Quito in fall 1966 to lay the groundwork for a youth exchange and a visit of diocesan leaders in 1967 to be led by Bishop and Mrs. Marmion. We would then entertain a visit of Ecuadorian young people in early winter 1968, with a return trip by the young people of our diocese, probably in summer 1970. This plan received the approval of the decision-making bodies in both dioceses. I saw its importance in meeting two specific goals. First, it would stretch the vision of our diocesan leaders to a worldwide perspective and thus help to lift us out of our provincialism. Second, it would be for our young people a cross-cultural experience with young people of a different ethnic and racial background. Ecuadorian kids were not black in the way that word was used in Virginia, but they were not white either, and if they had lived in America, they would have been considered black by the laws of our prejudice. If our young people could know these Ecuadorians as friends, then perhaps they could begin to leap over their own racial barriers and embrace their African American counterparts in Lynchburg as friends. That was my real goal. My hopes were built on ambitious, but not unrealistic, dreams.

I put flesh on those plans while in Ecuador. That was actually my initial journey outside the United States. My first stop was Bogota, Columbia, where the bishop of Ecuador and Columbia, the Right Reverend David Reed, lived. I was with him for only two days. David and his wife were gracious hosts, but what impressed me most was the luxury in which this missionary bishop lived, with several Colombian servants who cooked and cleaned his palatial home, which was guarded by an amazing security system of gates, fences, barbed wire, and burglar alarms. Ecuador was scheduled for an election convention in the next year, when its own bishop would be chosen. The Diocese of Ecuador would then be split off from that of Columbia. So David was more of a caretaker bishop presiding over that process than anything else. The task of choosing a bishop would, however, be more difficult than anyone could envision at that time. David hoped the companion diocese relationship would help the new diocese develop a sense of identity, purpose, and support. So did I.

On I flew to Quito, where Onell met me to begin the task of introducing me to Ecuador. I met Roman Catholic and Protestant leaders and embraced anew the need for ecumenical conversation and cooperation. I went to the mission compound of Radio Station HCJB (Heralding Christ Jesus' Blessings) and learned of a fortress mentality that colored some people's understanding of mission. I rode a train called the autoferrer from Quito at an elevation of 12,000 feet to Guayaquil at sea level. It was an all-day journey through beautiful but rugged country. It did not help the trip that the train killed both a cow and a horse on that journey. White crosses here and there along the tracks indicated that from time to time this train had killed human beings.

Once in Guayaquil, I again was taken to survey the work of our church. With Onell I met our other two priests, Ray Riebs, an experienced missionary who cared deeply for those he served, but who could not escape his own paternalistic personality, and John (Jack) Roen, who ran an effective social service agency. We visited the mission in the part of Guayaquil known as Puerto Cabezas. It was a picture of poverty more desperate than I had ever confronted before. Large concentrations of urban dwellers were living in squalid cardboard shacks with no running water, walking on flimsy paths above the mud. They were covered in their own filth and generally lived without medical attention.

Riebs, Roen, and Onell constituted the total number of Episcopal priests in Ecuador. Not one of them was Ecuadorian and only Onell was Latino. It was hard to imagine how so small a diocese would ever elect a bishop. There simply wasn't a large enough critical mass to impose traditional episcopal structure on the Anglican Church in Ecuador.

I looked forward to the proposed exchanges between our two dioceses, which I believed would feed into everything else we were doing internally and externally as a church. The balance of that program year simply unfurled in these previously laid directions.

Yet no church lives outside the moving events of history that quite literally carry us whether we realize it or not. During the summer of 1967 two things happened, one locally and one nationally, that were destined to impact me dramatically. The local event was the sudden resignation of the chaplain and sacred studies teacher from the faculty of Virginia Episcopal School, the boy's prep school in Lynchburg founded by Bishop Jett. This resignation, coming so near the beginning of the fall term, made it all but impossible for Austin Montgomery, the headmaster, to secure a replacement before the first of the year. That meant that some emergency provisions had to be worked out to cover the fall semester. Austin believed he could get retired clergy to handle the chapel services, but he did not want to entrust the teaching of the required sacred studies course to someone who might not be an effective or experienced teacher. He and his wife, Eleanor, were members of St. John's and they had been regular attendees at the adult class. When Austin discovered that the curriculum for the fall in sacred studies was an introduction to the Old Testament, he decided to ask me if I would be willing to take on this teaching assignment for three months. I was thrilled at the possibility and, when I discovered that he would condense the various sections of this class into one unit and schedule it for 8:00 to 9:00 A.M. Monday through Friday, it certainly became feasible. I then discussed this proposal with my vestry and got their approval. So a teaching opportunity stood waiting for me when the summer months were over.

The national event that occurred that summer was the eruption of racially tinged urban riots in Newark, New York, Cleveland, and Los Angeles, among others. At the time of these riots our presiding bishop, John Hines, had been attending a bureaucratic meeting of the World Council of Churches in Switzerland. Recognizing the gravity of this situation, he immediately flew home, organized for himself a private walking tour of Bedford-Stuyvesant in New York City and later one in urban Detroit. He talked person to person with urban dwellers. He heard their sense of disgust with organized religion, which seemed to meet them at no real point in their lives. They also experienced powerlessness, since they had little or no ability to exercise control over any part of their lives. John Hines was a student of history. He knew that wherever powerlessness existed, exploitation followed. The way to stop exploitation was quite simply to empower people. Aided by an African American on the church center staff named Leon Modeste, John Hines confronted the triennial meeting of the Episcopal Church that fall in Seattle with a new vision and a new vocation for the church. It was this church's task and privilege, he asserted, "to take its place humbly and boldly alongside and in support of the dispossessed and oppressed peoples of this country for the healing of our national life." John Hines knew full well that this was where Christ would be and a church that claimed to be the Body of Christ must be there as well.

The response of the convention was to adopt this vision, reorder the priorities of the church, redo the church's budget, and launch a series of empowering initiatives that would be known as the General Convention Special Program. This program was to have its impact primarily outside church structures. It was designed to break the cycle of poverty by freeing indigenous community groups to do what they were quite able to do for themselves if they only had the means, namely, to bring hope, integrity, self-esteem, and, yes, power to the traditional victims of our dominating prejudices. John Hines changed the agenda of the entire church's debate. This was a remarkable achievement for one man to accomplish. Here was a leader who knew something about leadership and who could actually demonstrate it. He was my kind of man. I looked forward to meeting him. It also heightened my sense of the importance of our Ecuador program, where race and poverty would be central issues.

I was obviously not a delegate to the general convention, since the representation from our diocese had been elected less than six months after I had arrived in Lynchburg. So with my attention fastened on Seattle, I met my first 8:00 A.M. class at Virginia Episcopal School. I loved the classroom and had unfulfilled desires to spend part of my life in an academic setting. In my fantasies, however, the setting was always a university or divinity school, never a boys' prep school. Yet if I could keep one hundred older teenage boys interested in the Bible at 8:00 A.M. in the morning five days a week, then I could teach anywhere. So the grand experiment began.

That semester was a tremendously expanding new adventure for which my work in St. John's adult class had prepared me rather well. I was sufficiently familiar with my material to be free of my notes. My storytelling approach found a ready audience. I deliberately opened this class by lifting from the biblical text a couple of bizarre stories, like Judah's sexual affair with his own daughter-in-law, Tamar (Genesis 38), and the account of the Levite's concubine who was gang-raped and murdered (Judges 19). These were, in the words of the old song, Bible stories "they had never heard before." It was an eye-opener for them, enabling them to see the Bible in a very different way from the view offered by their traditional upbringing.

Then I proceeded to teach the Hebrew Scriptures biographically, developing the characters of Abraham, Joseph, Moses, Joshua, Elijah, David, Solomon, Amos, Hosea, Isaiah, Jeremiah, Micah, and many others. It was my hope that one of these personalities would capture the imagination of these teenagers and lead them to do a paper on that person and thus to touch the sacred Scriptures more deeply than they had ever done before. I was not disappointed. I was thrilled at the response of my students and actually hated to see the semester end, though the time commitment this class took could not have been tolerated for much longer. My desire to develop my teaching skills received a mighty internal boost, however, from that experience.

As the year continued at St. John's, people began to comment on my love for the Hebrew Scriptures. The Jews seemed to me to be lusty people, life affirming and God-filled. God was for them a presence with which they wrestled, rather than a supernatural parent figure before whom they bowed in repressed obedience. I even began to attend the local Reformed synagogue enough to be known there.

But into the excitement of that year the Lynchburg newspaper once more injected its reactionary venom. The issue this time was a proposal I put before the vestry that we invite a Montessori school to occupy a portion of our unused parish house on weekdays and to make what this school could offer a gift to the young families of our community.

When these plans were made public, we were amazed at the active opposition from the local press about the dangers of the Montessori teaching methods to American values. It was not always easy to follow Carter Glass's argument, but it was based on the principle that the Montessori educational system represented something modern and different from traditional education. Traditional education in his mind meant rote learning of mathematical formulas, using flash cards, competing in spelling contests, and memorizing the basic facts of history. The Montessori process, on the other hand, it was said, was related to new theories of how children learn by experience and reeked of the insights of John Dewey, whose influence on American education was instrumental in breaking down the basic discipline of the family and making this nation ripe for a communist takeover. It was a strange, even weird, argument, but it had its effects. After these negative news stories and editorials appeared, the members of our vestry began to receive mail opposing the Montessori school. Threats to withdraw from the church if this school was housed there soon followed. Under this pressure the vestry folded, and the proposed school was voted down. It was Carter's victory this time. We would inevitably meet again.

Meanwhile, I was delighted and pleased to learn from Bishop Marmion that the Presiding Bishop, John Hines, was going to visit our diocese. He wondered if I would be kind enough to get a fourth and arrange a doubles match on the tennis courts of Lynchburg as part of the diocesan hospitality. At last I would have the chance to meet this man face-to-face. The match was arranged and the fourth, a better than average southpaw player from my congregation named Bill Fix became John Hines's partner against Bill Marmion and me. I discovered that Bishop Hines still had some of that skill that landed him in the number two spot on the Varsity Tennis Team at the

University of the South. Spong and Marmion lost 6–2, 6–2. But for me the hero became real and I discovered I admired him even more. I had no doubt but that the direction in which John Hines was leading was right for the church. It also raised in me a continuing desire to force our racial prejudices into consciousness and to deal with them overtly.

When the Ecuadorian young people came to visit our diocese, their presence focused the issues of race just as I had hoped it would. The young people got along wonderfully, as our teenagers engaged them both personally and deeply. However, some of the parents found the experience of watching the socializing of white and nonwhite teenagers more than their racial prejudices were able to tolerate. The young people ate together, played together, prayed together, and danced together. It was the dancing that really triggered the negative emotions. Dancing in every society is a kind of sexual ritual and people like Bunny Vaden seemed to understand that better than most. The ancient and elemental fears that linked race and sex emerged to cause the parents' negative reaction. Yet this Ecuadorian visit was, from my perspective, a great success, and the plans to send a youth delegation from our diocese to Ecuador within the next two years became a source of great energy among our own young people.[4]

As the status quo of Lynchburg's value system and prejudices was challenged, we discovered that our life among the social leaders of the town had all but come to an end. More and more Joan's orbit revolved around the marginalized. When we invited black couples to our home for dinner, we were made to understand just how deeply this violated Lynchburg's social taboos.

To complicate matters, a diocesan decision was made to close the small struggling black Episcopal church in Lynchburg and to integrate its congregation into other Episcopal churches. Most of these black Episcopalians chose to go to St. Paul's, the church downtown. One black family came to St. John's. Through that transfer St. John's became the first desegregated church in the affluent Rivermont section of Lynchburg. By today's standards that seems such a pitifully small step, but in the late 1960s it was a breakthrough.

As our involvement with St. John's social leaders declined, my activity and responsibilities in the Diocese of Southwestern Virginia and in the larger church began to expand. I was elected to the standing committee of the diocese and one year later became its president. By virtue of that office, as well as my close friendship with Bishop Marmion, I was invited into significant roles of diocesan leadership. Increasingly, I began to view the life of the church from a diocesan perspective, rather than a parochial one.

Bill Marmion was not an original theological thinker, but he was always open to new possibilities. On issues of social justice, however, he had no room for compromise. If the Christian Church did not support justice, inclusion of all, and fairness in the economic areas, it could not be the Body of Christ. I admired this man even more as I got to know him better. There was not a devious or dishonest bone in his body. He had quite consciously expanded his episcopacy to include the standing committee in general and its president in particular in wide-ranging ways.

I can still say today that the Diocese of Southwestern Virginia was the best diocesan experience I ever had as a priest. The bishop was clearly a leader. The clergy were deeply invested. The diocese depended on the leadership of both these clergy and the new generation of laypeople who replaced the ones who could not make the transition from the old segregated world of the past into the more open, less class-conscious world of the future. Indeed, it was the vision of a church that stood for truth and was willing to pay the cost of witnessing to it that attracted them. I was impressed by the fact that institutional integrity was more important than institutional success and, in the long run, integrity was essential to success. So many church leaders who elevate unity above truth never seem to understand that a unified church in communities where I lived would have been a segregated church. The gospel was not the story of God reconciling one church member to another, but rather of God reconciling all of the world to God. That meant that wounds, injustices, and falsehoods had to be opened up, that the pain of growth and truth had to be endured, and above all that the church should never be afraid of controversy. I came to the operative conclusion while in Lynchburg that the church would die of boredom long before it would die of controversy. There was great strength in that realization and, while John Hines modeled it for me nationally, Bill Marmion modeled it for me locally.

My calling to model this kind of courageous ministry was still developing. It was certainly enhanced as I got deeply involved in the life of my seminary and was placed on the search committee of the board when we had to find a new dean. That position enabled me to begin looking at the church from a national perspective. The job of the seminary dean as the head of the faculty was not just to educate, but to shape and form students who would become the priests and bishops of the future.

The search committee included trustees, student representatives, faculty representatives, and other alumni. The deanship was of first importance to representatives of the faculty and the political infighting there was most intense. The rise of what came to be called the religious right was already apparent in the life of our society. I was amazed to discover that this school, which had taught me to "seek the truth of God come whence it may, cost what it will" had turned so conservative by this time that they chose the three most right-wing members of the faculty to serve on this committee. They would make it difficult to elect a forward-looking candidate.

The faculty delegation was made up of Richard Reid, a fine but quite traditional New Testament scholar who bragged about the fact that the prayer book ought to be changed at the rate of one word every one hundred years. The second of the three was my former teacher Clifford Stanley, the theology professor whose earlier liberal leanings had been destroyed by the antiwar protests and who was already saying such things as, "The only hope for America is to elect the right-wing governor of California, Ronald Reagan, to the White House." This was, please note, twelve years before Reagan became the Republican nominee. The third faculty member was a longtime friend, C. Fitzsimmons Allison, who had in 1967 moved from Sewanee to Virginia Seminary to teach church history. He had been on the same Southern lecture track I had traveled. At one time we had been very close friends. However, now there was something in Fitz that I could not fathom. He was almost hysterically anxious about the church. He saw enemies everywhere. He wanted to purge the church of various heresies that seemed to him to be breaking out all around him. The new dean, he announced, must "hold the center" of the Christian faith, which Fitz clearly believed was being chopped away by something called "modern secular humanism." He became the dominant voice on that committee.

It was a revealing assignment, and for the first time in my life I began to wonder if the Christian faith, as I heard it being described, was still a virtue to which I wanted to be committed. Fitz was unbelievable. He pronounced "as no longer within orthodox Christianity" such people as Philip A. Smith, who later became the bishop of New Hampshire, Bennett Sims, who would become the bishop of Atlanta, and John Fletcher, who was destined to be named the ethicist at the National Institutes of Health. If these persons were heretics, then orthodoxy had become very thin. Fitz's candidate was Cecil Woods, his old friend from the faculty at the School of Theology in Tennessee. As the life of the committee developed, I became the primary counterpoint to Fitz and the tension between us grew. In the end he prevailed and Cecil Woods was nominated to the board of trustees by an eleven-to-one vote. I was the one dissenting vote. The board elected him dean.

My idea of an effective dean, and indeed of leaders generally, was found in two distinctly different styles. A leader could be a visionary who sees the future and by dint of his or her competence and energy can call the institution into that vision. A leader could also be one whose personal sense of security is so great that he or she can allow, without being personally threatened, the visions of those who serve that institution below the level of the head to become operative. Both styles could be effective. Cecil Woods, in my opinion, was lacking on both counts. He was an insecure man without a vision. He began, in my opinion, the decline of that seminary's reputation as a liberal evangelical school dedicated to good scholarship into one of a defensive faith community seeking to protect an outdated understanding of Christianity. To watch that decline was like watching the death of something very near and dear to me. But with Cecil Woods as dean every new faculty member that school added seemed to be one more insecure defender of the faith of yesterday. A theology professor named David Scott was, in my opinion, the nadir appointee, with Chris Hancock a close second, since neither of them seemed capable or willing to engage the issues of the day.

But nothing could finally divert my attention from the excitement that St. John's seemed to provide for me with regularity. It was not long, however, before I was back into conflict with the ever present Carter Glass III and his newspaper. In early spring 1968 I accepted an invitation to do a series of lectures at St. Luke's Church in the Mountain Brook section of Birmingham, Alabama, a community of luxurious mansions, cultivated yards, and gracious living. It was, of course, also all white.

It was in the midst of that lecture series that radio and television programs were interrupted to report first the shooting and then the death of Martin Luther King, Jr. He and other leaders of his organization, the Southern Christian Leadership Movement, like Ralph Abernathy and a young Jesse Jackson, were in Memphis, Tennessee, to support the primarily black garbage workers union in their strike. Dr. King had moved his crusade for black people from civil rights into areas of economic justice. He had also begun to speak out against the Vietnam war. Dr. King's public turn against the war was motivated by two things. First, the horror of the war offended his Christian pacifist convictions, which were based in large measure on the life and work of Mahatma Gandhi. Second, Dr. King was aware, as most

Americans were not, that the overwhelming percentage of soldiers fighting and dying in Vietnam were black Americans.

This new emphasis in the ministry of Dr. King exacerbated the editorial negativity of the *Lynchburg News*. In the minds of the editorial writers of this paper, labor unions, strikes, and all issues of economic justice were Marxist-inspired efforts to distribute wealth equally. Of course not to support the war effort in Southeast Asia was to be communist. This was especially so since the war was billed by our own government as a necessary stand against communism. Dr. King was clearly supporting the communist line, and the Lynchburg paper's voice against the civil rights movement in general and Dr. King in particular was increasingly strident.

His death in Memphis broke like a clap of thunder over this country. The pent-up frustration and despair present in the black community erupted in new riots across the nation. Enormous mourning was also apparent. In the white community there was a range of feelings that reflected the range in racial prejudice. I was impressed to discover among the business leaders I was addressing in the affluent suburbs of Birmingham a deep appreciation for Dr. King. These business leaders had seen the black population rise economically, become better trained workers, emerge into management levels, and begin to take their place as members of corporate America. They had realized that capitalism would never work unless industriousness and hard work were rewarded by promotions and increased pay. They knew that ambition must be encouraged by economic rewards. They had also come to realize that if half of a state's population was kept near the poverty level, the other half was dragged down economically. A society rises and falls together. Segregation finally hurt the dominant class also. This was a lesson the *Lynchburg News* could not embrace. I was fearful of what that paper's editorial comments on the death of Martin Luther King might do to the social fabric of our community.

When I got home, I addressed the meaning of Dr. King's death in my adult class, sharing some of the insights gained from my time with these Birmingham business executives. I thought the insights were well received. However, the editorial that came out in the newspaper came very close to stating, "The bastard got what he deserved." No, it did not use those exact words, but that was the tone the words communicated. One could almost feel the anger rising in the black community. We were sitting on a tinder box in the city of Lynchburg. The riots that marked so many cities of our land were now a real possibility for this small Southern town.

One of the few places where an honest dialogue between the white citizens and the black citizens of this community took place was in the Lynchburg Ministerial Association. As racial tensions rose around the country, and especially after the radically insensitive *Lynchburg News* editorial, an emergency meeting of the ministerial association was called by request of the black pastors. We met quickly to listen to their pain. Their plea was that we needed to confront that newspaper with community outrage and we needed to provide a proper channel for the black community to vent its feelings in a constructive witness. Their proposal was a planned march the following Sunday led by pastors walking arm in arm. The destination of the march would be a World War I memorial in the heart of the city. Long stairs approached this landmark, which would be ideal for the gathering of a crowd for a community service in honor of Dr. King. Not coincidentally, this monument was next door to the building housing the *Lynchburg News*. The black pastors stressed the fact that, for the sake of the black community, white participation in this march was essential. The black community needed to know that this newspaper did not represent the opinion of the white population. This march was to be the first community effort aimed at isolating the mentality of the *Lynchburg News,* or to have the citizens of Lynchburg say, in words that the editors of the newspaper could understand, that its corporate racism was no longer tolerable. It also raised the stakes for the white ministers. They needed to decide whether or not they would stand up and be counted. Jerry Falwell was conspicuously not present at this meeting.

I knew immediately that I would participate in this march. I also accepted some responsibility for getting that part of Lynchburg's affluent population and leadership represented by St. John's to understand the issues and support this effort. During the week I contacted by phone or in person the business and professional leaders of Lynchburg I knew personally to ask them to be present. I also went to see Dr. Magill to lay the plan out to him. He had, by this time, had a stroke that had impaired his walking ability. I had been privileged to be present with him through this personal crisis as his pastor, and he had shared with me a great deal of his life story. We had also discussed our various perspectives on Christianity. His sense of being replaced by me began to fade and he began to see me as building on what he had created. A growing friendship had developed, which I deeply appreciated. There is something about the onset of a critical illness that removes pettiness and causes the bigger picture to become visible. To share an hour with Dr. Magill in his home once a week became something to which I actually looked forward. I also learned that he had begun to speak positively of me and my ministry to those members of the congregation who were not so sure they appreciated their young rector.

On this occasion I explained to him where the idea of the march had come from, what it hoped to accomplish, and why its success was essential to the well-being of our town. Then, looking him straight in the eye, I said, "Bob, it would mean a great deal to me and to this community if you would join me in this march." I am sure he did not anticipate his personal involvement, but I believed he was a terribly important symbol. I explained to him that I knew he would not be able to manage the whole walk. I suggested that he be brought to a spot near the memorial steps where the service would be held, and that when the march came by he come out and walk those last few feet on my arm. I would have a chair for him at the memorial service site. It was a stretch for Bob to imagine doing this. I only asked him to think about it and to let me know by Saturday night. I told him I was going to talk about the march at the adult class on Sunday morning and urge the members of St. John's to join me in it. My plea would be enormously effective if I could also announce that Dr. Magill would be present with me. I did not press him further. I knew he would think about it and make his decision in his own way.

The newspapers obviously got wind of this proposed event. We had planned to publicize it through our churches and synagogues, but the news spread to radio and television. The youthful news anchor of the local Lynchburg ABC affiliate was a recent Princeton graduate named Charles Gibson, who would someday host *Good Morning America* on ABC-TV nationally. He would learn his craft and learn it well in this unique town. When the story announcing the march and the memorial service appeared in the paper, it was presented as "a black thing."

On Saturday night Bob Magill called. He would be with me on Sunday. He would meet me at the rendezvous point and accompany me on those final steps. My admiration for this man leaped. He had let himself grow into a new being. I asked him to keep it a secret until I could announce it on Sunday morning. He agreed.

The adult class was unusually large on that Sunday morning. I devoted my entire lecture to the dynamics of Dr. King's death and what it meant for our country. I referred to a national report, commissioned in the wake of the urban riots in 1967, by the Johnson administration on the status of race relations in America. This commission had been chaired by the governor of

Illinois, Otto Kerner. Its published findings, called the Kerner Report, stated
that America was drifting into two societies, separate and unequal, and it
spelled out the dire consequences for this land if that drift were not arrested.
It was a forceful document, but politically it was a too-hot-to-handle manifesto. President Johnson, consumed by an attempt to save his presidency from
the fallout of the Vietnam war, had ignored it. That abdication of leadership,
however, did not help this embattled Texan. Mr. Johnson was challenged in
the Democratic primaries, first by Senator Eugene McCarthy and later by
Senator Robert Kennedy. Their challenges were sufficiently successful that
Mr. Johnson withdrew and announced that he would not seek a second full
term. The Republicans had by and large castigated the Kerner Report with
the strange suggestion that the report encouraged violence. Bobby Kennedy
would be the only major American politician who would embrace this report
and its findings. It was also Senator Kennedy who had, during the riots after
Dr. King's assassination, gone into the streets to try to redirect the anger of
black Americans. As the closest brother of an assassinated president, he had
credibility, and the black leadership could hear what he was saying. His bold
political call was for a racially united country, and he would make the end of
separation, oppression, and violence a part of his presidential campaign.
Politically this man excited me more than any presidential candidate I had
ever known. I had a deeply emotional commitment to his potential presidency.
When he was murdered, my daughter Ellen wept for three days. I wanted to.

   Although the members of St. John's were not Bobby Kennedy fans, they
were also not fond of the idea that murdering people like John Kennedy and
Martin Luther King, Jr., was the way to settle political disputes, and so they
listened skeptically as I outlined the plans for that day. I went into detail
about how and why the march had come about. I announced that I would be
in the march and take part in the memorial service. I made it clear that the
editorial policy of the *Lynchburg News* was destructive to the well-being and
good order of our city. I urged them to join me in the march, to transform it
from simply a protest into a symbolic act of commitment to build a city
based on respect and goodwill. Then in conclusion I said, "Finally, I want
you all to know that Dr. Magill will be in the march with me. He will walk
the last few feet on my arm."

   The response was what I had imagined. At first they could not believe it.
Then one could almost see them visibly reprocessing their own responses,
challenging their own internal fears and prejudices, and reopening the possibility of their own decision about whether to participate.

The march and the memorial service met all of our expectations. It was made up in about equal proportions of black and white citizens. A group of black pastors, with arms locked, led the march and took the major roles in the memorial service. A line of white pastors made up the second row of the march. I was on the end of that row on the right side, so that when we neared the site of the memorial service, Dr. Magill could come out of the crowd on his cane and walk the final steps at my side. He was there, beaming, and the image of Bob Magill and Jack Spong walking together arm in arm in a memorial march for the slain civil rights leader Martin Luther King, Jr., was riveted in the minds of the people of St. John's. The mantle had finally been passed, and it had been done with Dr. Magill's blessing. I was enormously grateful to him.

Dr. Magill died shortly after this. I conducted his funeral service assisted by Bishop Marmion. His body was cremated and, according to his final instructions, I committed his ashes to their final resting place, which was inside the high altar of St. John's Church in Lynchburg. One had literally to crawl on one's hands and knees to get them into that site, but I did it. I would have done anything for him. I was touched that he willed to me his entire theological library with the words that I had been to him "like a devoted son."

For a period of time after the march the *Lynchburg News* did seem sobered by this experience. It certainly began to understand that it was not blessed with universal support, even in the white community. Perhaps the election of Richard Nixon that fall was consolation enough for the newspaper. George Wallace ran second in Lynchburg, with Hubert Humphrey a distant third. We were not mainstream America.

With the election over, the season of Advent drew near. I had announced all fall my intention to start an Advent series of lectures on the birth narratives of Matthew and Luke. In these lectures I would seek to answer the question of the historicity, or lack thereof, of such things as the virgin birth, the star in the East, the wise men, the shepherds, the Bethlehem birthplace, the angelic messenger, and all of the other symbols that make up the familiar Christmas stories. I finally felt that we had laid sufficient groundwork to allow some theological conclusions to be drawn.

There was some obvious excitement at this announcement for two reasons. First, I was finally, after three full years in this class, going to toe-dip at least into the New Testament. In a strange way, by avoiding the New Testament for so long a kind of keen anticipation had begun to build. There had been much repartee and humor about whether this church was turning into a synagogue and would only deal with the Hebrew Scriptures. Second, this announcement clearly signaled that the stakes were being raised in this class and that some of the traditional foundation stones of our faith story were being moved out of the category of the untouchable and into the category of the debatable. During the fall I constantly dropped provocative hints in the class about what was to come. These subliminal advertisements kept the subject alive and in the private conversation of our people. In retrospect, I find it almost unbelievable to recall the twin emotions of fear and excitement that seemed to be present in that church. But this was in the 1960s in the fundamentalist South. The only place the literal Bible was regularly challenged in that day in this region of the country was on the issue of whether each day of the six-day creation story stood for aeons of time or for twenty-four hours. I was planning to explore the story that told of God's miraculous entry into human history, which most people assumed to be necessary to the claim of the divinity of Christ and thus to the essence of Christianity itself. My willingness to raise these questions publicly was thought to be akin to playing with fire. For a church activity, this was high drama. Little did I realize that I was embarking on a way of life that would someday issue in my writing career and that would stamp me forever in the minds of traditional Christians as a provocateur.

On the first Sunday of Advent the adult class was significantly larger. There were, in fact, not enough chairs, and for the first time in this class's history about twenty people stood on the sides of the room. I entered my subject in a very direct way, by looking at exactly what the New Testament says about Jesus' origins and tracing the development of the birth tradition through the early years of the Christian Church's life, facing head on the nonliteralness of the birth narratives of Matthew and Luke.

We touched many other things in this group of lectures, which ultimately lasted seven Sundays. The response was beyond my expectations. There was little threat or defensiveness. There was instead enthusiastic reception. Far from "destroying Christmas," as some had suggested might happen, people said, in hundreds of different ways, that it had given them a new way to celebrate and appreciate the meaning of Christmas. It also emboldened me to recognize that people are capable of hearing anything I had to say, that they were not locked into religious stereotypes, conclusions, and patterns of yesterday. So I began to map my plans for a serious consideration of the New Testament in fall 1969. The groundwork had now been laid, and this congregation was ready to journey with me into new territory. I looked forward to the adventures that lay before me in this parish, in my diocese, and throughout the whole church. My leadership and my priesthood were clearly growing beyond the traditional boundaries of my profession.

Yet in the midst of this exciting career there were still shadows that continued to fall across my path in some form everyday. These shadows centered in the continued strange behavior of my wife. There seemed to be about her life the inevitability of a developing sickness that nothing I could do was able to change.

In early summer 1969 I began to receive visitors from Richmond at our Sunday services. They were members of the calling committee of St. Paul's Church, located in the heart of that city. By the end of June I had been called to be the rector of what is arguably Virginia's best-known church. It was rather soon to leave Lynchburg. I had been there only four years. I doubt if any other church in America could have enticed me to leave. But St. Paul's Church attracted me as no other position before or since has ever done. I knew that if they called me to be rector, I would accept. They did, and so the summer 1969 turned out to be not a time to prepare for a study of the New Testament, but a time for moving. Interestingly enough, at the same time, Carter Glass III's family decided that perhaps the time had come for a change in the leadership of the newspaper. So Carter stepped down, and a family member from Mississippi was brought in to replace him. Someone observed that Lynchburg lost its liberal voice and its conservative voice at the same time.

1. An external vestment worn by bishops in choir office services.

2. The Lambeth Conference is a gathering of the Anglican bishops of the world that meets once every ten years.

3. From the novel *The Shad Treatment*, by Garrett Epps (New York: Putnam, 1977). Though this is a novel about Virginia politics, there is no question that the author is commenting through the characters of his novel on the relationship between Senator Harry Byrd and Harry Byrd, Jr.

4. That visit occured in 1970, a year after I had departed from Lynchburg. It resulted in a tragedy. A mud slide struck a vehicle carrying our young people and some adult advisors into a river. Lives were lost, and the scars were real.

# 10

# *Something for Everyone in the Cathedral of the Confederacy*

❋

THE MOVE to Richmond was not easy. Joan had indicated that she was not willing to live in the present rectory, a large four-story residence that would have been burdensome to keep clean. The vestry agreed to sell that structure and let us choose another house. When the time came to go house hunting, however, Joan refused to accompany me to Richmond.

What I don't know about houses could fill volumes. Two members of St. Paul's, Canny Pasco and Mary Tucker, both the wives of vestrymen, agreed to assist me. I knew little about Richmond, including the image that certain neighborhoods projected. I had in mind only the needs of our daughters for a nice yard, separate bedrooms, if possible, and proximity to their schools. What a kitchen included or how it was laid out were things that simply did not enter my consciousness. Indeed, I could not imagine a less competent person than myself to take on such a task.

Since St. Paul's was in the heart of the city, the rectory could be anywhere, but the majority of the congregation lived in what was called "the west end." So we limited our search to that area. Finally I settled on several possibilities, got information on them, and returned to Lynchburg. My hope was that, having done this preliminary screening, Joan would come back with me the next week to make the final decision on which house to buy. When the time came to return to Richmond, however, I found myself responsible for making this important decision alone. With the continuing help of Canny and Mary, I settled on a relatively small house, both in terms of its external appearance and its square footage. Yet it had five bedrooms, a formal living room, a dining room, and a family room. The laundry was conveniently located just off the kitchen. Its many modern conveniences included an intercom system. There was, however, no protective porch or entryway over the front door, which I did not notice until months later when Ellen's first date to the spring cotillion was almost drowned along with her first corsage while he waited for me to open the door. Though this house was relatively new and sat on a large lot, it had little storage space unless we bought a shed for the backyard. I thought this house small enough to be manageable, and many a step would be saved by the intercom system that I, at least, thought was a nifty addition. So the vestry of St. Paul's purchased it, and the church now possessed a new rectory that at least two of the vestry wives thought satisfactory.

Our move to Richmond would actually take place during the general convention in South Bend, Indiana. This was necessary if the children were to enter on opening day the Episcopal day school known as St. Catherine's, where, as part of my salary, they were given scholarships. I would come three weeks later after I had discharged my duties as an elected deputy to this convention, a responsibility Bishop Marmion had asked me to take on as a final request. We had discussed this and Joan seemed agreeable to the plan. It was not ideal, but faithfulness to our children and to my commitment seemed to offer us no alternative.

The vestry at St. Paul's understood the difficulty we faced and the pressure it placed on Joan, so they agreed to assist by paying for all of the packing and unpacking. Also, Betty Giles, a close Lynchburg friend, had agreed to spend that first week with Joan to help with the children. She was much loved by our daughters and her presence would be a significant gift to them and to us. Nevertheless, I know I was not fully sensitive as to just how burdensome making this transition alone was. Joan was moving into a house she had never seen. I still had no idea why she had been unwilling to participate in the house decision, but it felt ominous to me. I called from South Bend on moving day and each day thereafter. The one impression that came through on every call was that Joan did not like the new house at all. I responded defensively by criticizing her for not participating in the choice. In typical male fashion I asserted that I had done the best I could and suggested that she would ultimately adjust. That clearly was not helpful.

Her list of complaints was lengthy. There were no trees in the yard. The kitchen was too restrictive. The rooms were all too small. Storage space was inadequate. But her special distaste was saved for the intercom system. She refused to use it and announced that no one else would use it either. It was the primary symbol of her distress. I was not able to understand, nor was I very sympathetic to her reaction. Even our cat, Herman, seemed to add to our transition problems. Our neighbors complained that he howled around their house at night when their cat was in heat. I arrived home from work the afternoon after this complaint had been lodged to discover that the vet had operated on Herman so that his desire to howl at the neighbor's cat was greatly diminished. At least one problem in our lives had proved solvable.

Since none of these problems lent themselves to easy solutions, I simply plunged into my work. The children were meeting new friends and getting established in a new school, the academic demands of which were greater than anything that they had experienced in the public schools of Lynchburg. So they and I settled into our respective roles, each of us clearly seeking to avoid the tense situation involving Joan's distress, which none of us understood.

Perhaps it was fortuitous that the reaction to reports about the South Bend convention was sending shock waves throughout Virginia. At that convention black militants had taken over the microphones and demanded reparations for the years of racial abuse they had endured. The convention had responded sympathetically by proposing that the church seek to raise a sum of money to be used to address the economic inequities and the root cause of poverty that separated black America from white America. The Richmond newspaper, owned by one of Richmond's oldest and most distinguished families, the Bryans, had already editorially condemned the decision of the general convention, referring to it as a surrender to terrorism and blackmail. The editorials went on to call on Virginia Episcopalians not only to refuse to contribute to this special fund, but also to withhold all funds from the national Episcopal Church until the leadership of the church got the message and, most especially, until the presiding bishop, John Hines, came to his senses.

The publisher of the paper at this moment in history was Tenant Bryan, a courtly man of the old South who bowed low and kissed the hands of women upon being introduced. He was a cultivated, conservative gentleman for whom segregation was simply a way of life, not something evil. He also was an Episcopalian who still attended the family church on the north side of Richmond, where Bryan Park was a major fixture in the landscape. His cousin Thomas Bryan was the former mayor of Richmond, a gregarious, folksy, and lovable man who was a top executive in Richmond's oldest department store, Miller-Rhoads. Tommy was as conservative as any other member of the family, but did not have a malevolent bone in his body. He was a member of St. Paul's and indeed sat on our vestry.

This newspaper's overt and hostile opposition to this national church initiative guaranteed that the battle about the church's response to the pain of black Americans was going to be fought out publicly in Richmond. In the interim, between the end of that convention and my arrival in Richmond, it had become obvious that neither Robert Gibson nor Robert Hall, the Episcopal bishops in Virginia, were planning to take any public leadership in this struggle. They were far more a part of the structure of the established social order than either realized. There was no Bishop Marmion in this diocese.

The letter I had sent to the members of St. Paul's to tell them about our fall plans stated that on the Wednesday before my first Sunday, I would address a special meeting of the congregation on the issues raised by the South Bend convention. I remembered saying that when Bishop Marmion arrived in Roanoke as the new bishop, he had been "forced to use his influence before he had any." I was facing the same reality. I would be defending an unpopular decision before I had been given a chance to build any relationships whatsoever. But having come, in that South Bend convention, to such significant new understandings of the price white racism had extracted from black Americans, I was determined to rise to this challenge. My Richmond world might as well know from the beginning who their new rector was. I had prepared an address on this convention for the people of Lynchburg as part of my report back to that diocese. It would take only minor adaptations to have it ready for Richmond. So on my third day in Richmond and my first Wednesday I came home early to handle some chores that the move required before going down that evening to meet my congregation for the first time.

My first task was to mow the lawn. While I was engaged in this activity in our front yard, Alison Gibson, the bishop's wife, dropped by to welcome us to town. She had actually come to visit with Joan and was surprised to find me in old clothes working on the grass. She was quite apprehensive about South Bend and about the reception she feared I would receive that evening. She assumed that I would be staying downtown to make sure that my speech was the very best it could be. The fact that I was busy in the yard did not jibe with her state of anxiety. She assured me that she would be in the audience that evening. I knew that both Bishop and Mrs. Gibson were members of St. Paul's, so that was not unusual. I was surprised to discover that Robert Hall, the bishop coadjutor, was also in the audience that night. I interpreted that to mean that he too was anxious and that he regarded this particular meeting as crucial for the whole diocese.

About 250 somewhat agitated members of St. Paul's assembled in Scott Hall that night. Clearly, reactions to the decisions of the South Bend general convention, while not informed, were deep, emotional, visceral, and real. One could almost feel the hostility when one entered the room.

My plan was to handle this evening alone. My conviction was and is that controversial issues need to be faced head on. I wanted my new congregation to see me as willing to deal with this crisis unafraid, willing to withstand the heat of their criticism.

At. 8:00 P.M. sharp I went to the podium, greeted the people, thanked them for coming, and told them not only who I was, but that I had been to the South Bend convention as a deputy from my former diocese. I went on to say that I had voted in favor of the most controversial of the resolutions adopted by that convention and that I welcomed this opportunity to tell people why and to lay the issues out before them clearly. If they had expected a defensive or apologetic posture, I wanted them to know quickly that they would not get that from me. Then I launched into the speech, concentrating on the pain and distress that had manifested itself in the actions of the black delegates, which most of them viewed as excessive. I tried to help them imagine themselves as black people, oppressed, marginalized, underpaid, and victims of discrimination. I asked them to embrace the fact that blacks were also Christians, who were told by their churches verbally that all people were created in God's image, and that as baptized Christians they were members of Christ, Children of God, and inheritors of the Kingdom of Heaven. Yet institutionally a message quite different was communicated to blacks. I portrayed the offering we agreed to make at South Bend as an opportunity to redress the evils of our segregated past. It was, I asserted, an investment in human beings who cried out for a boost. I claimed that the integrity of the gospel itself demanded this response.

Throughout the talk I watched the faces of the people in my audience. There was no doubt that I had everyone's attention. However, one woman, whom I guessed to be in her mid-seventies, sat in the front row and scowled at me, shaking her head negatively through the entire presentation. She was elegant and well appointed, dressed in black with her graying hair pulled tightly into a large bun behind her head. If she wore makeup, it was not discernible. She sat up straight as a ramrod. She had an austere air about her. I looked at her a number of times during the talk. She was, in fact, hard to miss, seated just to the right of my podium. I marveled at the muscle control it took to keep that scowl in place for so long.

When I concluded the formal talk, the applause was more than perfunctory, but less than enthusiastic. I announced my willingness to take questions. The major ones centered on the offering. How would it be raised? The South Bend decision was to leave it to dioceses, congregations, and individuals, which meant it would be voluntary. I added that I thought it was important to give everyone a chance to participate so that they could be a part of rebuilding racial trust in this land and creating an atmosphere of opportunity. I announced that Joan and I planned to support this offering and I hoped they would also. When there appeared to be no more questions, I thought it was time to close the evening.

At this moment, however, Bishop Hall raised his hand. I recognized him and he came forward to the podium. I suppose he felt these people needed to hear from their bishop. After thanking me for my presentation, he became defensive and unhelpful. He berated the press reports and assured people that none of the money they gave in their pledges would go to this purpose. It was a negative note that I regretted. When he sat down, our senior warden stood up, thanked me for my clarity, and said that I had demonstrated the kind of leadership that had led the vestry of St. Paul's to call me to be their rector. This time there was substantial applause with people rising to their feet, all save one. The scowling woman sitting in the first row remained seated. With them standing, I said the benediction. My sole detractor did rise for that, and finally the evening was over.

When the people began to leave, there was a buzz of general conversation. I immediately stepped down to confront that unresponsive, negative person in the first row. I stuck out my hand and said, "I'm Jack Spong. Who are you?"

"I'm Miss Helen Adams," she responded, as if all three words were significant; her scowl was undeterred by speaking. Whether inspired by the devil or the Spirit, I do not know, but, surprising even myself, I said, "Well, you'd be a hell of a lot more attractive if you smiled once in a while." She was as shocked as I at this comment, and there was a moment when her response hung in the balance. But a suppressed smile creased her lips and she muttered some words of welcome to St. Paul's and turned to leave. About three or four people in the audience had been close enough to see and hear this exchange, and the report of it spread more rapidly throughout the congregation than did the report on the South Bend convention.

Miss Helen Adams was an almost stereotypical spinster who had been a schoolteacher prior to her retirement. She had been the bane of every rector's existence through several administrations. She was critical of everybody. She was in church every Sunday, but disapproved of almost everything and would not raise her contribution to the church beyond twenty-five cents per week. She was known to one and all as a lonely, sad, and negative, but genteel woman. I could have finished my relationship with her forever with that first comment. Instead, I discovered that she had related this exchange herself to a number of people as if she had actually enjoyed it. When I saw her on the following Sunday, she indeed smiled. It was as if an iceberg around her had melted. She would prove to be one of the most unforgettable characters I have ever met. She also raised her pledge that fall to a dollar a week. It was a step in the right direction.

Following that talk, a member of the congregation named Bill Mann came to ask me if he could have a copy of my address. He wanted to see about getting it published, he said. Bill was a socially prominent bachelor and an advertising executive at the Richmond newspaper. I assumed he wanted to reproduce the talk for those who had not been able to be present and gave him my manuscript. That night, however, Bill called a few leaders of the church, proposing that they join him in buying a full-page advertisement in the *Richmond Times Dispatch* on which would be run the full text of my address. He also asked these leaders if they would be willing to sign their names to this advertisement and thus to commend it personally to the wider community. He argued that the cost of the full page would be minimal compared with the cost the church might have to absorb if the anger being generated by the conservative secular press were not confronted with positive influential voices.

The following week, after my first Sunday at St. Paul's, a full-page advertisement appeared in the Richmond press under the banner headline "A Message to All Episcopalians." An opening paragraph explained briefly who I was, the context in which the speech had been given, and the desire of the signatories to counter the distortion of those who were not present in South Bend by making available a factual report from one who was. In addition to Bill Mann's signature, there were the signatures, among others, of Mr. and Mrs. Sidney Buford Scott, arguably Richmond's most prominent family, Mr. and Mrs. Walter Craigie, a well-known investment banker and his wife, Mr. and Mrs. Robert Gordon, the CEO of a major Virginia bank and his wife, and Mr. and Mrs. H. Merrill Pasco, a top attorney at Richmond's major law firm and his wife, and Dr. and Mrs. Henry St. George Tucker, Jr., a highly respected physician and the son of the former presiding bishop of the Episcopal Church and his wife. The signatures read like a segment of Richmond's social register.

This page broke upon the Richmond reading public like a bombshell. The *Richmond Times Dispatch* was as close to being a statewide paper as Virginia possessed. This full-page advertisement served to introduce another Spong to public life in the state of Virginia, but its most important feature was that members of Richmond's old-line establishment had put themselves on the line for a more open and compassionate society.

The absence of public leadership from either of Virginia's bishops also meant that church leadership on issues before this society was rather suddenly vested in the rector of Richmond's downtown church. I had quite unknowingly filled a vacuum. I suspect it came as a surprise to the bishops and other clergy that a man who had not been in the diocese a full month had suddenly become the public spokesperson for the Episcopal Church. I learned once again the powerful lesson that to be the right person at the right time in the right place doing the right thing is a potent combination or, as another person observed, "The world stands aside for those who know where they are going."

But I also learned quickly that St. Paul's offered a powerful public pulpit that was respected and looked to for leadership. It was part of the heritage of this church stretching back to the days when Dr. Charles Minigerode, the rector between 1856 and 1889, became the only figure allowed to visit the imprisoned president of the Confederate States of America, Jefferson Davis, following the defeat of the South in the Civil War. Emerging from that prison cell, Dr. Minigerode would, each time, hold a press conference, and he thus became Jefferson Davis's voice during his imprisonment. This reputation of St. Paul's as a place of city and statewide leadership was further enhanced during the rectorship of Dr. Walter Russell Bowie (1911–1923), who became the national leader of progressive Christianity on a wide variety of social and theological issues. It would be my role to continue this tradition in ways I could not at that moment even imagine. For now I could only sense the power of the place.

That full-page advertisement quickly became a story in the national press, beginning in the *Washington Post* and going via the Associated Press across the country. It prompted a large number of requests for copies of the full statement and, of more significance to me, it brought personal letters of thanks not only from the presiding bishop, John Hines, but from the Reverend Dr. John Coburn, who was the presiding officer in the House of Lay and Clerical Deputies.

This rapid public beginning to my Richmond ministry vested the other things I began to do with new authority. For example, I had insisted during the search process that a Sunday adult Bible class had to be part of my life at St. Paul's. I wanted a forum in which I could continue to explore the edges of Christianity. That was not a universally popular decision. Thomas Boushall, the former warden and the grand old man of Richmond's business world, told me privately that it would never work. "We are a downtown church," he insisted. "No one will come to the heart of the city for a 9:15 family service or a 10:00 Bible class. Attendees at the 8:00 service," he went on to say, "were those who wished to be at church, but who wanted to keep the day free for other things." Among the eight o'clockers, I would discover, were a significant number of professional people, notably doctors and lawyers who, following the service, went to their offices within a few blocks of St. Paul's to put in full work days. It was a powerful argument from tradition that I would confront many times in Richmond. If I surrendered to it, there would be no progress, but to change it I had to recognize that these habits developed for good reasons, making the traditions of the past both deeply entrenched and formidable. Reasons even more compelling must be marshaled to confront the established practice. The leaders of St. Paul's agreed to allow the experiment, believing deeply that before Christmas this idea would be abandoned by me as simply unworkable. During the summer prior to moving, I had laid out the problem before a member of St. Paul's paid staff, Jean LeRoy, and asked her to help me design a Sunday morning program that would be both sensitive to our downtown reality and open to the things I was committed to doing.

Jean LeRoy was a remarkable woman. She was a professionally trained educator and a deeply committed and knowledgeable Christian. As a staff member, she possessed the best theological mind with which I would ever be privileged to work. As our relationship developed, I learned that I could tell her a month or so in advance about the subjects I was interested in treating in future sermons and within two or three days there would appear on my desk five or six books with pages marked in each. She would have distilled into fifty pages or so the best theological thought available on the subject I desired to address. The books came from the library of the Union Theological Seminary, a Presbyterian facility of great stature on Richmond's north side.

Jean was also a practical "can do" kind of person. She had been a missionary in Cuba during the early part of her career. Her perspective had been further broadened when she served as the director of Christian education in a parish in California under the rectorship of the Reverend George Tittman, a remarkable Episcopal priest whose life ended as a result of a bizarre and random act of murder. She had been for a number of years a valued member of St. Paul's staff, and I was pleased that she was excited about the possibility of working now with me. I knew instinctively that I was in for a treat.

When Jean returned with a proposal two days later, I knew that I was blessed with a genius. "We start by admitting that a downtown church has unique opportunities," she began. "We have a loyal congregation of people drawn from the suburbs who come to church downtown because it offers them something special. That specialness may be as pedestrian as the fact that this is a socially prominent church, but Richmond has several churches that could qualify on that score. Some of them are located conveniently in suburbs. Specialness for some of our members may lie in the fact that our music is of concert quality not normally replicated in the suburbs. Our music budget supports a full-time organist and a double quartet with an extra soprano. Specialness for others is found in the quality of our liturgy and preaching, which must be effective and consistent. Another special drawing quality of a downtown church may be that it is perceived to be a place where the issues of the whole city are addressed, or in which various outreach programs are sponsored. But," Jean summarized, "something draws them."

Driving to her conclusion, she continued, "We must, therefore, design an educational and Sunday morning program that will be second to none, making that program one more thing that will cause people to choose to be part of a downtown church. If they want safe traditional education, they have plenty of choices, but if they want a challenging program that will stimulate their minds, open their imaginations, and equip them for ministry in the twentieth century, then we want them to know that they can get it here. They must, however, be willing to make a commitment in order to reach that goal. Our responsibility is to make that goal not only a reality, but an exciting drawing card."

St. Paul's people did not normally come downtown for a church function at night. Even the vestry, made up exclusively of businessmen, met at 4:00 P.M. But given that limitation, our people might be willing to make a bigger time commitment on Sunday morning. "We should therefore load

Sunday morning with opportunities, building all of them into a two-hour block of time," she suggested, warming to her task and clearly sensing my agreement.

I listened as she described the plan. "We should upgrade the 8:00 A.M. service of holy communion to include a full sermon, the same one, not a précis of what would be preached later. A practice run would help the preaching quality," she added. There would be time to rewrite parts of it before its second run. "We should," she suggested, "return to the custom of Dr. Bowie's days of publishing the sermon. When the preacher knows that the sermon is to be published, he will inevitably work harder on it," she added. She also proposed that we add a continental breakfast and book discussion group for eight o'clockers. She would lead that book group, at least at the beginning. This would offer greater possibilities to those twenty-five to fifty people who made 8:00 their preferred hour of worship.

But her most brilliant plans were for the two-hour block from 10:00 to noon each Sunday. We were to promote that two-hour time span as a single unit for every member of our congregation from the cradle to the grave, asking our people to make this the minimum expectation of those who chose to be members of St. Paul's. The plan had several segments. For the youngest members of our congregation, the newly born through age three, we would provide full nursery care by competent attendants.

For children age three to about seven, we would run a two-hour modified daily Bible school format. That is, we would plan a collage of activities that would include children's worship, story time, activity time, rest time, refreshment time, and play time. These blocks would be in regular rotation so that the attention span of the children would not be taxed and the experience would be pleasurable.

For children in the second to the seventh grade, and thus able to read, we would run a normal church-school program from 10:00 to 10:50. These children would then join their parents in church for worship, departing at the sermon hymn to go into an activity period during which we would offer a choice of electives in music, drama, art, woodworking, or carpentry that would last until church adjourned at about 12:00. We would seek volunteers from our congregation to lead these activities, but our commitment to this variety would be so strong that if necessary we would hire people, especially in woodworking or carpentry, where skills might be difficult to locate. We would seek at least two public occasions a year—one at Christmas and the other probably in the spring of the year—to feature the gifts of the children involved in these programs. We also decided that we would display all our children's creative work in a public way on the final Sunday of the church-school year for their parents and friends to see and thus to build public awareness of the excellence of the church-school program.

For young people in the ninth through twelfth grades we would have a church-school class from 10:00 to 10:50 that would be issue-oriented; they would then be in church from 11:00 to 12:00, where many of them served as members of the junior choir and acolytes. From time to time for a special unit we might bring the high-schoolers into the adult class if the topic seemed appropriate. We also ran a junior- and senior-high youth program, which was mostly social, on Sunday evenings. A number of special events, such as cookouts, dances, and ski trips were part of this age group's life.

The adults would be invited to come to the adult Bible class at 10:00 A.M., which would be accompanied by coffee and tea. It would adjourn at 10:50 to get families together for church. I would teach the adult class each Sunday, and we would promote the whole Sunday morning as education and worship. The 11:00 service would remain formal, intact, and inviting. I would be in the pulpit as the preacher on almost every Sunday of the year from the Sunday after Labor Day to the last Sunday in May. We would offer consistency and try to build the downtown church on that basis. For the older members of the congregation who came only at 8:00 or at 11:00, there would be no discernible changes. For those who wanted more, a rich menu was offered. It was, I thought, a brilliant plan and, with vestry approval, it was adopted. It became operative on my first full Sunday in residence.

We intended to undergird this program with professional support. Jean would train the church-school teachers, meeting with them regularly. She would also pick the curriculum and be familiar with it on every level. My responsibilities would be the adult class, the sermons, and the pastoral dimensions of the congregation. For success we knew we needed to recruit a youth minister, an administrative person, and a person skilled not just in music, but in liturgy and worship who was able to work with both children and adults.

In time Walton Pettit became the youth minister; he had a talent for taking plans worked out corporately by the staff and shepherding them to fulfillment. Lucy Boswell Negus became the administrative person, managing the office and its personnel as well as the maintenance staff. She brought with her the additional talent of an unusual ability with words, sentence structure, and general editorial expertise. Raymond F. Glover became the liturgist, organist, and choirmaster. He was the best liturgical person with whom I ever worked. He also had great gifts with children, and the children's choir program bloomed under his tutelage. He would, as his life developed, go on from St. Paul's to be the general editor of the 1982 Episcopal hymnal and would complete his career as professor of liturgy, music, and speech at Virginia Theological Seminary in Alexandria, Virginia. When this group was fully assembled (and that took several years), it was a remarkable collection of unique and talented people, and we had a number of years to work together in what was the best-functioning staff, where all the pieces meshed harmoniously, I had yet experienced. But the initial key was Jean LeRoy, who helped me shape the vision and see the roles we needed to fill to make it a reality. We started, however, with what we had. So Jean and I put together the program for the 1969–1970 year, and we appeared to do it well since the parish responded with enthusiasm.

For the adult class I decided to begin with the book of Genesis and confront the issue of fundamentalism head on. Since I had worked on this material in Lynchburg, it was quite familiar and I needed that kind of resource to get through this year of enormous demands and a short-handed staff. The book of Genesis would open for this class theological topics like creation, the fall, sin, alienation, covenant, and redemption. I would treat this book far more deeply than I had done previously. That commitment was apparent when I chose Gerhard Von Rad's book entitled simply *Genesis, A Commentary* to be my own study guide. Before the year was over this massive book would be incarnate in me and my biblical and theological education would have taken a quantum leap forward. Indeed, so rich was my interaction with Von Rad that on the basis of that experience, I made the decision to live with at least one major theological or biblical book a year until I had mastered its content in a similar fashion. It was not quantity, but theological and biblical quality that I sought. My personal study and devotional life was at that time organized around the daily office of morning prayer. By making morning prayer the basis of my personal devotional time, I would regularly engage the Scriptures and for the sermon part of this prayer activity I would work through the study book I had chosen to master that year. It was the beginning of what would develop into a lifetime habit. In Richmond this study would feed first my adult class and secondarily my preaching. It would also in time come to feed my writing career, but at that time I could not even imagine that I might some day have a writing career. I only knew that I was in a new place, facing a new challenge and that I intended to do it well.

The adult class was launched with only about fifty people. Among them were the members of our vestry, who were present not by choice, but out of loyalty. Nothing had shaken their conviction that this young rector needed to try this thing in order to get it out of his system and then the life of St. Paul's could go back to normal. But encouraged by my Lynchburg experience, I believed I could win a faithful audience even in downtown Richmond. I also perceived a deep religious hunger in people that was not met by pious clichés or traditional Bible classes. I deliberately expanded the time available for questions at the end of each lecture in order to be more personal and to achieve a higher level of trust.

By early November class attendance was climbing toward eighty, and even Tom Boushall became enthusiastic. With the combination of the publicity that surrounded the South Bend presentation and the gossip that went through various social circles about this class, there was a growing sense of pride at St. Paul's that a new era had been born. As the adult class grew, so did the Sunday school. Indeed, the two-hour session was becoming quite popular. Parents were dragging their children to church at 10:00, attracted by the adult class. But the children were refusing to miss their wildly popular activity period during the last half of church, which meant that church attendance also grew. The woodcarving (and we soon added soap carving for the younger members) and carpentry classes appealed to boys in particular in a way beyond my imagining, and when we did the Christmas pageant in 1969, all of those activity groups began to shine. Our pageant was not just shepherds and wise men dressed in bathrobes with towels around their heads, but an original play that allowed all of our children's talents to find expression. They built props, painted them, provided music, and were stars in the play. It was so successful, the children could not wait for their spring event. Each part of our two-hour plan strengthened the other. By the time my first full-program year was complete, the adult class was averaging one hundred people per Sunday, the church school was bigger than it had ever been before, and church attendance was up significantly. A surge of life could be felt throughout the congregation. Even Miss Helen Adams would not miss a Sunday.

I wanted to be certain that I did not neglect the senior members of this congregation who might not be excited about our new program, which was geared primarily toward younger families, so I instituted a regular and intensive visitation program. These visits gave me the opportunity to build relationships and trust with our older members on a one-to-one basis. Beyond that, I discovered myself greatly enriched by these encounters. I learned the folklore of the parish, the history and interrelatedness of the families, the defining events in these people's lives, personally and corporately, as well as their fears and prejudices.

Embracing the culture of both Richmond and St. Paul's took quite a while. History and tradition were valued in both places. A person in Richmond in his or her eighties would have been the child of parents who, in their younger years, had witnessed firsthand the pain of the Civil War and the difficult period of Reconstruction. St. Paul's was so deeply a part of that Southern history. This church was known as the Cathedral of the Confederacy. Both Robert E. Lee and Jefferson Davis were members of the congregation. Indeed, the Civil War literally ended in St. Paul's on a Sunday morning when a messenger from General Lee interrupted the morning worship service to inform President Davis of the surrender at Appomattox. Jefferson Davis rose to leave the church. Dr. Minigerode knew what this meant, so he stopped the service at that moment and ordered the church bell to toll as it did at a funeral to announce to the entire community that the war was over. The South as a separate nation and the institution of slavery were both dead.

St. Paul's reveled in this history. There was in St. Paul's a stained-glass window dedicated to Robert E. Lee. In the early 1940s during World War II some sailors from the Norfolk naval base were partying in Richmond and got pretty inebriated. In an ensuing scuffle and rock fight with some Richmond natives, the Lee window was damaged. Because the offending persons were in the employ of the U.S. Navy, the federal government agreed to be financially responsible for the necessary repairs to the Lee window. It was a generous and appropriate offer, but it did not count on the memory of some of the older Daughters of the Confederacy in St. Paul's Church. Horrified by this suggestion, they boldly announced that "No Federal money will be allowed to pollute the Lee Memorial." So the offer of federal help was declined and the window was repaired by these true daughters of the South. People smiled about that story twenty-five years later, but it was repeated so often one knew that it touched something deep in the corporate psyche of this city.

There was, however, one battle based upon this history that I felt compelled to engage in my first year. St. Paul's had a flagpole on the front of the church that enabled a very large flag to wave at a 45-degree downward angle over the front entrance. On this flagpole during the weeks of Robert E. Lee's and Jefferson Davis's birthdays, the tradition had been to fly the battle flag of the Confederacy, the Stars and Bars. St. Paul's was a tourist stop and many visitors on the tour came regularly to St. Paul's to sit in the pews that had once been occupied by these two Confederate heroes. These pews were, of course, clearly marked. To me, however, that flag was nothing but a symbol of slavery and segregation. The KKK displayed the Stars and Bars at all of its rallies. It was carried by partisan crowds at football games in the deep South where those universities that sought to defy the law of the land and remain bastions of segregation were playing each other to the strains of "Dixie." I had no intention of being the rector of a church that would fly the Confederate flag on any occasion. I learned about this custom almost by accident in November of my first year and immediately took my concern to the vestry at its December meeting.

I saw no way this would be anything but a win-lose vote. My fallback position was that I would simply boycott the church the week that the flag flew around each of the two birthdays. I would be on vacation, but I made it clear that I would never enter a church flying the Confederate flag. My passion surprised the vestry, who had never thought much about this issue. But it roused considerable opposition in two sons of old Richmond aristocracy, Catesby B. Jones and James Rawls. Both felt that the honor of their families was being insulted. It also gave them what felt like a legitimate and socially acceptable issue with which to express their displeasure at their "liberal new rector." The debate was long and vigorous. I warned them that our city was half black and I could envision riots outside St. Paul's to protest that flag. I think that the introduction of that possibility had a salutary effect, for when the vote was taken, the Confederate flag would never again fly on that flagpole. It was, however, not a total victory. The flag would be retained, the vestry directed in a face-saving compromise, but it would henceforth be placed in a stand inside the church to mark the Lee pew during the week of his birthday and the Davis pew during the week of his birthday. This would be explained in a brochure given to the tourists. It was a compromise I could live with. The public affront was removed. The reason for its use was now historic and the fact remains that after one or two years the altar guild simply forgot to put the large and cumbersome flag out and so the custom died. Though I had on this issue used up a part of my reservoir of goodwill, I had also established myself as a person with deeply held convictions for which I was willing to do battle. Respect grew, I felt, even if the almost universal approval, which I had certainly enjoyed, began to diminish.

Several weeks after the flag battle, I experienced my first Lent at St. Paul's. It was like Lent in no other congregation I had ever known. Beginning on Ash Wednesday, the first day of Lent, and concluding on Good Friday some forty days later with a three-hour service, St. Paul's ran a daily Lenten preaching ministry. To this pulpit were invited the great leaders of the Episcopal Church and the ecumenical Christian community to preach at a service from 12:30 to 1:00 P.M. Luncheons were served in the parish house on both sides of the service so that people could get Lenten preaching and lunch in one hour. The weekly speakers would be invited at least two years in advance, and the invitees tended to be bishops, cardinal rectors, especially of New York churches, and academicians from seminary faculties. For an unknown speaker there might be as few as 100 to 150 people at the noontime service. But for one of the old favorites like Elton Trueblood, the great Quaker scholar, and Terence Finlay, the rector of St. Bartholomew's in New York City, the crowd would swell to 500 people a day. To be co-chairs of St. Paul's Lenten luncheons was still a coveted position that always made the social pages of the Richmond newspapers about two weeks before Ash Wednesday. The outside speakers that first Lenten season had been invited by my predecessor, but I knew many of them and looked forward to spending time with them.

Nothing about that excitement or busyness, however, could repress the increasing anxiety still present in my personal life. I lived with an ominous sense of the unknown in relation to my wife. No matter how hard I tried, I could not understand the dynamics that kept manifesting themselves in her life. My hopes that she would come to enjoy the house were simply naive. As the months went by, her agitation only increased. She would be visibly upset if anyone dared to use the intercom system. Our younger two daughters seemed to adjust well, but our oldest was having a difficult time. Breaking into the established social life in a girls' school in the ninth grade was not easy. But by the time the second September arrived, all were very much part of the system.

Joan, however, was not. She adamantly demanded that we move. I found this embarrassing. This would be the second rectory in less than a year that the church had sold, because it was not satisfactory, and it was widely known that she had not participated in the choice of our home. However, I had no alternative but to raise the issue with my warden. Once more I found the leadership of this church to be gracious. We put the house in Windsor Farms on the market. It sold within a week for a price $5,000 beyond what we had paid in August of the past year. We found a house on Three Chopt Road in the west end that was old, but large and gracious. Joan appeared to like it. It was on the market because the previous owner had committed suicide by hanging himself in its attic. I think that must have suppressed the price and salability a bit so that we were able to buy it for a price that equaled the selling price of the former house. Joan seemed visibly relieved. This new house had lots of trees, an attic, and a garage. Above all, it did not have an intercom system. It was convenient for the children, since it was located within three blocks of St. Catherine's school. I breathed a sigh of relief that we finally seemed settled and that first year was over.

My attempts to listen to what Joan was bothered by seemed to bring no answers. Some themes did appear. One was power. She spoke of herself as powerless, and she viewed the people at St. Paul's as powerful people. The other was privacy. Her response to the intercom system as an invasion of privacy was so emotional and so upsetting that it could not even be discussed. Even though we had moved away from that, it still came up from time to time. For the life of me, I did not understand how these things were interrelated. I was to learn.

# Pushing St. Paul's Outward While Inwardly Grappling with Prayer and Pastoral Tragedy

✳

T HERE IS a wonderful sense of being in a familiar place that marks the life of a priest after the first year in a parish. The sense of strangeness has largely departed and been replaced by a feeling of belonging. I was so satisfied and happy professionally that I began to think there must actually be something wrong with me. Clergy gatherings tended to be complaint sessions in which time was spent on how miserable, misused, and unappreciated the ordained person was and how dreadful the congregation's "old guard" was. I felt none of that. I was challenged, eager, and looking forward to the coming years with high hopes, ready to respond to new opportunities that would turn my life in new directions.

The only regret I had was that moving had forced me to give up my seat as a deputy to the next general convention. So I was delighted to get a letter from the editor of the *Episcopalian*, the national monthly church newspaper, asking if I would accept the temporary assignment of covering the upcoming convention. To see a general convention from the press gallery would provide a new perspective. The editor particularly wanted me to cover the debate around the overseas missionary policy of our church. It was not the most exciting beat, but it was one about which I was knowledgeable. A major focus of that debate would be the request by the ninth province of our church (Central and South American and the Spanish-speaking islands of the Caribbean) that the House of Bishops elect a bishop for Ecuador. Ecuador had tried and failed to elect a bishop on its own. With only three

Episcopal priests in the entire country, no two of them were willing to support the third. At the same time the overseas department of our national church, headed by Brooke Mosley, the former bishop of Delaware, opposed electing anyone bishop for Ecuador. He felt we needed to move away from hierarchical structures and rethink the role of a missionary bishop in a dramatically new way. Ecuador, in his mind, was not prepared to do that. The decision would focus the larger debate on the proper missionary strategy.

But before that convention beckoned me, there were many things to do to get the new year started. I did not want to suffer what people in the world of professional athletics call the sophomore jinx.

The educational program at St. Paul's was now a well-accepted reality. People actually seemed to miss it during the summer and look forward to it in the fall. For me this new year was a chance to branch out into some totally new material. I had now taught this class for five years in Lynchburg and Richmond without ever getting fully into the New Testament. But this year that would be my focus. I chose as my subject for the year the Gospel of Mark. It was not only the first Gospel to be written, by at least a decade, but it was also a short Gospel with only sixteen chapters. I must confess to some anxiety that I could make these sixteen chapters last for forty weeks, but that was to prove no problem at all. I chose D. H. Nineham's commentary on Mark to guide my work. I wanted to begin with introductory material on the style of this Gospel, the author, date, context, and its unique features. That alone would carry me into November. The Gospel breaks quickly into major units: the Galilean phase of Jesus' life, the journey section, then the Jerusalem phase, and the concluding Resurrection story. I would try to describe how the individual narratives of the text might have developed in the period of time between the death of Jesus around 30 C.E. and the time when Gospel writing actually began in the seventh, eighth, and ninth decades of the Christian era. Finally, I wanted my class to be able to separate the literal history behind the text from the portrait-painting interpretation in the text. I wanted them to distinguish between the authentic Jesus tradition and the church's theological development that had expanded the Jesus image beyond the one eyewitnesses could ever have recognized. This class was designed to shatter any latent literalism the people had brought with them from their church-school days. I wanted them to appreciate the uniqueness of Mark, to separate it from Matthew and Luke.

As I had been forced to recognize in Lynchburg, I knew that for some, perhaps many, I was quite deliberately embarking on a threatening course.

When teaching the Old Testament, one can suggest that certain things are not historically true. Talking about the Jesus story is riskier, however, because people have much more of their religious security invested in it. Yet so much of the Jesus story reflected long abandoned theological concepts and an unbelievable first-century worldview, which meant that for many the literal narratives had become a barrier to faith!

By and large, the church has never invited its members to pose these troubling questions. But I believed an unexamined faith or a religious system that did not confront the real issues of credibility would never endure. I sought to carry these people with me into something rare and new—religious intellectual integrity. I had no idea where this journey would lead. I only knew I was committed to this approach and the class seemed receptive.

Next I began to look at the total life of the congregation, to see what was missing. I did not want my succeeding years to be spent in simply continuing or even expanding things previously done. There were, I felt, still enormous gaps in the parish program that needed to be addressed. I now wanted to plan other programs for the parish that would be as dramatic and worthwhile as our educational program had proved to be.

The area that concerned me most was our lack of focused outreach in the poor and black communities of Richmond. We did, as a church, sponsor a school for hearing-impaired children and a center for handicapped adults. But St. Paul's, Richmond, was a wealthy, predominantly white congregation worshiping in the heart of a majority black city that had pockets of dire poverty and patterns of deep racial injustice all around it. Our church seemed not to engage those issues at all. The opportunity to address that area of our corporate life presented itself almost as if it had dropped from heaven.

My predecessor at St. Paul's, Joseph Heistand, later the bishop of Arizona, had expended much of his energy in Richmond on a major building program. The facility that housed our library, offices, vestry room, church-school rooms, and assembly hall, where the adult class was held, had been both expanded and beautified. St. Paul's sat on the top of a hill in downtown Richmond with its property dropping off steeply toward the James River to the south. This natural terrain had provided a unique opportunity to excavate underneath St. Paul's and build in that location a three-tier parking garage. That was probably the decision that guaranteed the health and continued vitality of this downtown church. This garage was available exclusively to the people of St. Paul's on Saturdays, Sundays, and evenings, but it was a commercially viable income-producing parking facility during the rest of the week. It had generated sufficient income over the years to retire the total debt incurred in the expansion program by 1971. We would, therefore, come into an unanticipated windfall of about $50,000 a year. My task was to design an outreach program to take advantage of those funds. The only claim against this resource was the vague notion that when the debt was paid, there would be sufficient income to maintain the entire structure in good condition forever.

My plan was to designate $15,000 a year for maintenance, request $35,000 a year for an outreach program, and then try to build that program aimed at relieving the strains of racism and poverty in Richmond. It was to be, at least in my mind, St. Paul's version of the General Convention Special Program, instituted by Bishop Hines in 1967. Of necessity, it would not be able to take the risks that the national church's program had taken, but with this sum of money, it could be developed into a significant and noteworthy ministry.

I discussed these ideas with my staff and we began to devise a plan that we called the "Isaiah 58:12 Program." When this program did become public, it sent people scurrying to their Bibles, where they read these words: "And your ancient ruins shall be rebuilt; you shall raise up the foundations of many generations; you shall be called the repairer of the breach, the restorer of streets to dwell in." That text embodied my dream for the kind of outreach ministry that St. Paul's should be about.

As we envisioned this program, an elected body would receive proposals from community groups for programs that could make real and long-term differences. The criteria for the Isaiah 58:12 board were: Does this proposal meet a legitimate need that will serve to repair the breach between races and economic groups in this city? Does it have local community support? Will it enable members of this congregation to get involved in outreach ministry in a hands-on way? Can the program, once begun, demonstrate sufficient value to be permanently funded from other sources in the city? Would it qualify for grants from local businesses, the United Way, or foundations?

Once the Isaiah 58:12 board made a recommendation, it would go to the vestry of St. Paul's for final approval before the funds would be allocated. This final step gave the vestry ultimate control and thereby power to cut out the daring projects, but my sense was that without this proviso, the vestry would not be willing to accept the program at all. In my mind half a loaf was better than no loaf at all.

With these pieces in place, I planned to bring the proposal to the vestry for approval at the December 1970 meeting. That schedule would also give me time to build a consensus on the vestry with one-to-one conversations. With the Isaiah 58:12 Program on the drawing table, I left for Houston and the general convention with my press credentials on display.

My journalistic beat at the general convention placed me most often in the press gallery of the House of Bishops, where the overseas debate would be initiated and where the election of a new bishop for Ecuador, if approved, would take place. Because of those circumstances, I was able to watch this body at work for almost two full weeks. That was a fascinating education.

It was an unpleasant convention. The fallout from both the Seattle convention in 1967, at which the General Convention Special Program was passed, and the South Bend convention in 1969, with its racial confrontation, was still intense. Anger abounded. John Hines had received so many death threats that he was compelled to wear a bulletproof vest and hire bodyguards. The mood of the convention was motivated by the desire to wrest back control of the church from its elected leaders in New York City and restore it to the local leaders and, most particularly, to the local bishops. In resolution after resolution the vision, brilliance, and risks of this church's attempts to put its very life alongside the poor and the dispossessed of our nation were curtailed.

The church was quite clearly rebuffing its leader. In the House of Bishops the opposition to John Hines was led by the bishop of Mississippi, John Maury Allin. He was not rude, just sarcastic, cutting, and pious. He filled his comments with sacred phrases designed to make his anger acceptable. Clearly this man was eager to gain points as the identified voice of opposition to John Hines. I have no doubt that this was an expression of Jack Allin's own values and his perceptions of reality, but it was also a well-recognized road to power to cast yourself as the leader of the opposition, particularly since John Hines's popularity had dropped considerably. Jack Allin was rewarded for his efforts by being elected by his fellow bishops to the executive council, where he would continue to oppose vigorously the Hines initiatives. I also watched the Hines supporters, people like Roger Blanchard, first of southern Ohio and later part of the Hines staff in New York, Robert DeWitt of Pennsylvania, Ned Cole of central New York, Paul Moore of New York, Tod Hall of New Hampshire, and Kilmer Myers of California. The middle-of-the-road bishops who would not stand anywhere until they saw which way the wind was blowing were also apparent. It was clear to me then whom I admired and whom I did not.

This convention also decided that women could be ordained to the sacred order of deacons, and immediately the debate was launched about women as priests. Again the sides were clearly identified, but I could also see new leaders like John Burt of Ohio, John Krumm of Southern Ohio, and Philip McNairy of Minnesota emerging. The initiative of the late James Pike, bishop of California, who had declared that all women who had been ordained deaconesses were in fact authorized to act as deacons, was now justified. Women would enter the ordained ranks of the church officially after this convention, even if it was only in what the prayer book still called "this inferior office." However, everyone—especially those most deeply opposed— knew that this was a decision that would forever change the life of the church.

When Ecuador did come up as an issue, it created only a minor debate on the nature of the episcopal office. Overseas bishops at this time were still predominantly white Anglo-Saxon appointees who carried with them the accoutrements of power and prestige and who lived the life of princes of the church. One thinks of such people as Heber Gooden in Panama, who was a benevolent colonial despot supported by the American military, economic, and diplomatic personnel in Panama City. There was in the House of Bishops no desire to perpetuate this style of episcopacy in yet another country. This was the argument Brooke Mosley articulated with great eloquence. But the change in consciousness had begun. The brothers Saucedo—Lupe and Melchor—in Mexico were living out another kind of episcopal presence, and the colonial mentality that assumed that bishops had to be white Americans was beginning to die.

When the debate was over, Melchor Saucedo had carried the day with his speech saying, "Look at me. I am a worker bishop," and so the House elected Adrian Caceres, a native of Bolivia and former Roman Catholic, who proclaimed that he saw the role of the bishop of Ecuador to be the primary missionary. I interviewed him after the election and filed my first story with the *Episcopalian.* I rather enjoyed my time as a journalist. I had moved from sports to the House of Bishops in my journalistic career. I wondered if that represented progress.

I returned to Richmond after that convention with a greatly enhanced sense of what this church of ours was like, how it operated, and who the major movers and shakers were. I also knew that my admiration for John Hines was immense. He was quite a man, with vision, courage, and tremendous oratorical gifts. He was a tireless leader with enormous personal integrity. I knew where my loyalties in this church were. John Hines made me intensely proud to be an Episcopalian. Once again, at this convention, I had a brief meeting with this man whom I regarded as larger than life. In that meeting he expressed personally his appreciation for what he called my "national leadership in the South Bend controversy." He also indicated a willingness to be part of our Lenten noonday preaching schedule at St. Paul's on a future occasion. I was delighted at this prospect and was determined to bring it about as soon as possible. That turned out to be in March of 1972 when John Hines made the first of his two Lenten visits to St. Paul's during my rectorship. For five straight days a packed church listened to his spellbinding preaching, and during those five days I had a rare opportunity to talk one-on-one with the person who, in my opinion, was destined to be the greatest and most significant twentieth-century leader in American Christianity.

With the fall season in full swing, I had about six weeks to get the pieces of the Isaiah 58:12 Program together and to meet one-on-one with members of the vestry in what was clearly a lobbying effort. We would be proposing a program that would stretch the vision of our congregation beyond any limits it had ever known, but this program was also tempered by the political realities of conservative Richmond. We were treading a fine line. I was, however, proud of what these plans represented and the potential they possessed and eager to sell it to the leadership of St. Paul's. In the process of presenting this proposal individually over lunch with the members of the vestry, I became aware that this would not be an easy sell. My most reactionary threesome, James Rawls, Catesby B. Jones, and Tommy Bryan, were still around and each was clearly opposed. They had lots of clout and at least one other member of the vestry was a subordinate at the bank where James Rawls was a senior executive. I wondered if he would vote against his superior in a public vote.

I had a crucial luncheon with Eppa Hunton IV. He was an attorney and the fourth-generation direct descendant of the first Eppa Hunton, who had been the cofounder of the law firm of Hunton and Williams, which was at that time and still is the largest and most influential law firm, not just in Richmond, but in the entire state of Virginia. Eppa IV was an ultraconservative, old Richmond kind of person. He was, in my opinion however, a person who could be appealed to under the rubric of "noblesse oblige." He came from that segment of old wealth endowed with a sense that it had a class duty to reach out in a benevolent way to the poor. It was a fascinating luncheon where, under the guise of socializing, tough negotiations were in fact taking place. Eppa's first line of defense was to state that $35,000 a year from the garage income for this outreach program was too much. He picked up the argument that the original plan had been to use the total income to provide maintenance for the whole facility. Maintenance money was never adequate, he observed solemnly. I thought to myself that museums have to be preserved, but not churches. Eppa, I was certain, did not recognize the difference. But by his words, "too much," Eppa had put himself on the line in favor of the program, but at a lesser figure. I immediately locked that position in by stating it. Seeking to be generous, I suggested that his concern could be met if we set aside $20,000 a year for maintenance and allocated the remaining $30,000 for the Isaiah 58:12 Program. This was still not sufficient for Eppa. I felt like Abraham in the familiar Genesis story, negotiating with the divine messenger over the number of righteous people in Sodom. So I tried $25,000.

But when I made that offer I dug my heels in deeply. I needed his support and was convinced that without it the program would fail to achieve a positive vote from the vestry. But I also wanted him to know that if it went under $25,000, it would be insufficient to do anything worthwhile and probably make the whole program just a waste of money. It would be, I said, like a government program that simply threw dollars at problems and never solved anything. I knew that was exactly what Eppa thought of all welfare programs, and it was a shameless attempt on my part to hook into the prejudices of his conservative rhetoric. It worked, however, and Eppa agreed to support the program at $25,000 a year and to divide the garage income at least for the next five years at 50 percent to outreach and 50 percent to maintenance.

I was now confident that I had the votes to win vestry approval. By a nine-to-three majority, the Isaiah 58:12 Program was soon born. It would be at least nine months before the money was available, but that would give us the time to set up the structure, elect the board, advertise the resource, and develop the program.

We now had in place all of the ingredients I believed essential to be an effective church. We had quality worship, buttressed by exquisite music. We had an educational program for all ages that challenged the brains as well as the hearts of our people. With this vote on the Isaiah 58:12 Program we also had a vehicle that would enable us to create a significant outreach program. Twenty-five thousand dollars a year seems unimpressive now, but in the early 1970s that would make a great difference. I prepared to celebrate

Christmas, but a telephone call came the next week that was destined to refocus my emphasis in a way I could not have imagined.

That telephone call had that out-of-the-blue feel about it. Cornelia Newton was a friend with whom I had worked closely in diocesan matters in Southwestern Virginia. She lived with her physician husband, two daughters, and one son in the little mountain town of Pearisburg, Virginia. I had not seen her for over two years and I had always enjoyed her company, but this call was obviously not social. It was from her room in the University Hospital in Charlottesville. She wondered if I could come to Charlottesville. She needed to talk to me, she said.

"What's wrong?" I asked, sensing a rather anxious tone in her voice.

She replied, "I don't want to talk about it on the phone. I will tell you all about it if you are able to come here. I will be here for at least a few more days."

"Of course I'll come," I responded, looking at my calendar. "Is tomorrow afternoon satisfactory, about 2:00?"

That next day at 2:00 I sat down beside her bed and said, "What brings you to the hospital, Cornelia?" She began her story.

A chronic cough that she could not seem to get over was her first symptom. General tiredness was her second. Her physician husband, finding a suspicious spot on a lung in an X ray, had insisted that she enter the University Hospital for a complete medical workup. The results were despairing. The spot on the lung turned out to be metastatic carcinoma that had already spread from the primary lesion. Tests revealed that this was an inoperable malignancy. Chemotherapy might delay death, but it could not prevent it. This lovely woman in her early forties, the mother of three children, one of whom was only twelve, living within a healthy marriage, was looking at death directly in the face. I recovered from the shock and invited her to tell me all about it. For more than two hours we roamed over the terrain of her life. She was, in effect, a condemned woman who was inviting me to enter into the depths of her being where she needed a companion. She had not allowed anyone to enter some of the episodes she shared with me. I was touched and honored that I was the one she trusted to help her do her painful grief work. At home she needed to be strong for her children and even for her husband, but she felt she could be weak and vulnerable with me. It was one of the most honest and difficult human meetings I have ever had with anyone before or since. I could only liken it to entering her very soul. Those hours of intense sharing were incredibly life-giving to me and apparently to Cornelia as well. We talked openly and freely as two human beings can talk only when the masks that protect us are laid aside.

When the time came for me to leave, not knowing quite what to say, I asked if I could pray with her. That was, I am sure, something I felt was a role expectation. She did not object, so holding her hand in mine, I said a prayer. I do not recall the words of that prayer, but I will never forget my feelings about it. It was phony and pious God-talk, made up of one religious cliché after another. I was embarrassed about it when it was over. It added nothing to the depth of our conversation or to the meaning of our relationship. Indeed, if anything, it detracted from both. I thanked her for the time we had shared and promised to visit her at least once a week while she was in Charlottesville.

On the drive home I kept coming back to the contrast between the reality present in the conversation and the lack of reality present in the words of that prayer. The former expanded both of our lives. The latter contracted at least my life and, I suspected, hers as well. If prayer contracted life, I wondered, was it still prayer? If conversation that was deep and genuine expanded life, then was that conversation not a prayer? I wondered if I had my designations all wrong. If I could not pray with honesty then, I asked myself, could I really pray at all? I have never had a more critical conversation with myself, and this issue simply would not go away. I vowed I would never again pray in a pastoral visit until I could pray with as much honesty as I could find in my ability to talk with and to the person I was visiting.

This internal conversation also forced me to confront my own growing faith crisis. John Robinson's probing theological questions just would not go away, and now they had become both personal and existential. I decided that I must figure out what, if anything, I really believed about prayer and that either I would act on that with honesty or stop pretending to be a person of prayer. When I say these words now, they sound rather dramatic, but it was an intensely real vow for me at that time. I began to recognize that what I had been doing in my ordained career was playing the role of the praying pastor, and I was not willing to do that any longer.

In my typical left-brained way I retreated to my library. I must master my inner debates intellectually before I can master them emotionally. I also told Jean LeRoy that I wanted to do some work on prayer for future sermons and asked if she would get me some good theological resources. I would address this issue in the way I had learned to address all other issues—I would walk into it and through it; I would never again seek to ignore the problem or dodge the questions. I also believed honesty required that I process this material publicly. If I could no longer parrot prayer clichés, then I wondered if anyone else in my profession could. Were we all hiding? Was prayer a kind of magic game that people didn't really value, but still would not relinquish? Would people welcome a chance to get out of this box? Would people be willing to let this fantasy called prayer go? Did it have a neurotic hold on them that would be tenacious? Could I show those captured by this fantasy that there was something better? But I knew full well that if people felt that they had no alternative to this magic potion called prayer, then I would be perceived as ripping away from them a piece of their security system. That behavior is always experienced as hostile. Prayer could never be redefined in the midst of hostility.

Where would I do this public study? Since our adult class was already set for the year, I decided that I must do this as a series of sermons at the 11:00 service. That would make it something quite new in my ordained life. I had deliberately tried to keep the 11:00 worship hour traditional and safe and, as such, quite distinct from the adult class. I had chosen to honor this distinction so as not to be insensitive to those who did not desire to raise questions about their faith. Perhaps, I thought, I might be able to organize this series of sermons around something familiar to the people. Then they would be able to hear only what they were capable of hearing. Jesus had talked about prayer, according to the Gospel accounts. His disciples were portrayed as coming to him on one occasion and saying, "Lord, teach us to pray!" He had responded, says the text, with the words of the Lord's Prayer. Perhaps I, following this example, could use the Lord's Prayer to frame my questions and to seek some new answers. This I proposed for Lent 1971.

I kept in touch with Cornelia during this time, once more in Charlottesville and then by phone when she returned to her home. Her health deteriorated rapidly. It never seemed appropriate to share with her the impact of that first visit. That was my problem and my reality. Cornelia had enough on her plate; she did not need my agenda.

I began to read deeply in preparation for this prayer series. I roamed through old classics like *The Imitation of Christ* by Thomas à Kempis, the writings of Brother Lawrence, and those of St. John of the Cross. I also sought out those authors who had achieved a more modern following, even if it was not yet certain that their work would become the classics of our day, people like Charles Whiston and George Buttrick. I was surprised to find how few recognized theologians actually wrote on the subject of prayer. I discovered two authors who finally moved me forward. The first was Louis Everly, a French Roman Catholic with a decidedly modern bent, whose two books, *Our Prayer* and *The Prayer of Modern Man*, were very provocative. The second was my old friend John A. T. Robinson whose brief chapter entitled "Worldly Holiness" in that pivotal book *Honest to God* still captivated me. In doing this study I began, for the first time, to grapple seriously with the theistic limits to the definition of God. I also began to realize that to process these themes as deeply as I felt I needed to would take more than just the six Sundays of Lent, so I began the series by introducing the subject in the three weeks before Ash Wednesday, and I decided that I would call it complete only when I felt that closure had come. The fact is that this subject dominated my preaching and thinking for more than twenty weeks in the late winter, spring, and early summer of 1971. Even I was amazed at the intensity of my commitment to this subject.

The response of the people of St. Paul's to this effort was also deeply gratifying. They had no idea what lay behind this endeavor, but they detected a particular passion and dedication. Perhaps all sermons ought to have those qualities, but some subjects are in fact more personal than others. I suspect the members of St. Paul's were responding to the existential quality revealed in these sermons. We had an unusually large demand for copies. Somehow this series was making contact with people more deeply than other things I had done. I was looking for answers in a very public way, and I was fascinated to discover that so were the majority of our Sunday worshipers. Churchgoers have somehow been taught that it is inappropriate to explore the truth that might lie behind the traditional formulations of faith. I was, in some sense, giving them permission to do so, and they were responding positively.

Several weeks into this series I began to hear people say that these sermons ought to be published as a book. That was a totally new idea to me and, though deeply flattering, it was, in my mind, completely out of touch with reality. I simply smiled appreciatively and accepted these comments for what I thought they were—"front door of the church talk" by those who had a special relationship with the preacher. But this talk persisted. I was touched, but since I did not have the slightest idea about how to pursue a publishing possibility, I made no effort to follow up. I was, however, willing to do what I knew how to do. I would take the whole series and edit it so that it could be read as a single work without the preacher's repetitious throat-clearing efforts that are present in sermons each Sunday. I could accomplish that during my summer vacation. Then I would make this edited version available in the fall in a mimeographed form. I had no plans to do anything beyond that.

The program year closed on that note. I was amazed to realize that the thing that had consumed most of my energy was an activity in response to something that I could never have anticipated. As I engaged the task of thinking theologically, I began to recognize that what people called the basic concepts of Christianity are not as secure as believers hoped. I also discovered that honest theological questions raised by the exigencies of life itself could be addressed, questioned, debated, and explored publicly without disturbing faithful believers. Whom, I wondered, had we been protecting in our fear of raising these questions openly in the church's life before? More and more I began to suspect that we were protecting only ourselves, the insecure ordained ones. This would be a premise I would test again and again, and every test led to the same conclusion.

A call one evening in August from Dr. Maury Claiborne Newton informed me that Cornelia had died. I drove to Pearisburg and met her family, especially her vulnerable and grieving twelve-year-old. I remember standing by Cornelia's open casket and gazing at a young adult whose dark hair had no trace of gray and recalling yet again the depth of our conversation. Cornelia, in her sickness and now in her death, had affected me profoundly. I never had the chance to share with Cornelia what she had meant to me and the rather dramatic role she would play in the unfolding of my life as an author. What I could do I did. I joined with my dear friend and former bishop, Bill Marmion, and together we conducted the burial office. After the funeral I started the long drive home, thankful that I would have about four hours on this journey to process my thoughts and pleased at the prospect of our upcoming vacation. I needed some downtime just to think.

# 12

# *Professional Highs, Personal Lows*

❋

WHEN WE returned from our vacation, I was excited to start the adult class again for two reasons. One was that I had chosen the book of Romans, which would inevitably send me into a vast range of theological topics like the nature of sin and grace, justification, and the second coming. It would be rich material. I had chosen books by C. H. Dodd, Martin Luther, and Rudolf Bultmann to guide my study.

The second reason was that WRFK-FM, the radio station located on the campus of Union Theological Seminary in North Richmond, had decided to broadcast this class live to a listening Richmond audience. This initiative was destined to magnify the impact of this class on the life of this city a thousandfold. Yet the freshness and excitement of these new things did not diminish the continuing conversation about publishing my series on prayer. Usually that kind of talk dissipates rapidly after the event becomes history. I began to realize that something deep had been touched and that I needed to take this talk seriously.

Having no idea how to determine whether a book is publishable, I decided to seek the advice of the one person I knew who understood both books and publishing, Paul Sorel, the manager of the bookstore at my former seminary in Alexandria, Virginia. Paul was a salty old character who had the ability to express himself in simple, direct, and sometimes four-letter words. But Paul knew books and dealt with publishers daily. He also knew how to sell books and which books would sell, which meant that he had the respect of the publishers. I told Paul the story and shared the comments I'd been hearing for about eight months by this time. I mustered the nerve to ask him if he would be willing to read the manuscript and give me his frank opinion. I was relieved that he did not laugh. Paul agreed to take the manuscript and let me know his thoughts. He never did.

Instead, in December of that year I got a letter from the chief editor of Seabury Press in New York, including a signed contract committing Seabury Press to publish this book. I was both stunned and pleased. I signed my part of the contract and posted the letter that same day. I thought I should get it back to them before they changed their minds. I think they offered me a $250 advance. The editor also made some specific suggestions for improving the manuscript and requested that it be rewritten and edited before June 1. I discovered that the kind of work being recommended took a concentrated period of time beyond a couple of hours a day or even one day a week. With the normal activities of a busy parish, the rigors of Lent, and my teaching load, there was no way I could get a week free to do this work before the early summer. I was quite discouraged.

Once more Paul Sorel came to my aid. When I explained this concern to him, he wrote a letter to my vestry announcing the proposed publication of the book and telling them that I needed some uninterrupted time to put the manuscript into publishable condition. The seminary, he said, had agreed to provide a guest room for a week and to give me access both to the library and to any other resources, including faculty advice if desired. I would not even miss a Sunday, so the adult class would not be interrupted. Paul knew exactly which buttons to push in that request. The vestry took up this request at its December meeting and were not just positive, but pleased. We found the best possible time for St. Paul's schedule and I left church after the services on February 6, returning on Friday, February 11.

I settled into my room in Johns Hall by 4:00 that Sunday afternoon and went to my assigned cubicle in the library to organize my work. I came out of the library for an hour for dinner and when it closed that night, but then I worked in my room until well past midnight. Even starting in the late afternoon that Sunday I put in eight hours of work. Monday through Thursday were equally intensive. I worked sixteen hours each day. I learned the fine art of rewriting a manuscript under the direction of the editorial suggestions and the tedious discipline of close, intensive editing. As a public speaker the only punctuation mark I had ever used was a dash. Before that week was over, I had found it necessary to revert to my high-school English grammar class and had diagrammed every sentence in the book. Every subject, verb, adjective, and adverb was clearly in the appropriate place, to say nothing of commas, quotation marks, periods, and semicolons. I made sure that there were no improper verbs, no dangling participles, no split infinitives, and no inappropriate modifiers. Out of that exercise came the simple, but not often consciously embraced, realization that a good book is nothing more than a collection of good sentences organized around a common theme.

I also took paragraphs that were crucial to the development of my thought and worked over them until they had the power required. I do not know that I have ever been as busy and as single-minded as I was for those five days. However, by 5:00 P.M. on Thursday, the work was complete, and I accepted an invitation to join the students in Johns Hall for a happy hour before dinner.

The happy hour occurred in the dormitory common space where daily newspapers and a television set could be found. It was a convivial, relaxed time with the local news from a Washington, D.C., television station in the background. My ear caught a promotion piece on the story that was to come after the next commercial. "An antibusing rally was held last night in Richmond, Virginia, on the steps of the state capitol," said the announcer. "We'll have the details next after this announcement, so stay tuned." Since the state capitol was literally across the street from St. Paul's, I quieted the room to hear this two-minute television feature.

In the following television clip a man named Howard Carwile, an attorney who had been elected to the Richmond city council, was addressing the antibusing rally. The crowd was angry and Carwile was playing on their negative emotions. Howard Carwile was a pulse-feeling politician. When his district had had a strong black minority presence, he had courted black votes. When, however, a recent annexation had been passed that greatly expanded the white, blue-collar constituency of his district, Howard decided that his political future rested on his ability to articulate the racial fears and anger of his white voters. These people found themselves caught between the rising demands of our black citizens for justice and full human rights and the threat to their economic security and sense of racial superiority that expressed itself in their prejudiced behavior.

Howard Carwile was also a showman, almost an evangelist for his causes. He turned phrases and used words in a clever and sometimes outrageous fashion, which only served to make him the darling of the media. The busing controversy of the early 1970s had come about because of a court order by a federal district judge named Robert Mehridge. Judge Mehridge had been appointed to the bench by Richard Nixon upon the joint recommendation of

Virginia's two senators, Harry Byrd, Jr., and William B. Spong, Jr., which hardly qualified him to be thought of as a liberal. But because he had ruled that Richmond's predominantly black schools could not achieve the court-mandated desegregation without a regional program, he ordered that busing be utilized until the predominantly white suburban schools in Chesterfield and Henrico Counties and the predominantly black schools of the city of Richmond achieved regional racial balance. The whites who had fled to the suburbs to escape integration were now confronted with the fact that their escape hatch was being closed down.

The fury of the people was heaped upon Judge Mehridge. His house was under constant guard, and guests invited to his home were frisked. Since the federal judiciary was beyond a referendum on the part of the people, there was in this fury the frustration of powerlessness.

Perhaps it helped this frustration that prior to 1969 the governor of Virginia, a Harry Byrd ally named Mills Godwin, had articulated this white anger and had given strong public voice to the opposition to busing. At least the people felt that their elected officials shared their anger and represented their fears.

However, the course of politics is never smooth, and the internal forces of modernization were tearing apart the traditional alliances. In the Democratic gubernatorial primary of 1969, the sitting lieutenant governor, Henry Howell, a self-proclaimed national liberal, was defeated by William Battle, Jr., a moderate son of a former old-line Byrd governor. The bitterness of that campaign split the party so deeply that Howell refused to support Battle in the general election, opening the door for the election of a moderate Republican named Linwood Holton, from Big Stone Gap, Virginia. His wife was Jinx Rogers, the granddaughter of old Bishop Robert Jett of Southwestern Virginia and sister of Bunny Vaden of Lynchburg. It's a small world.

Holton's first act shocked the public deeply. He enrolled his children in the almost all-black public schools of Richmond. He also refused to use the office of governor to articulate racial hostility against busing. This meant that lesser figures like Howard Carwile now became the voices of violence and opposition, and Linwood Holton increasingly became the political object of their abuse. Those were the realities that came across the television screen that night in the seminary dormitory. I had no realization then that this episode would force my political instincts to find a very public expression. As Carwile wound toward his oratorical climax not fifty yards from the governor's mansion, he was urging that euthanasia be used on the governor.

I was stunned. It was difficult to believe that even Howard Carwile would stoop to calling for the mercy killing of our governor. That kind of hostile political oratory was sufficient incentive to inspire some deranged person to an act of violence that people of every political opinion would surely regret. I consoled myself with the thought that this crude man had so overstepped the bounds of decency that he would be roundly condemned by responsible voices on both sides of the political aisle, as well as by Richmond's business and civic leaders. But returning home on Friday morning, I found nothing but silence, and this widely reported comment simply sat on the corporate life of our city as a kind of public wound, greatly diminishing Richmond's reputation as a decent place to live. Friday evening and all day Saturday passed without comment from any elected or business leader. It had not occurred to me that I should take on Howard Carwile, but silence in the face of this outrage seemed to me to say that it was now acceptable for a politician to call for the mercy killing of an elected official whose policies he opposed. I did not want to live in a place that had degenerated to that level.

In my study that Saturday evening I made the decision that if no one else would speak out against this man, then I must. So I wrote out a statement that I intended to read at the start of my adult class the next day. When it was complete, I put in a call to Staige Blackford, the governor's press officer and a member of St. Paul's. I told him my plans and asked whether the governor would be helped by such a statement. Staige indicated that the governor would welcome it and that, like me, he had wondered why no one in Richmond's business or political establishment seemed willing to call Mr. Carwile to accountability. He suggested that I might have copies of my statement available to hand out lest I be misquoted. He also indicated that he would alert the city and state press corps to the fact that they might want to go to a Bible class at St. Paul's the next day. They were there in force.

I began the class by saying that I wanted to read a prepared statement. That was so unusual that a hushed silence fell upon the room. I recounted the incident at the rally on the steps of the state capitol and expressed the affront I felt to the image of my city that this comment created. I talked about the bounds of propriety in political discourse and excoriated Howard Carwile for his tasteless and provocative remarks, calling his words "the cheap shot of an insensitive politician." I also called the political and business leaders of our city to task for their silence in the face of this insult to our city's image. The statement lasted less than five minutes. It was greeted with a standing ovation. Staige Blackford made the copies I had prepared available to all who wanted them, including the press. Members of the press left en masse. They did not remain for the lecture.

By noon the statement was being reported on every radio station in the Richmond area. It was on the local television news Sunday night and was a front-page story in the *Times Dispatch* on Monday morning. Carwile struck back in a way that indicated that my remarks were on target. He issued a statement dismissing me as a "pusillanimous preacher" and "ecclesiastical lickspittle." "When I look at some spiritually anemic preachers," he added, "I think of embalming fluid." But I had clearly hit a nerve, and thankfully the city rallied to my side. Editorials in the local newspapers and on the radio commended me for standing up to this man. WRVA, Richmond's 50,000-watt major radio station, said, "While many a statesman paused timidly at the threshold of this open door, the Reverend Mr. Spong passed through and illuminated the lamp of reason. . . . It had to be said." A censure resolution was introduced in the city council meeting the next day.

But the vitriol present in the body politic of our city also found public expression. My family began to receive a stream of abusive, threatening phone calls. By this time our daughters were old enough to answer the phone, so they got earfuls of four-letter words and heard their father called a "son of a bitch" and a "bastard" more than once. I reported the abusive calls to the local police, and our house was placed under police surveillance for a significant period of time. Even some weeks after this crisis was over, I was in the driveway of our home at 4:30 in the morning with the motor running ready to take one of my daughters to a bus for a youth trip into the mountains. She was a bit late getting out of the house. In that short time between starting the car and pulling out of our driveway, a police car was behind my car with its red lights flashing and an officer was at my car window demanding identification. It was a reassuring feeling. Even *Time* magazine got into the act in the February 21 issue with a story entitled "Bumpy Road in Richmond." It was my first appearance in this national magazine. It referred to me as the "esteemed rector" and identified me as the cousin of U.S. Senator William B. Spong, Jr.

Linwood Holton also called me on Monday afternoon to thank me. He became a very supportive person and was, in my opinion, a great governor. He was also the last liberal Republican to sit in the governor's chair. The old Byrd Democrats began to abandon their party and take over the Republican party of Virginia. Senator Byrd, Jr., declared himself an Independent. My cousin, Bill Spong, surely must have seen the handwriting on the wall. He called himself a moderate, but a moderate Democrat in Virginia was interpreted as a national liberal. This was not a winning hand at this moment in Virginia politics. That reality would become obvious later that year when Bill sought reelection for a second term in the U.S. Senate. It also set me on a path to being a more outspoken and public person. There were both pluses and minuses in that role, but it was something that I decided was unavoidable. If one accepts the vocation of leadership, then one is not free to avoid the painful issues. Honesty and integrity were more important to me than either popularity or tranquillity.

It was a rather dramatic way to return from that one-week absence from my parish. The time demands of the Carwile episode took most of that next week. The volume of my mail increased some 200 percent. It was now Lent, and the time for additional work on the manuscript was almost nonexistent. However, before Easter I gave copies of the manuscript to four gifted editors—Jean LeRoy, Lucy Boswell Negus, soon to be in our church's employ, Cyane Hoar Lowden, a gifted young woman with aspirations to be a poet, and Carter McDowell, a close personal friend and a new member of our church. Jean edited for content, Cyane for style, Carter for readability, and Lucy for all of the above. Lucy had a wonderful way with language. She rearranged my words so that the sentences had power, but they never ceased to be my words. After Easter, when I received each of their comments in writing, I retreated into my study to go over their recommendations simultaneously page by page. My trust in their abilities was not misplaced.

Finally, about June 1, the manuscript was mailed to Seabury Press bearing the title *Saying Our Father in a Religionless World*. I was told that I would not receive the copyedited version until early September and the book was scheduled for an April 1973 publication. I was also informed that my title was too long and too wordy. It would be the first of my titles, but not the last, to be rejected by the publisher. The people at Seabury Press proposed the title *Honest Prayer*. I did not object. The word "honest" lined my book up with the thought of John A. T. Robinson's *Honest to God*. John Robinson was, in fact, the grandfather of this book, and the word "honest" as a qualifier to the word "prayer" raised interesting and disturbing questions.

With the book in the mail, I turned my attention to our vacation, for which we returned to the Outer Banks of North Carolina, where we hoped to have two blissful weeks. Our daughters were now sixteen, thirteen, and eleven and, fortunately for us, they still enjoyed being together. Even Joan seemed at peace. I was excited by all the things happening to me and encouraged about Joan. It was a good holiday.

When we had four days of beach time left, I received an urgent message through the local grocery store at Nag's Head to call my editor at Seabury Press in New York as soon as possible. Our beach cottage had no phone, so I rushed to the local pay phone. The words I heard contained both good news and bad.

The good news was that my book was going to be designated the "Seabury Book for Lent 1973"! Joel Pugh, whose book was to have held this slot, had informed Seabury that he would not be able to meet its deadlines. I found it hard to believe what I was hearing. To be named the "Seabury Book for Lent" meant that my book would receive massive advertising in the church press and would be recommended by the church's own publishing house to all Episcopalians for their Lenten reading. With this designation, the initial press run would be raised from 3,000 to 7,500 copies. For a first-time religion author that was a very large and affirming commitment. I was excited beyond measure, for this also meant that the editorial staff at Seabury believed the book was quite good. I couldn't wait to rush back to tell Joan and the girls this news. But there was more.

The bad news was that if *Honest Prayer* was to be the Seabury Book for Lent, then its publication date had to be shifted from April to January 1, which meant that I needed to return home at once if I was going to meet the new deadline. My editor informed me that the copyedited version of the manuscript would arrive in Richmond by special delivery the next day and I needed to have it back to New York with all corrections in place within five days or lose the Lenten slot. I hung up and rushed to our cottage still excited, but feeling troubled at what this would do to our vacation and the sacrifice I would be asking my family to make.

Their response was wonderful, and we agreed to enjoy the rest of the day, have a nice dinner, go out to the carnival rides and climb the sand dunes after dinner, and then leave early the next morning. "Maybe it will rain the last three days," Jaquelin said. Katharine suggested that at least we "would not run the risk of being stung by jellyfish." It was raining when we pulled away early the next morning. This was the only time I ever gave thanks for bad weather at the beach! I worked hard on the copyedited version and met the deadline. Everything was now go. In time I got the "galleys" and the "blues." Each stage was a new first and thus for me a special joy. Finally, in December a package arrived with two copies of the final product. I opened it alone in my office and sat there for several minutes just fondling the book. I took in its maroon cover, yellow lettering, and white author's name. My first impression was that it was so small. It printed up to just over a hundred pages and that was accomplished with a generous use of white space and blank pages. In my fantasy, surrounded by so many pages of notes and print, I had imagined it to be as large as the *Encyclopaedia Britannica*. I will never forgive one reviewer who referred to it as "a booklet." Sheepishly I showed it to the members of my staff, and then that night to my family. Yes, I am sure I had delusions of grandeur and hints of immortality. A first book is an unrepeatable experience.

The Seabury Book for Lent was advertised widely in the church press and received favorable early reviews. Within six months it was in a second printing and in the course of its life it sold just under 10,000 copies. That does not strike me as a lot today, but it was a sufficient number to establish me as a successful author and that is the door-opener to getting future books published.

Indeed, the book was popular enough that before Easter I received by mail an unsolicited signed contract from Seabury Press to publish my next book. It was a book for which not only no manuscript existed, but also for which there were no ideas, no concepts, and no titles. Seabury wanted this second book to come out in fall 1974. After thinking about it for a while, I decided to take the material from my adult confirmation classes and shape it into a manuscript. I had always used adult confirmation classes not for indoctrination into an Episcopal ethos, but for wrestling with the substantial theological issues of our faith story. Those lectures focused on Jesus, seeking to find the power of the Jesus figure that caused Paul, among others, to say "God was in Christ." It would also be my first venture into seeking to place Jesus into the context of his Jewish background. My working title was *Jesus for the Non-Religious*. It would be the second book title rejected by my publisher.

If I had had eyes to see, I would have recognized that the three strands of my life defining my very being were now in place. In my adult class I was probing the biblical story deeply and beyond the traditional boundaries of interpretation. In my public life I was embracing issues, taking the flak of public debate, and daring to inject the values of my faith system into the secular and cultural arena. Now my writing career offered the potential of carrying my message beyond the orbit of those who knew me, where my books would be embraced, attacked, and debated. When these three elements are put together, a controversial life is probably inevitable.

When I was able to turn my primary attention back to my congregation, my focus was on our first recommendation of the Isaiah 58:12 Program. Inspired by the announcement of the availability of the Isaiah 58:12 money for grants aimed at addressing the needs of Richmond's poor and minority communities, Dr. Marigail Wynne, an internist completing her residency at the Medical College of Virginia, worked with community leaders to put together a proposal to open a full-time medical clinic in the area of Richmond known as "Fulton Bottom." This was the community that nestled quite literally underneath Church Hill, that part of old Richmond in which Patrick Henry had delivered his famous "Give me liberty or give me death" speech. Fulton Bottom, a minority and poverty community in Richmond, had not had a resident physician to serve its needs in thirteen years. Those who required medical attention had to go to the emergency room of the Medical College of Virginia. A visit there usually took a full day, posing a hardship for, among others, working parents. This meant that the citizens of this area literally sought medical care only when the situation had become critical; a pregnant woman in Fulton Bottom would, typically, seek medical care only when labor commenced.

A locally situated medical clinic with a doctor who might actually get to know the citizens of that community was a revolutionary idea. Dr. Wynne's proposal was also heavily weighted toward preventive measures and community health education and offered a significant opportunity for volunteers, perhaps from St. Paul's. This community needed education in basic nutrition, family planning, parenting skills, and literally thousands of other areas that people in St. Paul's had the ability to offer. The major initial funding for the project came from Isaiah funds, but it was a community-based effort. Its board of directors contained two members of St. Paul's, but was weighted toward Fulton community leaders. Other funding came from Richmond Community Action funds and local foundations. The clinic, open from 9:00 A.M. to 4:00 P.M. Monday through Friday, was staffed by a doctor, a nurse, and a rotating pharmacist. If this project worked, the Medical College of Virginia would become the referral center and not the primary care facility.

By the time vestry approval was sought, it was a foregone conclusion that this would be our first project, and we actually planned the dedication before the vestry vote. Governor Holton agreed to speak on this occasion, which guaranteed wide media coverage. That was important to me because it was essential to create pride in our outreach ministry and to make it part of a congregation's self-identity. We were clearly building on a new foundation.

That year was also one of heightened political activity everywhere. Richard Nixon was preparing to run for reelection against a badly fractured national Democratic party. At the same time Bill Spong's first six-year term was drawing to a close. Politics had changed dramatically since his victory in 1966. The Republican party had emerged as the new home for the conservative Old Virginia Democrats. The national Democratic party had been torn asunder by the Vietnam war, urban riots, and racial violence. The assassinations of Martin Luther King, Jr., and Robert Kennedy in 1968 had precipitated violent swings in political allegiances. Hubert Humphrey had been defeated by Nixon in 1968 primarily because he never could bring together the old-line Democrats with the followers of Eugene McCarthy and Bobby Kennedy. George McGovern, described by a labor union official as "a Methodist preacher who has never sweated," became in 1968 the Kennedy stand-in and, using the changed rules of the party, was destined to win the nomination outright in the summer of 1972. His campaign would prove to be a disaster. His acceptance speech was delivered in the wee hours of the morning when most Americans were asleep, because the undisciplined and raucous delegates tied up the convention with various demonstrations. The person chosen by McGovern for vice president, Senator Thomas Eagleton of Missouri, was forced to resign shortly after the convention adjourned when it was revealed that he had received electroshock therapy for a mental illness. After an embarrassingly long time of backing and filling, Senator McGovern named Sargent Shriver, a Kennedy in-law, to the ticket. It was, however, already too late. Even the first hints of what came to be called the Watergate scandal were not sufficient to resurrect to the status of viable contender the McGovern-Shriver ticket.

Virginia did not escape this fallout. Early in 1972 the Virginia Republican party practically conceded the Senate seat to the incumbent, Bill Spong. A realignment of congressional districts based on the last census meant that two Republican congressmen were placed into the same district. The most lackluster and ineffective of the two was William Scott. A compromise was worked out in which Representative Scott withdrew to avoid jeopardizing Republican control of that seat. As his reward William Scott was given the Republican senatorial nomination. It was an honor that most people assumed to be empty. But when the televised proceedings of the Democratic convention revealed the chaos of one pressure group after another vying for control of the party that climaxed in the nomination of George McGovern, there was a profound shift in the American electorate. That shift would prove to be a disastrous turn of events for local Democratic office holders around the country, and Bill Spong was one of them.

Bill distanced himself as far as possible from the national party. He tried to establish himself as an independent Democrat or even as a "Virginia Democrat." From listening to his speeches one had the sense that his opponent was named Charles de Gaulle. But suddenly this Senate seat was a horse race. Republicans who had written off this race earlier now began to sense that it was winnable.

Less than a month before the election, new money and national campaign expertise were poured into the Scott effort. Hard-hitting personal attacks, playing on the deep racial fears of this region, were launched against Bill, who was portrayed as an ultraliberal. Compared with William Scott, that was true, though from my perspective he seemed quite conservative. Scott never mentioned Bill's name except in connection with George McGovern. It was the McGovern–Spong party against which he ran. About a week before the election, Scott for the first time edged ahead in the polls. A big election-eve rally was planned for Richmond with Vice President Spiro Agnew coming to town to give Scott the final boost. It was an effective tactic for the public to see Agnew and Nixon embrace Scott while castigating the liberal "McGovern supporting" Senator Spong.

When the votes were counted, Nixon had carried Virginia by a 70–30 split in the vote. Bill had lost his Senate seat to Representative William Scott by a 51–49 percent margin. Virginia would now be represented in the Senate by a man that the Washington press corps, during his term as a senator, would vote "the dumbest man in the U.S. Congress." He was also so ineffective that Republicans and Democrats alike assumed that he would be a one-term senator, which indeed he was.

I was devastated by this defeat and felt a deep sense of personal rejection. I also determined that, as the only Spong remaining in public life in this state, I would cast aside whatever restraint I had exercised out of deference to Bill's political career. I was ready to be quite public.

Shortly after that election I was given an opportunity to serve my city in a political appointment. A call from the vice mayor, Henry Marsh, inquired if I would be willing to serve a term on the Richmond Human Relations Commission. This appointment was of sufficient importance that Henry Marsh and city councilman William V. Daniel came to my office to tell me about the responsibilities. They did not, however, tell me much about the background of this commission.

A black leader named JeRoyd Green was not to be reappointed. He was seen as having been too aggressive. Neither did they tell me that the way this commission was chosen was that each of the nine members of the city council had one appointment to the thirteen-member commission and the other four were chosen by majority vote of the council. The white majority on the city council was five to four, so they saw to it that the Human Relations Commission always had at least a seven-to-six white majority. The effective leader of the commission was a white attorney named John P. Ackerly III. He was aggressive and conservative. His role, it seemed to me, was to render the commission ineffective. He did this by his mastery of parliamentary procedure and by forcing the commission to deal with issues that he would shape. JeRoyd Green had challenged him significantly, so he had been removed. None of the other black commissioners had JeRoyd Green's particular skills. Among the newly appointed commissioners were a black assistant high-school principal, a black labor organizer, a rising black female political leader, the white chairman and CEO of the James River Paper Company, and the white rector of St. Paul's Church.

This commission offered me a public forum in the secular arena. In the four years I served, the commission dealt with discrimination against minorities, women, and gays and lesbians. My sense was that 85 percent of the complaints we investigated were racial, 10 to 12 percent had to do with women, and the gay/lesbian issues were almost nonexistent. Very quickly I emerged as the principal challenge to Jack Ackerly's leadership. I mastered *Robert's Rules of Order* and took him on in parliamentary procedures. I also discovered that if I voted with the black minority, they became the majority. Over the years we forced the commission into a high profile by being proactive. Prior to an election, we would do such things as call on the candidates publicly to avoid race-baiting politics and announce our intention to monitor the rhetoric of the campaign. We also discovered that neither of Virginia's two senators, by now Senator Harry Byrd, Jr., and Senator William Scott, nor any of Virginia's entire congressional delegation had a single black employee on their staffs. That seems incredible today, but in the early 1970s such discrimination was typical. We even gained access to a memo from Senator Scott in which he instructed those hiring for him to consider "whites only." By making that memo public we gained credibility, at least in the black community, for being something other than window dressing. We also incurred the hostility of many members in the white community, articulated with regularity by John P. Ackerly III.

My final coup d'état on that commission was when I assisted in the election of James (Duke) Stewart to be the first black chair to serve that commission. Duke was a massive man, with genuine, though not well-trained, intelligence, who had come up through the ranks of his union and the local chapter of the NAACP. When I discovered that he wanted to be the chair, I promised to help. The nominating committee appointed by the white chair proposed a slate that would have continued the same officers for another year. When further nominations were called for, I immediately nominated Duke to run against the incumbent. At that meeting we had both a gallery and representatives of the press. They helped to keep the deliberations civil. The chair allowed discussion, so I spoke about the fact that this commission had never had a black majority, even though the city of Richmond did, and that it had never had a black chair, which I regarded as inexcusable. Jack Ackerly spoke about the need for experience and suggested that the chairman had done such a good job that he had earned reelection. But Jack could count and he knew he was defeated. Duke received seven votes, six black votes and mine. The incumbent had six votes. A new day had come to the Richmond Human Relations Commission. Duke appointed me his unofficial parliamentarian, and he served with distinction.

Throughout that fall of 1972, as Bill's defeat became first a possibility and then a probability, I had been edging deeper into more politically aggressive activities, the chief of which was to give my full support to the second Isaiah 58:12 Program proposal that was at that time winding its way through St. Paul's decision-making processes. It would, however, not come to a final vote and thus to public notice until late November, when the Senate election would have been long over. This project had to do with funding an educational campaign to bring about open housing in the city of Richmond, a highly controversial issue in the 1970s. People could hide their deepest prejudices even from themselves in most areas of life, but when their neighborhoods faced integration, all of their fears fed real economic consequences and brought out the very worst in them. Yet it was so clear that so long as we remained segregated in our neighborhoods, progress would never be made toward building a just society. It was also obvious that housing segregation was a matter of both economics and racial prejudice and that one would never be solved without the other. We had as a Southern society faced the integration of our public schools. Now it was time to face the housing issue.

Operating in our city of Richmond was an organization calling itself Housing Opportunities Made Equal (H.O.M.E.). It was the brainchild of a

DuPont scientist named Dr. James Hecht, who was one of the most unusual and gifted human beings I have ever known. He and his family entered my life in a memorable and unusual way.

Some two years earlier, in August 1970, Jim Hecht, his wife, Amy, and their two children, Charlie and Margaret, moved to Richmond. Not long after their arrival, they visited St. Paul's and filled out a visitor's card. When I read this particular card, which indicated that a family of four had worshiped with us and that they had recently arrived in Richmond from Buffalo, I called the telephone number and soon found myself speaking with Amy Hecht. I told her I would like to drop by to welcome them, introduce myself, and to talk to them about St. Paul's. She seemed receptive and so I asked, "How about tonight around 7:30?" After being greeted warmly, I began to ask the gently probing questions necessary for getting to know strangers, like what he did at DuPont, why they had come to Richmond, and when they had actually moved from Buffalo. It was this last question that opened the floodgates on a remarkable story.

The Hecht family finished school and work in Buffalo at the end of May that year. They were not due to move to Richmond, where Jim had been transferred, until August. They had accumulated vacation time, which they planned to use on a great family vacation trip across the United States. Their plan was to put their house into the hands of a real estate agent, depart for this extended trip, and return to Buffalo the day before the movers arrived to oversee the move itself. But they, in fact, had told one and all of their Buffalo friends good-bye and did not expect to see any of them, not even during that one day of moving. They had already bought a home in Richmond, which was ready to receive them and their furniture when their home in Buffalo sold. The vacation trip included most of the natural beauty spots of the American West. The children were ecstatic with anticipation.

One stop on this grand tour was to be at Yellowstone National Park in the Grand Tetons of Wyoming. This family arrived at Yellowstone on the planned day with their three children—Charlie, Margaret, and Andy—in tow. But before they left this national park, Andy, their eight-year-old boy, had fallen into the open thermal pools and been scalded to death before their eyes. They could not even retrieve the body. Park officials came and told them that they would be able to recover the body, but it would take time. The shock and grief were numbing. They had no community of family or friends near them with whom to share their desperate pain and bereavement. They had left Buffalo; they could not return there. They had never lived in

Richmond and knew no one yet in this city. They had driven into Yellow-stone Park as a family of five and hours later driven out a traumatized family of four. There was no closure. Consulting one another in the midst of their grieving agony, they made the decision to continue their trip simply because they had nowhere else to go and would, at least, be visiting some members of their family before their journey was over. They needed that family contact now more than anything else. It was probably the darkest part of life each of these four people would ever know.

In early August they arrived in Richmond, where everyone they met assumed they were a family of four. It is hard to walk up to someone you are just meeting and say, "We just lost our son," so opportunities to talk about their grief had been very few. They had lived in Richmond for about three months bearing this incredible burden before they happened upon St. Paul's Church. When I opened the subject of their move, it enabled them to share their story with a person outside their family. In Buffalo they had been members of the Unitarian Church. It met the social and politically active sides of their lives, but now, in the face of this experience, they began to look for something that might sustain and heal their aching and broken hearts. Because they had known quite favorably Larry Scaiffe, the Episcopal bishop of Western New York, they decided to try an Episcopal church. St. Paul's had been their choice. That is how our lives first touched. That evening visit was one of the most moving events of my life. I did not leave their home before 11:00 P.M. I simply listened and grieved with them.

I saw the Hechts frequently over the next few weeks. It was a many-sided family. Amy was an educator and a nurse. Jim had been very active in the cause of open housing in Buffalo and had even written a book entitled *Because It Is Right*, published by Little-Brown, about the struggle that he and others, including Bishop Scaiffe and his coadjutor, Bishop Harold Robinson, had led to secure nondiscriminatory housing in the city of Buffalo. He was a passionate, articulate, brilliant man, deeply committed to living a life that would right the wrongs of society. He dealt with internal pain by external action. Andy's death had thus brought the cause of park safety into focus for him, and he would be instrumental in shaping public safety in all of the national parks of America through his work. That would be his ultimate tribute to his son. But at the moment it was hurt, grief, and an aching sense of loss that all but consumed this unique family.

It is hard to bring closure to the grief experience until there is a proper rite of passage, if you will. That is part of what a funeral service does for grieving people, but it is hard to have a funeral service until one has the body of the deceased to lay to rest. It was in the late spring of that year that the Hechts learned that Andy's bones had finally been recovered and the cremated remains would be sent to them soon. Together we planned a funeral, and on June 27, 1971, we interred Andy's ashes in the garden of St. Paul's Church after the 11:00 service. Many members of St. Paul's gathered with this family they barely knew to share in the grief. Each of the remaining members of the Hecht family took part in that service. It was a powerful bonding experience, and all of the Hechts were subsequently confirmed.

By the next fall the Hechts were actively involved in St. Paul's, and Jim's passion for justice and his incredible energy connected in a remarkable way with the commitment of St. Paul's to spend its outreach money on projects that would speak to poverty and racism in our community. It also led to what was for me the most crushing defeat I would suffer in Richmond. But that defeat would enable me to learn the great lesson that losing a battle in the cause of justice is never a loss, for out of the ashes of defeat the shoots of a greater victory are always springing up. The most important issue in life is not winning; it is being faithful to your core values. Remaining true to what you believe is right in the face of defeat is the only essential for God's service. To recognize that God shares in eternity makes one aware that being faithful publicly and consistently is the only way that both the future and eternity will reflect God's will.

Jim decided that he would try to do in Richmond what he had accomplished in Buffalo in the area of open housing. But he also recognized that times had changed and that he might now accomplish through education and goodwill in Richmond what confrontation and legal threats had secured in Buffalo. Segregated housing was actually illegal, but that did not stop real estate agents from "steering" black couples to "black" or "integrated" areas and refusing to show black couples homes in white sections even in the price range they were capable of paying. In Buffalo when a black couple dealt with an agent, white volunteers from H.O.M.E. would set up a session with the same agent. If discrepancies appeared in the houses shown or the neighborhoods visited, then a lawsuit was instituted. It did not take many such court cases to sensitize the Buffalo real estate industry, and progress was made.

What a witness it would be if community forces led by church and public officials would bring about through education and goodwill the removal of all barriers to open housing in the capital of the old Confederacy. That would bring Richmond enormous positive recognition. By 1972 Jim had begun the process of putting together both a coalition of Richmond's most prominent citizens and the details for a massive educational campaign to establish Richmond as an open-housing city. Engaging the help of the media, his coalition would appeal to the Isaiah 58:12 Program for funds to launch the citywide education campaign the next year.

In October the proposal won the endorsement of the Isaiah board. It was not unanimous, but it was a strong majority. It should have come to the vestry in November, but sensing a close vote in the vestry, I postponed the issue until the December meeting so that Jim and I could talk face-to-face with wavering vestry people.

Jim had done an impressive job. He had lined up the public support of economic leaders and had won the endorsement of Governor Linwood Holton. But as the day for the vote drew closer, vestry people were lobbied by more than Jim and me.

The day of the vote was December 11, 1972. Perhaps I hoped the spirit of Christmas, which was just beginning to dominate the consciousness of the city, might weave its magic spell over my all-white, all-male, deeply conservative Southern vestry. The debate lasted for two hours. It was well presented. The senior warden, Henry St. George Tucker, Jr., endorsed it warmly. My usual naysayers, Catesby Jones, James Rawls, and Tommy Bryan, opposed it. Their primary argument was that this was a political and economic issue, not a religious issue; second, they appealed to a favorite religious argument, namely, that it would divide the church, upset the people, and cause them to cut off their pledges. No matter how many times these threadbare arguments had been shown to be lacking both in power and integrity, they continued to be trotted out to give ignorance and bigotry the cover of respectability.

The uncommitted members of the vestry were in a difficult spot. They had to make a stand. My nose count before the meeting began was five to five with two still neutral. Under the canons of the Episcopal Church, the rector has a vote only in case of a tie. So since I was quite prepared to vote for this project, we had to win only one of the two neutral members. In the debate one of those two identified himself as a no vote, so it all came down to one man. I had great hopes that he would rise to this moment of history.

There was a request for this to be a roll-call vote—another pressure tactic. Those who voted positively would be subjected to whatever social retaliation could be mustered. That may have been the tactic that tipped the vote. My last remaining hope on the vestry joined the six negative voters to defeat the proposal by a margin of seven to five. It was the first and, to my knowledge, the only time the vestry vetoed the recommendation of the Isaiah 58:12 board. It quite divided the church, but in a way that conservatives had never anticipated. Conservatives tend to talk only to each other and to suspect that anyone who disagrees with them is either mentally unbalanced, immature, or under the influence of some un-American political philosophy. However, it was hard to dismiss people like Buford Scott, Henry St. George Tucker, or even the Republican governor of Virginia, who supported this initiative. They represented a solid part of Richmond's establishment and on this issue they were willing to stand up to be counted. That reality would ripple through our community in fascinating ways.

I was deeply, even bitterly, disappointed by the vote. In that state one is vulnerable to saying and doing things later regretted. So I said the benediction, closed the vestry meeting, and retired to my office to sit alone with my thoughts. Catesby Jones would later say in print that I pitched a temper tantrum and pouted. I often wondered how I could have done both at once. My primary feeling at the end of the day was a great sense of loss that a dream with such potential was not supported. Beyond that, I actually had a strange feeling of pride that this was the only church in Richmond that would have had the courage to take on such an issue and the only one that could have come this close to succeeding. Perhaps that is hollow consolation, but it was consolation nonetheless to me.

In retrospect, however, it became obvious that this vote was not a defeat at all. Indeed, when I referred to this episode as "my greatest failure in Richmond," Dr. Hecht corrected me by asserting that "in the end your fair-housing efforts were an enormous success." That was nothing, I was certain, but "Jim Hecht's pastoral care." Yet out of the ashes of that defeat great energy did come together to address the housing issue. Because of the defeat of the Isaiah 58:12 Program proposal, Jim decided to accept the presidency of the Richmond H.O.M.E. organization. To that task he devoted both his enormous energy and his rare competence. The positive resources that had been identified in the St. Paul's debate were brought into this fight. Richmond's largest and most creative advertising agency, which had been willing to develop the educational campaign pro bono if St. Paul's vestry had approved the program, now signed on to do the same for H.O.M.E., producing in time a widely used television spot that ridiculed discrimination.

Buford Scott publicly endorsed the H.O.M.E. agenda, signed many of the advertisements, and agreed to serve on its board. By the power of his

wealth and social standing these acts on his part made open housing politically and socially acceptable in conservative Richmond, and his example was
followed by others. Three members of the Richmond city council, including
Mayor Thomas J. Bliley (now a long-standing Republican congressman
from the Richmond Henrico district), Wayland W. Rennie, and Henry L.
Valentine II, all publicly supported H.O.M.E. Teaming with two black
members of the council, Vice Mayor Henry Marsh and Willie Dell, a bright,
articulate female leader, gave H.O.M.E. a majority vote on the city council,
a vote necessary to get government funding. This meant that between 1973
and 1977, by which time both Jim and I had moved from Richmond, the
budget of H.O.M.E. grew from $1,000 to $100,000, far more than the grant
from St. Paul's could have achieved. It would not be long before that budget
would grow beyond $1 million a year. A representative of the Richmond
Realtors, a group that had initially and vigorously opposed H.O.M.E.,
donated a house to be used as H.O.M.E.'s headquarters. Its office is still in
that house to this day. I like to think that the losing fight engaged by the
vestry of St. Paul's moved this issue forward, but, in my opinion, none of
this would have happened without the dedication of Jim Hecht. In a real
sense open housing in Richmond is a memorial to Andy Hecht and St. Paul's
role was to do what churches have always done—"bind up the broken-
hearted and make the streets safe places in which to play."

After the publication of *Honest Prayer* and even the arrival of the first
hints of spring in 1973, I was forced to recognize that my wife continued to
be a deeply troubled person. She had become more and more reclusive. I
found myself increasingly going to social events alone. She went to bed earlier and earlier and made it very clear that she did not want to be disturbed
by lights, the radio, or by me when I did come to bed. By this time Ellen
was dating and the other girls had very active social lives, so I would wait
up for them. The late-night talk shows, such as Johnny Carson's *Tonight
Show*, became regular features of my life during those waits. I finally
moved my bedroom to my study over the garage, where I had my desk,
books, writing equipment, and a sleeping cot. It was not ideal, but it
offered a place where I could wait up for the girls and read without disturbing Joan. When I put a portable television set in that room, it symbolized that I had moved to a new place. My professional life was so fulfilling
that I simply pursued it with such vigor that it met my emotional needs as
well. Joan was always sweet, but appeared to be consumed with something
I could not quite reach.

My anxiety about her began to be focused when some of the content of her mind finally became visible. We had agreed to go out to dinner at the home of Carter and Charles McDowell. Carter, one of my book editors, and Charles, a brilliant hand surgeon, were probably our closest social friends, or at least my closest social friends. This particular evening was rather informal; only three couples were present. The conversation was relaxed. I do not recall what we talked about, but the evening flowed in a very pleasant, low-keyed kind of way.

Shortly after 10:00 P.M. we left to go home. On our way Joan startled me by saying, "Did you know they taped our conversation tonight?"

"What?" I asked incredulously.

"They taped our conversation tonight," she repeated. "I wonder what they plan to do with the tapes."

Trying to take in this strange claim, I quickly thought over the conversation of the evening. I could not imagine why anything said that evening would have been of any interest or value to anyone if it *had* been taped. So I suggested that Joan had been watching too many spy thrillers on television. I put this conversation out of my mind, and the subject did not come up again until about two weeks later when I called home. Joan seemed particularly short. She answered my queries with a one-syllable yes or no. I asked her when I got home if she were feeling well.

"Yes," she said, "but you need to know that someone has tapped our telephone line." This time I suppressed my immediate desire to debunk these remarks and decided that I needed to listen closely to what she was saying. I inquired about the reason for her suspicion. She explained that she believed we were targets of a conservative group seeking to discredit me for my liberal stands. After listening to her full explanation, I tried to assure her that, in my opinion, her imagination was working overtime. When we finally changed the subject, I was left very disturbed at how consistent this comment was with her fear that her social conversations were being taped. I was trained enough to know that these were dangerous symptoms of very serious mental problems. Since Joan was unwilling to see a doctor, I really did not know what to do except to wait and wonder.

The wait did not last long. On a beautiful day in the early spring, I drove home from the office at about 5:00 P.M. to be greeted by a strange set of circumstances. I entered through the kitchen door from the garage and confronted a startling picture. Masking tape covered the chrome trim on the stove and refrigerator and a sign in Joan's handwriting was taped to the top of the stove. It read, "Danger—Leaking electricity." I walked through to the breakfast room to find all the electric outlets taped over with masking tape and almost every towel we owned employed to cover the radiators throughout the house. My first response was to assume that we had experienced some calamity in our home.

"What in the world is going on?" I inquired. Joan was very calm. It was as if she was very much on top of her world at last.

"Jack," she said, "our house has been under surveillance for some time. The Central Intelligence Agency and the Federal Bureau of Investigation have placed cameras into our electrical system that operate through our radiators. They have tapped our phone. Photographs from our home have begun to appear regularly in the newspaper." She had several papers in her hand to demonstrate this obvious truth. One had a picture of swans swimming in a nearby lake as a sign of spring. We had a ceramic swan on display in a cabinet in the living room. The other photographs were equally close to her claimed reality. It was more than I could absorb. I did not know what to say. It would have been easy to allow my feeling of threat to be expressed as anger, but that would have been totally ineffective.

Joan sensed my unease and responded that she knew it was hard for me to understand these things, but now that she understood them, she was able to take defensive measures. In her mind she was now engaged in an almost cosmic struggle against these alien forces invading our privacy. From her perspective, she was acting as my protector. Conservative forces, which she identified as working through our friends in Richmond, including those who were leaders of our church, were trying to mute the liberal voices of our society. In her mind I was clearly high on their list of targets. She had been fortunate enough to discover this and had acted to defend me.

When I could think rationally again, I recognized that, even in these delusions, her love for me came through. She was acting in my defense. However, that was not my first response. Our daughters were present for this conversation, and they listened silently in wide-eyed amazement.

After absorbing all that she had to say, I said, "Joan, please listen. What you are saying is not so. If you think it is real, that means that you are not able to separate reality from fantasy. That is a classic symptom of a serious mental illness. We need to consult a doctor at once." She listened without response.

I first called her psychiatrist in Lynchburg. I had not talked with him before, since Joan wanted her conversations with him to be private. I had respected that, but now I needed to make decisions and I needed to have accurate data.

Reaching him, I identified myself as Joan Spong's husband. He remembered his patient. I described the things that were going on now. He checked his files and his notes. "What you are describing is paranoid, perhaps schizophrenic, behavior. I find no suggestion of that in my notes. We dealt primarily with depression and with trying to explore sources of low self-esteem that appeared to be rooted deeply in her childhood. I will be glad to see her again, but you might find it more convenient to talk with someone locally. With the Medical College of Virginia in Richmond, there are some outstanding resources present in your community." He would be willing, he concluded, to consult with anyone we chose to share his knowledge and background material.

The conversation gave me time to think and to calm down. I returned to Joan and told her of this conversation and of his suggestion that we consult a local psychiatrist immediately. She did not seem to object. It was my first glimmer of hope.

Finding the right psychiatrist was my first task. I did not know any at that moment, but I had many friends in the medical community who did. None of my suggestions met with a positive response. It was obvious that consulting with Joan was leading nowhere, and that I would have to find the doctor without her help.

It was dinnertime by now, and we settled into the task of preparing to feed the children. I had no idea what was going through our daughters' minds but, if it was upsetting for me, I knew they must be experiencing similar feelings. I suspect their mother's behavior had been confusing to them for some time. Perhaps what happened that day clarified former experiences that they had not been able to understand.

After they were settled, I got into the car and went to visit Charles McDowell at his home. I told him what had transpired and asked him for help in getting a good psychiatrist. He was wonderful. He made a call that night, and an appointment was set for the next day. At the appointed time, we were in the psychiatrist's office. Joan was cooperative. She told her story. I sat almost speechless as the story poured out in more detail than I had imagined. The doctor responded to this tale of spying and persecution by saying that psychiatry was not an exact science and that he would need to see her for about six weeks before he could make a proper diagnosis and thus suggest a proper therapy. He would like for her to get a prescription filled that would simply lower her stress and anxiety so they could explore her situation in a bit calmer atmosphere. He did state that she was manifesting behaviors that pointed to a significant pathology, but he held out hope that it could be dealt with medically. It was the most encouraging word I had heard all day.

Returning home, we talked and I felt a great sadness when I realized the burdens Joan was carrying. Whether those burdens were objective or subjective, they were real to her and somehow I had not been sensitive to that for years. I tried to talk with our girls, but found that they did not wish to talk about these things. Denial, or at least ignoring this topic, seemed the easier path for them.

The six weeks of doctor's appointments seemed to go slowly. I tried to make the life in our household as normal as possible. When the towels and the masking tape were taken away from the radiators and electrical outlets, they inevitably reappeared in a day or so. The girls coped, I noticed, by being home as little as possible. I found myself turning for companionship to books, study, and writing. I took Joan for most of the appointments in that six-week diagnostic period. Sometimes I would be with her, sometimes she would see the doctor alone, and sometimes he would speak to me alone. I discovered by chance that she was not taking the medicine the doctor had prescribed, but was flushing it down the toilet in the exact dosages each day. I asked her why and she responded that she did not want the doctor altering her mind with drugs. That was exactly what the CIA and the FBI wanted, since she was now onto their schemes. They would work through the doctors to try to destroy her mind, so that she could not testify against them. I felt an ominous lump rising in my throat.

At the end of the six weeks, I asked the doctor to give his diagnosis not just to Joan and to me, but to our daughters as well. I wanted our daughters to hear whatever the doctor had to say directly from him, not secondhand from either Joan or me. It was a deeply disturbing day for us all, but especially for our teenage daughters. I wonder now if taking them to this meeting was wise, but at the time it seemed to be the only way to show them that all of us had to view this situation with informed and objective eyes.

The diagnosis was acute or true paranoia. In the acute paranoid personality a different reality has taken over the life of the victim, but once one assumes the truth of that reality, the behavior of that individual seems perfectly appropriate within that world. People can act in a completely normal way inside their reality until "the system" comes into play. That certainly proved to be an accurate description. Throughout the duration of this disease people who did not know Joan well would experience her as shy, somewhat withdrawn, but able to carry on a perfectly normal conversation unless it touched one of her fears, like the loss of privacy, the CIA, bugging devices, intercom systems, or mind-altering drugs. It was that aspect of this disease that confused people who would hear rumors of a mental disease, but who would meet her and find her conversation lucid and normal. Indeed, when the Watergate scandal broke, Joan believed that her public and private life had come together. The Nixon administration was behind this thing, she concluded, and I was obviously one of their targets. She spent hours each day watching those hearings with an autobiographical intensity.

For there to be much chance of effective treatment, a period of hospitalization would be required. Drugs would be used to lower anxiety. People create a different or psychotic reality because they find the reality they are facing intolerable. People become delusional about their importance in the scheme of things because their self-image has been so brutalized. That usually occurs in childhood and is survived by the building of effective coping devices. Sometimes the only coping device that works is to create a different reality into which one can escape. That is when the symptoms that mark acute paranoia develop. Success in treatment is not high. These were the conclusions we learned from the doctor.

I had two other pressing concerns I wanted the doctor to address. "Is this hereditary?" I felt great anxiety for our daughters.

"Absolutely not," said the doctor. "This is an environmentally produced trauma, usually related to something in early childhood. It cannot be passed on genetically. Your daughters are not at risk from that point of view." Suddenly, Joan's response at her sister's death of believing that members of her family and those who came to the funeral were looking at her and wishing she had died instead of Shirley began to make sense.

My second concern was, "What will happen if Joan refuses treatment or hospitalization?"

The doctor replied, "The chances of success in treatment will obviously be dramatically reduced. If she does not submit to voluntary hospitalization, you will have to decide whether to commit her legally." That statement had the force of a fist in my solar plexus. The idea that I would ever be in a position to be required to commit my wife to a mental institution did not enter my consciousness easily. Our daughters listened carefully, but asked no questions, even when specifically invited to do so. Some terrifying decisions clearly needed to be made.

When Joan and I met alone with the doctor, my worst fears were realized. She refused to be hospitalized voluntarily. She would fight any legal attempt to force her into a mental hospital. Life was closing in on both of us. The doctor said that he would try to treat her as an outpatient, but she would have to follow his instructions and take her medication in the way he directed. With her full cooperation it was not impossible for her to be treated outside an institution. His experience, however, was that patients with this diagnosis were both incapable of and unwilling to follow the directions of the doctor and that the doctor became almost inevitably a part of the paranoid system, usually working for the enemy. However, the idea of signing legal papers and committing my wife, against her will, to a mental institution was so anathema to me that I was immobilized at the prospect. With all the prospects of imminent failure, we settled on a six-month trial period of out-patient treatment. Joan promised full cooperation. I was sure she meant it. I was also sure she could never accomplish it, but it was better than the alternatives.

As the months dragged on we settled into a survival pattern. Joan withdrew more and more into the sanctuary of her private world. She cut herself off from life. She accepted no social invitations. I frequently would not know that we had been invited somewhere because Joan would decline for both of us. When I discovered this, I objected, informing her that I could not live her life, but I did insist on living mine. So, after that, Joan would normally decline for herself and leave me to explain why I was coming alone. A number of difficult and sometimes highly embarrassing episodes occurred when she would decline for both of us, unknown to me, and I would attend as an unexpected guest.

The treatment with the psychiatrist seemed to get nowhere. Joan consistently refused medication. It was clearly a waste of time and money, but I clung to it as the only chance we had that I could tolerate. I learned all I could about this disease. I talked with a doctor in our congregation named Eleanor Evans, who was at the Medical College of Virginia, and she got me everything she could out of medical books and journals to help me understand what I was facing. I also talked with an attorney about the legal process of a forced commitment. The idea that representatives of the sheriff's office would arrive to take my wife forcefully away was so repellent to me that I knew I could never do that.

The treatment stopped in six months, judged to be unsuccessful. The ballad "We live in two different worlds" could not have been more true. I shared this data of my life with my staff, my wardens, and an intimate group of about six couples who were my friends. Otherwise, I simply tried to live a normal life. I poured myself into my work with even greater intensity. To the degree that I was capable, I tried to be a sensitive parent, being available to my daughters as much as possible. Ellen entered the University of Virginia in fall 1973, so she only lived inside this strange world for about a year. They were busy social years for Ellen, who was a popular young woman. Katharine and Jaquelin were engaged in athletic activities, jobs, and horses. I became the shopper of record, and actually some of my favorite times were taking the girls shopping for clothes and sitting for hours while they tried on one dress after another. I would take my cue from their eyes when they emerged from the dressing room and could tell in a moment whether or not they liked the dress. Then I would affirm their choice with lavish praise. After a while I became quite good at picking out things they would like. In our own ways we each developed our individual lives. But for me life became lonelier and lonelier.

I worked long hours. I did not feel as comfortable going away to do lectures, since the children seemed to need me nearby, but I did not stop completely. Those away times were like an oasis of sanity for me, and I still did three or four a year.

When the summer came, I busied myself with the task of writing my second book. Some members of our congregation had offered me the use of their home while they were away that summer. I would go there from 10:00 A.M. to 5:00 P.M. each day with my notes and some reference books. I had there none of the distractions of either my home or my office. By the end of summer the manuscript of what came to be called *This Hebrew Lord* was completed. This book, remarkably enough, is still in print and continues to sell one to two thousand copies a year. In its twenty-fourth year of publication HarperCollins began to refer to it in advertisements as "a classic." Writing was clearly becoming more and more my activity of choice. I found solace, excitement, and a sense of worth in my writing that sustained me in this period of my life, which was marked by both loneliness and depression.

# 13

# *Breaking Tradition: Jewish-Christian Dialogue and Christpower*

✳

THERE IS something objectively real about institutional Christianity that sometimes serves to lift people out of their self-absorption. John Hines's announcement that he would resign from the office of presiding bishop had exactly that effect on me. I was stunned by this announcement and wondered about its effect on the church's life. It also meant that the general convention scheduled to meet in Louisville in the fall 1973 would be a crucial gathering for Episcopalians. The church was in a mood of negativity. John's resignation was his acknowledgment that he, rather than the changing world, had become the focus of debate for many people and that was allowing the real sources of pain and distress to be ignored. He did not believe he could continue to be effective in this atmosphere. Those of us who both admired and were inspired by him braced ourselves for what would come next.

The church was clearly moving into a period of reaction. The question was how much of a reaction would it be. Enormous forces of change were at work, but they simply created enormous forces of resistance. John Hines's style of uncompromising leadership had everywhere in his career produced reactionary figures as his successors. The nominating committee of the House of Bishops tried to moderate the reaction. The articulate leader of the younger liberal bishops was John Burt of Ohio. The reactionary leader was Jack Allin of Mississippi. The potential leaders who stood in the great gray center were plentiful.

John Burt was one of our Lenten preachers that year, and we had a dinner party in honor of him and his wife, Martha. Among our guests were Bishop and Mrs. Gibson. I looked forward to this evening as a chance to know the Burts better. At that moment he would clearly have been my choice for presiding bishop. The dinner, however, did not go well. John Burt talked incessantly. Aware that Bob Gibson was on the nominating committee, he perhaps hoped to impress him. If that was his desire, the result was exactly the opposite.

I have been told that the three bishops the nominating committee wanted to submit were John Burt, Robert Spears of Rochester, and Christoph Keller of Arkansas. In their minds that would give the church the choice of a liberal, a moderate liberal, or a moderate conservative. The conservative bishops, however, were well organized. Jack Allin of Mississippi was their candidate, and they made it clear that if he were not nominated, they had sufficient votes to embarrass the committee, even if they did not succeed in electing their candidate. So John Burt was dropped and Jack Allin was added so that the slate now contained a moderate liberal, a moderate conservative, and a hard-line conservative. I have wondered many times how much that decision to drop John Burt was shaped by that dinner party in my home.

When we arrived at this convention, my first impression was how many retired bishops had come out of the woodwork to vote. The swing of the church was destined to be to hard right. John Burt was nominated from the floor, but ran a poor fourth. Jack Allin was almost elected on the first ballot and was in fact elected on the second. Robert Spears was a distant second, Christoph Keller an even more distant third. The House of Deputies took three hours to concur with that election, but finally gave its approval over my objection. John Maury Allin would succeed John Elbridge Hines. It was like having George Wallace succeed Abraham Lincoln.

The reactionary mood of this convention was also expressed in its turning down a proposal to open the ordination process to women. It was a razor-thin rejection, but a rejection nonetheless. The women ordained to the diaconate in 1970 would now be forced to wait another three years, and there was no guarantee then. Indeed, the new presiding bishop made it clear that he did not support the ordination of women and was deeply committed to an all-male priesthood.

The liturgical renewal that resulted in the proposed revision of the prayer book also had a setback, for Jack Allin made it clear that he opposed prayer book revision. The fact that our prayer book now has Rite One, which is

98 percent identical with that in the 1928 book, is the result of his active lobbying.

The gay issue was around, but mostly in the corridors. It was assigned to the Standing Commission on Health and Human Affairs, chaired by Robert Spears. Its day had not yet come.

I had been elected a delegate to this convention from the Diocese of Virginia. But, even more important, I had decided to come to this convention intent upon seeking election to the national church's governing body known as the executive council. I felt that, with John Hines departing, it was time for his spiritual heirs to step forward. I was nominated by the wife of the bishop of Western Mexico, Catherine Saucedo, the result of my work in the area of overseas ministry. I was also endorsed by the liberal lobby known as Coalition E. There were some twenty nominees for three positions. On the first ballot Robert Parks of Trinity Church, Wall Street in New York City, was elected. On the third ballot Robert Royster of Colorado and John Shelby Spong of Richmond were elected. The next closest candidate was Paul Washington of Philadelphia. It was a six-year term. I would have almost a year to work with John Hines before Jack Allin was installed. Other priests who served on that body with me were Gerald McAllister of San Antonio, Rusty Kimsey of The Dalles, Oregon, Dillard Robinson of Newark, and Stewart Wood of Indianapolis. This position propelled me rapidly into national leadership in the church. The irony of that moment was that I had been elected to my national post by the same convention that made Jack Allin presiding bishop. Indeed, in a picture that appeared in the *Convention Daily* the next day, Jack Allin and I were standing side by side vesting for a service. This would add a new dimension to my life, but there was still no question that St. Paul's, Richmond, was the center of my world and the source of my deepest vocational pleasure.

As my assignment on the executive council, I was placed on the Christian Education Committee working with Werner Mark Linz, the head of the Seabury Press and thus my publisher. We decided the time had come to re-create in a new idiom a series of books prepared for the adult education needs of the church called "The Church's Teaching Series." This series had first been done in the 1950s as a resource to undergird the church's commitment to develop a Sunday-school curriculum known as the Seabury Series.

I was given the task of shepherding this decision through the executive council and was to be a member of the editorial committee. We worked hard to get the plans together, but before we were ready to present them, the changing of the guard in national leadership occurred and Jack Allin replaced John Hines. Ours was not the only initiative that felt the chill.

The transitional meeting of the council in spring 1974 at which the new presiding bishop would be installed was scheduled in our National Cathedral in Washington, D.C. By this time my relationship with John Hines had grown into a close mutual friendship. At the council meetings at Seabury House, Greenwich, Connecticut, we frequently played tennis together. I had been a regular visitor in his home and had treasured my time with both John and his wife, Helen. My admiration for him was deepened by this personal knowledge, for he was warm, open, and brilliant and possessed what I could only call an awesome personal integrity.

John's retirement was not easy for him. Not only did he feel that his attempt to call the church into a real engagement with the world as it was had been thwarted, but his successor was, in his opinion, a man who replaced creative vision with an unthinking reaction wrapped in the language of a dishonest and threadbare piety. I believe John Hines saw me as one who might continue his legacy. Since Richmond was so close to Washington, I prevailed on him to spend the night prior to the Allin installation with us. We had a lovely evening together and arranged a tennis foursome for the next morning, a very hot June day. When the match was over, we showered, dressed, and prepared to leave. John did not want to put his wet tennis togs in his suitcase, so we placed them in a plastic bag on the back seat of my car for the trip to Washington.

At the cathedral service of transition Jack Allin wore a very tall miter, something John had never done, and spent what seemed to me to be an undue amount of time in his sermon extolling the virtues of Mississippi. Mississippi was among the most backward and least progressive states in the nation. It was represented in the U.S. Senate by James Eastland and John Stennis, both of whom were, in my opinion, white supremacists. The idea that our church was to be led by one of the most conservative bishops in the House, who would spend his inaugural address extolling the virtues of Mississippi was difficult for me to comprehend.

However, with the transition complete, we went to the first meeting of the executive council chaired by the new presiding bishop, and John Hines had someone take him to the airport to fly back to Asheville and his retirement home in Highlands, North Carolina.

For some reason I had to return to my car to pick up something I had left. By this time the temperature was nearly 100 degrees Fahrenheit. My locked car, parked on the cathedral grounds in the sun, was stifling. When I opened it, I spotted John Hines's tennis clothes—his shorts, his shirt, and his athletic supporter. If they had been a bit spicy when he took them off following the tennis match, they were rancid now. I got what I needed from the car and then decided to take the plastic bag to see if perhaps I could find a way to get it to him.

As I walked back to the meeting, a young priest from Delaware spotted me and came over to introduce himself. This was the first time I met Jack Marston McKelvey.

I discovered that John Hines was already at the airport, but that his plane would not depart for at least an hour. So I grabbed Rusty Kimsey and Stewart Wood and asked them to go with me to deliver this smelly package to the former presiding bishop. The three of us zoomed out to the National Airport. We located John and with mock piety and high ceremony we presented him with our package of tennis goodies. We also had a chance to say good-bye to him yet once again. All three of us, who are today bishops, were then and are now Hines devotees. But it must have been the first time in ecclesiastical history that an Anglican primate was presented with a smelly jockstrap as the final gift of his episcopal career.

It was very clear that I would not be on the favored leadership team under Jack Allin. The first thing he did was reassign me from the Committee on Education to the Committee on Evangelism. Evangelism, despite its being talked about constantly by conservatives like Jack Allin, was a low-status activity. Its life was filled with pious platitudes and sacred mantras, which everyone voted for but no one really took seriously. But the more important thing was that this assignment took me away from my work on the church's teaching series. So I protested successfully and was subsequently reassigned to Education, though I think this episode awakened the new presiding bishop to the fact that something important was going on in the area of Christian education that would probably threaten him. That was itself dangerous, because there was such enormous distrust of any national initiative that Jack Allin talked about limiting the task of the national church to that of only supporting local initiatives. This was phrased to make it sound like he was not abdicating a national leadership role, but the fact remains that few or no initiatives ever emerge locally. He was supported in this vigorously by the bishop of South Carolina, my former rector, Gray Temple.

When the church's teaching series plans did come up, they were met not with overt opposition, but with tactics that would remove any worth from the project. In Jack Allin's opinion the books were to be simple enough for children. They had to confirm both the expectations and the faith that people brought to them. They were not to be controversial. They were to encourage, not to disturb, the faithful. I interpreted these guidelines to mean that the books in this series were not to be designed to allow people to grow. They were, in short, to be propaganda materials, not educational materials. They were to confirm the prejudice and ignorance that already abounded in this church of ours.

It was also clear that I would not now chair the editorial committee. That assignment went to Alan Jones, a safe, benign British Anglo-Catholic on the faculty at General Seminary whose interest was primarily in spirituality. It was also clear that I would not be chosen to be an author. I had anticipated that I might do the volume on the Bible, but that was not to be. The fact that I now had a track record of eight years as a fairly effective teacher of the Bible to laypeople was not given any consideration. I did retain my seat on the editorial board, but it was filled with sufficient conservative voices to mute my influence, or at least to keep it from becoming dominant.

Many of the authors were picked more for their ideology than their competence. The only good thing about this was that by and large these people either could not or did not do the work. Alan had asked his mother-in-law, Madeleine L'Engle, to be a coauthor with Urban T. Holmes III of the volume that was to introduce the series. Madeleine was a popular writer and a lovely person, but she and Terry Holmes got along like two crossed sticks. He regarded her as "straight out of *Ladies' Home Journal*." She regarded him as "arrogant, obtuse, and intellectually incapable of communicating to the average person." The partnership was finally dissolved, and Terry wrote the book alone. It was, however, twice as long as the series could manage, so John Westerhoff was employed to edit it down to size.

Philip Turner and Ruth Tiffany Barnhouse were asked to coauthor the volume on ethics. Both of them were, in my opinion, strange choices. Thankfully, both of them proved to be incompetent to meet any deadline or to complete the task. Finally the editorial committee dismissed them both, and Earl Brill was asked to write this particular volume, which turned out to be one of the better ones. However, the whole series was a good bit less than I, for one, had counted on. The anti-intellectual bias of conservative Christians, led by Jack Allin, was now in full swing. They never did understand the issues that needed to be addressed. Under the guise of undergirding "the faith of little people," the books were generally dull and they were never a major resource to the church.

My second major battle on the council was to determine whether or not the Episcopal Church would join in a new ecumenical church-school curriculum called the Joint Educational Development Series. The mood of the national church leadership was still reactionary. The only initiatives that could be affirmed were local. Every national initiative was viewed with extreme skepticism—it might create "disunity in the church." The unfortunate thing about that mentality was that a single parish or diocese does not usually have either the creative or the financial assets to produce an entire curriculum. If one were not produced nationally, it would not exist. That was, of course, the primary agenda. People could purchase private, "for profit" material in a range of flavors from fundamentalism to inane liberalism produced by various commercial groups. I felt strongly that we ought to join the Joint Educational Coalition and produce something that would be intellectually challenging, biblically stretching, and educationally professional. I was, however, on our committee a minority of one. It was clear to me that this was a fight that could not be won. The decision before me was whether it was a battle worthy of being fought at all.

I decided finally that it was. Such a fight would reveal publicly what was actually happening to our church's leadership. It would show the whole church where the values of the present administration were. Finally, it would, I hoped, expose the fact that the catch phrase "local initiative" (or "local option") was nothing but a euphemism for inertia and for allowing a conservative agenda to dominate our church. I prepared my argument well, and my inquiries certainly served to make the people at church headquarters nervous. David Perry, the paid educational executive, acted as if it might be exposed that his department had no agenda and no real purpose other than to fly around the country "consulting" on educational matters. No one seemed to recognize or care that I had created in a downtown church in Richmond a spectacularly successful total education program. When the day of decision making arrived, it was clear that I had the attention, if not the support, of the church center leadership. The report from our committee to the executive council contained the recommendation that we not enter this cooperative venture, but rather that our stance should be to continue our program of encouraging local educational initiatives. The motion was seconded and the discussion opened. Gray Temple gave the rationale for the committee's decision. It amounted to a defense of motherhood and an appeal to the good old days when churches studied the Bible as if it had dropped from heaven fully written and in the King James Version.

When I was recognized, I offered a substitute motion that we join the JED process and commit major funds and effort to its development, producing thereby a product that would help guide our church into a realistic future. My motion was seconded and so I was given the opportunity to speak to it. I outlined first the philosophy and goal behind this material, wondering in the process why it was not being embraced enthusiastically. Then I named the drift that was apparently enveloping the church as an "anti-intellectual bias." It was, I suggested, a manifestation of fear and revealed a lack of either leadership or creativity. I suggested that it represented the elevation into dominance of a mentality that set the highest priority on allowing nothing to disturb church complacency, but at the cost of sacrificing truth and opportunity. I urged the church's highest governing body to see what was happening and to reverse it. Participating in the JED process offered that kind of opportunity. I felt I made the best case I could and at least placed the proper issues before the church's leadership so that a debate could ensue. I also knew that this debate would be well covered by the church press and thus these issues would be heard across a wide spectrum of church life. It was my hope that the people of the church would at least learn that its leadership was not monochromatic.

When I finished this address, Gray Temple and his allies struck back. He spoke about the lack of trust that embraced everything "that comes down today from headquarters." It was one more slam against the heroic leadership of John Hines. When the vote came, my substitute motion carried about one-third of the council membership, a far higher percentage than I had reason to anticipate. But it also revealed that Jack Allin's election was no fluke. The conservatives had the votes to do almost anything they wished, at least at the executive-council level of leadership. Those of us who wanted to preserve the Hines legacy had our work cut out for us. History, however, is a funny thing. An idea whose time has come will not be repressed by dull minds, even those in leadership positions.

By this time Jack Allin had called the bishop suffragan of Atlanta, Milton Wood, to come to New York to be his executive assistant and in effect the vice president of the church. He would be typical of Jack Allin's appointees. Milton's greatest talent was, in my opinion, that he did not threaten Jack Allin or reveal any of his weaknesses. In his career he had been a quintessential professional assistant. I also knew that he was filled with prejudices. It was discouraging. Seeing no way to make a contribution nationally, I returned to my local projects, but kept an eye out for any opening on the national scene that might enable us to call the church into faithfulness.

John Hines had invited us to spend the Labor Day weekend with his family in Highlands. Joan would not go, but I decided to accept. Our girls would be away with friends, and it would be a nice way to end the summer. Robert Brown, the retired bishop of Arkansas, and his wife, Warwick, were also nearby in Cashiers, and I had wanted for some time to see them. Bob Brown had also been the rector of St. Paul's, Richmond, serving there from 1947 to 1955. This former rector's public and enthusiastic support of me and my ministry was deeply appreciated.

This late summer weekend was lovely in those tall Carolina mountains with bright sunshiny days and crisp nights. John, Bob, and I played golf together on the High Hampton Course in Cashiers, about six miles away, and had wonderful opportunities to talk on the course and over the evening meal.

I startled John at dinner on Saturday with the proposal that he commission someone to write his biography. He dismissed this idea at once as too improbable to consider. However, I pressed him, explaining as best I could the crucial role I believe he had played not only in the Episcopal Church, but in the American religious scene generally. I told him that such a book could be an analysis of the role of leadership. It would be easy to outline and illustrate with his life the elements found in an effective leader. He clearly had no zest for this idea. I perceived that he was still feeling defeated. He asserted that no one would want to take on this task, but I countered that idea immediately by telling him that I would. That was a surprise even to me. If he could get an experienced biographer, that would obviously be preferable, but if he was not willing to do that, then, I repeated to make sure it had been heard, I would be delighted to take on the task of seeking to tell the story of the Hines years. It was a story I was convinced needed to be told. I also was certain that the story of the person John Hines was and the influences that shaped him would make a readable narrative.

Bob Brown thought it was a wonderful idea, and he believed we could raise the money to underwrite this project without any difficulty. That support certainly pushed the project along a bit. Bob further thought I should write it primarily because I was enthusiastic about it. He added that I had already demonstrated a writing ability. Both of them were aware that my second book was complete. Furthermore, I could begin this task the next summer. Bob went on to suggest that he would put together an editorial committee made up of himself, John Coburn, and Scott Field Bailey, the bishop suffragan of Texas and John's former assistant. That committee would oversee the project both financially and editorially. They could even help in doing the research. John wavered. A slight smile crossed his face. He agreed at least to think about the idea over the weekend.

On Monday morning after breakfast, as I prepared to leave to make my way back to Richmond, I pressed him for an answer. He finally said he thought I was crazy and that no one would read such a book, but if I wanted to do it, he would consent. That was not enough for me, so I pressed him still further. Would he then commission me officially as his biographer so that I could, without hassle, gain access to his papers and correspondence? This would also open doors to me to interview friends and foes alike. Finally, would he subject himself to the interview hours required to get the oral history of his career on tape? I reminded him that I could only do this work during the summer, which would mean that it might take four or five years. He agreed to all the conditions. I was elated. My third book, I was confident, would be a biography of my special hero. It would also be fun to get to know him that much better. The idea of being named his biographer was not in my conscious mind when I left Richmond for this weekend. Now I could not wait to get home to share the news with my family and friends. My editorial volunteers might be interested, I thought, in becoming research assistants, if we could find enough money to cover their travel costs.

I was pleased to discover that both Lucy Negus and Carter McDowell shared my enthusiasm, and we began laying plans for the project. Bob Brown was true to his word. Shortly thereafter, I received a letter from Christoph Keller, Bob Brown's successor in Arkansas, saying that a family trust fund over which he presided would be pleased to underwrite the expenses of both travel and research to prepare material for a Hines biography. An initial check for $6,000 was included. I appointed Carter McDowell treasurer, and opened the account in the name of Hines Research Expenses. I began by sending out a flurry of letters seeking both data and permission to interview during the next two years. News stories in the church press announced the project, which was helpful since that meant I did not have to explain it from scratch each time. It was now quite official and in the public domain. Once that preliminary burst of activity was ended, I simply filed answers to my letters as they came in and basically put the project on hold until the next summer arrived. I returned my primary energy to the work of being rector of St. Paul's.

The year unfolded without a hitch. *This Hebrew Lord* came out early in 1974 and received a good amount of publicity; for a religious book it gained a solid sales record. It was clear that this book also was destined to be a success. Little did I dream of what doors the title would open to me.

In May 1974 I answered the phone to find myself talking to Jack Daniel Spiro, senior rabbi at Richmond's Reformed synagogue, Temple Beth Ahabah. It seems that over the weekend he had been invited to a cocktail party in his neighborhood with some of his Gentile friends. While there, he spotted a green book on the coffee table entitled *This Hebrew Lord*. The title had intrigued him. He borrowed the book and had just finished reading it. "I've never read a book by a Christian that paid such a tribute to Judaism," he said, "but of course I disagree with your conclusion."

I found that remark amusing. "Of course you do," I responded. "If you agreed with me, you would have to be baptized and there are few positions I know of open to baptized rabbis." He laughed. The conversation was both friendly and easy.

Then he got to the purpose of his call. "I would like to conduct a debate with you on your book before the members of my synagogue," he stated. "Would you be interested in doing that?" Nothing appealed to me more, and I said I would be delighted.

We agreed to meet for lunch later that week to discuss and, if it seemed feasible, to plan this event. The lunch lasted for four hours. Seldom had I met someone I instinctively liked that quickly and that deeply. Jack Spiro was a native of New Orleans, married, and the father of three. He had come to Beth Ahabah only that year. He was a brilliant man, a Ph.D. in Jewish studies from Hebrew Union College. He possessed a facile and wide-ranging mind and was a warm, articulate human being. His ready smile and open, upbeat personality made him quite accessible. We had been trained theologically in the same general era. We had Paul Tillich and Martin Buber in our mutual intellectual backgrounds. Despite the differences in our deepest religious convictions, we spoke a similar theological language.

The more we talked, the more it became obvious that "debate" was not the right word to use to describe what we were planning—a better word was "dialogue." We would do it not only at Temple Beth Ahabah, but at St. Paul's also. Our general plan was for Jack to open the dialogue with an address on the history of Jewish-Christian relations. Then, for three successive Sabbath evenings at 7:30 P.M., I would speak to the synagogue congregation in a dialogue format about my understanding of Christianity with Jack posing the questions. On the intervening three Sunday mornings at 11:00 A.M., we would simply reverse the process, and Jack, responding to my questions, would share his understanding of Judaism. Our efforts would not be to convert, but rather to explain, clarify, and destroy distortions, inaccurate perceptions, and deadly stereotypes. Following each service we would adjourn to a less formal room and respond to questions from the congregation. I would conclude this series in early December with an address on why Hanukkah could be and ought to be celebrated by Christians. With the format generally in mind, we went to our respective congregational decision-making bodies to lay our plans before them. At both church and synagogue there was an enormous positive response to the project. We had the summer to think about it, work on it, and prepare for it. It would be conducted in the late fall of the year. I was very excited at the prospect.

Life was becoming professionally almost more than I could manage. The parish, however, was thriving. We had finally broken the gender barrier in acolytes, lay readers, and vestry membership. It was not easy. The first female acolyte was a high-school senior and the daughter of one of our vestry members. Her first assignment after completing her training was to serve at the 8:00 A.M. Eucharist, where there would be only a small congregation. It turned out to be a disaster. Before the service was half over, our new acolyte had fainted dead away in the sanctuary and had to be bodily carried out. We listened to a chorus of male propaganda: "Girls were never meant to do things like that in the first place," and "Perhaps she was having her period. That's why girls ought to limit their activities." I suppose such comments were inevitable in that time in history. But unknown to this unconscious young woman, she had a very sensitive rector who understood quite personally that fainting at the 8:00 A.M. service was not gender-related. The gender integration of the acolytes continued.

The first woman lay reader whom I appointed to read the lessons at morning prayer and to administer the chalice at the communion services was Celia Luxmoore, a tall, attractive young Englishwoman who had been born in London. Her reading voice was exquisite, especially for a church with deep English roots. She also worked for my vestryman Tommy Bryan at Miller-Rhoads Department Store. I thought by choosing one whose ability to read in public was so obviously a gift and one who was known and admired by the leader of one of the most conservative and socially prominent families in our congregation the negativity would be minimal. That was not an accurate assessment. We went through a period in which people simply avoided her side of the communion rail so they would not be forced to receive the communion wine from a woman. Perhaps I should not have chosen for my trail-blazing female lay reader someone who was eight months pregnant! But we persevered, and soon other women were serving in this way.

When the summer arrived, I spent much of it making a number of short trips to research the life of John Hines. I went to Seneca, South Carolina, to talk to neighbors, school classmates, and former teachers. I visited the house in which he was born and the little Episcopal Church of the Ascension, where his job was to build the fire in the woodstove each Sunday morning. I saw the remains of a crude tennis court that John and his older brother, Edgar, had tried to build and on which John had begun his love for that game. I visited and interviewed his still living siblings about his childhood and especially about his mother and father. I wrote letters seeking information, stories, and anecdotes to a list provided me of college classmates, seminary classmates, and representatives from the various congregations he had served. I visited the University of the South at Sewanee and, with great help from the administration, I read the record of his years as a student, during which he had been class president, fraternity president, and editor of the *Sewanee Purple*, the university weekly. The young John Hines began to come into focus for me, the strands that would later be woven into his unique life.

I also had a week in Highlands with John and Helen, and spent about three hours a day with the tape recorder going. The story of this man's life, the decisions he had made, and the way in which he made them proved to be fascinating. I also got his opinions on a wide variety of church activities and church leaders with whom he had worked. Some, like Stephen Bayne, he respected enormously. Others who opposed him, when they did it fairly, also had his respect. I think of William Brady, the very conservative Anglo-Catholic bishop of Fond du Lac. The person with whom he appeared to have the deepest friendship was Roger Blanchard, the former bishop of Southern Ohio, who had resigned to join his staff. There were others—both supporters and detractors—who simply did not have his respect because he felt they lacked personal integrity. John Hines understood that his style of leadership was costly. People had to know who they were and what they believed in order to deal with the power of this leader's convictions, his unwillingness to be political in the sense of seeking compromise, and the strength of his personal integrity. After that visit I began what proved to be a lifetime habit. Once a week John and I visited on the telephone. The call was at my initiative on all but a very few occasions. I was just at the beginning of the biography, but the project began to have substance for me.

It was growing increasingly clear that my excitement with my professional life was in fact filling up an ever widening void in my personal life. Joan more and more lived in a world no one else understood. I increasingly took on the role of mother and father to the children. They were popular, smart, and athletic and had begun to move in ever widening social circles. I set aside one night a week and one full day a week, Saturday if possible, to be available to do whatever they wanted or needed me to do. They took over many of the household duties and helped to make life tolerable. Indeed, I perceived that our home was a relatively happy one. But I am certain that these children experienced the enormous tension that marked my relationship with Joan as her sickness developed, and that tension was destined to create scars that would inevitably have to be confronted.

Thanks to a generous vestry, I was given the entire summer off, so I divided it between my Hines research and my children. We made lots of small day trips that summer. Ellen was home from the University of Virginia and in a social whirl. Kathy had time in Tarboro with her beloved godparents, and Jaquelin spent lots of time at her favorite horse farm and was in several horse shows.

In the summer of 1974 three retired bishops, Brooke Mosley of Delaware, Ed Wells of Western Missouri, and Robert DeWitt of Pennsylvania, decided that they could no longer wait for the church to decide that women were created in the image of God and therefore could not be barred from ordination to the priesthood. These men, supported by Tony Ramos, the bishop of Costa Rica, determined that they would act to ordain women now without the proper ecclesiastical authorization. They argued that the canons did not prohibit this action if "men" was interpreted generically. So gathering together eleven female deacons who were, with one exception, seminary graduates, qualified in every way, who had served in the diaconate for at least the prerequisite one year, they planned to do what they called a prophetic act. In the Church of the Advocate, Philadelphia, where Paul Washington was the rector, these three bishops in July 1974 ordained these eleven women to the priesthood. They were willing to let the church deal with reality. They were also prepared to take the consequences if necessary. On that Saturday morning the Church of the Advocate was packed. The crucifer was a black woman named Barbara Harris; the preacher was the vice president of the House of Deputies of the Episcopal Church, Charles Willie, a Harvard sociologist.

The service caused a furor. Jack Allin was livid. He called an emergency meeting of the House of Bishops to deal with this act of ecclesiastical disobedience. But the deed was done and now the church had to respond. The House of Bishops censured by formal vote the offending bishops not once, but twice. It passed solemn resolutions declaring the ordinations null and void. But invitations to these new priests to celebrate the Eucharist in churches around the nation indicated that many did not regard their ordinations as invalid. Church leaders then proceeded to put several of the inviting rectors on trial, but it soon appeared too widespread a practice to discipline effectively.

The bishop of West Missouri, Arthur Vogel, argued that the ordination of the women was irregular, if not null and void, because the "consent of the ecclesiastical community had not been forthcoming." It was a strange argument, typical of Arthur on many subjects, but spokespersons for male preserves do strange things when their right to rule is challenged. The issue of the ordination of women was no longer academic, and clearly the convention of 1976 would have to face this new challenge. Several bishops, led by John Burt of Ohio, announced that until they could ordain both men and women, they would ordain neither. The pressure was mounting. Jack Allin discovered that the presiding bishop cannot impose his will on the whole church. The idea that women could be priests was an idea whose day had come, and a prelate from Mississippi who was out of touch with reality could not stop it. The ripples of this event spread quickly throughout the church.

I smiled more broadly as we went that summer to a more isolated vacation spot in South Carolina called Litchfield Beach. So did my daughters, who finally saw women like themselves becoming leaders of the church. Our beach time was marred only by the fact that Joan decided that the *Charleston (S.C.) News and Courier,* which was the only newspaper we could get at the newsstand in Litchfield Beach, was writing stories about her and that the Coast Guard helicopter that regularly flew over the beach was photographing her. As a result, she seldom ventured out of our cottage. The girls and I, however, had learned to cope with that kind of behavior and so, despite it, we had a wonderful time. After dinner each evening, with coffee in hand, we would walk the beach to a place where sunsets could be seen. Joan would even go with us on these walks since helicopters did not fly that late. Those moments remain today very pleasant memories.

That fall was a vigorous and exciting time. One of the "Philadelphia Eleven" came to the diocese of Virginia and concelebrated at the Eucharist at St. Peter's Church on Church Hill in Richmond. Bishop Hall sat in the pews of that church for that service, thus giving it tacit approval. When the howls of protest arose from conservative circles, Bishop Hall announced that his eyes were closed in prayer so he had not seen the offending act!

The "Dialogue in Search of Jewish-Christian Understanding," as we came to call it, was the big thing on our parochial agenda. Jack Spiro and I had assembled a working group. Assisting me were Lucy Negus and Carter McDowell, who had in effect become part of an editorial team for all that I did. They were now joined by Robin Valentine, a publicity expert who coined the slogan "Virginia Is for Lovers" and who had recently moved to town as the new wife in an old Virginia family. Jack asked Frank Eakin, a Bible professor and chair of the religion department at the University of Richmond, to assist us in our preparation. Though a Christian and an ordained pastor in the Baptist Church, Dr. Eakin was deeply sympathetic toward the Jewish Scriptures and the Jewish faith. Frank's wife, Frances, also joined the team and made a vital contribution. We worked on format, content, and questions. We sought to discover the average concerns, definitions, and stereotypes that floated around both congregations when each spoke about the other's God. We also dealt with issues of imperialism, evangelistic techniques, and that sense of condemnation and doom that so many Christians pronounce so ignorantly on Jews.

Lucy Negus and Robin Valentine began to feed publicity notices to both congregations and to the press, radio, and television. Interest was clearly rising. Jack Spiro's opening address on the history of Jewish-Christian relations was well received. There was, however, only a slight rise in attendance that Sabbath eve at the synagogue, certainly nothing that was unusual. I preached that Sunday on the plans and the hopes for the dialogue. I did not go into the content. It was, in effect, a twenty-five-minute commercial. Again, there was a slight bump in attendance, but nothing out of the ordinary. In the mind of the public the dialogue began on the first Sabbath/Sunday that both rabbi and rector would be together.

That occurred on Friday evening, November 1, at 7:30 P.M. at Temple Beth Ahabah. The synagogue was packed. Both congregations were present in great numbers, as were many other people from the community at large. The media were also present in abundance. WRVA, Richmond's major radio station that blanketed Virginia, had decided to tape the entire series for a delayed broadcast. The *Richmond Times Dispatch* made the dialogue a feature of its Saturday-morning front page. Radio stations played excerpts and reported it as a news event within an hour of its ending.

The format worked well. I had prepared very concise answers to Jack's questions, which were designed to expose Jewish misconceptions and Jewish prejudice about what Christians actually thought and believed. The congregational question period in the social hall of the synagogue also was lively. Some of the questions anticipated our plans for the future Fridays, so we gave hints only, thus building anticipation. The whole area of Christology was to be the substance of the second synagogue session. Our team met when it was over and pronounced it a great beginning. Indeed, we had set a standard that future sessions would need to meet if we were going to sustain this level of interest. It is frequently amazing how success requires that the encore stretch beyond what was previously anticipated. We had only one day to get ready for St. Paul's. Jack Spiro, who was not nearly as disciplined in his preparation as I, felt confident that he could "wing it" effectively, but all of us urged him to prepare meticulously. He was probably the best person on his feet I had ever heard, but he took our advice and worked hard over Saturday.

Sunday morning, November 3, 1974, was filled with excitement at St. Paul's. The adult class was on the book of Acts and touched on the conflict between Paul and synagogue leaders. It was a full room, but the 11:00 service looked like Easter Sunday. There were perhaps a thousand-plus people present. Jack Spiro was brilliant as my questions forced him to lay out Jewish concepts that had long been misunderstood or perhaps even deliberately distorted by Christians. We opened up the typical and popular Christian prejudices. People learned, for example, that the primary reason Jews had entered the banking and jewelry businesses was that Jews were precluded in the Christian West from owning land. Therefore, hard currency and precious metals and stones became the areas in which Christian prejudice forced them to develop expertise. Once again, after church the question period was lively and well attended. People did not just go home after the service.

This second session was on the radio stations as news by 2:00 that afternoon, on the local television news that night on all three channels, and was a feature story in the *Times Dispatch* on Monday morning. We had clearly touched a community nerve. The rebroadcast of the entire sessions in both synagogue and church got a very large audience according to the calls the radio station received. Our team met to evaluate and plan ahead. Once again, the stakes seemed to be rising. We felt compelled to keep the standards high.

By Friday morning negative letters to the editor began to appear in the local newspaper. Christian fundamentalists were sure that a dialogue that made no attempt at conversion of all Jews was not a Christian activity. Orthodox Jews were equally sure that Jack Spiro had polluted Judaism by even engaging Christians on these subjects. One Christian pastor stated in a letter that I was not the proper representative of Christianity for this dialogue and wondered how I was chosen for this task in the first place. He suggested a more literal Christian would be a better choice. He assumed it was a part of some larger ecclesiastical plan. Both Jack and I had a dramatic uptick in our mail.

Friday was on top of us before we knew it and back to the synagogue we went—this time to standing room only. "A Rosh Hashanah crowd," Jack observed. Press representatives were once again present. Microphones and cameras were part of the scene. It was on this evening that Jack was going to pose the Christology issue for me in the way that Jews would normally ask it. For Jews, God was wholly other. God could not be particularized. Yet at the heart of the Christian faith lay the claim that God had been incarnate in Jesus, that in Jesus God had come into human history.

I had worked on that answer more than on anything else. I wanted people to know that incarnational thought and trinitarian thought were not fully developed until the fourth and fifth centuries of the common era. Such claims were not in the original proclamation of the gospel. I tried to show how the Christ or messiah concept had developed in Jewish history, beginning with its being a title originally given to the king and its later becoming a mythological picture of an idealized future leader who would someday come to inaugurate the Kingdom of God. The Jews, while not admitting incarnational language, were in fact able to point to people whom they believed spoke God's word or acted out God's will. So I approached Christology from this point of view. I hoped that they might be able to see the original Christian claim that in Jesus the word of God was spoken and the will of God was being lived out, which then grew into incarnational language. It would for many of them be a doorway into a new way of viewing the Jewish Jesus of Nazareth.

I concluded that answer by asserting that the Gospels do not say in a simplistic way that Jesus is God. Jesus is portrayed as praying to God. He was not talking to himself. Jesus died. It is inconceivable to say that God can die. God did not get crucified. Jesus did. But when the disciples looked at the cross, they saw it as a portrait of the self-giving and ultimate love of God. What the Gospels do say, I went on to explain, was that Jesus revealed God. Jesus pointed to God and enabled people to see God when they looked at

Jesus. What God is, they were suggesting, Jesus is. The disciples of Jesus believed that in Jesus the word of God had been spoken and the will of God had been lived out. That is why, I concluded, at Caesarea Philippi it was said of Jesus, "You are the Christ, the Son of the Living God." I was pleased with my answer, and there was a good response. In the general-question period afterward a series of questions allowed me to clarify that narrow distinction. It was a wonderful evening.

The story in the *Times Dispatch* on the following Saturday morning announced, "Jesus Is Not God, Rector Asserts." It was the beginning of a new phase of my life. If the letters from the fundamentalists had been a trickle up to this point, they quickly became a flood. The security cages of the evangelical troops were clearly rattled. By Thursday of that week placard-carrying members of the Janke Road Baptist Church in Richmond were picketing St. Paul's. Within three weeks Carroll Simcox, the editor of *The Living Church*, was bemoaning the state of Christianity in Richmond and writing news articles about the dialogue that would bring a stream of letters to that publication debating my faith and my credibility. The national Episcopal newspaper ran a story on the dialogue, and the *Washington Post* became the first national newspaper to cover the dialogue in a major feature.

The local chapter of the National Conference of Christians and Jews came to ask us if the dialogue could be published. We referred them to Mark Linz at Seabury Press and discovered that he was interested. Once again, Jack Spiro had to build for his next Sunday's presentation at St. Paul's on this new place where we were in the dialogue. It had already far exceeded our expectations.

Sunday at St. Paul's was even bigger. Even the Bible class hit a record as I continued to open up early church themes from the book of Acts. Once again Jack Spiro rose to the challenge and did an electrifying job. The community of St. Paul's bonded with him. He was one of them, and more than one person began to wonder out loud about the discriminatory patterns, written and unwritten, that affected housing, private clubs, career advancement, and many other areas in which Jews had been traditionally treated as victims of prejudice.

Once again this dialogue was featured in the morning paper on Monday. We had another week to go, more issues to discuss, and a manuscript to prepare for publication. The public-service television station in Richmond wanted to know if Jack and I would do a televised dialogue with call-in questions.

My first formal portrait at age twelve. 1943

With (from left to right) my daughters Ellen, Jaquelin,
and Katharine and my first wife Joan. 1983

The Rt. Rev. William H. Marmion, Bishop of Southwestern Virginia and hero of the Lynchburg chapter.

The Rt. Rev. John A. T. Robinson, my close friend and mentor. The author of *Honest to God* and the Bishop of Woolwich.

A political cartoon by syndicated cartoonist Jeff MacNelly depicting the Gov. Holton–Howard Carwile–John Shelby Spong dispute. 1971

Senator William B. Spong (my cousin) to my left and the Rev. Dr. William C. Spong (my brother) to my right at my consecration as Bishop. 1976

With the presiding Bishop of our church (1964–1973) Rt. Rev. John E. Hines, my closest friend and my ultimate role model.

A photo that accompanied a newspaper article in the *Daily Mail* of London by the Bishop of London entitled "The Bishop Who Is Running the Church into the Ground" during the Lambeth Conference. 1988

With Phil Donahue and Dr. Ruth Westheimer after the *Phil Donahue Show* during the tour for *Living in Sin?* 1988

Picketers at the General Convention in Philadelphia. 1997

The ordination of Robert Williams, the first openly gay priest living in a publicly acknowledged partnership. December 16, 1989

Speaking at the
Omni Shoreham with
Ed Browning looking on
after the Disassociation
"victory." 1990

Speaking in Australia during a book tour for *Liberating the Gospels.* 1997

With my wife, Christine. 1998

With Christine, my daughters and their families, and my mother
at her ninetieth birthday party. 1998

They hinted that this might have longer-range possibilities of a regular program.

The final Friday and the final Sunday of our plan were carried out in the same high level of both interest and vitality. The press stories were vivid, and the ensuing dialogue marked this as a major community event. Seabury Press had agreed to publish the dialogue as a book, but only if we could do it on a quick schedule to take advantage of the energy around this event. The debate we engendered in the national religious press made the theological issues, especially concerning the Christological formula, hot items for discussion and dialogue. Our mail continued to increase, especially my abusive mail from small religious minds.

On the Sunday within the eight-day celebration of Hanukkah, I formally closed the dialogue by calling on Christians to incorporate Hanukkah into the Christian calendar, recognizing that had the light of true worship not been restored to the Temple under Judas Maccabeus, the Christian enterprise would never have been born. That too became a major news story.

We spent most of December getting the manuscript of the dialogue ready for publication. We asked Frank Eakin to write the foreword. He did so with such clarity and expertise that it helped the book to become an important contribution to the growing knowledge of anti-Semitism in our history. Frank's foreword showed in a very poignant way the prejudiced cultural background against which Jack Spiro and I had been doing our work. Our editorial team began to try to shape Jack Spiro's rhetoric. He would not prepare a manuscript and spoke extemporaneously, so his words didn't transcribe from tape to page very well. However, editors Negus, McDowell, and Valentine could turn oral rhetoric into effective written language and so they did. Frances Eakins typed it for us and Seabury planned publication for early in 1975.

One rather beautiful episode showed me a deeper truth that this dialogue had created. It occurred on Christmas Eve in St. Paul's. A well-known leader of Temple Beth Ahabah and his wife came to the midnight Eucharist. That was in itself not unusual—the two congregations had worshiped together on eight different occasions that fall. But when the time for communion came, these two came forward with their hands outstretched to receive the bread and wine that for us Christians symbolized the body and blood of Christ. I reject no one at the altar rail whose hands are open, and so this Jewish couple did receive the sacrament. I saw this temple leader about a week later on the streets of downtown Richmond. After exchanging the pleasantries of the new year, I said, "Joe, we were so pleased to have you and your wife at church on Christmas Eve. Thank you for coming."

He then said, "I'll bet you were a little surprised when we decided to receive communion."

"I was," I admitted. "Tell me what that meant to you."

"We thought about it a lot before we did it, Jack," he continued, "but let me ask you some questions to show you how we came to that decision."

"Okay," I responded, eager to hear.

"Was not the communion service of the Christian Church said to have originated in the Last Supper, which was supposed to be a Jewish Passover?" he asked.

"Yes," I responded, "that is a major strand of our tradition."

"Were not all those fellows who attended the Last Supper Jews?" he pressed on.

"Yes, they were," I affirmed.

"Were any of those disciples at that meal baptized or confirmed?" he continued.

"Not to my knowledge," I responded, interested in the direction he was going.

"Well, we figured that if unbaptized Jews could receive communion from Jesus at the start of the Christian faith, then we could receive it from you in thanksgiving for the dialogue that had brought us close together again!"

It was, to my mind, irrefutable logic and made me begin to realize that all the barriers we institutional people had placed into the life of the church as a way of keeping pure and exclusive our claims to be the sole agents of God on this earth were now inoperable. The idea that the only channels God would use to reach people with grace were the institutionalized Christian sacraments was itself strange. The claim that these sacraments could be celebrated and administered only by those who had been officially ordained and thus empowered by the church to accomplish the opening of these channels of grace suggests that God somehow works for the church or that the church somehow controls God. That was a concept I had never formulated before, but now that I had, I knew I must never lay it aside.

I also began to look at the creeds in a new way. An elementary study of the formation of the creeds in the third, fourth, and fifth centuries will reveal that the process that produced them was deeply political and highly compromised. The creeds were more about power than they were about truth.

That some came to be called "orthodox" and their version of Christianity designated "orthodoxy" was not necessarily a recognition of who was right, but a recognition of who had won. A primary purpose of the creeds was not to spell out the Christian faith, but to exclude competing groups and their competing versions of truth from the church's life.

The first creed of the church appeared to be "Jesus, you are the messiah or the Christ," which then evolved into three words, "Jesus is Lord." How he was "Lord" or what "Lord" meant was not defined. Clearly to the Jewish people, to call him "Lord" was to relate him to messianic expectations. Gentiles, however, used the same word with very different meanings. "Lord," to them, took on kingly and royal connotations.

The Apostles' Creed, which was basically shaped at the Council of Nicea in 325, incorporated the developing trinitarian formula. But over that century its use did not preclude a wide variety of interpretations that those who framed the Apostles' Creed to create unity in the newly recognized faith of the empire had not anticipated. Near the end of the fourth century, the Apostles' Creed was expanded to close loopholes and thus to exclude a wide variety of contending points of view. That is why phrases describing Jesus as "God of God," "Light of Light," "very God of very God," "begotten, not made," and "of one substance with the Father" were included in the Nicene Creed. The creed was becoming more and more convoluted.

Even that, it was discovered over the next century, did not rule out a variety of as yet unimagined ways to interpret those more and more rigidly exclusive phrases. This necessitated yet another creed known as the Athanasian Creed, which went on for several pages in the most convoluted, loophole-closing set of words I have ever read. Somehow, the Christian church had been infected historically with the idea that the truth of God could be fully revealed, that it could be reduced to propositional statements, and that it was the church's possession. That is idolatry, and idolatry will never be eternal.

The dialogue with the rabbi, the conversation with the temple member after the Christmas service, and my growing sense of wonder at the mystery of God began to move me slowly, but surely, into another theological place that would be characterized as one of unbounded openness.

The fallout from the dialogue lasted for weeks. We were debated in the Letters to the Editor section of the local newspaper for about six weeks and in the conservative national Episcopal journals for longer than that. The television program on cable TV received good reviews. It even won, we were told, a major share of viewers in the Richmond market the night it was shown. Frank Eakin served as the moderator for that program and a good part of it dealt with call-in questions from the viewing public. The impact of the dialogue was still expanding. One questioner wanted to know what the major effect of the dialogue had been on each of us personally. I responded that before the dialogue was first discussed about seven months ago, I had not known Jack Spiro at all, but today he was one of my closest friends. I should have stopped there, but I went on to add, "Indeed he is so close a friend that if I were to die tomorrow, he would surely be one of my pallbearers." A letter arrived the next week from a disturbed conservative Christian, saying, "I hope it will not be long before Rabbi Spiro has the chance to act in that capacity."

The final question in the television program was directed to me: "What do you mean by 'Christpower'?" That was a word I had developed to get underneath the explanations about who Jesus was or is that have been offered throughout Christian history and that were finally formalized into creeds, doctrines, and dogma. I sought to get people to meditate on the power present in the Christ experience. This was the power that required interpretive words first drawn out of the Jewish worldview when Jesus was called "Our Passover" who was "sacrificed for us," an image obviously lifted out of the Passover liturgy, and the "Lamb of God who takes away the sins of the world," an image lifted out of the liturgy of Yom Kippur. Later, Western doctrinal concepts like "Incarnation" and "Trinity" were used as explanations. But Christpower was the name of the sense of love, forgiveness, expanded life, and expanded being that seemed to have been associated originally with Jesus. As that power was experienced beyond the life of this Jesus, it tended to be called "Holy Spirit," but I tried to continue to call it Christpower, for that left it vague, undefined, and inclusive. It had helped me be open to the claims on truth brought to me by Jews in the dialogue. It was a good way, I thought, to close the television program, and it was the final word.

Seabury published the book that spring. It was not destined to be a great book, but it sold out its first printing primarily in the Richmond area. The public-service television station talked to the rabbi and me about developing for 1976 a twenty-session television series. We agreed we would work on that and present them with a model. My only wonder was where the time would come from to accomplish all these projects.

The final event in the dialogue did not occur until the following fall when Jack Spiro and I were announced as recipients of the Brotherhood awards of the Richmond chapter of the National Conference of Christians and Jews. The awards would be presented at a formal dinner held in the grand ballroom of the John Marshall Hotel. The newly elected Republican governor of Virginia, Mills Godwin, would be the speaker. Each of the nominees was invited with spouse to this black-tie affair, where we would have a small private cocktail party with the governor prior to the large dinner. We would then be seated with our wives on the dais on either side of the governor and his wife. I told Joan about these plans and was told quickly that she would not go. Mills Godwin, the governor, had been a hard turn to the right for our state, succeeding the moderate Republican Linwood Holton. Though they were of the same party, Godwin, a former Democrat, had been part of the ex-Byrd machine takeover of the heretofore progressive, but now conservative, Republican party. In Joan's mind he was part of the group spying on her. She would not be in the same room with him. To have her boycott this event was hurtful to me, but I did not know what to do about it.

I asked Kathy, my oldest daughter still at home, if she would attend with me as my family representative. She happily agreed, but I knew that Joan's absence would cause the rumors to fly after this dinner, where perhaps one thousand of Richmond's leading citizens would be present. I shared my distress with Jack Spiro, who knew about my wife's sickness. He responded in a way that was deeply touching and revealed the kind of person he was. Discussing this with his wife, he decided with her consent that he would take his teenage daughter, Hillary, to the dinner and when he spoke he would inform the assembled hosts that each of us had brought our daughter to this event because it was their generation who would be the ones to rid this nation of its prejudices. The people applauded. The gossip never developed. I was deeply in his debt. It was hard not to be excited by the opportunities that I was given.

I suppose it is inevitable that local success begins to get non-local attention. During the previous few years, I had begun to receive inquiries from individuals, sometimes from official nominating committees, asking about my willingness to be considered as a nominee for the office of bishop in a variety of dioceses as diverse as Tennessee, West Virginia, Nebraska, Olympia (western Washington State), and Mississippi. I was not interested at that time and wrote letters declining. I was touched by the fact that I was being thought of for this office, but I was not ready to leave St. Paul's.

A feeler from the diocese of Delaware arrived in late 1974 while the dialogue was in full swing. It was one I could not immediately dismiss. I had led the clergy conference for that diocese earlier in the year at the invitation of their bishop, William Mead, the same man under whose direction I had done my fieldwork assignment during my middle year in seminary. The conference was held in the Pocono Mountains of Pennsylvania and was based on my soon to be published book, *This Hebrew Lord*. The conference went well, and it was good to see Bill and Kate Mead again. Bob Smith, my former clergy mate and tennis partner in Lynchburg, was present as the rector of a Wilmington church. I was deeply distressed just weeks later to hear that Bill Mead had died in his sleep. I could not get to the funeral, but a week later I drove to Wilmington to pay my respects and to have a long visit with his wife, Kate. I had admired Bill immensely.

It was because of those connections that I decided I ought to at least consider this opportunity, so I did not decline. In January 1975 I received visitors from Delaware and later at their invitation went to Wilmington to meet with diocesan leaders. Ned Kimmel, the son of Admiral Kimmel of Pearl Harbor fame, was the chair of the nominating committee. The visit went well, and shortly thereafter I was informed that I would be one of their five official nominees. The others were James Moodey, William Clark, John Sanders, and Larry Whittenore. I was distinctly conflicted when I got this news, excited and depressed simultaneously. To have the possibility of succeeding Bill Mead was tremendously fulfilling, but to leave Richmond at this time was anything but a pleasant idea.

Having never been in this situation before, all I knew how to do was roll with the process. I went to Delaware and was given a tour all over the state. I met exciting people, learned about the issues they faced, experienced something of their history expressed in the ministry, not just of Bill Mead, but of their former bishops, two of whom were still alive. I also got to know better a group of young Delaware clergy led by Jack McKelvey, who seemed eager to elect me their bishop. I suppose I lived with my inner tension about the possibility of being elected bishop, because deep down I could not imagine such an election result. Returning home, I waited for the election date with mixed feelings.

Between my visit and the date of the election, I received letters from a majority of the clergy in that diocese informing me that they were positive about the possibility of my election. If they were representative and if they carried through, that meant that I was almost a sure shot to win. My emotional escape hatch was being closed.

I talked with my children, who were not opposed to a move to Wilmington. Joan was neutral. I had the slight sense she felt she might escape constant surveillance if she moved out of Richmond.

I wondered if I would have sufficient friends to sustain my personal life outside of Richmond. In Richmond I had a circle of friends who worked with me closely, who welcomed me into their homes and lives, who understood the vacuum at the center of my life. I did not feel I could replicate them in Delaware. I wondered if, as a bishop, I could write books or do things like the Jewish-Christian dialogue.

Professionally, being a bishop was not my ambition. I could see myself more in the mold of a Walter Russell Bowie or a Theodore P. Ferris, both of whom were priests, lecturers, and authors. That was for me lofty ambition indeed, beyond my grasp I was sure, but that was the direction that felt right to me.

Finally, I had a difficult time imagining myself living in Delaware. It felt off the beaten track to me. Outside of Wilmington, it was very rural and very conservative. It was basically a one-industry state. I wondered what it would feel like to live in an economy dominated by the DuPont Company. It was a one-university state as well, and the University of Delaware, though a fine school, did not seem to me to be a frontier place where the culture was either challenged or engaged. None of these feelings by themselves was substantial, but the cumulative effect was weighty. I do believe that we must listen to our feelings. My deepest concern, however, lay in the question that kept being raised about how I could cope with the role of bishop with Joan's health the way it was and whether I could make it without my Richmond friends. These were intuitive reservations grounded in selfish considerations surely, but they were determinative and inescapable.

As the day drew near, it was clearer and clearer to me that I was not of a mind to allow myself to be elected. The church in Delaware needed a bishop who was eager to serve them. It needed a person who had a vision for that state and an eagerness to bring that vision into being, not a reluctant bishop who was unable to appreciate the gifts it had to give because he preferred to be somewhere else. It became obvious to me that honesty required a withdrawal. I talked to John Hines at length about it. He had an enormously high view of the episcopate. In his mind the bishop of the smallest and most remote diocese could shape the church more effectively than could the rector of the largest and most influential parish. But John also understood the nature of vocation, and if there was no energy for a position, he thought that fact ought to have attention paid to it. Still he urged me to wait until the last minute, so that I was sure that my mind would not change.

On the day before the election, I called Ned Kimmel to tell him I was withdrawing. He was disappointed and, I suppose, could not avoid feeling the hurt of an affront. But he also knew that it is demeaning to one's own church or diocese to try to talk someone into loving it and wanting it if they did not. I told him I would send a formal statement via Western Union that could be read to the electing convention at the start of the next day.

There was both disappointment and anger among the people of Delaware. I understood that. William Clark, the oldest of the candidates nominated, was finally elected, but it took eleven ballots. I was roundly criticized in ecclesiastical circles and among certain conservative bishops who seemed to suggest that I had insulted the office itself by withdrawing. I honestly thought that this episode would end forever any possibility of my being a bishop. I was not unhappy with that conclusion. I remained on the executive council. My voice was increasingly heard in the national leadership debate. My third book, *The Dialogue*, had just been published. Mine was a rich life, and the Sunday morning after my withdrawal the congregation of St. Paul's made it very clear that they were elated with my decision and looked forward to a long rectorship. So did I.

My fourth book was to be published that fall. It was, strangely enough, a book I did not write at all. Yet all of its words were mine. My gifted editor and administrative assistant, Lucy Negus, had the task of preparing each Sunday's sermon for publication the following week. I preached from a full manuscript that I had edited many times before I delivered it. I even edited it between the 8:00 and 11:00 services, usually in response to Jean LeRoy's criticism. But we also taped the sermon, because a live delivery sometimes senses when ideas are not clear and expands them in an ad lib fashion. Lucy would type up the handwritten manuscript, listen to the tape, add in any ad libs, and finally edit it for clarity. I would go over her edited version for any final changes before okaying it for reproduction.

In early 1973 her edited versions began to appear with a one-page blank verse rendition of the major point of the sermon. My words, but her layout, design, and style. I looked forward to these synopses, and the file of them began to grow week by week. I was so enamored with her abilities that I began to write the sermons with this blank-verse rhythm in mind. For the Christmas service of 1974 I wrote the whole sermon in this style, calling it "The Birth of the Christpower." It combined my work in the dialogue, my developing new theology of God as a divine presence more than an external supernatural being, and my work on the birth narratives. The result was very positive. Lucy was bringing out of me and my words a communicating power I did not know I possessed.

By chance one day she showed her collection of blank-verse renditions of my sermons to a young man named Thomas Hale, who was doing some other work for her. Tom had his own local publishing company specializing in coffee-table books, with pictures and minimum script, that featured cities or regions of Virginia in which there was local pride. They were classy, slick volumes, expensive to purchase, elegantly designed, and meant to be gift books.

When Tom saw these seventy to eighty blank-verse pieces that Lucy had created over the last two or more years, he immediately envisioned it as a luxury coffee-table book for Christmas. He asked for permission to publish them. He believed that the publicity around the dialogue would provide him with sufficient market to guarantee a success. He showed us his plans—a large volume with a black cover highlighting the word "Christpower" emblazoned across it. High-quality, cream-colored, almost velvet paper would hold the words. They would be interlaced with expensive sheets of various colors. Large Old English artistic designs would mark the first letter of each of the poems. The cover would include my name as author and Lucy's name as "arranged by." We would share whatever royalties were involved. The book was to be out in late September, sell for $14.95, an enormous price in that day, and be pitched at the Christmas season. A sale of one thousand volumes would meet his costs; two thousand copies would turn a significant profit. We agreed, and my fourth book became a reality. It felt like the absolute justification for staying in Richmond.

That summer I was preparing to begin a number of trips to pick up my research into the life of John Hines. Together with my family I would spend time in New York reading his correspondence and papers. I would visit St. Louis, Missouri, where he began his ministry as curate to Karl Morgan Block, and Hannibal, Missouri, where he had served his first rectorship. Then I would move on to Augusta, Georgia, and Houston, Texas, to read the vestry minutes of the years John had served as rector in each of those places. That would be expanded in Texas to include his years as coadjutor and as bishop of Texas, where his papers, his addresses, and the diocesan journals were available. I would also go into the archives of local newspapers in each town in search of Hines stories and would seek out key people for interviews. At the end of that summer we also were looking forward to our family time at the shore.

Before departing on the first of these normally three-to-four-day jaunts, I went to Stuart Circle Hospital to pay a call on a member of St. Paul's. When I was leaving, the patient in the next room called out to me as I walked past his open door. I went in to meet my caller. His name was Francis Slade Danzoll, and he was a retired priest who had once been the archdeacon of Hudson County and rector of St. Paul's Church in Bergen, a section of Jersey City, New Jersey. I had not met this man before. He attended another Episcopal church in town and I gather played a lot of golf in his retirement. He knew me, however, because he listened to the adult class each Sunday morning on the radio. He informed me that the assistant bishop of Newark, the Right Reverend Kenneth Anand, had died. I knew that, for I had written the resolution of condolence passed rather routinely at the last meeting of the executive council. He went on to say that the diocesan bishop, George Rath, just three years short of retirement, had decided to call for a coadjutor bishop to be elected in 1976 who could work with him to bring about a smooth transition in 1978. The nominating committee had sent letters to all bishops and to all the clergy of Newark, active and retired, soliciting nominees. Slade had received this letter and wanted to submit my name. He could not believe I had just walked past his door. I appreciated his confidence, but I really did not want to go through that process again and told him so. He argued that at this stage there would be 150 names submitted to this committee and that the chances of anything coming from his nomination were remote. He hoped, he said, that I would at least allow him the privilege of sending in the nomination.

I had never been to Newark in my life except to land at the airport and to take a bus quickly into New York City. I did not think at this time that I knew a soul in New Jersey. The Diocese of Newark was part of the metropolitan New York area. It was far beyond my orbit of travel or life experience. Delaware still felt Southern to me. New York did not. I told Slade I would think about it and would let him know. I did look at the diocese of Newark in the *Episcopal Annual* that day and my memory was refreshed by the fact that this was the diocese to which Leland Stark had been elected from his rectorship at Epiphany Church in Washington, D.C., where I had known him while a seminary student. He was still there albeit retired. I also discovered two seminary classmates, Wayne Schwab, who had been a year ahead of me and who was now the rector in Montvale, New Jersey, and Herbert

Donovan, who had been two years behind me and who was a rector in Montclair, New Jersey. To my surprise, I also found the name of Philip Cato on that diocesan roster. He was associate rector of St. Peter's Church in Morristown. As a boy Philip had sung with me in the boys' choir at St. Peter's in Charlotte and he had been a close friend of my younger brother. He had gone to seminary at Episcopal Divinity School in Massachusetts and I had totally lost contact with him. That was the extent of my knowledge of people in New Jersey.

Slade called me on Tuesday of the next week and pressed me for a decision. It occurred to me that this might be an opportunity to make up publicly for my Delaware withdrawal. I could agree to be considered. I would probably not be nominated. If I were, I would surely not be elected. So I agreed. The election would not be until March 6, 1976, and that seemed an eternity away. To say I was a reluctant candidate would not be an overstatement.

The summer unfurled, and a busy one it was. My notes on John Hines kept growing. So did my tape recordings. I anticipated a final summer of research in 1976 and then beginning to pull the material together in a narrative form by summer 1977. Lucy Negus and Carter McDowell were also doing research trips. They interviewed a number of people in New York and actually revisited step by step the Hines tour of the Bedford-Stuyvesant district in New York City in their attempt to capture the passion that John had put into his General Convention Special Program address in 1967. This project was certainly developing on schedule.

Seabury Press had, in the meantime, suggested I look at doing a book on ethics based on the Ten Commandments. So I scheduled myself to start teaching the book of Exodus in the adult class that coming fall. I would work on Exodus until I arrived at Exodus 20 and then I would spring into a detailed analysis of the Commandments. They constituted rich material and opened the door to dealing with changing patterns of human sexuality, to say nothing of the moral issues present in abortion, war, capital punishment, and euthanasia. Having watched the ethics volume in the Church's Teaching Series come to such an impasse and to be over a year late in its publication, I was eager to do a study in this area. Books by Brevard Childs and Martin Noth became my two primary resources on Exodus. In our staff meetings we were also thinking about doing another dialogue series of sermons, this time on medical ethics as part of our education program. St. Paul's congregation had recently begun to do some serious work in the resettlement of refugees from Vietnam. That too was raising interesting issues. Finally, I was determined to do a series of sermons this year on the subject "This I Do Believe," based on the creeds. It was designed to state a modern faith in a positive manner, and I looked forward to it. So I plunged into the fall program with a sense of great expectations. I forgot about the process in the Diocese of Newark, which seemed so remote.

Returning from the beach in early September, I ran over a list of "while you were away" notes from Lucy Negus. Among the notes was a memo about a young doctor in our church who was having strange physical symptoms. His feet and ankles were swelling for no apparent reason. He was an anesthesiologist at the Medical College of Virginia named Jim Campbell. I went out that evening to see him.

Jim was in his early forties, married to a physician, and the father of two young children. I got to his home to discover an ominousness about the whole household. Jim was trying to believe he was having a reaction to some fertilizer he had been using on his roses, but everything about his manner revealed a lack of conviction. I was to watch the medical school faculty be unable to tell one of their popular physicians that he had acute leukemia, a hopeless diagnosis. They actually sent him to Duke Medical Center in Durham, North Carolina, so that those doctors could be the ones to inform him. I went with him to Durham and so became part of his family almost instantaneously. I saw him regularly over that first dreadful month. The treatment was almost as bad as the disease. Jim was forced to give up his medical practice at once. He became a part-time volunteer in our parish office during the last year of his life and I saw him almost daily. I even referred some people I was seeing in counseling to him when they needed to consult with an M.D. To walk inside the death experience of a friend is a rare privilege. It was to be rarer still, for though I did not know it then, Jim was destined to become my own pastor.

In late fall 1975 I received a letter from the chair of the Newark search committee informing me that the number of candidates was now down to twenty-five and I was among them. It asked for my consent to go forward. A month later another letter said they were down to twelve and I was still among them. They asked if I could come to Newark for an interview with the whole search committee in early January. I had a surprisingly good time on that interview. I recall making only one point to the nominating committee. Referring to my work on the adult class in my two most recent parishes, I stated that I would have to be convinced that I could be a teaching bishop.

If that were not possible, I would not be interested in the position. They responded to that idea with enthusiasm.

Returning home, I actually felt some excitement about this diocese. I discovered that the metropolitan New York area was a fascinating arena for all kinds of things from ideas to communication. To have the *New York Times* available at your door each morning excited me, given my treatment at the hands of the Southern press. To get New York television, which carried the Giants, the Jets, the Yankees, the Mets, the Knicks, and the Nets on a regular basis, was rich fare for this sports enthusiast. The diocese itself offered contrasts that were challenging. Its urban areas were quite depressed, with high unemployment figures. Its suburban areas were very affluent and vigorous, but the churches in them seemed with some obvious exceptions to be lifeless. New Jersey was second only to Connecticut in per capita wealth, but its five major urban areas were among America's most desperate cities. This diocese had a history of engaging the issues of its day. It sent women to the national convention of the Episcopal Church before women were allowed to be seated. It boasted among its clergy Nancy Wittig, one of the irregularly ordained women of 1974 who became known as the "Philadelphia Eleven." It had hosted a black-power conference in the midst of the urban riots of 1967. Its bishops, in previous administrations, had been active in the struggle against the war in Vietnam and in the civil rights movement. It boasted a cadre of outstanding clergy. It had, however, been in a holding pattern for about four years; one bishop had retired and the succeeding bishop's very short tenure due to his age precluded his starting things he could not finish. It had tremendous lay leaders who were veterans of many battles.

After this visit I felt that if one had to be a bishop, then the Diocese of Newark would be an exciting place. About ten days later a call came that I would be one of their five official nominees. Although still not eager to be elected, I did not feel any of the hesitancy I had felt in Delaware. I shared this story with Jim Campbell as it developed. He was one of the few I could talk with about it openly.

On a Sunday afternoon in February the five official candidates of the nominating committee and the three nominated by private petitions were introduced to the delegates to the election convention and invited to answer their questions. This formal assembly was held at the Marriott Hotel in Saddlebrook, New Jersey. Some six hundred clergy and lay deputies were present, divided into eight groups of approximately seventy-five each and assigned to eight different rooms. The eight nominees were sent to each of the eight rooms and given twenty minutes either to make a statement or answer people's questions. Since I had no statement I wanted to make and felt statements were themselves inappropriate, I went to each room, simply introduced myself as Jack Spong, and said "I'm here to respond to your questions." Others, I am told, spent half to three-quarters of their time on prepared remarks. I was certainly not interested in campaigning for the position, and I suppose that became obvious.

The big issues of that day were the ordination of women to the priesthood and the proposed revision of the *Book of Common Prayer*. When these apparently divisive questions were asked of me, I responded as simply and bluntly as I could. If I was to be elected, I certainly did not want it to be on some false premise. So when asked about the ordination of women, I said "I favor it. Next question." Others, I am told, sought to straddle this issue and promised to support pastorally those on both sides of this raging debate.

When asked about the revision of the 1928 prayer book, I responded, "I helped to write it, so of course I'm in favor of its adoption." I had, in fact, been invited to be a consultant to the Standing Liturgical Commission and had worked particularly on the initiation rites of baptism and confirmation. I was asked a wide variety of other questions that day that ranged from my churchmanship, to my personal relationship with Jesus Christ, to how I prayed. No one asked about the job I was doing in Richmond or about my family. I thought that was strange. So I concluded each segment by saying that I believed my greatest gift was the teaching of adults. If I could not find a way to be a teaching bishop, then I hoped they would elect someone else. I did not need the episcopacy for a full life in my career. When the sessions were over, I felt exhilarated. They were a challenging group of clergy and laity.

About ten days before the election, Philip Cato called and asked if I would return and meet with a group of clergy alone. They wanted to discuss some issues they could not address in a public session. The meeting in Phil's home in Morristown, at which there were no more than fifteen to eighteen clergy, was an emotional one; much cynicism and many morale issues surfaced. Primarily, I listened and occasionally responded out of my own parish experience. One priest opened the session by saying he had heard I was a bomb thrower. I wasn't sure what that meant, but it sounded hostile. I told him that I believed the church should meet the issues of our world head on and that truth was more important to me than church unity. Unity is a very secondary virtue. Faithfulness and integrity were primary. I shared with them briefly some of my learnings from the Jewish-Christian dialogue and the hope that if I were a bishop, these things would not disappear from my life, drowned out by administrative trivia. I also repeated my concern that the position had to offer me a teaching outlet and that if I could not find one here, I did not want to be elected. The fact that I had withdrawn in Delaware gave credibility to that statement.

This was the last contact I had with anyone from the Diocese of Newark until Joe Herring called me on March 6, 1976, to tell me that I was about to be elected the eighth bishop of Newark and Bishop Rath called later to confirm the election. When the news broke across Richmond with a front-page story in Sunday morning's *Times Dispatch*, the response was strange. Some were pleased and offered congratulations. Some were angry and felt betrayed. Some simply distanced themselves from me. There was only one person with whom I could talk openly. That was Jim Campbell.

He was dying and he knew it. In an unusual way what I was experiencing was also a death. I was dying to a city and a parish I had loved intensely. I was dying to a region of the nation that was native to me. I was dying to many projects that had been very important to me. I would have to resign from the executive council. I would probably never be able to write the Hines book. I would be leaving the friends who had sustained me as I wrestled with my personal family crises. My second daughter would enter the University of Virginia when I moved to Newark. My third daughter, a rising senior at St. Catherine's, opted to finish her senior year in Richmond, so I was losing my children. None of them would move with me. No one understood that except Jim Campbell, and so our talks together became shared grief. He helped me sort out the issues of my dying as I helped him sort out the issues of his. No one else could have done that for me.

On May 30, I conducted my final Sunday services at St. Paul's. Jim died on Monday, May 31. On Thursday, June 3, I conducted my final service of any sort at St. Paul's. It was Jim's funeral. In a real sense, it was mine also. I arrived in Newark on June 6. No one there was aware of the profoundly moving experience through which I had just walked. I was to them simply the new bishop. It made communication difficult.

# I 4

# *Transition to the Episcopate and Developing a World View*

※

T HERE IS an enormous emotional wilderness that occurs between the
day one is elected to the episcopate and the moment of consecration. It
is a time of wrenching good-byes and the breaking of pastoral relationships.
It is accompanied by feelings of bereavement and guilt. But it is also a time
of high anticipation, excitement, and dreams, which inevitably get tempered
by reality. For me it was also the beginning of that process in which my
integrity and my faith were to be challenged by an organized conservative
ecclesiastical campaign.

As soon as I became the bishop-elect of Newark, I began to encounter the
dreadful reputation the city of Newark and the state of New Jersey possessed in the minds of many. One of the standing jokes was that this election
satisfied everybody—those who liked me were glad I was to be a bishop, and
those who didn't were glad I was to be the bishop of Newark. My immediate
sense was that the very being of the city of Newark had absorbed enormous
negativity and was, therefore, a hurting city, desperately looking for love and
affirmation.

A delegation from the diocese, consisting of Hughes Garvin, the president of the standing committee and the rector of St. Peter's in
Morristown, Marge Christie, the president of the Episcopal Church
Women, and Phillip Cato, my longtime friend, arrived three days after the
election to extend to me in person the official invitation to become the
bishop of Newark. During their visit they also began to tell me about the
darker sides of the life of the diocese that had not been mentioned in the
election process.

There were deep conflicts in the diocese. The runner-up in the election was a priest named Tom Carson, rector of Christ Church in Greenville, South Carolina, who had been nominated by petition as a direct challenge to the nominating process. His supporters, led by the clergy on Bishop Rath's staff, projected him as one opposed to the major new initiatives being debated in the church at that time, namely, the ordination of women and the revision of the prayer book. I knew Tom Carson fairly well and found him to be a decent, open person with conservative, but not rigid, convictions. I suspect that his supporters were more conservative than he was. My chief anxiety attached to his candidacy was whether or not I would find a welcome among the members of Bishop Rath's staff who clearly had opposed my election, since, at least for the first two years, they would be my primary working colleagues.

I also learned that the dean of Newark's cathedral, Dillard Robinson, with whom I had served on the executive council of the national church, had been adamantly opposed to this "Southern white man" becoming bishop and trying to direct ministry in Newark, an overwhelmingly black city. Furthermore, I was informed that the old-line Anglo-Catholic churches were distressed that someone who, to say the least, was uncomfortable with Anglo-Catholic worship forms was now to be their bishop. The rectors of these churches were also all but universally opposed to the ordination of women and were preparing to protect their position at all costs. The more evangelical churches in the diocese were worried because the bishop-elect had been debated in the national church press as one who was not comfortable with such traditional Christological formulas as the Incarnation and the Holy Trinity. They wondered about my orthodoxy. Everywhere I turned there seemed to be another obstacle. I began to wonder how I happened to have been elected.

To my surprise, I learned that tapes of my very recent adult Bible classes had, since the election, been floating around in conservative circles in Newark, receiving on their journey something less than an approving response. In that class we had arrived at Exodus 20, and I had turned my attention to a unit on the Ten Commandments. My task was to open that ancient moral code to new knowledge and circumstances that would inevitably destabilize the power of what might be called objective ethical standards. In the class on the last Sunday in February (the Sunday before my election), I had concluded my series of lectures on the sixth commandment, "You shall do no murder." In that series I had gone into such issues as birth control, abortion, euthanasia, and capital punishment and spent some time challenging the theory of a just war. The dialogue on medical ethics that I was doing at the 11:00 A.M. service also fed those classes, particularly during the question period.

On the day after the election, as fate would have it, I started the series of lectures in the adult class on issues in human sexuality, with my point of entry being the seventh commandment, "You shall not commit adultery." I began by lifting the definition of women as the property of men out of the background of this commandment. I had proceeded to discuss whether or not sex inside marriage is always holy and to raise the possibility that, if marriage did not always make sex holy, then sex outside of marriage might not always be destructive. I could and did illustrate both of those principles with pastoral insights out of my own counseling experience. This kind of open and forthright discussion of issues had become commonplace in our class. It did not occur to me that outside the environment we had built in St. Paul's such an honest discussion of these ideas might be heard as radical, controversial, and even shocking. I was, in this teaching role, following the motto of my seminary, "To seek the truth of God come whence it may, cost what it will."

I was amused later when I heard that critics had reduced this exciting class to a one-line cliché by asserting that my election as bishop "came between murder and adultery." It was for me a new experience to have people, not out of ignorance, but out of a deliberate malevolence, attempt to violate my integrity and to smear my reputation by twisting and distorting my words.

All of these concerns cascaded upon me in that first contact with the delegation from the Diocese of Newark. I clearly had my work cut out for me.

I requested the opportunity of coming to Newark to meet with the clergy prior to accepting the election. This was granted, and in three sites around the diocese the clergy gathered to engage their bishop-elect in dialogue. My sense after these gatherings was that the clergy of this diocese were a depressed group with little sense of direction. Bishop Stark had been ill. Bishop Rath was, in effect, an interim bishop, and a sense of meaningless drift had embraced the diocesan leaders. The crucial and key rectors in such places as Madison, Morristown, Short Hills, and Summit were nearing retirement, so their ability to lead was diminished. The diocese had been in a steep membership slide since the mid-1960s. Many churches were simply no longer viable, and this was eating away at clergy morale.

I tried to convey to the clergy the sense that I was not coming to attempt to remake the diocese in my own image, but rather to seek a partnership so that together we could address the issues before us. I am sure that these words, however, sounded empty.

Joan, of course, did not accompany me on this trip. I stayed in the homes of two clergy families who, though they were kind and friendly, were nonetheless strangers and, whether I liked it or not, cast me in the role of an authority figure. I had my first sense of the intense loneliness that was going to mark my life in this new role. I also confronted among certain clergy overt rude behavior. It was focused in conservative, traditional circles. The surface issue was the ordination of women, but I suspect that this negativity would have been present even if that were not the issue. Within two years these negative clergy had left the diocese, some for membership in rightwing splinter churches, some for retirement.

Two of the clergy of the diocese had been among the official nominees for the office of bishop. They were David Gillespie, of Englewood, and Herbert Donovan, of Montclair. One diocesan priest, Robert Maitland, who was passed over by the nominating committee, had been nominated by petition. None of them came close to being elected, as the mood of the convention was clearly to elect someone from outside the diocese. I wrote to each of these clergy immediately after the election to tell them that I looked forward to working with them, that I would need their help, and that I hoped to be worthy of their friendship. Both Herbert and David responded with gracious letters and, in fact, proved to be wonderful and supportive friends. Later I was to preach the sermon at David's installation as dean of Grace Cathedral in San Francisco and to be one of Herbert's co-consecrators when he became bishop of Arkansas. Robert Maitland, however, never responded to my letter and organized his life from that day to the day of his retirement as my chief in-diocese critic. I felt sad that negativity engulfed his otherwise effective career.

When I returned home from these visits, I wrote my official letter of acceptance to Newark and my official letter of resignation to St. Paul's. I was touched that Bob Hall, who by this time had succeeded Bob Gibson as the bishop of Virginia, wrote a public letter first to St. Paul's thanking me for my ministry there and then to the Diocese of Newark to introduce me to them as one that he trusted, admired, and welcomed as a colleague in the House of Bishops.

Almost immediately after these official communications were written, I became aware that my election was destined to be challenged by conservative church voices around the nation, led by Carroll Simcox, the editor of *The*

*Living Church*, and Perry Laukhuff, the editor of a right-wing news sheet called *The Certain Trumpet*. These two men, in the company of about twenty of their supporters, wrote to each bishop and standing committee in the nation urging them not to concur with the election, which, under the canons, required a majority consent from both groups. Both men had identified their version of Christianity with Christianity itself, which is in my mind nothing short of idolatry. Once again I saw how deeply dishonest religious debate can be. For one to ascertain the truth is a legitimate concern, but to seek to darken a person's public character with slanted innuendos and quotations strangely out of context is not a legitimate tactic. It is, however, as I was to learn, frequently the tactic of religious debates. This is a manifestation of the same religious mentality that fed the horror of religious wars, the Inquisition, and church splits. I would never get used to this behavior coming from those who claimed that they were in the service of the God of love, and I would also never escape it.

As the consent process developed, I stayed in touch with John Hines. He understood the church and its pockets of hostility well, and he never doubted that the confirmation would be overwhelming. I did learn later that about a year before my election a man named Robert Terwilliger, an ultraconservative priest from New York, had been elected bishop suffragan of the Diocese of Dallas. His election had been vigorously opposed by some liberal elements in the church before he had finally been approved. That liberal opposition had not been forgotten, and my election provided the conservatives with an opportunity for payback time. I found this confirming procedure so demeaning and so dishonest I vowed I would never use it to foster any political agenda in the church, and so I have not only supported, but have actively and publicly campaigned for, the confirmation of the right-wing bishops duly elected in dioceses of our church, including Edward MacBurney, John David Schofield, Terence Kelshaw, Jack Iker, and Keith Ackerman. None of them ever reciprocated by trying to reach across to the liberal side of the church to build a community that could embrace our rich diversity. Indeed, every one of them later used his episcopal office to engage in activities designed to purge liberals like me from the church. Their behavior was consistently disappointing, as it always is when people confuse their own point of view and value system with God's will. Yet that is the weakness that seems to corrupt religious people constantly.

During the confirmation process three episodes were particularly noteworthy. One was that the standing committee of West Virginia voted not to concur with my election despite the fact that their nominating committee a year earlier had officially asked me to consider election as bishop of West Virginia. It was the election in which Robert Atkinson of Memphis, Tennessee, was ultimately chosen. The president of the West Virginia standing committee was Francis Wade, and he wrote to me the letter of rejection. He would someday apologize for that act and invite me to do a series of lectures in St. Alban's Church on the grounds of the National Cathedral in Washington, where he was later to be the rector.

The second memorable episode came when the standing committee of the Diocese of Arkansas also refused to give their consent. Their bishop, Christoph Keller, was in England when that vote was taken. Not only was the bishop, through his foundation, underwriting the expenses of my Hines research, but his daughter, Neil, was a member of St. Paul's in Richmond. Beyond that, Chris Keller had come on two occasions at my invitation to baptize his grandchildren and to preach at St. Paul's. There was also the fact that Neil had developed a brain tumor, and I had been privileged to be with that family through that crisis, which included a hospital-room Eucharist around her bed prior to surgery that most of us were not sure she would survive. We were all in tears that night, and the bonding grief experience had been intense. Bishops, I discovered, cease to be bishops and become fathers when the life of a daughter is at stake. She survived that surgery and the tumor turned out to be benign, but my relationship with Chris had that experience in its background. When Chris Keller learned of the action by his standing committee upon his return to Little Rock, he wrote a letter to his standing committee protesting their action and outlining his reasons why. At their next meeting the standing committee of Arkansas reversed the decision and voted unanimously to concur.

A telephone call from a man who introduced himself as "Father Wantland," the president of the standing committee of the Diocese of Oklahoma, ushered in the third memorable episode in the confirmation process. Bill Wantland was a self-educated former lawyer and family court judge in Oklahoma who had been ordained to the priesthood without attending an accredited seminary. He had taken courses here and there and read privately until he passed canonical exams in Oklahoma. His mind was perceptive, but bounded by rigid lines beyond which he could not think. He had the ability to recall massive amounts of irrelevant data from church history and to quote obscure sources that no one knew well enough to challenge. He was deeply rooted in the Catholic side of the Anglican Communion and seemed to believe that Christianity was to be identified with the ancient formulations of the church fathers. I'm sure Bill felt there was no significant church history after the sixth century. Dogmatic theology, which to me is an oxymoron, was for him the major discipline a priest needed to master. If one did not ascribe to the dogma of the church as the fathers articulated it, one simply was not a Christian in his mind. I thought this attitude was quaint and could not believe any citizen of the twentieth century could think this way. But I listened as he set about to check out my orthodoxy over the telephone.

He read me some passages from antiquity that I immediately recognized as the writings of Arius, the protagonist to Athanasius in the battle to formulate the creeds in the early fourth century. Then he asked me to comment on these passages. I found this tactic both arrogant and amusing. Bill would in the future elicit both words from me more than once.

I told him he was reading from Arius and why I believed that Arius's understanding of Christology was inadequate. He was pleased and Oklahoma's standing committee voted to concur with my election. I did not have a chance to tell him that I also believed Athanasius's understanding of Christology to be inadequate. Bill could only deal with one litmus test at a time.

By mid-April sufficient consents were in to know that confirmation would not be a problem, and so Bishop Rath began to gather a group of clergy together as a liturgical committee to plan the consecration service. Strangely enough, not once was I consulted on this matter either by the bishop or by the committee. Their first decision was to get permission to hold the consecration in the Roman Catholic Cathedral of the Sacred Heart in Newark, a beautiful Gothic structure that could seat up to twenty-five hundred people. It was not a venue I would have chosen. The Roman Catholic attitude toward women offended me deeply. The way this church dealt with its own most creative scholars seemed to me to preclude any serious theological debate on any issue. Its rejection of family planning and birth control was, in my mind, immoral. Its blanket condemnation of homosexuality in the face of the fact that so many of its priests and bishops were gay men was to me without character. It also concerned me that we would be consecrating a bishop in a cathedral where the Roman Catholic archbishop would decline to receive communion in a service he was hosting and in which I would not be welcomed to receive communion at one of their services. I would have preferred a secular setting like Symphony Hall in Newark or even the Meadowlands as a sign that the church I was leading would have every intention of engaging the world. But it was not to be. To change it after plans were made, however, would be rude, and so I acquiesced.

When the committee then went on to design the liturgy, sending to me their finished proposal without inquiring as to my desires, I was disturbed. When I read the outline of their proposed service, I was appalled. You would have thought a king was being crowned. It seemed to have everything in it except my being borne on a seat carried by four people with poles across their shoulders so that the crowds could bow and I could give them my episcopal blessing. If a consecration service is designed to introduce a new bishop to the diocese, this service would be guilty of violating the truth-in-packaging laws. I was ceremonially a low churchman. I was, in the grand sense of that word, an "evangelical." Unfortunately, that word had become identified with a narrow fundamentalist perspective that was also anathema to me, so I could not use the word without being misunderstood. I understood that there were some churches in the diocese where Catholic liturgy was their style, and I was prepared to meet their expectations as lovingly as I could. But I did not want to have that practice imposed on me or upon the diocese. Above all, I found it rude beyond measure that anyone would plan a service that would be perhaps the most significant moment in my ecclesiastical career without once consulting me. So I wrote a letter to the chair of the committee, with a copy to Bishop Rath, in which I thanked him and his committee for their work, but told them that I had other plans. I did not care for incense. I had no intention of chanting the service, and I would choose the music, the vestments, and the participants. I doubt if that letter made me any friends in a group I already knew as not disposed to be friendly.

I thought long and hard about that letter before I sent it. They had put me in a position where my only choices were to acquiesce or to reject. It was a clear power play in my mind. If I acquiesced, I would never have a chance to be myself in this office. If I rejected their plans, I would create a hardened core of opposition. I held George Rath responsible for placing me in that situation and told him so on my next visit. There was not a malevolent bone in George's body, I learned. He was as sweet and kind a person as I had ever met, but he was simply not a strong leader and bowed to pressure wherever it appeared. When he understood my feelings, he did everything he could to rectify the situation.

Up until this time I was open to trying to do whatever would be expected of me in this wonderfully diverse diocese. But now I concluded that I must establish my personal identity before I got lost in the trappings of the office of bishop. It was almost a survival issue for me. So I made difficult, but calculated, decisions. I would live out a style of episcopacy that was appropriate to me publicly and in diocesan services, but when I was the confirming bishop in a local congregation, I would try to conform to their liturgical style. Above all, I would try to be accessible, to meet regularly with congregations in settings where they could ask questions, express concerns, and hear me face-to-face. I would seek to communicate directly with the laypeople of the diocese, so that I would not be so distant that I had to be filtered to the congregation by way of the priest. After five years, it was my hope that my identity would be established and I could then more comfortably wear the symbols of the office. Whether this was a wise decision I cannot say. That it was a necessary decision to my personal well-being I have never had a doubt.

For five years I could not bring myself to wear the purple shirt of the bishop's office. It reminded me of someone trying to be Robin Redbreast. In Richmond I had frequently worn only a shirt and tie. I put that habit away and vowed that in my office and on every official occasion I would wear the clerical collar, even though the shirt would be black. My vestments of choice would be rochet and chimere rather than cope and miter. I had difficulty with the miter, because it was nothing but an ecclesiastical version of a king's crown. I was not interested in being "a prelate." It amazed me that a bishop could dress in a crown, wear a royal cape, sit in a chair called a throne, live in a house called a palace, wear the royal signet ring on his finger, which people would kneel to kiss, carry the ecclesiastical version of the royal staff known as a crozier in his hand, and still convince anyone that the business of the church and its clergy was to be servant to the people of God.

Furthermore, until people began to talk to each other in chants, I felt that this was not the proper language of worship. Genuflecting and incense seemed to me to be part of a liturgy that exalted not God, but the priest. Using the parental words "Father" to refer to the clergy and "Mother" to refer to the church encouraged, I believed, passive dependency among the people. In my mind the task of the church was not to keep people childlike, but to encourage them, as Paul said, to grow into "the fullness of the stature of Christ Jesus" that was within them. I was not enamored with clergy or congregations who in every detail of their corporate life seemed to me to play some ecclesiastical version of that game "Father Knows Best." The world I lived in was not the thirteenth century, where only the clergy were educated. My world was a dynamic, intellectually exploding world of space travel and subatomic physics, a world of modern medicine and overpopulation, in which resources were both limited and not distributed equitably even at minimum levels. I wanted the church to speak to that world.

So my consecration service as a bishop was reorganized. All the bishops wore rochet and chimere, even the presiding bishop. John Hines was my preacher and his sermon was a clarion call to involvement in the world and a wonderful introduction of me and my values as only John could rehearse them. The liturgy was out of the proposed revision of the *Book of Common Prayer*. I was, in that choice, affirming liturgical change. The canon of consecration was form "C," which spoke of galaxies and interstellar space. The hymns were my favorites anchored by Harry Emerson Fosdick's great poem, "Grant us wisdom, grant us courage for the facing of this hour," and the combined choirs sang a medley of my favorite choral pieces from my years as a boy soprano. My wife and children were to bring forward the elements. My brother, Will, was to be the litanist and my cousin Bill, the former senator, was to read the Epistle. Rabbi Jack Daniel Spiro was to read the Hebrew Scriptures, first in Hebrew, then in English. I was accompanied by two personal chaplains, Walton Pettit, my assistant from St. Paul's, and Phillip Cato.

It was appropriate to ask the Roman Catholic archbishop, Peter Gerety, to bring greetings since we were in his cathedral. So we did. He spoke, however, for forty-five minutes, making the service almost three hours long. It was my first experience of Roman Catholic insensitivity. Jack Allin also presented me officially to the congregation in polite, but brief and restrained, comments. I looked out on that congregation through misty eyes and saw people who touched me deeply. James "Duke" Stewart, the black head of the Richmond Human Relations Commission had ridden a bus all night from Richmond to be there. Elderly people, like Kitty Guy who was in her eighties and Elizabeth Scott Anderson in her seventies, from St. Paul's Church had come, and of course my core of special friends, Lucy Negus, Carter McDowell, Robin Valentine, and Jean LeRoy. Russell Palmore, who directed the acolytes at St. Paul's, and his wife, JoAnne, were also there.

Two unique events marked the service itself. One was that somehow my stole got misplaced and I found myself walking in without one, so Herbert Donovan took off his stole and gave it to me. I later told him that at least the right stole, if not the right man, was consecrated. He smiled.

The second was that demonstrators picketed the service carrying placards. The conservative Episcopal press reported this as a lingering sign of the controversial nature of my election. They should have investigated more closely, had they been interested in the truth rather than propaganda. The picketers were all conservative Roman Catholics picketing Archbishop Gerety for allowing the Roman Catholic cathedral to be used for a Protestant worship ceremony. It was one more bit of evidence that the conservative religious press would not act with integrity. I filed that conclusion for future reference.

Since we had had no time to look for housing, we simply sublet a furnished house for the summer, while its owners were in Europe. We would not actually move out of our Richmond home until September 1, so Joan and the children could remain there or visit in New Jersey as they saw fit. This arrangement served our purposes well, for I was not to be home much before September.

More than a year before my election I had been picked to represent our church at three "Partners in Mission" conferences, a program of the Anglican Communion to build a global identity by inviting delegates from abroad to assist in the mission planning of the host province. The team from the United States was to have been a priest, myself, and a bishop, the Right Reverend Wesley Frensdorff of Nevada. When I was elected bishop, it meant that our team suddenly included two bishops. Since it took about a year of preparation to get ready for these conferences, the decision was made not to change our team. The trip was to the provinces of Kenya, Mauritius, and Southern Africa. When I discovered that I was going to be a bishop, I felt that I needed an introduction to world issues, so I added visits to Geneva and Rome on the front of that trip and one to Israel on the back. In Geneva I wanted to get a briefing on the Christian Church globally through the offices of the World Council of Churches. In Rome I wanted to make contact with Vatican officials, discuss the worldwide ecumenical scene, and visit the holy sites of that city. In Israel I wanted to establish contact with Jewish leaders and, if possible, with Muslim leaders and to tour the Holy Land for the first time. I felt that a Christian leader had to be knowledgeable about the whole world's religious scene if he or she intended to speak effectively. It would be an expansive time for me, though it would also consume the bulk of the summer. The Diocese of Newark knew about this before the election and approved it. I contacted Wesley Frensdorff and he agreed to join me on the Geneva-Rome part of the trip, but I would have to go to Israel alone, since he planned a stopover in Botswana.

I had never met Wesley, but I got to the airport first and booked us together into the nonsmoking section of the airplane. He never forgave me for that. At least twice an hour, he felt compelled to go to the back of the plane to smoke. Despite that incompatibility, we became instant friends and were closely associated until his untimely death in a plane accident in the Grand Canyon in 1986. He had been born in a Jewish family in Germany. His real name was Wolfgang, not Wesley. He had escaped the Nazis as a child, first to England and then to the New York area, where he was raised as a Christian. He had a tremendous sense of humor, a story for every occasion, a lovely wife named Dee and five terrific children, whom I met on that occasion only through photographs. He was also, to my delight, ecclesiastically irreverent and stood loosely to many church traditions. In the trunk of his car he kept a three-legged stool, which he periodically removed and sat on, announcing that the Cathedral of the Diocese of Nevada was now open and ready to function. He also clipped off the two sashes from his miter for the simple reason that "they tickled my neck" and then announced that he had the "only circumcised miter in Christendom." With an attitude like that, I might even become favorably disposed toward miters.

We had a super visit to Geneva. Our briefing officer was a South African expatriate Anglican priest named Khotso (Walter) Makhulu, who would someday become the archbishop of Central Africa. He roamed over the world giving us background, but we focused on South Africa, not only because that was his home, but also because we were going to be there for about ten days. He went into the history of apartheid, the distinctions between black South Africans, colored South Africans, Afrikaners, and English South Africans. He discussed the political situation and told us of the roles being played by the African National Congress, the attempts at compromise on the part of the Zulus, the imprisoned black political leader Nelson Mandela, and the resistance led by Mandela's wife, Winnie. He also spoke of a rising star in South Africa named Desmond Tutu, who was, at that time, dean of St. Mary's Cathedral in Johannesburg, but who had recently been elected bishop of Lesotho, one of the Bantu lands set aside for "independence" for blacks by the ruling South African government. We were to be present for Desmond's consecration and Wes and I had been asked to be co-consecrators. We both found the time spent with Walter to be enormously worthwhile and felt particularly well prepared to visit South Africa.

The stopover in Rome was for just three days, but we accomplished all our goals. We spent time with the Vatican's ecumenical officer and discussed a wide range of issues with him; we also met the head of the Anglican Church in Rome, the Reverend Harry Smythe, and became conversant with his ministry. We were fortunate to meet an American seminary student preparing for the Roman priesthood who was willing to take us touring. We spent eighteen to twenty hours a day trying to take in everything from the Sistine Chapel to the ancient Roman athletic ruins. We missed very little.

Going on to Nairobi, we participated in our first Partnership in Mission conference. Kenya was in what came to be called the "Kenyatta" phase of its history. It had won independence from Great Britain with the Mau-Mau tactics, but had settled into a fairly progressive government headed by Kenyatta that sought to build a nation using basically a modified capitalist economic system. We visited tea and coffee plantations and ate in what were once private clubs reserved for "English only." It was in one of these clubs that I met Leonard Coleman, who was at that time a lay mission appointee of the Episcopal Church. He was a member of St. Luke's in Montclair and would become a good friend, a noted Republican leader in New Jersey, and ultimately the president of baseball's National League.

I also met clergy and lay Christians from all over Africa, as well as John Bothwell, a Canadian bishop from the Diocese of Hamilton, who quickly joined Wes and me, making a regular threesome.

Among those who impressed me were two very young bishops, Henry Okullu and David Gitari, clearly the future leaders of the church in Kenya. Henry was a member of the Luo tribe and thus the recipient of a great deal of suspicion from the dominant Kikuyu tribe of President Kenyatta. It was because of that tribal identity that Henry never became the primate of the Anglican Church of Kenya. That role was passed to a Kikuyu bishop named Manassas Kuria, a man who could not come close to Henry in ability. David Gitari would in time become the primate of Kenya, but would be, for me at least, a disappointment in that role. He appeared to stagnate intellectually and to be frightened by new issues.

The trip to Mauritius brought me to an island in the Indian Ocean that is arguably the most beautiful spot in the world. It boasts of poinsettias growing wild along the roadside. There I met one of the church's great heroes, the Most Reverend Trevor Huddleston, who was the acting archbishop of Mauritius. Trevor had been one of the courageous leaders of the struggle for justice in South Africa until he was banished by the apartheid government and forced to return to England. The leaders of the "Catholic Party" of the Church of England who were in charge of the missionary work in Mauritius sent him to this lovely spot when the archbishop of Mauritius died quite suddenly. Trevor was to guide them until a successor was chosen, but he was to become my friend and would later visit us in the Diocese of Newark.

With a short stop in the Malagasy Republic, we flew on to Johannesburg. The stop in Madagascar was required by the politics of the day. Mauritius had broken off diplomatic relations with South Africa over riots occurring in the region of Soweto that the South African police had put down with excessive and murderous force, so our plane could not fly directly from Mauritius to Johannesburg. We left Mauritius on an Air Mauritius plane and landed in Madagascar. The plane then changed the signs over its door from "Air Mauritius" to "Air Madagascar" and on we flew. It made me understand that diplomatic relations were far more often rhetoric and show than acts of substance. That is why diplomatic attempts to isolate and punish economically an offending nation seldom work. They serve only the needs of local political propaganda.

When we arrived in Johannesburg, the reality of those Soweto riots came home to us in poignant horror. The riots had been triggered by a government policy requiring that all children be taught in the language known as Afrikaans as well as in English and whatever their native dialect was. It was in one sense not a major requirement, but it turned out to be the straw that broke the camel's back. For black young people in the district of Soweto (which stood for Southwest Township), Afrikaans was the language of oppression. It was the language of apartheid, and the language of the cruel pass laws. These young people were now to be required to learn the language of those whose power had reduced them to living in a survival mode. It was the match that ignited the passions created by apartheid, and once it was struck, the explosion was instantaneous. Rioting teenagers poured into the streets, breaking auto windows, turning cars over, igniting them, and expressing their total revulsion with apartheid. They had reached the point where they would rather be dead than continue to live in oppression. This episode was the beginning of the end of white rule in South Africa, but that was not recognized by either side at that moment in history.

South Africa's white riot police moved into Soweto in force and, in the ensuing conflict, murderous firepower was used by the police on the teenagers, killing between two and three hundred of them. The crowds were finally dispersed, and the government sent trucks in to pick up the dead who were lying about the streets. I was told that the bodies of these kids had been hurled unceremoniously onto the back of flatbed trucks, two or three deep, and carted off to the morgue. Grieving parents had to go to the morgue to sift through piles of bodies in an effort to identify their own sons and daughters. It was a scene hard to imagine, and the anger that flowed forth in the black community was hard to overemphasize.

The first thing I did in South Africa was to attend a memorial service for the Soweto victims in St. Mary's Cathedral conducted by the dean, Desmond Tutu. He articulated the pain in the black community but, to my amazement, he also articulated the need for Christian forgiveness, for love and inclusiveness. He did not appear to be infected with black anger, no matter how justified it might have been. He was clearly a man I wanted to know better.

We did meet him soon, along with his wife, Leah, and two of his children, his daughter Mpho and his son Trevor, named for Trevor Huddleston. We spent lots of time with Desmond and genuine bonds of affection grew between us. I was pleased that I would be one of his co-consecrators. I had no idea at that time what greatness lay in store for this man.

Desmond was the star of the consultation, which was held at a campsite in Rosettenville, just out of Johannesburg. We roomed with black South African Church leaders, a practice we were told violated the apartheid laws. It felt quite noble to be guilty of such violations.

When the conference was over, we all went to St. Mary's Cathedral for Desmond's consecration service, which would be conducted by the archbishop of Capetown, Bill Burnet. The sermon would be preached by Lawrence Zulu. Wes Frensdorff, Shannon Mallory, then the bishop of Botswana, John Bothwell of Canada, and I would be non-African co-consecrators. It was a moving service. I did try to conform to the South African liturgical tradition by seeking to wear the cope and miter provided. It was the first time I had ever had such vestments on. This particular set was both heavy and musty, but I got into them and was standing in the crowd trying not to be noticed in my dreadful self-consciousness. But my former classmate David Birney, who was present as staff to the consultation, would not allow me the luxury of anonymity. When he saw me fully vested in the regalia provided, he could not contain his laughter. Perhaps I did indeed look that funny. Perhaps David simply could not embrace the fact that this classmate of his whom he had first met when the classmate was but twenty-one years of age was now a bishop. But his laughter was contagious, and before long I was the source of much amusement. I wanted to crawl into a hole. Not able to do that, however, I proceeded to remove these vestments and to put on my rochet and chimere. Wesley Frensdorff kept me company by doing the same thing. So two rochets and chimeres were present among the copes and miters at Desmond Tutu's consecration. But my hands were on his head, and I had a small part in presenting this incredible person first to the episcopal office and then to the world.

Desmond was consecrated to be the bishop of Lesotho (pronounced Lesutu). We had great fun with the juxtaposition of Tutu of Lesotho. To equal that I suggested I would have to become Spong of Hong Kong. On numerous occasions in our future life together, we would use this rhyming name combination when we introduced each other.

Desmond would in time be the winner of the Nobel Peace Prize. He would move from being bishop of Lesotho to being the General Secretary of the South African Council of Churches, to being bishop of Johannesburg, to being archbishop of Capetown. On two occasions he spent a month as my guest serving as assistant bishop of Newark. He has confirmed Episcopalians in sixteen of our churches. These trips served as a kind of "R and R" break for him from the tensions of his struggles for freedom in his native land. He spoke in our diocese in May 1984, just five days after receiving the Nobel Peace Prize. He was in New York when the announcement was made. He immediately flew to South Africa so that he could share that prize with all those he represented, and he returned to New York to fulfill the commitment he had made to us two years earlier. We felt we were part of the process that lifted this man into world stature. I know we were proud of him and that I especially treasured our long and abiding friendship.

When the South African conference and the Tutu consecration were complete, we prepared to leave for the final leg of our journey. I bade farewell not just to Desmond Tutu, but also to my long-time traveling mate, Wesley Frensdorff, and to my new Canadian friend, John Bothwell, and prepared to fly to Tel Aviv to spend a week in Israel. The flight was uneventful except that the security was overwhelming. My luggage and my person were searched as they had never been searched before. The procedure was repeated on landing in Tel Aviv and indeed at almost every stop in Israel. I stayed at the home of the bishop of Jerusalem and the Middle East, an Arab Christian named Faik Haddad. I also spent some time at St. George's

College in Jerusalem, where I met a young Episcopal priest named Philip Culbertson, who was working on his doctorate at Hebrew University. The contrast between these two people was striking. Faik Haddad was pompous, filled with hostility toward Jews, and enjoyed as no one I had yet met the trappings of his office. Whenever he went anywhere in his car, he not only had a driver, but he put flags on his front fenders to announce his importance. His chief complaint in life was that he had not been provided, like his English predecessor had been, with sufficient money to have a full-time gardener. He intended to be a prince of the church. He was also the most manipulative man I have ever met in his attempts to get people to send him money for one of his many projects. I had him to dinner with about eight of our clergy later when he visited the United States, and he put the bite on every one of our guests for money before the dinner was served. His technique was to determine what he would ask each priest to send to his work by going through a series of questions about the size of their churches and the size of their budgets. Then he would tailor his request to what he perceived the budget of that church could manage.

While with him in Jerusalem, I listened to him relate the story of how his Palestinian family lost their home to the Jews in the "eight-day war." He quite literally loathed all things Jewish. In a strange way he helped me understand the depth of the tensions in the Middle East, tensions even the Palestinian Christians could not relinquish. I spent a full day during my Israel week at the Museum of the Holocaust, known as Yad Vashem. When Faik Haddad discovered where I had gone and perceived the depth of my response to that experience, he began to berate the museum as nothing more than Jewish propaganda. I found this man to be shallow, bigoted, and deeply hostile. I developed, because of him, a lack of respect for the Palestinian leadership of the Anglican Church in Jerusalem that was not diminished even by his successor.

With the Reverend Philip Culbertson, however, the experience was deeply transforming. He took me on personal tours of Jerusalem in which we separated the wheat from the chaff, the true holy places from the tourist traps. I visited the holy sites with this archeologically informed graduate student, from the cave at Machpelah in the town of Hebron, in which Sarah and Abraham were supposedly buried, to the village of Nazareth and the Sea of Galilee, which played such large roles in the life of Jesus. I spent some time in Bethlehem, which was about as inauthentic as any spot I have ever visited. I had not yet done the work on the birth narratives of Matthew and

Luke that would convince me of the midrashic and legendary character of these ninth-decade stories, but the unreality of Bethlehem itself paved the way for that. When tourist guides showed me the place in the stable where Jesus was born and the exact spot where each wise man stood when the gifts of gold, frankincense, and myrrh were presented, I almost gagged. I am now convinced that Jesus was born in Nazareth and the whole Bethlehem account was designed to relate him to the Davidic expectation. The primary purpose of the Bethlehem tradition today, at least in Bethlehem, is to undergird the tourist industry.

But Jerusalem, the Via Dolorosa, and the attempt to locate the Garden of Gethsemane and the hill of Calvary were impressive. So was the Galilean countryside, with its rocky soil and its olive groves, and the out-of-the-way places that loomed so large in Judeo-Christian history, like Capernaum, Joppa, Jericho, and Masada. Philip showed me most of these and opened my eyes to a new dimension of biblical understanding. I was pleased that my life would cross Philip Culbertson's life many times and in unexpected places like Oberlin, Ohio, Fairlawn, New Jersey, Sewanee, Tennessee, and Auckland, New Zealand, before our respective careers came to an end. I never ceased to learn from this gifted man and to be grateful for him.

My trip, which I had deliberately designed to prepare me for my new episcopal duties, was now over. I flew home, and we finally moved into the rectory of Christ Church in Ridgewood, where we lived until February 1977, when the diocese bought a bishop's residence for $97,500 in Morristown, New Jersey. We then moved into that house, where I would live until retirement. Strangely enough, it was my old friend Phillip Cato who picked this house and who lobbied for us to buy it. It was four blocks from his house in an old section of Morristown that reminded me very much of Virginia. I was still homesick, so I am confident that nostalgia played a major part in that decision. It was a choice that would prove to be more crucial to the course of my life than I could have imagined at that moment, but I suppose that is the way most decisions are, and life turns on decisions that we make without knowing all the implications. My life was enormously expanded in those first months as a bishop in lands half a globe away. Now, however, the time had come for me to begin to sink my roots both into New Jersey and into the role of bishop.

# 15

# *The Heart Cannot Worship What the Mind Rejects: Entering a Dark Valley*

※

I PLUNGED into my episcopal career like an enthusiastic schoolboy beginning a new school year. My plate seemed incredibly full. Initially demanding my attention were the start-up activities in the diocese, my first general convention as a bishop, and a manuscript on the Ten Commandments that had to be at the publisher by January 1.

The first thing I did as a bishop in the diocese was to call a clergy conference so that we could plan for our life together. I discovered that there had not been a clergy conference in this diocese in eight years. Many ideas were placed on the table for discussion at that conference, but only one of them was to endure and make a lasting contribution to the quality of our life—the continuing education of the clergy as a resource to ministry.

We decided corporately that we would make a special effort to keep our clergy on the theological cutting edge of Christianity. This would be accomplished by reorienting our continuing education dollars, which had traditionally been used to send individual clergy away to various training conferences. We would shift them to bring world-renowned theologians and biblical scholars to our diocese to stimulate, challenge, and train our clergy and any laity who chose to attend. The format we adopted was a visiting lectureship we called the New Dimensions Series. After much experimentation, we decided to offer three lecture days per year. I was invited to be the lecturer each year for one of those days. Nothing could have pleased me more.

The preparation for this annual New Dimensions day, which continued throughout my career as a bishop, gave me a focus around which to organize my study life and allowed me to continue my writing career. Every book I have written in my years as a bishop, except this autobiography, was born as a lecture in this series.

The second of these New Dimensions days was to feature the best theologians and biblical scholars available. Our clergy and laity have had the opportunity of engaging and interacting with such people as Hans Küng, Mortimer Adler, Raymond Brown, Elaine Pagels, Keith Ward, James Forbes, Karen Armstrong, Buckminster Fuller, and many, many others. These scholars helped us expand our traditional boundaries, explore cutting-edge speculations, and engage our faith intellectually. It is hard to measure the impact of this program on our corporate life, but our willingness as a diocese to walk the edges of our faith and to probe heretofore unexplored ideas certainly was influenced by this constant series of opportunities.

The third day each year in this series was ultimately to be dedicated to the interface of science and theology. This particular lecture day attracted a small endowment from a still unknown source who admired what our diocese was doing. This anonymous donor also suggested that this science/theology lectureship be named for John E. Hines, my dear friend. We were happy to comply. That endowment has grown over the years and now has about $100,000 in its corpus. Our desire in this activity was to keep the dialogue between science and theology open so that our generation of Christians might never again have to face the conflict that marked the church's response to Galileo or Charles Darwin. This, of course, means that Christian theology must be open to radical change as new data that disturb the status quo are engaged. In this series we have presented physicists like Paul Davies, biologists like Arthur Peacocke, medical doctors like Lewis Thomas, and environmentalists like Daniel Martin. We have even invited people who challenged overtly every significant Christian claim, like Daphne Hampson, thereby forcing our clergy to defend their faith in public debate. I know of no other diocese in the Anglican Communion that has enabled its clergy and lay leaders to feast on such a diet of intellectual richness.

To maximize the experience, I would always entertain our visiting scholar at a dinner party the night before the lecture, inviting three of our clergy couples to join us. This meant that over the years of my episcopate, many clergy had the opportunity of intimate conversation over dinner with the most fertile minds of the Christian world. That tradition has proved to be wonderfully invigorating.

This series also gave notice that in the Diocese of Newark it would not be business as usual. In order to enhance the impact of this initiative, I announced that I would be willing during my first two years, while I was still bishop coadjutor, to do six teaching missions a year in six of our congregations. The format I used was to visit a congregation on four consecutive Tuesday evenings or to combine my confirmation visit with an intensive parish weekend that would start on Friday night, have two sessions on Saturday, and conclude on Sunday morning prior to the confirmation service. I had more invitations than I could accept, and I discovered that probing the essentials of our faith publicly in a setting where people could comment and raise questions was very popular. It also changed the image of the bishop dramatically. He was not the ultimate authority, but a fellow pilgrim walking publicly in dialogue with the people into the mystery of God. As I embraced more and more of the leadership role of the diocese, this New Dimensions resource and the concept of a teaching bishop were never far from the center of my life.

Departing for my first general convention of our national church as a bishop shortly after this clergy conference, I had a taste of what the House of Bishops would be like as an insider. The issues before us that year were terribly emotional, involving both the changing of the prayer book and the decision about ordaining women to the priesthood and the episcopate. As with every potential change in people's worship life, these proposals met with fearful hostility.

Inside the House of Bishops I quickly identified with the heirs of John Hines on the liberal side of the aisle. My first speech in that body was in support of ordaining women. Despite the opposition from the presiding bishop, Jack Allin, this convention not only authorized the ordination of women to the priesthood, but also endorsed the proposed new prayer book. It also initiated the first rather tentative discussions on issues of human sexuality, including homosexuality.

Returning to the Diocese of Newark on January 2, 1977, I joined Bishop Rath to conduct a service of recognition for Nancy Wittig, our local member of the "irregular" Philadelphia 11. We scheduled that service as soon after January 1 as possible since the canonical changes we adopted at the General Covention did not become law until that date. I ordained Martha Blacklock to the priesthood on January 18, 1977, my first priestly ordination. Then I settled into the routine activities of my office.

The part of my life that was not routine was that of my being an author. I had a contract to produce a manuscript on the Ten Commandments for my publisher by January 1, 1977. The primary content work had been done in Richmond, but editing and preparing the manuscript for publication had to be done in New Jersey, where none of my editorial advisers was present. I did not realize how dependent I was on those who formed my writing community. I tried to return to this Richmond group, but discovered that one does not go home once one has left. The bands of affection were broken by my departure. My editor at Seabury Press offered no real help. I had to do this work by myself. Editing your own material is not unlike trying to be your own doctor or lawyer. You cannot escape a distorting subjectivity. More than anything else in my new career, this activity brought home to me a sense of my radical aloneness.

When I read *The Living Commandments*, upon publication, I was deeply depressed. It was not that I disagreed with its content, but its editing was obviously inadequate. It remains today the only book I have written that is an embarrassment to me. It did not sell well, not going over five thousand copies, and did not go into a second printing. I really wondered at this point in my life whether I could combine being a bishop with being an author. If I could not, then I had clearly made a mistake in accepting this office.

These three facets of my life—Newark, the church's national life through the House of Bishops, and my work as an author—continued to interact with one another through the remainder of my coadjutor years. I spent that time getting to know the diocese very well, planning for my years ahead, interviewing potential new staff people, and helping the diocese say a proper farewell to my predecessor, George Edward Rath. The one decision I did make was not to ask for a permanent assisting bishop. At forty-five I was too young for a bishop coadjutor who would wait more than twenty years to succeed me. My sense was that a diocese cannot elect an effective suffragan or assistant bishop until it knows the diocesan bishop very well. That would take time.

Meanwhile, in our diocese every church expected a bishop's visit once a year. With 140 churches no single bishop could hope to accomplish that task alone. I also was aware that the state of New Jersey was a racially diverse area. Black people constituted the major ethnic minority, but the black community was divided into three distinct groupings: Africans, West

Indian Islanders, and American-born descendants of those who had emerged out of the shackles of slavery. Next there was a Hispanic group, again divided among Cubans, Puerto Ricans, Mexicans, and Central and South Americans. Finally, there was a growing Asian presence made up of Japanese, Chinese, Koreans, and Vietnamese, as well as Indian and Pakistani people. There was no doubt that the future of this area was multiethnic, and yet at that time the majority of the people in the diocese were still ethnically white descendants of northern Europeans. If I had called for the election of an assisting bishop at that time, the odds are the diocese would have chosen another white male. Before that occurred, I wanted the people of our diocese to see in the bishop's office some of the diversity that the state reflected.

As a worldwide Communion, the Anglican Church boasted gifted leadership in almost every country of the world. I would meet many of these people at my first Lambeth Conference, which would occur in 1978. I could invite four bishops a year from the Third World to visit us and to function as confirming bishops. We would learn much from them and our vision would be broadened. To these bishops we could offer an expanding opportunity and perhaps some restorative time that would give them a time of refreshment to enable them to return somewhat renewed to the quite difficult labors in their native lands. Our people would get to see African, Latino, and Asian faces in the episcopal role. It might condition them to consider the blessings of electing a person of color to the episcopal office in the future. So beginning in 1979, I embarked upon the visiting bishops plan and carried it out for twelve years. In those years we received African giants of our faith tradition such as Desmond Tutu from South Africa, Henry Okullu from Kenya, Dinis Singulane from Mozambique, George Browne from Liberia, and Peter Hatendi from Zimbabwe. From Latin America we welcomed Paco Reus from Puerto Rico, Melchor Saucedo from Mexico, Lemuel Shirley from Panama, and Tony Ramos from Costa Rica. From Asia came Peter Kwong of Hong Kong and James Pong of Taiwan. Many of these visitors came more than once; Paco Reus, a particular favorite, came nine times. All of them blessed our lives and lifted our vision. People in the Diocese of Newark knew they were confirmed or received into a worldwide Communion.

As I became more and more engaged in these activities, I became painfully aware that my wife, Joan, shared in none of the excitement. My hopes that she could leave her fears behind were clearly unwarranted. Instead, it became obvious that she retreated more and more into the world of her fantasies. Only once in a great while would she accompany me on a diocesan function or confirmation visitation. When she did, she was distant and aloof, sometimes sitting in the car until after the service had begun. People who did not understand her mental state began to think she was a cold and uncaring person. Nothing could have been further from the truth, but it was easy to see how that conclusion was drawn. In a short period of time, she stopped attending anything. It actually was easier this way. By the time I had become the diocesan bishop, it was clear to me that I would do my work alone. Even those things like the Lambeth Conference and the House of Bishops' meeting, which were filled with social activities and to which most bishops brought their spouses, were to be for me solo events. Increasingly Joan's retreat expressed itself in her refusal to answer either the phone or the door, so people could not reach her even if they wanted to. She moved her sleeping place into the attic of our home, where she believed she was safe from the cameras that, in her mind, continued to photograph her at every moment. This meant that frequently when I came home at night, I would not see her. I would most often leave in the morning before she emerged. I became a devotee of the New York Yankees, for they were my regular companions at night on television, at least from April through October. Increasingly, I found companionship in my books, study, and writing career.

At my first New Dimensions day I began a series on the Resurrection that I hoped would lead to a book. Though my Kanuga experience on this subject was in the background, this was my first effort at reconstructing the Easter moment as something other than a physical resuscitation. I wanted to address this primary Christian affirmation in a new way and, in the process, demonstrate that I could write an effective book while serving as a bishop. I projected three years to complete this task.

In my second year of work on that volume, I attended my second general convention, this time as a diocesan bishop, and found myself caught up in the first public debate in our church on the subject of homosexuality. This debate emerged from a report from the Standing Commission on Human Affairs and Health chaired by the bishop of Rochester, Robert Spears. I was troubled by these issues in that year 1979. The bishops I admired all supported a new openness to gay and lesbian people. The bishops who resisted every new idea were overtly negative about this subject. I did not want to be identified with that negativity and yet I was not ready either intellectually or emotionally to embrace homosexuality as anything other than an aberration, a distortion of normal behavior, or perhaps even a mental illness.

When Bob Spears brought forth his recommendations calling on the church to recognize and welcome homosexual people into its full life, I went to the sidelines and became a spectator in the debate. The opposition was led by Robert Terwilliger, the bishop suffragan of Dallas. Paul Moore of New York, Kilmer Myers of California, and Bob Spears of Rochester were the major positive voices. The conservatives won an overwhelming victory in that first skirmish on an issue that would dominate our church life for a quarter of a century. The report of the Standing Commission on Human Affairs and Health was scuttled and a substitute resolution was adopted that piously thanked the commission for its work and then dismissed its recommendations, reaffirming the traditional standards and recommending that only people living in faithful heterosexual marriages or committed to celibacy be considered by the church for ordination. This substitute passed by a 100-to-32 margin. I did vote with the minority of 32, but less out of any great conviction than out of a refusal to be identified with the conservative majority. Jack Allin voted with the majority, and I suspect believed that righteousness had prevailed. Righteousness that does not endure, however, is hardly righteous.

The unraveling of the authority this substitute resolution might have possessed, however, began the next morning when John Krumm, the bishop of Southern Ohio and an unmarried man, rose to read a statement of conscience to the House. He took note of the fact that the resolution passed the previous day was "recommendatory and not prescriptive." Then he announced that he could not in conscience obey it, and he invited others who were willing to stand with him to join their names to this statement. Twenty-one bishops did. I was not one of them. But the issue was surely drawn for me in this maneuver—I knew I had work to do and that the ancient prejudices of my own background would have to be examined. I returned to the Diocese of Newark open, but uncommitted.

Shortly thereafter a priest made an appointment with me to talk about what he called "a personal matter." After the initial pleasantries, he took a deep breath and said, "Bishop, I did not vote for you to be my bishop, but the convention did and I must live with that. I cannot abide a dishonest relationship with my bishop, so I have come to tell you I am a homosexual. I have been a homosexual, so far as I know, all the days of my life. It was not my choice. It is my being. I seek to live my life with honor and integrity, but I cannot and will not deny or seek to hide my identity from myself, my friends, or from you. I perceive that you are not comfortable with this issue. I would be willing to help you examine it if you wanted me to do so."

His honesty and composure were impressive. I asked him to tell me about his life, which he proceeded to do. He described his years of denial, his attempts to conform, his reflected self-hatred, finally his dawning acceptance, and now his overt celebration of who he knew himself to be. I listened with much internal conflict, but I listened.

This was a good priest—competent, faithful, and popular. My stereotypes of what constituted homosexuality did not have room for someone as impressive as this man, personally or professionally. He was clearly putting himself at risk. He asked nothing of me except that I be open to learn. I promised him nothing except that I would try.

Shortly after this meeting, I had the difficult task of informing a priest who had been working to revive a blue-collar church in a densely populated part of our diocese that we would not be able to extend his three-year contract and thus, in six months' time, he would no longer have a position. As a courtesy to him I decided that this conversation needed to take place in his home rather than my office.

I knew this priest was a single man, but it honestly had not occurred to me to think he might be gay. I discovered on this visit that he had a housemate, but again that did not ring bells. I sat in his living room, broke the news, and allowed sufficient time for us to discuss it. I promised my help in finding him a new position. It seemed to go well. Before leaving I asked to use his bathroom. Upon entering it I noticed "his" and "his" towels on the racks and pictures of male nudes on the walls. It was hard not to assume that this was a gay bathroom. I returned to the living room and asked him about what that meant. He was immediately open and honest. His roommate, he said, was his life partner. I said that as a bishop I would not allow an unmarried heterosexual couple to live in a church's rectory, and I could not do that for a homosexual couple either. I thought that was a fair and even-handed approach.

"But Bishop," he said, "heterosexual couples have the option of getting married. We do not."

His words represented simple logic and were, in my mind, irrefutable. I absorbed them like a body blow to my prejudices. I actually extended this priest's contract for an additional year so that at least he would not think his removal was because of his homosexuality. I salved my conservative conscience by saying, "You do need to know that if this becomes a public issue during the time you remain here, I do not have the power to protect you." I am sure he recognized that I also did not have the will to do so. I left that home that day knowing that I still had much work to do on this subject, but I also knew I could never again reflect the moralistic attitude of my unchallenged past.

My life was never one-dimensional, and each dimension demanded its due portion of my time. My manuscript on the Resurrection, entitled *The Easter Moment*, had by now been shipped to the publisher. The proposed and agreed on publication date was January 1, 1980.

I was very excited about this book when it was complete. I had opened it by sharing the story of my friendship with Jim Campbell as we walked together into the meaning of his death. In that narrative I could describe the enormous power present between human beings when barriers of fear and threat are lowered and a relationship of openness, freedom, honesty, and deep sharing called the two people beyond all of the limits of a human-imposed finitude. I closed this book with my first public probe into the question of life after death.

There was, however, a series of glitches in the production of this book that completely destroyed my confidence in Seabury Press as a publisher and created, even for this book, an initial sense of deep disappointment. My editors missed every deadline. Delays were commonplace. The result was that a book about Easter, due out around January 1, did not get to bookstores until Easter was over. It was, therefore, dead on arrival. It could not capture shelf space in bookstores until it was a year old. I began to think there was no way I could be both a bishop and an author.

Yet about fifteen months after *The Easter Moment* had been published and with it showing very low sales figures, it still opened a tremendous new adventure for my life. I was spending a part of my summer vacation in 1981 at home. Our children had come for a visit and we were together doing little more than chatting around the pool, cooking out on the porch, and reading nonprofessional books. On this particular July day I had come in from the backyard to get my favorite summer beverage, a tall glass of iced coffee made with skim milk, giving it the exquisite taste of liquid coffee ice cream. A phone call in the kitchen interrupted my anticipated palate pleasure.

"Bishop Spong," the voice on the line said, "this is Claiborne Pell." The name was familiar, but I could not immediately place it. So with my internal computer racing to identify the caller and to provide me with a context in which to place this voice, I responded guardedly, "Yes, what can I do for you?"

"Well, I've recently read your book *The Easter Moment*, and I wonder if you might have time to discuss life after death with me."

"That would not be very easy on the telephone," I responded, still trying to place the familiar name of Claiborne Pell.

"Oh, I didn't mean to do it now," he responded. "Do you ever get to Washington? If so, I wonder if you might stop by my office in the Senate Office Building and we could have time to do it then."

Washington. The Senate Office Building. Claiborne Pell. Suddenly, I put it all together. I was speaking to Senator Claiborne Pell, Democrat from Rhode Island, one of the senior members of the U.S. Senate, whose distinguished career had made him either the chair or the ranking minority member of the Senate Committee on Foreign Affairs. He was also the Pell of the Pell Grants. He had been among a small group of finalists in the vice presidential sweepstakes when Hubert Humphrey was the Democratic nominee in 1968.

Once my internal information system clicked into place, I was able to enter the conversation a bit more fully. "Yes, Senator, I do get to Washington from time to time. As a matter of fact, I will be passing through Washington next Thursday."

"That's wonderful. Could you stop by?"

"Well, I could, but it would be late in the afternoon and I will have my daughter with me." She was a second-year law student at William and Mary. We were moving some things into her apartment and would be returning to New Jersey late Thursday afternoon.

"We'd love to have your daughter accompany you. I will get some of my younger staff members to show her around so she won't be bored. Perhaps we can talk for an hour or so in my office and then we'll go out to dinner." I hung up the phone and went back to my lounge chair and book in the backyard, iced coffee in hand, wondering how this all could have happened.

"Who was on the phone?" my wife asked.

"It was Senator Pell of Rhode Island. He wants to discuss life after death with me. I made an appointment to see him in Washington next Thursday when I'm driving Kathy back home from Williamsburg." It sounded just as incredulous to her as it had sounded to me.

When the day came, Kathy and I made our way through the late afternoon Washington traffic, past various receptionists and secretaries, until we found the office door that announced its occupant was the senator from Rhode Island and said "Please enter." We did, finding ourselves in a reception room. As we opened the door, a bell sounded to announce our arrival. A male voice, calling from an attached office, invited us to be seated. He would be out as soon as he got off the phone, he said. We looked at book titles on the shelves while we waited a very few seconds before a thin, olive-skinned man, perhaps five foot eleven, emerged with outstretched hand.

"I'm Claiborne Pell," he said. "Thank you for coming by." I introduced myself and Kathy, and we began a rather awkward conversation.

"Please be seated," the Senator said. "I've invited a few people to come by to talk with us. I'm afraid I have to be here to vote on several matters until about 7:00 P.M., but I've made reservations in the Senate dining room for our group for dinner at 7:30.

With that, he opened a small refrigerator and took out several splits of champagne, which he proceeded to pour into flutes. The frosted, dry, bubbly beverage hit the spot.

In a short time about six people had joined us, and we sat in a circle while Claiborne Pell posed the agenda for the conversations. Is there life after death? Can we communicate with the dead? Is there such a thing as an out-of-body experience that might give some credibility to the claim that some part of us might survive our own physical demise? In a very short time the conversation was flowing freely as we each shared what we really felt about this intriguing subject, not just what we felt we ought to say we believed. Periodically, a bell would ring and Claiborne would go out to the Senate floor to cast his vote, returning within two or three minutes to rejoin the conversation. When the bell rang at about 7:00, he cast his last vote of the evening and we made our way to dinner.

Imagine discussing life after death with a group of people convened by a senator in the Senate dining room in Washington, D.C.! Yet, as part of this lively conversation, the idea arose that this ad hoc dinner group might convene an interdisciplinary conference in Washington to examine this subject from a wide variety of angles. I was asked if I would be interested in being part of the leadership of such an endeavor. Of course I would be interested, I responded. Carole Taylor, a member of this group and a close friend of Claiborne's, was asked to coordinate our efforts, and we agreed to meet again before too long to pursue our plans. By this time it was 11:30 P.M. and Kathy and I were still facing a four-hour drive to New Jersey. Claiborne and I stayed in touch over the next few years as these plans developed.

I found myself strangely energized in this encounter by the religious yearnings of people not unlike Claiborne who were no longer actually part of the church. They were searching for meaning but outside the traditional structures of religion. I admired their honesty and yearned to be in dialogue with them.

This project intrigued me, but for a variety of reasons, it would be years developing. So I returned to the more routine activities of my profession that seemed to wait for no one. Since I was still not willing to press both the church and society on the issues of justice for gay and lesbian people, I turned my energy toward becoming more aggressive in dealing with a prejudice about which my mind was absolutely clear, the full inclusion of women in the life of the church. I sought self-consciously to open all lay positions in the diocese to fifty-fifty participation of men and women. I began a vigorous attempt to get congregations to risk considering women priests for positions of rector and vicar. In my annual address to the diocesan convention, I called publicly for one church with sufficient substance to attract a priest to break the barrier and open its pulpit and altar to an ordained woman. At this time women clergy were still relegated to part-time cures or given difficult assignments in which no one else was interested. I wanted our diocese to demonstrate the gifts of ordained women openly, and I sought a high profile in my personal crusade to call the whole Communion to move toward opening ecclesiastical doors.

As a part of this strategy I made sure our visiting Third World bishops experienced the gifts of women priests. I received that year a letter from an Englishwoman who believed herself called to be ordained, but who, given the attitude at that moment in the Church of England, had no way to pursue that vocation in the land of her birth. She wrote to inquire if she might seek ordination here. "Will you allow me to test my vocation in your diocese?" she asked. "Will you ordain me if in the opinion of your discernment process I am qualified?" After looking at what this might mean to our diocese and to the church at large, I answered both questions with an enthusiastic yes. So Elizabeth Canham came to Newark, and a whole new chapter of our diocesan lives began to open.

Elizabeth was a member of St. Luke's Church in Charleton, a suburb of South London in the Diocese of Southwark. She was supported in her quest by her rector, the Reverend Tony Crowe, and her bishop, the Right Reverend Mervyn Stockwood. They both wrote to urge me to act for the Church of England, which was neither willing nor able to act for itself.

Elizabeth had sought the priesthood all of her life. Because that door was closed to her, she enrolled first in the evangelical ministry of the Church of England known as the Church Army. After additional training she pursued the role of a deaconess. Mervyn Stockwood had ordained her to that order. In a sworn affidavit to me he informed me that, at Elizabeth's ordination as a "deaconess," he had used the identical words and actions he used when ordaining male deacons.

Mervyn, who was one of the great characters of the Church of England, loved controversy. He had demonstrated that in his choice of suffragan bishops for the area of his diocese known as Woolwich. It was Mervyn who appointed John A. T. Robinson to that post. He also appointed David Sheppard (subsequently the outstanding bishop of Liverpool) and even the ultraconservative Michael Marshall, who later became the evangelism officer on the staff of the archbishop of Canterbury. Mervyn was an outspoken liberal, the champion of Britain's Labor Party, and a not very well closeted gay man. He was also a delight to know.

When our general convention voted to ordain women deacons in 1970, it also declared that any woman ordained a deaconess was now to be considered an ordained deacon without further ordination. Acting on the authority of that resolution, I received Elizabeth as a deacon in our diocese in the spring of 1981. I then had her screened by our Commission on Ministry, which tested her psychologically, physically, spiritually, and academically. She passed all tests with flying colors. They recommended her to the standing committee for ordination. She was unanimously approved. The stage was set for the dramatic ordination in the Diocese of Newark of the first Englishwoman priest in the Anglican Communion.

Mervyn agreed to be the preacher at this service and to join me in the ordaining act of laying hands on her head. She would be an Episcopal priest, but as such she was part of the Anglican Communion, which would qualify her to function sacramentally in England. Thus her ordination was a direct challenge to the Church of England.

The British news media were captivated by this cheeky attack upon the English church's decision-making processes. Both the BBC and the Independent Television Corporation of London sent television crews to cover the ordination. The major British dailies and the *New York Times* were also present. On Saturday morning, December 5, 1981, in our cathedral in Newark, Mervyn and I laid our hands on Elizabeth's head and made her "a priest in the Church of God."

The *New York Times* put her picture on page one of the Sunday paper on December 6. British television played the story prominently on Sunday morning. Her ordination sent a signal throughout the entire Communion that in Newark we were not prepared to honor oppressive traditions we believed immoral. Our international reputation was being formed. Elizabeth's ambition was to return to England to serve as a priest, but until that branch of our Communion would receive her, she accepted an assignment to serve as assistant rector of St. David's Church in Kinnelon, New Jersey. But when she returned to England on holidays to visit her parents, she was not averse to celebrating the Eucharist if the occasion arose.

The gauntlet was thrown down when the dean of London's St. Paul's Cathedral, Alan Webster, invited Elizabeth to do just that in the living room of the deanery for the London leaders of the Movement for the Ordination of Women, one of whom was Alan Webster's wife. That invitation got the attention of the bishop of London, the Right Reverend Graham Leonard, probably the most reactionary bishop in England. When he was not able to prevent the celebration of this Eucharist, his rhetoric became so excessive and his prejudice so obvious that he actually helped our cause. He attacked his dean, Elizabeth Canham, and me. He demanded that I "discipline Miss Canham." I do not quite know what he expected me to do, but I was amused by his archaic language. When Bishop Leonard announced in the mid-1980s that "women could not be priests in the Anglican Communion because God had created them just to be wives and mothers," I howled with delight. "These words," I said in a prepared statement, "are spoken by the bishop of London in a land where Elizabeth II sits on the throne and where Margaret Thatcher runs the government. Perhaps the bishop of London does not know either what country he is living in or what century he is living in."

Having raised the stakes of the debate in England, we moved to spread our crusade to other parts of our Communion. Henry Okullu of Kenya was so impressed with women priests when he visited the Diocese of Newark that he decided unilaterally to ordain women in his country. From my office he made the call to begin the process. When Liberia was moving from the jurisdiction of the American Episcopal Church to join the Anglican Province of West Africa, George Browne, the bishop of Liberia, another of our visiting bishops, wrote me asking if we could send a woman priest to Liberia. His new province had agreed to accept all of Liberia's clergy, and George wanted to have a female priest among his clergy so that he would never have to fight that battle. I responded and a woman priest from Newark joined the cathedral staff in Monrovia, and the church in Liberia suddenly had women among its clergy. It was a heady time.

Yet that exciting year closed for me on an ominous note. On Christmas Day 1981, my wife informed me that she might have to have some surgery. She had some mastitis, she said, in her left breast. She was very vague, however, when I asked for more information. Unable to get straight answers, I decided that I must talk to her doctor. When I called him the next morning, I received a shocking message.

He said, "Bishop, your wife is seriously ill. She has a malignant tumor in her left breast. It has been there for quite a while. It has festered and erupted and is now an open draining sore. The malignancy may already be too far advanced to save her life. I have tried to get her to agree to surgery for two months now, but I can't seem even to get her attention."

The doctor was clearly frustrated. He did not know the reality of this patient with whom he was seeking to communicate. When I placed her behavior into the context of her mental condition, he actually seemed relieved. We then focused on what we needed to do. Both of us knew, that even though we faced a life and death situation, it would not be easy to get her to act.

After that call, I spent about eight hours seeking to convince Joan that surgery was essential. When she finally agreed, I called her doctor once more and arrangements were made to admit her as soon as she had seen the surgeon, which was scheduled for the next day. Finally, the operation was set for the first week of January. The surgeon was equally adamant that this was a critical situation. It would be a complete mastectomy, he said. Clearly the doctors did not believe that anything less than that would be effective.

When the day of the surgery arrived, I drove Joan to the hospital and took her to the admissions desk. When she was asked to sign the standard papers to give consent for the surgical procedure, she refused. When told that X rays would be required, she would not agree to them. Both the surgeon and the radiologist, she told me, were working for the government. They would seek to destroy her, she argued, because they knew that if she lived, she would expose their criminal behavior of spying on her. Her paranoia had the classic dimensions of grand delusion. She would, she believed, someday be acclaimed a heroine for standing up to these oppressive elements of a government gone haywire. But at this moment her life was hanging in the balance. At each stage during this strange hospital rendezvous I quietly talked her past these fears and promised that I would be with her. It was, I assured her, the only chance she had to live and even to fight these dreadful enemies that so affected her mind. I think her fear more than my persuasiveness prevailed and the proper documents were finally signed. She entered the hospital and prepared to walk through this new valley.

The surgery was a technical success, though I have no idea what it means to a woman to lose a breast. The malignancy was not as extensive as her doctor had feared. The pathology report revealed that it had spread to only three lymph nodes. Chemotherapy would be required, and so we were referred to an oncologist. When the surgery was sufficiently healed to enable her to go to the oncologist's office, we went for the first appointment.

All kinds of questions emerged in my mind. Should I take her to New York's Sloan Kettering Hospital, the most highly regarded cancer treatment hospital in the world? It would be much less convenient, but if it made any difference to her life expectancy, I wanted to entertain it. I also knew that Joan would never go to the doctor on her own and so I must arrange my schedule to be available to accompany her. Visiting bishops, whom we were continuing to sponsor, cannot, by the nature of their visiting status, really do much more than the ceremonial tasks of the bishop's office, so I needed to seek other assistance.

Our visit to the oncologist answered most of my questions. The oncologist had trained at Sloan Kettering and assured us that he could give us the same care that Sloan Kettering offered. Since Morristown was far more convenient, that was enormously encouraging to both of us.

The treatment schedule in Morristown would be fourteen consecutive days of chemotherapy and then fourteen days off. That schedule would last a full year. He described the side effects of chemotherapy: chronic nausea, weakness, and potential hair loss. I would need to be with her at least half a day when she received a treatment. I asked him to assess the long-term prognosis. "It is not hopeless," he responded, "but it is serious. To discover malignancy in three lymph nodes is ominous. Our experience is that we have a good cure rate with less than three and a poor cure rate with more than three. Three is on the cusp, and it can go either way."

After this visit I laid out my reality before my closest advisers. We made a decision to ask the retired bishop of Massachusetts, John Burgess, a longtime friend with whom I had served on the national executive council, to become the assistant bishop in the diocese for one year. He lived in New Haven, Connecticut, and could spend five days a week with us. He agreed. This wise, experienced, and unflappable man was a godsend. I trusted him totally, and the fact that he was an African American was a wonderful serendipity in my quiet campaign to get people to appreciate a non-Caucasian in the office of the bishop. When Joan accepted this plan and agreed to cooperate with the process, I was elated and I entered every one of her chemotherapy sessions for a year into my date book. Next, I adjusted my schedule in almost every detail around that reality by canceling many things. I prepared to give Joan primacy in my life for that crucial year. The chemotherapy sessions were to begin in a week. I felt that we had weathered this crisis.

Two days before the first session was to begin I came home in the late afternoon to be informed by Joan that she had called the oncologist and canceled the whole program.

"Why?" I asked, astonished at this decision.

"That doctor works for the CIA," she responded, "and he will poison my mind. I must keep my mind clear so that I may testify against these people when this case is broken open."

I felt a lump in my throat and was engulfed by a hopeless sense of despair. I spent that evening using all of my skills of persuasion. I discovered that I had used up all my powers in persuading her to have the X rays and the surgery. I could not now dent her determination. I finally gave up, determined to try again the next day. I also wanted to talk to her doctors—the oncologist, the surgeon, and her personal physician—to discover what the risks were if Joan's decision was allowed to stand.

Those conversations were not encouraging. The doctors were convinced that the only chance she had to live was by engaging in this chemotherapy program. They were unanimous in suggesting that without it her chances of living as long as two years were slight. Yet I could force it on her only by committing her legally to a mental institution. I had faced that issue before and knew I could never do that. Ultimately, after consulting with our daughters, my decision was to allow her to do it her way, even though this meant that I might well be allowing her to commit suicide. Anything else, I concluded, would either violate her person or destroy what I believed was her fragile will to live. But the guilt and anxiety I experienced with that decision was total. It was the heaviest and most difficult decision I have ever had to make. When I finally accepted her decision, Joan assured me as her only concession that she would see her personal physician on a regular basis. Even though my schedule did not now require it in the way I had earlier anticipated, I was still glad that Bishop Burgess was around. Increasingly I recognized that I was in a state in which I desperately needed the support of this good man. The diocese also needed the stability he provided.

Despite the lack of the chemotherapy, Joan did remarkably well, and her personal doctor kept me informed of her status. He was encouraged as the weeks stretched into months and she still seemed to be fine. Before the year was over, she actually had a prosthesis built and then had her breast reconstructed surgically. That was a life sign, and I was delighted.

When we were well into the first year after the surgery, Joan was sure the cancer scare had subsided. But even though she showed no physical signs of illness, Joan's paranoid patterns continued. The tension in our household was palpable. Joan sank into increasing isolation. She would go once in a while to her church in Morristown, but Hughes Garvin, her rector, told me she always came late, sat in the last row of the chapel with her back to the wall, and left at the time of the passing of the peace. Hughes came to see her regularly, but only if I was at home did he get in. She would not answer the phone, since it was tapped, or the doorbell for meter readers or repairmen, even when I had called them to come. I dreaded any kind of home maintenance problem—plumbing, heating, electrical, and so on. I would call the required service person, but unless I stayed home to open the door, nothing was ever fixed.

Other behaviors also kept my anxieties very high. Joan once went down on the train to visit her mother, who was in a retirement home in North Carolina. But she came back in an enormous used Buick she had purchased. This meant that our two-person family now owned three cars! When I inquired why she felt the need to buy a car, she explained that the CIA was trying to kill her and make it look like an accident. Her car was a small Fiat. It would offer her no protection, she said, if she were lured into a bridge abutment. But she felt she would be safe in this massively large, tanklike Buick. Once she got it home, however, she never drove the Buick again. Finally, we gave it away.

Shortly thereafter I came home and thought Joan must be out since her car was gone. To my surprise, however, Joan was at home, so I assumed her car must be getting serviced somewhere. "Where is your car?" I inquired in a fairly casual way, suspecting nothing and simply seeking what I expected to be routine information.

"I gave it away," she answered calmly.

"You did what?" I asked.

"I gave it away," she repeated.

"Tell me why you did that," I inquired, and another chapter in this strange sickness poured forth.

"That car," she said, "has hidden recorders in it that have kept records of everything said inside its doors. I have frequently talked to myself while driving and now I know that those monologues were recorded. A person with a proper listening device could thus get access to everything that I have said."

"But why did you give it away? You need a car. That one was in good repair. It barely had forty thousand miles on it." I was still shocked.

It was, in her mind however, perfectly logical. She no longer wanted a bugged car. She could not sell it, she said, because everyone would know who the previous owner was and might be able to trace these recordings to her. In her mind, by giving it away anonymously, she circumvented that problem.

"To whom did you give it?" I finally inquired.

"To the rabbi at our neighborhood synagogue," was her reply. "He promised to keep my identity a secret, and they are planning to raffle it off at the synagogue fund-raiser." We did receive an official receipt from the synagogue, thanking us for our charitable contribution and informing us of exactly how much we could claim on our tax returns.

The loss of the car would not destroy our financial stability, but it did not help it either. I began to wonder, however, what would be next. We bought her another car, a new Volkswagen Rabbit, and I hoped it would not get bugged with listening devices.

A bit later I came home to discover both Joan and the Volkswagen gone. Waiting until she returned home proved unfruitful, for the whole night passed and she did not appear. I was frantic, but not sure what to do. I contemplated notifying the police, the Bureau of Missing Persons, or calling some of her friends. I considered checking the hospital and even the morgue.

I contented myself first simply by calling our daughters. Ellen and Kathy both reported that their mother had called each of them a couple of days before and said she was thinking about going out to see our youngest daughter, Jaquelin, in California. Jaquelin, who was working on her Ph.D. in physics at Stanford, but was living in an apartment in San Francisco, had heard nothing of this plan. With that much lead I decided to take no action and hope that this hint would, in fact, prove accurate. About five days later Jaquelin called and said, "Dad, Mom has just arrived for a visit. I wanted you to know that she seems to be okay." I breathed a sigh of relief. Jaquelin promised to let me know when she departed, so that we could be prepared to receive her back. About two weeks later Joan returned.

I asked her why she had not let me know. Her reply was simple. If she spoke a word, it was reported to her enemies, who would then follow her. She had to be secretive. She was, by this time, convinced that her dentist had placed hearing devices into her fillings so that she could not speak a word to anyone without her enemies recording it.

I asked her where she had stayed on this cross-continental trip. Her response did nothing to lower my anxiety. She slept in her car at truck stops, she explained. She made this same journey on two occasions. I worried about her safety. Life was completely unpredictable and sometimes bizarre. This level of tension and anxiety continued to shred my few remaining emotional resources.

I recognize now that I responded to this stress by leaning on anyone and everyone who had any strength to give. I know I became a difficult executive. In time this behavior would be a cause of major dislocations and resignations on my staff. I could not keep my domestic pain isolated. It began to flow into and to disrupt my professional life until that part of my life was also in disarray.

I tried to pull things together and was greatly encouraged when my mentor and friend, John A. T. Robinson, accepted my invitation offered early in 1982 to come to the Diocese of Newark the next year to lecture to our clergy and to spend some time with me. It was something to which I looked forward with great anticipation. Having things in the future that I could joyfully anticipate was a healing balm.

A break in the rising tension was also provided by the next triennial general convention of our church, which met in the fall of 1982. Since I had still no major responsibility in the House deliberations, I looked forward to going as an opportunity to see many friends. Jack Allin had continued to appoint me only to such assignments as the Committee on Miscellaneous Resolutions or the Committee on New Dioceses. There was not much action there. Any contribution I could make had to be via the floor debate, not the committee structure. But I was destined to discover that floor leadership can be decisive.

Jack Allin at this gathering was seeking to have the canons changed to transform the office of presiding bishop into an archbishopric. He argued that in ecumenical relations the title "presiding bishop" was misunderstood. He was more deeply into titles and ecclesiastical status than any national figure I have ever known. The hype that preceded the convention on this issue was very interesting. It spoke of what great ecumenical advantages would accompany this title change. There was no public talk against the idea. I assumed that the measure would pass, since it is very difficult for the House of Bishops to deny their elected leader something he so clearly desired. Opposition, indeed, was made to sound rather petty.

But when the issue was finally raised on the floor of the House, John Burt of Ohio rose and quietly, yet forcefully, spoke against this measure. It was the symbol, not the substance, he said that he opposed. The church has been moving away from hierarchical symbols into a more collegial mode of leadership, and this change would fly in the face of that. Burt's stand emboldened the rest of the House, who felt general discomfort with the proposal, but did not quite know why. Over time I am confident that, if we had acquiesced and made the presiding bishop the archbishop, we would have changed dramatically the very structure of our church, which is now a confederation of dioceses. The title of archbishop would have been defined in terms of the long Anglican Church history of this title as a hierarchical office. Throughout the Anglican Communion an archbishop in fact has authority over local bishops. In our part of this Communion, where no archbishop titles are used, the diocesan bishop shares authority only with the clergy and laypeople of his or her diocese as they live under the order created by the canons and advised by the collegial discussions of the general convention.

It soon became clear in the discussion of the House of Bishops, that the title of archbishop was not going to make it, so a move was made to wrap some meaningless titles, like primate, around the presiding bishop's office to soothe Jack Allin's sense of rejection. Jack interpreted this string of titles in the watered-down version of his original request to mean that he was authorized to use the form of address generally reserved for an archbishop, "The Most Reverend." That honorific was, however, specifically not authorized. But suddenly "The Most Reverend John Maury Allin" appeared on stationery and all official documents. When Jack was being interviewed at his retirement, a reporter asked him what specific differences would mark his retired life. To my amazement he responded first by saying he would no longer be called "The Most Reverend." I thought, "How pitiful."

Once that form of address was employed, however, its status appeal seduced the next occupants of that office, and the next two presiding bishops have chosen to use it. One must constantly be vigilant to prevent common usage from conveying a meaning never intended. So I do not, have not, and will not use "The Most Reverend" for anyone and hope that its basic silliness and patriarchal power gamesmanship will someday be recognized and abandoned. A superlative word like "Most" is indeed a strange title to confer on any human being.

At this same general convention we were told one morning that later that day the House of Bishops would be called into executive session. This strange and rare procedure immediately set off speculation about what dire reality we would have to confront. Was there a critical diagnosis in someone's life that would cause major shuffling of structure? Was there a scandal brewing that we needed to know about before it became public? Had the church inherited a fortune that we needed to plan on how to use before we announced it to the public? Rumor, jokes, and anticipatory conversation filled the corridors that day.

When the appointed hour came, the press, visitors in the galleries, priest assistants, staff to the secretary of the House, wives of the bishops, and anyone not an actual bishop was invited to leave. It took a few minutes for the marshals to clear the House, close the doors, and stand guard outside. We all prepared to listen to the moving agenda that would require the extraordinary procedure of an executive session.

Imagine our surprise when Jack Allin spoke from the chair in tones that were designed to sound somber, but to me sounded more like whining, and asked the House to consider legislation authorizing the continued use of the 1928 *Book of Common Prayer*! He spoke of the pain that countless numbers of laypeople had felt when, in 1979, the new prayer book had become mandatory. He related stories in which faithful people were buffeted by such disturbing changes as the ordination of women, the revision of the prayer book, and our attempt in the John Hines years to include minorities in the mainstream of the life of the church. Now all these people ask, he was saying, is to be given the security of being able to cling forever to the treasured words of the traditional prayer book. I was astonished at this tactic. Here was the church's elected leader once again asking us to be sensitive to a group of people with whom he personally was identified. How can a member of the House deal with that kind of abuse of power without seeming to be rude?

When his brief plea was completed, the floor was then thrown open for discussion. Ned Cole, the bishop of Central New York, was the first to speak. In a delicate manner he tried to inform the chair that the new prayer book was creating a new church, more open, more inclusive, and that the move the presiding bishop was proposing would represent a new barrier in that evolutionary process. Paul Reeves, the bishop of Georgia and one of the most reactionary members of the House, who once proclaimed that the church had been off track and had done nothing positive since the Reformation had begun, rose to quote John Wesley and announce that "his heart had been strangely warmed" by the presiding bishop's call to reinstate the old prayer book. Paul was himself closely aligned with a group known as the "Society for the Preservation of the 1928 Book of Common Prayer."

There were a few questions about how such a proposal might work and some other neutral comments, but the discussion seemed to be going nowhere. So I rose and approached the microphone. When the presiding bishop recognized me, I immediately got his attention by saying, "Jack, you have seriously misread the mood of this House and of this church." The use of the informal first name was appropriate in a closed session. Had we been in public debate, I would have addressed the chair as "Mr. Chairman," but it served to put him and the members of the House on notice. Attention surely perked up.

I went on to speak of the trial process through which the church had gone publicly to bring about liturgical reform. That trial process had begun in the 1960s with the introduction of worship books we called by such titles as "The Green Book" and "The Zebra Book." I spoke of the enormous numbers of people who in good faith had given countless hours to the task of liturgical revision in committees, on the task force for prayer book revision itself, as readers, and in experimental congregations. I talked of those creative clergy who had used this opportunity to educate their congregations about the meaning and history of liturgy. I mentioned those negative clergy who never engaged the issue, who castigated every new idea, creating in their churches a fortress-like mentality of hostility.

I went into the two votes at general convention that had authorized the new prayer book by substantial majorities. I reminded Jack Allin that to accommodate his own conservative sensitivities, the Committee on Prayer Book Revision had revised the new prayer book to include Rite One services for morning prayer, the Eucharist, and the Burial Office that included in large measure the material most people treasured from the 1928 book. I suggested that his proposal would be viewed as pulling the rug out from under those who had engaged the issue so creatively, while it would reward the most negative behavior of those who resisted all change. This would be a disastrous setback for the whole church, I stated. I concluded my remarks with another personal statement. "I am both disappointed and amazed at your suggestion. It is an absolute abdication of effective leadership." I returned to my desk and there was a stunned kind of silence. Seldom are words that harsh said in public debate to the chair in that House. It certainly was not designed to heal our strained relationship.

But there was, I detected, also relief in the House that someone had spoken bluntly to this pious attempt at manipulation in the name of "church unity," and the consideration of this request was clearly destined to go nowhere. The discussion, however, went on for perhaps another thirty minutes before it died of its own inertia. There was no vote. There was simply the recognition that this bad idea was unworthy of more time. Jack Allin never brought it up again, and the Society for the Preservation of the 1928 Book of Common Prayer began its slow but inevitable retreat into oblivion. After this day Jack Allin and I both knew that any leadership I might exercise through the normative structures of the church would not come until we chose another presiding bishop in 1985.

I returned home to find Joan still doing well physically, but less and less open to any communication. But the energy of that convention carried me for a while.

A letter arrived shortly after my return that caused me great anguish. It was from John A. T. Robinson informing me that he had received an almost certain fatal cancer diagnosis and would have to cancel his proposed trip to Newark in May. He did not believe he would still be alive at that time. He also sent me a copy of the sermon he preached at Cambridge after he received the diagnosis in which he spoke about the meaning of his own death. It was a powerful witness that brought tears to my eyes. He had loomed so large in my growth and development that I was not prepared to lose him. I also felt some responsibility to carry on in the directions he had set. A bishop who is engaged in a theological reformation is rather rare. I did not feel prepared to take his place, but I saw no one else ready to do that either. At that time I was working on the manuscript that would be published in about a year entitled *Into the Whirlwind: The Future of the Church.* It was in many ways a Robinsonesque book and would presage every direction my intellectual life would take for the balance of my career. I am confident that in my grief over losing John Robinson I deliberately sought to make this book rise to the level that would keep the issues he had addressed before the church.

John died in early 1983. I was pleased to be asked to write the American tribute to him that appeared in *The Christian Century*. It was an essential part of my grief work. He was buried in the church cemetery near his home in Arncliffe, West Yorkshire. I stayed in touch with his widow, Ruth, and would in 1996 make a pilgrimage to his grave. I would also on that visit sit at his desk in his study and, while looking at a sculpture of his head, with his pen in my hand, write the chapter on prayer in what was my most provocative theological book,[1] which was dedicated to posing the issues before the church in my generation as John had done in his books in his generation.

But aside from these escapes into the world of study and ideas, Joan's mental condition and my remaining emotional resources both seemed to be headed downhill. I appeared powerless to impede that journey.

At the next meeting of the House of Bishops, however, I found myself cast in a new and unique role. Jack Allin had decided to organize the 1983 yearly meeting of the bishops around an acrostic he called the "SWEEPS Program." SWEEPS stood for stewardship, worship, evangelism, education, pastoral care, and service. To me it was so gimmicky it constituted a public admission that the presiding bishop had decided to tinker around the edges of the church's life, because either he did not recognize or did not understand the driving issues the church was facing.

In Jack Allin's typical style of operation, he chose six bishops, one might even call them cronies, to head each theme, instructing them to develop a day at the meeting of the House of Bishops based upon the assigned topic. The bishop asked to chair the day on worship was Harold Robinson of Western New York (Buffalo). Harold was a decent man, relatively conservative, who loved the trappings of the bishop's office and the delusions of power that these trappings produced. He saw himself as a bishop called primarily to "guard the unity of the church," so he was oriented to be an establishment player, quick to condemn any action that might rock the church's boat. He was a member of the same province in which I served, so I had come to know him fairly well.

I had also been invited to be a guest lecturer at the Chautauqua Institution, located in his diocese about an hour's drive from Buffalo. This conference center, which had its roots in Methodism, attracted nationally known speakers in every discipline of human knowledge. Conference keynoters were regularly political leaders, world-class scientists, best-selling authors, or famous poets. Over the years, for example, I have been present at Chautauqua with such people as Buckminster Fuller, John Ciardi, Karen Armstrong, and James Galway. Many people in Harold Robinson's diocese, including his secretary, had attended lectures I had given at Chautauqua, and they had made him aware of my competence, as revealed in these lectures, as well as my popularity with these audiences. Perhaps this is what encouraged him to ask me to be one of four or five bishops who would help him plan, shape, develop, and carry out the day on the subject of worship.

When this committee met to begin work on this project, I set the agenda by asking why worship was having such difficulty in our day. What was going on in our world that rendered the words and the forms employed in worship difficult to understand? What were the elemental needs in human life to which the activity of worship spoke? What were the primitive roots of worship and how were those primitive roots expressed in contemporary liturgy? As our committee began to address these issues, it became apparent that none of the other bishops had raised these questions before and that the vague dis-ease they sensed in themselves and in their clergy and congregations about worship found illumination in this discussion.

Perhaps I had thought about this more than others because I had recently given a New Dimensions lecture on prayer that had raised these issues. After some discussion Harold asked the committee how they would feel about assisting the entire House of Bishops in small groups to have the kind of discussion on worship we had had that morning. There was enthusiasm for that idea. But the bishops could not have that discussion unless the issues were posed for them in the same manner that they had been for this small group on this day. How the content was to be placed before them was our question.

Harold Robinson turned to me and asked me if I would be willing to prepare a paper to deliver to the House of Bishops focusing on the issues. Then we would divide the House into small groups, each with an appointed leader who would have a copy of my address and some questions to elicit discussion. These small groups would last for two hours and be concluded with a plenary session in which the thinking of the small groups would be shared and in which I, as the author of the paper, would have the opportunity to respond to questions that had been raised. The others confirmed the plan and I was, in effect, elected to the task.

In all of my years in the House of Bishops, I recall no other time when the House would be asked to give as much as four hours of a single day to interact with the thought of a single bishop. It was a rare opportunity, and I was pleased at the confidence this group of my peers expressed in me. Only afterward did it occur to me to be amused that the one Jack Allin had sought to keep in very secondary and minimum assignments in the House was now being asked to play a role in his SWEEPS week that he hardly anticipated. I am confident that when he heard of these plans, he was not pleased, but felt he could do nothing about it. After all, Harold Robinson, one of his lieutenants, had arranged it.

I worked hard on this lecture. I read much about primitive religious practices and how various powers of nature, like the sun, the moon, and the sea, had been deified and what happened when this deification had been abandoned. I looked at elements common in all religious traditions, like a sense of being chosen, a sense of divine revelation, the development of holy sites, sacred traditions, the ideas of guilt and sacrifice, and what causes the sense that someone is, in fact, a holy person, whether called a prophet, a messiah figure, or a founder of a new religious practice. I examined the defensiveness found in all religions, the excessive claims they make for their particular truth, the various attempts to posit inerrancy and infallibility that seem to mark every religious tradition. Above all, I sought to understand and identify the change element in a developing religious tradition that causes both worship practices and creedal beliefs to be abandoned. I also sought to examine the forces that enabled new practices and beliefs to be born. I wanted to establish the fact that all religions are lived out in a dialogue between spiritual insight and new knowledge and are thus always in flux and always evolving. My presentation was designed to break open the sacred mantras we are taught to repeat in worship but are not, in fact, based upon accurate history. For example, the idea that Jesus founded the church, ordained and empowered the Twelve, and intended for certain institutional forms to journey through history is historical nonsense. So is the suggestion found in our liturgy that we pray the Lord's Prayer because "Jesus himself taught us to do so." The Lord's Prayer embodies a definition of Jesus that did not develop until well after his death. I wanted to open worship to the challenge of the knowledge revolution in our century. My recurring theme would be "The heart cannot worship what the mind rejects."

The lecture went through many revisions, but when I left for the meeting, I carried with me some three hundred printed copies of the talk. They were to be given out to the bishops after the lecture was delivered orally. In addition, copies were also to be provided to group leaders and the press immediately prior to its presentation, so that they could follow it and be able to quote it accurately if they chose to do so.

The first day in this gathering of the House of Bishops was dedicated to stewardship. It was like the fall fund-raising event in every congregation, that is tips on how to meet financial goals were shared, covered with a bit of pious rhetoric. Success stories from around the country were related, but nothing more than the obvious was said. As the days of this week wore on, things did not improve as the bishops struggled to give substance to Bishop Allin's hapless cliché. The day on evangelism hit a new low both in content and in attendance. Bishops do vote with their feet, and while our conservative evangelical bishops droned on about how they sought souls for Christ and how we should follow their good example, the crowds around the coffee tables in the hall grew larger and larger. This caused the second day, which was dedicated to worship, to stand out in clear, if controversial, relief.

The day began, as it normally does, with the experience of worship. Bishops appear unable to work without a daily Eucharist. Then we moved into some brief routine House business that took us until about 11:00 A.M. Finally, the day was turned over to Harold Robinson, who outlined our plans and introduced me. This was the first time I had ever stood before this House in a formal way, outside floor debate. I felt quite self-conscious.

The House, however, listened attentively. I watched the facial expressions of the bishops, all of whom I now knew by name. I saw encouragement on some faces, wonderment on others, anxiety and fear, even shock on still others. Some bishops live in strange isolation from the world in their secure religious ghettoes, where no questions are ever raised. Interestingly, I saw no anger. That would come later. When I finished this presentation, there was appropriate applause and copies of my text were immediately handed out for use that afternoon in the discussion groups. The press asked for interview time, which I granted immediately. I was delighted to discover that even the secular media treated this effort as newsworthy. That indicated to me that the honest search for the truth of God did have a continuing appeal. The complete text of my paper was published in two installments in the national Episcopal newspaper, then called the *Episcopalian*.

At lunch and in the discussion groups that afternoon, the reaction was mixed, and negativity came from surprising sources. Those who act as if there is something called "the faith once delivered to the Saints" were forced to some attack mode response, for their security systems were badly damaged. Their favorite tactic was to attack my credibility. "He is no scholar," was their refrain. "We don't need to listen to him." As the years went by, that became the primary conservative line of defense. This wing of the church has taken shots at me, calling me unlearned, naive, an amateur theologian, "at the low end of the intellectual curve," and many other similar aspersions.

It was an interesting charge. I have authored more books than any other bishop of our church. These books have sold more copies than all other books by all other bishops in that House combined. I was elected to Phi Beta Kappa at the end of my sophomore year at the University of North Carolina and was chosen to be the Quatercentenary Scholar at Cambridge University in 1992. I am today an honorary fellow at Emmanuel College, Cambridge. I have been invited to be the William Belden Noble lecturer at Harvard University. I have been awarded two honorary Doctor of Divinity degrees and one Doctor of Humane Letters by recognized institutions of higher learning. All of these are academic honors none of my critics has ever thought about achieving, and yet they have constantly sought to minimize my credentials as their way of opposing my challenge to the church's traditional theological stances. I have not responded to these demeaning comments. I have only observed that time after time I have posed the issues on which the church has, in its decision-making assemblies, been forced to concentrate.

The most surprising response, however, came from the liberal side of the aisle. Otis Charles, the former bishop of Utah, who had left that post to become the dean of the Episcopal Divinity School at Cambridge, Massachusetts, was strangely negative and very vocal. He was also like a dog with a bone—he could not let it go. He gnawed at it for several days. I never quite understood where his negativity came from, but it centered around what was almost a refrain in the presentation, "The heart cannot worship what the mind rejects." I had, in keeping with this theme, illustrated the ways in which both our worship patterns and our God concepts have changed throughout human history. The sun was an object of worship, for example, until the mind determined that this object of worship was a material substance burning at an incredible rate and putting out an enormous amount of heat and light. With that knowledge, the ability to sustain the worship of the sun disappeared. This was an essential theological and liturgical principle that would be a cornerstone of all my future work.

Jack Allin survived the day. He never said a word to me about that address. Out of SWEEPS week emerged no memorable ideas that anyone I have interviewed can recall. I am sure the content I developed in that lecture has also been forgotten by most bishops, but their image of me, created by that day, remained vivid. I was regarded as thoughtful, articulate, well read, and able to defend myself in a public arena or debate. That was not a bad image to see developing. But after that meeting I settled back into my marginalized role, serving on powerless and insignificant committees, entering into the House of Bishops debate only from the floor, a pattern that would continue until Jack Allin's retirement.

When I returned home, *Into the Whirlwind* hit the bookstores. Seabury Press had been sold to Winston Press, which published this book. I was pleased with its professionalism. In this book I addressed three revolutions with which the church must deal if it is to engage the real world: the intellectual revolution, which threatened the church's orthodox formulas; the sexual revolution, which threatened to expose the repressed sexuality, especially the repressed homosexuality, that abounded in the church's life; and finally the revolution in tribal identity, which threatened the nationalistic definitions that had so deeply informed our church life. I pulled no punches in laying out the details of each revolution.

It did become my best-selling book thus far, reaching for the first time beyond the ten-thousand-copy limit that my books seemed unable, heretofore, to transcend. It revealed my changing, but not yet fully worked out, new understanding of homosexuality and surely pointed to directions I was destined to walk. But it also suggested that repressed homosexuality in the priesthood was the primary cause of the church's continued discrimination against women. I suggested that the church's commitment to celibacy had turned the priesthood into the largest closet in which homosexual males could hide from the pressures to get married and that the vestments of the clergy were overwhelmingly feminine. The old saw "Why do we call him father if he dresses like mother?" came into play. I even suggested that the almost nude figure on the crucifix that adorns the cells of monks was erotic if you were a homosexual male. I looked at the items that were kissed liturgically by the priest, the stole, the altar, the missal, and raised questions about misplaced sex symbols. It was a passionate attempt to raise to consciousness the church's incredible duplicity about sexual matters. It certainly got people's attention. In my own church it created a visceral reaction among those repressed gay males, both in the United States and in the United Kingdom, who so totally rejected the possibility that women could be priests by suggesting their real fear was that women would make their closets no longer safe. The most vehement opponents I knew in both America and the United Kingdom to the ordination of women were self-denying gay males. So the battle was joined in those circles. It also brought to a flash point my already troubled ecumenical relationships with the Roman Catholic Church in New Jersey.

During our church's fight to open the priesthood to women, the pope kept playing what I called "the ecumenical card," suggesting that the

Anglican ordination of women injected "grave difficulties" into the quest for ecumenical unity. At the same time he announced his willingness to receive disgruntled Anglican clergy into the Roman priesthood, even allowing them to maintain their married status so long as they opposed the ordination of women. The Roman Catholic Diocese of Paterson had in fact been quite public in reordaining two married Anglican priests in Madison, New Jersey. So I concluded that if one had to fight the might of Rome to secure women priests in the Anglican Church, I was quite willing to do just that.

Earlier, I had fired a shot across the bow of the local Roman Catholic leadership by breaking off our ongoing ecumenical dialogue. My reason for doing that was the removal of Hans Küng from his position as a Catholic theologian at the University of Tübingen. If Rome could not allow the theological dissent of one of its own most creative scholars, then I deemed it a waste of time to carry on an ecumenical dialogue in which no real issues were ever discussed because Rome would not allow them to be debated. So losing our ecumenical dialogue on a diocese-to-diocese level was an insignificant loss to me. But breaking the dialogue was considered an unprecedented step and received front-page news coverage. It created protest in both Roman Catholic and Episcopal circles and was characterized as a "rash" decision. "Rash" it was not. Calculated it was, and the result was to raise issues to consciousness and debate. The Roman Catholic bishops acted hurt and aggrieved and expressed the hope that the talks could be resumed before too long. Of course, no progress is ever made in ecumenical talks when Rome sets the agenda, but the impression of continued work in these difficult areas is nonetheless an important part of their image. However, underneath that polite response was anger destined to come to the surface sooner or later.

I responded by inviting Hans Küng to be one of our New Dimensions lecturers. I later invited Charles Curran when he was removed from his seat as professor of ethics at Catholic University in Washington for refusing to keep private his questions about mandatory birth control and the Roman Catholic attitude toward homosexuality. I also invited Matthew Fox when Matthew was being harassed by Joseph Cardinal Ratzinger for questioning the theological system that assumes original sin and the fall as the primary building blocks in a theology of control, and Rosemary Ruether when Rosemary was raising issues about the Virgin Mary and the place of women in the church. All four spoke to large audiences, and each attracted a significant number of Roman Catholic visitors. The archbishop of Newark viewed all these actions with both silence and dismay.

When interviews with me generated by *Into the Whirlwind* began to appear in the New Jersey and national religious press, the façade of detached politeness finally broke and the anger of Rome flowed freely. Finally, the archbishop of Newark, Peter Gerety, exploded in a letter sent to me, marked "personal," dated November 9, 1983. It read in part:

> I must confess that your confrontational style has made me personally and many of our clergy, religious and laity very uncomfortable about your desire in this regard (for ecumenical cooperation).
>
> I have not reacted in any public way to your more spectacular comments which seem to be, at least, full of baiting statements about the Roman Catholic Church. The enclosed clipping [a resumé of some of my suggestions that the priesthood is significantly made up of gay males in hiding and that their negative attitudes toward women rise out of this fact], however, contains remarks attributed to you which are not only expressions of doctrinal and disciplinary disagreements. They are simply crude insults which question our integrity.
>
> It was my hope that you would repudiate these press reports of your remarks. Many days have passed and you have not done so. Therefore, I am forced to conclude that they are all indeed accurate.
>
> Accordingly, I protest vigorously these attacks upon the integrity of the clergy, religious and laity of the Roman Catholic Church. How any ecumenical relations can be conducted in this atmosphere escapes me.

Archbishop Gerety also wrote to the Lutheran bishop Herluf Jensen, who was at this time the president of the New Jersey Coalition of Religious Leaders, protesting these comments. Bishop Jensen called me, asking what the fight was about. He apparently had not found these public statements anything more than interesting.

I could not tell the archbishop how many Roman Catholic priests had written me supportive letters and spoken encouraging words to me when I met them in local communities because that would have violated their confidentiality. So I simply acknowledged the letter expressing my sorrow that he had been upset. Later, I accepted the archbishop's invitation to lunch at his home in Newark to discuss these matters. The lunch was pleasant and the conversation was honest. I think he understood my feelings, if he did not fully appreciate them. I really liked Peter Gerety. He was an open and thoughtful person. However, the idea that ecumenical relations were so important that my church or I would tolerate anti-intellectual, antifemale, and antihomosexual sentiments without objection as the price of ecumenicity was incredible to me, and in time I think the New Jersey Roman Catholic hierarchy began to understand that they could play those cards no longer.

But the fact remained that any serious ecumenical discussion between the Roman Catholic archdiocese and our diocese came to a grinding halt when the Roman Church, under the ultraconservative John Paul II, continued the practice of making each bishop and archbishop more conservative and less cooperative than the last, which certainly occurred when Peter Gerety was replaced by Theodore McCarrick. The official and public Roman Catholic–Anglican dialogue simply disappeared from view in New Jersey and would do so eventually both nationally and internationally. It is today the deadest of all ecumenical conversations in the Christian world.

Outwardly *Into the Whirlwind* produced a flurry of activity that seemed to be effective and purposeful. But though I could engage that debate with great energy, when 1983 ended I was emotionally drained and very near to being a broken man. Three members of my staff upon whom I had depended so deeply, indeed on whom I had leaned for emotional support, had decided that they did not want to continue to work for this diocese and departed, leaving me almost incapable of running the diocese. I felt like I was on the way to being a failure in my episcopal activities. I did not know where to turn. My wife's sickness continued to dissipate my energies at home. My publishing career had now become a source of enormous hostility in right-wing religious circles, which I could only absorb. None of my fellow bishops, least of all Jack Allin, was eager to be supportive. My fuse had become quite short and my temper was spoken about openly. It was the nadir. There was no more room on the downside. I had clearly hit bottom.

1. *Why Christianity Must Change or Die* (San Francisco: HarperSanFrancisco, 1988)

# 1 6

# *Rising from the Ashes*

※

I AM A survivor.

I never realized that as completely as when I came to the transition year of 1984. I made some critical personal decisions that were, I now recognize, survival decisions. First, I moved physically into a small apartment over a garage adjacent to my office in downtown Newark. It was in a high-crime urban neighborhood and therefore dangerous, but I felt a peace of belonging in those three small rooms and a bath. My days at work were long, and constant reading became my primary companion at night. Although the move did not do much to change the personal issues with which I was dealing, it relieved stress and I began to discover a new energy.

The most helpful person to me during this time, serving not just as my friend, but in a real sense as my pastor, was a priest named Denise Haines. She had joined the diocesan staff as an interim measure when the resignations began, but ultimately stayed five years. A brilliant woman with a great deal of energy, she became the first female archdeacon in the Anglican Communion. During this time she was also nominated for the office of bishop and, though she ran well, was not elected. I am quite sure that I could not have survived that time of transition without her support. She was primarily responsible for my hiring one Wanda Hollenbeck to be my executive secretary, a decision that introduced me to a most remarkable human being who would work with me for ten years.

The other crucial appointment to our staff was that of Christine Barney to be the chief administrative officer of the diocese. This unique woman had been a personal friend primarily to my wife, but to some degree to me as well. She had also become an active lay leader in our diocese. When this core of three unusual women began to function at Cathedral House, a new sense of competence returned to the life of the diocese. In time two additional priests, James W. H. Sell and Leslie Smith, joined our staff to create a working environment that began to remind me of my days in Richmond. It became obvious to me that in these moves I had both stabilized my working environment and secured a nondraining home environment. Life began to flow again, if not into my almost lifeless body, at least into the life of the diocese.

It probably helped that no major issues came before us in that rather quiet year. The Conference on Life after Death was taking shape, but was not scheduled until fall 1985. Claiborne wanted to get through his reelection of 1984 before going public with this conference. It would be his last term and that gave him an enormous new sense of freedom, allowing him to act out the role of elder statesman and pursue interests that might not have any political cachet.

The members of the faculty for this conference were, however, already invited and included intellectual superstars that would be the envy of a great university. Paul Davies, a rising young physicist at the University of Newcastle on Tyne in the United Kingdom, whose book, *God and the New Physics*, was his most popular offering at the time, and Rupert Sheldrake, a British biologist, had agreed to join us. Sheldrake walked the edges of his scientific discipline as he sought to demonstrate the ability of animals to communicate across barriers as great as the Atlantic Ocean. To balance these frontier speculators, we also secured Anthony Flew, the well-known British philosopher and atheist who helped keep a creative and skeptical tension in the conference. Next came Sogyal Rinpoche, a Buddhist mystic; Stanislav Grof, a psychiatrist who had pioneered the use of psychedelic drugs in therapy; Candace Pert, the chief of biochemistry at the National Institutes of Health; Kenneth Ring, a psychology professor at the University of Connecticut whose specialty was near-death experiences; Charles Tart, a professor at the University of California at Davis who without apology called himself a parapsychologist; John Hick, the radical British theologian, then at Claremont in the United States; Jacqueline Damgaard, an Atlanta psychologist who specialized in multiple personality dysfunction; and Willis Harman, the president of the California-based Institute of Noetic Science. Claiborne and I were the amateurs in a spectacularly impressive group of leaders. Through Claiborne Pell's connections and influence the conference was to be hosted by Georgetown University at the invitation of its Jesuit president, Father Timothy Healy. Its other cosponsors were the Smithsonian Institution as part of the Smithsonian Symposia and the Institute of Noetic Sciences. We looked forward to this high-profile event in fall 1985.

Meanwhile, other things demanded my attention. In January 1985 I had presided over an annual convention of our diocese that clearly expressed our new upbeat mood. My depression had lifted significantly. Minor irritants did not bother me as they had earlier. I could ignore a couple of destructive, perhaps emotionally disturbed, clergy. In my convention address I urged our diocese to authorize my recommendation to appoint a special task force to study and report on changing patterns in family life, a study that had been called for by the general convention of our national church as early as 1982.

I asked this task force to address three questions that pointed to signs of change in our understanding of both human sexuality and family structure. First, why do the majority of our young people today initiate sexual activity long before marriage? Is this simply an attempt to accommodate immorality, or is it a response to other issues we have neither articulated nor understood? Second, why do so many postmarried adults (divorced and widowed) elect not to be married again, but also not to remain apart from sexual activity? Third, is the church or the society in which we live ready to respond in a new and nonjudgmental way to the sacred partnerships being formed by an increasing number of gay and lesbian people?

It did not seem to me or to anyone else that this would be a terribly controversial study. The convention endorsed my proposal by a unanimous vote, a sure sign that they regarded it as being in the same category as motherhood and apple pie.

When the convention adjourned at about 5:00 P.M. on that January Saturday, a number of people gathered around the podium. They brought various things to my attention or wanted to comment on some aspect of the convention. One of these people was a priest in our diocese named Nelson Thayer, whose transfer from New York I had only recently received, though he had lived within our geographical boundaries for some time as a professor of pastoral theology on the faculty of the Methodist Seminary at Drew University in Madison, New Jersey.

"Jack, I would be quite interested in serving on your task force to study changing patterns in sexuality and family life," Nelson said. "I am doing a great deal of work in my classes on that subject and would love to put the academic and the experiential sides of this issue together."

I did not know Nelson well enough at that time to know what he thought about any subject. I liked his mild manner. I respected his obvious academic skills. I had read a recent book he had published. But, above all, I yearned to tie seminary and congregation together, and Nelson offered that opportunity.

Without giving it a thought, I responded, "Why don't you chair this task force for us, Nelson?" I gave that crucial decision absolutely no advance thought, yet it was one of the most fateful and, I might add, brilliant decisions of my career.

Nelson and I met in about a week to flesh out the membership of the task force. By that time I had received a number of calls and letters from people expressing interest in serving. We formed the membership of the task force from that source. Indeed, we appointed everyone who asked to serve. I met with them once at their initial gathering to give them my charge. Then I stayed out of their lives and let them do their work. It would be two years before they made their study public. I moved on to other things, not the least of which was another general convention of our national church during which we were scheduled to go through an interesting transition.

Jack Allin's time of mandatory retirement had finally arrived. He had been a heavy presence in the life of this part of the Body of Christ, repressing its initiatives more than even he understood. He kept trying to keep the church related to a world that was passing away. Progress had to be achieved over his active opposition. Undoubtedly, the church needed a time of resting and absorbing after the dynamic Hines years. Jack Allin's election represented just that kind of reaction. If he had served only three years, he might have provided a quite effective breather for the church, but he served for twelve years, and that meant that he was left behind the church in almost every dimension of its life.

He found himself on the wrong side of every major issue and was in fact defeated by them. The church had authorized the ordination and had actually ordained women over his objection. The church had revised the prayer book over his objection. The church had begun the dialogue on human sexuality over his objection. The significant leadership of the church had long since departed from the presiding bishop's office and was vested increasingly in diocesan bishops, where church and society began to collide. When Jack Allin finally lifted his dead weight off the life of the church by his retirement, new possibilities began to emerge.

The nominating committee, made up of equal numbers of bishops, clergy, and laity, had placed four names before the church for its consideration as his successor. However, only the bishops had the power of the ballot.

The nominees were, in alphabetical order: Edmond Browning, the bishop of Hawaii, a quiet liberal, but not a person of imposing leadership gifts; William Frey, the bishop of Colorado, probably the most naturally talented man in the group, but rooted so deeply in the theologically conservative wing of the church that he could never have been the church's leader; Furman (Bill) Stough, the bishop of Alabama, known as a Southern liberal, but thought of as a national moderate; and John Walker, the bishop of Washington, head of the Urban Bishops' Coalition and the first African American person ever nominated to head the Episcopal Church.

As the election neared, no clear favorite emerged. Bill Stough was regarded as an acceptable, if lackluster, candidate, and Bill Frey was not a major contender.

I was torn in this election. John Walker was my seminary classmate. He had been the first black preacher ever introduced into the noontime preaching series at St. Paul's in Richmond. He was a trustee with me at Virginia Seminary and active with me in the Urban Bishops' Coalition. He was articulate and urbane, clearly a good bishop of Washington. John, however, had one disconcerting habit that gave me pause, at least momentarily. He accepted positions, titles, and offices, but attended to the duties these required very poorly. His attendance record, for example, at the meetings of the board of trustees of Virginia Seminary was not good. Most of the work of the Urban Bishops' Coalition was actually done by John Burt of Ohio even when John Walker was president, because he was consistently unable to be present at the planning meetings. He did attend the public meetings and conducted them brilliantly. He was a gifted African American and I suspect everyone sought to secure him for their activity, and John could not decline, but no one could have carried well that heavy a load of responsibility. However, I admired his ability and I coveted for my church the witness of an outstanding black leader.

On the other hand, Ed Browning had been a close personal friend of mine over the years. He too had been a visitor in our Lenten preaching schedule in Richmond. Because of my wife's health, I was normally a single person in the meetings of the House of Bishops, which involved a significant number of social events. I was deeply touched that Ed and his wife, Patti, together with Wes and Dee Frensdorff, took particular care to see that I was included at those otherwise lonely activities. Ed Browning would also bring a wide range of experiences to the presiding bishop's chair. He had served as a missionary bishop in Okinawa, being consecrated at age thirty-seven. He understood cross-culturalism and even spoke Japanese. Later he headed our overseas work at the national headquarters in New York, so he was familiar with the ecclesiastical bureaucracy and how it worked. Still later he was the bishop for Europe, gaining diplomatic experience there. Finally, he was a very effective diocesan bishop in the multiethnic diocese of Hawaii and was also consistently liberal on all the issues that mattered. He was not, however, a leader in the House of Bishops. I never recall his taking part in any debate on the floor of the House prior to his nomination.

I made my decision on whom to support based on my assessment of the candidates' abilities rather than sentiment. John Walker had the chance, I believed, to be a great leader for our church. So while Ed Browning had my affection, John Walker received my vote on every ballot.

The day of the election was beautiful. The general convention was meeting at the convention center in Anaheim, California. For the actual election, all of the bishops were transported to a nearby church, where we were sequestered until the choice had been made and the House of Deputies had concurred with our decision. It was a fascinating vote count. John Walker led the first ballot by a significant margin with seventy-five votes. Ed Browning edged out Bill Stough for second place by the slender margin of forty-eight to forty-seven. Bill Frey was a distant fourth. That one vote margin for Ed on that first ballot was enormously important. It meant that he would be the alternate to John Walker's candidacy. There were those who looked upon a possible primacy for John Walker with disfavor, and they had to have an alternative. On the second ballot the support for Stough and Frey dissipated, and it became even more clear that this would be a two-person race. It also became obvious to old political hands in the House that Browning had more second-choice votes than did Walker. Walker still led on the second ballot, but by a smaller margin. On the third ballot Browning pulled ahead and he was elected on the fourth ballot. This slight, red-headed, sensitive man, originally from Corpus Christi, Texas, with his lovely, but shy and introverted wife, would now step into the office that, in my opinion, had been filled to its ultimate capacity by only one person in my lifetime and his name was John E. Hines.

I called John Hines to tell him the news as soon as I was free to do so. He too liked Ed Browning, but he too had questions about whether Ed was strong enough to be creative in the position. We wondered how this man who was in fact a gentle and genuinely good human being would thrive in this high-profile, deeply political position. The next twelve years would answer that question. It would not be easy for him, and he would discover that his sweet nature and gentle spirit would not win him the applause and support he so deeply desired.

However, a shift in leadership at the top of any organization causes all of the other pieces in the puzzle to reconfigure. Jack Allin's conservative friends would clearly fall from their influential positions. But would Ed Browning use the power of this office to lead or would he interpret his mandate to be that of simply presiding over a dynamic organization in an attempt to keep it moving forward? Would he sacrifice truth for unity? I was asked to write an article on Ed for an in-house publication. I interpreted him as one who believed like John Hines and thus as one who would not seek to impede the church, but who would, like Jack Allin, not be a dynamic leader.

My first opportunity to speak with him alone after his election came the next day in a chance meeting on our way to some event. I congratulated him and pledged my support and friendship. I did say that I hoped I might be given a meaningful committee assignment for a change, rehearsing quickly the positions Jack Allin had assigned to me. He assured me that my talents, which he said he admired greatly, would be utilized. He was true to his word. When the committee assignments arrived early in 1986, I had been placed on the Standing Commission on Human Affairs and Health. The agenda before this commission consisted of such issues as homosexuality, abortion, family planning, genetic engineering, and active and passive euthanasia, including physician-assisted suicide. This was the commission that had forced the general convention of 1979 to debate homosexuality for the first time. Despite the fact that its resolution had been overwhelmingly defeated on that occasion, the issue of homosexuality would not go away. The chair of this newly appointed commission was to be the bishop of Rhode Island, George Hunt. He had been my seminary classmate, and we were very compatible on the issues. I looked forward to this assignment and felt that finally, after almost ten years as a bishop, I might be able to find a way to work inside the system rather than outside it. This commission would prove to be my only opportunity, but it would be the vehicle through which a radically different agenda would come before the decision-making bodies of our national church.

The Pell conference convened shortly after the general convention concluded. More than seven hundred people crowded into Gaston Hall at Georgetown University to listen to our star-studded faculty look at life after death from every angle. The attendees asked questions. The leaders dialogued with each other. The boundaries of every mind present were expanded. The conference was covered by the *Washington Post*, the *New York Times*, and the Voice of America. It was one of the most intriguing intellectual experiences of my life. I did address this conference more to pose the issues to be explored than to do the exploration. I contributed an article and served as the overall editor for the book that grew out of the conference, which bore the weighty title *Consciousness and Survival: An Interdisciplinary Inquiry into the Possibility of Life Beyond Biological Death*.

This experience also led me into a long and rich study of life after death in both the scriptures of the Old and the New Testaments, as well as among the great religious traditions of the world. I spent some time examining the way in which both confidence in and doubt about life after death had shaped the very history of Western civilization. At one point I believed that this area of study would actually constitute my major life work, but it proved to be only a fascinating detour. This study did not find expression in the book that grew out of this conference, nor did the great volume on this subject that I once contemplated ever see the light of day. The reason was not the absence of conviction, but the inability of my frail human words to capture that conviction. The subject of life after death never narrowed for me into a manageable focus. It always expanded in an apparently endless way, so drawing conclusions that would be book worthy became increasingly impossible. That study was not lost, however, for it was destined to shape new chapters on life and death in books of mine that would appear in 1994 and 1998.

Later serendipities in my life were a direct result of this conference. Claiborne and I remained in close contact until he retired to Rhode Island in 1991, when seeing each other became more difficult. Carole Taylor went on to marry a retired editor of *Time Magazine*, and they hosted several gatherings in their lovely home overlooking Central Park in New York City, to which Christine and I, along with Claiborne, were invited to discuss such exotic subjects as unidentified flying objects.

Paul Davies and I stayed in touch through letters, communiqués, and an occasional visit when we discovered ourselves in the same place, such as Oxford in the United Kingdom or Adelaide in Australia. We also continued to read each other's writings. His endorsement on the back of my book *Why Christianity Must Change or Die* meant a great deal to me. Rupert Sheldrake popped up in my conversations many times, the last one being with a New Jersey psychiatrist, and he later coauthored a book with my friend Matthew Fox.

I discovered in this episode that my primary audience was increasingly outside the walls of the church. Within religious circles I regularly came to be regarded as the skeptic who was not willing to affirm what traditional religious leaders needed to affirm. But I was not then, nor am I now, ready to give up on the church. I only wanted to have the people of the church recognize that beyond the walls of sacred buildings lived an audience significantly turned off to the church's traditional message, but nonetheless made up of people on a spiritual quest for transcendent dimensions to life. That audience with which I came in contact through these nonchurch experiences, became quite visible to me and it would shape the direction of my life dramatically. In time, I would name these people "Believers in Exile" and I would become one of them, but that would not be for more than a decade.

I would try, however, one more time to work within traditional church structures to see if we could reform this institution from within. At last I had a vehicle for that attempt in my membership on the Standing Commission on Human Affairs and Health.

The first meeting of this commission came in the spring of 1986 and was convened at my former seminary in Alexandria, Virginia. Under the polity of the church, a standing commission is made up of bishops appointed by the presiding bishop and priests and lay members appointed by the president of the House of Lay and Clerical Deputies, which was the other half of our bicameral decision-making national structure. The head of that second body was the Very Reverend David Collins, dean of St. Philip's Cathedral in Atlanta, a classmate and soul mate of Jack Allin. He was an enormously competent man, but his roots were in the emotional, evangelical, conservative wing of our church. He participated in what was called the charismatic renewal movement, which, in my opinion, always degenerated into a pious kind of biblical fundamentalism that invested the Bible with an authority that belonged only to God. His appointments to this commission reflected those attitudes.

Collins appointed a woman from Arizona who was the vice president of a body called the National Organization of Episcopalians for Life (NOEL), the pro-life, anti-abortion lobby in our church, and a layman from Florida named Harry Griffith, who headed something called the Episcopal Bible Reading Fellowship and later the Anglican Fellowship of Prayer. Harry, a Southern fundamentalist, would make his stand, and a visceral one it would be, against homosexuals and something he identified as "the gay lobby" or "the gay agenda." These, I discovered, were code words that stood for anyone whose point of view differed from his. Next there was a layman from Eau Claire, Wisconsin, who was surprisingly liberal, violating my stereotype of that diocese, and a priest, Robert Cooper, who was a professor on the theological faculty at the Episcopal Theological Seminary of the Southwest in Austin, Texas. The third bishop Ed appointed to the commission was William Swing of California, a man liberal in his spoken words, but one who did not always follow those words with any action. There were others appointed, but these were the principals and this commission proved to be the context and the location in which our church's struggle with the issue of homosexuality was to be fought out. It would also be the arena in which the scope of my career as a bishop would ultimately be determined. The section of my 1983 book *Into the Whirlwind* that dealt with issues of human sexuality had placed me squarely, if still conservatively, into this debate.

From the very beginning, all issues paled before the debate on sexual matters. The primary definition of homosexuality in the church's past, which called it a mental sickness, a moral depravity, and the chosen behavior of deviant and evil people, was being challenged by new knowledge emerging from the world of medical and scientific research, especially in what came to be called the brain sciences, as well as reproductive studies and the field of biochemistry. The idea that one's sexual orientation was a moral choice had come to be seriously questioned. Studies began to reveal that the number of homosexual people in the human population was consistent and steady in all times and in all cultures, making it look like a natural statistical norm. Where cultural acceptance was present, homosexuality emerged from the shadows and expressed itself quite creatively. Where cultural opposition and persecution were heavy, homosexuality tended to be repressed, denied, and deeply closeted. I never will forget an African bishop who said to me, "We don't have any homosexuals in Africa." But the fact remains that homosexuality is as real and present in Africa as it is anywhere else in the world, as both my mail and a recent study published by St. Martin's Press in 1998 have surely documented.[1] Scientists also had become indisputably aware that homosexuality was not limited to human beings, but was present in the natural order among mammals[2] and perhaps even among some reptiles. Thus, the argument of the conservatives that homosexuality was "unnatural behavior" was compromised significantly.

Driven by public awareness of these academic conclusions in the 1960s, 1970s, and 1980s, an increasing number of people, certainly including me, began to recognize that the prevailing stance of condemnation and moral judgment that marked the church's attitude toward gay and lesbian people was inappropriate. It was based on a false premise.

In the public mind, homosexuality was still identified primarily with the male population, and, strangely enough, it tended to be associated with promiscuity and child molesting. That was, of course, nothing more than the conclusion of a prejudiced irrationality, but it colored attitudes nonetheless. Statistical studies made it obvious that children were far more at risk of being sexually violated by heterosexual adults than by homosexual adults, and promiscuity certainly marked the heterosexual world, as prostitution, called the oldest known profession, certainly made clear. But prejudices feed on fear and ignorance and the mystery and minority status surrounding homosexuality lent themselves to the manipulation of fear and ignorance.

As this commission settled into its work, the personalities settled into their roles quickly. The vice president of NOEL had little interest in any subject save abortion. Harry Griffith had little capacity to grow beyond his pious Southern biblicalism and could relate to homosexuality only as a sin completely condemned by Holy Scripture. Bob Cooper recognized no hiding places for anyone on any issue and used his quick wit to puncture pomposity at every point. The gentleman from Eau Claire was quiet, but surprisingly supportive of what came to be called the liberal side of the issues. George Hunt tried to act as an impartial chair, but could not deny his own convictions or his experience. He was a positive force, but the neutrality of the chair placed real constraints upon him. Bill Swing never engaged an issue, sometimes leaving meetings to play golf at a local course. The others tended to be silent participants. By a process of elimination I was clearly chosen to be the point guard in the debate to create a new climate in this part of the Christian Church in regard to the issue of homosexuality. That new climate called for justice first, then acceptance and affirmation second. It was a daunting task.

It took us a while to orient ourselves to this task and to face the question of how we might address this issue churchwide. We did not want to present another report that would be dismissed by another general convention as quickly as the 1979 report had been. The mistake of the commission in that year was to forget that a large decision-making body like the general convention could not engage this issue on the same level as the members of the commission had done. So when the members of this convention were confronted with controversial data they had had no chance to process, they inevitably voted according to both their fears and operative prejudices. How to engage the whole church in this debate became a question high on my agenda. My conviction was that when people discuss an issue openly, they cannot help but take in new data and grow.

Ed Browning had decided to give this commission and this subject one full day at the interim House of Bishops meeting, but we could not get that day until the fall of 1987, since the interim meeting of 1986 had already been scheduled. To have our commission plan a day for the House of Bishops was a particularly easy task because the three bishops on this commission— Hunt, Swing, and Spong—who would be in charge of that day were generally in agreement, and so we did not have to expend great amounts of energy in debating how we would use this opportunity. We knew the House well. Since I was the senior bishop, I was probably more deeply aware of the tactics we needed to develop. Our task was quite simply to provide a forum in which the whole church could discuss this issue openly. Since our day with the bishops would not come until 1987, we realized that we would have to seek to reach the people in the pews first and then the bishops. That was not, in my opinion, the preferred order, but it became the necessary order, given the pressure of having a report ready by the general convention of 1988.

As we thought about the easier assignment of dealing with the House of Bishops, I urged, above all else, that we use the technique of small-group discussion that had been employed when my paper on worship had been presented four years earlier. Since most bishops take quite seriously their role of chief pastor to their dioceses, it was my conviction that if we could organize this day to focus on the pastoral rather than the political approach to homosexuality, we could move the members of this body forward.

By this time the AIDS epidemic was coming out of the shadows and into intense public awareness. The death of a well-known public figure, Rock Hudson, and the subsequent revelation about his homosexuality even got the attention of our conservative president, Ronald Reagan. So long as faceless categories like "gay men" and "drug addicts" were the primary victims of this disease, little public attention or funding was directed toward it. But, increasingly, personal faces were being placed on the disease.

The Stonewall Uprising, which occurred in New York City in June 1969, had also made the public aware of the lack of protection gay people received from law enforcement agencies and galvanized gay people's response to these attacks by urging a more aggressive stance in their own defense. My sense of history had taught me that whenever any oppressed people begin to say "Enough is enough. I will not tolerate abuse any longer. I would rather die protecting myself than die a passive victim of prejudicial aggression," then no force in the world can keep them in bondage to either prejudice or fear any longer. This was true of the Jews in Egypt, people in slavery, women seeking equality, and blacks in a segregated society, and it would prove to be true of homosexual people in our day. When that attitude is born in history, the moment of freedom has arrived. It is also worth noting that history never moves backward for the people who claim the right to define themselves once that new definition has emerged. All of these things were working for us as we sought to find a way to bring the members of the Episcopal Church into both the reality of this debate and a new cultural awareness.

Slowly a plan of action was worked out. For the House of Bishops meeting in fall 1987, we would open the day with a preliminary report made by the standing commission. Robert Cooper, the vice chair and ranking priest on this commission, would be invited to make that presentation. Then the bishops would be broken into groups of eight to discuss their pastoral approach to and support for gay and lesbian people, both lay and ordained, within their dioceses. After lunch we would have a plenary session in which the small groups would report back, sharing the highlights of their discussion. The three of us who served on this standing commission as bishops would preside over that plenary session. This session would be designed not to lead to legislation, but to open the conversation among the bishops. This fact would be stated early to remove anxiety and to facilitate discussion.

With that plan, at least in outline form, we turned to the bigger issue, namely, how to initiate the conversation among the people of the church at large. The people of our churches never gathered in a single place, nor could they receive information in a consistent manner, so access to them was not easy. But the church did have a national monthly newspaper called at that time the *Episcopalian*. It went to all the clergy of the country and to a significant number of the laity, especially the lay leadership of our church. It was not a perfect vehicle, but it was the best we had.

I was asked to approach the publisher, Richard Crawford, with the request that he allow the Standing Commission on Human Affairs and Health to seek to initiate a dialogue in our church early in 1987 on the subject of human sexuality through the pages of this newspaper. This project would involve, first, an introductory article that would simply pose the issues that were before the church. This article was anticipated to be generic in nature, unsigned, and nonargumentative. It would appear in the February 1987 issue. Then three topics would be debated with pro and con articles in three subsequent issues. Those three topics were the same ones I had asked our diocesan task force to consider at our convention in 1985, namely, the predominance in our society of sexual activity prior to marriage; the increasing number of postmarried people, either divorced or widowed, who chose to live with a partner but not to get married another time; and finally, the reality of homosexuality and the growing desire on the part of gay and lesbian couples to receive the church's blessing on their committed partnerships.

The commission discussed at length who the authors of these contrasting articles would be. They needed to be good representatives who could present their points of view in provocative and powerful ways. To be effective, these articles needed to be clear and well written. Finally, we arrived at a decision. Two of our outstanding women priests, the Venerable Denise Haines from Newark, known as a liberal, and the Reverend Fleming Rutledge from New York, known as a conservative, would square off on the issue of understanding premarital sexual activity. The Reverend William R. Coats, an articulate liberal priest who wrote frequently for a publication called *Plumbline*, and the Reverend John W. Yates, an articulate conservative priest with deep Southern roots, were chosen to examine from both sides the postmarried phenomenon. Lastly, John Fortunato, a clinical psychologist and a gay man from Chicago, would be pitted against Dr. Ruth Tiffany Barnhouse, a conservative psychiatrist from Dallas who would later become a priest, to debate the gay issue. These articles would appear on opposite pages of the *Episcopalian* clearly identified as a "yes" response and a "no" response. The introductory preface article was designed to announce the series and urge the readers to utilize the Letters to the Editor section to join the debate. We expected that debate to rage in that forum for most of 1987, certainly until the House of Bishops meeting in October. We were not disappointed.

The basic outline of this proposal was adopted by the commission in June 1986, and we set to work pulling together both the churchwide discussion and the day for the bishops. Harry Griffith was the most vocal opponent of our plans. His opposition came primarily from the assumption that there was nothing to discuss, that none of these issues should be opened to any response except that of condemning those who refused to abide by the church's historic standards as affirmed, in his mind, by the Bible. But the majority prevailed and the church-wide debate began to come into focus.

I did not realize how much Harry's recalcitrance would affect either this project or my life. I set about to get commitments from our chosen authors. I

also volunteered to draft the proposed introductory piece and to have it ready
for the commission's approval. The deadline for both of these tasks was the
next meeting of the commission in the fall. When that meeting date arrived,
I brought my introductory article to share it with them for their suggestions,
since it was to be written in the name of the entire commission. It was what I
regarded as an innocuous piece of writing. I did not advocate anything in
particular. I simply set the stage for the debate. Though Harry Griffith had
been vocal in his opposition earlier, he was absent from this fall meeting. The
article was generally approved by those present but, in the interest of fairness,
I was urged to seek to reach Harry by phone and to run this statement by him.
If it was to be from the commission, it seemed appropriate that every member of the commission should at least hear it in advance.

When my call got through to Harry, I was shocked at his response. By
opening the question, he said, we were implicitly legitimizing that which the
Bible abhors. I did not know what to do with his response. It was so typical
of evangelicals who live in a world of unchanging truth and divine magic. I
told him that I would try to meet his objections by making this piece sufficiently bland and morally neutral, but I could not fail to introduce the debate
that, I reminded him, the commission had already voted to conduct. Returning to the group, I shared the problem with them and excused myself to seek
by editorial excisions to try once more to make the piece one that all of us
could agree to sign. It is not easy to address changing patterns in sexual
behavior unless one admits that changing patterns exist. When I had it as
bland and noncommittal as I could get it, I read it to the group once more
and then placed a second call to Harry. I told him I believed I had gone as far
as I could go to meet his objections in this article. I also repeated its purpose,
which was to introduce a debate that the commission had decided the whole
church needed to have. If I cut this article any more, people would wonder
just why it had ever been published at all.

Harry continued to be totally negative. He would not be a party to this
piece. If it appeared as an unsigned article from the commission, he would
write a letter to the editor and distance himself from it. This conversation
was, in my opinion, like talking to a member of the Flat-Earth Society after
the astronauts had orbited and photographed this round planet.

However, Harry's words did give me an out. If this could not be an agreed
upon article from the whole commission, then I would write it and sign it as
one member of the commission. This way the project would get launched
and nobody's integrity would be compromised. I could certainly speak as

one member and I clearly had majority support. I proposed to Harry that we give up our attempt to have the article come from the group and I would own it publicly. I think he was glad to get off the hook, so he said he would not object to this if it were clearly my article, but he wanted to be in no way personally identified with it. He certainly had the right to join the debate on any side he wished, I told him, certain that he would.

Returning to the group, I reported our conversation and my proposed compromise. Everyone seemed satisfied with that, and so the decision was made. Without Harry to worry about, I rewrote the article to pose the issues a bit more boldly. During the fall I collected the proposed papers from all our pro and con contributors and the whole series was delivered to the editor of the *Episcopalian* by November 1. The die was now cast. On or about February 1, 1987, an article would appear in the official publication of the Episcopal Church, signed by the bishop of Newark, calling the church into a discussion and debate on issues of human sexuality, including homosexuality. This was in and of itself unprecedented. I felt that we had moved this issue forward in a significant way, and I looked forward to the energy that was sure to be loosed when the February through May issues of the *Episcopalian* arrived at the homes of our people and when the House of Bishops met in the fall. Quite satisfied, I turned my primary energy back to the Diocese of Newark.

Our diocesan Task Force on Changing Patterns in Sexuality and Family Life, chaired by Dr. Nelson Thayer, made its first report to the diocesan council on December 10, 1986.[3] The purpose of that report was not to get approval, but to inform the council of the major issues that would be before our January convention. We were concerned that the leadership of the diocese be prepared for the debate. The report stated clearly its purpose in the introduction. "The intent of the Task Force has been twofold: to prepare a document that would help the clergy and laity of the diocese to think about the issues, and to suggest broad guidelines for the church's pastoral response to the three groups previously identified—young adults who choose to live together, postmarried people who choose to remain unmarried but not to remain partnerless or sexless, and homosexual couples who choose to form sacred partnerships. We also want to engage those who are not in those groups, but who are concerned about the issues raised." They went on to define the church as a "community in search," not a "community in perfection." Building their case, they listed the factors that have brought on changes in this area of life:

1. The secularization of America as it moved from a rural to an urban sense of itself
2. Social, economic, and geographical mobility
3. Technological advances in disease control and birth control
4. A reduction in the age at which puberty begins
5. The reality of adolescent dating without chaperons
6. The postponement of both marriage and careers to a later age
7. Changes in the cultural attitude surrounding the body from shame to celebration
8. The decline of exclusive male economic hegemony
9. The existence of a better-educated society and the subsequent diminishment of traditional authoritative definitions
10. The clash between traditional authorities dedicated to repression and order and the new values of self-fulfillment in a pluralistic society

The report further examined the biblical, theological, and ethical considerations involved in these issues and made a strong case for the legitimacy of relationships that represented alternatives to marriage.

Then, in startling clarity, the members of the task force recommended in relation to premarital sexual activity that "all relationships are to be assessed in terms of their capacity to manifest marks of the realm of God: healing, reconciliation, compassion, mutuality and concern for others, both within and beyond one's immediate circle of intimacy." In regard to postmarried adults, they stated: "When mature adults choose to celebrate their love and live their lives together outside of marriage, provided that they have considered and responded sensitively to the public and personal issues involved, we believe that their decisions will be blessed by God and can be affirmed as morally acceptable and responsible by the church."

Moving on to look at the issues of committed homosexual relationships, the report suggested that, "Ideally homosexual couples would find within the community of the congregation the same recognition and affirmation which nurtures and sustains heterosexual couples in their relationship including, where appropriate, liturgies which recognize and bless such relationships."

This blockbuster report, with its fresh and startling resolutions, was received, strangely enough, with no great emotional upheaval by the diocesan council. Perhaps that was because it was presented as a study document

rather than one on which to vote. Indeed, the suggestion was made that the
only resolution that might be proposed by the task force to the convention
was that this report be referred to the churches of this diocese for their consideration. In many ways this seemed a reasonable route to go, and so the
council received the report with appreciation but with almost no emotional
notice. I do recall one older single priest named John Owen, who was relatively quiet in his manner, being positively animated by this report. It clearly
had spoken to him.

After Christmas 1986 this report, along with other materials prepared
for the consideration of the convention, was mailed out to all our clergy
and lay delegates. Three delegates elected from each congregation and all
our canonically resident clergy, a total of about 600 delegates, form the
membership of the convention. During the three weeks prior to the convention, meetings were scheduled in each of the different convocations of
the diocese where the opportunity was provided to discuss all materials
before coming to the convention. Members of the Task Force on Changing
Patterns in Sexuality and Family Life would be present at each convocation to present the substance of their report and to answer any questions.
Yet when these convocation meetings were completed, no major energy
had developed around this sexuality report and certainly no protest. I did
not get a single letter about this report from anyone until after the convention had acted to receive it and the press had interpreted it to the public at
large.

A week before our convention met, packets of material were sent to the
New Jersey press and to the radio and television stations that normally covered our convention. In these packets were copies of every report on which
our convention would be asked to take action. On Monday of the convention
week, the religion writer for the *Bergen Record*,[4] the second major daily
paper that served our part of the state of New Jersey, contacted our press
officer and made arrangements to interview me on the issues coming before
our convention. The appointment was made, and he came on Tuesday afternoon. The only thing I recall he asked about was the sexuality report. He
also, I discovered later, followed up this interview by contacting Nelson
Thayer and several other members of the task force. He then sought out the
opinions of those who might be opposed to the recommendations of this
report. On Thursday morning, in a front-page story headlined "Dissent on
Sexual Doctrine," this reporter broke the story for the secular population of
our state. His story carried a color photograph of the bishop of Newark with

a quote from our interview, "You can't take an ancient rule and apply it willy-nilly in the midst of radically different social structures and still have morality" (Bishop Spong).

The article said that this task force would call on the church "to approve nonmarital sexual relationships, including those between homosexuals." It went on to say that this task force recommended "that Episcopal pastors develop marriage-like ceremonies to recognize and bless homosexual relationships," and described this fifteen-page report as concluding that the church's "longtime ban on sex between unmarried people is outdated and no longer workable."

This religion writer had also sought reactions from those in the national Episcopal Church office, who obliged him with comments on a report they had never read by calling the report "unusual" and saying that it was "the first thing of this sort that I am aware of." Those were inane comments, but they fed the excitement created when anyone challenges headquarters and therefore suggested that this report was a prelude to great controversy. In many ways that was exactly what this report was, but that idea was not a powerful motivator of the task force. Truth was.

That same day the Associated Press picked up the *Bergen Record* story and sent it out across its network wire services to all of its news sources in America. The story was also filed by Reuters, and so it played across the news of the world on Friday morning. I was surprised at how much national and local energy now gathered around these issues. I had press interviews over the telephone that Thursday with newspapers across the country. I had been dealing with these questions so regularly they were hardly news to me.

When I arrived at my office that Friday morning needing to do last-minute preparation for the convention, which would convene at 1:00 P.M. in the Robert Treat Hotel just four blocks away, I discovered myself caught in a sea of television cameras, many with national networks, and the wires of radio microphones. I tried to be fair to the members of the fourth estate and to grant each an interview. Some of them were willing to do the interview together, which certainly helped the time pressure.

Contrary to many members of my profession, I have generally regarded the members of the press as friends, and I seek to cooperate with them unless and until I discover them to be untrustworthy. They have their job to do and their deadlines to meet, and I try to honor that. They also help me to get my message into the larger world, and I welcome that assistance. I make it a habit to introduce myself to the entire crew. I learned long ago that if the radio or television crew is interested in the interview, so will the audience be for whom it is being taped or filmed.

By and large the secular press has been supportive of my ministry. The religious press has not. Many of my critics have sought to portray me as chasing publicity. I suppose it has looked like that to some, because the press has certainly covered me in my career. But the truth is that the totality of my "courtship of the press" could be summed up by my personal commitment. I try to be polite to the media. I seek to serve their needs. I thank them for their interest. If possible, I give them the time and the information they want. I return their calls. Off camera, if they request it, I provide them with background material that will make their story effective. I offer to be available later if they want to clarify a point in their story, and when they do a good job, I drop them a note of appreciation. That is my credo for press relations. I do not regard reporters as my enemy. On more than one occasion a reporter I have known, doing a story on some religious or ecclesiastical matter not connected with me at all, has nonetheless called me just to clarify issues of polity or to learn of official church stands to be able to do the story properly. My name does not appear in their news piece, but reporters respect their sources and learn through experience which are trustworthy. If the members of the press are treated fairly, they tend to reciprocate.

I had ample opportunity on that Friday to demonstrate that attitude. I was clearly under pressure, and they appreciated that and honored it by assisting me. I also invited the representatives of the media to attend the convention, told them exactly when in the proceedings this report and the debate on it would take place, designated a member of my staff to look after their needs, answer questions, and identify speakers, and provided them space at the convention hotel in which to do their work. Coffee and tea were in that room to refresh them.

Our convention began with the Eucharist and sermon in the grand ballroom of the hotel. As fate would have it, our two invited guest preachers were John E. Hines and the new presiding bishop, Edmond L. Browning. But we discovered at 9:00 that morning that John Hines's travel agent had booked him on an 8:00 P.M. flight to New York rather than an 8:00 A.M. flight as he had presumed, and so when he arrived at the airport, there was no morning flight. He could get there in the afternoon, but not in time to deliver the opening sermon. He did, however, send us the text of that address by fax, and archdeacon James W. H. Sell delivered it for him. His absence at that service was disappointing, for his spirit and power were so great, but he did arrive before dinner.

One of the great attractions of the convention for Ed Browning, which helped him to accept our invitation, was the chance to spend that time with his predecessor. It would still happen, but it would be diminished by at least half a day. Ed would learn, however, if he had not known it beforehand, that it is not the retired, but the active, presiding bishop whom the press seeks to put on the spot when controversy appears. Ed Browning would be the focus of their attention. This debate would take place under the glare of the light from national television cameras. It would be reported on the wire services across the land and to the world. He would surely be interviewed. There was to be no hiding place in the primate's office. When he accepted my invitation shortly after his election in 1985, neither of us knew that this barrier-breaking report on human sexuality would be before this part of the Christian Church, nor that he would be required to respond to it. That would, however, not be the assumption made by either his critics or mine, who saw collusion in almost everything.

At approximately 3:15 P.M. on Friday, January 30, 1987, from the presiding officer's podium I introduced the Reverend Dr. Nelson Thayer, who came to the platform microphone to present the work of the task force to the assembled delegates. The other members of the task force were asked to come forward and to sit on the stage so that the members of the convention could see those responsible for this report. It was a body of twelve people, six priests and six laypeople. Three of the priests had been through a divorce. Two of the priests were homosexual persons, one out of the closet and the other deeply closeted. Two of the priests were women and four were men.

The parochial settings of the clergy members varied widely. One was an academic on a theological faculty, another the assistant in a very affluent suburb. There was a rector of an inner-city, predominantly black congregation, a rector of a small, solidly middle- to upper-class white parish, and a rector of one of our largest churches, located in a bedroom community to New York City, whose previous rector had left to become a bishop. These clergy were surely diverse, and yet they were representative of this diocese.

Indeed, so were the laity. Among the laypeople, four were women and two were men. Two were professional counselors. One worked for Mobil Oil. One was an African American educator, and one was a well-to-do woman whose intellectual curiosity had led her to take courses at a theological seminary just to expand her horizons (and make her husband wonder where this might lead). It was these people's interest, not their point of view, that landed them on this task force. Certainly there was no attempt to pack the committee on any side of these issues, as our critics would later claim. I believe in utilizing the interest and positive energy already present in persons in the service of an issue. I do not worry about seeing that balance is maintained on a task force. Balance will come from the members of the convention itself if they feel challenged by a report.

Dr. Thayer made his report to the convention with clarity and enthusiasm. At the end of it, he indicated that the task force had decided only to move that the report be received and commended to our churches for a year of study and that no resolutions to adopt come until that year of study was complete. That decision certainly made it possible for the delegates to engage these issues boldly. That resolution was offered and, following our rules of order, it was seconded and referred to an open hearing to be held from 4:00 to 6:00 P.M. that day. Dr. Thayer would preside at that open hearing, and the commission members would be seated at a table in the front of the room.

I do not attend open hearings so as not to impede anyone, but especially those who might have a negative opinion of me. The task force members would hear the comments and answer the questions of those delegates who wished to make their opinions known. The press would also be invited to the open hearings, but only to listen and identify those they might seek to interview later. Needless to say, that room could not hold the people who attended, so the hearing was moved from that room into the grand ballroom of the hotel, where the convention itself was being held. This open hearing would, in effect, be a meeting of the committee of the whole. The issues were aired with great intensity. More than forty persons spoke their minds and countless others asked questions for clarification. Following that hearing, the members of the task force would meet and, in the light of the hearing, decide whether or not to amend the report or their resolution. If they decided to do that, the task force would come back to the convention with the amended motion or a substitute motion from the commission itself. That would be the motion placed on the floor for debate.

It was an incredible hearing. The courage this report gave to gay and lesbian Christians, and to parents, relatives, and friends of gay and lesbian people, was breathtaking. There were, of course, voices of fear and words of discomfort from those caught off guard and forced to think about a series of issues they preferred to leave buried in their subconscious. The commission members listened to every voice patiently. Nelson Thayer's calm and forthright demeanor set exactly the proper tone.

It was Nelson Thayer who convinced any who wished for more decisive action that this report had already moved beyond the boundaries of the Episcopal Diocese of Newark and into the public arena across the nation and throughout the world. He understood better than most that forcing the issue into public debate legitimized it as much as a positive vote would do. He argued that both education and the raising of consciousness were achieved simply in initiating the dialogue, not in determining the outcome. If they tried to force a vote and it failed, the dialogue would cease. "Truth," he said persuasively, "does not need a majority vote to achieve its purpose." So this nonpro-active approach was affirmed, and the resolution that came out of the open hearing was the same one that was previously proposed. That night, in my convention address, I did what a leader must do. I endorsed the report and urged it to be studied seriously in all of our churches.

In the deliberations the next day, the task force resolution was placed on the floor of the convention. It called for the convention to receive the report with thanks, to commend it to the congregations of the Diocese of Newark for a year of study, and to ask the members of the task force to monitor that study and to bring recommendations and resolutions out of that study to the convention of 1988 for debate and possible adoption at that time.

The great debate was destined not to be repeated in the convention itself, since it had clearly taken place in the open hearing, and the people believed they had been heard. This resolution therefore elicited almost no discussion on the floor. One amendment was added, accepted by the members of the task force, that a study guide "reflecting the theological diversity of the diocese be prepared to assist the study." I put the question to a voice vote. I cannot therefore be certain of the exact count, but considering that about 600 delegates were on the floor, my guess would be that the vote was something like 590 to 10. The press referred to it as an overwhelmingly positive vote. After the vote was taken, television cameras turned off their lights, the radio crews packed their equipment, the press people gathered their notes and briefcases, and the convention moved on to consideration of the recommendations of the Standing Committee on Church Structures and then to the issue of clergy salaries. It was a wonderfully odd and even amusing order.

When the convention adjourned on Saturday afternoon and following a dinner served in a local Portuguese restaurant with diocesan leaders to express our appreciation for the work they had done at this convention, I drove to our home in Morristown bone tired. I needed to check on Joan, having not done that for five days because of the convention pressures. She had, of course, shared in none of this drama. Indeed, she probably was not even aware that it was occurring. She had spent this weekend, as she did most of her time, in her private world with neither radio nor television disturbing her peace. On the twenty-five-minute drive west from Newark to Morristown, I turned on WCBS, the all-news flagship station of Columbia Broadcasting System in New York City, to hear that the Episcopal Diocese of Newark had become the first unit of a mainline church in the United States to endorse premarital sex and homosexual marriage. It was but the first of many similar news reports that would flow out across this land. Arriving home, I watched the 11:00 local ABC news on Channel 7 to learn from the reporter that "Episcopal bishops meeting in Newark had endorsed same-sex marriages." I was startled at this inaccuracy. By the time the vote was taken on Saturday afternoon, Ed Browning and I were the only nonretired bishops in the gathering, and all this convention had voted to do was to refer this report to our people for a year of study. Truth, I was to learn, can hardly be allowed to get in the way of a good story. I sank into the sleep of the weary.

On Sunday morning the New Jersey papers made our convention and this report a front- page story. "Liberal sex view urged," said the *Elizabeth Daily Journal*. "Episcopal report challenges dogma on nonmarital sex," screamed the *Camden Post*. The Newark, Bergen County, Passaic, Jersey City, and Morristown papers displayed similar headlines to greet those awakening to a quiet winter Sunday. The *New York Times* made the headline personal and put it on page three. "Newark Bishop seeks to bless unwed couples," it proclaimed. The Associated Press sent the story across America. CNN's Headline News covered it in many of its thirty-minute segments during the next twenty-four hours. The national debate was on for sure, and it had begun in the Diocese of Newark.

The *Bergen Record*, having broken the story, moved further ahead by getting an exclusive interview with Ed Browning and running it complete with a two-column picture of the presiding bishop. In his very circumspect manner, Bishop Browning declared the debate healthy, but declined to endorse the report, calling it only "an important contribution to the whole life of the Episcopal Church."

That would be a tactic this good man would try again and again, but it would always fail. The right-wing of our church knew where he stood in his heart of hearts, so these efforts to seek to keep his person and his office above the fray placated them not one whit. Those of us pressing for change would finally become so frustrated with his unwillingness to put himself on the line for any issue in which he believed that we lost admiration for one who was our colleague. The ultimate loser, however, was Ed Browning himself, who, seeking unity, found that both his soul and his body were compromised. In the last year of his primacy, he finally recovered and stated clearly what his convictions were. It was too late. Once again, the church had moved beyond its designated leader, but the venom dumped on this man by the losing right-wing of the church would know no bounds.

My Sunday assignment on that next day would take me back to the city of Newark for a confirmation visitation to a church called the House of Prayer, located in one of Newark's most difficult crime-filled neighborhoods. This inner-city church was made up of African Americans, Hispanics, and Caucasians. They were generally poor and tended to live in a wide variety of family patterns, including gay and lesbian couples, which meant it was also a gathering of people who had heard a welcome word of good news or gospel coming from their church through the witness of that convention. So they received me warmly. We prayed and shared the Eucharist together. I confirmed ten candidates, most of them young, black adolescents, and preached on a text from Micah 6:8, which reads "What does the Lord require of you, but to do justice and to love kindness and to walk humbly with your God?"

It was a wonderful, affirming service of worship and provided me with a window of quiet calm before the storm of reaction would break on Monday morning.

1. *Boy-Wives and Female-Husbands: Studies in African Homosexualities,* ed. Stephen O. Murray and Will Roscoe (New York: St. Martin's Press, 1998).

2. See article in *Time,* April 26, 1999.

3. The full text of this task force report is found in my book *Living in Sin? A Bishop Rethinks Human Sexuality* (San Francisco: HarperSanFrancisco, 1988), pp. 230–48.

4. The reporter's name was Michael J. Kelly.

# 17

# *The Battle Lines Form*

※

As the story of our convention, interpreted by the press, began to echo across the land, I was called by reporters in cities from coast to coast and from Canada to Mexico. I was asked to be on radio talk shows in some thirty cities. My mail increased four-hundredfold. Some of it was incredibly hostile and provided me with my first personal insight into the prejudice with which homosexual people must deal constantly.

But what I had not counted on was that, while the secular press and radio told the story of the Diocese of Newark's initiative in the sexuality debate, the bishops, clergy, and active laity of the Episcopal Church would be receiving their February copies of the *Episcopalian,* in which, thanks to Harry Griffith, there would be a signed article by the bishop of Newark laying before the church the same issues about which the secular press was proclaiming Newark had already decided. It looked to many conservative church leaders, in their religious paranoia, like a liberal takeover. This introductory piece promised that in the March, April, and May issues of the *Episcopalian* the debate would be continued. There, some members of our church would actually be heard speaking in favor of premarital sexual relations inside a relationship of mutual commitment, older postmarried people forming sexually intimate relationships without remarrying, and the possibility of committed gay and lesbian relationships receiving the church's blessing within a liturgical setting.

For many people not yet awakened out of their traditional defining prejudices, this was more than they could embrace emotionally. The old adage "When you can't deal with the message, attack the messenger" took over. The press had already identified me in right-wing religious circles as the primary source of these disturbing insights and, thus, as the betrayer of the

Episcopal Church. The *Episcopalian* invited letters to the editor as a way of enabling people to engage the dialogue, and the letters poured in. It did not take an invitation from the secular press that had covered our convention to elicit a torrent of reader reaction. So in both the secular and the religious press across the land the debate raged. In the religious publications, letters to the editor would continue until October, when we would have the opportunity of bringing these concerns to the House of Bishops. The plan we had adopted on the Standing Commission on Human Affairs and Health was working brilliantly—indeed, because of the task force report in the Diocese of Newark, better than any of us had anticipated. Yes, of course we had created some tension in the church, but that was essential if we were going to force people into dialogue in which destructive stereotypes could be laid to rest forever.

I found myself in receipt of invitations to lecture far beyond Episcopal circles. I delivered a series of lectures to Methodist clergy in Oklahoma and Kansas. Invitations came from the United Church of Canada, the only national faith community of which I knew that was wrestling publicly with these same issues. Seminary and university audiences in Illinois, Indiana, Oklahoma, and Colorado requested my presence. Community churches not significantly bound by denominational loyalty began to invite me to their congregations.

The most far-reaching result, however, came with a telephone call from Michael Lawrence, the senior editor of Abingdon Press, the United Methodist publishing house, in Nashville, Tennessee. Michael called to propose that I write a book for Abingdon Press on the changing patterns in human sexuality. He wanted the book out by April 1, 1988, in time for the annual conference of the United Methodist Church in the United States, where issues of human sexuality would be on the agenda. The completed manuscript would need to be ready by September 1, just six months away. "Are you interested and is this time line possible?" Michael wanted to know.

I had never before had a publisher call to ask me to write a book on a pre-determined subject. It raised many issues for me, but the time limit in which the book had to be completed was not one of them. I had invested myself deeply in reading on this subject while our diocesan task force had been working. The research, for all practical purposes, had thus already been done. The three issues I had asked our task force to look into were issues I also had probed. They would constitute three major segments of any book. A scriptural analysis of the various texts so often used to bring about religious condemnation of sexual behavior other than that expressed in heterosexual married fidelity would constitute another major segment. That, with an introductory chapter, some proposals on how to transform the revolution, and a concluding chapter would complete the book. I was confident I could finish that assignment in six months.

I had a contract, however, with Harper Collins and would need a release from it if I were to do this book for a minor competitor. I hung up the phone and thought about what steps I needed to take next.

I called John Hines to seek his advice and to tell him the news. He was, as always, supportive and excited for me. Talking to him clarified my issues.

Next I called my editor at Harper Collins. Getting a release proved to be disappointingly easy. It was clear that I was too minor a member in their stable of authors to cause them to express any great concern about either losing me or having me write for a competitor. They indicated that they had no desire to do a book on this subject and would therefore be delighted if I wanted to work on this with Abingdon. It was almost a "Here's your hat. What's your hurry?" kind of response. In retrospect, nothing I had published with Harper by that date had sold as many as twelve thousand copies, and my most recent work, *Beyond Moralism* (coauthored with Denise Haines), had died after a first printing of five thousand. The only salve for my sense of being so totally marginalized was that my editor did say that Harper would reserve the right to exercise its first-refusal clause from my contract on any future manuscript I might write. Hanging up, I realized that my relationship with Harper hung by the slenderest of threads.

Next I discussed this project with my secretary and members of my staff. They saw this as an affirmation of the work of our diocese and were all supportive. "We could manage the workload," they asserted. I knew they could. Within an hour I called Michael Lawrence back and verbally accepted his offer. He put a contract in the mail, and I began to organize my writing schedule to meet the requirements of this book.

In order to clarify and test my message, I began to preach on these subjects in my confirmation visitations around the diocese. I used the book of Jonah as my biblical text, developing a sermon to expose the prejudice of homophobia. The theme of Jonah was that God's love always breaks open the boundaries we place both on our own love and our understanding of God's love. This text enabled me to tell the Jonah story, in which most people took delight, and to look at the various boundaries the church had overcome in the past: our prejudice against Gentiles, women, people of color, divorced people, left-handed people, and mentally ill people, to name just a few. Then I focused on the one prejudice still considered socially acceptable, namely, the prejudice against homosexual people. Examining it, I made simple points: No one chooses their sexual orientation; gay and lesbian people are not strangers from a distant planet, but our sons and daughters, our brothers and sisters, our aunts and uncles, our friends and neighbors. Finally I concluded by guessing the size of the congregation and then saying that if 10 percent of the population is homosexual (a number widely discussed at that time), the statistical probability was that the number of gay and lesbian people in the congregation that morning was . . . (and I would state the number). "Look around," I exhorted the congregation, "and see if there is anyone you see whom you fear or hate or want to reject." The response was usually thoughtful and positive. A pattern also began that would be repeated every time I used these themes; namely, that at the front door of the church, as people departed, several worshipers would whisper to me that they were included in the number of homosexual people present in my statistical analysis.

In early June 1987, when I was already deep into the first draft of this manuscript, I preached that sermon at St. Elizabeth's Church in Ridgewood, New Jersey, an affluent and traditionally conservative congregation. At the coffee hour one gentleman was more than eager to get through the crowd to speak to me. Normally that kind of eagerness is an expression of hostility, and so I braced myself for his onslaught. To my amazement, however, this man was incredibly positive. "I have waited for years to hear someone in the ecclesiastical hierarchy say what you have said this morning. I agree with you and I can help you document your conclusions."

"Who are you?" I inquired, a bit taken aback.

"My name is Robert Lahita," he responded. "I am a research doctor at the Cornell Medical Center in New York City."

Bob Lahita was more than that. He not only had his M.D. degree, but a Ph.D. in microbiology as well. He was also the closest thing to a Renaissance man that I have met. Not only was he brilliant in his field, but he had a wide-ranging array of interests, from sports to music to food to good wines to directing the rescue squad's activities in his spare time in one of New Jersey's poorest counties. He was in demand as a medical lecturer all over the world. He was and is America's leading expert on the disease lupus erythematosis, a disorder of the immune system that appears to afflict women more frequently than men. His research on this disease had brought him into a new frontier of learning called the science of the brain, in which studies seek to understand why some diseases appear to be sex-related. Probing that biological boundary in the brain between male and female and seeking to understand sex-related differences was the topic that was at that moment consuming his time and energy.

Raised a Roman Catholic, Bob Lahita had actually served for a period of time as a member of the development board for the archdiocese of New York, where he had come to know John Cardinal O'Connor, the Roman Catholic leader in New York City. In this capacity he found himself constantly disillusioned by the fact that most Roman Catholic ethical teaching was based on badly outdated scientific conclusions. Eventually, that disillusionment led him to resign from that position and move to Ridgewood with his wife and two sons, where he began to attend the nearby Episcopal church. That is how he happened to be there that morning, and that was the context in which his enthusiastic words were framed. We chatted as long as possible without being rude to others at the reception. I told him about the book I was writing and he offered to help in any way he could.

The following week I went to his home in Upper Ridgewood at 7:30 P.M. and did not leave until midnight. We chatted easily and reached a level of trusting friendship quickly. His wife, Terry, was present and helpfully engaged the conversation. Bob gave me his perspective on the origins of sexual orientation. It was above all else the brain, he said, that determined the object of one's affection. All human beings have one sex organ, he suggested—the brain. All else is equipment. A process known as the "sexing of the brain," he argued, took place in utero and was connected to the level of testosterone, the male hormone, present in the pregnant female. The hypothalamus played a role that had not yet been fully determined. Above all, he indicated, none of the doctors at the Cornell Medical Center believed that sexual orientation was a choice or was changeable once set. They were even experimenting with laboratory animals and could produce homosexual behavior in white mice, which would demonstrate that homosexuality is of the natural order and not a human distortion. It is of one's being, not of one's choosing, was his confident conclusion. If these two things could be established beyond reasonable doubt, then all of the traditional negative attitudes of the church toward homosexual people would need to be reconsidered because they would clearly have to be seen as wrong.

Bob Lahita promised to make available to me whatever pertinent study papers he could lay his hands on at the Cornell Medical Center. He also agreed to read the final manuscript of my book for its scientific accuracy and to write a preface for this book that would, in effect, put his scientific impri-matur on its contents. In time Bob Lahita decided to identify with the Episcopal Church, and I had the privilege of receiving him officially about two years after the book came out. He, in turn, chaired the diocesan science/theology task force and was given the official title of "Science Consultant to the Bishop of Newark." He and his wife came to be among our most enjoyed and intimate personal friends. I am ever so pleased that Cardinal O'Connor of New York was not receptive to Dr. Lahita's scientific advice since it did not undergird traditional Roman Catholic sexual preju-dices, for that was the catalyst that began this doctor's shift into another faith community.

Encouraged by this assistance, I completed the first draft of the manu-script on July 28, giving me almost five weeks for editing and checking details. Then, with the Lahita imprimatur and preface ready, I met the Abingdon deadline of September 1, 1987.

Michael Lawrence was quite enthusiastic about this book on first reading. He suggested some minor changes and the addition of a more affirming stance for those people, homosexual and heterosexual alike, who choose to be celibate or whose circumstances mandated single status. It was easy to incorporate these good suggestions into the text. The staff at Abingdon Press also seemed to share in Michael's excitement.

While the book was in the process of being written, a letter arrived in my office from a man in Dallas, Texas. He was responding to the newspaper accounts about the work of our diocesan task force and things that I had said in the media in regard to the church's acceptance and affirmation of honest, open homosexual persons. His name was Robert Williams, a Master of Divinity graduate of the Episcopal Divinity School in Cambridge, Massachusetts. Robert had not sought ordination because he was an out-of-the-closet gay man who lived in what he described as a permanent, committed relationship of several years duration with his partner, Jim. His diocese, the Diocese of Dallas, would not consider him for ordination on that basis alone. In this let-ter, Robert, in effect, said to me, "If you really mean what you say, why don't you test it and act on it by considering me for ordination in your diocese?" I responded to his letter by indicating that if he wanted to enter the process and be screened for ordination in the Diocese of Newark, the only way to do that would be to move to this diocese, become involved with one of our con-gregations, and be recommended to me by the vestry and rector or vicar of that congregation. If he wanted to talk to me about this process, I told him that I would be happy to have an appointment with him. He accepted that invitation and before the summer had ended, Robert Williams walked into my office for the first time.

He was a large man, well over six feet tall with a strong, healthy-looking build. His tanned and ruddy face showed the influence of the Texas sun. I could imagine him in a cowboy hat, riding his horse into the sunset. Robert was articulate and bright. If he could be ordained, he hoped to open a diocesan ministry for gay and lesbian people. He believed that homosexual persons had been so badly violated and abused by institutional religion through the years that few of them would ever darken the doors of the church again without some prior assurance of welcome and love. What was needed, he said, was a safe place, a kind of oasis, where gay and lesbian people could come, talk about their issues, feel acceptance, explore their spiritual natures, and gain both the strength and resolve to return with integrity to a church, if they could find one, that expressed in deeds, as well as in words, a message of welcome. Our diocese had, in effect, expressed just such a welcome in the report of the task force. What Robert Williams was proposing was that we build a diocesan-sponsored ministry that would deliberately reach out to the homosexual population more than half way. It was an intriguing concept.

His long-range plans were even more appealing. He wanted to be the first openly gay, male theologian of the church who would specifically help the church look at theology through the eyes of an authentic gay male experience. He argued that the church historically had failed to incorporate the gifts of black people during the days of slavery and segregation. When the doors of the church were finally opened to the full inclusion of African Americans, enormous enrichment flowed into our understanding of both God and Christ. The slave experience had helped black Americans to develop a faith that redeemed both their suffering and their rejection. He cited, to illustrate his point, not only the role of black music that we refer to as "Negro spirituals," but also to that school of thought known as "liberation theology," which, though begun by Roman Catholics in Latin America, was significantly shaped in the United States by the black experience and was thus a black gift to the church. How poor and bereft the church was in that era of prejudice because it defined black people as subhuman and therefore as not possessing gifts that the church considered worthy.

The same thing, he continued, could be said of the church's attitude toward the contributions of women. So long as women were kept in second-class positions in the life of the church, the feminine dimension of human experience was denied to theology, liturgy, and spirituality itself. Look at the gifts that have come to Christianity from the Rosemary Ruethers, the Elisabeth Schüssler Fiorenzas, the Elaine Pagelses, and the Phyllis Tribles, he said, just to name a few. In the same way, he continued, the homosexual experience has also been excluded from both Christian knowledge and Christian spirituality. If the doors of the church can be opened to receive the spiritual insights of gay and lesbian people, a new source of Christian enrichment would be available. There was a sense, he said, in which Carter Heyward on the faculty of his seminary was doing that from the lesbian perspective. It was his hope to obtain a doctorate and become the Christian theologian who would bring to the church an awareness of the spiritual insights of gay men. It was both an ambitious plan and a deeply convincing one.

I was very impressed with this man. He had a genuine sense of who he was, could communicate his vision, and had the intellect capable of accomplishing his dreams. I did see some anger in him but, given what he had experienced from the church and society alike, it seemed to me both in bounds and appropriate. All he needed and all he was asking was that we screen him for ordination honestly and fairly without prejudging him as unfit for ministry based on his self-affirming, open homosexuality. That was exactly what our diocesan task force report had urged us to do. I told him that it would be a long route and there would be no guarantees of success and no promises. Robert would need to qualify on his own merits. However, if he were willing to move to this diocese and to support himself while seeking the endorsement of a rector and vestry, I believed that our diocesan decision-making processes would screen him fairly. Robert Williams accepted the challenge.

The next week at a diocesan Christian education conference held on the campus of William Paterson College, I gathered together in a private session the five priests whom I believed would be open and supportive of this gay initiative. They were Lucinda Laird of St. Mark's, Teaneck, and Craig Burlington of St. George's, Maplewood, both of whom had a gay social group meeting in their respective parish houses and from that contact a number of gay and lesbian persons had joined their congregations; Elizabeth Maxwell of St. Matthew's, Paramus, a strong supporter of gay rights; Alex MacDonell of St. Luke's, Haworth, the father of a gay son; and finally, Gerard Pisani of Trinity Church, Bayonne, who was at that time my only fully out-of-the-closet gay priest, living openly with his partner of many years.

I told this group of five about Robert Williams and my positive impression of him. He needed a supportive rector, and in my opinion this group of five represented the best chance of identifying that person. To be supportive did not mean that the priest had to endorse Robert for ordination at that moment. It only meant that he or she would not be closed to such a possibility, would be willing to open the door of opportunity so that his possible vocation to the priesthood could be tested, and would make certain that the vestry of the sponsoring church would be willing to treat him fairly. Robert needed to be outstanding in order to get through the screening process. He would be under enormous pressure as the first openly gay male seeking ordination. His position in the church would not be unlike the one faced by Jackie Robinson, the first black major-league baseball player, who managed that barrier-breaking transition magnificently and who was later elected to the Baseball Hall of Fame on the basis of his outstanding ability. It is very difficult to crash through powerful barriers of prejudice with a mediocre candidate. We needed to determine that Robert Williams was capable of being a superior candidate and of bearing the pressure. I concluded that session with these five priests by asking, "Will any of you consider the possibility that you and your church might give this man a chance by having him become a member of your church and being open to the possibility of sponsoring him for ordination if in your judgment he shows that he has the necessary qualifications?" The question rested heavily on that assembled group.

I had placed a tremendous challenge and opportunity before five of my finest priests. I waited to see what their response would be.

It was a response of fear, not faith, that came back to me. Theory had just become reality. Their decision and action would potentially cost them something. It was a moment of truth, and I waited to see what their level of commitment was. None of them jumped at the opportunity. I saw what I would learn to recognize as the ultimate weakness of most liberals. They can't walk the walk nearly as easily as they can talk the talk. The rationalizations began, and a variety of reasons why it would not be a good time in each of their respective churches emerged.

I admired all of these clergy, but there is, I have discovered, something in the character of most of those who become ordained that makes it difficult for them to do the things that will bring them conflict and pain, no matter how deeply they are committed to a cause. Having said that, I do understand that clergy are vulnerable to this pressure in ways that bishops are not. There is a sense in which a bishop by virtue of his or her very office has no further career goals. That is hardly ever so for a priest. I came to realize on that day that I, as a bishop, would need to exercise strong public leadership on this issue if I expected the clergy to risk their careers. I would also have to take the brunt of the criticism that would be forthcoming. Clergy in time would be able to do it, but only if the bishop gave them protection and demonstrated how to lead without either fear or bitterness.

Finally, after a conversation that none of that group would today be proud to remember, it was my one gay priest, who probably had the least to lose and the least to gain, who was willing to be the sponsor. I appreciated Gerry Pisani's offer, but felt it provided Robert with the weakest of all of the possible supports. Gerry would be seen as self-serving, while the others would have been perceived as doing it out of principle. But one takes what one is offered and moves on. So Gerry Pisani and his church, Trinity, Bayonne, agreed to provide Robert with the opportunity to enter our process.

In September, Gerry met with Robert and worked out with him a schedule to follow in becoming part of this congregation and assisting at worship so that he could get to know the people and to gain their endorsement. It would be six months before any recommendation from Gerry and his vestry would enable me to start the diocesan screening process.

Life, however, went on at quite a pace, and I endured one of the most defining experiences in my life that November when I returned to my Newark apartment on the rare occasion of a free Sunday afternoon. I had completed my confirmation assignment in Leonia by 2:00 P.M., picked up the Sunday paper at a newsstand, and was looking forward to watching the Giants play football on television. Rather nonchalantly I pulled into my enclosed parking lot and prepared to enter my apartment, only to discover that I was not alone.

A young African-American male about thirty years of age, obviously high on something and ominously wielding the jagged glass of a broken liquor bottle, accosted me. Not another person was in sight and the street was hidden from our view. This was to be a one-on-one confrontation. His approach was menacing. My only weapon was my ability to talk. "What do you want?" I inquired.

"Twenty dollars," was his response.

"If you put that bottle down, I will give you twenty dollars," I responded, trying to keep my composure.

He looked at me quizzically and, to my amazement, he asked, "Do you promise?"

"I promise," I repeated almost instantly, but a sense of relief overcame me. He was holding the lethal weapon and he was asking me to promise to be true to my word. I was dressed in the full street wear of my profession: a dark suit, a purple vest, and a clerical collar. I had on my finger my bishop's ring and a gold pectoral cross was around my neck, both of which had a street value at any pawnshop far beyond twenty dollars. This man, I thought, needs a quick fix, for which only immediate cash will be helpful.

So I said again, "Yes. I will give you twenty dollars, but you must throw that bottle into the dumpster and walk with me out to the street. I will not give it to you here." That was a strange tactic I realized, when I later thought about it. He had the weapon, and I was setting the terms of our settlement. I then added the reassuring words, "I give you my word. You will receive twenty dollars."

To my immense relief he heaved the broken bottle into the dumpster, and we walked toward the street. About ten yards before we entered the street, I reached to take out my wallet to find a twenty-dollar bill. The man lunged for me and tried to snatch the wallet. I had no time to think, but only to react. I discovered in that moment that I was not a pacifist.

I resisted him physically. Suddenly, I was engaged in a rather undignified schoolyard brawl. We rolled over and over on that paved parking area, struggling for the advantage. At some point I became convinced that I would prevail. I was a bit larger than he, although thirty years older. I emerged from that struggle sitting astride him. I pinned his arms with my hands and his body with my legs. He looked at me as though he was certain I would kill him. I suppose that in the value system of his world that would be the rule. Yet he did not beg or whimper. I still had my wallet, so I stood up with him still on the ground. I took a twenty-dollar bill out and, putting my wallet away, I offered it to him.

"I gave you my word that I would give you twenty dollars and here it is," I said.

He looked at me as if I represented something his world had never encountered. He rose, came close enough to snatch the bill from my outstretched hand, uttered a torrent of profanity, and ran out of the lot, disappearing behind the YMCA across the street.

I looked at myself. I was a sight to behold. My trousers were torn at the knees. One knee was bleeding profusely from a large scrape that would soon form a beautiful scab. My coat had dirt all over it. A slight cut over my eye sent blood down my face, where dirt and sweat were already present. My heart was beating at a rapid pace. But I was alive, and not hurt or scarred in any permanent way. I made my way into my apartment and called the Newark police. They managed to arrive forty-five minutes later. I was glad it was not an emergency!

I cleaned myself up, changed clothes, and called my daughters in Richmond. I needed to talk with someone about this incident in order to process it. They reacted with more fear than I had anticipated. They wondered when this man or one of his friends would return to complete his unfinished business. They had never been comfortable with my living alone, even on a part-time basis, in this apartment in Newark. But they also understood how upsetting my very presence was to their mother's sense of security. They urged me to think about moving Joan to Richmond, at least temporarily, where they could care for her, and I could return to the bishop's house in Morristown. I agreed to consider that possibility.

I had long been worried about whether I could ever give Joan the care she needed. I tried to spend time in Morristown at least twice a week, including almost every weekend. When I was away, however, as much as five days would go by with no one checking on how she was or whether she had everything she needed. She had a car and could get groceries, for example, but whether she did so adequately, I could not tell. It did not help to ask a friend to call on her, because Joan would never answer the door. I could not check on her by phone, for Joan would never answer the phone. With two daughters who were much concerned and with both of their husbands' extended families in Richmond, someone could be in touch with her regularly. Her safety and well-being, and now mine, seemed to be well served by this plan. After thinking about this for a week and talking with my daughters in more detail, I went out to see Joan to propose this possibility.

To my surprise and delight she was very positive about the idea. She now remembered Richmond far more fondly than she had ever cared for New Jersey. I called our eldest daughter, Ellen, and had Joan talk to her about apartments in Richmond near our daughters. Our second daughter, Katharine, was expecting her first child and our first grandchild in April. Joan wanted to be there for that. She also was still convinced that the forces that plagued her life were by now all in New Jersey, so if she returned to Richmond, they might cease and desist, at least for a period of time. It would be for her a preemptive strike that would force them into a major adjustment. In reality she believed they followed her to Richmond the day she moved, but the hope of at least a momentary escape played a part in the decision-making process. By early December an apartment had been rented, and Joan had moved to Richmond. She had been so little a factor in the public life of the diocese for so long that there was almost no notice of her departure. I did tell our closest friends and the members of the standing committee. Joan moved with everything she wanted from our house. Her comfort and pleasure were the only criteria. I sent her a check each month to cover all her expenses.

In retrospect I wish we had never encouraged this move. That is not because it did not work well. Indeed, Joan was quite happy. Our two Richmond daughters and their extended families cared for her lovingly and well. She shared in the joy of the birth of our first grandchild and spent much time holding and loving that baby. It also provided an opportunity for our daughters to understand fully and firsthand the state of their mother's mental health. From that point of view the move was positive. My regret, and it is a deep and continuing regret, stems from the fact that she had only nine more months to live. I, of course, had no way of knowing that when the move took place. The malignancy had passed the five-year mark with no recurrence. The doctors were amazed, but pleased. The only real problem was her mental condition. But hindsight always has twenty-twenty vision. We made the decision based on what we knew at the time. Nonetheless I have wished a million times that I had endured those final months without abdicating my responsibility to care for my wife, "in sickness, and in health, till death us do part." I did not do that. I cared for her during a mental illness that lasted over fifteen years and a physical illness that lasted six and a half years, but I did not run the full course. I reached the stone wall of my ultimate limits just nine months before her death. I now returned full-time to our home in Morristown.

The people at Abingdon Press flew me to Nashville before Christmas, where I met with and received the red-carpet treatment from the president and chief executive officer on down. They were clearly excited about the proposed book, which they had now had for three months. I had the sense that most of them had read the whole manuscript. They had changed the title from my rather pedestrian *Sex and the Bible* to their more provocative *Living in Sin? A Bishop Rethinks Human Sexuality*. They had planned a twelve-city publicity tour to launch the book in April. Part of the agenda for my visit was to coordinate these plans with my schedule. I met with the marketing, publicity, and design people. They proposed a bold cover for the book of black, red, and white with brush strokes being the style for all the chapter headings. They showed me a side of publishing I had never seen before. I had never realized, for example, that authors went on book tours and that media opportunities for authors are overtly sought by publicists working for the publishers. I assumed these things just happened. My education was just beginning.

Most of the following January I spent preparing for our diocesan convention, at which we did, in fact, adopt the report of our Task Force on Changing Patterns in Sexuality and Family Life. By this time, more than half of our churches had engaged these issues, and we were quite comfortable with its conclusions.

During February, as part of a sabbatical study program of one month a year for three years, worked out by the diocese to fit my peculiar circumstances, I was a Monday-to-Friday student at Union Theological Seminary in New York, working on what has always been a passionate, but unfocused, area of academic interest—the interface between the physical sciences and theology. I identified pivotal figures in the development of modern Western thought, such as Copernicus, Galileo, Newton, Darwin, Freud, Einstein, and Stephen Hawking and began to read not only their primary works, but also biographies about them. I did not know where this study would lead, but I knew it was something I could not avoid. I also used some of that time to do final editing on the galleys and "blues" from Abingdon Press. Things began to run together upon my return from Union, for Abingdon had waiting for me in the mail copies of the covers of the new book, advertising T-shirts sporting the title "Living in Sin?" across the front in bold letters with "Abingdon Press" on each shoulder, and copies of prepublication advertisements they had already begun to run in religious journals, notably in a publication aimed specifically at United Methodist clergy called the *Circuit Rider.* Everything was on schedule for an April publication date. Excited by these artifacts of the publishing world, I turned my attention back to the struggle the leaders of our diocese were having over whether to ordain an out-of-the-closet gay man who lived openly with his partner.

Gerry Pisani's endorsement, along with that of his vestry, arrived, and I turned Robert over to the commission on ministry, so that they could obtain the preliminary reports deemed necessary prior to the decision-making screening conference. Robert was, for example, required to complete a full psychiatric evaluation at the Princeton Career Development Center. That evaluation concluded by recommending Robert for ordination. A physical examination by his doctor was also required. Upon review, the screening committee judged the medical report to be incomplete, so they requested a second opinion. In neither report were there red flags that would cause any concern. Every sign indicated that he was in good health. The recommendation from his faculty at Episcopal Divinity School was also received and it was glowing, probably the most laudatory report on a seminary graduate I have ever read. All the members of the faculty had personally signed this letter. That was in itself a rather unusual procedure.

Finally, on the last weekend in February 1988, the time of decision arrived. The format of that weekend was to place each aspirant into a number of two-on-one interview situations. The commission formed its two-person teams of one priest and one layperson to conduct this series of interviews until all the members of the screening committee had spent about forty-five minutes with each candidate. It was a grueling, informative, and revealing process that started on Friday evening and concluded at noon on Saturday. When the interviews were complete, there was a Eucharist, followed by lunch, after which the aspirants departed. The commission members then began the arduous task of saying yes or no to each prospect. Normally I would arrive in time for the Eucharist and would sit in on the evaluation session without participating. I needed to know the basis for each acceptance or rejection in order to be a good pastor to these people, either when they returned, disappointed, to their congregations or when I made the decision to enter them onto the ordination track.

Robert was one of five aspirants being screened that weekend. When his turn came, I discovered that the members of this committee were all over the place. His ability had attracted many, but his openness about his sexuality had frightened others. The debate on him was the longest and most emotional that I can ever recall. I said not a word. The group normally discusses each candidate until a consensus emerges. No consensus was ever to emerge in Robert's case. Finally the issue was put to a vote. There were four categories that they could choose. Category One was "recommended without qualifications." Category Two was "recommended with qualifications," which would then be listed and an appropriate action to address the concerns would be recommended. Category Three was "not recommended at this time." The implication here was that some specific action had to be undertaken before a positive vote might be given at some future date. Category Four was "not recommended." This category had a more final note about it and suggested that the aspirant did not, in the opinions of these people, appear to have a priestly vocation. All of Robert's votes were in categories one and four. He had twelve "ones" and eight "fours." There was at that time no requirement beyond a majority vote, so Robert was recommended to me to be enrolled as a postulant for holy orders and thus started on the path toward ordination. The second barrier on the long journey toward priesthood had now been passed.

I met with Robert a week later and then wrote him a formal letter making him a postulant for holy orders in the Diocese of Newark. We also talked about how he could best use his postulancy to enrich his preparation for ordination. He agreed to continue to work with Gerry Pisani in Bayonne. About seven months would pass before he would be required to come before the standing committee of the diocese. The commission on ministry reflected the bishop's appointments, but the standing committee was fully elected. So in that body the will of the diocese would be representatively tested. I had told Robert that the vote of the standing committee would be his most difficult hurdle. Meanwhile, with this first goal achieved and with postulancy requiring a minimum of six months, Robert moved once more off the front burner of my attention.

I had the sense that I was sitting on a potential volcano. New activities and life-changing events seemed to cascade on top of one another. I needed a pause and thought I would have it now, since the book would not be out for at least another month. I would, in its pages, be advocating the recognition by society and the blessing by the church of committed monogamous same-sex relationships; the establishment of covenants, that is, the acts of betrothal, as I would call them, by young people who choose to live together prior to marriage; and the development by the church of a liturgy to recognize the end of a marriage and to allow divorced people to go through that emotionally complex trauma, without guilt and alienation being the only things the church added to their experience. I settled back to wait for its April launch. That anticipated pause was not to be granted to me, however, for about a month prior to the publication date of my book, I received an unexpected call from Michael Lawrence.

"Jack," he said when I picked up the phone, "I don't know how to tell you this, but we have decided to cancel your book."

"Cancel my book?" I asked as if I did not believe what I was hearing. "What do you mean?" My incredulity was overwhelming. They had had the manuscript now for more than six months. They had approved it, printed the covers, and set the type. Advertisements were already rolling, the tour, with its scheduled personal appearances, planned, and the publication date carefully targeted. What could possibly have happened to change their minds at this point? I was stunned to silence.

So Michael Lawrence continued. "We have had a number of complaints since the *Circuit Rider* ads began to appear." I learned later that most of the disapproval had come from Texas, where a very popular Methodist bishop had recently been exposed, after his AIDS-related death, as leading a double life. He was a prominent bishop with a wife and children by day, but an active homosexual by night. The wounds of this scandal were still raw in Methodist circles. In such an emotional setting, for the official Methodist publishing house to publish this book was deemed by these critics to be ludicrous. "If we refuse to cancel your book," Michael continued, "we have been told that a resolution will be introduced at the St. Louis National Assembly of American Methodism to appoint a committee to oversee the publications of Abingdon Press. We cannot run the risk of censorship. So with great apologies, I've been asked to communicate this decision to you at once." Michael went on to express his personal anger and despair at this decision. He recognized, as I did, that this decision meant that censorship had already been imposed on Abingdon Press. He clearly believed that his integrity as an editor had been compromised.

I felt sorry for Michael, but my head was reeling and I could not deal with his pain until I had done something about my own. I asked Michael if I could call him back in an hour. He agreed and I hung up the phone and sat at my desk for at least ten minutes in a kind of uncomprehending anguish. I was angry, embarrassed, and frustrated. Months of hard work were now aborted. I saw only despair in these events. No silver lining was apparent to me. Finally, after speaking with my secretary, Wanda Hollenbeck, I went down the hall to share this news with other staff members.

When I called Michael back, the reality of their decision had set in. We only repeated our previous conversation. Abingdon now released a statement to the press. The Associated Press ran the story of that announcement in papers across the country under a variety of local headlines that proclaimed something like, "Methodist Publishing House Cancels Episcopal Bishop's Book on Sex." The story indicated that the content of this book was deemed to be too controversial for the Methodist Church to be placed in the position of appearing to be endorsing it through its official publishing house. This achieved for me and the book, I learned in retrospect, literally thousands of dollars worth of free publicity. Some of my critics would later suggest that I had masterminded this series of events as a publicity stunt. That was true only in their imagination. I was in fact personally devastated and began the process of living into what felt like a black hole.

In a week's time, however, I discovered that being banned by the United Methodists was almost as good as being banned in Boston. By the following Friday I had offers from nine publishing houses willing to compete with each other for the privilege of being the owner of this manuscript. One of those nine was Harper, whose publisher Clayton Carlson called me personally to urge my return to the house of Harper. He made it clear that they wanted both this book and my future writing career to be under their imprint. My stock had clearly risen. I did not want to spend time dealing with competing offers, so I told Clayton that if Harper wanted the book, I would prefer to stay with the publishing house that now owned my previous titles. Without further ado the manuscript went to Harper under my standard author's contract. I made no attempt to make them sweeten the pot.

Harper moved the publication date back to June 1 and planned a multicity media tour. They raised the list price on the book two dollars, anticipated an advertising budget beyond anything I had ever imagined, and projected a minimum sale of fifty thousand copies, more than the total sale of all my other books put together. Suddenly I was in a different league of authors. On the media tour arranged by Harper, I appeared on more than one hundred radio and television programs, many of them, like Tom Snyder's show and William Buckley's *Firing Line*, with national audiences. The book was written about in newspapers and magazines across the nation, in Canada, and in the United Kingdom. Its publication created for me the busiest June in my life. I worked frantically to meet the obligations of my episcopal office while not neglecting the demands of a very well-planned media tour. Many a time I held press conferences in the airport since that was the only time left on the schedule. On one of those frantic trips back to the diocese during that month, I was surprised to find Joan back in our home in Morristown.

I fear that the press of my life did not allow much time on that occasion for a significant visit. She seemed to be doing well physically, though she complained of pain in her hands, which she attributed to carpal tunnel syndrome. She was very excited about the first grandchild and brought me pictures of her holding the baby. I treasure those pictures to this day. We had one brief, but tender, evening together before I had to depart the next day for another event, this time a diocesan one. I remember her standing at the back door to wave good-bye as I drove away. I had no idea that this would be the last time I would ever see her alive. She had left for Richmond before I returned home. During the last week of June I made trips to Chicago, Pittsburgh, and Philadelphia for major media events and did a two-hour call-in talk show in West Palm Beach, Florida. Then I was off to Detroit for the triennial general convention of our church.

I collapsed in Detroit. Contracting some virus, I was in bed with raging fever and nausea for about a week of that convention. I barely remember it, although I managed to make an appearance on the *McNeil-Lehrer News Hour* near the end. I also did a Tampa radio program and had press interviews with both the *New York Times* and the *St. Louis Post Dispatch*. The convention ended on July 10. I returned home, packed, and departed two days later for the United Kingdom for my second of the Anglican Communion's once-a-decade Lambeth Conference of bishops.

The Lambeth Conference in 1978 had bored me beyond measure. Its one saving grace had been my getting to know John A. T. Robinson so well. I had no agenda at this second conference that was compelling to me personally. Whether women could be bishops without breaking up the Anglican Communion was the big issue, and I was convinced that nothing Lambeth could do would stop that from occurring. So I viewed this 1988 conference as downtime; I would enjoy meeting Anglican leaders from around the world, renewing previous friendships, and allowing my somewhat weary body and mind to rest. It was a pleasant prospect, but one that turned out to be totally removed from reality.

When I checked into my room in Eliot College at the University of Kent in Canterbury, I found press requests attached to my door from the *Times*, the *Guardian*, the *Independent*, and the *Daily Telegraph*. I could not believe that in the face of the issues confronting Lambeth, my book had stirred up so much interest in the United Kingdom that this much press attention was going to be required. When I checked out these requests, however, I discovered to my amazement that it was not my book, but a very hostile personal attack made on me by my old adversary, Graham Leonard, the ultraconservative bishop of London, that had piqued their interest. For reasons I had not anticipated, Bishop Leonard had decided that I must be countered if Lambeth was going to stop women from being elected to the episcopate. He had, furthermore, decided to accomplish this by a vehement attack on me that was published prior to the opening of the conference. In a signed column in the *Daily Mail*, Bishop Leonard identified me as the primary problem in the Anglican Communion. I found that strange indeed, for many reasons.

First, the *Daily Mail* is generally referred to as part of the "gutter press" in Great Britain. Second, the intensity of this personal attack gave me a status that was both surprising and inappropriate. The article covered a full page and contained a picture taken of me jogging at the Lambeth Conference ten years earlier. I projected a remarkably well-preserved youthful countenance! The headline proclaimed me to be "The Bishop Running the Church into the Ground." The four major British newspapers wanted my response.

That episode began a whirlwind Lambeth Conference for me. After I read the article, I was willing to answer questions about it. The questions centered on the fact that many parts of the Anglican Communion now ordained women, but England, Wales, Australia, Scotland, and much of Africa did not. This created what Graham Leonard called an "impaired Communion." What his attack did, however, was to identify me as the chief instrument of change in the entire Anglican Communion on the issue of the ordination of women. Since this was the dominant issue at this Lambeth Conference, Graham Leonard had projected himself and me as the polarities of the Communion, which of course meant that the press fastened onto both of us.

The fact that my book *Living in Sin?* with its controversial proposals, had just been introduced into the United Kingdom only added grist to their mill. Over the three weeks of Lambeth I was interviewed by the media—television, radio, and print—more than anyone else at the conference. BBC Television sought in vain to get a televised debate between Graham Leonard and me, because he was not willing to engage me in that format. So what the BBC did was interview me in their studios and then go to his office to interview Graham. They asked us identical questions, then cut and spliced the tape to make it appear that we had, in fact, been in a face-to-face meeting. It was ingenious, and well done.

When Lambeth was over, my name had become a household word throughout our worldwide church, respected in some circles, anathema in others. An interesting serendipity was that from that day to this, religion writers of the British press have called me on a regular basis when doing stories on the life of our church and at least one of these writers and his wife have become personal friends.

Despite this fury of activity, Lambeth, however, ended on a very difficult note for me.

Two days before its conclusion, I received an urgent call from my daughter Katharine, in Richmond, Virginia. When she had gone to visit Joan, she had found her dead. Realizing the truth of what she was saying was so difficult to embrace that I responded by asking her to tell me again what she had just said. This time there was no doubt about her message. Death had come with a suddenness that surprised us all. The pain in the hands and fingers had been not carpal tunnel syndrome, but the first sign of a massive metastasis in her bones, a familiar pathway on which breast cancer travels. I learned later that even as the pain increased in the last days of her life, she had refused to see any doctors for fear that they were still in the employ of the CIA and FBI. She did, however, accept the visits and ministrations of Dr. John B. Catlett, Katharine's father-in-law. He called on her as family, not as a physician, but knowing the situation, he managed her pain during her final few days with drugs that he "just happened to have with him." It was a kind, caring, and sensitive thing to do, and I was deeply appreciative. She seems to have taken these medications as she felt a need for them, but the fact remains that when she died, she died alone. The pain of that realization haunts me to this very moment.

I could not get a plane to the United States until the next morning so I decided to continue the activities of that afternoon and evening without making the death of my wife public. I told only Ed Browning, but I asked him not to reveal this until I had departed. I had visions of five hundred bishops trying to be pastorally supportive. That was more than I could have endured. I retired to my room to be alone to grieve and to pray. Then, washing my face, I went down to dinner, which I shared at a table filled with Canadians. We engaged in the normal chit-chat of the conference.

I had previously agreed to be on a BBC radio program that evening to summarize the Lambeth Conference, so I decided to honor that commitment. Two other bishops, David Gitari, of Kenya, and Donald Robinson, the archbishop of Sydney, Australia, were the other guests in what was designed to be a kind of roundtable discussion. David represented the young Church of Africa. Donald was a deeply conservative evangelical, and I was clearly the voice of the liberals. The BBC always seeks balance. The thirty-minute program went well, and when it was over the other two bishops departed.

Since I had been interviewed on the BBC many times during that gathering, I had gotten to know the reporters quite well. That particular program was produced by Beverly McAinsch and the radio hostess was Ruth

Peacock. The two of them asked if I could stay when the program was over and have a gin and tonic with them in the mobile unit to celebrate the end of their Lambeth assignment, since this was to be their final broadcast from Canterbury.

It was while sitting in that makeshift studio in a BBC trailer that I talked for the first time quite openly and for more than an hour about the death of my wife. These two professional journalists were absolutely wonderful pastors. They listened, they allowed my tears, they offered their support, and they became my friends. Both of them would come in and out of my life on other occasions and no Christmas goes by, even now, that I do not hear from the two of them. Indeed, I would, the next year, return to the United Kingdom to preach at the marriage of Ruth Peacock to another BBC world correspondent named Tim Mabey, which was held in a small Anglican church in Wales.

The next morning, as I left early with my luggage in hand to get to Heathrow for the flight home, two other bishops, recognizing that I must be leaving early because something unusual had occurred, reached out to me in wonderful life-giving ways. They were Don Taylor of the Virgin Islands and Frank Gray of Northern Indiana. They were pastors in the great sense of that word, and I was deeply appreciative.

My journey home was incredibly long. I flew to JFK in New York and then transferred to a plane to Richmond. On the final leg of that journey I ran into an old Richmond friend, L. Douglas Wilder, who had shared some of our struggles for racial justice in Richmond back in the early 1970s. He had gone on to be elected state senator and lieutenant governor. The world was changing. Doug was now a candidate for the governorship of Virginia. He would be elected, making him the first black governor since Reconstruction. Later, he would even become a candidate for the Democratic nomination for president of the United States. I enjoyed our trip down to Richmond together. He allowed me to talk as much as I needed to about Joan. He was, however, another symbol that a whole new order inclusive of both racial minorities and women was emerging in our society. I was riding the same tide in the life of the church that he was riding in the political order. Doors were being opened. Our own daughters would be the beneficiaries of those changes. I landed in Richmond to plan for the burial of the one who had been my wife for thirty-six years.

Joan's funeral had two poignant moments that brought home the fact that I would never be able to escape my public image.

While seated with my daughters in the first pew of St. Paul's Church beside Joan's pall-draped coffin, I was amazed to feel myself being struck across the back and shoulders with a cane in a manner that was clearly not accidental. My assailant was an elderly woman. I turned instinctively to respond to this blow. This woman then said, in a voice audible to anyone within ten yards, "You son of a bitch." Continuing her journey down the aisle, she went through the side door where the pallbearers, all but one of whom were priests of our diocese,[1] were waiting to come into the church. To them she said, "I've been wanting to tell that bastard what I think of him for a long time, and I finally got the chance." She then disappeared from my life to live in the shadows of anonymity forever.

The second episode occurred when I went to thank the man who had carried the cross leading the choir into the church. I had not anticipated either choir or acolytes for this mid-afternoon service. This man was in his early thirties and I presumed he must have taken time away from his work to be there. In fact, the number of adults who constituted the choir amazed me for the same reason. I had not lived in this city for over twelve years. When I approached this young man to express my appreciation, he responded, "Bishop, you don't know us, but we know you. All of the acolytes and choir members here today are members of Integrity (the Episcopal organization for gay and lesbian people). We would do anything for you because you have done so much for us." I was touched to the point of tears.

A memorial service was also held at St. Peter's Church in Morristown, New Jersey, the following Saturday. The church was packed. I sat with my secretary and her husband, Wanda and Dick Hollenbeck, and we listened to a sermon preached by the Reverend Alex MacDonell, who, uniquely among the clergy of our diocese, had been allowed into Joan's life. She was devoted to him. Those liturgies closed the door on that chapter of my life that had been both wonderful and despairing, and I settled into the real grief work, which involved not just bereavement, but the guilt of having been so inadequate to this lovely, but disturbed, woman, and for not having been able to carry her to her final days and most of all for the aloneness of her death.

I went, just a week later, to our summer place at the beach. We treasured our time and our friends in that community. This year, however, all I did was to walk through those three weeks like a zombie. I found myself almost incapable of conducting a memorial service for another member of that community who had died. I went to few parties, preferring to be alone for most of that vacation time. Harper, however, forced me to stay in touch with reality by setting up telephone interviews on the book with nine radio stations throughout the nation. So I had to get myself psychologically up for those. It was a helpful exercise. When September arrived, the press of public activity resumed. I was interviewed for major features in the *New Jersey Magazine,* the *Baltimore Sun,* and the *Richmond News Leader,* and I led the clergy conference for the Diocese of New York at the invitation of its bishop, Paul Moore.

It now seemed like the media tide unleashed by *Living in Sin?* was carried by its own momentum. I no longer needed a publicist. I made an appearance on CBS's *This Morning* program. It was there that I discovered the presence of secret allies in the gay underground. An assistant producer named Eric Marcus[2] had worked behind the scenes to make sure that I was interviewed on that television program by Kathleen Sullivan. It was, I was told later, the first time that the subject of homosexuality had ever been broached on this show. Getting that interview was not easy. Clearly an internal debate was raging. I was booked twice and canceled twice. Then I was booked a third time and bumped from a live interview to a taped interview. Kathleen Sullivan was, however, wonderful. The interview went well. As we left the set, she said "I wish we had bishops like you in my church." I gather the producers and directors reviewed that segment before making the final decision to run it. But Eric and Kathleen lobbied hard, and it played in full the next day. Another barrier had crashed.

"Dr. Ruth" Westheimer, the popular sex therapist, called me about the book and praised it highly. Later, she and I appeared together on the *Phil Donahue Show.* It was a smash hit. Phil Donahue has always been a supporter of justice for gay people. I got hundreds of letters from that appearance. So did Phil Donahue, and that particular program was rerun a time or two during subsequent summers.

Life does go on. When November arrived, I found myself, through plans set up at least a year earlier, flying with members of our Companion Diocese Committee to Hong Kong at the invitation of its bishop, the Right Reverend Peter Kwong. Dr. Deborah Brown, the chair of that committee and senior warden of the Church of the Epiphany in Allendale, also made that trip with about a dozen other lay and clergy leaders of our diocese. Almost inevitably this trip was a bonding experience for all of us. We shared this common adventure and ate most of our meals together as a large family. It was for me a further time of genuine healing, as the members of this group, I believe, recognizing my continuing fragility, cared for me in sensitive and loving ways. We also had special times in Shanghai and in the New Territories of China, when I engaged a Buddhist monk named the Reverend Kok Kwong in a deep and meaningful dialogue on what lies at the core of our respective religious traditions. I also learned experientially that the God I worshiped was also clearly present in a Buddhist temple and that a Buddhist temple could be for me a holy place of prayer.

When we returned to the United States, I had the joy of a second visit with my Richmond family over Thanksgiving, and returned to my office ready for the first time in months to resume, with full energy, my role as the elected leader of that diocese. The cloud of grief was finally lifting.

The item foremost on our agenda was the decision of the standing committee about whether we as a diocese could proceed with the ordination of Robert Williams. The commission on ministry was now prepared to recommend him to the standing committee to be enrolled as a "candidate for holy orders." It would be, as I had anticipated, Robert's most difficult hurdle. The standing committee, made up of four clergy and four laity, took its responsibilities seriously and acted very independently and conscientiously. I knew they would look at this decision from every possible angle. I had no idea how they would finally decide. My political assessment going into that meeting was that there were two members ready to champion Robert and his cause powerfully and two who were vigorously and unalterably opposed to ordaining Robert. The other four members of this body were open, but so far as I could see uncommitted. They could go either way. Robert would need to win the support of three of these four to be recommended. I thought the odds were against his achieving that, and I had tried to prepare him for that possible eventuality.

The standing committee and Robert had lunch together and then the whole group interviewed him for almost an hour, which seemed to go well. Then Robert was asked to leave and the real deliberations began. Emotions swayed back and forth throughout the debate. The fears of the uncommitted members were expressed. The concerns of those adamantly opposed were heard, together with their predictions of the dire consequences for the life of our diocese if we were to go through with this ordination. The hopes of the two who believed that this was the time and Robert was the person to strike a blow for justice and to build an inclusive church were also heard. The discussion continued for over two hours, as consciences were formed and minds were either newly convinced or hardened. Finally, I perceived movement among the clergy in that middle group. They began to see more pluses than minuses in proceeding. It was Wade Renn, the rector of Grace Church, Nutley, who finally slapped the table and said, "Hell, let's do it! The time has come." He carried every undecided vote with him.[3] The final tally was six to two in favor of ordaining this man and this vote moved Robert Williams into a position to be ordained deacon in early June 1989. Only some weird or bizarre happening would normally stop the process once this decision was made. The last major barrier had been overcome. He had passed all of his exams and had been recommended by all of the necessary decision-making bodies. I called Robert to give him the news. We both rejoiced, even as we knew that each of us was embarking on a difficult path.

As the new year dawned, my first assignment outside the diocese was to give a lecture at a conference in Kirkridge, Pennsylvania, entitled "I Remember John A. T. Robinson," to mark the anniversary of his death. I was delighted to have been chosen for this responsibility and reveled in the times my work was associated with this man. My principal lecture at this conference sought to outline the theological crises the church was facing in the last decade of the twentieth century. It would, I discovered much later, form the basis of my book *Why Christianity Must Change or Die.* At this point it was simply an articulation of what the church must struggle against to understand its life.

In early 1989 Charles Gibson had me on ABC's *Good Morning America* with Jerry Falwell. Falwell had been publicly critical of me and had quoted the Bible at length to condemn both my writing and my conclusions. Charles Gibson had scheduled us for the normal five-and-a-half-minute segment. It was a dynamic and spirited debate. To Jerry's surprise, I knew the Bible better than he did. When we broke for the commercial, Charles Gibson made a unilateral decision to cancel his next segment and keep Falwell and Spong on for five and a half minutes more. It was a rare opportunity to go head to head with the obsequious Jerry Falwell. People watching did not realize that all three of us had known each other in Lynchburg, Virginia, when Jerry and I were pastors and Charles Gibson was the local television news anchor for the ABC affiliate.

When this program was over, I wrote Jerry a public letter urging him to engage me in a series of national debates on the Bible. "We could between the two of us," I suggested, "turn this country into a Bible reading nation once again." Jerry responded not personally, but through the press, that he did not want "to lift Mr. Spong out of his anonymity."

This idea, however, was not lost. In conversations about this with my editor Jan Johnson, at Harper, she suggested that I answer my religious critics by writing a book that would claim the Bible as my ally in the struggle for gay rights and point out the fallacies in conservative fundamentalists' use of this holy text as a weapon of prejudice. It was so easy to organize. All of those adult classes in Lynchburg and Richmond came back and almost formed whole chapters. My tentative title as this manuscript developed was *Rescuing the Bible from Fundamentalism*. It proved to be my only working title that made it into print. I would not budge from that title after a professor introduced me to a packed auditorium of undergraduates at a Florida college by saying, "The proposed title of his next book is *Rescuing the Bible from Fundamentalism*" and the audience applauded. Any title of a book about the Bible that gets the applause of an auditorium full of college students is a title no publicity department should ever change.

Later that year, as a direct result of my challenge to Jerry Falwell, the Reverend John Ankerberg, a second-tier television evangelist, did accept the invitation to debate, and we did six thirty-minute television programs together that played on a cable network across the country. My reputation as a major liberal religious voice in the public arena was clearly building.

I spent February 1989 at Yale Divinity School as the second month of my sabbatical program. I was now focused on the Bible book. At Yale I worked mostly on Paul, but I continued to be drawn to that apologetic task that seemed to consume me. It could best be summed up in the question, "How can premodern creeds be recited with integrity in a postmodern world?" Once again I returned home each weekend for confirmations, and I tried to run the diocese on two days a week, obviously aided by an extremely competent staff.

In March 1989, a member of my staff, Christine Barney, celebrated her fiftieth birthday at a dinner party given by some of her Morristown friends. I was invited. It was the first social event I had attended as a single person since Joan's death. It felt good. It was a comfortable evening. Chris was a friend of long standing. I enjoyed her company. Two weeks later Addison Groff, the rector of St. Peter's in Rochelle Park, invited me to his retirement dinner. I discovered that he had also invited Christine Barney, since she had worked closely with him in her position of diocesan administrator. So I suggested that I would pick her up and drive her over. It was the closest thing to a "date" in which I had participated for thirty-seven years.

My youngest daughter, Jaquelin, got married in Richmond that May. I discovered in that experience what the mother of the bride has to do for a wedding. I could not have managed without the help of my Richmond daughters. The wedding was, however, a huge success. Chris Barney and her two children were on the guest list, since they had been close both to Joan and to our daughters. Though not together as a couple, we nonetheless shared that additional social event.

On June 3 at 10:30 A.M. at St. Peter's Church in Morristown, I ordained Robert Williams, along with four other candidates, to the sacred order of deacons. There was no publicity, no news stories, no objections, and no fanfare. I assigned him to assist at All Saints' Church in Hoboken and to begin to pull together his dream of a diocesan ministry to reach the alienated gay and lesbian population. All Saints' was willing to sponsor this ministry, since the estimates were that at least 30 percent of Hoboken's population were homosexual persons. I then set out on a series of outside engagements—a clergy conference in Rupertsland, Canada, lectures at the Perkins School of Theology at Southern Methodist University in Dallas, a rally in Trenton for gay rights, and the keynote address to the national Integrity gathering in San Francisco. All of these were quick trips. I took no days off from my work at that time, or perhaps it would be more accurate to say that I used my normal day off to do these outside things. There was nothing that gave me more pleasure, so it was not a sacrifice. Indeed, it filled what would otherwise have been lonely days for me.

Late in June the *New York Times* got word of the ministry to gay and lesbian people, named the Oasis, that Robert Williams was beginning to set up in Hoboken and decided to do a feature on it. The story appeared on the metro section's first page with a picture of Robert in clerical collar standing in front of an altar. In the article Robert was identified as an openly gay man and his partner was named. The article closed with the words that his ordination to the priesthood would take place in mid-December. Several days later I received a letter from John Howe, the bishop of Central Florida, inquiring whether he had read the article correctly and objecting strenuously. He sent a copy of his letter to the presiding bishop. I responded that Robert was indeed on a track leading toward the priesthood, that the canons had been scrupulously followed, and that our church had never forbidden this action. I referred him to the Statement of Conscience that John Krumm had drawn up in 1979. The fact that we had elected Edmond Browning, one of the signatories on this Statement of Conscience, to be presiding bishop in

1985 certainly indicated that this position was a legitimate one. I sent a copy
of my letter to the presiding bishop. This is how the proposed priestly ordination of Robert Williams first entered the public arena.

That summer, as part of my vacation, I had accepted an invitation from
the Episcopal church on Bainbridge Island in the Puget Sound across from
Seattle to be the "Scholar in Residence." My duties were to deliver four lectures, one a week for four weeks. In exchange I was provided with a house,
fully furnished, overlooking the Sound, where I could write the final text of
*Rescuing the Bible from Fundamentalism.* The temperature was always a pleasant seventy degrees. I could sit at my desk on the deck in shirt sleeves with
paper, pens, and books spread out before me. It was almost a paradise. I was
scheduled to leave Newark on the morning of Friday, June 29. On Thursday
morning, June 28, Christine Barney came by my office to tell me that she
needed to see me some time during that day. I told her I would call her when
I was free. She left and, in the rush of doing the final things, I never thought
about her again. At 5:00 P.M. she came once more to my office, this time
clearly angry.

"I told you I needed to talk to you today," she said, with quite visible tears
streaming down her face. I apologized for my insensitivity and invited her to
sit down. I felt even worse when she told me that at her annual physical exam
her doctor had discovered a lump in her breast. Her mother had died of
breast cancer in her early fifties, and Christine was concerned that the hereditary pattern of her family had now caught up with her. She had an appointment with a specialist the next Monday morning. She needed me to know
that she would be out of work at least on Monday and longer if surgery was
required. The more ominous reality that this could be serious also permeated the conversation. Since I had not even responded to her request for an
appointment until it was forced upon me at the end of the day, and since I
was leaving for the state of Washington the next day, it was hard to express
my concern with credibility. So I listened and tried to be sensitive to her not
very well hidden fears. I promised that I would call on Monday. It was very
little, but it was all that I could do.

That night before departing for Bainbridge Island I called each daughter
to tell her how to get in touch with me. When I got Katharine, I discovered
a very depressed young woman. She did not want to worry me with her
problems, she said, but slowly, as we talked, they began to creep out. She was
the extremely conscientious mother of Shelby, a very demanding fifteen-
month-old daughter. She did not get enough sleep. She had lost a lot of

weight. Her father-in-law, Dr. Catlett, had become concerned and had sent her to see a specialist. Tests revealed that her pituitary gland was not functioning properly. Further tests had been ordered. The range of possibilities went from something very minor all the way to cancer of the pituitary gland. That news was more than I could manage. My heart sank.

"Do you want me to come to Richmond," I inquired.

"No, Dad, we won't know anything for a couple of weeks. If I need you, I'll call you then."

Never had a trip seemed so ill-planned. But the next morning I flew to Seattle, took the ferry to Bainbridge Island, and settled into my home for a month. I was, however, in a very real depression. My focus, much to my surprise, was at least as much on Christine as it was on Katharine. I could get neither off my mind and constantly tried to imagine life without either one of them. It was like having a nightmare all day long followed by a restless night. On Saturday I found it impossible to settle into a writing routine. I could postpone that until Monday, since I had agreed to preach at the host church that Sunday as a way to introduce the visiting scholar lecture series. A concrete assignment does require the brain to become objective. So I simply wasted Saturday doing what authors frequently call "getting ready to write."

I did call Katharine that afternoon to discover that she was feeling better. Her own doctor had dismissed any possibility of a malignancy and was quite irritated at the specialist for even raising that fear. Kathy was much relieved.

On Sunday, following the services at church, I called Christine to wish her well. She was being brave and stoical, but obviously knew no more than she had known the previous Thursday. Strangely enough, my depression did not lighten with Katharine's good news. I had not realized that Christine was this important to me. I was not conscious of the fact that she had entered that inner sanctum of relationships so special that the threat to such a person was experienced as a threat to oneself. I promised to call her Monday evening. She told me who to contact to get a message if she was not home.

It was a dreadful Monday. Once more I tried to write, but nothing flowed. I rearranged my notes endlessly. I tried to read some of the resources I had with me. I would read the same paragraph ten times without ever comprehending what it was saying. Finally, I gave up and went for a long walk. Coming home about 2:00 P.M., I fixed a simple lunch and prepared to wait until 3:00, which was 6:00 Eastern time, which seemed the earliest possible moment that I might reach Christine.

At 2:45 I could wait no longer. I dialed her number and got a cheery voice of one neither hospitalized nor fearful.

"Are you okay?" I asked.

"Yes," she responded. Their first procedure was to probe the lump with a needle, drain the fluid from it, and analyze that. It revealed no sign of cancer, so no surgery would be necessary. I did not know how to interpret the wave of relief that swept over me. I would not get home for three and a half weeks, but I knew that Christine had become someone very important to me. That afternoon the writing began to flow, and it continued until I prepared to board a plane for Newark.

The thing I needed to work out especially was my section on Paul. I envisioned two chapters, one an external view of Paul and the other an attempt to understand the inner Paul, the emotional drives and hidden agendas of this man. At Yale Divinity School I had read a book published in the 1930s by Arthur Nock that raised the possibility that Paul might have been a deeply repressed gay man, suggesting that this was the "thorn in the flesh" he had besought God to remove to no avail. To that insight I added a conversation I had had with a gay man who said that when he read Paul, he was reminded of himself before he had accepted the fact of his homosexuality. He too had hated himself and felt that a war was going on inside his body. With his mind he followed one set of values, but with his body he followed another. He resonated with Paul's desire to keep the rules so vigorously that he was driven to persecute anyone who seemed to weaken or deemphasize the necessity of the rules. Next I examined in great detail the one place where Paul undisputedly condemned homosexual activity (Romans 1). He described it as God's punishment on those who did not worship properly. In Paul's few autobiographical notes, he had referred to himself as zealous for the law and blameless before God. Was Paul being autobiographical in the Epistle to the Romans? I wondered. This text, Nock's suggestion, and the conversation with the gay man played on my mind in fascinating combinations.

I decided to test this possibility in the only manner I could imagine. I would assume it to be true. I would then reread the entire corpus of Paul's writing to see if this possibility illumined these texts in a new way. Second, I decided that the way to reread this Pauline material was in the order in which scholars think it was written, not in the order in which it appears in the New Testament. I wanted to see if I could pick up growth and change in Paul's thinking. This experiment proved to be a wonderful experience, filling an entire day. I took notes on the points where Paul's words seemed to undergird my hypothesis. Overwhelmingly it clicked for me. My assumptions surely made sense of the texts. His bitterness became understandable. His rigidity could now be explained as a defense mechanism. His passion first for the law and then for the grace of Christ became insightful. His persecuting personality and cataclysmic conversion fitted. Hidden clues like Paul's phrase that even his "nakedness" could not now separate him from the love of God took on new meaning. The idea that sin dwelt in his "members" (a Greek word that meant bodily appendages), causing his "members" not to obey the law of his mind, became revelatory. His dismissal of women and his unwillingness to marry to satisfy his passion now seemed to point to my assumptions.

It was a revealing day. But should I write this speculation in a book for the public to read? Was this not something that would best be done in dialogue, lest misunderstanding and prejudiced images overwhelm readers and create a destructive hostility? I decided to write the chapters first and to face those questions later. The writing poured out. My notes based on a chronological reading of Paul almost leaped off the pages. In forty-eight hours the two Paul chapters were complete.

I knew then that my inclination would be to use this material in the new book. The primary reason that this possibility angered people was that they carried in their subconscious minds such repelling stereotypes of homosexuals that to apply those stereotypes to Paul was considered to be so sacrilegious as to be inconceivable. But if homosexuality is a given, not a chosen aspect of one's being, then homosexuality is not abnormal, and no better way could be found to combat that uninformed prejudice than to go public with this speculation. Would it not also be worth a great deal to recognize that the dark, or shadow, side of human life that Carl Jung stated was in every person, might be loved and thus made acceptable and whole in the God experience? I thought so, and to me this is exactly what Paul's life demonstrated. Since Paul framed the primary Christian concept of grace, would it not be a life-giving insight to suggest that all of us received that sense of grace, understood as the unbounded love of God who loves us just as we are, from one who had been a repressed and self-hating homosexual man? These possibilities were both intriguing and satisfying. I decided that I would go with this material in the book if a test of this thesis on the clergy of the diocese got a good reception during the New Dimensions lectures in October.

After this, the book almost completed itself. I loved writing it. The manuscript needed to be in Harper's hands by early 1990. I was well ahead of schedule.

The flight home was one of high expectations. I had asked Chris if she might meet me and suggested that we go to dinner together. I looked forward to seeing her.

I had committed myself to a media tour of the United Kingdom, organized by HarperCollins, London, for ten days in early August, so I was not home long. The London tour was quite worthwhile. I managed to escape the religion beat and was handed over to one of Britain's best-known profile journalists. The result was a full-page profile in the *Times*.

Returning home I prepared to go to our favorite beach retreat for the final three weeks of the summer. My children would each be present with me for a part of that time. I invited Christine to come out when the children were there. The blending was easy. All my daughters knew her, but they clearly were meeting her now in a new way, though we had not yet discussed the possibility of marriage. It was nonetheless obvious that a bond between us was growing.

On September 4, 1989, my first day home from the beach, Chris and I had dinner in Morristown. There for the first time we discussed the possibility of life together. It was still a frightening prospect for me. We analyzed where each of our children were, how our relationship might impact them, our financial realities, the fact that she would have to leave her job, which she loved very much, and the financial impact that this would have. The Church Pension Fund had a rule that if an ordained person got remarried after the fifty-seventh year of his or her life, the new spouse would not be fully covered by the fund until the couple had been married for three years. We would have to risk that. It was an easy, wide-ranging conversation. It never occurred to me to ask if she would marry me. I guess I just assumed that. As we left the restaurant to walk to my car, Chris asked, "Does this mean that we are engaged?"

I don't know why that idea startled me. It just was stated more bluntly than I was yet ready to do. There was no ring, no proposal, no kiss. It was, when I looked at it, a strange way to approach the reality of marriage. I had thought of none of those things. So I responded lamely, "I guess so," hardly a dramatic or affirming statement of commitment.

Because of the public nature of my life, we needed to guard our plans and our privacy until we were ready for the world to know.

We told our children first. I did it by phone. Since each of my daughters had been with us at the beach, none was surprised, and they each expressed their hope for our happiness together. Chris did it in person. She picked up her daughter, Rachel, from high school and drove to Burlington, Vermont, where her son, Brian, was in school, so that she could tell the two of them together. Rachel wanted to visit a friend and was not eager to stay in the motel as her mother had requested, but Chris insisted that she had something urgent to tell them. Rachel's response was, "You're not going to tell us you have cancer, are you?" Teenagers are blunt, if nothing else. Chris assured her that her health was not the issue.

Brian's girlfriend, Jen, was there, so it was not just the family gathering that Chris had intended. But when Chris finally got their attention, she said, "I'm going to get married." Rachel and Brian's only response was "To whom?" But Jen, who had come to visit Chris with Brian a bit earlier in the summer, had intuitively picked up enough to know who it was at once, and so she told the others. All of our children were sworn to secrecy. We had not yet picked a date, but we hoped it would be over the Christmas holidays.

In October, Richard Grein, the new bishop of New York, was installed in the longest church ceremony I have ever attended. Chris went with me and, since I was vested and part of the service, she was seated in a pew reserved for the bishop's wives. The inspection process had begun.

Charles Gibson of ABC News and his wife, Arlene, invited me to dinner about a week later. They also asked if I would like to bring a guest, so, happily, Christine accompanied me. Both of us enjoyed the Gibsons immensely. We would see them from time to time in our married life. On October 28 the rector at St. Paul's in Englewood, Jack McKelvey, celebrated his tenth anniversary with a dinner dance. Chris and I attended and danced together. We could almost see the heads nodding.

Finally we invited some of our closest diocesan friends, four couples, to dinner at my house. I sat at one end of the table with Chris at the other. The meal was exquisite. But after dinner, to accompany dessert, I brought out the flutes and opened a bottle of champagne. When the glasses were filled, I proposed a toast: "To Christine, who is willing to change her name to Spong." They all pretended that they had known all along, but I think they were as surprised as anyone else.

The following night at Chris's home, we reversed roles with her closest personal friends. She proposed the toast. We had managed to tell our families and closest friends first. The public was notified in my November column in *The Voice*, our diocesan newspaper. After describing the things you learn when you become a widower, such as the heretofore unknown-to-me fact that a clothes dryer had a lint filter that needed to be cleaned regularly lest the dryer burn itself up and perhaps the house with it, which had come perilously close to being my experience, I said that Joan's death and my bereavement had taught me many things, not the least of which was a profound respect for what a true partnership in marriage really means. I closed the column with this final paragraph:

> I hope that is true, because over the New Year's Day weekend, I will take the vows of holy matrimony and will once again become a husband. The one who will become my wife is Christine Mary Barney. We ask your prayers and your good wishes. I trust that for all of us it will be a happy new year.

Little did I know that it would be the most tension-filled year of my life.

1.   That one was the Reverend Loren B. Mead, classmate, godfather to my daughter as I am to his son, and my longtime friend.

2.   Eric Marcus later interviewed me in my office for a book he was writing on those who had helped move the gay agenda forward. I was featured in a chapter entitled "The Bishop."

3.   In 1977 Wade Renn had asked the convention of the Diocese of Newark to pass a resolution condemning the action of the bishop of New York for ordaining to the priesthood Ellen Barrett, who was a lesbian living in a committed relationship. This vote on the standing committee represented a significant shift in his views.

# 18

# *Marriage and the Year of Years*

\*

T HE NEWS of our proposed marriage spread slowly, but surely. About a week after the *Voice* column was published, I received a call from Ed Browning congratulating me on my coming marriage. I appreciated his call, but I also took this opportunity to remind him of our correspondence last June about Robert Williams.

"He is tentatively scheduled to be ordained on Saturday, December 16, in Hoboken," I said. "We still need the final official recommendation for priestly ordination from the standing committee, but that is almost perfunctory in this diocese unless there has been some overt trouble in the diaconate. Robert has, in fact, been exemplary and his developing ministry of the Oasis is growing. I do not anticipate any problems at all this time around. He has justified our confidence. We do not plan to advertise this service in the media, but we do not plan to be dishonest about it or seek to hide it either. The gay community will certainly know about it and will be present in large numbers. We are ordaining him as a sign that the church in this diocese is ready to acknowledge and affirm monogamous, faithful, same-sex unions, so it must be open." We were acting, I told him, on the Statement of Conscience that he signed with twenty others in 1979. We were also acting consistently with our own task force's recommendations adopted by our convention in 1988.

Ed listened patiently. Then he offered what I thought was a strange suggestion. "Why don't you write the bishop of Dallas and make him aware of your plans, so that if there is some publicity, he will not be caught off guard."

"Why should I do that?" I inquired. "Robert has never applied for ordination in that diocese, and even though that is his home, he will have lived in this diocese as a communicant for almost two years prior to his ordination."

I was baffled by the suggestion. Ed's concern was that Donis Paterson, the bishop of Dallas, not be caught off guard.

"If that's the situation, Ed, I'd be glad to write every bishop and give them the background." Ed thought that would be helpful. He was eternally hopeful that the right-wing bishops of our church would, if given proper information, act reasonably and rationally. It never worked.

I discussed this with Robert and we proposed two letters: one from me outlining the canonical process, which we had meticulously followed, and one from Robert talking about his life, his call, and his hopes for ministry. I wanted to put a human being into their minds, challenging the stereotype contained in the pejorative phrase "a practicing homosexual." The letters were mailed by the first of December. I thought no more about this matter until about a week before the proposed ordination.

A telephone call from a BBC reporter in London sought my response to a statement issued at a press conference held in Texas by the Right Reverend Clarence Pope, the bishop of Fort Worth. Since Clarence had not followed the normal courtesy of sending me a copy of his statement before releasing it to the public, I had no idea what the reporter was talking about. So he read it to me on this transatlantic call. In his statement Clarence condemned the proposed ordination, called on me to cease and desist from following through on this plan, and proclaimed that the general convention had ruled definitively on this question in 1979. This meant that in his mind I would be violating my vows to uphold the doctrine and discipline of the church if I proceeded with this ordination. When I heard these comments, I almost laughed out loud.

Clarence Pope was one of the ultraconservative male chauvinist bishops of the church. Despite the changes in the canons passed in 1976 to open the ordination process of the Episcopal Church to qualified women, he had steadfastly refused to obey those canons. No woman was allowed to test her vocation in that diocese, celebrate the Eucharist, or be eligible to serve any church there as its rector. The general convention resolution about homosexuality, to which he referred, specifically called itself "a recommendation." With a minority statement issued the next day stating the inability of the signers to be bound by this recommendation, a position not in accord with the "recommended position" could hardly be called prohibited by the church. So I responded in a rather flip manner by saying, "Any bishop who refuses to obey the canons of this church can hardly be critical when another bishop is unwilling to obey a recommendation of general convention."

Clarence Pope would someday, like the bishop of London, leave Anglicanism for the Roman Catholic tradition, except that, in Clarence's case, he would return six months later when he came to the conclusion that Rome did not treat him as if he were important enough.[1] I had known Clarence for more than twenty years. He had a rigid, uptight personality, but I genuinely liked him. I had no intention, however, of stopping this ordination to keep Clarence happy.

What Clarence had done, however, was to turn the ordination into a media event. Our diocese had hoped to avoid making this a spectacle, but we were prepared to accept that alternative if it became necessary. The church had ordained gay men for centuries, but had never admitted it—a colossal game of denial. We in the Diocese of Newark had no interest in continuing that ecclesiastical charade. Our desire was to send a public message to the homosexual population of our metropolitan area that this church welcomed them. We wanted it to be communicated in a normal and routine way, but we were quite ready to defend it publicly if attacks came. Clarence Pope was but the tip of the iceberg of negativity we would have to confront. Ed Browning's strategy of informing the bishops in advance had clearly backfired. It had, in fact, created the storm that we now had to be ready to endure.

Clarence's statement issued to the press and my response became part of an Associated Press account proclaiming that the first openly gay man living publicly with his partner was going to be ordained a priest in the Diocese of Newark. Religion and sex had combined to make a powerful story. We had press calls every day of the week prior to the ordination. The public began a countdown, in effect. I needed a full-time press office. The Venerable Leslie C. Smith, one of our archdeacons, served in that capacity, but his job description also included running the Department of Missions, working in deployment, and editing *The Voice*. Public relations and press relations were a miniscule part of his responsibility. Nevertheless, he handled this load magnificently. He was calm, rational, and firm.

When December 16 arrived, I actually had two ordinations—one in Jersey City at 10:30 A.M., the other in Hoboken at 5:00 P.M. The 10:30 service involved a woman to whom Christine had been very close, and so she planned to attend. She also knew that the Hoboken ordination could be chaotic, and she wanted to be with me. So we planned a day of churchgoing.

We arrived in Hoboken two hours early, about 3:00 P.M. The rector, Geoff Curtiss, said that various representatives of the media had called all day. Some were there already. He and Leslie Smith suggested that Robert and I be available for a press conference before the service. It would cut down on the number of individual interviews greatly. We both agreed.

By 4:15 P.M. we had all of the major national and local television networks present—as well as the microphones from many area radio stations. We also had the journalists from the print media with their ballpoint pens and spiral notebooks. The place was a zoo. We answered their questions as honestly and as low-key as we could. Most of them focused on what the response of the church hierarchy was going to be. Was I courting trouble? Could I be impeached? The press insisted on using that political term instead of the ecclesiastical word "deposed." I tried to explain the authority under which I was operating, but Ecclesiology 101 had not been a course any of them had taken. At 5:00 the procession began. About forty of our clergy were present. There were also three bishops attending and vested. The retired bishop of Maine, Fred Wolf, was the preacher. My assisting bishop, Walter Righter of Iowa (retired), was there just to be supportive. Both bishops joined me in the laying on of hands.

There were hostile demonstrators outside the church and one protester inside who spoke loudly when we asked if there were objections. He appeared to have been a Pentecostal preacher. I heard his objections and ruled that he had said nothing we did not already know about Robert Williams, and Robert had satisfied the canons and been approved by every authorized decision-making body of this diocese. "This ordination," I ruled, "will go on." There was sustained applause. The protester continued to heckle until the ushers removed him.

In the midst of television cameras with their long cords, we tried to maintain the sacredness of this moment. Robert had prepared for this ordination for over ten years. The service reflected his rather catholic-leaning spirituality. I sang the Veni Creator Spiritus, and we observed a long period of silence. Then the ordination prayer was offered to God with our hands laid on Robert's head. "Make him a priest in your church," we said. The deed was done. Robert was vested in a red chasuble. We shared the peace, and Robert concelebrated the Eucharist with me. I would guess that one-third of the congregation was gay and lesbian. We had sent a powerful symbolic message to this world that we were an open and affirming church. Tears were shed by people who never thought they would live long enough to see their church welcoming them just as they were or welcoming their sons and daughters. I was proud of this diocese and proud to be its bishop. I remember the emotions of that moment quite vividly to this day. This was one of the exquisite times of gospel proclamation in my life. The love of God broke into circles and crevices of life where it had generally not been thought of as present before.

It was almost midnight when I got Chris back to her home and fully midnight when I pulled into my garage. We listened to the radio on that homeward journey. The ordination was on every station. That New York station whose slogan was "Give us twenty-two minutes and we will give you the world" treated this story every twenty-two minutes for most of the next twenty-four hours.

When I got to my bedroom, I turned on CNN's Headline News and found the story there every thirty minutes. I was amazed that the media treated it as so large a story, and I often wondered why. Without Clarence Pope's protest, my guess is it would have been as quiet as Robert's ordination to the diaconate, but I will never know.

The next morning the ordination was a major story in the papers of the nation. Reporters had called the presiding bishop, Ed Browning, for his comments. In his initial response he indicated that I had operated within the canons of the church and thus had done nothing illegal. It was, I thought, the best I could hope for from him at that moment, hardly supportive, but not negative.

My confirmation services the next day were quite routine. The people of our diocese seemed undisturbed.

On Monday our office was overrun with telegrams, letters, and telephone calls, many of which were quite abusive. Our secretaries were instructed to ask callers to write, to promise that we would respond to their letters, and to listen, but not to allow themselves to be abused. They did a wonderful job. By Tuesday the volume of mail reached over one hundred letters a day. About 80 percent were negative. That volume would rise each day for ten days before it began to slow.

On Wednesday morning I received a night letter from the presiding bishop that had been sent to all of the bishops of the church. His tone was radically different. I found it hard to believe this was the same man. He accused me of violating the collegiality of the House of Bishops. He stated that the position of the church was articulated clearly in that 1979 resolution of the general convention that said that it was not appropriate to ordain anyone unless they were living in a faithful heterosexual marriage or were pledged to celibacy. He announced that he was calling together the provincial presidents, who constituted his Council of Advice, to deal with this crisis in the church.

I could only read that letter as coming from one who had collapsed under the weight of hostility. It was particularly galling to see Ed lean on the authority of the 1979 resolution, which he had personally and publicly indicated he could not and would not obey as his authority. By this time I had learned that the best way to deal with a storm was to maintain calmness, not to react until its fury was spent. Ed Browning had violated each of my rules.

The bishop of California, Bill Swing, went on national television to ask me to apologize to the church for this action. The gall of that man was appalling. He had ordained countless gay people and a gay couple was on the staff of his cathedral. If he was not aware of that, then he was incompetent, for everyone else knew about it. Bill Swing was, at that time, a candidate to be bishop of Washington, D.C., and somehow, I assumed, was trying to "de-Californianize" himself so as to have a better chance at election. The strategy failed. The gay community in Washington made it very clear after hearing his television message that Bill Swing would not be an acceptable candidate to them. His candidacy fizzled. Calls for my resignation came from the typical sources—those who always seek to purge the church of everyone except themselves. The threat of a trial to remove me if I did not resign was heard. The center of the House of Bishops was dreadfully silent. I had only one vocal supporter in that body, the bishop of New Hampshire, Doug Theuner.

In the midst of this swirling turmoil Chris and I planned the final details of our marriage. We had decided on the date of January 1, 1990, a Monday, primarily because I had a confirmation service in Hackettstown on Sunday, December 31. I could actually get three unencumbered days for a wedding and a short honeymoon trip if we had the ceremony on Monday. So at 2:30 P.M. on Monday, January 1, 1990, accompanied down the aisle by all our children and our one grandchild, we stood at the altar to hear the words that bound us as husband and wife. Leslie Smith was the preacher. Jim Sell, celebrated the Eucharist, and David Hegg, the rector of St. Peter's, did the actual marriage. Petero Sabune and Susannah Hobbs, a clergy team from Jersey City, read the lessons and assisted in the communion. Cynthia Black, a young assistant priest in Essex Fells, played the trumpet to add to the magic of the day. Nelson Thayer and five hundred and fifty other guests filled the church. We sent no invitations. We just said "come if you want to," and come they did. We were told that the wedding would be interrupted by protesters, but they never materialized. We were, however, prepared. We planned a reception for three hundred, so it was something like the loaves and fishes. About 5:30 P.M. Chris and I drove off to a site never revealed to anyone for two blissful days without mail or phone.

I was back in the office by Thursday morning. The tide of hostility was still rising. Ed Browning had invited the angriest bishops to come to New York to meet with him early in January. I called him to say I would like to meet with them—a request that was denied. This had the feel of a kangaroo court. I was later told by Harold Hopkins, the presiding bishop's pastoral officer, that I was considered "too powerful." These angry bishops needed to be able to ventilate, not listen to my explanation, I was told. Their minds were clearly made up, and they did not wish to be disturbed with facts. It was a strange way to handle hostility. My respect for Ed Browning was badly battered.

Things did not improve in January. Robert Williams was also in the eye of the hurricane. The television talk shows all wanted him to be their guest. Robert was young, volatile, and inexperienced with the media. No one had time to work with him to advise him. Leslie Smith had his hands full managing me and the diocese. We were simply not prepared or equipped for this onslaught.

Robert also had a short fuse when he was badgered by reporters. The shortness of that fuse was more often than not the story. The press began to portray him quite negatively. My attempts to advise him were suddenly unwelcome. I did warn him that we were in a political battle to change hearts and that how each of us conducted ourselves was vital to that struggle. He felt quite adequate to continue in his aggressive style. Gerry Pisani had been so irritated by Robert's manner, I learned later, that as a personal protest, he declined to be present at his ordination to the priesthood. He had served as one of Robert's presenters at his ordination to the diaconate.

Stories about Robert began to be commonplace. Even the gay community became concerned and tried to offer help. It was to no avail. It was as if in achieving his goal to become a priest, his personality had undergone a change.

On the Wednesday before our diocesan convention the last weekend in January, Leslie Smith brought to the staff meeting the most distressing news yet. Robert had been speaking in Detroit. A reporter from the *Detroit Free Press* began to interrogate him rather aggressively. Robert responded with increasing anger, asserting in the process that homosexual people need not be faithful to their partners. Faithfulness and monogamy were, he asserted, part of a scheme to impose heterosexual standards on the gay community. The very basis upon which the Commission on Ministry and the standing committee had endorsed his application for ordination was that he could model a committed monogamous relationship as an alternative to promiscuity, on one side, and to mandatory celibacy, on the other. On no other basis would we have been willing to support his ministry at the Oasis. Robert had cut the ground out from under those who had placed their lives and careers on the line to support him. But as bad and damaging as those comments were, in this same interview Robert had refused to bridle his anger.

The reporter continued his relentless questioning.

"Are you saying that sex is good for everyone?"

"Yes, that is what I am saying," Robert asserted.

The reporter continued, "Are you saying that Mother Teresa would be better off if she had sex?" In exasperation Robert uttered the words that would echo around the world.

"Yes. Mother Teresa would be better off if she got laid."

The man I was being pilloried for ordaining was making it almost impossible for anyone to come either to his support or mine. My heart sank when I heard this. The grand experiment, based on the hope of developing a new consciousness in the church, was going up in flames.

I called together the board of the Oasis and laid the problem before them. "Unless Robert reaffirms the basis on which he was ordained, I cannot in conscience continue to support his work at the Oasis or to ask the diocese to underwrite it," I told them.

I met with Robert to discuss ways to get out of this situation. I suggested an apology to the Roman Catholics for attacking one of their icons. He responded that to ask a gay man to apologize to the Roman Catholics was like asking a Jew to apologize to Nazi Germany. I felt the despair of encircling gloom. Robert did not know how to deal with public relations. He was now an empowered victim who needed to give as good as he got. That might create good feelings in the victim, but it does not win hearts. This man, I concluded, was no Jackie Robinson.

The situation came to a head at our convention. While I held off a resolution to cut the funding to the Oasis, the Oasis board, most of whom were homosexual persons, meeting with Bishop Righter, finally voted to inform Robert that they no longer had confidence in his leadership and that they were requesting his resignation. A severance package was agreed on and, with advice from Carter Heyward, Robert resigned.

That, however, was only raw meat thrown to my critics. This incident only proved how incompetent I was in allowing this ordination to take place in the first place. I had, in their minds, violated the church, the collegiality of the House, and the resolution of the general convention. Pressure for my resignation continued to mount. It was in this jolly mood that February 1 arrived and my third sabbatical month, this one to be spent at Harvard Divinity School, was set to begin. This year, with Walter Righter on board, I was not planning to return home each weekend. Chris, whose resignation was not effective until June 30, could not be with me except on weekends. I really questioned whether I should not forego this study month, but I had made various commitments to speak in the Boston area and at the Episcopal Divinity School, and life had been so harrowing that my friends prevailed upon me to honor this sabbatical time.

The first week I was there I went out to a newsstand to get *Time* magazine. I had been told I would be featured in it this week. While there, I also picked up *Newsweek* to discover that I was the featured religious story there also. Neither story was positive.

About halfway through that month the presiding bishop called to tell me that the Council of Advice, made up of bishops who were presidents of the nine provinces of our church, had voted to take a specific action against me. He wanted me to come to New York so that this message could be given to me in person. He did not want me to read about it in the newspapers.

"You can tell me on the phone, Ed," I insisted. He declined to do that, saying it would not be appropriate to our longtime friendship. I told him that his behavior was not appropriate to our longtime friendship either. I declined to go to New York, and the conversation ended.

I thought about this phone call for several hours and then called him back. I will be there by 4:00 P.M., I said. I am still not sure that was wise, but I had so little support I could not afford to alienate Ed further. He had crumpled so badly I sometimes wondered what was holding him up.

When I arrived, Ed was not alone. Herb Donovan, the bishop of Arkansas, a classmate and former priest in my diocese, now serving as the secretary of the House of Bishops, was present. Before being elected in Arkansas, he had been an outspoken liberal on this issue. Also present was Harold Hopkins, the presiding bishop's pastoral adviser and former bishop of North Dakota. They described the meetings they had held with angry bishops and with the Council of Advice. Something had to be done to cauterize the bleeding, they felt. If they had done nothing, their rationale was that something worse would be forced upon them and me. I told them that it struck me as strange that all these people had come together to discuss me, but no one had provided me with an opportunity to confront my critics face-to-face. I was being manipulated to save something idolatrous called "the unity of the church." A church united in ignorance and prejudice could never be the Body of Christ, I said. It was in vain. This threesome was not willing to listen to my preaching on that afternoon. I was handed a letter. They said it was "a letter of disassociation." The presiding bishop and the provincial presidents had officially disassociated themselves from my action in ordaining Robert Williams and from my diocese for agreeing to that ordination. Why that could not be communicated to me over the phone I will never know.

I did not bother to read the letter. I said something about how history would validate my initiative and cover their response with shame. I also indicated that I would take this battle on the road and appeal over the heads of the bishops to the people of the church. Those were brave words spoken by one who could count only on one supportive bishop in the entire country and whose mail was running four to one against his action. Ed walked me out to the elevator, trying I am sure to be supportive. "I want to thank you for driving down from Cambridge," he said.

"Anything to serve the church's homophobia," I responded unrepentantly.

Ed looked as if I had kicked him in the stomach. I wanted to say, "You will die, Ed, if you are not true to what you deeply believe. Be a leader, not a bureaucrat." But the elevator closed with both of us looking at each other in silence as we parted.

I drove home to Chris. I spent the rest of my time at Harvard plotting a national campaign to deliver the church from the peril of seeing its prejudice against homosexual persons become a perceived virtue.

When I returned to the office, I outlined my plans to our staff. The concept of the "Oasis Ministry" must be preserved, even if its founder did not continue to head it. This diocese must defend its integrity and do it self-consciously. I must be allowed to speak everywhere I was given the opportunity or the invitation. We must be aggressive in seeking to turn this negativity around. With staff approval I then approached the lay and clergy leaders of the diocese. The leadership agreed. The standing committee, led by its president, Richard Shimpfky, and its senior clergy, Jack McKelvey and Jack Croneberger, requested and received a meeting with the presiding bishop to express their protest. The standing committee sent a letter to every bishop and standing committee of the church explaining our action. A search committee for a new head for the Oasis was formed, and in time the Reverend David Norgard was called to be the executive director and missioner. A more effective priest would be hard to imagine. His partner, Joseph, was also a great asset. Finally, I took my media experience and appealed to contacts in radio, television, and newspapers to get our story out. This diocese was committed to the full inclusion of homosexual people in the life of the church. We would not be deterred from that goal by the setback with Robert Williams.

I went to the meeting of the bishops of our province early in 1990 and confronted a rude Richard Grein of New York and a hostile Harold Robinson of Western New York. Dick Grein simply did not speak. Harold, on the other hand, spoke, but never said a kind word. I discovered later that he had received into our priesthood a completely uncloseted gay man who had formerly been a Roman Catholic priest. I told him I was glad he had changed his mind on this subject.

"I didn't know he was gay," Harold claimed.

"Well, then you are incompetent," I asserted, "for everybody in the gay community knew him well." It was a stinging and unkind retort. Harold was not malevolent. He just could not escape certain interior barriers. Homosexuality was one of them.

That year I addressed the National Conference of High-School Science Teachers in the Washington, D.C., area and the student body at Rollins College in Winter Park, Florida. When John Howe disinvited me from an invitation to preach at his cathedral, Barry Levas, a professor, opened the Rollins Chapel to me on that Sunday and I spoke to a packed house, including some members of the staff of the disinviting cathedral. Both John Boswell, of Yale's Department of History, and Krister Stendahl, then the chaplain at Harvard Divinity School, came powerfully to my aid quite publicly. I spoke in Edmonton and Manitoba. I led the clergy conference for the Diocese of Virginia. I stayed on the telephone with media people and call-in radio shows across the country. I defended our action in my columns in *The Voice,* which clearly became the best-read bishop's column in the United States, and I nurtured as best I could a hurt diocese and a hurt gay and lesbian community.

The person most caught in this struggle was our second openly gay candidate for holy orders, Barry Stopfel. Barry and his partner, Will Leckie, were both graduates of Union Seminary in New York. Barry was preparing to be ordained deacon in June 1990. He had the unanimous support of the decision-making bodies and was working as a part-time lay assistant to Jack Croneberger, our rector in Tenafly. Jack Croneberger's teenage son Tim had, in one of life's strange twists, made his contemplation of suicide known to his parents. Later Tim said that the reason for this threat was that he was gay and he did not believe his parents would ever accept him. That fear proved to be unfounded as Jack Croneberger dealt with this subject openly with his congregation during his sermons. Barry was a significant pastoral support to their family during this time. I believed he would make a superior priest. When he was ready for ordination, he was called to be an ordained assistant in that parish with the full knowledge that he and Will were a couple. I could not refuse to ordain him and still have any credibility left in the gay community I was so desperately seeking to win back into the church.

I communicated this to Ed Browning and got the sense that he went into apoplexy. He urged me to postpone Barry's ordination, at least until after the meeting of the House of Bishops in September. He would, he promised, ask me to postpone it no further, but he made it clear that he could not protect me if I proceeded. I discussed this with Barry and with the standing committee. No one was happy about this postponement, but everyone felt that it could be tolerated. I learned later that Barry was actually devastated by this decision and saw it as one more slap by an insensitive and unloving church. My actions in his view did not give integrity to my words.

When I ordained the deacons that year on the first Saturday in June, Barry was not present. Some of our clergy worked out their protest over that omission by coming to the altar, but refusing to receive the communion bread from my hand. Louie Crew, now a part of our diocese and earlier the founder of Integrity, announced that he would conduct a public fast from the communion table until this church was open to people like himself. It would be a long fast, but Louie came faithfully to the altar even as he went away hungry for what he called the Bread of Life.

In the midst of this struggle Nelson Thayer, whose task force had ignited the whole church, died tragically of a raging kidney malignancy that seemed to run in his family. In that death the church lost one of its finest priests and I lost one of my best personal friends. One graceful note that entered our diocesan life during this period of turmoil was that Richard

Shimpfky, president of the standing committee that approved Robert Williams for ordination, was elected bishop of the Diocese of El Camino Real (San Jose and Monterey to San Luis Obispo). No more appropriate symbol of the fact that those who stick by their principles finally win respect could be imagined. Our diocese was very proud of him and we were present in good numbers when he was consecrated in San Luis Obispo, California, on September 8, 1990, just prior to the first meeting of the House of Bishops since the ordination of Robert Williams.

That meeting was scheduled for September 14–20, 1990, in Washington, D.C. It would be Chris's first meeting with that body. We knew it would be a hostile gathering, but we decided we would go in with our flags flying. No matter what its outcome, I planned to ordain Barry Stopfel when it was over. I would rather be forced to resign with my integrity intact than to continue to serve as a bishop without it. Chris chose her wardrobe well for that gathering. She was in bright reds, oranges, and yellows. We would not play the role of either victim or wimp. She was actually magnificent. It was, however, a bit strange for her. She was never officially introduced or welcomed.

A motion was introduced by Bishop Wantland of Eau Claire, Wisconsin, to have the House of Bishops join in the action of official disassociation already pronounced by the presiding bishop and the provincial presidents. By this time both Ed Browning and most of the provincial presidents had changed their minds and were not willing to support this new action. They argued, weakly I thought, that the situation was different now from what it had been in February. The February action was appropriate to those circumstances, but it would not be appropriate eight months later. I did not understand that argument, but read it as their attempt to redeem themselves. But the "pound-of-flesh" bishops would have none of that. I came prepared not to defend myself, but to speak if a negative resolution was passed. The resolution came on the floor on about the fifth day. The advocates were familiar names: Clarence Pope, Maurice Benitez, Gordon Charleton (probably the most irrationally homophobic man I have ever met), Bill Frey, and John Howe, among others.

I had an agreement with Ed Browning that I would take no part in this debate. If I won the vote, I would say nothing. If I lost the vote, I wanted to be able, as a personal privilege, to address the House. Ed promised to accommodate that request. For two hours the debate raged. I got the sense from listening to those who spoke that it was going to be closer than my critics believed. I was ready no matter how the decision went.

Finally the time came for the vote. A request that it be by roll call was made. My critics wanted no anonymity. Everyone must be on record. The roll call began. When my name was called I voted "present." So did the retired bishop of Delaware, who certainly supported this cause, but felt strongly that retired bishops ought not to vote. Only one of the provincial presidents voted to support their own letter. Down to the last vote the issue was in doubt. When the suffragan bishop of North Carolina, Hunt Williams, voted to disassociate, the issue was decided. His was a vote I had thought would be positive. He had been a friend for many years and this stance was both disappointing and lacking integrity. The secretary of the House, Herb Donovan, announced that the House had disassociated itself from me and the Diocese of Newark in the action of ordaining Robert Williams by a vote of seventy-eight to seventy-four with two abstentions. If Hunt's vote had not been negative, a majority would not have been achieved.[2] I was actually quite pleased with the vote. From one supporter in February to seventy-four in September was a remarkable transformation. My critics could not believe the closeness of the vote. Since they talked only to people with whom they agreed, they thought that they would win this vote hands down.

I immediately stood up and asked to be recognized, requesting the personal privilege of addressing the House. Ed gave me the floor. I walked to the chair where he was presiding, placed my notes on the lectern, and began forty-five minutes of what surely must be described as passionate purple oratory. I recounted the history of our diocese's involvement with this issue, my studies at the Cornell Medical Center, and the willingness of our gay clergy to work in the most dangerous ghettoes in our inner cities and transform those places into communities of hope. I cited the people won back to Christ and the church by the work of the Oasis, which was finally counteracting the church's discrimination and abuse of gay people over the centuries. I described the priesthood in the Western Catholic tradition of Christianity as the primary closet for gay people. I raised to consciousness the gay influence on vestments, crucifixes, church appointments, and even theology. I urged the bishops to own the realities and to embrace what was now thought of as "this dark side" of Christian history. I dismissed the argument used against homosexual persons from the Scriptures as woefully inadequate in the light of modern science. I called ex-gay organizations fraudulent. I spoke of my own pride that I headed a diocese that would dare to reach beyond the traditional barriers of our classical prejudice, and I vowed that I would someday be just as proud of my whole church. I thanked them for giving me their attention and stepped down.

Walking to my desk, I received a "semi-standing ovation." That is, those who "ovated" stood to do so; those who did not "ovate" remained seated. The mood in the House had certainly changed. At least a dozen bishops gathered around my desk and said some version of "If I could have heard that speech before I voted, I would have changed my vote." At that moment I knew I finally had a majority in the House. It was not a majority I could count on to vote positively. It was, however, a majority I could count on to prevent the House from voting negatively. That majority has held in every general convention from that day to this, and it is growing.

My speech was reproduced for the media and distributed to the press. I was asked to hold a press conference. The mood was positive. My address, not the vote of disassociation, was the story of the day. I felt that victory had been snatched out of the jaws of defeat. My critics acted as if they had been defeated, and they were furious. I had incurred their unending hostility. I welcomed it.

That night two bishops came to me quietly and separately to tell me that they were gay. Both were married. Both had children. One had voted to associate, one to disassociate. The one who voted to disassociate had tears in his eyes. "I am so afraid," he said, "that I will be exposed. I cover that fear by being negative and harsh on this issue on every public occasion." Obviously I do not respect that attitude, but I do observe that it occurs frequently. The church is far more compromised on this issue than laypeople can ever imagine. That is why dishonesty about homosexuality in the church is so intense and is covered by such fearful hostility.

Also that night the only provincial president who had continued to support his earlier action to dissociate himself from me and the Diocese of Newark asked to speak to me. He was William F. (Dub) Wolfrum, the bishop suffragan of Colorado. I wondered what he wanted. "Jack," he said, "I have a gay priest in the Diocese of Colorado who needs to move and I don't think there is a chance we can move him in Colorado. Would you consider recommending him for a place in Newark?" I cannot relate here what I wanted to say at that moment. I just filed this conversation away, so that someday my readers would get an insight into how the church's bishops actually acted.

I still needed to make my intentions about Barry Stopfel known. I did not want to ask permission, because I was not planning to obey if permission were not given. I did not want to put Ed Browning in the position where he would be held accountable for my decision. So I did not talk to him directly. I talked to his two closest associates. They, I am certain, cleared this with Ed and the next day proposed that Barry's ordination to the diaconate proceed as planned. It might be worth considering to ask Walter Righter to do the ordination since the press was following me too closely, they suggested. "It would defuse it a bit," they continued, "if you were not the ordaining bishop. You could then ordain him to the priesthood some six months later."

It was an interesting solution. My primary concern was to get Barry ordained, not who did the ordaining. I returned home, spoke to Walter, who agreed at once, and then to Barry, who was elated. The date was set. It took place in the church where Barry worked and where Jack Croneberger was the rector. One man objected. The press was strangely absent. The strategy had worked. Little did I realize that some six years later Walter Righter would be put on trial for "heresy" for performing this ordination, which he could not have done without my permission and at my request. Why they picked Walter for this honor and not me, I do not know. If they thought they had picked a softer target, they would learn what I had always known about Walter—that he was made of steel.

The conservatives then announced that they would seek to amend the canons at the general convention of 1991 to prohibit the ordination of any additional homosexual people to the priesthood unless they took the vow of celibacy. The fight was not over yet. It would go on in the setting of the lay and clerical deputies, who are generally more liberal than the bishops. I was convinced we could win in this setting. I looked forward to this battle.

My heart sank, however, when Ed Browning called and asked me if I would be willing to postpone Barry Stopfel's ordination to the priesthood until after the 1991 general convention was convened in Phoenix. This man's ministry was destined to be the one on which the whole struggle of the church turned. Our standing committee, however, believed that this was a reasonable request. Since Barry was the assistant in Tenafly, the congregation would not be deprived of the Eucharist for waiting a few extra months. Barry was not pleased, but by this time he had accepted his role of an agent of change.

As we settled into a relatively normal diocesan routine after Barry's diaconal ordination, a call from Ruth Peacock of the BBC in London announced her desire to come to America to do a series of radio reports on me as a controversial American bishop. I agreed to this request, and both Chris and I looked forward to having her with us. She went with me on my two

Sunday visitations. In the morning I was in a vibrant, but quite formal, West Indian parish. That afternoon I was in a less dynamic, waspy suburban parish. Both of them, however, were vital and alive by British standards. Ruth seemed moved by both, but especially by the West Indian congregation.

Following the afternoon service, Ruth indicated a desire to be confirmed. It was hard to do in Britain, she said, because she needed to preserve a sense of objectivity in reporting religious news. But she had long ago moved out of the evangelical tradition of her father, a free-church pastor. In that suburban church in the early evening, we relit the candles, revested, and I confirmed this very special person. She is today a member officially of the Episcopal Church, so she is in communion with the Anglican Church in England. She has since served as church warden for St. James', Piccadilly Circus, in London. It was a wonderful touch with which to balance the events of that critical year.

We also elected a suffragan bishop that November. Jack McKelvey, president of our standing committee, was chosen on the sixth ballot. The runner-up was Mary Adelia McLeod, later to become America's first female diocesan bishop, in Vermont.

My last event of that year was to lead a clergy conference in the Diocese of Georgia at the invitation of one of our most conservative bishops, Harry Shipps. I was surprised to receive his invitation, but accepted it as a gracious and healing gesture. I did this conference on the content of my soon to be published book on the Bible. When the conference was over, I received a standing ovation from the clergy of south Georgia. Miracles never cease.

Chris and I celebrated rather quietly the first Christmas of our married life together and then we observed our first wedding anniversary at a service in St. Peter's Church in Morristown. I doubt if I could have survived that year had I not had her with me at every point. It was a bonding year for us both. We had descended into valleys and scaled heights in that twelve-month period that many people never achieve in a lifetime. We held each other closely and looked forward to whatever lay ahead.

---

1. Former Bishop Pope had a hard time making up his mind, for I learned that after more than a year back in the Anglican Communion, he once again defected to Rome, only to return a second time. Headline writers in religious journals loved to proclaim, "Pope Becomes Catholic Again," or "Pope Leaves Roman Catholic Church Again."

2. That would have made the vote seventy-seven to seventy-five with two abstentions. Seventy-seven would not have been 50 percent plus one of the total vote.

# I 9

# *Triumphs:*
# *The Koinonia Statement,*
# *Victory in the Heresy Trial,*
# *and Worldwide Invitations*

※

I F 1990 was the critical year of my professional life, then surely it could
be said that 1991 was the beginning of the longest and most creative
period of my career. The year began with the publication of *Rescuing the
Bible from Fundamentalism,* a book that zoomed to the top of the religious
books best-seller list,[1] claiming the number one position for eight straight
months. It sold more copies in its first year than all of my books, including
*Living in Sin?* had sold in their entire history. This made it one of the
best-selling religious books offering a liberal perspective in recent memory.
The media tour arranged by HarperCollins and directed by a publicist in
Chicago was incredibly successful. Major newspapers across the country
covered this book, including the *Wall Street Journal,* which gave it a rather
remarkable front-page story. Magazines, such as *Time* and *People,* did features. I was on every major television talk show and spoke with more than a
hundred radio stations, including my favorites on National Public Radio.

We made two trips to the United Kingdom in that year, the first to spend
the sabbatical month of February at Magdalen College, Oxford, and the second, for ten days in May to respond to the British media's interest in this
book. These visits continued to expand my horizons and open new doors to
me professionally. During the time at Magdalen, for example, I was introduced to the thinking of two great scholars—a University of Birmingham

New Testament professor named Michael Goulder and the radical Cambridge theologian Don Cupitt. Both of these men would become mentors and friends. Goulder's work was brought to my attention by the dean at Magdalen, the Reverend Dr. Jeffrey John.

Goulder's life and story were unique. He had been a priest of the Church of England and even a candidate to be bishop of Hong Kong, but in the early 1980s he had resigned from the priesthood and began to call himself an atheist. He even wrote a book in which he defended his newly minted atheist position.[2] Nonetheless, he continued to teach the New Testament and his work was so fresh and so innovative that I was captivated by it. I had not yet met Michael, but I would a year later, and his thought was destined to shape my study life for five years, during which time I would write three books, each of which reflected his influence.[3] It was not easy to locate Michael's books, since most of them were out of print save for a commentary he had written on Luke in 1989,[4] which I bought to take home with me. It would be one of the great reading experiences of my life.

I became aware of Don Cupitt when a London cousin of mine, a serious Christian, asked me to read a Cupitt book entitled *The Sea of Faith,*[5] which obviously had disturbed him greatly. I read this book with increasing enthusiasm and with the same response that I had to *Honest to God* more than fifteen years earlier. It moved me to a totally new place. Cupitt focused what had been for me only a vague sense that the problem facing the church was a fundamental inability to use our traditional religious words any longer. These words had become meaningless jargon or expressions of irrelevant piety. He outlined with remarkable clarity the apologetic problems, created by the knowledge revolution in the Western world, that now faced every traditional Christian creedal understanding. He chronicled the intellectual, scientific, and philosophical mountaintops dotting Western history that rendered most of our ancient theological formulas inoperative. Yet Christian leaders continued to parrot these phrases as if they still communicated great meaning. I had more difficulty embracing Cupitt's prescription for dealing with this crisis, but I was stunned by the brilliance of his analysis.

Above all else, I knew I wanted to know this man better and engage his thought more deeply. So I simply went to the phone and called him at Cambridge, happy to discover that my public reputation meant I did not have to explain who I was. He invited me to come to Cambridge and a relationship of great admiration and affection began with this remarkable man whose intellectual journey had taken him so far beyond his religious roots that he was almost driven to build a whole new place that religion might inhabit. Most of his critics had minds so circumscribed by traditional dogma that they could not even imagine Don's new place, and so they condemned him as "an atheist theologian." An atheist theologian is one who does not affirm the God concept of his critics. Don shared with me the fact that only three Anglican bishops in the world still spoke to him. It is strange how religious disagreement so often brings about personal rudeness.

I was to have an opportunity to engage Don much more extensively when I was notified of my election as Quatercentenary Fellow of Emmanuel College, Cambridge, for the spring term 1992. The opportunity to spend a full semester at Cambridge as an elected fellow was an enormous honor. I looked forward to it with great relish. Indeed, the anticipation brightened every day from my election to my arrival.

The year 1991 was also the year in which our newly elected bishop suffragan was consecrated, and for the first time in my career I had a full-time episcopal assistant. Jack Marston McKelvey, was one of my favorite clergy leaders in the diocese. A competent giant of a man, he not only undergirded my career, but through his own gifts and talents expanded the office of the bishop dramatically. I often wondered how I had managed to work without him. He cut the frenzy out of my life and that allowed both of us to do better the things each of us was capable of doing. I, for example, decided to use the resource and presence of this good man to enable me to offer more public lectures in the diocese, so that our clergy and laypeople could grapple with the same issues I was studying. In this manner I found the means and the opportunity to externalize my own internal debate within a very open community of faith. So, from that year until my retirement, in addition to my annual New Dimensions lectures, I delivered three Lenten lectures and two fall lectures each year.

These opportunities enabled me to test, prior to publication and among people for whom I cared deeply, the ideas that later would be found in my books. I discovered, reminiscent of my experience in both Lynchburg and Richmond, that laypeople are far more open to this exploratory enterprise than are clergy. The greatest resistance to my intellectual challenges to the traditional Christian formulations would always come from the ranks of the ordained, both bishops and priests, many of whom were simply unable to see, much less to appreciate, the vision out of which I was speaking. That fact always worried me, for I saw no way this kind of defensive ordained leadership could ever direct the church that I loved into the future it must inhabit if it was going to live in the world that was being created before our very eyes. Our world is not one of miracle and magic in which virgins give birth, wise men follow a wandering star, or resuscitated bodies walk out of a tomb three days after burial. Literalized, those stories are nothing but religious nonsense. Yet I remain convinced that those symbols of our faith story could each still be opened to new meaning for those of us who have a real desire to worship God with our minds. Unfortunately, I discovered that the majority of ordained people appear to live inside a secure network of traditional propositional statements that by and large had only "mantra" power for them. A mantra is certainly not capable of being explored intellectually unless it has been broken dramatically out of its literalistic frame of reference. Listening to a conservative biblical scholar like N. T. (Tom) Wright try to make a case for the literalness of the legend of the virgin birth, for example, at the beginning of the third millennium was simultaneously amusing and depressing.[6] He was a propagandist rather than an educator. A church in which the outdated thought of Tom Wright was given either honor or credibility was not a church that would endure into many tomorrows. Yet so many of our ordained leaders, like Tom Wright, speak to a world that no longer exists.

The reality of this dilemma would create the environment in which my professional life would be lived for the balance of my days. I became increasingly committed to fashioning a diocese that allowed our clergy the freedom to risk, the ability to envision the future, and the capacity to experiment with liturgy, theology, and ecclesiology. My goal and my vocation was to open doors through which some people could make the transition into the future of our faith story. Without that transition, I was convinced Christianity would die.

In my continuing battle to encourage an inclusive church where gay and lesbian people would be treated with justice and respect, 1991 was also a crucial turning point.

The general convention of our church held its regular triennial meeting that July in Phoenix. It was, at least up to that time, the most acrimonious church gathering I had attended in my entire career. Because of my public positions and actions, I was clearly at the center of that acrimony. The conservatives vowed to push for what came to be called the "Frey Amendment," sponsored by the now resigned bishop of Colorado, William Frey. This proposal sought to amend the canons of the church to prohibit specifically any further public ordinations of open and partnered homosexual persons.

Around that central debate were many smaller ancillary battles. Church leaders, in what I had come to recognize was typical of institutional religion, wanted to address this issue by appointing a special task force to study yet again the whole subject of sexuality and especially homosexuality. The fact that we had already done that through the Standing Commission on Human Affairs and Health on two separate occasions—one in 1979 and the other in 1988—did not seem to be noticed. No matter how we sought to dance around this issue, it was an idea whose time had come, and it simply would not go away. Ed Browning had by this time removed me from the Standing Commission on Human Affairs and Health by not reappointing me to that body after the 1988 convention, so ending the only opportunity I would ever have to work for change inside the ecclesiastical structures. Ed salved his conscience by appointing me to the Pastoral Letter Committee and the Theology Committee, both of which had status but little effective power.[7] From that day until I retired I would influence the church solely through my personal external challenges.

Thus the first great battle at the Phoenix convention was over who would constitute the membership of this newly proposed ad hoc task force on sexuality. The issue was whether open, self-accepting homosexuals should be appointed. The bishop of West Texas, John McNaughton, argued strongly against such a possibility, saying that openly gay people would be nothing but lobbyists for a cause and would have no objectivity. He implied that homosexual people had no gifts to bring to any enterprise other than that of their sexual orientation, which in his mind defined them.

In the subsequent debate I called that mentality nothing short of blatant homophobia and countered that it would be today unthinkable in this church to appoint a task force to consider racial issues without giving it a racially diverse membership; nor would we appoint a task force to look into women's issues with no women on it. The bishop of West Texas took great umbrage at being called homophobic, and the debate degenerated into open hostility. Most religious people are nervous nellies when it comes to genuine conflict. The House of Bishops was no different. Led by the bishop of Connecticut, Arthur Walmsley, the suggestion was made that this angry House go into executive session to deal with the hostility that seemed to be tearing the bishops apart. Ed Browning agreed and for several days in that convention, he tried to turn this raucous and deeply divided gathering into a confidential, sharing therapy group. It was about as confidential as a radio broadcast. Within ten minutes after I had spoken in this "confidential setting," a ranking member in one of the most conservative lobby groups in the church told me, almost verbatim, what I had said.

Ed kept trying, however, and this tactic resulted in a series of bishops' meetings apart from spouses and the press that would be convened at Kanuga for the next seven years. In these nonlegislative sessions Ed tried to lower the decibels. He brought in a priest monastic to serve as chaplain to the bishops and to lead our daily meditations, which were to be part of a process in which we would "worship together, pray together, study the Bible together, and seek to build across our differences a sense of episcopal community"—nice words, but out of touch with reality. In fact, never have I been part of more dishonest gatherings where, in the name of piety, attempts were made to repress differences rather than to deal with them. So I clenched my teeth, listened to pious words, went through the motions of worship, and endured massive amounts of thinly veiled hostility being pronounced in the name of Bible study. So ineffective were these gatherings that, far from building community, they resulted finally in an attempt on the part of our right-wing bishops to purge the House of those whom the conservatives had identified as the primary "troublers of Israel."

None of this, however, stopped Ed Browning from trying to heal this breach in community until about a year or so before his retirement, when he finally gave up and faced the fact that there can be no compromise between those who regard homosexuality as a sin that cannot be accepted and those who regard it as an aspect of our humanity that needs to be affirmed. At the Phoenix general convention the House finally refused to mandate any category for those who would be appointed to that task force, leaving the issue to the presiding bishop, and openly gay persons were made members. Chaired by Richard Grein, the bishop of New York, the task force was directed to report to the general convention of 1994. The church loves to pretend to deal with an issue by studying it for three more years.

At this same tension-filled gathering an attempt was also made by the bishop of Oklahoma, Gerry McAllister, to censure Walter Righter, the assistant bishop of Newark, for ordaining Barry Stopfel to the diaconate and Ron Haines, the bishop of Washington, for ordaining a lesbian to the priesthood. Again, there was passionate debate filled with righteous rhetoric. More and more bishops, however, began to share their experiences in dealing with individual gay and lesbian clergy. It was self-evident that the policy of the church did not prohibit the ordination of homosexual persons. It was more an ecclesiastical version of "Don't ask, don't tell" and, above all, don't raise questions or act honestly. At least three bishops—Robert Anderson of Minnesota, George Hunt of Rhode Island, and Edward Jones of Indianapolis—stated on the floor that if Righter and Haines were censured, they should be also, for they had all knowingly ordained homosexual clergy living in monogamous relationships. This public testimony clearly expanded the issue, and as a result the censure resolution failed.

When the proposed amendment to the canons that would prohibit the ordinations of noncelibate homosexual people finally came up, it was not in the form of a canonical change, but rather of a mandated resolution. It was also proposed not by Bishop Frey, but by John Howe of Central Florida. A roll call vote was requested. By a ninety-three to eighty-five margin, with five abstentions and two absentees, the House of Bishops refused to write this prohibition into the guidelines of our common life. The majority that I believed was created after my address on the vote of disassociation a year earlier had held. I was elated. I called Barry Stopfel immediately, and we set the date for his ordination to the priesthood for the first mutually convenient Saturday after my return to the office in September. I insisted on doing this ordination personally. I would never again step aside for political reasons to avoid conflict, no matter who requested it. As this convention came to an end, my deep sense was that I had won. It would take the church almost a decade to pass the positive legislation, but the war had been won, even if there were battles still to be fought. I felt totally vindicated.

One other event occurred during that convention that once again forced me to recognize that I was now a very public person. Christine and I received an invitation to bring greetings to the national convention of the Metropolitan Community Church, also meeting in Phoenix. The MCC was a church founded by a Pentecostal pastor, Troy Perry, when he was removed from his ministry after his homosexuality was discovered. This was to be a church for gay and lesbian people who found themselves no longer welcome in their various congregations, and it cut across the spectrum of Christian traditions. We were pleased to accept their invitation.

Troy Perry and his top aides entertained us at a small dinner party prior to the meeting. The place was under heavy security. It made me deeply aware of the environment of hostility in which openly homosexual people are frequently forced to live. When the time came for us to go to the convention center, Troy divided his top aides, and they went in separate cars. If the leader was killed, the others knew how to step up and keep the movement going. Most heterosexual people have never had to function in such a combative atmosphere. We arrived safely and walked into an assembly of twelve hundred homosexual persons. As Christine and I appeared at the door, with no announcement and no introduction, the assembled host rose and gave us a thunderous ovation lasting about ten minutes. Both of us were deeply touched. When Troy finally got their attention, he introduced me. Again the applause was overwhelming. I spoke for a very few minutes, relating some of our experiences in the Diocese of Newark. Then I introduced Christine, who also spoke. She told them what it meant to her to be present at this gathering with her life partner and urged them to cling to, rejoice in, and uphold their commitments to their life partners. It was so simple, so direct, and so affirming for the people of this gathering, most of whom were with partners neither the secular society nor the mainline churches were willing to recognize. But Christine did recognize them, and again they applauded while we, holding hands, fought back tears. I embraced Chris and thanked God silently that I was blessed with such a wife.

With this latest battle now won, we left a day early and flew to Los Angeles and then on to Sydney to begin our first tour of the lands we refer to as "down under." It was an incredible visit. The HarperCollins Australian publicist who arranged the itinerary for us was Andy Palmer, one of the most remarkable young men I have ever met. We made more than two hundred public appearances in Australia and New Zealand over the next six weeks.

In Australia every major newspaper interviewed us, and almost every televised talk show had me as a guest. That included morning television, late-night television, and the Australian version of *Meet the Press.* The national news magazine did a feature. Radio stations, both national and local, including "teen radio," clamored for interview time. I spoke to packed auditoriums in Sydney, Brisbane, Melbourne, Canberra, and Perth. Of course I raised up a mighty tide of conservative Christian opposition. Two people took over the microphones in Perth, where more than a thousand people had gathered in a school auditorium during a rainstorm. These two, who identified themselves as evangelicals, proceeded to scream incoherently at me and the crowd. A conservative religious columnist in a national paper wrote not one, but two columns condemning me and my point of view. Finally, the leaders of the very conservative Archdiocese of Sydney spewed forth what could only be called venom. None of them could deny, however, that we had raised into public view a mighty following of spiritually hungry people that their conservative institutions were not feeding. That did not stop them from stooping to attacks on my being, my faith, and my sincerity.

The positive response, however, was such that a second tour was planned for 1994, and indeed a third tour was ultimately scheduled for 1997.

Moving on to New Zealand, we encountered the same hunger for faith combined with integrity and honesty. Here the tour was directed by the talented and competent Elizabeth Boys Robinson, at that time the director of the Anglican Bookstore of Wellington. She and her husband, Geoffrey Robinson, the morning voice of Radio New Zealand, were destined to become close friends. By now the fundamentalists had begun to strike back publicly, so I had to walk through picket lines to give a lecture in Wellington. We crisscrossed this exquisitely beautiful, small country, speaking in every major population center on both islands.

We were deeply drawn to the people in New Zealand, including that nation's great liberal Christian voice Lloyd Geering, whose earlier endorsement of my 1983 book, *Into the Whirlwind,* on his radio program had first created excitement about my work in that part of the world. On a per capita basis, sales of my books have been better in those two nations in the South Pacific than in any other English-speaking country in the world.

While in Wellington, we crossed paths with Don Cupitt and his wife, Susan, on a lecture tour. Radio New Zealand arranged for Lloyd Geering, Don Cupitt, and me to do a two-hour trialogue hosted by Neville Glasgow. As strange as it seems, I was the only one still affiliated with the institutional church. My vocation was then, as it is now, to be an agent for the reformation of the church. Both Lloyd and Don no longer felt the institution was either willing or able to be reformed. That difference produced the tension in this program, making it fascinating listening and resulting in the sale of more copies of the tape of this program by Radio New Zealand than any other program they had ever broadcast up to that time. It was also later voted the "Radio Program of the Year" in New Zealand. Once again, I was made aware of the vast audience of searching, but not institutionally related, people by and large ignored by the church.

We returned home leaving a host of friends, new readers, and new respondents in both countries. We looked forward to our return. As we refreshed ourselves from these strenuous activities at our favorite beach retreat, we knew that our lives were now different, that we were no longer private citizens, and that we inhabited a new place in life. It was filled with both opportunities and dangers.

Encouraged by my editor at HarperCollins, Jan Johnson, I began to draw into readiness my book on the birth narratives of the New Testament and their impact on the role of women throughout Western history. This was a book motivated by a deeply personal agenda. I wanted to write it so that my daughters might be helped to escape the negativity with which the Christian church has traditionally viewed women. Those three young women, Ellen, Katharine, and Jaquelin, plus Chris's daughter, Rachel, were almost visibly before my eyes as I wrote every word of that final text. It was due for publication in fall 1992 just in time for Christmas!

That book set the pattern that my life would follow for the next few years. *Born of a Woman: A Bishop Rethinks the Virgin Birth and the Treatment of Women by a Male-Dominated Church* came out in 1992. Its companion piece, *Resurrection: Myth or Reality? A Bishop's Search for the Origins of Christianity,* came out in 1994. *Liberating the Gospels: Reading the Gospels with Jewish Eyes,* the book that most profoundly reflected my indebtedness to Michael Goulder, followed in 1996. Harper introduced each book with a ten-city media tour, which was often expanded to about twenty cities by incorporating my own lecture circuit.

With each book we would also spend at least a week in London doing media events as well as time in Toronto. Invitations to speak in Great Britain and Canada were plentiful. My schedule was both heavy and deeply fulfilling.

My ultimate commitment, however, was not to this ancillary career, but to the Diocese of Newark. My vocation and conscience dictated that my work as a bishop inside the diocese must get not only the lion's share of my time and energy, but that it must be quality time. That diocese made everything else possible. I struggled daily to make sure that I was faithful to this trust. Sometimes that commitment made for very long hours.

Developing the lives and ministry of our clergy was my highest responsibility as a bishop. That sometimes meant supporting such obvious things as seeing to it that clergy salaries were raised with regularity, adding benefits such as dental insurance to the clergy package, monitoring the health insurance provisions to make sure that there was quality care, making scholarship funds available for the college education of clergy children, developing an equity-sharing program so that when clergy retired from a lifetime of living in church-supplied housing, they would have a sufficient down payment to buy a home. Beyond these things, bishops are always a role model for the clergy simply by what they do, what principles they are not willing to compromise, and how they confront issues, pursue truth, refuse to tolerate abuse, engage in study, and are faithful to the demands of the profession.

Those are powerful, if unconscious, teaching moments. I rejoice today when I realize that from the clergy ranks of our diocese, during my years as a bishop, have come five new bishops, six cathedral deans, and the cardinal rectors of such diverse dioceses as Western Massachusetts, Western Michigan, Kentucky, Connecticut, Rhode Island, New Jersey, Washington, D.C., and Southern Virginia. At the same time our own diocese continues to be stocked with outstanding young clergy talent, among whom are clearly more bishops, more deans, and more cardinal rectors.

Additionally, it was my responsibility as the bishop to make certain that we managed for the long term the financial assets of the diocese. During my tenure in office, through incredible lay leadership, changes in our investment policies meant that the diocesan investment account grew from $5 million to $40 million. In addition to that, we raised in three capital-fund campaigns a sum that stands today at more than $8 million, while at the same time we were placing into our structures and programs almost an equal amount produced by the income from these funds.

We also did the hard work of combining small and, in some instances dying, churches to provide a critical mass of people and thus to enhance life in places where congregations over the years had been reduced to nothing more than holding operations. But though these things represented the core duties of my office and on these issues I spent the majority of my time, none of these activities will form my legacy. The world would little note, nor long remember, who did these things, though to me they were a privileged opportunity and among those who stood at the core of the life of the diocese, there has been appreciation that I did them well.

My legacy was, however, created in the public response that arose from my teaching and writing life. Each book seemed to open up new audiences. *Born of a Woman* carried me first to Ann Arbor, Michigan, for a series of lectures at St. Andrew's Church and at the University of Michigan. Next I flew to the Montreat Center in the mountains of western North Carolina to address a group of Presbyterians, and finally to California to lead a clergy conference in the Diocese of El Camino Real. My contacts with the Metropolitan Community Church in Phoenix opened other invitations to address various parts of that faith tradition, including a regional gathering in Tampa, Florida, where I experienced incredible anger and rudeness from the Episcopal bishop, Rogers Harris, for what he regarded as an invasion of "his territory." Absorbing the abuse of threatened conservative bishops became almost my daily bread.

Early 1992 found me at my seminary before an absolutely packed dining hall debating the issue of homosexuality with my old nemesis John Howe of Central Florida. That experience fascinated me on several levels. First, John was visibly nervous, muttering beforehand that he was "not very good at this sort of thing." He urged me not to flip a coin to determine the order of speaking, but to allow him to be the second speaker.

When John spoke, he used the evangelical party line about the Bible condemning homosexuality to diminish the insights I had sought to develop during my presentation. The audience had the opportunity to be challenged by me and then to have their prejudices reinforced by John. In his closing remarks after the question period, John tried to be cute by caricaturing some of my book titles and lifting me up for ridicule. It was not cleverly done and fell with an embarrassing thud on the audience. In my closing remarks, I simply ignored his gaffs and spoke to the issues. The audience applauded our efforts, and I went out to have a late-night snack with a group of that seminary's closeted gay and lesbian members, whom the faculty supposedly did not know existed, along with a few gay people from Washington, including a Roman Catholic priest whom I greatly admired.

John Howe and I had both agreed that the entire debate could be audiotaped and the tapes made available at cost to anyone who wished to have them. Imagine my surprise when I discovered that the tapes had been doctored to make John Howe's closing statement more positive! It was one more demonstration of the fact that evangelical religion appears to breed dishonesty and that the more overtly pious people attempt to be, the more they must hide their anger and their lack of character, not just from others, but from themselves.

As my orbit of influence continued to expand, I received invitations to carry my message to university campuses in the United Kingdom, Canada, and the United States. These opportunities were always invigorating, because the audience frequently brought both openness and religious ignorance into the dialogue. That at least was true unless some college fundamentalist organization, like Campus Crusade for Christ, decided to use the occasion of my visit to organize a "witness for Jesus" against the infidel.

That happened at the University of Maryland, where I addressed a large audience of what seemed to be appreciative students, at least until the question period, when I began to be aware that at each of the four or five microphones that had been placed in the auditorium aisles to facilitate dialogue with students, campus fundamentalists were standing three or four deep. I never got a question that escaped the presupposition of literalness. I heard the historicity of Adam and Eve upheld as well as the contention, voiced rather stridently, that the original Greek of the Gospels was, in fact, the language Jesus spoke and that it had been literally recorded. I went from microphone to microphone in recognizing questioners, but it was to no avail. All of them were fundamentalists. The majority of the audience voted with their feet, and when the question period came to an end, only about a tenth of the original audience remained.

I discovered that appreciation and opposition played off each other. As invitations grew in number, so did the number of those threatened by things I had to say. I encountered individual hecklers in many places, especially in the United Kingdom, where there is a kind of evangelical subculture that infects the established church. It has power beyond its numbers because most people in the United Kingdom do not go to church anymore. Leaders of the establishment kept the lid on this ecclesiastical subculture over the years by choosing bishops who were generally out of the Oxford/Cambridge axis of English social life. The evangelicals had local pastors, including well-known preachers and evangelists, like John Stott, pastor of All Souls', Langham Place, in London. But by and large the key ecclesiastical positions were filled with English gentry or at least with bright, gentry wannabes from Oxbridge. That safeguard was violated by Margaret Thatcher, who late in her political career appointed a thoroughgoing evangelical named George Carey to be archbishop of Canterbury. He would prove to be both an embarrassment and a disaster to the efforts of the Anglican Communion to be a bridge church into the future.

In July 1993, I was invited to join the faculty of the Vancouver School of Theology summer school while, by coincidence, John Stott was also lecturing at Regent College, the evangelical wing of the University of British Columbia. With our deeply contrasting views of Anglicanism, we were invited to debate changing sexual values at the Anglican cathedral in Vancouver.

Arriving some twenty minutes before the appointed hour, I was amazed to find a long line of people waiting to get in. The cathedral, which seats about a thousand, was already packed and a room in the parish house had been opened to take care of the overflow. Sex appeared to be an exciting subject in Vancouver that summer.

The moderator for this event was the dean of the cathedral, the Very Reverend Michael Ingham.[8] John Stott and I each made opening statements reflecting well our differing perspectives. Then we responded to a series of questions from the audience. These questions could be addressed to either of us, and the other could comment on the answer. I became aware during the question period that John Stott was finding this a very different audience from those he normally addressed. Evangelicals hardly ever enter the world in which their critics live. My presence on the ticket had attracted a significant number of people who had been hurt by the church, disillusioned ex-fundamentalists, divorced people, and, obviously, gay and lesbian people.

Among the homosexual members of the audience were those who continued to be affiliated with the church as well as those who counted the church as their primary oppressor. Many of these people challenged John Stott with questions he had never faced before, making him articulate some rather outrageous positions in which it was apparent that neither John's love nor God's love could embrace those who were assumed to be outside the boundaries of a controlling sexual propriety. Divorce was a sin, he suggested, and remarriage barely possible. Homosexuals would have to repent and change if they wanted to get to heaven. As the drumbeat of challenging questions continued, John became more and more uncomfortable and his answers more and more bizarre. He even spent time defending his single status as not reflecting homosexuality, an issue no one had raised. He was clearly relieved when the question period was brought to a close.

Both of us had been asked to prepare five-minute closing statements, which I had done. John, however, believed that he could do that on the spot, drawing on the events of the evening. His closing remarks reflected both his shock and his lack of preparation. He resorted to name-calling, claiming that I could not be a Christian while holding the ideas I had advanced, which were, in his mind, so totally condemned in Holy Scripture. I was disappointed, but not surprised by his behavior. I had long come to expect that of conservative, evangelical Christians.

In my statement, which came last, I defended a new openness on the church's part to women, divorced people, and homosexuals. I stated that we had uncloseted homosexual priests living with their partners and serving with distinction in the Diocese of Newark. I went into some of the scientific data that required a new nonjudgmental approach on the part of the church and expressed an appreciation that my part of the church had clearly moved in that direction.

I had agreed to have a complete transcript of the debate published by the Regent College magazine. It did not occur to me that they might alter the text. Imagine my surprise when I discovered that I faced another John Howe–type episode. The college actually extended to John Stott the privilege of writing a new conclusion to cover his dreadful performance. They justified this subterfuge with the incredible claim that I had violated the rules of the debate by introducing new ideas in my concluding remarks to which John Stott did not have an opportunity to respond. They were, therefore, in the name of fairness giving their champion an opportunity to address this imbalance. I was amazed yet again to discover the basic lack of integrity and honesty in conservative evangelicals. My respect for John Stott dropped substantially. This episode, however, seems to have been widely reported in Anglican evangelical circles around the world, for evangelicals' intense anger toward the one who was thought to have embarrassed their hero would flow toward me from Africa, Australia, New Zealand, and Canada, and I would confront it in every subsequent visit to the United Kingdom.

Early in the following year, while doing a series of lectures at Christiana Hundred, Delaware, the rector, Adam Lewis, suggested that I might consider starting a videotape library of my lectures for rental or sale. "You are carrying out a one-man crusade," he admonished, "and one man can never travel enough to be present in all the places necessary to give the crusade momentum. Videos and tapes, however, could." That was true enough, but I had neither the interest nor the time to organize one more activity. Such a project would require the raising of money to finance the operation, and I really was at the limit in my attempt to balance my dual vocations. So I responded with gratitude, but with neither enthusiasm nor desire.

Several weeks later, while conducting diocesan Lenten lectures in Englewood, New Jersey, the same issue arose during the question period. "Have you ever considered the possibility of videotaping these lectures, so that they could be used in places where you might never get?" I was asked. In response I told my questioner that this idea had recently come up in Delaware and that I had neither the money nor the time to give to such an activity. When the evening ended, a man and his wife (who asked that their names not be used in this book), both doctors, he an M.D. whose life had been dedicated to medical research and she with a Ph.D. in physiology, presented me on the spot their personal check for $20,000 to launch such an enterprise.

I was amazed. I did not know these people, though I had seen them at previous lectures in the diocese. He was raised as a Roman Catholic; she had been nurtured in one of the mainline Protestant traditions. Both had been unable to combine their childhood religious training with their enhanced education and knowledge, and yet their religious interests were still intense. They were associated informally with a Unitarian fellowship and had heard about me through a friend. They attended my nearby public lectures. They were quite eager to build a new religious consciousness and had been greatly encouraged by the things they perceived me to be saying.

I was appreciative of their interest, but declined their $20,000 offer, since I had no structure set up for it and therefore no way to be accountable.

"Why don't you create such a structure?" they asked.

"I would be glad to cooperate if there were a structure, but I don't have the time or the desire to engage in an activity that would feel like self-promotion," was my response.

These two doctors replied, as they took back their check, that if such a structure were ever created, their offer still stood.

I thought about the possibility for about a week, primarily because Christine seemed to think it was a good idea and had a personal desire to pursue it. I suggested she talk with Adam Lewis and a few others and see if any interest lay in developing it. I should have known that, given Chris's thoroughness and competence, there was no chance it would remain a disincarnate idea.

Within six months Christianity for the Third Millennium came into being, with Adam as its first president, one of the doctors as vice president, Christine as secretary, and the other doctor as treasurer; the last of whom wrote checks on their joint gift, for that was, at that time, all the money we had. That organization continues to exist and flourish today and now has a part-time executive director. Over the years CTM, as it has come to be called, has produced videos of my lectures, sold countless numbers of audiotapes, bought up all copies of my out-of-print titles, republished some of them, issued study guides on my books, and networked with other progressive Christian groups throughout the nation to build a movement far bigger than anything I could have done alone. I have donated to CTM the rights to audio- or videotape anything I do anywhere. I have never accepted a cent from this organization. Indeed, over the years Christine and I have contributed, as part of our tithe, thousands of dollars to its work. The organization now appears strong enough to outlast my career and to continue to make the resources of frontier Christian thinkers available to ordinary Christians all over the world who are working for the reformation of Christianity. There is

no doubt in my mind but that Christine and the two doctors have been the
driving force behind this organization.

In these struggles to change hearts and minds in the life of both church
and society, one develops a sensitivity toward those who are or have been
bearing the burden or "taking the heat." In our travels to the United
Kingdom we had often touched the life of an organization known as the
Lesbian and Gay Christian Movement (LGCM). Its executive director, the
Reverend Richard Kirker, was a Church of England deacon whose bishop,
Graham Leonard of London, had refused to ordain him to the priesthood
because he was a gay man living with his partner. Richard then helped to
found the LGCM as an ecclesiastical lobby group, which meant that he lived
his life in the eye of the storm without support from any bishop. Even gay
clergy, frightened by Richard's confrontational style, which threatened the
silent accommodation they had worked out with the church, joined in regular attacks upon him. To provide Richard with some badly needed sabbatical time away from the stress and tension of his job, we invited him to spend
three months working as an assistant in the Oasis ministry under the leadership of David Norgard. In this manner we joined together the primary ministries with and for gay and lesbian Christians in our two countries.

A couple of years later the network grew once more when David
Norgard's partner was promoted and transferred to San Francisco and
David resigned in order to accompany him to the West Coast. There he
founded Oasis California, and so our work for the acceptance of homosexual people into the full life of the church stretched not just from London to
Newark, but also from coast to coast in America. To bring these outposts
together, not by linking dioceses, but by creating a chain of Oasis congregations across both this nation and the United Kingdom that would advertise
publicly their commitment to inclusivity, became a stated joint goal. Christianity for the Third Millennium joined this effort, convinced, as I am, that
congregations open on the issue of gay and lesbian people might also be
open to exploring deeply the intellectual revolution and the faith crisis of
our time. We sought to build congregations that would welcome people
who came, in the words of the old hymn, "just as I am without one plea,"
and that would also invite the spiritual seekers and searchers of our world
to join in the journey into the mystery of God that would be offered in
those places.

Despite these initiatives I still had to recognize that institutional
Christianity moves at a snail's pace. Change seems to scare religious people

who appear to have a major investment in the status quo with which they have made peace. To bring a new consciousness to a religious mentality requires both time and vigilance, for the institution is always prone to drift back into the patterns of oppression. Watching our church move through the regular cycle of the triennial general conventions seeking to develop a new consciousness on issues of human sexuality made that quite obvious. The battle won on the roll call vote in 1991 would have to endure the undermining not just of the defeated minority, but also of its weaker supporters in 1994 before it finally got established in 1997.

The 1994 crisis came through the report of the task force on this subject, which generated such heated debate in Phoenix. The appointed chair, Richard Grein, the bishop of New York, was anything but effective. The first draft of this task force report reached our hands several months before the general convention was to convene in Indianapolis. It was a pale, uncommitted, and weak, but not destructive, report. It did not move the church forward, but it did appear to protect the progress we had made. I felt it was probably the best I could hope for as the church absorbed the changing world. However, many on the conservative side of the aisle engaged this report with vigor. Indeed, so fearful were these bishops, located primarily in the South and Southwest and led by my 1991 adversary, John McNaughton of San Antonio, that they sought to preempt the official report of this body by issuing their own statement in advance. Their statement was a clarion call into yesterday, a reaffirmation of what they called traditional family values. "Traditional family values," I was to learn, was political and religious code language for deeply homophobic attitudes. This document was signed by about a hundred bishops, perhaps 40 percent of whom were either retired or on the verge of retirement. Of the signatories, one suffered from Alzheimer's disease and two were men in their nineties. The typical reader of the religious press would not know these things, but would be impressed only with the number of signatures. It was clear that this was one more conservative attempt to reassert a point of view that was both uninformed and dying.

Liberal Christians, however, tend to be emotionally soft, and Richard Grein and his task force members were prime examples. They decided that the way to handle this challenge was to incorporate some of the insights of this conservative statement into their report in order to preserve that "idol" of most ecclesiastical gatherings—"the unity of the church." A second draft of the report, turning significantly in a conservative direction, was issued. It was not yet so negative that it would destroy my willingness to support it as an interim statement of where the church was on these emotional topics. It still kept the doors open to progress and change.

The dialogue, however, continued between these conservative bishops and task force members, resulting in a third draft that was even more conservative and traditional, pushing my willingness to support it to the very edge. I let it be known through contacts that I was certain would get back to Bishop Grein that if this report were revised again in the same direction, I would no longer be willing to vote for it and, if necessary, would create a more positive minority report. My sole purpose in that communication was to strengthen Richard Grein's obviously weak backbone.

We arrived in Indianapolis for that 1994 gathering to discover that the press reports of our debate on the homosexual issue had drawn to our convention the most hostile picketers imaginable. Non-Episcopalians from places as far away as Kansas and led by one of that state's most viscerally homophobic ideologues were present with very young children carrying hate-filled placards about "queers" and quoting biblical sources like Leviticus to inform passers-by that God wants all homosexuals put to death. AIDS, they proclaimed, was God's punishment on queers! One sign announced "Spong and Tutu are fag lovers." The messages were filled with such hate that it was difficult not to believe that some of the demonstrators might be prone to violence. My sense is that their rhetoric was so vicious and excessive that it actually swayed the center of our church toward a more progressive stance. Very few people wanted to be identified with the level of prejudice they manifested.

When Integrity, the national gay and lesbian organization for Episcopalians, held a public worship service in the Episcopal cathedral, Indianapolis police kept the picketers away. Even so, there was a note of apprehension and danger inside, because clearly some had come not to worship, but to observe—conservatives scouting out the opposition. I was one of a small group of bishops who were invited by Integrity to vest and take part in the service. Sitting in the congregation, Christine found herself behind a couple not participating in the service. As she stood to sing a hymn, she glanced down and spotted a message on a piece of paper cradled in the hand of one of the apparently hostile men in front of her. The note read, "Which one is Spong?" A little later this man left his seat and moved toward a door at the front of the church. Christine presumed that I might be in danger, and so she acted immediately. Ed Hasse, one of your young diocesan clergy, was a row behind her, and without explanation she asked Ed to follow this man. It is a tribute to Chris's integrity and to Ed's trust that he unquestioningly did as she requested. Both disappeared outside the church. Then she alerted the ushers, all of whom were Integrity members she knew, and they in turn alerted the security people. All of this was going on as I, oblivious to the crisis, sat in the sanctuary. The service ended without incident, and we do not know to this day whether it was Chris's excessive apprehension or a very real danger that was present in that hostile atmosphere. We were only glad to have averted an incident. Ed Hasse was an athletic young man who had played tackle on a college football team. Perhaps his tailing presence was all it took.

When the report of the special task force on homosexuality came up on the floor of the House of Bishops, the performance of Richard Grein and his task force members was the weakest and most inept that I have ever observed in that House. Conservative critics, mostly from Texas, offered amendment after amendment, which Bishop Grein accepted without debate or vote. The essence of the report had been gutted. The final and most galling moment came when John McNaughton moved that the statement issued by the Southern bishops with its episcopal signatures be appended to the task force report. That too, incredibly enough since it violated the open thrust of the official report, was accepted by Bishop Grein without debate or vote. It was total capitulation—and by the bishop of New York, in whose diocese were arguably the largest number of gay priests in the whole church with the possible exception of the Diocese of Chicago. The church plays amazingly duplicitous games in public.

The motion to adopt this now well-amended report and to commend it to the church for study passed. I was clearly in a minority once again. Dejected, I left the meeting at the time of adjournment and was confronted by a group of gay members from our diocese, including Louie Crew, Kim Byham, and several of our homosexual clergy. They were not just depressed, they were devastated—they felt beaten up and abandoned by the church they were just beginning to trust. They expressed grief and anger, and their tears revealed enormous hurt. Their pain registered on me deeply, but I did not know what to do about it. We had just seen a total liberal leadership collapse.

That night was a restless one for me. The pain the House of Bishops had inflicted on the gay population would not go away. By this time my identification with these people was so complete that I could feel their pain. The abuse I had endured when I ordained Robert Williams had made me aware of how much latent and overt hostility there is in our society just waiting to erupt toward homosexual people. I knew the cruel and false stereotypes that branded gay people as "child abusers," "promiscuous sex addicts," and "people incapable of forming bonded relationships." I knew the fear of physical attacks with which gay men in particular constantly live. I searched my mind for a way that I, as one person, could recall this reluctant church to a more balanced and forward-looking stance. In the early hours of the morning, still awake, I took out my pen and legal-size tablet. I could at the very least write a personal statement that would serve to separate me from the hostile resolution of the previous day. Though it was my own protest, perhaps it would give others a rallying point, but at that moment that did not matter. I knew that I had to do this even if forced to stand alone.

Before 5:00 A.M. I woke my sleeping wife and asked her if she would be willing to go to the hotel office center to type this statement on the computer so that we could edit it and prepare copies of it to distribute at the appropriate time. Sleepily she agreed. We both put our editorial skills to work until we had a text of which I could be proud. We went back to the office center to run off enough copies to hand out to all the bishops and the press. We kept every copy in our personal possession and erased the material on the computer, so the statement would not get leaked. Step number one was complete.

The second step was to find a way to put this statement officially on the floor of the House of Bishops. I contacted the secretary of the House, Herbert Donovan, the resigned bishop of Arkansas, now working in New York City, and my longtime friend, with whom I had struggled over this issue in Ed Browning's office years earlier. I shared my plan with him and asked if he would bring it to Ed's attention and ask Ed if he would be willing to recognize me at the beginning of the day's session on "a point of personal privilege." I would then read the statement and say it was at this point my personal testimony and I was willing to stand alone if necessary, but I felt others might be willing to stand with me. Herb agreed to bear this message, and the word came back that Ed had agreed to this plan.

It was in this manner that the document that came to be known as the "Statement of Koinonia," a title given to it by Martin Townsend, the bishop of Easton, came into being. In this document I asserted the essential givenness of both homosexuality and heterosexuality. I pronounced each of them to be morally neutral and suggested that people of both orientations had the capacity to live out their sexuality either in holiness or in destructive patterns. I asserted that gay people have always been in our priesthood and that the only difference today was that increasingly they were honest about it. I claimed for the screening process of each diocese the right to determine which candidates for ordination were to be acknowledged, in the words of the prayer book, as "wholesome examples to the flock of Christ." But I stated overtly that I, as one bishop of this church, would not reject a gay or lesbian candidate who lived in a partnered relationship that was faithful, monogamous, and intended by both partners to be lifelong. I said I wanted no one to be under the illusion that the nonbinding recommendations of the resolution passed yesterday would be operative everywhere. I concluded with an invitation for any bishop who wished to do so to join me in signing this statement.[9]

To my chagrin, when the session of the House of Bishops opened that day, Ed Browning was not in the chair. The presiding officer was our vice president, James Ottley, the bishop of Panama, who had not been clued in as to what was happening. I felt betrayed and assumed that one more time Ed Browning was ducking an issue. I now do not believe that to be the case. Herbert Donovan managed the process as secretary of the House. I was recognized. Fudging a bit, I stated my purpose to be that of reading a personal statement that would take only a couple of minutes. I was given the floor. Quite deliberately, once again, I went to the podium to make this presentation. I was not going to read it from a microphone on the floor. In fact, the statement took a bit more than ten minutes. Jim Ottley tried to interrupt and call time on me after about eight minutes, but I raised my hand to him like a policeman stopping a car and he backed down. My critics, obviously disturbed at this turn of events, were constantly clicking the rings of their notebooks, but I persevered.

When I finished, Christine distributed copies to the press, and to my delight a significant number of bishops, led by Mary Adelia McLeod, the bishop of Vermont, lined up to sign it, disrupting the ongoing business. Others had clearly felt what I felt, but they had no vehicle around which to rally. Before the day was over, we had just under fifty signatures. In time eighty-eight American bishops would sign the Statement of Koinonia. It was never a majority, but it did contain the bishops from most of the metropolitan areas in our nation, except for the deep South and Texas, and these signatories in fact represented the majority of the Episcopalians in the nation. We had once again gathered a critical mass that could neither be dismissed nor denied. The playing field on which this debate would be engaged suddenly became a bit more even. There were surprising signatories on this document, like Larry Maze from Little Rock and Ted Gulick from Louisville, both of whom would be castigated by some in their dioceses for this stand. The day after he retired, Ed Browning signed it. So did John Hines in his retirement.

During that day the House of Bishops wrestled with what to do with this statement. It did not really matter to me. The press had already trumpeted its message throughout the nation. In the interest of fairness, it was suggested by the bishop of Easton that this statement also be attached to the task force report to balance the statement initiated by the Southern bishops. That idea was fiercely resisted in conservative circles lest this to them totally unacceptable point of view, receive even a hint of official recognition. The compromise was to remove the conservative statement from the official task force report and authorize each group to publicize its statement as it saw fit; the official position of the church was to be the gray, vague product of the task force. I was quite content with this solution, for I knew the secular press would ignore both of the other two statements. The conservative statement said nothing new. The task force report said almost nothing at all. Once more we had turned an apparent defeat into a victory. I was delighted and learned again the valuable lesson that people need leadership to help them focus their higher selves. Without it, liberal voices are always weak and tentative and will ultimately collapse. I hoped the younger members of the House would go to school on this experience.

My conservative critics were seething. I was so clearly their most obvious and hated foe. They would, however, need to find another way to attack their designated enemy. They did. It took them a while to get the process going, but when their counterattack came, it was quite clearly a direct response to the Koinonia Statement.

Recognizing that they were losing in the gathered assemblies of the Church in the United States, where a majority vote was required to prevail, this group of ecclesiastical puritans, in a last-ditch attempt to defend their eroding position, decided to abandon the legislative processes and exercise their power through the judicial procedures of the church. Under the canons of the Episcopal Church, only ten active bishops were required to sign a presentment, the first step in the procedure for bringing formal charges of heresy, against another bishop. Once ten bishops had made the formal presentment, then their charges, together with the response of the bishop accused, were circulated to all bishops for their judgment. If only 25 percent of the bishops, including retired bishops, agreed that the charges needed to be investigated, an ecclesiastical trial would be ordered. A small minority could, therefore, hold the whole church hostage to their agenda.

These conservative bishops seemed to believe that the threat to time, energy, and reputation inherent in this procedure was so onerous that they could use it to intimidate and thus to continue to control the situation even with their declining minority. It was a radically hostile tactic, but once more they miscalculated seriously. They chose my assistant, Walter Righter, the retired bishop of Iowa, a white-haired, grandfatherly man of tough German heritage, to bear the brunt of their presentment rather than me. Perhaps they thought he was a softer touch. If so, they were dead wrong. He was made of steel and became stronger the more he was abused. Perhaps they did not want to give me the publicity that such a heresy trial would inevitably engender, knowing that I, by this time, had access to the media in a way that none of them did.

In any event, the four bishops of our church who still refused to obey the canons in regard to the ordination of women joined six other bishops, mostly from the South and Texas, to charge Walter Righter with heresy. His heresy was revealed, they said, in his action of ordaining Barry Stopfel to the diaconate in the Diocese of Newark and in his willingness to sign the Koinonia Statement!

These were strange charges. Walter had no authority of his own to ordain anyone in the Diocese of Newark. He acted quite obviously at my request, with my permission and authority, and with the consent of the Diocese of Newark's decision-making bodies. Also, by this time in history, I had personally already ordained Barry Stopfel to the priesthood, a far more serious charge. In this same time span, the bishop of Washington (Ron Haines) had ordained a partnered lesbian in a service reported on page one of the *New York Times*. The conservatives thus had a number of possible targets who were more appropriate for their wrath than Walter Righter, but he was their choice. If they succeeded with him, they announced that the bishop of Washington and the bishop of Newark would be their next targets. It was an amusing and even pathetic performance. In effect they were attempting to hurt me by putting my assistant on trial. Moreover, if the signatories of the Koinonia Statement were all guilty of heresy, as they implied, then the church would lose 40 percent of its active bishops, including those in New England, New York, Newark, Washington, Philadelphia, Chicago, St.

Louis, Minneapolis, San Francisco, Los Angeles, Louisville, Little Rock, and many other metropolitan areas.

Since only active bishops could sign the presentment, they rushed the process so that Maurice Benitez, the bishop of Texas, could sign just hours before his retirement rendered him ineligible. Probably no more irresponsible and expensive act has ever been done by a bishop in the last week of his active ministry. That trial cost the Diocese of Newark and the national church approximately half a million dollars. But Ben Benitez, who as a diocesan bishop refused to support the national church except in a token manner, was typically closed-minded and unrepentant. He seemed not to care for the financial well-being of the church that had provided him his livelihood. Later, even in his retirement, Bishop Benitez made reckless charges about the endowment funds of the national church, forcing that body to spend another $400,000 to demonstrate its integrity.

The heresy hunters based their heresy case on the "recommendation" of the 1979 general convention that Clarence Pope had claimed was the ultimate authority in the church on this subject when I ordained Robert Williams. Once again we had the anomaly, laughable outside the church, that bishops could disobey the canons of the church in regard to opening up the ordination process to women, but bishops who ignored a "recommendation" of a general convention could be purged from the House. There was no way we could lose this case, but a great deal of energy would be wasted and much destruction would be absorbed in the church by this mischief. I concluded that these conservative church leaders cared little about anything other than establishing the righteousness of their prejudices. I would see the same mentality acted out some years later when a conservative minority in the House of Representatives would almost destroy the Constitution in their attempt to impeach and remove the president of the United States. Something deeply destructive is unleashed in some threatened human beings when they cannot keep the world from changing and in the process diminishing their power. They inevitably seek to destroy what they can no longer control.

So the Episcopal Church moved toward a formal indictment of Walter Righter. A week before the deadline that would cause the presentment to expire, the necessary 25 percent was still lacking. However, the phones clearly hummed between Walter's presenters and wavering bishops until the exact number was found. To reach that total, a large percentage of signatories were retired bishops, including an Alzheimer's victim whose son signed the document for his senile father. Ed Browning's legal counsel, David

Beers, actually allowed his name to be included to reach the final count. My trust in David Beers's judgment was never repaired.

The church was thus forced to have a heresy trial that the vast majority of its people, ordained and lay, did not want. So unpopular was this trial that the leaders of the church had a hard time finding a place willing to host it. Walter, by this time, lived in New Hampshire, but the bishop there was not willing for his diocese to be used for its venue. Neither was the bishop of Connecticut or the bishop of Chicago. The Diocese of Newark would have been quite willing to act in that capacity, but church authorities feared that if it were held in a place too friendly to Walter, the decision would lack credibility. The court finally settled on Wilmington, Delaware. The nine bishops who sat as judges had been elected to the ecclesiastical court by previous general conventions. It was thought to be an empty honor, since the court had not been convened since the 1920s when a retired bishop of Arkansas was deposed for advocating evolution and ostensibly being a communist.

Religious bodies do become hysterical from time to time, as the history of Salem, Massachusetts, can attest. I looked at the list of judges, all of whom I knew well, and believed we could count on positive votes from six of the nine. Michael Rehill, the chancellor of our diocese, agreed to serve as Walter's attorney. Hugo Blankenship, Jr., the son of the former bishop of Cuba, represented the presenting bishops. The trial dragged through several postponements and finally reached a verdict on May 15, 1996. By this time it had drained the energy from the life of Walter Righter, Michael Rehill, Barry Stopfel, and Stopfel's partner, Will Leckie. It had also demoralized the people of the congregation at St. George's Church in Maplewood, to which Barry, as an openly gay man living in a committed relationship, had by then been called to serve as rector. But their life was restored when the verdict was announced. Walter was exonerated by a seven-to-one vote, gaining all but one of those three votes I had thought would be negative. The ninth judge, Fred Borsch of Los Angeles, recused himself because in the middle of the trial he had ordained a gay man living in a partnered relationship in his diocese. That was a good reason, I suppose, to step down, but it also revealed as nothing else I can imagine the absolute absurdity of this charade.

As fate would have it, my regular confirmation visit to St. George's Church was scheduled on the Sunday afternoon after the trial ended. Our diocese needed a time to rejoice together and this public church service provided it. St. George's was packed. Many of our clergy were present. Walter Righter assisted, to the enormous applause of the people. Another battle to

build an inclusive church in which ancient prejudices would be routed had
been won. The church had decided, in a strange inverted way, that there was
no ecclesiastical impediment to the ordination of a homosexual person, even
one living in a relationship of monogamous commitment. As most ecclesiastical institutions seem to do, we had backed into the future, not heroically,
but effectively.

My book entitled *Liberating the Gospels: Reading the Bible with Jewish
Eyes* was published shortly after this, so that the publicity surrounding this
trial fed the publicity generated by the book. The media tour planned by
HarperCollins returned me to places where I was by now well known. This
book also expanded once again my list of invitations, this time to include
synagogues in various communities around the world. I had by now already
turned my attention from the homosexual issue, which I believed to be
largely over, at least in my church in the United States. Now I sought to raise
consciousness on another of Christianity's great sins—the violence of anti-
Semitism, which is a uniquely Christian gift to the world.

But I also began to recognize that the stress under which my life had
been lived in recent years had taken its toll. In a routine physical, internal
bleeding was discovered, requiring a battery of additional tests. An endoscopy
revealed a diseased esophagus and stomach lining. There was no malignancy, but the history of this disease indicated that if not monitored carefully, malignancy could develop. I began a period of rigid dietary practices—
no caffeine, no alcohol, no fried or spicy foods, no citrus, no chocolate, no
carbonation, no mayonnaise, vinegar, or salad dressings. I became an aficionado of decaffeinated tea! I adapted well to my new regimen, put its
warning behind me, and picked up the pieces of my life. I was not yet ready,
even with this intimation of mortality, to slow my pace.

My last five books had all been quite successful and HarperCollins proposed that I now sign a two-book contract, one to be written on the creeds
and the other to be an autobiography. Harper clearly wanted to tie me down
for the balance of my active career, and I felt my relationship with them was
one of mutual appreciation. I began to work on the book that I had been
thinking about and wrestling with for years. I would finally seek to address
the topic of how one can say the premodern words of the creeds and still be
citizens of a postmodern world that had rendered most creedal concepts
bankrupt. My working title was "For Believers in Exile." It was due at the
publisher's by September 1, 1997, for publication in spring 1998. My speaking engagements, where I tested these ideas, found me first in the Diocese of

Newark and then once again across this nation, Canada, and the United Kingdom. I was even invited to conservative seminaries like St. Luke's School of Theology in Sewanee, Tennessee, which was balanced by two addresses I made to the scholars of the Jesus Seminar in Santa Rosa, California. Working on the content of this book, I once again drew more than a thousand people to a public lecture at Chautauqua Institution in New York. I spoke on university campuses in Berkeley, California, Anchorage, Alaska, and again in Vancouver, British Columbia. I made three appearances on a popular late-night television program called *Politically Incorrect*. One of those appearances was a rare one-on-one program with the host Bill Maher. People also began to recognize Christine's gifts and so invitations began to arrive for both of us to lead conferences at Kanuga, in North Carolina, and in Meridian, Mississippi. Later we were invited to be keynoters at clergy gatherings in the Dioceses of North Carolina, Oregon, and El Camino Real, California. Once, in the middle of a conference in Canada, I was felled by influenza and laryngitis. Christine stepped in and did my lectures for me for three straight days. A new dimension was added to our lives. Media opportunities continued to pour in. Presbyterian, Congregational, Unitarian-Universalist, Unity churches, and an occasional bold Episcopal congregation invited me into their corporate lives all over the United States. I continued to press the edges of both my faith and energy and to work at a frantic pace to accommodate this demand while not neglecting the task of being the bishop of the Diocese of Newark. My gracious diocese granted me a second three-month sabbatical leave in 1997 that, of necessity, had to be sandwiched around the general convention, but when complemented by my vacation, enabled us to extend the time significantly. I left the office in early June to study first at the University of Edinburgh. When my presence there became known to the Anglicans in Scotland, I was invited to address the national gathering of the Scottish Episcopal Church in Oban. I then spent a month as "A Scholar in Residence" at Christ Church, Oxford University. In those two great centers of learning, the manuscript for my book on the creeds came into its final form. Then I returned home to attend the last general convention of my career as an active bishop. It would meet in Philadelphia. There we would choose a new presiding bishop to succeed the retiring Ed Browning.

By this time I had already announced my own intention to retire early in the year 2000. This meant that I did not plan to return to official church meetings after that time. So I viewed the 1997 general convention as a kind of swan song, at least to this national ecclesiastical aspect of my public career.

This Philadelphia convention solidified in many ways the revolution in sexual values at whose center I had lived for so long. It passed a resolution to provide benefits for partners of homosexual employees of the church. This did not yet extend to the clergy covered under the Church Pension Fund, but that was inevitable. A resolution failed by a single vote in the lay order and a single vote in the clergy order that would have mandated the preparation of liturgical forms for the blessing of same-sex unions. But this convention responded to that close vote by appointing a special commission to bring a recommendation on that subject to the general convention in the year 2000. When one of our most outspoken conservative bishops, John David Schofield of the Diocese of San Joaquin in California, inquired if this meant that there would be a moratorium on this activity until 2000, Joe Morris Doss, the bishop in South and Central New Jersey, responded with one word—"No." Walter Righter was honored at this convention for his service to the church. We elected Frank Griswold, the bishop of Chicago, to be the new presiding bishop. His was a somewhat belated signatory, but a signatory none the less of the Koinonia Statement, which established that document as now mainstream.

I kept a low profile at this convention, becoming a kind of elder statesman, feeling that my days in the trenches were over and that younger bishops were quite able to carry this issue and to win. I spoke only one time. My beloved friend and mentor, John Hines, died in the middle of that convention. It was not unexpected. Christine and I had flown to Austin, Texas, that spring for the specific purpose of telling him good-bye and thanking him for what he had meant to me. His wife, Helen, had died a year before and I had preached at a memorial service in New York, over which Ed Browning presided, to honor her. John Hines's tenacity, however, kept him in life, if not always in consciousness, until July. I received the news of his death from his daughter, Nancy Hines Smith, by phone. Ed Browning was also notified. We remembered him at the convention Eucharist, and Ed asked me to prepare the resolution honoring him to be adopted by the House of Bishops, which I did, using that opportunity to address that House for the final time as I reminisced about this hero and friend of mine. I thought it fitting that those be my last remarks, so, quite by design and intention, I never spoke again on that floor.

When the convention adjourned, Chris and I set off to complete my sabbatical leave with our third lecture tour of Australia and New Zealand, with a stopover in Hawaii. Though once again I made more than two hundred public appearances on this trip, it was still far more leisurely, and we spent much time hiking on trails, through mountains, and even on a glacier in those beautiful lands with special friends whom we had grown to love over the years. In the relaxed moments of that journey I began to write my autobiography. My cousin Bill Spong died while we were in New Zealand. He left instructions that he was to be cremated and buried at any time that was convenient for me. I did that sad task over Christmas that year. Ed Browning also had postponed a memorial service for John Hines to be held in the Church Center in New York until my return, so that I could deliver in person a final and proper tribute to this great human being. This took place in November with all of John's children present.

While in New Zealand, I experienced continued stomach distress, lived on Prilosec, and knew that this esophagus and stomach problem would have to be addressed sooner or later. My doctors informed me that a laproscopic surgical procedure was on the horizon that offered a better prognosis than the continued reliance on acid-blocking drugs. It was, in their opinion, not yet fully tested, but it provided a hopeful possibility if I could just wait a while longer.

Throughout this journey into the South Pacific, I stayed in contact with my editor at HarperCollins. E-mail proved to be a wonder. My manuscript, still entitled *For Believers in Exile,* was in San Francisco, having already undergone significant copyediting. The staff at Harper was clearly excited by this book and ultimately urged, or perhaps even required, me to change its title to something more forceful and provocative. *Why Christianity Must Change or Die: A Bishop Speaks to Believers in Exile* was the final compromise. The edited manuscript was sent to us in New Zealand by Federal Express, arriving the day before our scheduled departure. Christine and I would use the nineteen hours in flight to complete the reading and to okay the final editing.

Already by this time in the Diocese of Newark nominations were being sought from which to choose my successor. Transition time on many fronts had clearly arrived. There was only one final major battle left that I was certain I would have to engage. That would occur at my third gathering of the Anglican bishops of the world at Lambeth during the summer of 1998. The homophobia that we had finally defeated in our own church after a national struggle that began in 1976 and seemed to be, if not concluded, then at least set in the proper direction by 1997 was now rearing its head throughout the

world, especially in cultures where prejudice and fear on this subject had yet
to be challenged by the medical and scientific data that had redirected
Western thinking. So once again I prepared to struggle for justice on this
issue, but this time on a world stage. It would prove to be the bitterest and
most unpleasant experience of my life.

1.  According to the charts in *Publishers' Weekly*.

2.  *Why Believe in God?* Michael Goulder and John Hick (London: SCM Press, 1983).

3.  *Born of a Woman* (San Francisco: HarperSanFrancisco, 1992), *Resurrection: Myth or
Reality?* (1994), and *Liberating the Gospels: Reading the Bible with Jewish Eyes* (1996).

4.  *Luke: A New Paradigm*, M. D. Goulder, two vols. (Sheffield: Sheffield University
Press, 1989).

5.  *The Sea of Faith*, D. Cupitt (London: BBC Publications, 1984).

6.  See *The Christian Century*, early winter, 1998.

7.  The Theology Committee was an interesting assignment. The leader of the conservatives, Fitz Allison, who considered me a heretic at best and a nonbeliever at worst, lobbied
for the remainder of Ed's career to have me removed from sitting on the official Theology
Committee of the Church. Ed responded by removing Fitz. There was hope.

8.  Later the able bishop of the Diocese of New Westminster in British Columbia.

9.  The complete text of the Koinonia Statement is found in Appendix A.

# *From Lambeth's Ignorance and Fear to Harvard's Promise of a New Career*

I AM CONVINCED that a graceful exit from a position of power and honor is as important as a graceful entrance. For this reason I began planning for my retirement almost ten years ago. It was the process prior to the election of a bishop suffragan in 1991 that forced the issue. The prospective candidates rightly wanted to know my plans. Under the canons of the church I could retire at age sixty-five (in 1996) and must retire at age seventy-two (in 2003). Since a bishop suffragan works as a permanent assistant to the bishop, no one would accept such a responsibility without knowing how long the bishop might remain in that post. So during that election process I had to begin to contemplate and articulate my future plans.

Three things entered my thinking and shaped my decision in determinative ways. There was first my writing schedule. If I was going to challenge the church theologically to rethink its primary symbols, I must do so as a sitting bishop. My book on the creeds was not only designed to do that, but was actually a call for a radical new reformation in Christian thought. That book was scheduled to come out in the spring of 1998, and my experience was that it takes about eighteen months to see a book through the phase I call its "publication impact."

I was also going to write this autobiography, which was scheduled to be published about the time I retired. An autobiography did not require my active status in the way that a challenging theological book did. Indeed, to bring it out near the retirement date would be ideal. From the standpoint of my writing career then, somewhere around the year 2000 seemed appropriate.

The second determining factor was the 1998 Lambeth Conference. It was inevitable that the issue of homosexuality and the church's response to it would dominate that international gathering. Gay leaders in our diocese and across the nation made it clear to me that, in their opinion, I must be a presence at Lambeth. I had, after all, been at the epicenter of this debate for so long that they felt I must not stop short of bearing witness at the Lambeth Conference. The war was all but won in the national Episcopal Church, but I was well aware that on the international level our church in America was far ahead of most other national bodies of the Anglican Communion.

Canada was still putting clergy on trial for being gay. In 1992, I had been to Toronto to testify on behalf of the Reverend James Ferry, a priest who, under threat of blackmail, had confided in the bishop of Toronto, the Right Reverend Terence Finlay, Jr., that he was gay and that there was someone he loved. Bishop Finlay responded to this confidence by firing James and outing him to the press when he refused to leave his partner. Subsequently, after a public outcry, the bishop called into being a medieval structure known as Bishop's Court and ordered Mr. Ferry to be put on trial for disobeying his bishop. No Canadian bishop was willing to come to his defense or to speak a word on his behalf. I had never met Jim Ferry, but when he wrote eloquently asking me to testify on the gay issue generally, I agreed to go to Toronto.

For four hours I was on the witness stand being interrogated by Jim's attorney and then cross-examined by his bishop's hired prosecutor, who was later to become the chancellor of that diocese. The packed galleries forgot courtroom decorum and applauded my words more than once, only to be warned by the presiding judge. But there was no way this court would exonerate Jim Ferry. When the verdict was guilty, his license to function as a priest was revoked. Bishop Finlay was actually one of Canada's more progressive bishops, but he was caught, as bishops are prone to be, by his vow to guard the unity of the church, which has usually meant blessing the status quo. So I had to assume that if a liberal bishop like Terry Finlay had acted this way, it meant that the total vote of the Canadian bishops would not be positive on this issue. Certainly the Anglican primate of Canada, Michael Peers, remained strangely silent.

England was even worse than Canada. The bishops of the Church of England had issued a study booklet on homosexuality that was designed to blunt the discussion and again to preserve the noble cause of church unity. It was a weak report, advocating a begrudging acceptance of gay and lesbian relationships as "not on a par with marriage" and proposing a two-tiered approach that enabled the church to support, at least passively, commitments between two same-sex laypeople, but denying that option to clergy couples since, as the report suggested, clergy had to be bound by a higher standard. Homosexuality was talked about a great deal in England, and evangelicals issued dire warnings about any proposed acceptance. It was enough to intimidate most bishops. When this report came out, only one bishop, Peter Selby, an area bishop in the Diocese of Southwark, was viewed as publicly supportive of gay and lesbian relationships. Certainly England presented a negative vote.

I could identify only one Australian Church leader, Peter Carnley, the archbishop of Perth, who might be counted on to vote positively on this issue, while the leaders of the Archdiocese of Sydney, probably the most reactionary part of the Anglican Communion, at least among First World Christians, could be counted on to oppose any step that looked like an accommodation. Roger Herft in Newcastle was leaning toward a positive position, but he had not yet achieved much notice.

It was no better in New Zealand, where again only one bishop, Murray Mills of the Diocese of Waiapu, was positive; David Coles, the bishop of Christchurch, was certainly thinking about the issue publicly, since he chaired the study commission of the church in New Zealand on human sexuality. The others, with the possible exception of David Moxon in Hamilton, were neutral to negative.

Only in Scotland, where the primus, Richard Holloway, was outspoken in his endorsement of gay rights, was there the possibility that a majority of bishops would be supportive. But the Scottish Episcopal Church counted only seven bishops in its entire ecclesiastical structure.

When one added to this mix the Third World bishops who were almost universally opposed to any openness to homosexual persons, there was no way that a positive statement could come out of the Lambeth Conference. It did not take a genius to recognize that. The political task facing those who shared my perspective was to minimize the negativity. My gay friends felt that my experience in that area would be helpful, so I promised them I would not retire before this conference. It was not just the conference itself, but its aftermath that had to be placed into my calculations. Again, adding about eighteen months pushed the date forward to around the turn of the millennium.

The third, but very minor, reason was the romantic appeal of the millennium itself. I had walked the frontiers of church life. I had interpreted my episcopal role to be that of preparing the church to enter and to live in the future. I at least wanted to lead this diocese, no matter how briefly, beyond the year 2000. From every angle a retirement date early in 2000 seemed appropriate.

Since our diocesan convention regularly meets on the last weekend of January, that time when the diocesan family was gathered for worship and its corporate deliberations appeared to me to be the proper context in which the transition should take place. So my plans were laid well in advance, but keyed to February 1, 2000, as the projected time of retirement. It actually turned out to be January 29, 2000. At that time I would be closer to my sixty-ninth birthday than my sixty-eighth, and I would have been bishop for almost a quarter of a century. Those plans had a nice feel to them.

With this schedule in mind, my successor, the Reverend Canon John P. Croneberger, a priest of our diocese, was elected in June 1998 and consecrated the following November, giving us fourteen months to effect a smooth transition. This meant that my book on the creeds was due out prior to his election, and the Lambeth Conference would be concluded prior to his consecration. With this time frame set, I began to live into my final professional events.

As early as 1996, before we had even departed for our sabbatical leave of 1997, which would take us to England, Scotland, Australia, and New Zealand, the first shot in the battle for the inclusion of homosexual persons was fired across the bow of the Anglican Communion's life. In that year a group of "Southern Hemisphere" Anglican bishops came together in Malaysia to take counsel on the state of the Anglican Communion. It was obvious that the growing inclusion of gay and lesbian people in parts of the West was disturbing to their understanding of Christianity itself. They issued at this conference a battle-worthy statement that they named after the capital of Malaysia, in which this gathering had convened. Thus, the Kuala Lumpur Statement made its debut in Anglican circles. The tone of this statement was both ill-informed and hostile.

These bishops represented some of the indigenous voices of the Third World, who were in many instances dealing with war, atrocities, famine, and fear in admirable and heroic ways. But the vast majority of them had not had the opportunity to engage the scientific data available in the Western world, which had eroded many of our traditional religious presuppositions and stereotypical definitions. These data were in the process of creating a secular worldview, removing from life so many of the typical appeals to religion, miracle, magic, and the intervention of a supernatural deity that had marked antiquity. People in Africa had, in large measure, not engaged this thought revolution. Many African Christian leaders, for example, still appeared to interpret individual deaths in terrorist activities as occurring according to some divine plan based upon God's assumed will. I listened with amazement to one African bishop who asserted that his response to a telephone call, which took him away from his home for about an hour, was part of God's plan to enable him to escape the terrorist murder that had victimized his wife and son. One wondered why it did not occur to this sincere but simple man that the God who had arranged for his safety could have quite easily done the same for his wife and son. He was content to give thanks for his "miraculous" delivery. It would have been blasphemy for him to blame God for the deaths of his wife and son, but that was what his theology suggested. It was a strange, almost magical, even diabolical, kind of religious understanding. Yet it is commonplace in many parts of the underdeveloped world.

It was hardly surprising that all of the definitions of that premodern cultural point of view would also be operative among these bishops in Third World societies, where women are still regarded as inferior to males. Women are judged not competent enough to be educated and thus systematically prohibited from entering the world of power through economic opportunities or political decision making. The status of women is therefore immorally low. Polygamy is still practiced in many African cultures, and so is the barbaric, patriarchal practice of female circumcision.

In these emerging nations, the traditional definition of homosexuals as either mentally ill or morally depraved people who chose to live out a distortion of God's creation was not only still operative, but was, as yet, almost unchallenged. Homosexuality was quite clearly a sin and an abomination to God. It was unquestionably condemned in a literalistic view of Holy Scripture. People knew nothing about the role of the hypothalamus or the level of testosterone in the pregnant female as factors that might determine one's sexual orientation. They were not aware that homosexual behavior is documentable in the animal world where, presumably, freedom of choice is not operative. They even suggested that homosexuality was a depravity or a disease limited to white Europeans[1] and that it had been introduced by European conquerors and colonial powers into the Third World. These people even seemed to believe that by prayer, counseling, and the gay or lesbian person's intense desire to change, homosexuality could be "cured." They did not appear to be aware that there is not a shred of medical or scientific data to support that claim. It was certainly affirming to this ill-informed mentality that conservative traditional Christians in the Western world shared most of these outdated, premodern prejudices.

Vast numbers of Anglican Christians in the Third World were primarily the product of English evangelical missionaries who had invested their converts with the same biblical fundamentalism that marked their religious fervor. They were taught by these mentors that eternal, ethical principles were written in the pages of a book they called the "Word of God," about which there could be no debate. Obviously they had not yet embraced cultural relativism. Nor did they seem to recognize that the system of slavery that had devastated the continent of Africa was a system that received its justification from their white oppressors with appeals to the same "Word of God."

The tone of the Kuala Lumpur Statement reflected this mentality, these prejudices, and this level of knowledge. It was also religiously aggressive. It condemned anyone who might disagree with its point of view on homosexuality, and it threatened to break off communion with any fellow Anglicans who might be motivated to ordain gay and lesbian clergy or to bless the sacred unions of gay and lesbian people. The Kuala Lumpur Statement suggested that any Christians who disagreed with its pronouncements must either be silenced or expelled from the church.

The two chief architects of this document, I am told, were Moses Tay, a man of Chinese origin who was the archbishop of Southeast Asia and the bishop of Singapore, and Maurice Sinclair, a transplanted English evangelical who was the archbishop of the Southern Cone and a bishop in Argentina. Archbishop Tay had been a medical doctor before changing his career. Not well trained theologically, he reflected an uninformed biblical fundamentalism and, strangely enough, an absolute ignorance of contemporary scientific knowledge on this subject. I would have hated to have been his patient! Archbishop Sinclair was a typical product of evangelical thinking who was sure that all the problems of contemporary life could be solved with authoritative pronouncements from Scripture.

Despite this non-African leadership, most of the signatories to this offensive, destructive document were the bishops of the young and vigorous churches of Kenya, Uganda, Nigeria, Rwanda, and other underdeveloped African nations. Significantly, very few bishops from South Africa, either white or black, lent their names to it.

When the statement, with its judgmental and insulting rhetoric, was made public, I felt sure that someone somewhere would raise a contrary point of view. I was, however, disappointed to discover that this statement lay on the body politic of the whole Anglican Communion for almost a year with no public response from any leader or body in our church. Once again, the silence of the liberals was deafening.

But while the liberals slept, the conservatives in America leaped on this new source of support for their discredited and defeated point of view and began plotting a way to turn the Episcopal Church away from its liberal agenda at the Lambeth Conference. They should at the very least be given credit for possessing political wisdom.

In spring 1997, a number of these same Third World bishops were invited, all expenses paid, to a conference in Dallas, Texas. This conference was financed by American money, and its ostensible purpose was to discuss the issue of Third World debt, which many, including the archbishop of Canterbury, seemed to hope would be the major issue at Lambeth. When the Third World bishops arrived, however, they found themselves in the company of the bulk of the conservative Episcopal bishops of America, who turned the focus of this conference away from Third World debt[2] and into another public condemnation of homosexuality as immoral, sinful, and rejected by sacred Scripture. The clarion call of this conference was to unite conservatives of the Western world with Third World bishops to force the Lambeth Conference to adopt the Kuala Lumpur Statement. This aggressive attempt to impose their point of view on the whole Communion guaranteed that homosexuality would be the principle topic of debate at the conference. The agenda had been hijacked. People would protest this shift. They would even suggest that liberal Americans had forced this item to the top of the church's list of concerns. The facts are otherwise. This was an attempt to force upon the whole Communion an outdated definition present in the Third World, but clearly dying in the Western world. To resist this imposition seemed to me to be an essential task. But once again, when the statement from the Dallas conference was issued, no voices anywhere spoke publicly in opposition.

The Lambeth Conference was thus set on a path to adopt a position violently opposed to homosexuality and by a formidable vote. The combination of Third World bishops, conservative Americans, evangelical English bishops, and their allies in Canada, Australia, and New Zealand would constitute a clear majority of those who would be delegates to the Lambeth Conference.

Although Lambeth had only advisory power, such a hostile resolution would be a major setback in our efforts to build a nonjudgmental, inclusive church where all of God's people would find a welcome.

I took only one action when the Dallas statement was issued. It was signed by the usual cast of characters in America with whom I had battled for so long. There was, however, one African signature that surprised me, David Gitari, the archbishop of Kenya. David was a man I had known and respected for many years. He had had a broad enough education to know better, I thought. So I wrote him to express my disappointment that his name had appeared on this hostile and poorly informed document. He did not respond. That was my sole contribution to the debate at the time. I was still sure that someone would arise to counter the spirit of condemnation developing in our church. I really had come to believe that I was too battle-worn and scarred by previous fights on this issue to be the effective leader at this international gathering. I would be present and I would support a continuing effort, but I hoped someone else would lead it.

However, nothing but silence came back to me. No Western primate and no American, Canadian, or British bishop stepped forward to offer a contrary point of view. It was déjà vu. The willingness of the liberals to surrender piece by piece to the aggressive conservatives at our general convention in 1994, which forced me finally to produce the Koinonia Statement, seemed to me to be exactly what we were now experiencing internationally. I perceived my church to be sinking once again into prejudice and premodern ignorance because no one was willing to pay the price that effective, out-front leadership required. My energy at that time was far more intensely directed toward my writing career. But I thought if I am the only one willing to give leadership on this issue, then the Anglican Communion is in a difficult place.

While visiting in Scotland in 1997, I had the chance to confer on this subject with Richard Holloway, the primus of the Episcopal Church in Scotland. He was someone I had known and admired for years and was, in my opinion, the most outspoken and courageous primate in the entire Communion. He was bright, articulate, well read, and well published. He shared with me on this occasion the fears that had been expressed on matters of sexuality at the periodic meetings of the Anglican primates, of which he, of course, was a member. According to him, the archbishop of Canterbury, George Carey, wanted to push the subject of homosexuality off the Lambeth agenda and into a decade-long international task force that would be asked to study this issue and report back in 2008. That had been the way the issue of women in the episcopacy had been handled by Lambeth ten years earlier. It was a familiar ecclesiastical tactic, but now was being proposed specifically as a way to block negativity. It was designed to buy time, enable knowledge to grow, and perhaps allow the problem to be solved locally before the international body could take a premature and foolish stand. The fact that close to a dozen female bishops would be in attendance when Lambeth convened bore witness to the fact that decisions tended to get made at the local level when waiting for an international advisory gathering of bishops to share its wisdom. Thinking that this was George Carey's plan, Richard had refrained from stepping forward to counter the Kuala Lumpur Statement.

I listened carefully to that proposed strategy. At that moment it appeared to me that this would be the best solution we could possibly achieve, since the votes were simply not present to defeat a negative resolution. However, given the deafening silence that emanated from the liberals in the West, the active organization going on among the conservatives, and the votes lining up around the world to affirm the Kuala Lumpur Statement, my sense was that something like the proposal of an international task force study would not have a chance to pass. That strategy would work only if there were two diametrically opposed positions, each with sufficient strength that a victory for either would disrupt the unity of the church. A strong counterweight to the advocates of the Kuala Lumpur Statement simply did not exist. Without it there would be no desire to seek a compromise. Richard did not seem to agree with this, but that idea found lodging in my mind and began to grow.

Later on our tour of Australia and New Zealand, I once again sought out local bishops to get a sense of where the debate lay in those lands. I found no one willing to offer significant leadership. Peter Carnley, the archbishop of Perth in Western Australia, was doing some creative things on sexual issues, but he had not thought beyond his jurisdiction. Roger Herft in Newcastle was designated to be the chaplain at Lambeth and so was neutralized, since leadership on this issue was not appropriate for the conference's worship leader. New Zealand's David Moxon had a wife fighting a difficult medical diagnosis and, though a man of great courage, he did not have the time or the ability to lead an international effort. David Coles, the bishop of Christchurch, was moving in a positive direction as he worked on sexual issues, but he was not ready to lead a charge. He had, however, conferred with the archbishop of Canterbury during the past year, and he shared with me insights that helped me know more about George Carey's way of thinking. The idea of establishing a task force where these issues could be studied for ten years was still operative.

As my sabbatical time stretched out in the lands down under, sexual debate was never far from the surface. At every question period, in every interview with print media, radio, and television, the question of the church's stand on homosexuality inevitably came up. In the minds of the media this was the defining issue of my life. The conservatives used this issue to seek to discredit my theological probings and my nonliteral biblical conclusions. It was clear that they felt they could win a debate on homosexuality better than they could on theological or biblical issues, about which they were generally ill-read.

Finally, while in New Zealand, after many more interviews on this subject, I came to the conclusion that if the Lambeth Conference was going to derail the effort to make the Kuala Lumpur Statement the official position of the Anglican bishops of the world, and if we were to have any chance to move this debate into an international study commission, I would have to assume, once again, a major role of leadership. It occurred to me that it might already be too late to mount an effective challenge. I also was deeply aware that my writing career, which had cast me in the role of the disturber of the church's theological and institutional peace, certainly compromised my ability to gain moderate votes, but no one else seemed willing to step forward. I was confident that this was not a winning fight. At best it was a neutralizing fight, but it was a battle worth undertaking, even if the final result was simply to create a strong international minority point of view within our Communion. That had been the path to victory in the United States, and I could travel that route again. But somehow I could not escape the feeling that I had been elected to this responsibility by default and that I had very few followers. Nonetheless, I emotionally accepted this assignment and began to draft a statement that could stand against the Kuala Lumpur Statement—and, I hoped, produce enough energy to make a majority of our bishops duck the issue in favor of a "ten-year study."

I first made contact by fax with Dr. Louie Crew in the United States and the Reverend Richard Kirker in the United Kingdom. A straight man must never presume to speak for homosexual people without their consent any more than a male should presume to speak for females or a Caucasian should presume to speak for people of color without their consent. Together the three of us began to discuss the draft of a paper that would be in the form of a letter from me to the Anglican primates of the world, but would be designed to build a fire on the positive side of this debate in preparation for Lambeth. When the first draft was complete, I submitted it by fax to my press officer, Dale Gruner, who proposed that the document be separated into "a white paper on homosexuality" and a letter to the primates introducing it and explaining its purpose. I was still to be the only signatory.

Once I had returned home to my office, the Lambeth project became my dominating issue. Talking almost daily with Richard Kirker in London, we debated the proper time to release this statement so as to gain maximum press coverage. We wanted to avoid Christmas. Early January was also no good since our new presiding bishop, Frank Griswold, would be installed on the tenth of that month and that event would certainly preempt at least the religious press of America. Operating as we were from a minority position, we felt a tremendous need to guarantee full international coverage. We finally picked the date of November 20, deliberately designed to coincide with the opening of the general synod of the Church of England. We wanted to make certain that the conversations at that synod would be on our desire to build and to demonstrate the power of a positive position for the inclusion of homosexual people in the church that might neutralize the Kuala Lumpur document.

With Richard Kirker in the United Kingdom and Dale Gruner in the United States providing copies of the statement to trusted members of the media, embargoed until 12:01 A.M. Greenwich mean time on November 20, we prepared to break this story with all the power we could muster, including on the Internet. I wanted the leaders of our Communion to believe that we constituted a mighty force, when in reality we were one bishop and three advisers. As a matter of common courtesy, we took special care to see that the primates and especially the archbishop of Canterbury received copies of this statement before they read about it in the press. So it was mailed to them by November 10. We indicated to none of them that this was destined to be a very public event when the embargoed date arrived.

I had phrased this paper quite self-consciously to be a hard-hitting, attention-getting document. I pulled no punches in its text. I called the Kuala Lumpur Statement both unworthy and highly prejudiced, while taking the archbishop of Canterbury to task for his weak and ineffective leadership, which I suggested reflected his own rampant homophobia.[3]

I did not have to wait long for a response. By fax Archbishop Carey fired off a steaming letter referring to my paper as "hectoring and intemperate" and telling me how destructive this action was for the very people I was seeking to help. There was no question that I had gotten his attention. The BBC sent a television team to my office to tape a personal interview for the evening news, to be presented on the date the paper was made public in the United Kingdom. When that story was run on television, the archbishop of Canterbury asked Richard Harries, the bishop of Oxford and an English moderate, to go on BBC television as his official spokesperson.

I responded to Archbishop Carey's strident rhetoric with a second letter, with copies again sent to the primates and again posted on the Internet, in which I suggested that his silence over the outrages of the Kuala Lumpur Statement compared with his white-hot anger in response to my paper revealed once again how deeply his prejudice against homosexual people really was. I also pointed out that his call to the bishops coming to Lambeth to be prepared to listen to those who disagreed with them was considerably cheapened by his own steadfast refusal to meet with any members of the Lesbian and Gay Christian Movement in England at any time during the entire tenure of his term as archbishop of Canterbury.

In his second response Archbishop Carey defensively asserted that he had met with Richard Kirker and that they had even had lunch together. I knew that was not so, but wanted to make certain I had the facts. So I called Richard immediately, and he reiterated his absolute denial of such an event. In my third letter to George Carey I called him on this point of fact.

In the archbishop's third response, which strangely enough was considerably softened, he penned in his own hand a postscript admitting that he had "misspoken" about having had lunch with Richard Kirker. He had, he said, confused Richard Kirker with Jeffrey John. It was an incredibly weak cover for his dishonesty. However, I chose not to comment on that further and allowed him gracefully to get off the hook of an obvious lie. There was, however, no way that George Carey could ever have confused these two English clerics. Jeffrey John, my friend from Magdalen College, Oxford, is a somewhat introverted, but brilliant, young English New Testament scholar. Richard Kirker is the highly visible, political director of the Lesbian and Gay Christian Movement, whose name and face were frequently in the public arena. George Carey had to have known him. There was no way he could have honestly mistaken these two for each other.

After the first two exchanges between the archbishop and myself, Peter John Lee, a South African bishop joined the debate, taking me to task for suggesting that Third World bishops were uninformed, thus injecting race into the debate. He went on to suggest that criticism of African biblical understanding or theological comprehension was racist. It was an interesting tactic and one that I would hear again and again. But Peter John Lee appeared to be a person open to reason and of a good heart. So I responded to him graciously and further letters flowed on that front. In a subsequent letter to George Carey I said in an offhand comment that I thought Peter Lee and I could draft a proposal on homosexuality with which most of the Lambeth bishops could agree. That idea appealed to the archbishop and he suggested that we try. By this time the tone of our correspondence had warmed considerably. Instead of the greeting "Dear Bishop" and the signature of "George Cantuar," the letters were now addressed "Dear Jack" and signed "George." Peter John Lee and I accepted this challenge and worked for a month to draft our paper. I went so far as to entertain the idea of flying to South Africa if and when we reached agreement so that we could issue the paper jointly from a Southern Hemisphere country, but time constraints ultimately precluded that possibility. We mailed it to the primates and again posted it on the Internet. In the finished document, entitled "A Catechesis on Homosexuality,"[4] we urged the Lambeth Conference to affirm three things: (1) that gay and lesbian people must receive the full protection available to them under the law, (2) that marriage was important and must be undergirded by the church in a powerful way, and (3) that promiscuous or predatory sex was almost always destructive to human life and should be opposed by Christians whether engaged in by homosexual or heterosexual persons.

Next we stated the three things upon which we could not agree and on which we did not think we could get a consensus from the Lambeth bishops. They were: (1) the blessing of same-sex unions, (2) the ordaining of homosexual people who live in publicly acknowledged, monogamous relationships, and (3) the role of the Bible in the solving of this and other contemporary ethical concerns. Here we faced the fact that where no agreement was possible, we had an obligation to describe the contending positions fairly with both honesty and integrity and thus to assert that these positions, so deeply in conflict, one with the other, are both in fact held by Christian believers. That itself was not easy since a fringe group of bishops actually believed that anyone who supported gay people was no longer a Christian at all. But as we faced these differences, our conviction was that we should not challenge the church to reach a compromise that would violate any bishop's conscience or integrity; rather, our task was to stretch the boundaries of the way we defined truth and allow the Christian institution the freedom to live, over the next decade, into a consensus that was not at this time available to us. I wrote my point of view on these issues, and Peter J. Lee wrote his. I thought we had produced a challenging document that could offer the Anglican Communion a way forward.

Before the ink was dry, George Carey faxed us that we should add a plea for the whole Communion to wait until a worldwide consensus was formed on these issues before any province acted on its own. That was totally unacceptable to me. It was also a familiar conservative delaying tactic. It had been used by traditionalists during the ecclesiastical debate on the ordination of women. I had met this argument first when conservatives were playing the ecumenical card. No part of Catholic Christianity such as Anglicanism, it was said, should proceed to ordain women until all of Catholic Christianity, including Roman Catholicism and the Orthodox tradition, agreed to do so. That, of course, would have postponed the ordination of women for eternity. When that argument was dismissed for what it was, it was next suggested that all the various provinces of the Anglican Communion must come to unanimity on this issue before any single province could proceed to ordain a woman. Given the status of women in some Third World nations, that would have given veto power to the most backward areas of the world and so once again was dismissed for the stalling tactic it was.

George Carey was now asking us to include this tired and threadbare stalling tactic in our paper as the price of his support. It was quite simply too high a price even to consider. So I responded immediately that I could not agree with this proposal. It was clear to me that from that moment the archbishop began to distance himself from our paper, even though it had been his suggestion that we prepare it. His spokespersons began to say things like the archbishop has asked "lots of people to be in dialogue on lots of subjects." Hence, there was nothing special or official about this paper.

Peter John Lee, I learned, began to be attacked by some evangelicals for even participating in this project with me. Evangelical bishops began to suggest that he had been hooked or snookered by the "sinister" bishop of Newark. Nothing could have been further from the truth. He and I had each worked together from our different perspectives while respecting the integrity of the other, a rather rare process in this church of ours.

In late April this debate was both impacted and complicated by the publication of *Why Christianity Must Change or Die*. This book made waves almost immediately. I had dedicated my May monthly column in *The Voice*, our diocesan newpaper, to introducing this book to the people of our diocese;

the title was "A Call for a New Reformation." I concluded this column with
Twelve Theses, which I would also post on the World Wide Web, calling
Christian leaders everywhere to debate a new way to define Christianity for
a postmodern world. The Twelve Theses were drawn from the book and
were stated as provocative conclusions, with none of the supportive material
or background published with them.[5] That was of course available when one
read my book, which was designed to be my contribution to the debate. This
column was deliberately intended to be a bold and daring thrust, and it
undoubtedly hooked the conservative and evangelical elements of the
church quite emotionally. It also opened me to their abuse, which, given my
high profile in the sexuality debate with the archbishop, was designed to tar-
nish my theological reputation and to minimize my voice at Lambeth. I
launched this book with a media tour of the United States organized by an
outstanding book publicist in Chicago hired by Harper. I did public events,
radio, and television across the nation. Four syndicated columns reviewed
this book in countless newspapers. The book took off like a rocket and was
in a third printing by July 1. By early June, conservative bishops in America
had published a letter proclaiming me no longer a Christian and disassociat-
ing themselves from my apostasy. To my knowledge none of them had read
the book. They only reacted to the Twelve Theses. My mail began to run
about one hundred letters a week. By the time we left for England some two
weeks before the Lambeth Conference, the debate on this book had clearly
leaped the ocean. A canon dedicated the entire Sunday sermon in St. Paul's
Cathedral, London, to condemning me and this book. Conservatives called
for me to be disinvited to Lambeth. Evangelicals clearly planned to use this
book to discredit any initiative I might take on the homosexual issue. Just
prior to the Lambeth Conference, the British evangelical church paper
known as the *Church of England News* sent Andrew Carey, the archbishop's
son, to interview me, ostensibly on the book. I had been interviewed by this
young man on previous books and he had always distorted my thought. I had
also described this religious journal quite deliberately in my correspondence
with the archbishop as "the worst religious newspaper in the world." It
had run vicious stories about me in the past, suggesting that the Diocese of
Newark was collapsing under my leadership. However, because I believe that
I have a responsibility to speak to the press on all sides of the issues, I agreed
to this interview. Andrew Carey's first tack was to say that by calling the
Kuala Lumpur Statement prejudiced and uninformed, I was insulting the
intelligence of Third World bishops. That was his prelude, and his opening

to turn this into a racial confrontation. I responded that all people who sought to speak to the ethical concerns of the whole world had a responsibility to be informed on the issues. The Kuala Lumpur Statement, I repeated, was simply not informed. Running through my familiar litany, I went on to say that this statement appeared to have no knowledge of the scientific data that suggested that homosexuality was not chosen, but was a part of some people's very being, that the overwhelming majority of scientists and doctors do not believe it is amenable to change, that homosexuality is documentably present in higher mammals, and that it appears to be a consistent part of the human experience in all times and places. He was not willing to engage these data since it did not serve his sinister purpose.

He then made some rather cynical and ill-informed comments about how the African churches were growing and the Diocese of Newark was shrinking. His knowledge of the Diocese of Newark was nonexistent. His assumption was that if we in Newark would only believe and act the way the Africans believed and acted with clear evangelical preaching, we would be a growing, not declining, church.

I responded that the two worlds were so different as to be not capable of comparison. In the Western world we face a secularized society, well informed by science and technology, where the old symbols of Christianity have been dismissed. In the parts of Africa that I had visited, the conversions to Christianity came primarily from uneducated people who were moving from animism into a rather superstitious form of fundamentalist Christianity. I believed that this transition was a step in the right direction, but not something that the West could ever emulate. The West begins with different assumptions. He kept pressing the suggestion that I was implying that Africans were ignorant. While denying such intentions, I went on to say that a moral issue like justice and the end of the oppression and murder of gay people was as important to me as the issue of slavery had been in a previous century. When people argued, as they had in the nineteenth and early twentieth centuries, that blacks were inferior or that Africans had simply not evolved to a status of equality as a justification for slavery or segregation, I would feel justified to dismiss that argument as prejudiced ignorance and would not be willing to be respectful of it no matter who made it. When people defined homosexuality as morally depraved, mentally ill, or as similar to bestiality or pedophilia, I would call that ignorant no matter who said it.

The story that appeared in the *Church of England News* was distorted and evil. I was appalled at its deliberate malevolence. The words "witch doctor," never mentioned in the interview, were in the headline, setting a pejorative tone. The text of the article suggested that I had called all Africans ignorant and superstitious, one step away from witch doctors, and that I had likened their attitude on homosexuality to slavery. The fact that among the most outspoken defenders of homosexuality in the world was a black African named Desmond Tutu was beside the point. The journalistic hatchet job of the evangelical press had been accomplished. When I read the story, I was dismayed at its deliberate dishonesty. I also recognized that the reporter had given the conservatives a socially acceptable weapon with which to pummel me, and they were quick to use it. There was no way I could counteract its pernicious influence because too many people had a deep desire to keep that story going. His story was designed to cover with respectability the most distorted African ideas on homosexuality that I had ever heard. To counter this ignorance was to open oneself to the charge of racism. Andrew Carey had begun the public assassination of my character and credibility at Lambeth.

The second attack came as the secular British press, taking notice of my book, referred to me on two occasions as an "atheist bishop." I was now, in their minds, in the category of my friend Don Cupitt. Obviously seeking to talk about theology to theologically untrained reporters had its risks. My attempt in the book and in the Twelve Theses to say that "theism" was no longer an adequate category to use to define God had been interpreted by them to mean that atheism was the only alternative.

The third attack came from a surprising source. The bishop of Monmouth, the Right Reverend Rowan Williams, one of our Communion's ablest scholars and one generally open and liberal on the gay issue, was asked to write an article on my posted Twelve Theses for the Lambeth issue of the *Church Times*, the closest thing to an official church newspaper in England. He did so in a very hostile way, suggesting that these Twelve Theses were juvenile and unworthy of serious consideration. Amazingly, Rowan appeared not to be aware that the Twelve Theses were based on my book *Why Christianity Must Change or Die,* which he had never read and presumably did not know existed. So, in typical classroom fashion, he argued in his piece that I had never defined theism. That was true in the Twelve Theses, but I did in two chapters of the book, specifically writing there that I was using a definition of theism drawn from the work of an English theologian named Richard Swinburne. Rowan's hostile attack certainly gave legitimacy, as well as aid and comfort, to those who wanted to dismiss me as unworthy of anyone's attention. I thought his words were irresponsible, unprofessional, and lacking in integrity, and I told him so. Given his theological standing as both a scholar and a liberal, however, I could not do more than absorb this new attack and wonder what would come next. Rowan was, in my opinion, eager to win the approval of the evangelical elements of the church who were blocking his advancement in the life of the church. Like so many bishops in the United Kingdom, he yearned to wind up in Canterbury, York, or at least London. All were light-years away from Monmouth. An unprincipled attack, which his article was, on the favorite target of the evangelicals would thus serve him well.

When I met with the sexuality section of Lambeth, I found the situation as bad, if not worse, than I had anticipated. Ugandan bishops said that homosexuality was "a white problem." They, along with their conservative and evangelical allies, objected even to hearing from a gay person in our section, suggesting that we should not give homosexuals special treatment, since we were not going to listen to wife beaters, people who practised bestiality, or child molesters either. The sexuality section of the conference was about two-thirds negative. Again, the combination of Third World bishops who had never really engaged the meaning of homosexuality from a modern perspective or who had never had their stereotypes challenged, were joined by evangelical bishops who saw the gay issue as an attack upon the family, morality, and Scripture, to form a powerful majority. The conference seemed once again headed for a negative gay-bashing resolution. Even Richard Harries of Oxford now appeared to be a liberal and he was still suggesting that we distinguish between orientation and action, a point of view we moved beyond in the United States decades ago. I had been so assaulted by a negative press that my leadership role was visibly diminished, even among the liberals. After all, one who was an atheist, who insulted Africans, and who questioned the basic tenets of Christianity would hardly be worth following on any issue. I kept encouraging others, such as Charles Bennison of Pennsylvania and Richard Randerson of Canberra, to come forward to lead. There was some reason, however, why each could not step up to the plate. It was a depressing time.

The American liberals made it clear that they were not willing to follow my lead even on tactics. I understood that, since I obviously carried the baggage of much conflict both here and over the years. Prior to departing for Lambeth I had received a very strange letter signed by the bishops of New England—Doug Theuner of New Hampshire, Mary Adelia McLeod of Vermont, Chilton Knudsen of Maine, and Tom Shaw and Barbara Harris of

Massachusetts—telling me that if I planned to use the Koinonia Statement at Lambeth, they would like to remove their names from it. They argued, feebly I believed, that the Koinonia Statement was limited to the debate and time in our church that produced it. It had no authority outside that context, they said. Theirs was a new version of the liberal waffle I had seen so often. Shortly thereafter I got a similar letter from Frank Griswold, using the same argument and making the same request. I was deeply disappointed by this lack of either commitment or courage.

The conservatives again and again picked up on the idea that I had insulted all Africans. They then tied it to their assessment of my writing, which they asserted had abandoned every aspect of Christianity, and sought to make me a pariah. African bishops who had never read a word I had written quoted these things in their speeches as if they were gospel truth. One bishop even suggested that I be censured by the conference. I supposed that if that had come to a vote, it would have passed. Even Frank Griswold got into this debate in a unhelpful way. He sent me a note asking if I would meet with three African archbishops who had asked for an interview to see if we could find some way to move away from the negativity they credited me with, so we could deal with the issues of sexuality itself. Frank naively assumed that somehow this brouhaha was not deliberate and did not understand that its continuation served quite well the specific political agenda of many people who were determined to keep it going. It could, therefore, never be cleared up, no matter how much we tried to resolve it in private conversation. It was clear to me that Frank had not had any significant experience dealing with either controversy or the media. Nonetheless, I agreed to meet with the archbishops. They were Njongokulu Ndungane of Southern Africa, who was Desmond Tutu's successor and very open on all issues of discrimination, Simon Chiwanga of Tanzania, who was also president of the Anglican Consultative Council, and French Chang-Him of the Seychelles, whom I had known quite well from Lambeth 1988. Frank Griswold and Arthur Williams of Ohio, the vice president of our House of Bishops, also sat in with us.

After discussing the matter for a while, all of them seemed to feel that some act of apology was necessary to keep this conflict from negatively impacting our struggle over homosexuality. They actually believed that this was a factor in the incredible negativity we were facing. I did not object to expressing regret that my words had been misinterpreted by the archbishop's son in such a deliberate manner to serve his political agenda and

that this misinterpretation was being carried on by others for the same reason, but I thought that if such words were to be offered, it should be done
privately and personally with those African bishops who felt offended. The
chance to be in dialogue so that stereotypes and distortions of truth could be
countered was appealing. However, there appeared to be no time for that,
since the numbers of African bishops were so large and the conference was
so fully scheduled. I suggested then that the three archbishops convey my
thoughts to the other archbishops from Africa, but that I was unwilling in
any way to indicate that this irresponsible evangelical reporter had been
accurate. They agreed to do that. I assumed the matter was closed.

While these conversations were going on, the rhetoric of certain African
bishops against homosexual people continued to be both crude and offensive. One suggested that if this conference did not condemn homosexuality,
that in 2008, when we met again, the bishops would be asked to approve sex
with dogs and cats. These bishops also continued to speak of God as an
intervening divine Mr. Fixit who served their agenda. The vastness of the
universe had not tempered their view of God as sitting on the divine throne
just above the sky and keeping tabs on all human activity. They espoused a
view of Scripture that was uncomplicated by the last 150 years of biblical
scholarship, asserting that God had written every word of the Bible and
endowed it with inerrancy. Before the conference was over, one African
bishop would assault Richard Kirker by trying to lay hands on him to purge
him of the demon that made him a homosexual person.

These African bishops were demonstrating again and again the truth of
my suggestion that much of African Christianity was expressed in a superstitious form of fundamentalism. That was not a racial comment. It was a
statement of obvious discernible fact. They exhibited a strange premodern
expression of theology that one met in the West only in Pentecostal churches.
It was foreign to everything I knew and treasured about the Episcopal
Church, but was clearly operative in these committed, evangelical voices
from Africa.

This same theological understanding, only a bit more perfumed, marked
the evangelical and conservative bishops of North America and Europe. They
used a slightly higher level of theological sophistication, but did not escape the
premodern mind-set to justify their negativity. Emboldened by their ability to
discredit me as prejudiced racially, these voices began to attack my faith and
to ridicule me personally. They asserted that I did not believe in God, denied
the Resurrection, and was seeking to destroy the church. They attacked my

integrity and my character as well as my faith. Again and again I began to hear the refrain that I was one who not only supported homosexual people in clear opposition to Scripture, but was a racist and "a not well-closeted atheist" wearing the robes of a bishop. My continuation in the office of bishop appeared to represent an intolerable affront to some of them, it was said. The suggestion that I issue a public apology to these people in the midst of this kind of character assassination was ludicrous to me.

Frank Griswold continued to press me to issue such an apology. I found his eagerness strange. I had not supported Frank for the presiding bishop's role, not because of his views, which were quite similar to my own, but because in his years in the House of Bishops I had never seen in him strength of either character or leadership. He was unwilling to engage issues in floor debate or stand for anything more serious than observation of a long pause at the asterisk when we recited the Psalms. In 1990 when the House of Bishops was voting on whether to disassociate themselves from me and the Diocese of Newark for ordaining a gay man living in a committed relationship, Frank, who had ordained more gay clergy than I could even contemplate, had been strangely absent. He had signed the Koinonia Statement, but not until there was a critical mass of signatures to enable him to feel relatively anonymous. Frank also had little understanding of the press. His naïveté on this subject had just recently been revealed in his "private" visit in jeans and plaid shirt to a Roman Catholic church in New York City where he received the Sacrament. He was observed and this was reported in the press. Frank fumbled through two weeks of semidenial before he admitted rather lamely that he wanted a private moment with "just Frank and Jesus."

With this kind of expertise in media relations, Frank nonetheless pushed for some action that would "get this problem behind us" so that "it would not distort the debate on homosexuality," as if that were the problem. I steadfastly refused. The word came back to me that the regret expressed through the archbishops had not been well received and that the Africans, encouraged by their conservative allies, wanted a public apology. I communicated to Frank's overseas ministry head that I was not willing to do that. Little did I realize how badly I was being manipulated at that moment, if not by my own presiding bishop, then by his staff.

I had received a press notice from the *Convention Daily*, a public-relations propaganda news sheet totally controlled by those running the conference, of which Frank Griswold and his press aides were a part, that they sought an interview with both Peter John Lee and myself on our Catechesis on

Homosexuality. They also wanted us to be photographed together. I agreed. I was surprised when I arrived at the media center to discover that I was being interviewed alone. Peter, I was told, was coming in later and I would need to return the next day for the joint photograph.

The interview ranged over the Catechesis, my book, and some of our experiences with homosexual priests in the Diocese of Newark. Then the interviewer said in what seemed an offhand way, "I know that comments attributed to you about religion in Africa have been a problem for you. Is there anything you would like to say about that?"

I replied that I had already expressed my regret to the archbishops of Africa about the way my views had been misrepresented and I did not want to say any more about it. "Has that been a difficulty for you?" he continued.

"Anytime my words are interpreted to be hurtful to anyone, I am sorry, but this was such a distortion that I will not dignify it further."

The next day I began to hear from people close to Frank Griswold that my public apology was forthcoming. When I returned the next day to the media office for the picture with Peter John Lee, I was told about my "message to the Africans." I replied that I had sent no message to the Africans. A member of the news team went to check out the story and returned to inform me that all she was referring to was my expression of regret that would appear in a story tomorrow. "If you folks portray that as an apology, I will be livid." I responded.

The next day the headline in the *Convention Daily* read "Bishop Spong Apologizes to Africans." I had been done in first by an irresponsible and malevolent reporter and second by a naive presiding bishop and his staff. Now I lived with an insult I never uttered and an apology I never offered. It was a surreal world.

I simply absorbed it, though I let Frank know how disgusted I was with his behavior and I would never again be prepared to trust either his character or his integrity. He seemed even more pathetic and inept as the conference went on. Not once did he rise to a role of leadership. From this moment on the Lambeth Conference was, for me, a place of overt dishonesty and rampant hostility. Nonetheless, even as a pariah, I continued to urge the liberal or progressive bishops to prepare a minority statement to have ready when the inevitably hostile Lambeth resolution condemning homosexuality was passed. I even drafted a possible statement that might begin to focus on the things that would need to be said. No one else was preparing a draft. The liberal caucus led by Doug Theuner of New Hampshire refused even to let me read my proposal to the assembled gathering of about 150 bishops. To these liberal bishops a minority statement prepared in advance would be seen as inherently unfriendly. It would assume that we had already lost the battle. My sense was that they did not know how to count. I warned them that the day after this hostile resolution was passed, the media would abandon Lambeth in droves and no minority statement would ever be heard by the very people most wounded by this ecclesiastical rejection. If we did not offer a minority statement on the same day immediately after the negative vote, it would be worthless. I also urged them to provide this statement in advance as a rallying point to give wavering moderate bishops a place to stand. My pleas fell on deaf ears. My ability to lead even my liberal friends had been destroyed. I did not mind that, for I recognize that this happens in all political struggles, but for none of the others to step up and provide any leadership whatsoever was deeply disillusioning. I was reminded once again how inept liberals can be when their actions require them to put their lives on the line. Liberal talk is cheap. Liberal action is frequently so costly it never gets engaged. I thought about my fearless friend John Hines, who combined word and action in breath-taking integrity. I searched in vain for an example of that among these bishops of our Communion. We were headed for a massive, embarrassing defeat, and my colleagues seemed oblivious to that probability. They reminded me of those who were busy rearranging the deck chairs on the great ship *Titanic.*

That night I did the only thing left for me to do. I wrote a personal statement and had it prepared to issue after what I felt would be a disastrous vote. At least I did not have to compromise my integrity to get anyone else to sign my statement.

The debate went as I had anticipated. The fragile document forged in intense debate for two weeks in the sexuality section of the conference, which satisfied no one, but which also insulted no one, simply could not hold. The archbishop of Capetown, Njongokulu Ndungane, made a plea that the conference support this fragile compromise, but he was ignored. George Carey was absolutely silent. He chose to sit on the stage, where his vote (which was by hand) could be seen by the whole assembly. The motions to amend our inoffensive resolution in unacceptably negative ways came up for one vote after another and each hostile amendment was passed overwhelmingly. Homosexual practice of any sort was pronounced sinful and "nonscriptural." The earlier version had contained a condemnation of homophobia, but that was removed. It was presumably okay to be publicly negative about homosexual people. The word "abstinence" was substituted for the word "chastity" to rule out the definition of chastity that meant faithfulness and thus to prohibit faithful homosexual couples from claiming chastity in their relationships. On each vote George Carey raised his right hand high and visibly in support of an increasingly hostile stance.

This document was now something insulting to me, to say nothing of the feelings of the vast numbers of homosexual Christians in the world. So was the process that went on at this conference. It was also insulting to the Anglican churches that had struggled on this issue in the United States, Canada, Scotland, South Africa, and New Zealand. Yet I could still be amazed at the silence of those who were themselves being compromised. Frank Griswold never said a word. Rowan Williams never left his seat. The heroes of the debate were one Canadian bishop, David Crawley of British Columbia, and two women bishops from the United States, Catherine Waynick of Indianapolis and Catherine Roskam of New York. They were, history might note, the first two women ever to speak at a Lambeth Conference, and they spoke brilliantly on behalf of the oppressed homosexual population. Before the vote was actually taken, incredibly, George Carey rose, approached the microphone on the stage, and endorsed this amended resolution as protecting traditional values and guarding biblical truth. He then asserted that he could find no biblical justification for any sexual activity outside marriage. It was a strange and inappropriate intervention at the final minute of this chaotic debate. The vote was then taken. It was a rout. The count was 540 yes votes, 70 no votes, and 45 abstentions. Frank Griswold was one of the abstainers, a tactic that I respected less than I did a negative vote. I saw liberal bishops who had opposed every one of these negative amendments vote yes on the final motion. One explained lamely to me that he felt that if this resolution did not pass, a more drastic resolution would be adopted. That was one more example of liberal incompetence. I wondered how out of touch with reality this bishop could actually get, since every amendment had passed by a two to one margin. There was no way this resolution was not destined to win approval. Gay and lesbian people had once more been abused and violated by a portion of the Body of Christ.

With the vote now over, I went out to meet a promised interview with the BBC. I distributed to the press corps fifty copies of my personal statement. It was a pitiably weak and feeble response to a major defeat, but it was all that I could do. In the press conference the primus of Scotland, Richard Holloway, expressed great anger, using such words as "betrayed, lynched, and raped." When asked about the speech of the archbishop of Canterbury, he termed it "pathetic." To the end he had thought that George Carey would seek a compromise, but George Carey had the votes to support his own negativity toward gay people. He did not need to compromise because there was no effective opposition.

I spoke next. After making reference to my written statement, I tried to find the silver lining in this dark cloud. "This debate has at least placed on the agenda of every province of this Communion the issue of homosexuality and the way homosexual people have been treated by the church," I said. "Once a prejudice has been lifted into public debate, it is doomed." I am confident this is correct, but at that moment it did not feel consoling. As we walked back to our rooms, we met liberal bishops in various states of shock, a couple of them even in tears. It was too late.

The conference continued down its disappointing path. It passed a resolution opposing the requirement by the Episcopal Church in America that no bishop can prohibit women priests from functioning in that bishop's diocese and no church in that diocese can be refused the right to call a woman priest to be rector. This resolution was passed to ensure that the church was "being fair to traditionalists." The conference moved to increase the authority of the archbishop of Canterbury and it expressed continued hostility toward modern biblical scholarship and any accommodation with the realities of the twentieth century. It was clear that the American Church was treated like a demon-possessed entity, a stance that American conservatives actually encouraged. The last big public battle that I would engage for what I believed was the cause of Christ was a massive defeat. I took my only consolation from the fact that history would inevitably turn this judgment around, and this Lambeth Conference would in time be a cause of great embarrassment, but its dark cloud would not be lifted from our corporate life within my active career. If any good came out of this, it was that moderate American bishops saw for the first time the discrimination and evil that homosexual people absorb every day. Several decided it was time to jump off the fence and stand for something.

Christine and I decided to leave Lambeth a day early to visit her family. All the major issues had been decided. Most of the remaining votes would be all but unanimous and the atmosphere was not just stifling, but reminded me of a mental institution where people lived inside many different realities.

On our last day at my last Lambeth Conference several rays of sunshine appeared. The conference defeated further attempts to give new status to the Kuala Lumpur Statement. At least that document was never endorsed. Peter John Lee of South Africa, speaking on another subject, paid an enormous compliment to me while he castigated the "demonization" of people with opposing points of view. Finally, as I walked out to the car carrying my suitcase, an African bishop approached me and said, "I've wanted to speak with you all during this conference. I support what you are doing. I want to know about the organization called Integrity and the possibility of getting a chapter of Integrity established in Africa." I was stunned. I think he was trying to tell me that he was gay, but I can never be sure of that. I asked him to write and he promised he would. I will not speak of that correspondence or use his name in this book, for that would surely place him at risk.

We received an e-mail our first night away informing us that the *Christian Challenge*, an ultraconservative publication, had put out a story that I was dying from stomach cancer and that the African bishops had refrained from introducing a resolution censuring me for my support of gay and lesbian people lest they turn a dying man into a martyr. The news of my fatal sickness was something that my doctors had never communicated to me, but perhaps the paper's reporter had other sources of information. At this point it was one more example of an irresponsible and dishonest conservative communication system.

From London I filed an op ed piece with the *New York Times*, calling this conference a sign of the death of Christianity. To my delight, it was accepted and ran the next week. Later, Frank Griswold, still trying to justify his weak Lambeth performance, wrote a long piece to rebut my editorial. The *Times* declined to run it.

We visited family and friends for a week or so before returning to the United States. Among these friends was a couple who had a gay son. We saw firsthand the devastation wrought on their lives and the life of their son by their church at Lambeth.

There was a time when I claimed for myself the title "evangelical." To me it meant one who lived on the Protestant and low church side of our Communion. It did not mean ill-informed, prejudiced, close-minded, and doctrinaire in a fundamentalist direction. After Lambeth I no longer wished to be identified with that word. The evangelicals I have met in public debate are frequently dishonest, manipulative, and unworried by any commitment to truth, fairness, or justice. If that is the evangelical future of Christianity they talk about so gleefully, then I want no part of it.

I saw the death of the church visibly at the Lambeth Conference. The evangelical fundamentalist takeover of the church internationally was apparent. It is not, I am confident, that this right-wing form of Christianity is growing, as they claimed, so much as it is that thinking people in the mainline modern churches are departing, leaving these distorted evangelicals as the sole remaining voices of Christ in the public arena. I had labored through all of my career to give a credible voice to a Christianity that was in dialogue with the real world. At Lambeth that possibility seemed to be a losing cause. If the Anglican Communion can turn this far to the right, then it joins a strident fundamentalist Protestantism, an antiquated Roman Catholicism, and an irrelevant Orthodox tradition as the major expressions of Christianity at the dawn of the twenty-first century. There is no leaven in that ecclesiastical lump and no candle left to shine in that ecclesiastical darkness. I see no hope for a Christian future in any of them. There is very little in any of these conservative traditions with which I could identify. If the church was not dying, objectively then I needed to face the fact that it was surely dying for me.

Bruised, defeated, and depressed about the future of the enterprise to which my life had been dedicated, I returned home to the diocese I loved, where no matter how small we might be in the scheme of things, we had managed to build a community of faith that was inclusive, where we were able to deal with any social and ethical question and demonstrated a willingness to explore both the Bible and the world of theology from any angle. *Why Christianity Must Change or Die* was still exploding across the American scene. Letters of deep appreciation for the freedom and hope my readers found in this book came in droves. I had only seventeen months to go before retirement.

Because of a bout with viral meningitis and finally the laproscopic surgery on my esophagus, I was out of the reaction phase to Lambeth for most of the fall. There were many voices now raised in protest. Mine was no longer necessary. Finally my health returned to normal, and I began the process of advising my successor and withdrawing from the role of episcopal leadership. It takes a lot of grace to lay down one's professional life. I was determined to do it with both dignity and integrity. I wanted to spend that period of time among my people and teaching across this nation wherever I was invited. The invitations poured in. Obviously that activity would continue beyond retirement, as my schedule for the next three years began to fill up.

The days of trying to participate in ecclesiastical structures in an attempt to make those structures responsive to reality, however, were over. I no longer

cared to fight that fight. Someone else who was less disillusioned by institutional religion and less bruised by hostile conservatives than I would have to
take on that chore. I was now convinced that the church of my dreams and
visions, the church I had glimpsed periodically, the church I loved, was being
drowned in a sea of dated theological irrelevancy undergirded by biblical
ignorance. The signs of rigor mortis were present if one only took off the
blinders and looked. The need to address the themes of a people in exile,
which my most recent book sought to outline, was overwhelming. I would
spend the final days of my professional life working on that frontier.

As the months passed bringing my day of retirement closer, Chris and I
basked in the love and appreciation of those among whom we had lived and
worked for almost twenty-four years. The positive mail on my book continued at an unbelievable pace. I had clearly struck a chord in the religious
yearnings of many modern people. This book remained on the *Publishers'
Weekly* top ten best-seller list for religious books for the balance of that
year. It was designated by *Publishers' Weekly* as one of the top fifty books of
all varieties published in the United States in 1998. It was singled out for a
similar notice by the *Christian Science Monitor*.

The audience for whom I wrote and to whom I spoke was obviously
responsive. They are Episcopalians, Lutherans, Methodists, Baptists, Roman
Catholics, and Unitarians. They are church hangers-on and church drop-
outs. They are atheists and agnostics. They are those who quite simply are
seeking meaning, integrity, and God. They are people on a spiritual journey,
and they allowed me to walk with them. I did so quite publicly and quite joyfully.

My homosexual friends felt badly damaged by Lambeth, but they appreciated my work even in a losing cause, and they said so repeatedly. At the
final diocesan convention over which I presided as bishop, our delegates
affirmed resolutions condemning the Lambeth vote, endorsing liturgical
services for same-sex unions, and calling on the Church Pension Fund to
provide pensions for partners of gay clergy. None of these resolutions had
one negative vote. We also had a resolution authorizing the appointment of
a poet laureate for the diocese. Out of approximately six hundred votes that
resolution received four no votes. It appeared that there was now more negativity to having a diocesan poet laureate than there was for blessing same-
sex unions. At least the people of the Diocese of Newark had moved to a
new place. The whole Anglican Communion would inevitably follow, but it
would take a few years.

I have enjoyed my episcopal career and my writing career. I have walked through my personal valleys and survived. I am married to a partner whom I love deeply and passionately. Spending my retirement with her is a wonderful and much anticipated source of joy. Our children are reaching the midpoint of their lives and careers, and our grandchildren are growing in a wonderful way.

My episcopal role has allowed me to know a host of lay leaders and clergy who have shared my vision. It has provided me with the joy of watching a faith community confront issues, devise solutions, stand up for truth, and willingly accept abuse as the price of their corporate witness. I have loved the process of selecting, training, and ordaining future clergy leaders and recruiting from across the land outstanding ordained persons to serve in our established congregations. I have never tired of looking into the eyes of children and adults alike whose life journeys have brought them to confirmation or reception in one of our churches. I have enjoyed learning new skills like money management and investment policies and being part of a process that enabled our endowed resources to increase by 800 percent during my years as bishop. I have treasured my opportunity to chair the board of Christ Hospital in Jersey City and to learn about the joys and perils in the lives of doctors, nurses, administrative people, and other employees in an institution squeezed by government regulations and the bottom line of managed-care companies. Being a bishop is a special opportunity, but being the bishop of Newark has been a peculiar, special, and high honor.

I have relished also my life as an author and the opportunities it created. Counting all of my various book titles, a total of between 500,000 and 1,000,000 copies of Spong books today float around the world, inspiring some, infuriating others, but above all creating debate. These books in turn have opened the lecture circuit to me, covering the English-speaking world. Between 1990 and 2000 I made almost three thousand public addresses. I have savored the opportunity given to very few bishops to speak on university campuses throughout the United States, Canada, England, Scotland, Wales, Australia, and New Zealand. I thought of myself many times as an evangelist, but one doing that evangelistic work by opening the possibility in people's minds that Christianity and the spiritual search were both still worthy of their time and attention. It was in the midst of my struggle to enlighten my church at Lambeth that I received from officials at Harvard University an invitation to come to that great center of learning as the

William Belden Noble lecturer for the semester beginning February 1, 2000. It was a deeply affirming opportunity that I accepted with delight and great pleasure. If I could have named the one thing I most desired to do when I retired, it would have been to teach at Harvard. Soon thereafter, representatives on the faculty of Harvard Divinity School expanded that privilege by asking me to teach a course at the Divinity School in addition to my university responsibilities. Still later, the title "Scholar in Residence" was offered by the people at Lowell House, which meant that we would not only live on campus, but also have the opportunity to eat our meals and interact daily with 400 undergraduates at that university. Increasingly, my life and interests had been turning toward an academic setting. It began with my appointment as a fellow at Cambridge University in 1992. On three separate occasions I served on the faculty of the Vancouver School of Theology of the University of British Columbia. Twice I taught classes for credit at the University of Alberta in Edmonton, and in the summer of 1999, I was a visiting lecturer at the Graduate Theological Union in Berkeley, California. I lectured in the United Kingdom in the fall of 2000, and will be lecturing in South Africa, Australia, and New Zealand during 2001. In addition to that I have been approached by theological seminaries and other colleges and universities here and abroad about the possibility of spending time as a visiting lecturer on their campuses. These opportunities represent a whole new career that now appears to be opening for me.

I am indebted even to my severest ecclesiastical critics, who have helped more than they might ever realize to cause people to pay attention to the things I have said and written. Their criticism was not always comfortable, but I came to realize the wisdom spoken by my friends at HarperCollins—critics and bad reviews sell more books than supporters and good reviews.

My life has been enriched by the opportunities I have had to engage in a personal way public figures in a wide variety of fields of endeavor, including the political leaders of both New Jersey and Virginia, but also including national leaders like Claiborne Pell. I have been touched by authors like Clarissa Pinkola Estés, Robert Funk, Marcus Borg, Dominic Crossan, and Karen Armstrong, by theologians like Hans Küng, Keith Ward, and Don Cupitt, by biblical scholars like Jeffrey John, Phyllis Trible, and Michael Goulder, by ethicists like Charles Curran, by media giants like Peter Jennings, Charles Gibson, Kathleen Sullivan, Phil Donahue, Bill Maher,

Oprah Winfrey, Dr. Ruth Westheimer, and Bill Press, and even by such reactionaries as William Buckley, Jr., and Pat Buchanan. Mine has been a tremendous ride around the course of life.

I entered the priesthood, I now recognize, seeking security for my anxious and insecure soul. I discovered in that vocation not security, but the expansion of life, and the radical challenges that life brings when one is open to the depths of the God who is for me the very Ground of All Being. Christianity ultimately provides no one with real security. Rather, it gives to me and others the capacity to embrace the radical insecurity of life as free, whole, and mature persons. The passive dependency that I meet in so many religious people is surely an aberration of what true Christianity is. I would not change my life path in any way. I have learned the wisdom of that prayer in the 1928 *Book of Common Prayer* that ultimately we must come "to give thanks for all things"—not some things, but all things.

Life has been sweet indeed. But above all else, I was throughout my life and am still today deeply convinced of the reality of God. Indeed, I am more deeply convinced of this reality at this moment than I have ever been before. I walk inside the wonder of this God in every experience of life. I have become more of a mystic than I ever thought possible for a rationalist like me. I still meet this God in the life of the one I call Lord and Christ, who is supremely important to my spiritual journey. I still love the church, at least as an idea if not in its corporate institutional form. The church of tomorrow will be radically different from the church of today, so different that some will not even see the continuity. But I take courage from the observations of history that the church of the catacombs did not look much like the Gothic cathedrals of the thirteenth century, and yet it was the same church. The church of the third and fourth millenniums will inevitably not look like the church of our day. So I urge my successors in faith to embrace, not to fear, the changes necessary to enable the church of the future to be born, for its birth pangs are being felt at this moment. I think a radical reformation is on our doorstep.

Despite all the opportunities in which I have had the privilege of being engaged with real life, the issues I have championed, the lives I have been able to touch as a priest, bishop, and author, I can still say that the accomplishments of which I am proudest are my marriage to Christine and the chance to be a father to three wonderful daughters and two exceptional sons-in-law. To enrich that with two terrific stepchildren and four beautiful grandchildren has been icing on the cake. I am ready now to pass the mantle of ecclesiastical leadership to the next generation and to allow the passage of time to determine what, if any, lasting contribution I might have made. History is a more adequate judge of eternal value than those who inhabit the time in which we actually live. I am therefore at peace. To all who in any way have shared my journey, I wish for you nothing less than the Shalom of God.

1. I suspect they learned that from the behavior of white missionaries.

2. Topics like forgiving the international debt of the Third World are very appealing to ecclesiastical groups. The topic is weighty and worthwhile. However, church leaders possess little political or economic power to bring to bear on this subject. So talk is cheap, costing the leaders nothing.

3. Copies of this statement and all the correspondence with the archbishop of Canterbury are available from Christianity for the Third Millennium (see address on the copyright page of this book), or look on my Web site http://www.dioceseofnewark.org/jsspong.

4. Available through Christianity for the Third Millennium.

5. The full text of the Twelve Theses, drawn from *Why Christianity Must Change or Die,* is printed in Appendix B.

# A Statement of Koinonia

by the Right Reverend John Shelby Spong, Bishop of Newark

T O the Members of the House of Bishops and through them to the whole church:

We the undersigned bishops want to thank the committee that created the Pastoral Study Document on Human Sexuality. That document in its various drafts forced the whole church to wrestle with issues that affect vitally the lives and hopes of a sizable number of the members of this church. This document also made our faith community better able to deal with the subject of human sexuality, around which there has always been great fear, great misunderstanding, great misinformation, and great prejudice.

We also value the collegiality of this House of Bishops and want to continue the mutual respect for our differences that is certainly part of the meaning of collegiality.

We are aware, however, that in its history this convention by various resolutions has taken stands on very emotional subjects such as capital punishment and abortion and has called this church to various boycotts of products to achieve what the majority believed was a moral agenda. On the role and place of women in the total life of this church, this body has spoken by amending the constitution and canons to give the decision of general convention the force of law. We are also aware that even with these official actions no one has suggested that those who hold contrary opinions are somehow violating the collegiality of this house or that they were not welcome to continue to bear witness and indeed to act on their consciences in these matters. Collegiality has meant that we have agreed to respect each other and to live with our differences. It has never been a straitjacket that we forced one another to wear in order to pretend that a consensus existed where in fact one did not exist.

In the discussion on what was first called "A Pastoral Teaching on Human Sexuality," we heard hints that collegiality was being interpreted in a more restrictive way. Perhaps, even more importantly, we heard voices of discouragement from some members of our Christian family, who had begun to trust that their church would share with them more of God's love and less of the church's judgment. This discouragement was produced primarily by press reports attempting to interpret the meaning of the action of this House in adopting the amended statement. It seems to hinge on the decision of this House to circulate with the committee's document a second statement produced by a group of bishops from the Southwest. It is their perception that this statement has had the effect of tilting the carefully crafted work of the committee back to a place where some members of our church no longer feel included, where those living in nontraditional relationships might no longer expect to find a place or a welcome in the Body of Christ, and where gay and lesbian clergy might question whether or not their gifts are still wanted by the church they love.

It is for these reasons we feel that this statement must also be made from a different perspective to this convention and to the whole church as part of the dialogue, lest anyone think consensus has in fact been reached on these issues or that there is no change occurring in this vital area of our life.

We believe that sex is a gift of God.

We believe that some of us are created heterosexual and some of us are created homosexual.

We believe that both homosexuality and heterosexuality are morally neutral, that both can be lived out with beauty, honor, and integrity and that both are capable of being lived out destructively.

We believe that wherever sexuality is lived out destructively, this church must witness to its negativity. We oppose all forms of promiscuous sex, predatory sex, sex that does not honor one's partner, or sex that does not hold that partner in commitment and love.

We believe that marriage is to be held in honor and that marriage represents the highest form of human commitment a man and a woman can make to each other. We believe that through marriage both the husband and wife are called to holiness.

We believe that celibacy is an honorable vocation for some of God's people and that those who have chosen to live in celibacy for whatever reason have gifts to give that will enrich both the church and the social order.

But we also believe that those who know themselves to be gay or lesbian persons, and who do not choose to live alone, but forge relationships with partners of their choice that are faithful, monogamous, committed, life-giving, and holy are to be honored. We will continue to relate to these couples with our support, our pastoral care, our prayers, and our recognition, in whatever form is deemed appropriate, that God is indeed present in their life together.

We also believe that the ordained ranks of this church are open to all baptized Christians and that through our regular screening process we will determine who is both called and qualified. We are aware of the presence in the church of gay and lesbian clergy. We bear witness to the fact that they have served and continue to serve this church with effectiveness and integrity. Some of them are single; many more of them are living in committed partnerships. They serve this church today as bishops, priests, and deacons. In all these orders they have won the respect of their ecclesial communities. Like the gay and lesbian population as a whole, many of our gay and lesbian clergy have gravitated to urban areas, where they live out their priestly vocations. In some urban areas the number of gay and lesbian people exceeds 35 percent of the total population. These gay and lesbian clergy work heroically and successfully in difficult assignments. By their willingness to accept and acknowledge their own sexual orientation and by the very witness of the committed nature of the lives they live with their partners, they have brought both the hope and love of Christ to communities of people long oppressed, long denigrated, and long judged by various religious authorities to be inadequate human beings in whom the image of God is somehow flawed.

We pledge to these clergy, whom we honor as part of this church, our support and protection, and we will continue to hold them to no standard higher than that to which we would hold any heterosexual priest whether he or she is single or married.

We also recognize that by canon law the choice of fit persons to serve in the ordained ranks of the church is not the prerogative of bishops alone, but of the whole church. We pledge ourselves to ordain only those persons whom the testing and screening process reveals to be wholesome examples to the flock of Christ. But let there be no misunderstanding, both our lives and our experience as bishops have convinced us that a wholesome example to the flock of Christ does not exclude a person of homosexual orientation, nor does it exclude those homosexual persons who choose to live out their sexual orientation in a partnership that is marked by faithfulness and life-giving holiness.

We want this House and the whole church to know that we can be faithful to Christ and to our ministries as bishops in no other way than by affirming these principles. We trust this dialogue on human sexuality will go on, for all of us have more to learn. But we make these comments publicly, not just to prevent future misunderstanding in this House, but also to send a message of hope to a significant part of the Body of Christ, which in our own inadequate way we try to represent.

## Those Who Have Signed the Statement of Koinonia*

1. Robert M. Anderson, Bishop of Minnesota
2. George W. Barrett, Bishop of Rochester, retired; Assistant Bishop of Los Angeles
3. Allen L. Bartlett, Jr., Bishop of Pennsylvania
4. Lane Barton, Bishop of Eastern Oregon, retired
5. George E. Bates, Bishop of Utah, retired
6. Charles E. Bennison, Jr., Bishop of Pennsylvania
7. Charles E. Bennison, Sr., Bishop of Western Michigan, retired
8. Roger W. Blanchard, Bishop of Southern Ohio, retired
9. Frederick H. Borsch, Bishop of Los Angeles
10. David C. Bowman, Bishop of Western New York
11. Edmond L. Browning, Presiding Bishop, retired
12. John M. Burgess, Bishop of Massachusetts, retired
13. William G. Burrill, Bishop of Rochester
14. John Harris Burt, Bishop of Ohio, retired
15. George L. Cadigan, Bishop of Missouri, retired
16. Sergio Carranza, Bishop of Mexico
17. Otis Charles, Bishop of Utah, resigned, Dean of Episcopal Divinity School
18. Stephen Charleston, Bishop of Alaska, resigned
19. David R. Cochran, Bishop of Alaska, retired
20. Ned Cole, Bishop of Central New York, retired
21. Daniel Corrigan, Bishop of Colorado, retired
22. Walter D. Dennis, Jr., Bishop Suffragan of New York

23. Robert L. DeWitt, Bishop of Pennsylvania, retired
24. Jane Holmes Dixon, Bishop Suffragan of Washington
25. Herbert A. Donovan, Jr., Bishop of Arkansas, resigned, Secretary of House of Bishops
26. Joe Morris Doss, Bishop Coadjutor of New Jersey
27. A. Theodore Eastman, Bishop of Maryland
28. William H. Folwell, Bishop of Central Florida, retired
29. J. Gary Gloster, Bishop Suffragan of North Carolina
30. J. Clark Grew II, Bishop of Ohio
31. Frank T. Griswold III, Bishop of Chicago
32. Edwin F. Gulick, Jr., Bishop of Kentucky
33. Sanford Z. K. Hampton, Bishop Suffragan of Minnesota
34. Barbara C. Harris, Bishop Suffragan of Massachusetts
35. Donald P. Hart, Bishop of Hawaii
36. John Elbridge Hines, Presiding Bishop, retired
37. Harold A. Hopkins, Office of Pastoral Development, Presiding Bishop's Staff
38. George N. Hunt, Bishop of Rhode Island
39. Robert W. Ihloff, Bishop of Maryland
40. Carolyn Tanner Irish, Bishop of Utah
41. James L. Jelinek, Bishop of Minnesota
42. David E. Johnson, Jr., Bishop of Massachusetts
43. Robert C. Johnson, Jr., Bishop of North Carolina
44. Edward W. Jones, Bishop of Indianapolis
45. Rustin R. Kimsey, Bishop of Eastern Oregon
46. Chilton A. R. Knudsen, Bishop of Maine
47. John M. Krumm, Bishop of Southern Ohio, retired
48. Edward L. Lee, Jr., Bishop of Western Michigan
49. A. Heath Light, Bishop of Southwestern Virginia
50. William H. Marmion, Bishop of Southwestern Virginia, retired
51. Larry E. Maze, Bishop of Arkansas
52. Coleman McGehee, Jr., Bishop of Michigan, retired
53. Jack M. McKelvey, Bishop Suffragan of Newark
54. Mary Adelia R. McLeod, Bishop of Vermont
55. Rodney R. Michel, Bishop Suffragan of Long Island
56. James W. Montgomery, Bishop of Chicago, retired
57. Paul Moore, Bishop of New York, retired
58. James H. Ottley, Bishop of Panama

59. Vincent J. Pettit, Assistant Bishop of Albany
60. Quintin E. Primo, Jr., Bishop Suffragan of Chicago, retired
61. Jose Antonio Ramos, Bishop of Costa Rica, resigned
62. Thomas K. Ray, Bishop of Northern Michigan
63. Francisco Reus-Froylan, Bishop of Puerto Rico, retired
64. David E. Richards, Bishop of Central America, retired
65. Walter C. Righter, Bishop of Iowa, retired
66. Hays Rockwell, Bishop of Missouri
67. Catherine S. Roskam, Bishop Suffragan of New York
68. M. Thomas Shaw, Bishop Coadjutor, Diocese of Massachusetts
69. Richard L. Shimpfky, Bishop of El Camino Real
70. Bennett J. Sims, Bishop of Atlanta, Emeritus, retired
71. Robert R. Spears, Jr., Bishop of Rochester, retired
72. John S. Spong, Bishop of Newark
73. Daniel L. Swenson, Bishop of Vermont, retired
74. William E. Swing, Bishop of California
75. Chester L. Talton, Bishop Suffragan of Los Angeles
76. Frank Jeffrey Terry, Bishop of Spokane
77. Douglas E. Theuner, Bishop of New Hampshire
78. Richard M. Trelease, Jr., Bishop of Rio Grande, retired
79. Frank H. Vest, Jr., Bishop of Southern Virginia
80. Orris George Walker, Jr., Bishop of Long Island
81. Leigh A. Wallace, Jr., Bishop of Spokane, retired
82. Arthur E. Walmsley, Bishop of Connecticut, retired
83. Catherine M. Waynick, Bishop of Indianapolis
84. O'Kelley Whitaker, Bishop of Central New York
85. William W. Wiedrich, Bishop Suffragan of Chicago
86. Frederick B. Wolf, Bishop of Maine, retired
87. R. Stewart Wood, Bishop of Michigan
88. Stewart C. Zabriskie, Bishop of Nevada

* The status listed was the status the bishop possessed when he or she signed this statement.

# *Twelve Theses*

Drawn from my book *Why Christianity Must Change or Die:*
*A Bishop Speaks to Believers in Exile*

\*

## A Call for a New Reformation

1. Theism, as a way of defining God, is dead. God can no longer be understood with credibility as a Being, supernatural in power, dwelling above the sky and prepared to invade human history periodically to enforce the divine will. So, most theological God-talk today is meaningless unless we find a new way to speak of God.

2. Since God can no longer be conceived in theistic terms, it becomes nonsensical to seek to understand Jesus as the incarnation of the theistic deity. So, the Christology of the ages is bankrupt.

3. The biblical story of the perfect and finished creation from which human beings fell into sin is pre-Darwinian mythology and post-Darwinian nonsense.

4. The virgin birth, understood as literal biology, makes the divinity of Christ, as traditionally understood, impossible.

5. The miracle stories of the New Testament can no longer be interpreted in a post-Newtonian world as supernatural events performed by an incarnate deity.

6. The view of the cross as the sacrifice for the sins of the world is a barbarian idea based on primitive concepts of God that must be dismissed.

7. Resurrection is an action of God, who raised Jesus into the meaning of God. It therefore cannot be a physical resuscitation occurring inside human history.

8. The story of the ascension assumed a three-tiered universe and is therefore not capable of being translated into the concepts of a post-Copernican space age.
9. There is no external, objective, revealed standard writ in Scripture or on tablets of stone that will govern our ethical behavior for all time.
10. Prayer cannot be a request made to a theistic deity to act in human history in a particular way.
11. The hope for life after death must be separated forever from the behavior-control mentality of reward and punishment. The church must abandon, therefore, its reliance on guilt as a motivator of behavior.
12. All human beings bear God's image and must be respected for what each person is. Therefore, no external description of one's being, whether based on race, ethnicity, gender, or sexual orientation, can properly be used as the basis for either rejection or discrimination.

*Author's Note:* These theses posted for debate are inevitably stated in a negative manner. That is deliberate. Before one can hear what Christianity is one must create room for that hearing by clearing out the misconceptions of what Christianity is not. *Why Christianity Must Change or Die* is a manifesto calling the church to a new reformation. In that book I begin to sketch out a view of God beyond theism, an understanding of the Christ as a God presence and a vision of the shape of both the church and its Liturgy for the future. When I publish the Harvard Lectures sometime in 2001, which I will deliver as the William Belden Noble lecturer in 2000, I plan to present a fuller, more positive understanding of what the Christianity of the future will be like.

# INDEX